*An Introduction to the*
*Hebrew Bible*

# An Introduction to the Hebrew Bible

## A THEMATIC APPROACH

Sandra L. Gravett
Karla G. Bohmbach
F. V. Greifenhagen
Donald C. Polaski

Westminster John Knox Press
LOUISVILLE • LONDON

*Book design by Drew Stevens*
*Cover design by Mark Abrams*

*First edition*
Published by Westminster John Knox Press
Louisville, Kentucky

This book is printed on acid-free paper that meets the American National Standards Institute Z39.48 standard. ∞

PRINTED IN THE UNITED STATES OF AMERICA

08 09 10 11 12 13 14 15 16 17 — 10 9 8 7 6 5 4 3 2 1

**Library of Congress Cataloging-in-Publication Data**
An introduction to the Hebrew Bible : a thematic approach / by Sandra L. Gravett . . . [et al.]. — 1st ed.
    p. cm.
    Includes bibliographical references.
    ISBN 978-0-664-23030-2 (alk. paper)
    1. Bible. O.T.—Introductions. I. Gravett, Sandra L.
    BS1140.3.I58 2008
    221.6'1—dc22
                                    2008006091

*To our families*

# Contents

Acknowledgments     xi

Introduction     xiii

A Guide for Readers     xiv
*The Main Players* xiv
*Place and Time* xv
*The Text* xv

Final Notes     xvii

## 1. Space and Time     1

Space     1
*A Geographical Tour around the Cisjordan* 1
*Context for Understanding the Hebrew
    Bible's Geography* 16

Time     19
*Earliest Periods (The Stone and
    Copper Ages)* 21
*The Bronze Age
    (ca. 3200–1200 B.C.E.)* 22
*The Iron Age
    (ca. 1200–600 B.C.E.)* 27
*The Babylonian Exile
    (587/586–539 B.C.E.)* 36
*The Persian Empire
    (539–333 B.C.E.)* 37
*The Hellenistic Period
    (333–164 B.C.E.)* 38

Conclusion     39

## 2. Reading the Hebrew Bible     41

Getting Started: The Hebrew Bible as
Translation     42
*Translation and Its Discontents* 42
*Before Translation: The Work of Textual
    Criticism* 46

Ways of Reading the Hebrew Bible     53
*The Synagogue's Book / The Church's Book:
    Reading for Theology* 53
*The Historian's Book: Reading
    for Data* 58
*The Literary Critic's Book: Reading
    for Art and Beyond* 68

The Book at the End of Modernity:
Reading Conflict and Difference     76

## 3. Introducing Identity     79

Beginnings     81

Next Steps     85

More Complications     86

Final Thoughts     90

## 4. Family     95

Family Structure     98
Bet 98
Av 102

"Marriage"                                      103

Children (Sexuality, Inheritance)               107

Other Functions of the *Bet Av*                 114
*Law* 114
*Education* 115
*Religion* 117
*Death and Burial* 120

Identity and the *Bet Av*                       122

Other Social Networks: Clans
and Tribes                                      125

Conclusion                                      128


**5. Gender                                     131**

Masculinity and Femininity in the
Hebrew Bible                                    134
*The Hypermasculine: Samson* 135
*The Tempered Masculine: Jacob* 140
*The Hyperfeminine: Esther* 145
*The Tempered Feminine: Jael* 149

Gender Anxieties                                151
*Women in Masculine Gender Roles:*
    *Ruth and Naomi* 151
*Other Examples of Gender Anxiety* 154

God and Gender                                  155
*God as Masculine* 156
*God as Feminine* 156
*God as Masculine and Feminine* 157

Reading the Garden: An
Exemplary Tale                                  158


**6. The Body                                   165**

The Human Body in the Hebrew Bible              168

The Normative Body in the Hebrew Bible          179

The Normative Social Body                       184

Body Practices                                  186
*Eating and Food* 186
*Clothing and Nakedness* 188
*Body Modifications* 189
*Sexual Intercourse* 191

God's Body                                      192

Conclusion                                      195


**7. Ethnicity                                  199**

Ethnicity                                       200

Idealization of Differences:
Ethnic Diversity                                202

Ambiguous Coexistence:
Israelite Ethnicity                             205

Violent Rejection and Exclusion:
Genocide                                        209

Ethnic Others                                   211
*Egyptians* 212
*Canaanites* 216
*Philistines* 221
*Edomites* 223
*Moabites* 224

The Problem of the "Inside-Outsider"            227

The Scandal of Particularity
and Anti-Semitism                               234

Conclusion                                      236


**8. Class                                      239**

The Small Landholding Class:
The *Bet Av* Ideal                              244

The Elite Class                                 249
*The Emergence of Elites* 250
*The Prophetic Perspective on the Elites* 255
*The Wisdom Perspective on the Elites* 261

*The Imperial Context and Its Shaping of the Elites* 264

**The Poor**     266
*Prophetic Sympathizers and Defenders of the Poor* 268
*Wisdom's Blame and Condemnation of the Poor* 269

**Conclusion**     271


**9. Introducing Power**     275

**An Image of the King**     276

**Entering the Power Web**     278
*The Mythic Life* 279
*The Anointings* 281

**Surfing the Power Web**     284
*Jerusalem, the Capital* 284
*Moving the Ark* 285
*A Dynastic Legacy* 287
*Conclusions* 288

**Webmaster**     288


**10. The State**     291

**Solomon and the Conjuring of the State**     293
*Solomon's Court* 295
*Conclusions* 303

**Opposition to Monarchy and the Dissolution of the State**     303
*Bet Av and Local Rule* 306
*Prophets* 308

**Israel after the State: The Politics of Empire**     316
*Yehud as a Colony* 316
*The Elite as a Collaborator Class* 318

**Conclusions**     319

**11. Ideology**     323

**The King-Zion Complex**     324
*Relating the King and Zion: 1 Kings 5 and 8* 325
*Relating the King and YHWH: Psalm 89* 326
*Relating YHWH and Zion: Psalm 48* 328
*Living with the King-Zion Complex: Hezekiah* 330
*The King-Zion Complex after the Monarchy* 333

**The Sinai-Nation Complex**     336
*Ancient Treaties, Covenants, and Ideology* 337
*The Sinai-Nation Complex: Rewriting the Treaties* 339
*Sinai versus Zion: Jeremiah and Revolutionary Impulses* 345
*Deuteronomy: A Mediating Position between Sinai and Zion?* 346

**The Sage-Order Complex**     347
*Creation as Ideology: Genesis 1* 348
*Wisdom as Ideology: Proverbs* 349
*Wisdom, Ideology, and the Empire: Qoheleth's Dissent* 352

**The Empire-Colony Complex**     353
*Esther: Playing with Power* 355
*The End(s) of Power: Daniel and Apocalyptic Thought* 355

**Conclusion**     359


**12. Media**     361

**Zion and Temple**     362
*A Tour of the Temple* 362
*A View of the Temple in Action* 368
*Holiness: The Temple's Way of Working* 374
*Conclusion* 377

Writing as a Material Practice    378
*Writing in the Ancient Near East
    and Israel  378*
*Early Steps: The Prophets and
    Durable Writing  383*
*Beyond Durability: Jeremiah's Scroll  384*
*Birth of a Canon? Josiah and
    Deuteronomy  385*
*Ezra: Another Scroll Appears  386*
*Writing and Empire: Esther and Daniel  389*

## 13. Deity    395

Divine Identities    397
*Elohim and El  397*
*Baal  399*
*Asherah  400*
*YHWH  400*
*Conclusions about the Identity
    of This Deity  404*

Identity to Power: How Many Gods?
Whose Gods? And What Does
It Matter?    404

Metaphorical Identities of the Deity:
Embodied and Enacted Power    408
*God, Jealousy, and the* Bet Av  *409*
*YHWH the King and the
    Divine Assembly  415*
*God as Emperor  419*

Conclusion    425

## 14. Considering Job    427

Job: A Case of Identity Theft    428
*Family Man  428*
*Man's Man  431*
*Disembodied Man  433*
*The Other Man  434*
*Rich Man, Poor Man  436*
*Conclusion  437*

Job: Power Plays    437
*Living in God's Kingdom  438*
*Thinking Through Job's Predicament:
    Ideological Approaches to Job  440*
*Expressing the Order of Job: Creation
    as Medium  443*
*Picturing God's Power  445*

Restoring Job    448
*Reviving Job's Identity  448*
*Renegotiating Power  450*

Translating Power: Job's Final Ambiguity    454

Conclusion?    457

List of Illustrations and Credits    459

Glossary    463

Index to Citations of the
Hebrew Bible    469

Index to Subjects    484

# Acknowledgments

We received assistance and support from many people as we wrote this book. When we met as an editorial group in Richmond, the William Smith Morton Library of Union–PSCE provided us with meeting space. We offer thanks to the librarian, Joe Coalter, and the staff. The Polaski family hosted us in Richmond, so our deep gratitude goes to Sandra Hack Polaski for cooking and cleaning and making things hospitable, as well as Will and Hannah for sharing a bedroom during the meetings. For a meeting in Greensboro, Bill and Mona Gravett, Sandie's parents, abandoned their house to us. Many thanks are due to them. The Irving Park United Methodist Church (Brian C. Allen, pastor) also provided meeting space. To attend these meetings, Karla relied on funds from a Faculty Mini Grant for Research Support (2006) from Susquehanna University. Volker received financial support from the President's Research Fund at Luther College, University of Regina, without which his participation in this project would not have been possible. At all meetings, Sandie served as group sommelier. Thanks are also due to Susan Cherland and John Lathan for artwork in the text, as well as to Laura Lengel for preparing the indices. Funding for Laura's work came from the Alice Pope Shade Fund, Susquehanna University. Michael Blum, director of the Faculty Digital Center at The College of William & Mary, provided invaluable assistance with the processing of images used in this text.

As we produced pieces of this text, we used much of the material with our students. Special thanks are due to the students in "The Old Testament" at Susquehanna University; in "Biblical Literature—Hebrew Bible" at Luther College, University of Regina; in "The History and Religion of Ancient

Israel" at The College of William & Mary; and in various classes at Appalachian State University.

We could not have written this work without the support of our friends and families, who tolerated absences and other milder forms of inattention for the past several years as we put this book together, especially Tom Martin, Linda McMillin, Bill and Mona Gravett, Sheri Gravett, Parker Williams, Susan Cherland, Isaak Cherland Greifenhagen, Jakob Cherland Greifenhagen, Sandra Hack Polaski, Hannah Polaski, and Will Polaski.

Karla Bohmbach
Sandie Gravett
Volker Greifenhagen
Don Polaski
January 2008

# Introduction

We do not read the Bible the way it is; we read it the way we are.
— Evelyn Uyemura, *Universal Salvation: The Current Debate*

The book to read is not the one which thinks for you, but the one
which makes you think. No book in the world equals the Bible for that.
— James McCosh, in *The Westminster Collection
of Christian Quotations*

---

The Bible permeates western culture. Its teachings support the decrees of
moral decision makers. Its themes provoke commentary and interpretation
in literary works. Its stories serve up material for dramatic renderings in
films, plays, and musicals. Its places appear in the news, in the wars and conflicts involving people who bear biblical names. And, of course, several religions organize themselves around the Bible, finding sanction for their
beliefs and practices in a book they consider divinely inspired. It might
sometimes seem as if the Bible is everywhere. As a matter of fact, the Bible
is the most read, most published, and most translated book of all time.

But the Bible's pervasiveness can trick readers into assuming a false
familiarity with it. Turning from cultural uses of the Bible and delving into
the actual text itself, one enters a strange and rather peculiar world. The
Bible often puzzles even its regular readers by pointing to practices and values far different from a modern, western context: slavery, camel riding,
polygamy, concubinage, animal sacrifice. Then there are all the tongue-
twisting names over which readers so frequently stumble: Zerubbabel,
Jehoiachin, Asshurbanipal, Nebuchadnezzar, and many others.

Yet an even more vital issue looms. What exactly does the term "Bible"
designate? To Jews, "Bible" is Tanakh, or Torah; to Christians, the Old and
New Testaments. These texts vary in number, order, and sometimes even
content. Beyond religious communities, the "Bible" functions as a cultural
touchstone or a historically interesting document. So what "Bible" means
varies depending on who is using it. This textbook focuses on a document
known variously as the Hebrew Bible, the Tanakh, or the Old Testament. It
reads the Hebrew Bible as a cultural artifact rather than as a source of

information about a people far removed in time or for present religious inspiration.

How, then, should we proceed? After two chapters introducing the biblical world and the text itself, this textbook builds around two themes: identity and power. The section on identity begins by providing an overview of identity issues both in the Hebrew Bible and for readers today, using the biblical story of Moses to illustrate. Subsequent chapters then treat distinct aspects of identity including family, gender, the body, ethnicity, and class. Each chapter explores how the Hebrew Bible constructs these features by examining the biblical texts that speak to them—looking both for main themes as well as the ways in which these are called into question, challenged, or undermined. Throughout, a focus emerges on how cultures of different times and places construct these identity features—and how those constructions relate to the Hebrew Bible. The second part of the book takes up the theme of power. Again, a short overview opens the section, this time using the biblical presentation of David to set forth the central concerns. The succeeding chapters then expand on this theme by treating specific topics pertaining to, and expressive of, power: nation, ideology, media, and deity. Finally, by way of a summary, a reading of Job brings to bear every aspect of both identity and power investigated in the course of the book. A glossary at the end of the book provides definitions for technical terms helpful in understanding the Hebrew Bible and its contexts. (The first time these terms appear in a chapter, they are presented in boldface.)

## A Guide for Readers

Before beginning, consider these several basic, key points pertinent to studying and understanding the Hebrew Bible.

### The Main Players

*The Deity.* For the deity featured in the Hebrew Bible, this textbook most often uses the terms "God" and "YHWH." While "God" is a familiar and generic name for the deity, "YHWH" will be new to many readers. Known as the *tetragrammaton* (Greek for "four letters"), this term generally functions as the biblical deity's proper name. Most scholars provide vowels for it such that they pronounce it Yahweh. Chapter 13 discusses traditions about whether or not one should speak this name aloud. The majority of English translations of the Hebrew render YHWH as "Lord," with three small capital letters.

*The People.* The Hebrew Bible tells the story of a people that it most commonly names "Israel" or "the Israelites." However, this term can invite confusion since it also has several other referents. Specifically, "Israel" can also refer to (1) the whole region inhabited by this people; (2) the single ancestor of this people, otherwise known as "Jacob"; (3) just the northern part of the region and its inhabitants, who comprised a separate kingdom for about two hundred years' time; and (4) a modern nation, established in 1948, inhabiting parts of the biblical territory. Its citizens are generally called Israelis, not Israelites.

This textbook normally uses "Israel" or "the Israelites" when referring to the entire ancient biblical people. The terms "the kingdom of Israel" or "northern kingdom" refer to the northern kingdom or its inhabitants. On a related note, the terms "Jews" and "Judaism" rarely occur. These designations come into play only after the writing of the last texts of the Hebrew Bible. Applying them to the Hebrew Bible is anachronistic.

*Place and Time*

*Israel or Cisjordan.* While the term "Israel" sometimes names the land inhabited by the biblical Israelites, it also names a presently existing state, which can lead to problems. Specifically, some people interpret the biblical use of the term as a divine mandate justifying claims to the land in the present day. Using "Israel" as a territorial designator reveals its politically fraught nature. Hence, although this textbook will at times refer to the biblical homeland as Israel for historical reasons, it will more readily use a more politically neutral term: Cisjordan. For more detail on both the meaning of Cisjordan and the reasons for employing it, see chapter 1.

*B.C.E./C.E.* The temporal framing of the Hebrew Bible occurs within the era of time conventionally known in western culture as B.C. Yet that abbreviation points to a specifically Christian way for marking time: B.C. = before Christ; A.D. = anno Domini (in the year of the Lord). Since this textbook does not promote any one particular religious viewpoint, it uses the more neutral terms of B.C.E. = before the Common Era, and C.E. = Common Era to demarcate eras of time. The years reckoned are the same as under the B.C./A.D. system. Again, chapter 1 provides additional explanation for these terms and the choice to use them.

*The Text*

**Books**

Although the Hebrew Bible generally comes to modern readers as one book (or part of one book), it is more accurately seen as a collection of books. Indeed, the very name "Bible" gestures toward that fact; it comes from the Greek *ta biblia*, meaning "the books." However, the exact number of books counted as belonging to this collection varies from 24 (Jewish), to 39 (Protestant Christian), to 46 (Roman Catholic and Orthodox). Considerable overlap does exist; still, one does not find every book in every collection. Most notably, the Jewish and Protestant Christian collections do not incorporate those works otherwise known as apocryphal or deuterocanonical books (e.g., Tobit, Judith, 1 and 2 Maccabees, Susanna) and found in Roman Catholic and Orthodox Bibles.

Each book also has a name, which scholars often abbreviate, making it easier and faster to refer to them. The following table provides these abbreviations. Familiarization with them will assist in the reading of this textbook.

## ABBREVIATIONS OF BOOKS IN THE HEBREW BIBLE

| | | |
|---|---|---|
| Amos = Amos | Hos = Hosea | Mic = Micah |
| 1 Chr = 1 Chronicles | Isa = Isaiah | Nah = Nahum |
| 2 Chr = 2 Chronicles | Jer = Jeremiah | Neh = Nehemiah |
| Dan = Daniel | Job = Job | Num = Numbers |
| Deut = Deuteronomy | Joel = Joel | Obad = Obadiah |
| Eccl = Ecclesiastes | Jonah = Jonah | Prov = Proverbs |
| Esth = Esther | Josh = Joshua | Ps/Pss = Psalm/s |
| Exod = Exodus | Judg = Judges | Ruth = Ruth |
| Ezek = Ezekiel | 1 Kgs = 1 Kings | 1 Sam = 1 Samuel |
| Ezra = Ezra | 2 Kgs = 2 Kings | 2 Sam = 2 Samuel |
| Gen = Genesis | Lam = Lamentations | Song = Song of Songs |
| Hab = Habakkuk | Lev = Leviticus | Zech = Zechariah |
| Hag = Haggai | Mal = Malachi | Zeph = Zephaniah |

### Chapters and Verses

In addition to having a name, each book (except for Obadiah) also is subdivided into chapters. These chapters further subdivide into verses. This chapter-verse system, developed centuries ago, functions as the standard way for referring to a particular biblical passage. For instance, "Gen 1:3" serves as a reference to the passage that reads, "And God said, 'Let there be light'; and there was light." "Gen" is the abbreviation for Genesis, the first book in the Hebrew Bible. The first number that follows indicates the chapter number where the passage can be found. The number following the colon is the verse number within chapter 1, where this passage appears.

This system of scripture citation also employs several other markers. A dash (–) indicates that you should read through from one chapter or verse to another. Thus, "Gen 1:3–2:4" refers to a passage running from verse 3 of chapter 1 through verse 4 of chapter 2. "Gen 1–11" denotes the first eleven chapters of the book of Genesis in their entirety. Small letters specify part of a verse, since verses do not always constitute just one sentence or unit of meaning. For example, "Gen 2:4a" tells the reader to consider only the first half of verse 4. The abbreviation "ff." (which means "following") functions as a general reference to several verses beyond just the one cited. For instance, "Gen 1:3ff." identifies a passage beginning with verse 3 of chapter 1 of Genesis and extending onward through the next several verses.

### Hebrew to English

Most western readers of the Hebrew Bible read it in translation. This textbook generally uses the New Revised Standard Version (NRSV). Citation of any other translation or of the authors' own translations will be noted. Most English translations follow a chapter-and-verse system that occasionally varies from the Hebrew versification. All citations of passages will assume the English versification unless indicated otherwise.

Some knowledge of Hebrew language terms assists in clarifying concepts. All Hebrew transliterations occur in simple forms with no diacritical markings.

## Final Notes

Four authors wrote this textbook. Each of us drafted chapters of the textbook—or parts of chapters—based on our interest and expertise. We then came together in a series of regular meetings over the course of several years to read, revise, and edit, so all of us had a hand in every part of the content.

Moreover, we first came to know one another in the same graduate program in religion at Duke University. Thus, we share common academic training that certainly shapes our perspective on the questions and the issues we address. Additionally, each of us grew up in a Protestant Christian tradition, and such a background affects the ways in which we approach the interpretive process—both consciously and unconsciously. Yet we do not offer readings as members of religious communities or for religious meaning. We simply acknowledge that our histories influenced how we thought about this text and the materials we selected to aid our readers in its interpretation.

Keeping in mind the basic guiding points and knowing something of who is taking you on this journey, let us now begin with a survey of the biblical world.

# 1. Space and Time

Tell me the landscape in which you live, and I will tell you who you are.
—Jose Ortega y Gasset,
"La pedagogia del paisaje"

What seest thou else
In the dark backward and absym of time?

—Shakespeare, *The Tempest*

**Space**

Where do you live? When meeting someone new, that question is often one of the first ones asked. It speaks to how significantly spatial location shapes identity. As the above quotation by Jose Ortega y Gasset asserts, where people live proves fundamental to how they understand themselves and how others view them.

Think about your own spatial location and how it compares to others you have seen or heard about. When you look out your window, do you see multistory buildings, suburban tract housing, open fields, or something else? What fills the horizon: high mountains, dense forests, flat deserts, rolling prairie? Can you hear water, and if so, what kind: gurgling rivers, melting snows, thundering ocean waves? Now think about how your geography influences your thinking, activities, beliefs, values, and lifestyle. For instance, what clothes do you wear to accommodate the weather? What do you need to guard against: floods, droughts, blizzards, earthquakes, tornadoes, prairie fires, hurricanes? Have you ever wondered how you might be a different person if you had grown up in a different place?

*A Geographical Tour around the Cisjordan*

Geography also shaped the experiences of biblical peoples. Imagine living in Jerusalem around 900 B.C.E.

Standing upon the city's walls and scanning the landscape brings into view reddish-brown limestone and chalk hills. Occasional stands of oak, terebinth, and juniper dot the hills. Among these trees roam deer, oxen, and boar, as well as predators such as foxes, wolves, cheetahs, and leopards. One might even glimpse a bear or lion. But human activity is also altering the

1

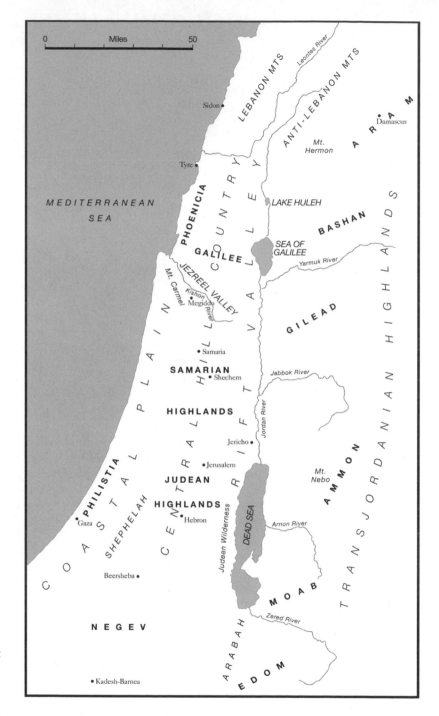

**Fig. 1.1: Map of Ancient Cisjordan and Its Immediately Surrounding Regions**

**Fig. 1.2: The Judean Hills around Jerusalem**

landscape. The trees here are giving way to agricultural terraces. These artificial shelves, cut into the sides of hills, support grapevines, olive trees, and small plots of barley and wheat.

In summer the hot, dry conditions feel oppressive. The sky arcs overhead a cloudless blue, for no rain falls now. The twenty-six inches (660 millimeters) of annual rainfall all comes between October and April, with the heaviest downpours in November through February.

That amount of rain in Jerusalem is just enough to support crops. Yet it falls erratically. Droughts occur about every three years out of ten. And no

### Rainfall Comparisons

The following chart lists the average yearly rainfalls for a number of the world's cities. Note that Jerusalem lies toward the drier end of the spectrum. Yet Jerusalem actually receives more rain per year than London—rather surprising, given London's reputation as a rainy city. But whereas London is subject to frequent light mists, Jerusalem experiences rare but intense downpours.

| City | Rainfall |
| --- | --- |
| Cairo | 1 inch / 25 millimeters |
| Los Angeles | 12 inches / 360 millimeters |
| London | 23 inches / 585 millimeters |
| *Jerusalem* | 26 inches / 660 millimeters |
| Johannesburg | 29 inches / 720 millimeters |
| Rio de Janeiro | 42 inches / 1086 millimeters |
| New York | 43 inches / 1190 millimeters |
| Sydney | 48 inches / 1220 millimeters |
| Tokyo | 60 inches / 1519 millimeters |
| Calcutta | 62 inches / 1582 millimeters |
| Hong Kong | 89 inches / 2200 millimeters |

rivers wind their way through the landscape around the city. Instead, only wadis appear. These dry riverbeds capture the winter runoff down the hills and into the valleys. All water thus comes from rainfall, springs, and wells dug into the ground. The dryness in the air gives a crystalline clarity to the sky. And at night the heavens glitter with millions of stars.

These geographic details all find their way into the Hebrew Bible in how the biblical writers image God, the world, and their relationship to God. A few examples suffice, all from the book of Psalms, the Hebrew Bible's songbook.

> I lift up my eyes to the hills—
>   from where will my help come?
> My help comes from the LORD,
>   who made heaven and earth.                    (121:1–2)

> Praise him, sun and moon;
>   praise him, all you shining stars!
> . . . . . . . . . . . . . . . . . . . . . . . . . . . .
> Mountains and all hills,
>   fruit trees and all cedars!
> Wild animals and all cattle,
>   creeping things and flying birds!        (148:3, 9–10)

> Save me from the mouth of the lion!
> From the horns of the wild oxen you have rescued me.        (22:21)

> O God, you are my God, I seek you,
>   my soul thirsts for you;
> my flesh faints for you,
>   as in a dry and weary land where there is no water.        (63:1)

> For day and night your hand was heavy upon me;
>   my strength was dried up as by the heat of summer.        (32:4)

> The LORD is your keeper;
>   the LORD is your shade at your right hand.
> The sun shall not strike you by day,
>   nor the moon by night.                    (121:5–6)

> You make springs gush forth in the valleys;
>   they flow between the hills,
> giving drink to every wild animal;
>   the wild asses quench their thirst.        (104:10–11)

> When I look at your heavens, the work of your fingers,
>   the moon and the stars that you have established;
> what are human beings that you are mindful of them,
>   mortals that you care for them?                    (8:3–4)

Positioned on Jerusalem's city walls on an especially clear day and gazing off to the west, one might see all the way to the Mediterranean Sea, a distance of about forty miles (sixty-four kilometers). Along this sea runs a nar-

**Fig. 1.3: The Coastal Plain near Ashkelon**

row strip of land known as the coastal plain. Mostly flat, it has sandy fertile soils especially good for growing all sorts of crops.

The ocean air makes the region more humid and so less pleasant a place to live. Not that **Israelites** are likely to visit it anyway, much less live there. Their enemies—the **Philistines**—inhabit it. And further north along the coastal plain live another foreign people: the Phoenicians. Besides farming, both the Philistines and the Phoenicians gain much of their livelihood from the sea: they fish and send out ships both to explore and to engage in trade. But the Israelites, largely landlocked, look upon the sea as a powerfully chaotic, fearsome force. Again, the Psalms provide potent images.

> Yonder is the sea, great and wide,
>   creeping things innumerable are there,
>   living things both small and great.
> There go the ships,
>   and Leviathan that you formed to sport in it.          (104:25–26)
>
> Some went down to the sea in ships,
>   doing business on the mighty waters;
> they saw the deeds of the Lord,
>   his wondrous works in the deep.
> For he commanded and raised the stormy wind,
>   which lifted up the waves of the sea.
> They mounted up to heaven, they went down to the depths;
>   their courage melted away in their calamity;
> they reeled and staggered like drunkards,
>   and were at their wits' end.          (107:23–27)

**Fig. 1.4: The Elah Valley**
*Traditional site of the David-Goliath fight*

**Fig. 1.5: The Samarian Hills**

You rule the raging of the sea;
    when its waves rise, you still them.       (89:9)

Note how the writers of these texts portray the sea as a dangerous and forbidding place. They likely never traveled by ship and probably never learned how to sail, fish, or swim.

Also to the west, between the highland area around Jerusalem and the southern part of the coastal plain, lies the Shephelah. This zone of low foothills functions as a natural buffer, as well as an arena of conflict,

**Fig. 1.6: The Jezreel Valley**
*A panoramic view of the Jezreel Valley (also known as the Esdraelon Valley) taken from Megiddo, an ancient city overlooking this valley from the southwest.*

between the Israelites and the Philistines. The biblical text narrates many battles fought in this area: here, for instance, is where 1 Sam 17 situates the story of David's killing of the Philistine giant Goliath.

But rather than journeying to the west, one might consider traveling northward. A day or two of walking brings a sojourner well into the Samarian highlands. The mountains here look less steep than those in the south, and with more open and flat valleys in between. The land appears more lush and green, since it receives more rainfall. Barley and wheat grow in the valleys, and intensive terracing on the hills supports grapevines and olive and fig trees. The people here recently broke away from Jerusalem's political control and formed their own kingdom, called **Israel** (as opposed to the kingdom of **Judah**). But despite the political separation, the two states share a broadly common language, religion, history, traditions, and social customs.

To the north of the Samarian highlands lies the Jezreel Valley (also called the Esdraelon Valley), a huge flat plain about twenty by fifty miles (thirty-two by eighty kilometers) in size. Featuring rich alluvial soils and plentiful water, it attracts many settlers. But kings, military generals, and caravan owners also prize it. As the only major east-west valley in the entire highland area, it is the favored place for transporting people and materials from

### Armageddon

The writer of the New Testament book of Revelation locates the final end-time battle in the Jezreel Valley, naming it Armageddon (Rev 16:14, 16). The name comes from *har*, Hebrew for "mountain," and Megiddo, the name of the city located at one end of this valley. In subsequent times Armageddon has sometimes taken on a more symbolic meaning, thus severing its link to a particular geographical spot. Now, for instance, the term more generally refers to events leading up to, or marking, an end of the world.

the coastal plain to regions farther east. Through the years many armies have fought over it. The story of Gideon defeating the Midianites and Amalekites, for instance, is set in this valley (Judg 6:33–7:23). Likewise, 1 Sam 29 tells of an Israelite army encamping here the night before suffering a terrible defeat at the hands of the Philistines.

Continuing the journey northward brings one to Galilee. At least fifty miles (eighty kilometers) from Jerusalem, this region would be much farther than most ancient peoples would travel at any time in their entire lives. The people living here are a rather mixed bunch: some share with Israelites a similar language as well as related beliefs and customs; others do not. The topography is similar to that of the Samarian highlands: hills and mountains interspersed with fertile, east-west valleys. But its northern location means it receives even more rain and so has an abundance of varied plant and animal life. Also, the hills of southern Galilee are less steep, with more open and flat valleys in between. But northern Galilee is quite mountainous and includes the highest mountain in the region (Har Meiron, 3937 feet/1208 meters above sea level). And to the north beyond Galilee the topography becomes even more steep and forbidding. Here the mountains of Lebanon—occasionally snowcapped—define the landscape.

But still if a Jerusalem traveler decides not to venture north, other directions beckon. Heading south into the Judean highlands, for instance, eventually brings one to Hebron, about twenty miles (thirty-two kilometers) away. (The city is home to the traditional cave tomb of Abraham.) Journeying southward, however, means facing increasingly difficult traveling conditions. The land becomes progressively hotter, more arid, and with ever steeper hills and valleys. The people living in this region find growing crops challenging; many emphasize the herding of sheep and goats instead. And even further to the south lies the Negev (whose name means "south" in Hebrew). A harsh land receiving scarcely any rainfall, one finds here forbidding mountains, deep rifts, and intense desert heat. Some wanderers pasture flocks in certain parts, but most sections cannot sustain habitation.

Consider, then, another direction. East of the city a road descends rather steeply from Jerusalem to the ancient site of Jericho. At a distance of about fifteen miles (twenty-four kilometers), one can easily make the journey in a day. Almost immediately after starting out, the terrain becomes dry, rocky, and barren. No trees or bushes (except at occasional springs) appear, and there is only sparse grass. No one lives or farms here, though shepherds sometimes pasture their flocks after the winter rains. Also, bandits haunt the area.

After reaching Jericho, another seven miles (eleven kilometers) of walking brings one to the Jordan River. This river runs along the great Rift Valley, a huge crack in the surface of the earth. The rift itself extends north-south from Turkey all the way to central Africa. Modern geologists know that a fault line between two tectonic plates caused this crack; the area experiences

**Fig. 1.7: The Galilean Highlands**

**Fig. 1.8: Mount Hermon, a Prominent Mountain Northeast of Galilee**

occasional earthquakes. The songs of the Israelites again speak of such phenomena.

> The voice of the LORD shakes the wilderness;
>   the LORD shakes the wilderness of Kadesh.
> The voice of the LORD causes the oaks to whirl,
>   And strips the forest bare.                    (Ps 29:8–9)

> Then the earth reeled and rocked;
>   the foundations also of the mountains trembled
>   and quaked, because he was angry.             (18:7)

**Fig. 1.9: The Negev**

**Fig. 1.10: Part of the Ancient Road from Jerusalem to Jericho**

> You have caused the land to quake; you have torn it open;
>   repair the cracks in it, for it is tottering.    (60:2)

Somewhere far to the north, in the Lebanon mountains, the headwaters of the Jordan emerge. Before its waters reach to the south, they pass through Lake Huleh and then the Sea of Galilee. The latter, also known as Kinnereth, is actually a huge freshwater lake some twelve miles (twenty kilometers) long and seven miles (eleven kilometers) wide. People living around it fish its waters.

**Fig. 1.11: The Sea of Galilee**
*A panoramic view taken from the north*

**Fig. 1.12: The Transjordanian Highlands from the Rift Valley**
*A view of the Transjordanian Highlands in the background. The Rift Valley, with the Jordan River flowing through it, is at the center of the picture.*

Across the Jordan, straight to the east, one sees the land rising quite sharply from the Rift Valley. At the top it levels out into a broad plateau, called the Transjordanian highlands. Running north-south, it parallels the highland area on the opposite side of the Jordan River. And although slightly higher in elevation, it receives somewhat less rainfall. Still, its climate allows for crop farming and the herding of sheep and goats (except in the extreme south). Several east-west ravines and gorges cut through the plateau, subdividing it into a number of smaller territories. These are, from north to south, Bashan, Gilead, Ammon, Moab, and Edom. The peoples of Bashan and Gilead generally share beliefs and traditions similar to the Israelites. For instance, they too claim ancestry from Abraham and worship a deity named YHWH. But the peoples of Ammon, Moab, and Edom identify themselves otherwise; in particular, they worship gods other than YHWH. Yet their customs and lifestyle also have many points of contact with the Israelites, such as subsistence agriculture, extended families grouped into small villages, and animal sacrifice in worship of their deity. Nevertheless, numerous and varied clashes have occurred between the Ammonites, Moabites, and Edomites, and the people of Israel, driven partly by competing claims for territory. Consider especially the accounts of David's campaigns against Ammon (see 2 Sam 10–11).

**Fig. 1.13: The Jordan River Just South of the Sea of Galilee**

Venturing into the Transjordan requires crossing the Jordan River, and that can be tricky. Although <u>only about ten feet (three meters) wide</u> and three feet (one meter) deep here, its current runs swiftly. Reaching the plateau on the other side requires a long, steep climb up from the valley floor.

Turning to the south and following the course of the Jordan River brings one to the Dead Sea. Here the landscape is bleak and blasted, evoking awe and wonder in those who view it. Cream, tan, and reddish rocks rise up, shimmering in the heat. No greenery is visible. And nothing moves; the land seems entirely lifeless. The surreal appearance of it all makes it more akin to a moonscape than a terrestrial landscape. According to modern scientists, it took several extreme factors coming together to produce this place: (1) its location 1,293 feet (394 meters) below sea level, making it the lowest spot on the earth's surface; (2) its extreme dryness, receiving as it does only 3 inches (89 millimeters) of rain a year; and (3) the acute heat, such that in summer the temperatures can top out at 140 degrees Fahrenheit (60 degrees Celsius). And then there is the high mineral content of the Dead Sea. With a 25–30 percent salt content, this sea is the saltiest body of water on earth.

## only about ten feet (three meters) wide

The Jordan River's small dimensions often surprise those who view it for the first time. Most likely certain Christian hymns extolling its grandeur contribute to mistaken assumptions about its size. Consider, for instance, the lyrics from stanzas three and four of a hymn by Isaac Watts, "There Is a Land of Pure Delight":

> Sweet fields beyond the swelling flood
> Stand dressed in living green:
> So to the Jews old Canaan stood,
> While Jordan rolled between.

> But timorous mortals start and shrink
> To cross this narrow sea;
> And linger, shiv'ring on the brink,
> And fear to launch away.

Or look at the first and last stanzas of "On Jordan's Stormy Banks I Stand," by Samuel Stennett:

> On Jordan's stormy banks I stand,
> And cast a wishful eye
> To Canaan's fair and happy land,
> Where my possessions lie.

> Filled with delight my raptured soul
> Would here no longer stay;
> Though Jordan's waves around me roll,
> Fearless I'd launch away.

The real Jordan River rarely, if ever, floods. Nor does it call forth comparisons to a sea. Further, however modest its dimensions in the past, in recent decades it has shrunk even further. Competition over the rights to its waters—chiefly involving Syria, Lebanon, Israel, Jordan, and Palestine—has led to its marked depletion. At many times now scarcely a trickle flows in Jordan's riverbed south of the Sea of Galilee.

**Fig. 1.14: The Terrain Surrounding the Dead Sea**
*The Dead Sea in the distance is bracketed by barren hills.*

**Fig. 1.15: Swimmers Floating in the Dead Sea**
*The high mineral content of the Dead Sea allows these four swimmers to stay afloat in the water without any use of either their arms or legs.*

(Valuable minerals such as rock salt and bitumen come from it.) In fact, when people swim in it, the high mineral content actually buoys them up.

Continuing southward leads one along the western shore of the Dead Sea. On the right, rocky, reddish-brown hills rise sharply from the plain. Among these hills numerous ravines and gorges thread their way.

**Fig. 1.16: The Judean Wilderness on the West Side of the Dead Sea**

**Fig. 1.17: Salt Formations at the Dead Sea**

According to many tales, the caves pocketing this area serve as a favorite refuge for outlaws. Some stories tell about how David, before becoming king, hid out here when Saul, ruler at that time, was trying to kill him (see, e.g., 1 Sam 24). The salt formations emerging from the shores of the Dead Sea also provoke comment. Here what especially comes to mind is the tale of how God changed Lot's wife into a pillar of salt for looking back at the destruction of Sodom and Gomorrah (Gen 19:26).

South of the Dead Sea lies only the Arabah (Hebrew for "desert plain"), which extends southward some 103 miles (165 kilometers) to the Gulf of Aqaba on the Red Sea. An arid flatland covered with alluvial sand and gravel, its vegetation comprises largely just sagebrush, camel thorns, and acacia. Its heat and aridity make it impossible for agriculture, and the region is largely devoid of people. Yet the area does have value insofar as it contains the only deposits of iron and copper ore accessible to those living in the **Cisjordan**. Further, the Gulf of Aqaba, with its port of Ezion-geber, serves as a gateway for sea trade with Egypt, Africa, and Arabia. But it is very, very hot.

*Context for Understanding the Hebrew Bible's Geography*

Most of the Hebrew Bible's stories played out in the landscapes described above. Bounded on the west by the sea, on the north by mountains, and on the east and south by deserts, the land possessed a hemmed-in quality. It was also small, its total size about that of New Jersey or Vancouver Island (about 256 miles [410 kilometers] north-south and 75 miles [120 kilometers] east-west). But contiguous territory also contributed to the Hebrew Bible's geography, particularly northeastern Africa and western Asia. Of most significance were two great river valleys, both supporting huge centralized states. In Africa the Nile River valley gave rise to the various Egyptian kingdoms, and in Asia the Euphrates and Tigris Rivers nourished Mesopotamia, an area that birthed the ancient states of Sumer, **Babylonia** and **Assyria**. (Mesopotamia, Greek for "between the two rivers," approximates present-day Iraq.) In addition, Syria, also called Aram and situated northwest of Mesopotamia, functioned as a sort of buffer between Mesopotamia and the biblical heartland.

In ancient times this whole region demarcated an arc of green. One could trace it starting at the mouth of the Euphrates and Tigris Rivers, follow it northwest through Mesopotamia and west through Syria to the Mediterranean, pursue it as it turned south through Palestine and then into northeast Africa, and finally reach its end by following the Nile River south. Called the **Fertile Crescent** by geographers, this arc marks the preferred zone of human habitation. The Cisjordan, situated in the middle of the arc, provides the only passable land routes connecting Africa to Asia; it thus serves as a land bridge connecting the two continents. As such, it often found itself caught up in the rivalries and power struggles of the various polities throughout the area.

Today this region is recognized in terms of the nation-states that control it: Egypt, Israel, Palestine, Jordan, Syria, Lebanon, Turkey, Iraq, and Iran. The label "Middle East" refers to the area as a whole. (Scholars, following older practice, often use the term "Near East.") The use of such terms depends largely on those who originate and utilize them. For instance, "Middle East" or "Near East" reveals a European perspective picked up by those who live in North America. During times of colonization, these peoples defined this area of the world from their own positioning and then

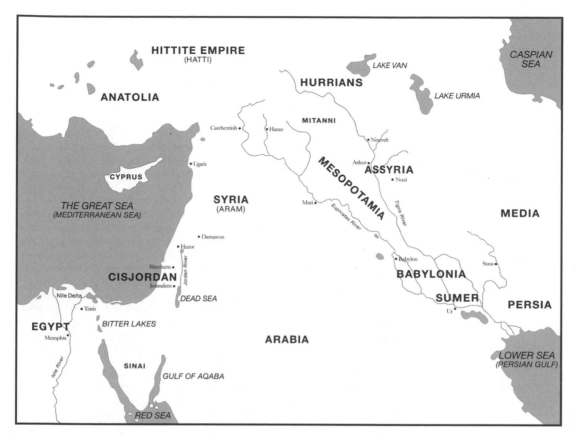

HITTITE EMPIRE
(HATTI)

ANATOLIA

HURRIANS

LAKE VAN

LAKE URMIA

CASPIAN
SEA

MITANNI

Carchemish •    • Haran

• Nineveh

• Ugarit

Ashur •
ASSYRIA
• Nuzi

CYPRUS

THE GREAT SEA
(MEDITERRANEAN SEA)

SYRIA
(ARAM)

MESOPOTAMIA

• Mari

Euphrates River

Tigris River

MEDIA

• Damascus

• Hazor

Shechem •
CISJORDAN
Jerusalem •

Jordan River

DEAD SEA

Nile Delta •

• Tanis

• Babylon

• Susa

BABYLONIA

SUMER

PERSIA

• Ur

EGYPT

BITTER LAKES

Memphis •

ARABIA

LOWER SEA
(PERSIAN GULF)

Nile River

SINAI

GULF OF AQABA

RED SEA

**Fig. 1.18: Map of the Ancient Near East**
*Map of the ancient Near East shows those states and regions that shaped the broader geography of the biblical world.*

imposed it on others. The pervasive use of both "Near East" and "Middle East" thus illustrates the ongoing hegemony of the so-called "West." This example demonstrates how names carry meaning and how place names typically lack political innocence or cultural neutrality. Think about the names for your own city, state, or country. Where did they come from and what do they mean? What claims, political or otherwise, do they make? How else have they been named, and by whom?

A variety of designations labeled the land serving as the immediate back-drop for the Hebrew Bible; all of them reflect particular human interests in the land. *Canaan* appears in many ancient writings (including the Hebrew Bible) beginning about 1400 B.C.E. It comes from a Semitic word meaning "reddish purple" and seems to refer to a valuable dye produced in the area from a certain type of seashell. *Palestine* derives from the biblical Hebrew word *peleshet*, meaning "the land of the Philistines." Its common use began with the Romans after 135 C.E. in the form *Palaestina*. After World War I the British revived this nomenclature, which continues to the present, naming the political entity Palestine. *Israel*, also a Hebrew term (*yisrael*), means "strives with God," or "God strives." Appearing in the Hebrew Bible, it names both the family descended from Jacob—renamed Israel in Gen 32:28—and the territory they inhabited. Like Palestine, its modern revival now names the modern state of Israel, formally created and recognized in 1948 C.E. "Holy Land" finds usage among the religiously devout, resonating with this land's sacredness to the three religions of Judaism, Christianity,

## Naming Places

In North America many names currently used for cities, bodies of water, and land areas actually derive from Native American, or First Nations, tribal words. For instance, Minnesota comes from a Dakota word meaning "sky-tinted waters." One of the Great Lakes, Huron, recalls the name of an east coast Native American tribal confederacy. And Manhattan, a borough of New York City, derives from the Lenape word *manna-hata*, meaning "island of many hills." In these cases, new political and cultural contexts have taken over terms used in older contexts, while also sometimes applying them in new ways. Other names, however, mark a more profound change in how a particular place is referenced. For instance, most people know of Philadelphia as the city of "brotherly love." The name, of course, derives from two Greek words meaning "loved or friendly" and "brother." But the Native Americans referred to the locality using a different name: *Coaquannok*, meaning "grove of tall pine trees." Regina, a city in Canada, received its name in honor of Queen Victoria. But before that naming, the Cree, as well as the first white settlers, knew the place as *Oscana*, meaning "pile of bones." (The reference was to piles of buffalo bones.) Similarly, early European settlers named the territory—and eventually state—of New York in honor of the English Duke of York. But the Iroquois referred to upstate New York as "the endless forests." But perhaps the best example of this politics of naming comes from Russia. In 1703 the Russian tsar Peter the Great founded a city on the Baltic Sea to serve as Russia's new capital; it was named St. Petersburg in his honor. In 1914, spurred on by anti-German sentiment, "burg" was modified to "grad" (a Slavic word for town or city); the religious connotation was also voided by dropping "saint." And so the city became known as Petrograd. However, in 1924 its name changed again—to Leningrad—in honor of Vladimir Lenin, founder of the Soviet Union. But with the collapse of communism in 1989, the name of the city changed yet again, reverting back to St. Petersburg (although some old-timers still refer to it as Leningrad).

## a certain type of seashell

The murex seashell, found along the eastern Mediterranean coast, contains a certain secretion that yields purple dye. However, actually obtaining the dye requires a multistep and labor-intensive manufacturing process. In ancient times laborers first gathered the shells from the sea, then crushed them, then boiled them in salt, and finally placed them in the sun to dry. Only at that point did the shells' secretion turn purple. Note further that it took eight thousand shells to produce just one gram of dye. That, along with the demanding processing, made this particular dye precious and rare. Only the very rich could afford clothes or other woven materials dyed this color. Even today it persists as a marker of wealth and status in the custom of coloring royal robes purple.

and Islam. "Promised land" functions similarly, though it expresses the more specific belief that God gave this land as a divine gift to the ancient Israelites.

In this textbook certain specific contexts will demand use of the terms *Canaan*, *Palestine*, or *Israel*. But given the particular cultural and/or political perspectives carried by each of them, the more general label *Cisjordan*, meaning "this side of the Jordan River," will most often be used instead. Though still reflecting a certain standpoint—one privileging the west side of the Jordan River—specific religious, cultural, or political agendas attach themselves less obviously to it.

## Time

The relative nature of space, linked to human naming processes, extends to ideas about time. Upon first consideration, claiming that time is arbitrary might seem ridiculous. After all, the ordering of time relies on unvarying natural phenomena: for example, a day measures one rotation of the earth on its axis, and a year recognizes the time it takes for the earth to circle once around the sun. Yet beyond these fixed elements, much about time depends on human decisions. For instance, dividing the day into twenty-four units (hours) originated with the ancient Egyptians, who based it on the rising of certain stars at different "hours" of the night. And when does a day begin? Hindus say at sunrise, Jews and Muslims say at sundown, and the modern west points to midnight as the beginning.

When it comes to enumerating years, even more variability rules. The year that many identify as A.D. 2000 the Jewish calendar identifies as 5761 A.M., the Muslim calendar designates as 1378 A.H., and the geological calendar calculates as however many years have elapsed before the present year.

This textbook follows a B.C. reckoning (along with its A.D. counterpart) with one modification. Along with many other scholars, the more neutral designation B.C.E. (before the Common Era) replaces B.C. (before Christ) and C.E. (Common Era) serves instead of A.D. (anno Domini, "in year of the Lord"). This system follows common western practice over many other possible systems. Of course, the peoples of the Hebrew Bible neither knew nor used it. They numbered their years in a much more localized and particular way, depending at times primarily on the regnal years of kings. Such reckonings occur frequently in the biblical books of 1 and 2 Kings (e.g., "In the thirty-eighth year of Asa king of Judah, Ahab the son of Omri began to reign over Israel" [1 Kgs 16:29]; "In the fifth year of King Rehoboam [of Judah], Shishak king of Egypt came up against Jerusalem" [1 Kgs 14:25]). And even that might have been too sophisticated and out of reach for many of the people; they accounted for years simply according to the life spans of family or village members, or notable events of their world (e.g., a famine, earthquake, military conquest; see Amos 1:1).

## The Making of Different Calendars

The tradition of marking dates in the western world as A.D. or B.C. goes back ultimately to a Christian monk, Dionysius Exiguus (Dennis the Small), who lived during the passing away of the Roman Empire. Around A.D. 525 he suggested a new method for dating events, choosing as time's fixed point the birth year of Jesus Christ. All years subsequent to that event he designated as A.D. (for *anno Domini*, Latin for "year of the Lord"); as a result, the further forward in time one went from that year, the larger the year numbers would become. Not until the early eighth century, however, did the English historian and theologian Bede begin marking years prior to Jesus' birth date as B.C. (before Christ); here the year numbers become larger the further back in time one goes (e.g., 1000 B.C. is earlier in time than 500 B.C.). Although Dionysius's calendar did not win immediate acceptance, eventually it came to dominate much of the world.

Meanwhile, the Jewish calendar reckons years according to its dating of the world's creation. By reading the Hebrew Bible rather literally, it computes the beginning of the world as 3761 B.C. (under the B.C./A.D. system). All its year-numbers thus count forward from that date. The Islamic calendar bases itself on the date the prophet Muhammad fled from Mecca to Medina, an event called the *Hegira*. According to the B.C./A.D. system, the *Hegira* took place in A.D. 622. An Islamic calendrical reckoning thus counts forward all year dates from that year, and it marks them with the abbreviation A.H., which stands for the Latin phrase *anno Hegirae*, "in the year of the *Hegira*." Anthropologists and geologists who deal with extremely remote times count years backward from the present year, identifying a certain date as B.P. (before the present). This last calendar is fluid since the present year date is always changing. But the difference is superfluous since the times dealt with are so remote (i.e., thousands if not millions of years ago). When dealing with such immense spans of time, a variation of tens or even hundreds of years makes no real difference.

## Absolute Chronologies

Dating a certain event according to the B.C.E./C.E. calendar means fixing it according to an absolute chronology. But how do historians correlate events reported in ancient texts as, say, occurring in the fourteenth year of the reign of so-and-so with our calendrical reckoning? The process is akin to putting together a huge jigsaw puzzle with many of the pieces either missing or broken. The pieces include data from ancient texts, particularly the regnal years of named kings (or, rarely, queens). These texts often also list the order in which the kings ruled, which aids historians in fitting some of the puzzle pieces together. But finishing the puzzle often depends on synchronisms of at least two sorts: (1) information that correlates the reign of a king in one country with that of another (e.g., 1 Kgs 14:25 synchronizes the fifth regnal year of the Judean king Rehoboam with the military campaign of the Egyptian king Shishak), and (2) astronomical observations recorded in ancient texts, such as comets or solar eclipses, which modern astronomers can often date precisely according to our calendar. Still, lack of information presents many challenges to the process. So does potentially unreliable data, such as mistakes in the text and coregencies that are not identified. Currently there are good absolute chronologies for much of the ancient Near East only through the first millennium B.C.E. (i.e., as far back as 1000 B.C.E.). Earlier than that we must approximate, marking those dates with *ca.*, which stands for *circa*, meaning "around, about."

From today's perspective, a person living in Jerusalem in 900 B.C.E. lived long, long ago. But from that person's perspective, a long, long history preceded him or her. In 900 B.C.E. the Egyptian pyramids were already almost two thousand years old, and human habitation in the area had started almost a million years previously. However, what, or how, this ancient Jerusalemite knew about the past remains unknown since the Hebrew Bible did not emerge until several hundred years later. (Chapter 2 gives more detail about how the biblical text was produced.) Of course, the Hebrew Bible does include accounts about times in the distant past. Yet its authors composed them within their own frames of reference and according to their particular knowledge and concerns.

The next section compares how scholars look at the earliest periods of human history with how the writers of the Hebrew Bible depicted the remote past. Such a comparison helps in thinking about biblical perspectives on time and history.

*Earliest Periods (The Stone and Copper Ages)*

Archaeologists categorize time for the earliest periods of human history according to the material out of which humans crafted their tools. The Stone Age thus characterizes the first main period of time; it falls into three main subdivisions: old, middle, and new. The Old Stone Age, or Paleolithic Era (*paleo* = old, *lithic* = stone), began almost a million years ago and ended about 18,000 B.C.E. In the Cisjordan this era includes the emergence of the first human life (of a type related to the Neanderthals of Europe). Archaeologists have found their remains in caves at Mount Carmel on the Mediterranean seacoast. The Middle Stone Age, also called the Mesolithic Era (*meso* = middle), comprises a period of time from ca. 18,000 to 8500 B.C.E. At this time excavations reveal the first semipermanent settlements, with notable burials, at places such as Jericho. The New Stone Age, or Neolithic Era (*neo* = new), dates to ca. 8500–4000 B.C.E. In it human innovations accelerated, prompted especially by the so-called agricultural revolution. That is, up to this point in time humans had sustained themselves largely by gathering wild foods, whether that meant hunting wild animals or collecting wild plants. But now they begin producing foods, both by deliberately planting and nurturing certain grains, and by caring for and breeding such animals as sheep and goats. A more secure food supply led to other inventions, such as intentionally manipulating clay into pottery. Neolithic peoples also built what some scholars recognize as the first city in the area, at Jericho.

In the Copper Age (ca. 4000–3200 B.C.E.), or Chalcolithic era (*chalcos* = copper), people innovated further. They discovered how to process copper metal into tools, weapons, and jewelry. They evinced a more sophisticated artistic aesthetic—painting frescoes on building walls and fashioning figurines out of ivory, stone, copper, and pottery. They also made use of material artifacts in their religious observances, as exemplified by a collection found at Nahal Mishmar, near the Dead Sea.

**Fig. 1.19: Neolithic Jericho**
*A tower at Jericho; its construction dates to Neolithic times.*

When the biblical writers imagined humanity's beginnings, they did so in terms of stories. (They obviously lacked access to contemporary methodologies of scientific investigation and reporting.) And in their stories they envisioned all of humanity originating with one family: Adam, Eve, and their sons Cain, Abel, and Seth. But as they narrate the stories about this "first family" in Gen 4, the writers allude to some of the same innovations of early humankind discerned by archaeologists. For instance, the story of Cain and Abel's rivalry in Gen 4:1–5 recalls the beginnings of agriculture, as well as the religious practice of sacrificing to a deity. In the continuation of Cain's story, the text narrates the building of the first city (Gen 4:17). A bit later the text mentions the development of metallurgy, as well as the beginnings of pastoralism and music (Gen 4:20–22).

Moreover, the genealogy in Gen 5 communicates, among other things, the notion of a huge expanse of time stretching far into the past. This resonates with the archaeological record and its reckoning of the Stone and Copper Ages as together encompassing upward of a million years. But the biblical writers operate not with a geological or archaeological frame of reference, but rather with a human-centered one. Hence, they imagine this immense span of past time by attributing unbelievably long life spans to the first generations of humans: according to Gen 5, anywhere from 777 to 969 years for a single individual. Yet modern forensic studies of the skeletal remains of the earliest humans tell us they lived brief lives, averaging perhaps only twenty years or so.

When biblical writers and modern archaeologists articulate the ancient past, they each frame it in distinctive ways. All are constrained by what they know, how they know it, and how they value what they know. In each case, though, the past they reconstruct spans an immense period of time: all the years stretching from humankind's beginnings to, say, 3200 B.C.E. add up to many more than all the years from 3200 B.C.E. to the present.

*The Bronze Age (ca. 3200–1200 B.C.E.)*

In the next period of time humans first made use of bronze, a metal alloy of copper and tin that is much stronger than copper alone. Historians subdivide it, too, into early (3200–2200 B.C.E.), middle (2200–1550 B.C.E.), and late (1550–1200 B.C.E.) ages. This period marks the beginning of the Israelites,

## The Heroic Past and Human Life Spans

A number of the world's cultures tell stories in which they imagine the first humans living incredibly long lives, crediting them sometimes with life spans of hundreds of years or more. Various reasons probably explain this phenomenon. For instance, later writers, looking back toward all the significant cultural achievements of their ancestors, perhaps felt the need to create a span of time immense enough, as they thought, for all those innovations to emerge. Also, to honor those early rulers who ruled with great wisdom, justice, and mercy, the people sometimes deified them; or, if not going so far as to actually esteem them as gods—and so as immortal—they at least envisioned them with immensely long life spans. Stories about the early days of humans on earth also often envision that time, when the world was fresh and young, as somehow especially blessed and good. The Greek poet Hesiod (ca. 750 B.C.E.), for instance, wrote in *Works and Days* about earlier times: ". . . and they [people] lived like gods, with carefree heart, remote from toil and misery. Wretched old age did not affect them either, but with hands and feet ever unchanged they enjoyed themselves in feasting, beyond all ills, and they died as if overcome by sleep. All good things were theirs, and the grain-giving soil bore its fruits of its own accord in unstinted plenty, while they at their leisure harvested their fields in contentment amid abundance." Such thinking resonates with how people even today sentimentalize "the good ole days."

Hesiod, *Theogony; and, Works and Days*, translated with an introduction and notes by M. L. West (Oxford: Oxford University Press, 1988), 40.

relative latecomers on the stage of ancient Near Eastern history. They are the people on whom the Hebrew Bible focuses.

The one thousand years of the Early Bronze Age saw the rise of impressive civilizations in the two great river valleys of the ancient Near East: Egypt and Mesopotamia. Strong leaders emerged in both places, centralizing their power in palaces and temples. They organized large-scale irrigation-based agriculture, developing complex networks of canals and channels that brought water up from the rivers; these enhanced the land's productivity in an otherwise arid climate. They also invented writing to better track the collection, storage, and trade of goods. Eventually scribes used writing also to record their cultures' myths, hymns, law codes, epics, proverbs, and other wise sayings. Surplus wealth enabled the leaders to sponsor huge building projects. In Egypt they built the great pyramids; in Mesopotamia the people constructed similar sorts of structures known as ziggurats (see fig. 1.20).

The Hebrew Bible evokes this time period in, most likely, only two stories: Noah and the flood (Gen 6–9), and the tower of Babel (Gen 11:1–9). The biblical flood story reads similarly to several accounts coming from Mesopotamia at this time that also tell of an immense and destructive deluge. The detailed similarities suggest that the biblical version borrowed from, or was influenced by, one or more of the Mesopotamian accounts (e.g., the Atrahasis Epic, the Epic of Gilgamesh). And Gen 11 not only locates the building of the tower of Babel in Shinar (the biblical term for southern Mesopotamia), but the description of its features also corresponds to those of the Mesopotamian ziggurats.

**Fig. 1.20: Model of the Ziggurat at Ur (in Southern Mesopotamia)**

## Sumer and Old Egypt

Mesopotamia's first civilization was the work of a people known as the Sumerians. Emerging in the south in the late fourth millennium B.C.E., they founded a series of city-states along the lower Euphrates and Tigris Rivers. The Sumerians are especially notable for a number of human "firsts": kingship, slavery, law codes, writing, schools, ziggurats, irrigation, the standardizing of weights and measures, the use of capital for investment purposes, and a base 60 (sexagesimal) system of counting and computation. Many Sumerian achievements found parallels in ancient Egypt, though the Egyptians may have lagged behind by a century or two. In some instances the Egyptians probably borrowed from the Sumerians, though at other times the Egyptians perhaps developed new technologies and institutions on their own.

Both the Sumerian and old Egyptian kingdoms were remarkably long-lived. The Sumerians lasted from before 3000 B.C.E. to about 2000 B.C.E., except for an interregnum of about 150 years (ca. 2300–2150 B.C.E.) when the Akkadians ruled them. Egypt's dynasties began in about 3000 B.C.E. when a man named Menes unified both Upper (the southern) and Lower (the northern Delta region) Egypt; he also founded the capital city of Memphis. An Archaic period, about which we know little, followed from roughly 3000 to 2700 B.C.E. During the next period, the Old Kingdom, many of Egypt's great early achievements took place, notably the building of the Great Pyramids. It lasted until the central government collapsed in about 2200 B.C.E. The First Intermediate Period then followed, a time of decline and disarray lasting about two hundred years.

The civilized splendors of the Early Bronze Age eventually gave way to a time of disarray and chaos. The unified empires broke apart; many of the cities collapsed. Sparse written records communicate few specifics, but excavated remains indicate that for several hundred years many peoples turned to a pastoral existence, living in seasonal camps or small hamlets and villages. Although some cities survived, they were generally of a more modest nature than those of the preceding Early Bronze Age. However, by around 2000 B.C.E. many of the old cities began to revive and new ones emerged. These became the centers of a new series of city-states and kingdoms throughout the Cisjordan, Syria, and Mesopotamia. In Egypt, meanwhile, the collapse into the chaos of the so-called First Intermediate Period ended. Strong pharaohs established a series of dynasties known today as the period of the Middle Kingdom (ca. 2050–1550 B.C.E.).

The Hebrew Bible locates Israel's immediate ancestors in this approximate time period. Sometimes called the patriarchs and matriarchs of Israel, they include Abraham and his wife, Sarah, their son Isaac and his wife, Rebekah, and finally Isaac and Rebekah's son Jacob, along with Jacob's many women and children. Their stories appear in Gen 12–50. But though Abraham and his family loom large in the Hebrew Bible, no texts outside of it testify to their existence. Nor do the outside texts mention any of the few foreign leaders named in Genesis. Making specific correlations between the biblical text and surviving written records of the time thus proves impossible. However, the ancestors' general lifestyle of wandering from Mesopotamia throughout Palestine and into Egypt does make some sense within the early part of this time period. Also, some of their sociocultural practices may parallel practices

### When Did Abraham and His Family Live?

Many earlier biblical scholars placed Abraham and his family in the Middle Bronze Age on the basis of three main lines of evidence. First, a number of their personal names—such as Abram and Jacob—were common in both Mesopotamia and Cisjordan in the early second millennium. Second, their sociocultural practices parallel those reported in texts from fifteenth century Nuzi, a city in Mesopotamia. Third, a number of cities in Cisjordan linked with Abraham's family were occupied and flourishing in the early second millennium, such as Shechem, Bethel, Hebron, Gerar, and Beersheba.

However, more recent archaeological discoveries have cast doubt upon many of the above findings. First, the names used were not limited to just the early second millennium. They also readily appear in a number of texts from later times. Something similar operates for the second point. That is, the sociocultural practices of Abraham's family have parallels also in texts from the first millennium. And finally, more recent and careful excavating has revealed that many of Cisjordan's urban centers were actually unoccupied in the early second millennium—even those supposedly visited by Abraham and his family. (For further discussion of the historicity of Israel's ancestors, see chapter 2, in particular the section "Writing History with the Hebrew Bible.")

evident from the city-states and kingdoms of Mesopotamia: for example, adopting a slave as heir, substituting a slave woman for an infertile wife, favoring a younger son over the elder, and possessing and utilizing household gods. But the connections are far from assured or convincing.

In any case, the biblical book of Genesis highlights how God chooses Abraham and his family, from all the peoples of the world, as the people of God. In doing so, God also makes them two promises: (1) they will eventually burgeon into numerous descendants (as many "as the stars of heaven and as the sand which is on the seashore" [Gen 22:17]), and (2) they will possess the land of Cisjordan as their own.

Just as the Early Bronze Age ended with established political entities collapsing, so too does the Middle Bronze Age end. A people known as the Hyksos invade Egypt and establish control over Lower Egypt (the northern region) for about one hundred years (ca. 1650–1542 B.C.E.). The Hurrians, who seem to have originated in the mountains of Armenia, sweep into northern Mesopotamia and Syria, and even the Cisjordan. In southern Mesopotamia, Kassites appear; they come from further east, from the highlands of Iran. By 1550 B.C.E., though, some political stability again takes root with new empires emerging. The Egyptians expel the Hyksos, and the many powerful pharaohs of the Egyptian New Kingdom (ca. 1550–1069 B.C.E.) arise; they come to rule an empire encompassing all of Egypt, the Cisjordan, and southern Syria. In northern Syria the kingdom of Mitanni, dominated by Hurrians, holds sway. Still further to the north, in central Asia Minor, the Hittites, whose origins remain obscure to us, establish their dominion. And in northern Mesopotamia the **Assyrians** first emerge as a political presence.

## The Collapse of 1200 B.C.E.

What ultimately caused the catastrophes that overwhelmed the Mediterranean and Near East regions around 1200 B.C.E.? The question both fascinates and challenges those interested in the ancient history of this region. Egyptian and Hittite records both describe Sea Peoples invading. Many scholars tentatively identify these Sea Peoples as a mix of displaced Mycenaeans, "professional" bandits and raiders, and disaffected mercenary soldiers. But where did these peoples come from, and what prompted them to leave their own territories? And why did they so aggressively advance on the kingdoms of the Late Bronze Age? Were they fleeing famine? Plague? If so, what caused such a presumably massive outbreak of famine and/or plague at just this time? Did the region experience a climate change? That is, did a series of drier or cooler years cause crops to fail and make the population vulnerable to sickness and disease? Or were the Sea Peoples themselves fleeing attacks from yet other peoples coming in from farther to the north or west? If so, who were these other peoples, and what caused them to abandon their homelands for new places to live? This huge population upheaval near the end of the second millennium B.C.E. easily provokes more questions than answers.

It all ends in a spectacular collapse that engulfs the region beginning in the thirteenth century B.C.E. The Hittite kingdom disappears and Egypt's New Kingdom fails. (Mitanni had been destroyed a century earlier.) Farther to the east, the Assyrian kingdom declines. To the west, the Mycenaean civilization, centered in southern Greece, collapses. Homer's *Iliad*, which narrates so dramatically the fall of Troy, may well creatively elaborate on a real event symptomatic of the fall of the Mycenaeans. Egyptian texts from this time report "Sea Peoples" attacking; coming from the west, they are perhaps the last remnants of the Mycenaeans.

Within this chaotic time period many scholars place the origins of the Israelite people. In the Hebrew Bible, the story follows naturally upon that of the ancestors. That is, Abraham's third- and fourth-generation descendants have come to live in Egypt to escape a severe famine in the Cisjordan. But when their numbers multiply, the Egyptians enslave them; the people then cry out to God to save them. God, identified by the name "YHWH," then commissions Moses to deliver the people and lead them through the wilderness to their "promised land." On the way, according to Exodus, they stop at Mount Sinai. Here YHWH and the people enter into a covenant, a type of ancient pact in which both parties make solemn promises to the other. The Ten Commandments, as well as the other laws found in Exodus, Leviticus, Numbers, and Deuteronomy, constitute one element of this covenant.

The spectacle and drama of the exodus and wilderness wandering have fired the imaginations of many through the ages. Yet few, if any, of their elements correlate with extrabiblical events, persons, or places. The voluminous Egyptian records of the time never mention Moses. The Hebrew Bible leaves unnamed the pharaoh of the exodus. And the text traces out so vaguely the route taken by the people upon leaving Egypt and then through the wilderness that we cannot surely identify it (though not for want of trying!). Even the identification of Mount Sinai rests more on later pious tradition than secure historical or geographical evidence.

*The Iron Age (ca. 1200–600 B.C.E.)*

The next major archaeological period, the Iron Age, lasts some six hundred years and frames much of the political history of the Israelite people. In outline, the account in the Hebrew Bible begins with the people establishing themselves in Cisjordan. After some generations, they adopt a monarchy as their form of governance (ca. 1020 B.C.E.). But by ca. 922 B.C.E. the kingdom thereby created splits into two: the northern kingdom of Israel and the southern kingdom of Judah. Israel exists as a separate polity for another two hundred years before the Assyrians destroy it in 722/721 B.C.E. After that, Judah continues on until 587/586 B.C.E., when it too meets with disaster; this time it is the **Babylonians** who devastate the land and exile a portion of the populace.

Because the Hebrew Bible focuses on events and persons from approximately 1200 B.C.E. onward, this period will receive detailed attention. In doing so, the biblical texts themselves will serve as the primary guide, allow-ing readers to gain a sense of the sweep of the biblical retelling of the story of Israel. As well, this survey will provide some key names of figures who appear later in this textbook. The Hebrew Bible's retelling, though, should not be mistaken for a historically accurate presentation of the people and events of the period. Hence, on occasion, additional data will supplement (and, in some cases, contradict) what appears in the Hebrew Bible, thereby helping the reader contend with some of the difficulties in understanding this period historically.

### The Settlement Period (ca. 1200–1020 B.C.E.)

The Hebrew Bible claims that when Moses died, the leadership of the people devolved to Joshua. He functioned primarily as a military general, leading the people in conquering the land. Joshua 1–11 presents the campaign as quick, ruthless, and thorough. Afterward, the narrators show Joshua and the tribal elders overseeing the division of the land among the different tribes and their clans (Josh 12–22). The book of Joshua ends with these clans reaffirming their covenant commitments during a ceremony at Shechem (Josh 23–24).

With the death of Joshua, the text identifies no single leader arising in his stead. Instead, a series of leaders, known as judges, emerges that includes such individuals as Gideon, Samson, and Deborah. The English word "judges" is somewhat misleading, since these leaders did not, in the main,

---

### Various Subdivisions of the Iron Age

Unlike the Bronze Age, archaeologists disagree about how to subdivide the Iron Age. G. E. Wright argues that it consists of three main periods (Iron I [1200–1000 B.C.E.]; Iron II [1000–600 B.C.E.]; Iron III [600–330 B.C.E.]); he also extends it down to 330 B.C.E.. William Dever and Amihai Mazar both posit only two main periods and end it at 586 B.C.E. They also agree that Iron I includes two main subdivisions: IA (1200–1150 B.C.E.) and IB (1150–1000 B.C.E.). However, they disagree on the sub-divisions within the second main period. The three subdivisions of Dever's Iron II period run as follows: IIA (1000–900 B.C.E.); IIB (900–800 B.C.E.); IIC (800–586 B.C.E.). Mazar's Iron II period is slightly different: IIA (1000–925 B.C.E.); IIB (925–720 B.C.E.); IIC (720–586 B.C.E.). Eric Meyers, meanwhile, resurrects Wright's three main peri-ods for the Iron Age, although he proposes distinct subdivisions for both Iron I and II. He also concludes the Iron Age at 520 B.C.E. He thus fashions the chrono-logical structure for the Iron Age: IA (1200–1125 B.C.E.); IB (1125–1000 B.C.E.); IC (1000–925 B.C.E.); IIA (925–722 B.C.E.); IIB (722–586 B.C.E.); III (586–520 B.C.E.).

These different configurations arise partly from the extent to which textual influence—particularly the Hebrew Bible—is brought to bear on archaeological dating. It also depends on how one analyzes the evidence from material remains, particularly the pottery. Near Eastern archaeologists rely heavily on pot-tery changes for dating purposes. Hence, how one reads the sometimes subtle alterations in the forms and styles of Iron Age pottery will affect how one sees and structures the subdivisions of the Iron Age.

hear legal cases. Rather, these biblical judges acted as martial captains, coming forward at times of military crisis to inspire and lead the people, or at least some subgroup of them.

Besides judges, the narrative also refers to priests leading, guiding, and teaching the people. Some stories locate these priests at certain shrines scattered throughout the land, where they officiated at animal sacrifices and other religious ceremonies. One shrine in particular stands out: the one at Shiloh. A number of texts identify Shiloh as the site of the tent of meeting (Josh 18:1; 19:51b; 1 Sam 2:22b) and the ark of the covenant (1 Sam 1–3). This ark is described elsewhere as a small wooden chest overlaid with gold, holding the stone tablets inscribed with the Ten Commandments (Exod 25:10–22; 37:1–9; 1 Kgs 8:21). Shiloh also served as the home of Samuel, a priest who acted also as judge and prophet. The biblical texts depict his time, the latter part of the eleventh century B.C.E., as especially perilous for the Israelites. Not only did internal dissensions divide them (Judg 19–21), but also the Philistines, a people who had settled on the coastal plain around 1200 B.C.E., were menacing territories the Israelites claimed for themselves. The Hebrew Bible insists that, given these threats, Israel needed a stronger, more centralized leadership to survive.

### The United Monarchy (ca. 1020–922 B.C.E.)

Considerable tension exists in the Hebrew Bible about adopting a monarchical form of government. First Samuel 8–12, in particular, goes back and

### The Philistines

In the twelfth century B.C.E. Egypt experienced a wave of attacks from outsiders. Because they came from the sea, the Egyptians referred to them as Sea Peoples. Among the more than twenty groups who made up this collective of attackers were the Peleset, or Philistines. Their dress, architecture, and pottery styles suggest they came from the Aegean region; some scholars thus infer that they are the last remnants of the Mycenaeans. Although he drove them from Egypt, Pharaoh Rameses III did allow the Peleset to settle in the southern coastal region of Cisjordan. Here they set up a coalition of five cities: Gaza, Ashkelon, Ashdod, Gath, and Ekron. From this position the Philistines significantly challenged Israelite control over the area.

They thus feature broadly in Israel's imagination of its past. The book of Judges, for instance, tells stories about how Samson skirmishes with the Philistines, ultimately dying after toppling one of their temples onto himself and a crowd of Philistine revelers. First Samuel, meanwhile, involves the Philistines in the rise of David: chapter 17 portrays a youthful David proving his heroism by defeating the Philistine giant, Goliath. The Philistine military threat also more generally prompts the establishment of the Israelite monarchy, first under Saul and then under David and his descendants. Later, Philistine history broadly parallels that of Israel and Judah. For instance, like the Israelites, the Philistines were attacked and subdued first by the Assyrians and then by the Babylonians; they also at times served as vassals to Egypt.

forth on the pros and cons of kingship. Still, the narrative eventually depicts YHWH as directing Samuel to anoint Saul as the first king. More of a great warrior chieftain than a true king, Saul initially succeeds in stemming Philistine incursions. But then he runs afoul of Samuel and, according to the narrators, God as well.

David eventually emerges as the next king, with the text portraying him as the ideal Israelite monarch. In light of the text's claims concerning his military successes and his political astuteness, he certainly seems to deserve that reputation. Not only did he confine the Philistines to their coastal territory, but he also dominated Syria, Ammon, Moab, and Edom. Under his rule Israel supposedly expanded its territory to its greatest extent, from the Euphrates River to the northern Sinai desert, and from the Mediterranean to much of the Transjordan. In the political arena, the text depicts David's choosing for his capital Jerusalem, which was centrally located between north and south and did not belong to any of the Israelite tribes.

David also set up an administrative apparatus and prepared to build a temple to YHWH. Second Samuel 6 elaborates on how, with much fanfare, he paraded into the city with the ark of the covenant, thereby bringing under his control an artifact resonating with many of the traditions of the people. A follow-up text presents the zenith of his glory when YHWH makes a covenant with him in which YHWH promises David peace and prosperity and that his family line will reign in Jerusalem "forever" (2 Sam 7).

### David, Solomon, and History

Scholars recognize that the text's repeated assertions of greatness for David and Solomon and their achievements are problematic historically. A number of reasons support their claim:

1. In a number of places the biblical accounts exaggerate obviously (e.g., silver as common as stone [1 Kgs 10:27]; see also 1 Kgs 10:23–25).
2. Archaeology has demonstrated that David and Solomon's supposed base of power, the southern highlands, was thinly populated in the period. It could not have supported such a widespread empire.
3. At the supposed time of David and Solomon's rule, the records of the surrounding peoples contain absolutely no references to them.
4. Archaeologists have yet to discover significant remains from Jerusalem for the time period of David and Solomon.
5. Other supposed monuments to the united monarchy's power outside of Jerusalem, such as the fortifications at Megiddo and other cities, probably derive from later periods.

Thus, when reading the biblical accounts, keep in mind that much of the material may stem from later writers manufacturing a golden age for their people. In doing so, they project back upon the beginning wealth, institutions, and social structures that belong to a later period.

However, the text also reports that David's reign almost ended abruptly with a narrowly averted coup by his son Absalom. Moreover, the succession of another son, Solomon, faced a serious challenge from a third son, Adonijah. (At least seven sons were borne to David, probably more; see 2 Sam 3:2–5 for an early listing.)

Solomon's reign, in the way the Hebrew Bible pictures it, demarcates an Israelite "golden age." A peaceful time, it allowed Solomon to devote himself to further enhancing the kingdom he ruled by engaging in international diplomacy and commissioning monumental building projects. His foreign policy, the writers claim, he enacted largely through his relationships with women, most notably his hospitality toward the Queen of Sheba and his marriages to foreign princesses. (According to 1 Kgs 11:3 he had seven hundred wives and three hundred concubines!) His building projects enhanced various cities throughout the land. The text has him in Jerusalem constructing both his palace and a richly adorned temple to YHWH. Elsewhere he supposedly built a number of fortress cities, such as those at Megiddo, Hazor, and Gezer. All these accomplishments that the text asserts for Solomon have fostered his reputation as one of the wisest men who ever lived (see 1 Kgs 4:30–31).

## Choosing a National Capital

When it came time to choose a capital for the newly constituted United States of America, strategizing similar to that attributed to David came into play. Rather than choosing an existing city located within a current state, the architects of the new nation decided instead to create a separate federal district governed by Congress. The site chosen for this district needed to mollify both northern and southern states. After much wrangling, members of Congress agreed on a site somewhere along the Potomac River, about equidistant between north and south. They charged President George Washington with the actual site selection. Thus, in 1791 Washington found himself mapping out an area of ten square miles taken from Maryland and Virginia. The precise area he selected was determined as the point on the Potomac River where oceangoing vessels could no longer navigate upstream. (At the time an ocean-connected port was deemed a necessity for the capital.)

In more recent times, similar kinds of geographical and political considerations have governed the choices of other national capitals. For instance, in 1908 Australia decided on a new national capital, situating it at a neutral, inland site and giving it its own separate federal district. After a design for it was approved, construction began in 1913; today Canberra is Australia's largest inland city. A few years later, in another part of the world, an independent Turkey emerged out of the ruins of the Ottoman Empire. In 1923 Kemal Ataturk, the man who did the most to forge this new Turkey, chose Ankara, in the center of the country, as the capital. This choice displaced Istanbul, along the western seaboard, and long the most renowned city of the entire country. More recently, Brazil chose an uninhabited inland site for its new capital. Government leaders intended it to replace an overcrowded Rio de Janeiro, promote development of the interior, and be more readily accessible to all parts of the country. In 1957 builders broke ground on it; in 1960 the government officially declared Brasilia the nation's new capital.

But many of Solomon's achievements required imposing heavy taxes and forced labor on his subjects. Although the biblical text largely muffles whatever dissenting voices did exist in his lifetime, after his death the dissent gained traction. The story of the many glories of the united monarchy comes to a crashing end with the kingdom's splitting in two.

### The Two Kingdoms (922–722 B.C.E.)

Notwithstanding Solomon's many wives and concubines, the Hebrew Bible reports only one son: Rehoboam. Upon his accession to the throne, the text describes his traveling to Shechem, a leading city in the north, to receive confirmation for his rule from the tribal elders there. But Rehoboam refuses to heed their request that he lighten the taxes and forced labor levied on them by his father. That intransigence fans the flames of rebellion. Led by Jeroboam, a former supervisor of labor gangs who had unsuccessfully rebelled against Solomon and then fled to Egypt, the ten northern tribes break away from the rule of the Davidic monarchy and subsequently found their own kingdom, called Israel. Rehoboam retains a hold over only the tribes of Judah and Benjamin, reconstituted as the kingdom of Judah.

For the next two hundred years the kingdoms of Israel and Judah co-existed. At times they were antagonists, even taking up arms against one another; at other times they related peacefully, going so far as to ally themselves against common outside foes. In many ways the northern kingdom enjoyed favored status—with a larger population, more abundant natural resources, and easier access to international routes of trade and communication. But these advantages came with a price, for they also made Israel more attractive and vulnerable to aggressive foreign powers. Meanwhile, these same threatening forces often ignored or bypassed Judah; its smaller population, less agriculturally productive land, and more isolated geographical position made it less appealing. Judah also benefited from greater political stability; in its 335 years of existence (922–587/586 B.C.E.) twenty monarchs ruled it, all from the Davidic line. Israel's tumultuous political fortunes, on the other hand, stand in sharp contrast; in only two hundred years (922–722 B.C.E.) it had nineteen kings from five different dynasties. In addition, only one city functioned as Judah's capital, Jerusalem, while Israel's capital moved about among several cities (Shechem, Tirzah, Samaria).

Understanding the historical dynamics of these two kingdoms also requires specific acknowledgment of the biases of the Hebrew Bible's writers. Coming from the south, they markedly favored the southern kingdom. For instance, the writers judge negatively every single king of the north, while granting positive evaluations to some, though not all, of the southern kings. The writers also privilege religious concerns. For example, they condemn Israel's king Ahab for going after other gods while largely ignoring his political and military achievements, which are clear in extrabiblical documents and archaeological remains. Given these special interests of the biblical text, its historical truth claims demand cautious assessment. How the text characterizes a certain person or event depends greatly on the writers' interests and concerns.

For both kingdoms these years centered largely on confronting and responding to various foreign aggressors. Whatever peace the Cisjordan may have experienced in the previous time period may well have been due at least in part to a power vacuum resulting from the weaknesses of other ancient Near Eastern countries at the time. This calm came to an end when Pharaoh Shishak and the Egyptians invaded Cisjordan in 918 B.C.E. Further, a resurgent Syria engaged in border skirmishes with Israel off and on from about the mid-ninth to the mid-eighth centuries B.C.E. And the various Transjordanian states of Ammon, Moab, and Edom also periodically challenged Israel, Judah, or both. Finally, a militarily fierce Assyria based in northern Mesopotamia began initiating, in the early ninth century B.C.E., almost annual campaigns toward the lands on the eastern Mediterranean; it coveted the region's natural resources (wood, precious metals, minerals, agricultural produce) as well as its position astride a number of important land and sea routes.

The Hebrew Bible claims that prophets rose to prominence in both Israel and Judah at this time. One source, the books of 1 and 2 Kings, narrates the activities of such prophets as Elijah, Elisha, and Micaiah ben-Imlah. Other books are named after the individual prophets whose words and deeds they

---

### Land and Sea Routes

The eastern Mediterranean region has long functioned as a key transit point for the movement of people and goods. By land, the region's position made it a bridge linking, in ancient times, Egypt and Mesopotamia. As a consequence, not just one but two international highways traversed it. The Way of the Sea, mentioned in Isa 9:1 (8:23 Heb.), ran along the Mediterranean coastline from Egypt's Nile Delta north to Mount Carmel; there it turned inland, crossing the Jezreel Valley before passing north to Damascus and then on to Mesopotamia. The King's Highway, referred to in Num 20:17, ran north-south along the whole spine of the Transjordanian plateau; it extended northward as far as Damascus, while terminating at its southern point at the Gulf of Aqaba. From there a number of smaller highways led both west and south. Both international highways regularly conveyed armies and trading caravans.

Travel by water served mainly to expedite the movement of trade goods. Along the eastern Mediterranean seaboard a number of excellent harbors functioned as significant conduits of this sea trade. Most notable, perhaps, were the harbors at the two Phoenician cities of Tyre and Sidon. The Phoenicians ranged widely in their ships, eventually establishing colonies as far afield as Spain and north Africa. They brought in from the west such highly prized goods as silver from Spain and fine pottery from Greece; from the east they welcomed rare spices arriving from India and southern Arabia, which they then shipped elsewhere. Since these harbors brought in so much wealth, and thus power, any number of empires in ancient times coveted possession of them. At various times overt threats came from the Assyrians, the Babylonians, and the Greeks.

purport to record, such as Amos, Hosea, Micah, and Isaiah. According to these sources, the prophets in general advocated a turn (or return) to covenant faithfulness to YHWH. This advocacy shaped their pronouncements on foreign policy, their advising on military strategy, their championing of the poor and powerless, and their condemnation of supposedly non-YHWHistic religious practices. Questions exist, though, over how much these emphases are attributable to the prophets themselves and how much to the theological agendas of the people editing these texts.

### Judah Alone (722–587/586 B.C.E.)

By the late eighth century B.C.E., political and military disaster hovered near both Israel and Judah, for Assyria increasingly menaced all the lands along the eastern Mediterranean seaboard. In 722/721 B.C.E., after a three-year siege, Samaria, the capital of the northern kingdom of Israel, fell to the Assyrians. In effect, this ended the northern kingdom of Israel. The Assyrians relocated many of the Israelites to places elsewhere in their empire. (From this action originated mythic traditions about <u>the ten lost tribes</u> of Israel.) Other Israelites, especially the rural poor, no doubt stayed in the land, while still others fled south to Judah (or elsewhere). Meanwhile, the Assyrians shifted other populations to Israelite territory, including those of their own people who functioned as the new ruling class. Eventually the land and its people recovered from the devastations of the Assyrians, and a renewed society emerged. Unfortunately, sparse evidence exists for the details of this process. The strongest data perhaps relates to the Samaritans, a group who carried on with religious and cultural practices similar to those of the citizens of Judah, though differing in some of the specifics. Politically, however, Israel now operated as an Assyrian province.

In the meantime, Judah had to decide how to respond to Assyrian aggression. King Ahaz acceded to Assyrian demands for loyalty by sending tribute monies. Others, such as Hezekiah, rebelled with only limited success. From about 700–650 B.C.E., however, Assyria sat at the zenith of its power and

### the ten lost tribes

The displaced Israelites gradually melded into the peoples of the Assyrian Empire among whom they lived. Despite that, a belief persisted that one day these Israelites, the so-called ten lost tribes, would again be found. For instance, Eldad ha-Dani, a ninth-century C.E. Jewish traveler, reported locating the tribes "beyond the rivers of Abyssinia" on the far side of an impassable river called Sambation. Another Jew, Manasseh ben Israel, used the legend of the ten lost tribes to convince Oliver Cromwell to admit Jews into England in the seventeenth century. Joseph Smith, founder of the Church of Jesus Christ of Latter-day Saints (also known as Mormonism), believed the Native Americans descended from the lost tribes. Other peoples too have been identified at various times as descendants of the lost tribes, and a few immigrants to the state of Israel since 1948 have also claimed descent from the ten lost tribes.

## The Samaritans

Historians continue to debate exactly when and how the Samaritans originated. Scattered references in texts written after 587/586 B.C.E. agree that Mount Gerizim, in the central highlands, served as both a geographical and religious focus. Many Samaritans lived in its environs, and at some time between the fourth and second centuries B.C.E. they built a temple on it. This latter act was no doubt prompted by their belief that Moses, at God's command, instructed Joshua to build an altar on that spot. This tradition finds support in the Samaritans' version of the Pentateuch. Known as the Samaritan Pentateuch, it reads somewhat differently from the **Masoretic Text**. But although Samaritans hold to their own version of the Pentateuch, and deem only it as canonical, they do share with Jews many other basic beliefs and practices. For example, both believe in the one God, YHWH; both have a high regard for Moses; and both groups observe the Sabbath and such other holy days as Passover and Yom Kippur. Several hundred Samaritans still practice their faith today; most live either in Nablus at the foot of Mount Gerizim or in Holon, a suburb of nearby Tel Aviv.

## An Assyrian Siege of Jerusalem?

When Sargon II, king of Assyria, died in 705 B.C.E., the empire he had ruled erupted into turmoil. The Judean king, Hezekiah, exploited this situation and rebelled, supported by alliances with Egypt and Babylon. However, within a few short years Assyria responded: in 701 B.C.E. its new king, Sennacherib, mounted a siege against Jerusalem. But then, rather mysteriously, the king withdrew his troops before taking the city. What happened that caused him to withdraw his troops? Once committed, the Assyrian military did not normally disengage from its campaigns. The biblical text complicates the matter by suggesting three seemingly unrelated reasons for the withdrawal. Second Kings 19:7 (also Isa 37:7) records Isaiah's prediction that Sennacherib will "hear a rumor and return to his own land." Perhaps this rumor pertained to political dissent back in the capital city of Nineveh. Sure enough, two of Sennacherib's sons did eventually assassinate him, although the killing did not occur until 681 B.C.E., rather later than the supposed 701 B.C.E. date of the Jerusalem siege. Another biblical text reports that God sent an angel of death who struck down 185,000 soldiers in a single night (2 Kgs 19:35; Isa 37:36). This account resonates with a report by the Greek historian Herodotus, which states that Sennacherib's army was overrun by mice (rats?) near the Egyptian frontier. Since rats spread the bubonic plague, which can quickly decimate a population, perhaps the angel of death is to be connected with a quick-moving plague. However, scholars characterize Herodotus's report as generally garbled. Moreover, the location is off: the Egyptian frontier is not the same as the environs of Jerusalem. Yet another biblical passage relates that Hezekiah submitted to the Assyrians—that is, he paid the demanded tribute by stripping both the palace and temple of its gold and silver (2 Kgs 18:14–16). Presumably the Assyrians withdrew after receiving the payoff. The textual existence of several different reasons for the withdrawal has prompted some scholars to posit two separate attacks by Sennacherib against Jerusalem: one in 701 B.C.E., cut short by the deaths of his troops, and the other in 689 B.C.E., abruptly ended by a summons back to Nineveh. But most scholars see a two-campaign solution as far-fetched and overly strained.

domination, and the Judean kings of that time, notably Manasseh (ca. 687–642 B.C.E.), accommodated themselves by submitting to Assyrian demands.

The decline of Assyria culminated in 605 B.C.E. when, at Carchemish on the upper Euphrates, Babylonia defeated the combined military forces of both Assyria and Egypt. Led by **Nebuchadnezzar**, the Babylonians not only claimed all the regions previously held by Assyria but also extended their reach further. Again, Judah faced the conundrum of deciding how to respond to an aggressive foreign power: submit or resist? King Jehoiachin, in a politically and religiously complicated decision, resisted. In 597 B.C.E. Nebuchadnezzar and his army responded by swooping down upon Judah, capturing Jerusalem, and deporting both its king and many of the leading citizens. A few years later when the ensuing Judean puppet king, Zedekiah, fomented another rebellion, Nebuchadnezzar returned. This time, in 587/586 B.C.E., he exacted a more terrible retribution: he destroyed and burned the city (including its Temple to YHWH), killed the king's sons before his eyes, blinded him, and forcibly removed both the king and a considerable portion of the Judean people to Babylon.

*The Babylonian Exile (587/586–539 B.C.E.)*

How does one measure devastation? How can one quantify trauma? The events of 587/586 B.C.E. shattered Judah, challenging and changing its political, social, and religious ways of being. Six hundred years of political autonomy came to an end. Key elements of religious, social, and cultural life, mediated through palace, temple, and urban centers, collapsed. Many of the people, exiled from their land and homes, now struggled to fashion a life for themselves hundreds of miles away, in Babylonia or elsewhere. No doubt thousands of others lost their lives, whether to warfare, famine, and/or disease. All these things the survivors felt and experienced at both the individual and the corporate level. Comparable scenarios have unfolded in the world more recently—in places such as Bosnia, Rwanda, Sudan, Afghanistan, and Iraq.

In such times, numerous dislocations and questionings occur. For the Judeans, some of these centered on YHWH. Many perhaps believed that

## Remembering in the Aftermath of Genocide

The dynamics of remembering show similar patterns in the aftermath of recent genocides. The remembering, whether in print, on film, or in other types of media, does not take place right away. Those subject to such horrors need time to absorb the initial shock of it all. Only after some time has passed can they more fully confront and attempt to wrest meaning from it. Elie Wiesel's *Night,* for instance, one of the more renowned memoirs of the Holocaust, came out in 1960, a good fifteen years after that genocide ended. (Another famous work about the Holocaust, *The Diary of Anne Frank,* does not work in the same way, for Anne wrote it during the war.) Or consider the movie *Hotel Rwanda,* about the 1994 genocide of Tutsis in Rwanda. The release of the movie occurred near the end of 2004.

YHWH had somehow failed them, either because YHWH had proved weaker than Marduk, the high god of the Babylonians, or because YHWH had simply turned away from them. Or perhaps the disasters proved that YHWH did not exist at all. Yet alongside such despair, others hoped and worked for renewal and a better future. Some dreamed of a renewed Davidic monarchy set in a magnificent far-off future. Others reshaped worship practices: with animal sacrifices and temple observances unavailable, some may have emphasized observing the Sabbath and other holy days. Still others, attempting to understand and find meaning for the destruction and exile, delved into the past. They called up old stories and traditions, preserved them in written form, and brought them together into a new whole. They thus spurred on a process eventually resulting in the written text of the Hebrew Bible.

The exilic period thus functioned as a starting point for a redefinition of the people's identity. The many changes experienced, both tangible and intangible, ended up finding acknowledgment in a name change: after the exilic period instead of being referred to as "Israelites" or "Hebrews," these people were now called "**Judeans**" or "Yehudites" (after **Yehud**, the name of the Persian province around Jerusalem). The Hebrew word for Yehudites, *Yehudim*, is the source for the term "Jews." Further, beginning with the exilic period, scholars identify the emergence of many of the emphases and structures represented later by Judaism. Beginning at this time, too, scholars frame periods of time not according to archaeological reckonings but rather in terms of political dominions: the Persian period, the Hellenistic period, and (after the Hebrew Bible is completed) the Roman period. In light of these many and various changes, many academics identify 587/586 B.C.E. as the most significant date in all of ancient Israelite history.

*The Persian Empire (539–333 B.C.E.)*

For all its fierce aggression and ruthless control, the Babylonian Empire lasted a strikingly short time. In less than one hundred years (in 539 B.C.E.) Cyrus of Media, allied with the **Persians**, captured Babylon without a fight. The ensuing Persian Empire held sway over the ancient Near East for the next two hundred years. The Persians gained the reputation (at least early on) of ruling benignly. As long as subject peoples paid taxes and tribute and expressed at least a nominal loyalty, the Persian overlords permitted them a certain independence in their local affairs. This policy manifested itself early, when Cyrus signed an edict (539 B.C.E.) allowing exiled peoples to return to their homelands and reestablish their lives. This edict included the Yehudites.

So in 538 B.C.E., Sheshbazzar led a group back to Judah (also called Yehud), intending to rebuild the Jerusalem Temple. But the difficulties and challenges proved insurmountable, and they soon abandoned the task. In 520 B.C.E. another group, under the leadership of Zerubbabel, the governor, and Joshua, the high priest, attempted something similar. This time they met with more success, building a new Temple and dedicating it in 515 B.C.E. Later still, sometime in the fifth century B.C.E., Nehemiah, a Jewish official working in the

Persian court, garnered permission to return to Jerusalem and oversee the rebuilding of the city's walls. Also in this century, Ezra, another Jewish official in the Persian court, returned to Jerusalem and played a key role in defining the postexilic Yehudite community. He helped decide both who should be included and who should not, and how they should live. And throughout this period a continuing literary outpouring of various kinds took place: novellas (Ruth), wisdom books (Proverbs), historical memoirs (Ezra, Nehemiah), and lyric literature (Song of Songs, Psalms).

*The Hellenistic Period (333–164 B.C.E.)*

In 336 B.C.E. Alexander the Great inherited the throne of Macedon (northern Greece) after his father, the king, was assassinated. Two years later, having raised an army of 40,000, he crossed into Asia and challenged Persian rule. Within a few short years he routed the Persian army (several times) and claimed all former Persian territories as his own. He then continued eastward, asserting his control over additional lands in present-day India and Afghanistan. Alexander did not stop, though, with the political-military conquest of the largest area ever yet held by a single empire. He also settled his retired soldiers in large numbers of settlements throughout his empire. This practice ensured continuous contact between the descendants of his Greek mercenaries and the residents of the ancient Near East. The contact produced a cultural mixing that scholars call **hellenization**.

As a consequence, in this period the Greek language began serving alongside Aramaic as the region's lingua franca. Distinctive Greek structures also began to emerge: the Greek city (the *polis*), temples, theaters, libraries, and gymnasiums. And in these structures Greek literature, philosophy, and religion found expression. But the ancient Near Eastern cultures also exerted their own pull on the Greeks who ruled them, through both their particular practices (including the worship of various deities such as YHWH) and their local traditions (such as those recorded in the Hebrew Bible). What emerged was a cultural mixture. The whole process was uneven and often filled with tension, as both the Near Eastern and the Greek peoples contended with how much they would accept of the others' social, political, and cultural beliefs and practices.

During this time of cultural interchange and tension, Alexander's successors reigned. One general, Ptolemy, ruled Egypt, Syria, and the Cisjordan. Another general, Seleucus, held sway over Asia Minor, Mesopotamia, and, at least initially, territories farther to the east. In 198 B.C.E. the Seleucids (after a century of almost constant warfare) took control of the Cisjordan from the Ptolemies. The Seleucids, however, quickly ran into difficulties that produced a "perfect storm" in the area around Jerusalem. Their need for funds encouraged the Seleucid ruler, Antiochus Epiphanes IV, to sell the office of the Judean high priest to Jason, who was more enamored of Greek culture than were many other Judeans. But Antiochus then turned around and found an even more Greek-friendly

Judean, Menelaus, who would pay even more for the office. The resulting bidding war set off civil conflict around Jerusalem; Antiochus eventually intervened to support Menelaus. Then, in 167 B.C.E., in an attempt to crush Menelaus's opponents, Antiochus apparently proscribed a number of cultural practices: circumcision, keeping kosher food regulations, and Sabbath observance. A revolt broke out, led by a family known as the Maccabees, and after twenty-five years of guerilla warfare and clever diplomacy, the Judeans won their independence. Early in the revolt (probably in 164 B.C.E.), as a way of protesting the persecution and encouraging the faithful, an anonymous scribe penned the apocalyptic sections of the book of Daniel. This material represents the last written work taken up into the Hebrew Bible. Thus, it also marks, in some ways, the end of the story of the people responsible for the Hebrew Bible. But, of course, the texts continue on in an afterlife of reading and interpretation even up to the modern day. Some of the specifics of that story will apear in the next chapter.

## Conclusion

About a hundred years ago Einstein's theories of relativity revolutionized science by demonstrating that neither space nor time are fixed. His theories have unsettled many, yet one can also safely ignore them insofar as they pertain to spaces and times immeasurably removed from everyday realities. But what about those spaces and times closer at hand? How often and to what extent do people recognize their fluidity and impermanence?

Consider some of the many spaces people inhabit: cities, states, provinces, countries. Their borders depend largely on lines drawn on a map, and although occasionally these borders follow a waterway or some other natural phenomenon, most have no external reality at all. Some person(s) drew them up at a specific time and place and for certain purposes; no doubt they will eventually pass away and others will be created in their stead. The spaces thus traced out by these borders derive from the changeable needs and desires of humans. Or consider forces in the natural world and how they, too, shape space. Floods, earthquakes, volcanic eruptions, and other climactic events can profoundly alter the landscapes they impact. Just think about a recent natural disaster that made the news and compare the before and after pictures of the area it affected. Space—because of the actions of both humans and the natural world—never stays the same.

Even as space fluctuates, so too does time. Consider some of the countless ways humans measure and value time and how they often clash with one another: solar versus lunar calendars, academic versus religious calendars (and various religious calendars), the business day versus a holiday. Or reflect on how experiences of time often hold surprises: "How time does fly!" "Is it time already?" "I've totally lost track of the time." No matter how much people try to capture time, it remains elusive.

Space and time both prove impossible to grasp and comprehend fully. The same holds true for the specific spaces and times of the biblical world; thus, reconstructions of biblical Israel and Judah necessarily remain provisional. Over the centuries the territories signified by these two terms varied, their boundaries shifting according to social and political circumstances. Of course, at least in some fashion they operated within the milieu of the ancient Near East during the first millennium B.C.E. But although the sources allow glimmers of these processes, much still remains unknown. This chapter outlines some of the spaces and times identified as most pertinent to an understanding of the Hebrew Bible. Yet the portrayal remains tantalizingly incomplete, just as the ability to grasp the detailed workings of modern spaces and times can also challenge and sometimes even baffle readers today.

**Discussion Questions**

1. How does this account of the biblical world compare to others you may know? What does this account seem to emphasize? What does it minimize or downplay? What does that imply about the particular interests of its authors?
2. Think about the temporal rhythms of your own life. What days mark beginnings and/or endings for you? What days or weeks signify high points in your life? How does this calendar compare to "official" calendars used by your culture, and what does this say about how individuals and societies variously shape time?
3. Draw a map of your world in which you highlight those places of most significance to you. How might your map be similar to and different from what others might draw of that same area?
4. Without going back and rereading this chapter, make a quick list of the ten most significant points you recall from it. How does your list compare to those drawn up by others in the class? Can your class come to any consensus about what goes on such a list and in what order?

**Suggestions for Further Reading**

Coogan, Michael D., ed. *The Oxford History of the Biblical World*. New York: Oxford University Press, 1998.

Dever, William G. *Who Were the Israelites and Where Did They Come From?* Grand Rapids: Wm. B. Eerdmans Publishing Co., 2003.

Isserlin, B. S. J. *The Israelites*. Minneapolis: Fortress Press, 2001.

Matthews, Victor H. *A Brief History of Ancient Israel*. Louisville, KY: Westminster John Knox Press, 2002.

Noll, K. L. *Canaan and Israel in Antiquity: An Introduction*. London and New York: Sheffield Academic Press, 2001.

# 2. *Reading the Hebrew Bible*

Took me four years to read the Bible. Reckon I understand a great deal
of it. It wasn't what I expected in some places.

—Karl, in the movie *Sling Blade* (1996)

Readers bring certain expectations to a text. When consulting a microwave
manual, one anticipates instructions on how to use the various features on
the keypad. Readers do not expect entertainment, ethical advice, or musings
on the meaning and purpose of life. The questions a person brings to a text
help determine how that person will read it. So a person "asks" the
microwave manual about how to do certain things, knowing better than to
"ask" other questions. The answers that readers obtain from a text largely
result from the questions readers pose.

The Hebrew Bible proves somewhat more complicated than a microwave
manual. Different groups of readers bring different expectations and different questions to the Hebrew Bible. Some readers ask many sorts of questions, depending on the need at hand. This chapter considers three basic
types of questions readers ask. First, given the Hebrew Bible's role as sacred
Scripture for Jews and Christians, theological concerns motivate many
readers. Second, given the Hebrew Bible's development through a long
period of history and in different cultures, some readers seek information
on historical issues. Third, given the Hebrew Bible's existence as literature,
still other readers raise questions about the way these texts "work" as literature. These three basic types of inquiry overlap; a theologically motivated
reader could read the Hebrew Bible in a historical or literary fashion, for
example. But keeping these ways of reading separate should help demonstrate how these various ways of reading the Hebrew Bible work.

**Getting Started: The Hebrew Bible as Translation**

Before examining the various ways of reading the Hebrew Bible, two basic problems must be addressed. First, most readers experience the Hebrew Bible as a translation. Since they do not know classical Hebrew, they are always at the mercy of translators. Second, no original manuscripts of the Hebrew Bible exist. All the manuscripts come from long after the period in which they were written, and these manuscripts often differ. So scholars must make their best efforts to determine the most likely original reading of a text, a job they call **textual criticism**.

*Translation and Its Discontents*

### Problem 1: Not Knowing the Words

When encountering an unknown word, most people simply look it up in a dictionary. A dictionary distills the way that word gets used in various contexts. But suppose all the known English came from the plays of Shakespeare? Or all the French came from the writings of Rousseau? English and French dictionaries would be much thinner, and the definitions would lack the richness that examining a word in many different settings brings.

The Hebrew Bible itself contains most of the world's surviving classical Hebrew. This makes defining words with precision and with sensitivity to various shades of meaning difficult at times. Consider a word that appears only once (a hapax legomenon) or one that occurs only a few times in the Hebrew Bible. In Song 1:10, the lover's neck is adorned with *kharuzim*, but no one can be certain of what they are, since *kharuzim* is a hapax legomenon. Since words similar to *kharuzim* in other ancient Semitic languages can mean "strung together," scholars conclude that the Hebrew word refers to a necklace of beads, jewels, or shells.

### Problem 2: Dealing with Ambiguity

The Hebrew itself frequently reads ambiguously, presenting several options for rendering the phrase at hand. Translators, of course, can use only one of those options in a translation. In Song 6:13 (7:1 Heb.), the female figure asks, "Why should you look upon the Shulammite, as upon a dance before two armies?" The relation between the two words of the phrase *kimkholat hammakhanayim* ("like a dance" and "the armies camps") is not clear. So translators can either attempt to give the reader the most information possible with their rendering ("dancing as though between two rows of dancers" [Jerusalem Bible]) or allow the text's obscurity to stand, more or less untouched ("in the Mahanaim dance" [Jewish Publication Society Version]).

At other points, translators reduce the ambiguity of the Hebrew. The angels Jacob sees ascending and descending do so literally "upon him" (Gen 28:12). A number of possible antecedents appear in the text, including Jacob and God. But the most obvious, the ladder (a masculine noun in Hebrew), leads a majority of English translators to render "upon him" as "upon it." While other readings might prove fruitful, English demands a choice, and the translator reduces the openness of the Hebrew text.

### Problem 3: Losing the Art

Finally, anyone who attempts to translate a document, especially an artfully constructed one, knows various features of the source language (e.g., alliteration, assonance, rhymes, and puns) only rarely survive the move to the target language. The beautifully assonant statement in Isa 7:9, *im lo taaminu ki lo teamenu*, uses the verb *aman* twice, though in two different constructions, which provide different meanings. The NRSV renders this poetry rather prosaically as "If you do not stand firm in faith, you shall not stand at all"; the reuse of "stand" at least points to the reuse of the same Hebrew root. The reuse of the same word with different senses comes out in Moffat's rendering: "If your faith does not hold, you will never hold out," although to do so he abandons the strict meaning of the verb *aman*. Neither version captures the almost musical quality of the Hebrew.

### Watching Translators at Work

Translators also determine how much of the original text's qualities they wish to maintain. A translation that maintains too much of the original language's style could be well nigh unreadable. But a translation that seeks to be easily readable may lose touch with the original's style. Translations seeking to replicate the source language and its structures accurately in the target language seek "**formal correspondence**" in word-for-word translations. Moving toward the other end of the spectrum, translations attempting to render the source language by matching idea for idea depart from the precise wording of the source text, making the results easier to understand. Scholars label these translations "**dynamic equivalence**" translations. Finally, **paraphrases** come at the far end of the spectrum; these renderings, while based on the source text, take great liberties with original wording to deliver an understandable (or more gripping) result.

Translations of the Hebrew Bible also reveal the theological interests of the translators. As an example, note these translations of Gen 1:1:

> In the beginning God created the heaven and the earth. And the earth was without form, and void. (King James Version)

> In the beginning when God created the heaven and the earth, the earth was a formless void. (New Revised Standard Version)

> In the beginning God created the heaven and the earth. Now the earth was formless and empty. (New International Version)

> When God began to create heaven and earth—the earth being unformed and void, . . . (Jewish Publication Society Version)

All of them make sense of the first word, *b<sup>e</sup>reshit*, differently, and Hebrew grammar permits each possibility. But theological assumptions enter in as well. The Jewish Publication Society translation implies that something "unformed and void" existed before creation, thus contradicting the Christian doctrine of creatio ex nihilo—that God created the world from nothing. (Of course, the Jewish Publication Society need not express concern for Christian theology!) Likewise the NIV, translated by conservative Protestants, leads the reader clearly to see that the "formless and empty" world results from divine creation. The translators here act out of both theological concern and a desire for a dynamically equivalent translation. The NRSV, translated largely by mainline Protestants, reveals less interest in holding a theological line but rather works to represent in English the ambiguity of the Hebrew (formal correspondence). Thus, its rendering lets

---

### How Translations Vary

These four translations of Gen 22:1–2 represent the diverse ways different translators, given their needs and presuppositions, render the text.

**Everett Fox, *The Schocken Bible* (seeks to replicate the Hebrew words and grammatical forms)**

Now after these events it was that God tested Avraham and said to him: Avraham! He said: Here I am. He said: Pray take your son, your only-one, whom you love, Yitzhak, and go-you-forth to the land of Moriyya/Seeing, and offer him up there as an offering-up upon one of the mountains that I will tell you of.

**Revised Standard Version (formal correspondence)**

After these things God tested Abraham, and said to him, "Abraham!" And he said, "Here am I." He said, "Take your son, your only son Isaac, whom you love, and go to the land of Mori'ah, and offer him there as a burnt offering upon one of the mountains of which I shall tell you."

**New International Version (dynamic equivalence)**

Some time later, God tested Abraham. He said to Abraham, "Abraham!" "Here I am," he replied. Then God said, "Take your son, your only son, Isaac, whom you love and go to the region of Moriah. Sacrifice him there as a burnt offering on one of the mountains I will tell you about."

**The Living Bible (a paraphrase)**

Later on, God tested Abraham's faith and obedience. "Abraham!" God called. "Yes, Lord?" he replied. "Take with you your only son—yes, Isaac, whom you love so much—and go to the land of Moriah and sacrifice him there as a burnt offering on one of the mountains which I'll point out to you."

# A Selection of English Translations of the Hebrew Bible

Translation styles resist easy categorization. The categories tend to flow into each other. Some translations are strong examples of a particular style, while others only tend toward either formal correspondence or dynamic equivalence.

| Translation | Year | Style | Authorizing Body for Translation |
|---|---|---|---|
| King James Version (KJV) | 1611 | formal correspondence | James I, King of England |
| Revised Standard Version (RSV) | 1952 | formal correspondence | National Council of Churches (mainline Protestant) |
| New American Standard (NASB) | 1971 | formal correspondence | Lockman Foundation (evangelical Protestant) |
| Living Bible (LB) | 1971 | paraphrase | Tyndale House (evangelical Protestant) |
| Today's English Version (TEV) | 1976 | dynamic equivalence (simplified language) | American Bible Society |
| New International Version (NIV) | 1978 | dynamic equivalence | International Bible Society (evangelical Protestant) |
| New King James Version (NKJV) | 1982 | formal correspondence | Thomas Nelson, Inc. (evangelical Protestant) |
| Tanakh: The Holy Scriptures (NJPS) | 1985 | dynamic equivalence | Jewish Publication Society |
| New Jerusalem Bible (NJB) | 1985 | dynamic equivalence | Roman Catholic Church |
| New American Bible (NAB) | 1986 | formal correspondence | Roman Catholic Church (U.S. Conference of Catholic Bishops) |
| Revised English Bible (REB) | 1989 | dynamic equivalence | Protestants and Catholics in the U.K. |
| New Revised Standard Version (NRSV) | 1989 | formal correspondence | National Council of Churches (mainline Protestant) |
| Contemporary English Version (CEV) | 1995 | dynamic equivalence (simplified language) | American Bible Society |
| New Living Translation (NLT) | 1996 | paraphrase | Tyndale House (evangelical Protestant) |
| English Standard Version (ESV) | 2001 | formal correspondence | Good News Publishers (evangelical Protestant) |
| The Message | 2002 | paraphrase (by Eugene Peterson) | NavPress (evangelical Protestant) |
| Holman Christian Standard Bible (HCSB) | 2004 | dynamic equivalence | Holman Bible Publishers (Southern Baptist) |
| Today's New International Version (TNIV) | 2005 | dynamic equivalence | International Bible Society (evangelical Protestant) |

### the reader determines their value

Today this value-determining reader functions as a consumer. A trip to a local bookstore reveals a vast number of Bibles in a variety of translations: *The Life Recovery Bible*; *Holy Bible, Woman Thou Art Loosed Edition*; *Precious Moments Bible*; *Chicken Soup for the Soul Bible*; even *Immerse: A Water-Resistant New Testament*. In general, these Bibles feature specialized notes or features appealing to a certain kind of audience, a "niche market." Additionally, the last twenty years has seen an explosion not just of "repackaged" or "rebranded" older translations but also of whole new English translations and paraphrases designed to address the needs of some group. Translation of the Hebrew Bible is now clearly an economic, as well as an intellectual and spiritual, exercise.

the reader decide whether the "formless void" preceded or followed the initial act of creation. None of these translations rates as more "accurate" than the others; rather, the reader determines their value, based on the assumptions the reader brings from his or her community to the text.

*Before Translation: The Work of Textual Criticism*

Today, books are mass-produced. Each copy of this book looks just like every other copy. But imagine the situation of a resident of Jerusalem in 180 B.C.E. At this point, most of the texts of the Hebrew Bible exist in written form, but when he reads his copy of Genesis, he cannot be certain that his friend next door has an identical copy of Genesis. His cousins in Alexandria, Egypt, have Greek texts that claim to be translations of the Hebrew Bible,

### The Work of the Masoretes

The Masoretes, who worked during the last half of the first millennium C.E., developed many ways to ensure the accurate copying of Hebrew Bible texts. The Masoretic notes to the Hebrew Bible included lists of words, noting places where spellings differed, as well as detailed statistics concerning word frequency and usage. All this information could be used to check the accuracy of their material by a means other than proofreading.

Before the Masoretes, the texts of the Hebrew Bible were consonantal, that is, only the consonants appeared in writing. The reader knew from tradition what vowels came where and where to accent words. The Masoretes, interested in preserving this oral tradition, invented a system of signs (placed around the consonants in the text) to represent Hebrew vowels and accents. This system represented, in written form, the received tradition of how the texts should be vocalized. Interestingly, where oral tradition mandated a reading (or *qere*) that did not match the written text (the *kethib*), the Masoretes allowed both to stand. They preserved the written text but inserted the "correct" vowels (frequently producing unpronounceable words). They then provided the "corrected" consonantal text in the margins of the text.

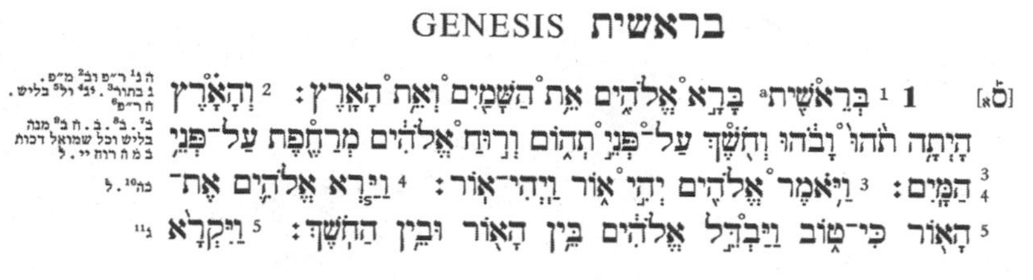

**Fig. 2.1:** *Biblia Hebraica Stuttgartensia*

*The* Biblia Hebraica Stuttgartensia *(BHS), the basis for most English translations of the Hebrew Bible, follows the Codex Leningradensis closely. The picture shows the first few verses of Genesis. This modern printed version includes, in its margins, notes originating with the Masoretes. And in and around the letters of the text, it displays the dots and lines that the Masoretes used to represent vowels and accents.*

GENESIS בְּרֵאשִׁית

[ס*א] 1 ¹ בְּרֵאשִׁית בָּרָא אֱלֹהִים אֵת הַשָּׁמַיִם וְאֵת הָאָרֶץ: ² וְהָאָרֶץ הָיְתָה תֹהוּ וָבֹהוּ וְחֹשֶׁךְ עַל־פְּנֵי תְהוֹם וְרוּחַ אֱלֹהִים מְרַחֶפֶת עַל־פְּנֵי הַמָּיִם: ³ וַיֹּאמֶר אֱלֹהִים יְהִי אוֹר וַיְהִי־אוֹר: ⁴ וַיַּרְא אֱלֹהִים אֶת־הָאוֹר כִּי־טוֹב וַיַּבְדֵּל אֱלֹהִים בֵּין הָאוֹר וּבֵין הַחֹשֶׁךְ: ⁵ וַיִּקְרָא

but are they like his version of Genesis or his neighbor's? A real problem arises here: unlike books today, no single standard edition of the texts of the Hebrew Bible existed in the ancient world.

The question now becomes what version modern translators use as their foundation. In the first century C.E., Jewish leaders (rabbis) began to develop a standardized version of the Hebrew Bible. By the last half of the first millennium, a group of these rabbis known as the Masoretes took up the work of maintaining a standard text. Known as the **Masoretic Text** (MT), its oldest complete copy, Codex Leningradensis, dates from 1007 C.E. Most modern translations, including the NRSV, start with an edited version of this codex, the *Biblia Hebraica Stuttgartensia* (*BHS*) (see fig. 2.1).

So the oldest existing complete text of the Hebrew Bible dates from at least 1,100 years after the composition of the final texts in the Hebrew Bible! Thus, no one can assume that the MT perfectly represents the original form of the Hebrew Bible. Indeed, other, older manuscripts offer different readings of biblical passages, bearing witness to the time before textual standardization. Complete existing copies of the **Septuagint** (abbreviated "LXX"), a collection of Greek translations of Hebrew Bible texts, as well as other works outside the Jewish canon, date from the third to fifth centuries C.E. Existing fragments of these Greek texts (see fig. 2.2) date as far back as the second century B.C.E. In many places the LXX parallels the MT; it represents what we might call a proto-Masoretic text (the MT before the Masoretes came along). But in many other instances, the Greek translators apparently misunderstood or reinterpreted their proto-Masoretic source text. And in some other instances, they translated a different text than the standardized MT. For example, in the LXX, the book of Jeremiah lacks a sixth of MT Jeremiah's bulk and arranges the contents differently. Apparently the LXX translators had before them an alternative early Hebrew version of Jeremiah. Likewise, the LXX's story of David and Goliath

### abbreviated LXX

The Septuagint gets its name from the number seventy in Latin, *septuaginta*. Thus, it is abbreviated using the Roman numeral LXX. The association of these Greek translations with the number seventy comes from a legend that claims seventy-two men translated the Hebrew into Greek.

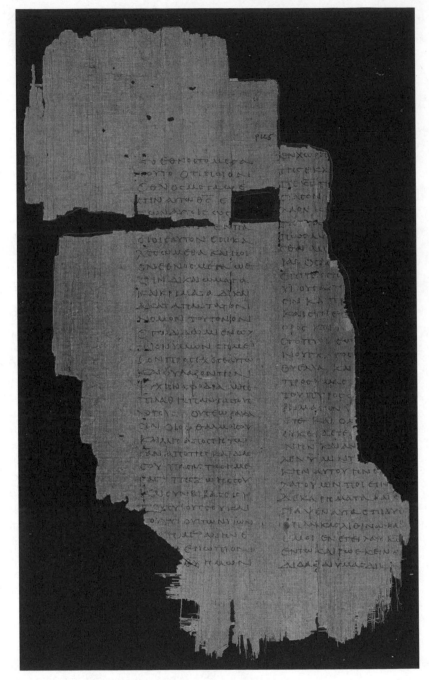

**Fig. 2.2: Chester Beatty Biblical Papyri VI (Rahlfs 963)**
*This comes from a set of fragments from a Greek translation of Numbers and Deuteronomy, written on papyrus in Egypt in the second century C.E. This particular fragment contains a version of Deut 4:6–23. Notice that there are no spaces between the words, nor is there any punctuation.*

**Fig. 2.3: Qumran, Cave 4**
*Bedouins (and, afterward, archaeologists) discovered the Dead Sea Scrolls in caves such as this one. The exceedingly dry climate helped preserve them, though many were torn in small fragments. Cave 4, pictured here, produced manuscript fragments from thirty-five of the thirty-nine books of the Hebrew Bible. Some include little more than a few verses, but others are more extensive. When all the caves near Qumran are taken into account, there are fragments of every book in the Hebrew Bible except Esther.*

(1 Sam 17) does not relate the episode of Jesse's sending David to visit his brothers in the army (vv. 12–31), or the ending in which Saul inquires about David's identity (vv. 55–58). And while Goliath in the LXX is still over six feet (two meters) tall, the Goliath of the MT measures over nine feet (three meters). Again, the MT and LXX tell strikingly different stories.

The scrolls found near Qumran (the Dead Sea Scrolls) provide the earliest copies of Hebrew biblical texts of any significant length (see fig. 2.3). In most cases, the scrolls exist as fragments, yielding only a few verses of a particular book (see fig. 2.4). One scroll, however, covers almost the entirety of the book of Isaiah. That scroll looks very much like the text of Isaiah in the MT (see fig. 2.5). Other biblical manuscripts from Qumran, however, read like Hebrew versions of LXX texts. Other texts prove hard to classify, representing even more variety in biblical manuscripts.

How do modern translations relate to all these old manuscripts? Before translating the Hebrew Bible, scholars engage in textual criticism. Textual critics rely on close examination of the differences between manuscripts as well as assumptions about the behavior of scribes to determine the most likely original reading of a text. For example, a scribe's eye could skip, either forward (leaving out material) or backward (duplicating material). An example of the latter occurs in Lev 20:10 (MT). The material underlined exactly copies the material directly before it reading right to left:

וְאִישׁ אֲשֶׁר יִנְאַף אֶת־אֵשֶׁת אִישׁ אֲשֶׁר יִנְאַף אֶת־אֵשֶׁת רֵעֵהוּ מוֹת־יוּמַת הַנֹּאֵף וְהַנֹּאָפֶת

Some textual critics eliminate the duplication as an unintentional error, translating the phrase only once (as in the RSV and NRSV), while some attempt to fit the phrase in twice (as in the NIV and NJPS).

**Fig. 2.4: Qumran, Cave 4 Scroll Fragments**
*These leather fragments from Cave 4, pieced together by scholars, contain 2 Sam 3:23–4:4. The text here, while similar in many respects to the MT, is not identical. It thus provides evidence for the textual critic who attempts to determine a probable earliest reading of 2 Samuel.*

*(Photograph courtesy of Israel Antiquities Authority)*

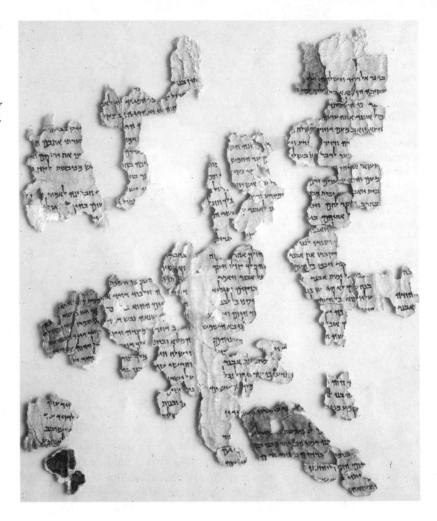

## Seeking Originals

Like the texts of the Hebrew Bible, no originals of the movie *Star Wars* exist, although there are a number of versions of *Star Wars* in circulation: a 1997 remastering with some changes, a digitally remastered 2004 version also including some significant alterations, and a version claiming to represent the "original" movie, issued in 2006. Taking matters into their own hands, some fans have used digital technology to edit their copies of the movie to remove later alterations, creating what they feel to be a plausible representation of what they remember seeing (and seeing and seeing) years earlier. These fans are doing something like what textual critics do. A major difference is that while *Star Wars* fans know there was once an original "master" of the film, Hebrew Bible scholars cannot be certain that there was a single original "master" of any book in the

**Fig. 2.5: Great Isaiah Scroll from Qumran, Cave 1**

*This is Isa 41:26–42:10 from the Great Isaiah Scroll from Qumran, Cave 1. Notice that it lacks the system of dots and lines around each word that the Masoretes later supplied to mark vowels and accents. While similar to the MT's version of this passage, the scroll's version has several differences in spelling and in the use of the divine name.*

## Errors: Unintentional and Intentional

It is clear that scribes made unintentional errors such as eye skips while copying the Hebrew Bible. Early Jewish tradition also claims that, on rare occasions, scribes made intentional changes in the text, calling certain passages *tikkune sopherim* (corrections of the scribes). For example, in the MT Zech 2:12 (v. 8 in English) reads, "For thus said the Lord of hosts (after his glory sent me) regarding the nations that plundered you: Truly, one who touches you touches the apple of his eye" (authors' translation). According to the tradition, the original version of Zechariah read, "the apple of my eye." Scribes then changed that text to read "the apple of his eye," producing the current MT. The NRSV translates the supposed earlier version, while the NIV relies on the present MT reading.

It is impossible to know how frequently the scribes copying the Hebrew Bible may have added, altered, or removed material for theological or aesthetic reasons. Some scholars assume such activity was common and see its traces in explanatory comments that interrupt a story's flow. Thus, in the story of Jacob's vision, the explanation that "the name of the city was Luz at the first" (Gen 28:19) could have been added later by a scribe seeking to explain the location and history of the site.

This determination proves a rather "easy call," but some offer much more of a challenge and significantly alter the understanding of a text. Note the vastly different translations of 1 Sam 10:26–11:1 in the NIV and the NRSV:

### NRSV

Saul also went to his home at Gibeah, and with him went warriors whose hearts God had touched. But some worthless fellows said, "How can this man save us?" They despised him and brought him no present. But he held his peace. Now *Nahash*, king of the Ammonites, had been grievously oppressing the Gadites and the Reubenites. He would gouge out the right eye of each of them and would not grant Israel a deliverer. No one was left of the Israelites across the Jordan whose right eye Nahash, king of the Ammonites, had not gouged out. But there were seven thousand men who had escaped from the Ammonites and had entered Jabesh-gilead. About a month later, *Nahash* the Ammonite went up and besieged Jabesh-gilead; and all the men of Jabesh said to Nahash, "Make a treaty with us, and we will serve you."

### NIV

Saul also went to his home in Gibeah, accompanied by valiant men whose hearts God had touched. But some troublemakers said, "How can this fellow save us?" They despised him and brought him no gifts. But Saul kept silent. Nahash the Ammonite went up and besieged Jabesh Gilead. And all the men of Jabesh said to him, "Make a treaty with us, and we will be subject to you."

The differences here show how translators make differing text-critical decisions. A text from Qumran contains the longer reading; the MT provides the briefer version. The NRSV translation committee determined the version from Qumran was original, while the NIV translators opted for the MT. But why? Many points favor the Qumran reading: it is the oldest attested version, and it seems to prepare the reader well for the mention of eye gouging in 11:3. And the translators theorized that the MT's shorter reading developed when an ancient scribe's eye skipped from one "Nahash" to another (the NRSV text above has these words in italics to make this easier to see), thus eliminating a large section of text. But the MT reading has the advantage of being shorter and stranger. Textual critics frequently assume briefer or more difficult readings are older, believing that scribes tended to add to texts and also tended to smooth matters out (rather than intentionally adding complexity). So the Qumran version could represent an addition made by a scribe to smooth the transition to the events of chapter 11.

Neither side in this debate can be perfectly certain of how 1 Samuel originally introduced King Nahash; the best either can do is to construct an argument concerning what is more *likely* original.

Sometimes only small differences arise between ancient versions, but these distinctions affect the meaning of a verse. In 1 Sam 15:32, Agag the Amalekite king receives a summons to appear before Saul, the Israelite king. The MT states that Agag says to himself, "Surely the bitterness of death is past." In other words, Agag anticipates a beneficial interview with Saul, perhaps because Saul at least hinted at the possibility of an agreement. At the very least, he does not expect the summary execution that YHWH has demanded. The LXX, however, along with a text from Qumran, reads, "Surely this is the bitterness of death." In this version, Agag comes across as fully aware of his deserved punishment and hence, it seems, has better insight into YHWH's demands than Saul. The NRSV relies on the LXX here, while the NIV uses the MT, both assuming that their version makes better sense and that, hence, their reading more closely reflects the original. The text-critical work behind these two translations shapes the presentation of Agag and, in turn, reflects directly on the characterization of Saul. This chapter proves crucial to the tragic narrative of Saul's loss of divine favor and the kingdom. Thus, understanding YHWH's displeasure rests, at least in part, on the choice to translate the MT or the LXX. The fact that two major English translations differ here shows that textual criticism does not resolve all the difficulties with the texts of the Hebrew Bible. Value judgments about fit and sensibility always enter the decision-making process of textual criticism.

## Ways of Reading the Hebrew Bible

To look at the various questions (theological, historical, and literary) that readers ask of the Hebrew Bible, this chapter focuses on three texts: the story of Jacob's vision in Gen 28, the story of Isaiah and the Immanuel oracle in Isa 7, and the Song of Songs. One of these texts serves as the primary example for each reading method considered.

### The Synagogue's Book / The Church's Book: Reading for Theology

For most of the last two millennia, theologically focused readings dominated the interpretation of the Hebrew Bible. Communities asked theological questions of this document such as What is God like? How does God deal with people? How does God deal with our community? What does God want us to do? These inquiries, pondered over hundreds of years by thousands of Jews and Christians, produced volumes of varying and contradictory answers. Such variety comes as no surprise; Jews and Christians read the same document and yet differ over theological presuppositions related to interpreting the text.

The distinctions in reading emerge easily when we think about the fact that each faith community calls the Hebrew Bible by different names. Jews call the text **Tanakh**, an abbreviation drawn from the initial consonants of its three sections: **Torah** (Law/Instruction), **Neviim** (Prophets) and **Kethuvim** (Writings). In typical Jewish practice, the Torah (Genesis to Deuteronomy) takes precedence. Congregations read the entire Torah in weekly sections (*parshaot*) over the course of a year, while only short portions from the prophets (*haftarot*) appear in the liturgy. To summarize very broadly, conformity to the Torah in some sense dictates the understanding of texts from the Tanakh.

Christians call the Hebrew Bible the "Old Testament," immediately marking it as something "old," in relationship with something "new" (the New Testament). The New Testament tends to take precedence over the Old Testament as an authoritative source for Christian doctrine and ethics. In other words, Christians ask "New Testament" questions of the Old Testament and conform their readings of the Old Testament to what they already "know" from the New Testament.

The story of Jacob at Bethel demonstrates some ways people of faith read the Hebrew Bible. No "right" way to read the text emerges, but watching readers interpret Gen 28 assists in understanding the debates people of faith engage in concerning the Hebrew Bible. And attending to these readers also reveals what "stakes" various communities hold in what seem at times perplexingly trivial and breathtakingly emotional acts of interpretation.

### Theology on Jacob's Ladder

Jacob's vision of a ladder reaching to heaven, with angels ascending and descending, powerfully imagines God relating to a particular human being. As early as the New Testament, Christians appropriated this image. According to the Gospel of John, Jesus asserts that "you will see heaven opened and the angels of God ascending and descending upon the Son of Man" (John 1:51). The reference to Jacob's vision, while not expressed through a direct quote, comes across clearly. Here John's Jesus understands himself to function in the place of the ladder, the place where divine and human meet. So the Hebrew "upon him" proves right—the ladder is no "it" but a "him"! In early Christian interpretation, this kind of reading became known as typological interpretation: the ladder prefigures or becomes a pointer toward (a "type" for) Christ. And understanding the ladder as a type for Jesus does not preclude its service as a symbol in other ways. In the Christian folk hymn "Jacob's Vision" the ladder represents the cross (or the work Jesus accomplished on the cross).

This kind of interpretation is not the only option in theological reading. Rabbinic interpretation (midrash) in Judaism did not make extensive use of "types" to understand Jacob's ladder. Rather, the rabbis assumed the interrelationship of all texts in the Tanakh. In this way, images and words from far distant passages offered options for uncovering the ladder's significance.

## "Jacob's Vision"

The hymn "Jacob's Vision" (also called "Jacob's Ladder" and "As Jacob with Travel") originated in England in the eighteenth century. There was no standard set of lyrics in a hymnal, so the words often changed to fit the preferences of the singers. The version here concludes the memoir of an ex-slave, George Washington Offley, published in 1859. Whether he learned these words while still a slave in Maryland or after he moved north to Connecticut is not clear, but they represent ways the story of Jacob's vision was interpreted in the early nineteenth century. It is especially interesting that, in this version, both Jesus and the salvation Jesus brings are the "ladder."

As Jacob on travels was wearied by day,
   At night on a stone for a pillow he lay,
A vision appeared—a ladder so high,
   With its foot on the earth, and the top in the sky.

*Chorus*
Hallelujah to Jesus who died on the tree,
   To raise up his ladder of Mercy for me.
Press forward! Press forward! The prize is in view,
   And a crown of bright glory is waiting for you.

The ladder is long—it's strong and well made—
   Stood thousands of years, and is not decayed;
It's so free of access, all the world may get up,
   And angels will guard you from bottom to top.

This ladder is Jesus, the glorious God-man,
   Whose blood rightly streaming from Calvary ran,
On his perfect atonement to heaven we rise,
   And sing in the mansions prepared in the skies.

Come let us ascend—behold! never fear—
   It stood every tempest and always will bear;
Millions have tried it, and reached Zion's hill,
   And thousands by faith are climbing it still.

Our fathers upon it have mounted to God,
   Have finished their labors and reach'd their abode,
And we are a climbing, and soon will be there,
   To join in their raptures, their happiness share.

G. W. Offley, *A Narrative of the Life and Labors of the Rev. G. W. Offley, a Colored Man, Local Preacher and Missionary* (Hartford, CT, 1859). The entire work is available online at http://docsouth.unc.edu/neh/offley/offley.html.

## Types for Jesus

If Jacob's ladder can point to Jesus, other images could likewise denote his presence. Early Christians found numerous parallels between the story of Isaac's near sacrifice (Gen 22:1–19) and the story of Jesus' life and death (understood by Christians as a sacrifice). In both cases fathers give up only sons, the son carries wood, and the events occur in the same place. Thus, Isaac points toward Jesus.

   Similarly, the manna in the wilderness comes down from heaven at God's command to address the material needs of the people wandering in the wilderness. In a parallel fashion, God sent Jesus down from heaven to provide for the spiritual needs of a people in a spiritual wilderness (John 6:32–33). Thus, the manna points to, or is a type of, Jesus. Early Christian interpretation of the Hebrew Bible is full of examples of such interpretation.

# Differences between the Tanakh and the Old Testament

The Tanakh and the Old Testament include the same texts, but in different orders. The particular listing here of the Old Testament is that typically accepted by Protestant Christians. Catholic, Orthodox, and Anglican Christians include other books (the **Apocrypha** or deuterocanonical works) and place them in a different order:

## Tanakh

**Torah (Law/Instruction)**
Genesis (Bereshit)
Exodus (Shemot)
Leviticus (Vayyiqra)
Numbers (Bemidbar)
Deuteronomy (Devarim)

**Neviim (Prophets)**
Joshua (Yehoshua)
Judges (Shofetim)
1 Samuel (Shmuel A)
2 Samuel (Shmuel B)
1 Kings (Malakim A)
2 Kings (Malakim B)
Isaiah (Yeshayahu)
Jeremiah (Yirmiyahu)
Ezekiel (Yekhezqel)
Hosea (Hoshea)
Joel (Yoel)
Amos (Amos)
Obadiah (Ovadyah)
Jonah (Yonah)
Micah (Mikah)
Nahum (Nakhum)
Habakkuk (Khavaquq)
Zephaniah (Tsephanyah)
Haggai (Khagai)
Zechariah (Zekaryah)
Malachi (Malaki)

**Kethuvim (Writings)**
Psalms (Tehillim)
Proverbs (Mishlei)
Job (Iyyov)
Song of Songs (Shir Hashirim)
Ruth (Rut)
Lamentations (Eikah)
Ecclesiastes (Qoheleth)
Esther (Megillat Esther)
Daniel (Daniel)
Ezra (Ezra)
Nehemiah (Nekhemya)
1 Chronicles (Divre Hayamim A)
2 Chronicles (Divre Hayamim B)

## Old Testament

Genesis
Exodus
Leviticus
Numbers
Deuteronomy
Joshua
Judges
Ruth
1 Samuel (1 Kingdoms)
2 Samuel (2 Kingdoms)
1 Kings (3 Kingdoms)
2 Kings (4 Kingdoms)
1 Chronicles (1 Paralipomenon)
2 Chronicles (2 Paralipomenon)
Ezra (2 Esdras)
Nehemiah (2 Esdras)
Esther
Job
Psalms
Proverbs
Ecclesiastes
Song of Songs (Song of Solomon, Canticle of Canticles)
Isaiah
Jeremiah
Lamentations
Ezekiel
Daniel
Hosea
Joel
Amos
Obadiah
Jonah
Micah
Nahum
Habakkuk
Zephaniah
Haggai
Zechariah
Malachi

Such a practice opened up a myriad of possibilities for assigning significance to any one image, depending on the other passages, words, or even letters one chose (or thought obvious) to use. So, for example, the ladder might represent the ramp to the altar in the Temple, since (1) Jacob's ladder sits on the earth, while the altar also came from the earth (Exod 20:24) and (2) God's standing above the ladder in Genesis finds a parallel in God's standing by the altar in Amos 9:1. In this reading, the angels of God stand for the high priests. Other rabbis understood the ladder as Mount Sinai, using numerous parallels including Moses, like Jacob's angels, ascending (Exod 19:3) and descending (Exod 19:14) the mountain. This identification gains added support when noting that the numerical value of the Hebrew letters in the word for "ladder" (*slm*) equals the same value as the Hebrew letters in the word "Sinai" (*syny*). The very letters in the Hebrew Bible thus prove vital for interpretation.

Not only do Jews and Christians divide over numerous issues of interpretation, but both traditions also include subgroups or smaller communities who ask different questions of the text and bring to it different cultural and theological expectations. As a result, Jews and Christians produce all sorts of interpretations of the Hebrew Bible. And religious groups differ, not just simply over the results of interpretation but over the very way interpretation is to be done. While the Hebrew Bible is understood as authoritative, there are also multiple authoritative, legitimate means to gain meaning from the text.

### the very letters

The rabbis used a variety of techniques to ascertain a text's meaning or explain an odd detail in a text. One of these was *gematria*, a system that used the assigned numerical values of each Hebrew letter (the first letter, *alef*, =1, the second, *bet*, =2, etc.). As an example, it is puzzling why Abraham takes 318 men with him on his rescue mission in Gen 14. This large and precise number would tend to draw commentary. But rabbis noted that letters in the name of Abraham's servant Eliezer added up to 318! Thus, the rabbis claim that Abraham took only Eliezer with him on the expedition!

The rabbis also used a method called *atbash*. This ancient method is, in essence, a letter substitution code in which the Hebrew alphabet is reversed. *Alef*, the first letter, is substituted for *tav* (the last letter), *bet* (the second) for *shin* (the penultimate), and so on. So in Jer 25:26 and 51:41, the text speaks of Babel as "Sheshach" and 51:1 refers to Kasdim (Chaldea) as "Leb-qamai." The methods here can be combined. In one instance, the rabbis offer explanations why one is supposed to remember the exodus on the Sabbath. They take the word used for the "hard labor" the Egyptians forced upon the Israelites, use atbash on it, then total up the resulting word's numerical value, getting thirty-nine. In Jewish tradition there are thirty-nine kinds of labor banned on the Sabbath. So when the Israelites were redeemed from the "hard labor" of Egypt, they were reminded not to engage in the thirty-nine kinds of labor on the Sabbath.

In both these methods, the rabbis assume that the Hebrew Bible is meaningful down to the very level of the letters. Thus, the letters themselves can be helpful in determining possible meanings for a text.

## Midrash

Midrash as a kind of Jewish scriptural interpretation flourished in the first millennium C.E. While *midrashim* (midrashic interpretations) focus on a particular text as a basis, the reasons for interpretation vary. Some interpretations deal with legal matters (*halakah*), others not (*haggadah*). Some collections of *midrashim* follow a text verse by verse (expositional); others link interpretations together for other reasons, sometimes claimed to be sermonic (homiletical).

The earliest surviving collections of *midrashim* (third to fifth centuries C.E.) are all expositional, following texts from the Torah. The Mekhilta of Rabbi Ishmael offers halakic and haggadic readings of Exodus, Sifra provides halakic readings of Leviticus, and Genesis Rabbah is haggadic. Perhaps the earliest surviving homiletic midrash collection is the Pesikta de Rab-Kahana (fifth century C.E.), which collects interpretations of readings assigned to be read in synagogue worship.

*The Historian's Book: Reading for Data*

Historians assemble data on certain times and places, evaluate the data as to its usefulness, and produce a reasonable and defensible construction of past events, persons, and cultures. Historians have used the Hebrew Bible as a source for evidence for their reconstructions of events in ancient Israel. More recently, historians have shown more interest in using the Hebrew Bible as a resource for describing the sociohistorical reality of the cultures from which the Hebrew Bible emerged. Scholars label reading the Hebrew Bible for these purposes, which includes a variety of methods, **historical criticism**.

In evaluating the Hebrew Bible as a source for history, historians frequently attempt to determine the time and place of the text's authorship. For modern literary works, that process is fairly straightforward, often as simple as finding the copyright information on the work's title page. But the Hebrew Bible lacks such a convenient system. The books of the Torah, for example, have no named author. In the Jewish tradition, their titles are simply the first words of the text (Genesis is *Bereshit* ["In the Beginning"]); in the Christian tradition, their titles serve to indicate their contents (Numbers begins with a census). The Psalms often feature notes, called superscriptions, that seem to name an author (e.g., "Psalm of David"), but these were added long after the psalm's composition. Indeed, the superscriptions may really indicate the psalm is in a style associated with David rather than being his literary expression.

Some books in the Hebrew Bible clearly name an author; the book of Jeremiah claims the prophet Jeremiah composed the book during the reigns of Josiah, Jehoiakim, and Zedekiah (Jer 1:2–3). But closer examination reveals that the book of Jeremiah emerged over a long period and includes a great deal of material that describes Jeremiah in the third person. According to the book of Jeremiah itself (e.g., Jer 36:1–4, 32), Jeremiah first spoke his message before others collected and wrote the words we now read. In short, one author did not write the books in the Hebrew Bible at one particular moment. These books result from a lengthy process, a process that began (as the book of Jeremiah indicates) with oral composition.

### Form Criticism: Looking for a Text's Oral Beginnings

Considering the nature of ancient Israelite society, assuming oral composition makes sense. Few ancient Israelites could (or needed to) read or write. The reliance on oral communication extends to the origins of biblical texts; people first *heard* many of these biblical stories, oracles, and laws. Although the spoken words have long since passed away, the written texts still betray, in many places, their oral origins.

When looking for the marks of the oral beginnings of a biblical text, scholars do **form criticism**. Form critics claim that oral literature exists in various set or established forms that express a certain kind of content in a particular and familiar manner. Think of these forms as equivalent to genres. For example, "sitcom" denotes one kind of television show, while "reality" means something else altogether. Simply isolating the oral origins of a particular biblical text does not reveal much about that text's development, however. Form critics go on, then, to claim that these oral forms emerged from distinct social settings (since the early form critics were German, biblical scholars still call a form's social setting its *Sitz im Leben*).

---

### Literacy in Ancient Israel

It is difficult to know with any degree of certainty how many ancient Israelites could read and write at a particular time. In fact, it is best to see literacy as a continuum from sophisticated use of writing to utter ignorance of written texts. The number of Israelites at any given time who could both read and write well (the current definition of "literate") was small, perhaps 1 to 2 percent of the population. These highly literate individuals were almost entirely scribes or others who worked for the court (although it is probable that kings in ancient Israel, as the kings of Israel's neighbors, were marginally literate at best).

A larger number of Israelites were "literate" in the way modern western preschoolers are. Some could write their names reasonably well. A good number, impossible to quantify, could recognize (and perhaps write) some words, such as *lmlk*, which indicated that an object belonged to the royal court (for a picture of such a stamp, see fig. 12.9). This is similar to children recognizing a stop sign. It does not make them "readers," but it does help them with certain tasks (and makes travel more interesting).

But the large majority of Israelites did not need to write or read to do their daily work. Societies and families that do not require a high level of literacy are not apt to take time away from productive activities to teach reading and writing. Thus, most Israelites experienced the contents of the Hebrew Bible as oral, either recited as part of an oral tradition or as read out by a literate scribe.

Form criticism can work on oral forms of expression from present western culture:

| Form | Markers of the form (structure and content) | Possible social setting (Sitz im Leben) |
|---|---|---|
| Pickup line | Frequently a question<br>Claims interest in the party being questioned (e.g., "Come here often?")<br>Not "deep"—tends toward the trivial | Bar, party |
| Relationship talk | Dialogical<br>Begins with "We need to talk"<br>Includes some disagreement over whether the discussion is needed<br>Often ends with "Let's just be friends" | Most frequently, a private space (dorm room, apartment, automobile) |

### The Song of Songs and Form Criticism

As a collection of poems, the Song of Songs betrays obvious oral origins. Form critics find a variety of oral forms in this book. In fact, it is easy for even someone not trained in form criticism to read through the Song of Songs and pick out certain poems that have similar structure and content.

One form will serve as an example here. Four poems (4:1–7; 5:10–16; 6:4–10; 7:1–5) have very similar content and structure. They describe the beloved's body in detail, using exotic **metaphors** ("Your teeth are like a flock of shorn ewes that have come up from the washing, all of which bear twins," 4:2; cf. 6:6). Their descriptions proceed either from top to bottom (4:1–7) or bottom to top (7:1–5). So in 7:1–2, the male begins with his lover's feet and proceeds upward to the thighs and then her pelvic region. These poems are similar to *wasf*s, modern Arabic poems often sung at weddings. This parallel provides a good guess at the social setting of these poems in ancient Israel: wedding celebrations.

Form criticism considers the historical origin of these songs. In this case, though, the precise time of origin remains unclear. No one knows exactly when ancient Israelites began singing these songs. So no definite relation of the songs to any particular point in Israelite history is possible. But the songs do point to celebrations within the household or village, disclosing something of the lived experience of typical Israelites.

### Source and Redaction Criticism: Accounting for the Writing of a Text

Someone, somewhere eventually wrote down this oral material, and someone else assembled it into a larger collection of various love songs. When scholars seek to discern the way biblical texts were edited together, they practice **redaction criticism**. When scholars attempt to isolate (and focus on) hypothetical documents that were incorporated into biblical books, they practice **source criticism**. The story of Jacob's vision provides an entry into the way source critics read the Hebrew Bible, while texts from the book of Isaiah will help illustrate how redaction critics work.

### The Sources of Jacob's Vision

Readers have long noticed peculiarities, odd shifts and jumps, in the stories of the Hebrew Bible. The story of Jacob's vision provides an excellent example. Jacob wakes up terrified and says he is in an extremely holy place (Gen 28:16–17). But he then, apparently, goes back to sleep, since he rises early in the morning (Gen 28:18). Where is the sense in having Jacob drift back into an unnarrated nap until dawn? There is also a bit of a "stumble" between verse 12 and verse 13. Verse 12 focuses on the stairway to heaven as central to Jacob's dream, but this amazing scene vanishes once God appears in verse 13. After God finishes speaking, the stairway reappears; Jacob notes that he must be at the very gate of heaven (v. 17). Removing verses 13–16 leaves a coherent story, a story perhaps more sensible than the full version.

Source critics attribute these peculiarities to the text's combining two sources: one focusing on a "stairway" and one in which God speaks. Some of these source critics then separate these two different Jacob stories and unite them with other pieces in the Torah that have similar characteristics. Through this process, the critics create lengthy narrative sources that they believe were later combined to form the **Pentateuch** as it now stands. The source dealing with the stairway is a part of "J," named for its common use of "YHWH" (known in German as "*JHWH*") as God's name, while God's speech comes from "E," which uses *elohim* as God's name. In other places in the Torah, source critics find the P (Priestly) source and the D (Deuteronomic) source, each with its own characteristic concerns and language. Many source critics are now less certain that these long narrative sources existed, preferring instead to see the Torah's origin in the gradual assemblage of a host of fragmentary sources.

The source critic then attempts to explain how these sources would have been written in their own historical contexts and, thus, helps readers to understand those contexts. For example, E focuses on Jacob's establishing this place as a religious site. E (unlike J) elaborates Jacob's vision of communication between earth and heaven via the ladder, marking this place as the very gate of heaven. E also emphasizes the pillar that Jacob erects and uses the phrase "house of God" (Heb., *bethel*) twice. These emphases suggest that Bethel functioned as a shrine to YHWH at the time E was written (ninth to eighth centuries B.C.E.). E, unlike other Hebrew Bible texts (e.g., 1 Kgs 12:25–13:5; 2 Kgs 23:15–18; Amos 5:4–7; Hos 10:15), does not criticize Bethel but accepts it. One could thus see this story being used originally to support Bethel as an ancient and worthy cult site, perhaps over against other sites such as Jerusalem.

## Two Stories of Jacob's Vision

Here is the story from Gen 28, divided into its two supposed sources, J (in italics) and E (in bold):

<sup>10</sup>*Jacob left Beer-sheba and went toward Haran.* <sup>11</sup>*He came to a certain place and stayed there for the night, because the sun had set.* **Taking one of the stones of the place, he put it under his head and lay down in that place.** <sup>12</sup>**And he dreamed that there was a ladder set up on the earth, the top of it reaching to heaven; and the angels of God were ascending and descending on it.** <sup>13</sup>*And the L*ORD *stood beside him and said, "I am the L*ORD*, the God of Abraham your father and the God of Isaac; the land on which you lie I will give to you and to your offspring;* <sup>14</sup>*and your offspring shall be like the dust of the earth, and you shall spread abroad to the west and to the east and to the north and to the south; and all the families of the earth shall be blessed in you and in your offspring.* <sup>15</sup>*Know that I am with you and will keep you wherever you go, and will bring you back to this land; for I will not leave you until I have done what I have promised you."* <sup>16</sup>*Then Jacob woke from his sleep and said, "Surely the L*ORD *is in this place—and I did not know it!"* <sup>17</sup> **And he was afraid, and said, "How awesome is this place! This is none other than the house of God, and this is the gate of heaven."** <sup>18</sup>**So Jacob rose early in the morning, and he took the stone that he had put under his head and set it up for a pillar and poured oil on the top of it.** <sup>19</sup>*He called that place Bethel; but the name of the city was Luz at the first.* <sup>20</sup>**Then Jacob made a vow, saying, "If God will be with me, and will keep me in this way that I go, and will give me bread to eat and clothing to wear,** <sup>21</sup>**so that I come again to my father's house in peace, then the L**ORD*** shall be my God,** <sup>22</sup>**and this stone, which I have set up for a pillar, shall be God's house; and of all that you give me I will surely give one tenth to you."**

*"YHWH" appears here where source critics do not expect it. This is the E source that uses *elohim* as God's name. Perhaps a later scribe or editor added the name "YHWH" here. More probably, this is evidence that source criticism is not perfect and that its system of divisions is hardly incontestable.

Anthony F. Campbell and Mark A. O'Brien, *Sources of the Pentateuch: Texts, Introductions, Annotations* (Minneapolis: Fortress Press, 1993).

### Editing Isaiah's Oracle

Redaction critics focus on the way editors put texts together from their various sources. The point of interest is not what purposes the text's parts originally served, but how the editor's work relates to his or her historical context. Isaiah 7, like the story of Jacob's vision, is a composite. It does not, however, break easily into two separate stories. Like most of the prophetic literature, it appears as a mixture of the voices of various speakers whose precise relation to each other is not entirely clear.

Isaiah 7:18–25 presents a good example of such a lack of clarity. These oracles do not fit perfectly with what precedes them in Isa 7:10–17. In verses 10–17, Isaiah, though frustrated with Ahaz, gives a sign that indicates Aram and Israel would not succeed in their attack on Judah (Isa 7:16). But Isaiah also intimates that Assyria (apparently YHWH's chosen instrument to destroy Aram and Israel) should not be relied upon. Ahaz's apparent strat-

## Characteristics of the Sources of the Torah

Scholars who support the notion that the Torah was composed of long narrative sources buttress their claims by pointing to the sources' distinct qualities, here listed in table form.

| Source | J<br>Yahwist | E<br>Elohist | P<br>Priestly | D<br>Deuteronomist |
|---|---|---|---|---|
| Divine name used | YHWH | Elohim | Elohim | YHWH |
| Other special terms | "Sinai" for Mount Sinai; "Canaanites" for indigenous population; "to lie with" and "to know" (= intercourse); "Sheol" as abode of dead; "suffer" (*tsb*) | "Horeb" or "Mountain of God" for Mount Sinai; "Amorites" for indigenous population | Prefers "Sinai" for Mount Sinai; "in that very day"; "gathered to his people" (= death); "be fruitful and multiply"; "prince" (*nasi*); "congregation" (*edah*); "possession, holding" (*akhuzzah*); "generations" (*toledot*); "priests and the Levites" | "Horeb" or "Mountain of God" for Mount Sinai; prefers "Amorites" for indigenous population; "Listen!"; God has "a mighty hand" and "outstretched arm" and has done "signs and wonders"; "the place where YHWH will choose as a dwelling for his name"; "Levitical priests" |
| Geographic focus | Judah | Israel (northern kingdom) | Judah | Whole land, centered on Jerusalem |
| Emphases and concerns | Blessing; God speaks directly; leadership | Fear of God; dreams; angels; prophets | Numbers (ages, measurements); genealogies; itineraries; careful instructions; cult and cultic arrangements | Centralization of cult at Jerusalem; rejection of nonstandard worship and other gods; obedience to covenant |

Anthony F. Campbell and Mark A. O'Brien, *Sources of the Pentateuch: Texts, Introductions, Annotations* (Minneapolis: Fortress Press, 1993); and Richard Elliott Friedman, *The Bible with Sources Revealed* (San Francisco: HarperSanFrancisco, 2003).

egy to seek Assyrian aid in this crisis rejects faith in YHWH (7:9) and thus courts disaster (7:17).

While Isaiah is far from specific about the results of Ahaz's faithless alliance with Assyria, the four oracles in Isa 7:18–25 are much more dire, focusing on the consequences of this act for the people as a whole. In these oracles, YHWH uses Assyria and its king as an instrument not for Judah's benefit but for its punishment. The images are extreme: Assyrians will settle over the land like bees (7:19), humiliate Judean men by shaving them (7:20), and reduce Judah's vineyards to trackless briar-filled waste (7:23–25).

Why has an editor added these oracles? They make Ahaz's lack of trust in YHWH an almost cosmic error. Ahaz's move is no mere political miscalculation; it violates the relationship between king, people, and their national deity. Inserted at this point, the oracles emphasize Ahaz's extreme failure just before another oracle from Isaiah (8:1–4) offers Judah release from its current dire circumstance by relying on YHWH's, not Assyria's, might. But, once again, Judah and its leaders opt for Assyria (8:5–8). The addition of the oracles connects these two rejections of divine help (7:10–17; 8:5–8) with a bridge detailing the editor's view of the inevitable results of such faithlessness.

But these oracles, as they emphasize the miserable consequences of Ahaz's faithlessness, also prepare the reader for the image of the faithful king in Isa 9:2–7. Either Hezekiah or Josiah, both of whom opposed Assyria, could be the king the editor has in mind. So the editor responsible for the hymn of praise to the current "good" king (Hezekiah or Josiah) may also have added material to chapter 7 to contrast the "bad" Ahaz with the "good" Hezekiah or Josiah. Where Ahaz's decisions caused destruction, the present faithful king will secure peace and prosperity.

### Looking More Broadly for Historical Context:
### Social and Anthropological Readings

Historians use the methods just described (form, source, and redaction criticisms) to locate texts and their component parts historically. Historians also make use of sociological and anthropological models to help draw out from the Hebrew Bible what may have been happening on a broad cultural or economic level in ancient Israel (these methods are sometimes called "social-scientific" to distinguish them from the older, more text-focused, methods).

### *The Song of Songs and Sociology*

The Song of Songs presents a good test case for sociological readings, since the poems seem to have nothing much to say about Israelite political or military history. Nor does the Song appear to have been used in worship. Rather, these poems seem to be intended to entertain. So modern readers can learn about Israelite culture by watching Israelites amuse themselves.

Anthropological studies indicate that in agrarian societies such as ancient Israel, female agency expresses itself primarily in the domestic sphere, so it is significant to note that the Song includes two references to a "mother's house" (Heb., *bet em*; Song 3:4; 8:2). Both these texts associate the "mother's house" with procreation. In Song 3:4, the singer mentions the mother's "chamber" where she was conceived, while in Song 8:2, the singer speaks of "the chamber of the one who bore me [*t<sup>e</sup>lamm<sup>e</sup>deni*]." The second may also refer to the mother teaching; the verb *lmd* here could mean "teaches" instead of the NRSV's rendering as "bore."

Here are arenas in which women could have had some responsibility and authority: ensuring proper prenatal care, assisting in births and their surrounding rituals, and instructing children in a variety of tasks. The Song fails to mention the "father's house" (Heb., *bet av*), the basic unit of Israelite social organization (see chapter 4). The song could thus suggest that in ancient Israel there was some locus of female power within the household.

Other glimpses of Israelite social organization may appear in the Song. The female figure's brothers, for example, express concern about her as she approaches the age for marriage:

> We have a little sister,
>     and she has no breasts.
> What shall we do for our sister,
>     on the day when she is spoken for?
> If she is a wall,
>     we will build upon her a battlement of silver;
> but if she is a door,
>     we will enclose her with boards of cedar.          (Song 8:8–9; cf. 1:6)

The brothers promise a reward for their sister if she acts as a "wall," perhaps a reference to her remaining a virgin until marriage. If she attempts to evade their control, they will cut her off from potential lovers. Chapter 4 discusses the reasons for this interest in female virginity. For now, it is enough to note that this text demonstrates some concern with how Israelites practiced family life.

But readers of the Song must exercise some caution in making sociological claims. The poems here could be more fantasy than description, so interpreters can read too much into these images. And it is not always clear that a particular anthropological model, derived from cultures in different times and places, can validly apply to Israelite life. Nonetheless, sociological and anthropological readings may provide some data for understanding the functioning of Israelite households, and this data may, in turn, help readers understand the Hebrew Bible itself.

### Writing History with the Hebrew Bible

As the discussion of various methods has demonstrated, the texts that make up the Hebrew Bible relate to their historical context(s) in complex ways. There were all sorts of forces in action in ancient Israel that generated this material, organized it, wrote it, edited it, and copied it. Any attempt to understand the process inevitably smoothes it out, so readers must not sell its complexity short. Moreover, attempting to understand that process helps scholars evaluate data for writing a history of ancient Israel—a goal of historical criticism.

When scholars evaluate the textual evidence, they cast doubt on the historical accuracy of the narratives in the Hebrew Bible. Jacob serves as an example. No certain evidence, archaeological or otherwise, exists for Jacob outside the Hebrew Bible. The stories about Jacob are stories; they are not contemporaneous archival records. And a figure such as Jacob, the supposed ancestor of the people Israel, would naturally attract all sorts of legendary material, material that relates cultural values rather than historical truth.

Can the stories of Jacob relate anything about events in ancient times? Some historians note that "Jacob," or names much like it, appears in several texts from the eighteenth to fifteenth centuries B.C.E. among Semitic peoples. In addition, several of the customs seen in the stories in Genesis, such as the head of household's use of a servant to produce an heir, also appear in Mesopotamian texts of this period. So other ancient material here may shed light on the Hebrew Bible.

While scholars who analyze these parallels do not argue that the stories of the patriarchs and matriarchs are "history," they claim that these stories may speak of actual historical individuals buried under a load of legendary accretion. Some call this position "maximalist." The maximalist historian gives the biblical text as much historical credit as is reasonably possible. (This is not the same as believing the Hebrew Bible is perfectly accurate historically.)

Other historians claim that the Jacob narrative tells us nothing of the early history of Israel. Texts from a variety of historical periods provide parallels to names and customs in the patriarchal stories. There is thus no need to assume the stories of the patriarchs and matriarchs are extremely early. At best, these tales give evidence of the way Israel constructed its own identity in the period of the monarchy (or even in and after the exile, depending on when one wishes to date the texts). In short, the "history" one finds by reading the Hebrew Bible is the history of the development of the *idea* of Israel—its ideology of national existence—rather than the development of the people Israel itself. Historians taking this position, or positions like it, are often called "minimalists" (often used, it should be noted, as a negative accusation). Scholars on these ends of the historical-critical spectrum often engage in heated, if not uncivil, discussions.

Historians ask the Hebrew Bible to tell them about the past, but this is no simple process. The texts of the Hebrew Bible must be placed in a historical context, analyzed to see what kind of evidence they reasonably present, compared with other ancient sources, and put into dialogue with the results of archaeological excavations. The particular needs and assumptions of the historical reader help determine what that reader "finds" in the Hebrew Bible.

## ends of the historical-critical spectrum

The terms "maximalist" and "minimalist" obscure more than they reveal, often serving as labels to dismiss rather than examine someone else's view. But the intense debate about the relation of the Hebrew Bible to history, expressed in these terms, continues, largely because

- many believers, Jewish and Christian both, take the historicity of the Hebrew Bible as an article of belief;
- the debates (and bloodshed) over who should control the present-day Cisjordan involve historic claims; and
- institutional interests are "in play" both inside the academy ("What should count as 'real' scholarship?" "Who counts as a 'real' scholar?") and in the broader world ("How can we sell more books/magazines?").

As a student of the Hebrew Bible, be prepared to see in the media various accounts of fights over the historicity of the Hebrew Bible. And be prepared to watch accusations of theological bias, Zionism, lack of scholarly credentials, intellectual incompetence, and anti-Semitism fly.

## Archaeology and the Hebrew Bible

**Archaeology** attempts to reconstruct the former culture(s) of a particular site or region, and archaeological excavations in the Cisjordan have provided much information on the material culture of the people who lived there in ancient times. Since this textbook introduces a particular cultural artifact, the Hebrew Bible, and not the cultural history of the ancient Near East, it will not provide a detailed introduction to the practice of archaeology. But when scholars, journalists, or even politicians use archaeological data, keep in mind the following:

1. Archaeology does not exist to "prove" or "disprove" the Hebrew Bible. Archaeologists address and evaluate the Hebrew Bible only in the context of delineating the region's cultural history.
2. Since archaeology focuses on material culture, it will often tell about cultural developments the Hebrew Bible texts either are not interested in (e.g., what women did in the household) or wish to suppress (e.g., nonstandard ways of worshiping YHWH).
3. While archaeology with its material bent makes full use of scientific tools, at its base it is still an interpretive enterprise. Archaeologists develop an argument concerning a culture; they do not write a mathematical proof concerning a culture.
4. Archaeologists argue with each other over the details, and archaeologists and biblical scholars are prone to disputing each other's work while guarding their respective "turf."

*The Literary Critic's Book: Reading for Art and Beyond*

Historians focus on the author of a text as the key to its meaning and significance. Dating the author's creation of the text and locating it socially and geographically are vital. Literary readers focus on the text itself or the reader's interaction with the text as keys to meaning. They need not raise questions of authorship or of the text's history of development. Rather, the text's use of language, its characterization, plot, and effect on the reader (ancient or modern) are at the fore.

### Narrative and New Criticism

As biblical scholars began reading texts from the Hebrew Bible in a literary manner during the 1970s and 1980s, they relied upon a style of reading known as **New Criticism**, especially when reading narrative texts. The New Critics dominated English studies in the 1930s, and their methods continue to thrive in English classrooms throughout North America. They held that neither the intention of the author nor the subjective responses of the reader determine a text's meaning. Rather, the text itself is the focus. To read a text appropriately demands entering deeply into its own structure and reading closely its use of language. Not all literary readers of the Hebrew Bible adopt this particular line of thinking or its ideological underpinnings, but the methods used even by more current narratologists still feature a strong focus on the text itself. Several features of the story of Jacob's vision invite a New Critical investigation.

### *Reading Jacob's Vision as a Story*

First, look at the uses of language in the story. The frequent use of the word "place" (*maqom*) stands out. Such repetitive use of the term here may seem wooden or dull to modern ears. Are all these references to "place" necessary? "And he came to a certain *place* and stayed there that night, because the sun had set. Taking one of the stones of the *place*, he put it under his head and lay down in that *place* to sleep" (28:11 RSV). By such repetition, the author wishes to alert the reader about this location and wants, from the start, for the reader to have "place" in mind.

---

### Tools for the Non-Hebrew-Reading Literary Critic

A reader of classical Hebrew can note all the occurrences of a particular Hebrew word in the text fairly easily. Readers of English translations cannot be so certain, however, since translators do not always represent a Hebrew word with the same English word. There are tools that help the non-Hebrew reader examine texts for use of Hebrew words. Interlinear translations place a simplified, highly literal, translation of the Hebrew below a copy of the Hebrew text. A concordance lists all the occurrences of a particular English word in a particular translation. Analytical concordances reveal the Hebrew words behind the English words in a given translation. The one pictured on the next page presents the RSV. Here we can see that in Gen. 28 the translators of the RSV used "place" to represent the Hebrew word coded "13," which is *maqom*. In Gen 30:2, however, "place" translates word "23," the Hebrew word *takhat*, while in Gen 40 "place" translates the verb *ntn* (word "15"). In Gen 42:15; 43:30; and 50:11, the translator supplied the word "place" to make a clearer English translation. There is no word meaning "place" in the Hebrew of those verses; this analytical concordance marks these occasions with an asterisk.

| | | |
|---|---|---|
| 28:11 | he came to a certain place, and stayed there | 13 |
| 11 | Taking one of the stones of the place | 13 |
| 11 | his head and lay down in that place to sleep. | 13 |
| 16 | LORD is in this place, and I did not know it. | 13 |
| 17 | was afraid, and said, "How awesome is this place! | 13 |
| 19 | He called the name of that place Bethel; | 13 |
| 29: 3 | and put the stone back in its place upon the mouth | 13 |
| 22 | Laban gathered together all the men of the place | 13 |
| 30: 2 | and he said, "Am I in the place of God | 23 |
| 32: 2 | he called the name of that place Mahana'im. | 13 |
| 30 | Jacob called the name of the place Peni'el | 13 |
| 33:17 | the name of the place is called Succoth. | 13 |
| 35: 7 | built an altar, and called the place El-bethel | 13 |
| 13 | went up from him in the place where he had spoken | 13 |
| 14 | a pillar in the place where he had spoken with him | 13 |
| 15 | Jacob called the name of the place where God | 13 |
| 38:21 | he asked the men of the place, "Where is the harlot | 13 |
| 22 | men of the place say, 'No harlot has been here.' | 13 |
| 39:20 | the prison, the place where the king's prisoners | 13 |
| 40:11 | Pharaoh's cup, and placed the cup in Pharaoh's | 15 |
| 13 | and you shall place Pharaoh's cup in his hand | 15 |
| 21 | and he placed the cup in Pharaoh's hand; | 15 |
| 42:15 | you shall not go from this place | * |
| 43:30 | and he sought a place to weep. | * |
| 50:11 | Therefore the place was named A'bel-mizraim; | * |
| 19 | Fear not, for am I in the place of God? | 23 |

**Fig. 2.6: Selection from *The Eerdmans Analytical Concordance to the Revised Standard Version of the Bible***

Second, examine the role of the **narrator**. Here (as in much of the narrative in the Hebrew Bible) the narrator, third person and omniscient, does not actively participate in the story as a character. But the narrator still controls the reader's level of knowledge. Readers can learn of Jacob's thoughts and dreams (Gen 28:16–17, 20–22) and can even hear YHWH speak (Gen 28:13–15), but only via the narrator. And this narrator discusses matters only when appropriate. In verse 11, for example, the narrator reveals that Jacob slept at "a certain place" but fails to report the place's name until much later (Gen 28:19). If the narrator had told all at the start, the story would be quite different. The readers would immediately equate the place Jacob sleeps with a holy place, thus making YHWH's appearance much less surprising. Noticing the ways the narrator controls information helps readers understand this story.

Also, notice how the narrator controls Jacob's speech in the story. Although the subject of the tale, Jacob remains silent for the first five verses (in fact, Jacob has said nothing after lying to his father in Gen 27:24!). When he speaks, he offers two brief exclamations of awe (Gen 28:16, 17) that affirm what the narrator has already intimated: Jacob has encountered YHWH. The narrator allows Jacob's voice to dominate the end of the story, with a three-verse-long vow (Gen 28:20–22).

Finally, note the pace at which the narrator narrates. The story begins with a series of verbs that proceed rapidly:

> *And* Jacob *left* Beersheba *and he went* toward Haran *and he arrived* at a place *and he stayed* there (for the sun had set) *and he took* one of the stones of the place *and he put* it under his head *and he lay down* in that place. (28:10–11, authors' translation)

This translation points to the speed at which Hebrew narrative, which tends to connect chains of verbs with "and" (note the italics), can move when the narrator wishes. The pace slows abruptly with nightfall (28:12), then resumes in verse 18 ("Jacob rose and took and set and poured"). These shifts of pace may be a clue to the narrator's emphases. The relatively slow narration of the vision scene invites the reader to slow down and pay close attention to it. And the speedy succession of verbs before and after the vision endows Jacob with an almost manic energy.

Tracking the way a story uses language, how it describes various figures, and how the narrator functions is basic to New Critical and many other forms of literary reading. Such observations would serve as building blocks toward a literary reading of Jacob's story, a reading that would need to explain how all these details work together to produce a meaning for the tale.

### Reader-Response

There are other ways to make literary sense of biblical texts than close reading in New Critical style. Some critics look at how texts affect readers and how readers draw meaning from texts. While New Critics look to the text as the arbiter of meaning, these critics look to the reader. In this pursuit, they are part of a diverse movement called **reader-response criticism**.

---

### Trusting the Narrator

Can readers trust the narrator to tell us the truth about a character or event? (Here "truth" does not refer to absolute truth, such as whether the narrator offers correct historical and scientific data.) Rather, within the confines of the story, does the narrator mislead readers, intentionally or unintentionally?

Modern fiction features many narrators who, it turns out, cannot be trusted. The narrator in Henry James's *The Turn of the Screw* is a good example. The narrators in the Hebrew Bible are generally reliable—that is, they tend not to lie to the reader's face. But that does not mean the narrators are impartial. Readers should be alert to the narrators' possible agendas regarding characters and events.

**Fig. 2.7: Marc Chagall's**
*Le Songe de Jacob*
*Artists have to interpret stories from the Hebrew Bible in order to render them visually or musically. In* Le Songe de Jacob, *Marc Chagall focuses on the mystical nature of Jacob's experience, inviting the use of vibrant colors and figures. In addition, Chagall places Jacob's dream in dialogue with two other images. In the lower right, he has placed an image of the sacrifice of Isaac. In the upper right, Chagall presents a crucified Christ floating in midair. The viewer of Chagall's painting is left to suggest what this dialogue might mean.*

*(Marc Chagall,* Le Songe de Jacob *[1960–1966], Réunion des Musées Nationaux / Art Resource, NY © 2008 Artists Rights Society [ARS], New York/ADAGP, Paris)*

### Readers' Responses to Isaiah 7

A reader-centered reading of Isa 7 could proceed in a variety of ways. Some reader-response critics look carefully at the way the text, through its own structure, pushes a reader toward certain conclusions. These critics often speak of "gaps" in a text that leave the reader to determine responses, which may be affirmed, contradicted, or never answered with certainty as the reader proceeds.

In Isa 7, for example, readers learn in the first verse that Judah's enemies failed, so they know something of the story's eventual outcome. Isaiah himself (v. 4) and YHWH (v. 7) also express this view. So readers join Isaiah and YHWH in the knowledge elite. Yet much remains unknown. In verse 3, Isaiah's son, Shearjashub, enters the narrative. The strange name begs for commentary. It means "a remnant will return," but is Isaiah's son a positive sign (there will be a remnant that survives this crisis) or negative (only a remnant will survive this crisis)? The strong statements of Isaiah and YHWH, coupled with the knowledge granted readers in verse 1, could lead readers to understand Shearjashub positively. God will protect the people; a remnant will return. The Davidic monarchy, under dire threat, will remain.

Isaiah later gives Ahaz yet another multivalent sign, a "gap" for the reader: Immanuel (Heb., "God with us"). Does God being with "us" mean that God is on "our" side? Perhaps yes. God says that he will soon destroy the other kingdoms threatening Judah (7:16). Does God being with "us" mean that God is close at hand to punish us? Perhaps yes. God intends to use Assyria to wreak havoc on Judah (7:18–25). So which meaning is it? The text never forces the reader to make the decision as to the significance of Immanuel or Shearjashub, and this play of meanings continues into succeeding chapters (8:8, 10; 10:21–22). By leaving the question open, by making the reader consider different ways of filling that "gap," the text moves the reader to accept Isaiah's assertion that God supports the nation and its monarch (positive) while also demanding complete loyalty on pain of dire punishment (negative).

While some reader-response critics claim the text guides the reader (perhaps unfailingly) to a particular meaning, others, following the lead of literary theorist Stanley Fish, claim the reader creates the text. By this, Fish means that interpretive strategies exist for readers prior to their reading a text; meaning is located in those strategies, not in the text itself. These strategies, developed by interpretive communities, create "text" from the marks on a page. Communities with different assumptions find completely different meanings, since their reading strategies have generated different "texts."

Theological readings provide good examples of such reader responses (although those readers would certainly claim that the "text" controls the reader, not the other way around). For example, Jews and Christians read Isa 7 differently. They do so because they as readers bring different expectations and ways of reading to the text. Christians tend to see verse 14 in connection with Jesus Christ, in some way being fulfilled in his birth (Matt 1:22–23), with the <u>young woman</u> being identified with the Virgin Mary. Jews tend to see Immanuel as the future king Hezekiah or another child of Isaiah. Isaiah 7 can be made meaningful in as many ways as there are distinct interpretive communities; readers control the process.

### Postmodern Readings

Fish's openness to diversity of interpretation provides a useful bridge to a set of literary reading techniques labeled "**postmodern**" or "poststructuralist." As with "reader-response," these terms cover a diversity of methods. But in general these techniques serve to reveal texts as points of contestation, as unstable vessels for meaning.

---

### young woman

The differences between Jews and Christians regarding Isa. 7:14 also derive from different translations of the Hebrew word *almah*, used to refer to the pregnant woman. Jews have rendered this word as "young woman," and this is the best translation, since the word carries no reference to sexual experience. Christians, who early on used the LXX, found in Isa 7:14 the Greek word *parthenos*, which frequently has the meaning "virgin." This traditional reading has been so strong among Christians that the word "virgin" appeared in Isa 7:14 in every major English translation of the Hebrew Bible until the RSV in 1952. This new rendering was quite controversial, and, to this day, different translations deal with this issue in a variety of ways.

Of the ways of reading in this broad group, deconstruction stands out as one of the more popular (and controversial). As a reading practice, deconstruction looks very much like New Critical close reading. Both methods feature intense, analytical approaches to the minute details of a text. But deconstruction makes some very different claims about the nature of language and meaning. While the New Critics claim the text itself bears a meaning, deconstruction claims that texts can never divulge a single, complete meaning. Meaning arises from the differences between signs in a text. Since these meaning-making differences continue to pile up as readers make their way through a text, any final meaning must be deferred. (This is Jacques Derrida's notion of *differánce*, a French word simultaneously meaning "difference" and "deferral"). Nothing need intervene to stop the endless play of signs; any end of meaning is an imposition.

Rather than reading the details of a text in order to come to "the" meaning, deconstructionists pay attention to the places where a text reveals the impossibility of closing off meaning. A deconstructive reading does not destroy the text; it analyzes the text to show that the text is not, finally, its own master (and neither is the reader, whose understandings of a text await inevitable undermining).

### Deconstructing Jacob's Vision

Now return to the word "place" in Jacob's story. Jacob takes time to rename the place of his amazing vision: "He called that place Bethel; but the name of the city was Luz at the first" (Gen 28:19). This detail is odd. The story presents Jacob in a rural setting. He sleeps outside; the only noteworthy feature of the area is a large rock for use as a pillow. But the text here indicates he is in the city of Luz, a city he now renames. Just what is "that place [*maqom*]" anyway? To what might it refer?

The story reveals some information about this "place." Jacob came to "the place" and took one of the rocks "of the place" for a pillow (28:11); YHWH appears "in this place" (v. 16); and "this place" thus inspires awe (v. 17). Despite the repetition, the identity of the place remains vague. "This place" exists somewhere between Beersheba and Haran. But Jacob attempts to resolve this vagueness by marking this place, using both a rock and a word. Both markers have a sense of permanence: the place is now called Bethel (it used to be Luz); the rock will wait around until Jacob gets some confirmation of YHWH's good faith (v. 22).

But the note of an alternate name for Bethel, indeed a more ancient name, calls into question Jacob's ability to mark his "place." Names change. Stones can change as well, from a pillow to a pillar and then, if God keeps his part of the deal, it will (oddly) become the thing that Jacob has claimed the place already is: Bethel (Heb., "the house of God"). The transitory nature of word and rock makes one wonder about the inheritance plans enunciated by YHWH (vv. 13–15). In this place where names are not what they seem, perhaps all language, especially promises, will remain unfulfilled.

### Ideological Criticism

Texts and readers serve as arbiters of meaning in literary readings. Readers' assumptions and needs shape their readings, while texts attempt to impress certain views upon the reader. These views, assumptions, and needs are all ideological in nature. Texts and readers hold certain perspectives—ideologies—that come to expression. Chapter 11 will discuss this idea in detail. For now, note that there are no nonideological texts and no non-ideological places from which to read. Ideological critics simply claim their perspective (all readers being in some sense ideological) and their social location (all readers being in some sense defined by where they dwell economically, religiously, culturally, sexually, etc.). Given their perspectives, ideological readers interrogate the way a text either presents an ideology or may be read ideologically.

### *The Song of Songs and Ideology*

The Song of Songs provides an example of an ideological reading. This text features women in a variety of roles—including speaking roles—so something may be going on in this text regarding gender.

Some scholars celebrate the Song as a place (if not *the* place) in the Hebrew Bible that portrays women as free (or relatively free) from male domination. In other words, the text could invite women to think of themselves as actors in the world, as pursuers of sexual pleasure (Song 3:4) capable of having power over men (4:9). The female figure in the Song certainly seems to have a robust self-concept, extolling her own beauty: "I am black and beautiful, O daughters of Jerusalem, like the tents of Kedar, like the curtains of Solomon" (1:5; cf. 8:10). As we have seen, the references to the "mother's house" in the Song may speak to a sociological reality in ancient Israel. But also, in terms of ideology, the use of the term could demonstrate that the "woman's world" is the "destiny" of the male figure (3:4; 8:2). The Song could thus be a useful resource for the reader attempting to find voices of liberation from oppression in the Hebrew Bible—in this instance, gender-based oppression.

But readers may also question this ideological perspective by asking to what end the female figure appears as "free" or "powerful." In places, male figures clearly control the female figure, even abusively (1:6). And the female dreams of being beaten and stripped by the town guards (5:7). These episodes could be an invasion from the text's patriarchal context—a "reality" that even the ideological point of view taken in the Song cannot finally ignore. Or one could read the combination of violence, control, and exposure of the female (5:7; 7:1–5) as pornographic. The Song narrates a male fantasy of being desired by a beautiful young woman who has nothing else better to do than wait for her man, imagining sexual encounters with him (5:2–6). Taken that way, the Song undergirds a patriarchal construction of femaleness: women serve male needs.

# Reading from Various Ideological Perspectives

The stories of the exodus and the conquest are stories of the liberation of the Israelites from oppression. But "liberation" is a political and cultural term; its meaning is closely related to the ideological perspectives and social locations of the reader looking for liberation. What do readers in a variety of contexts hear ideologically in these stories?

> The obvious characters in the story for native Americans to identify with are the Canaanites, the people who already lived in the promised land. As a member of the Osage Nation of American Indians who stands in solidarity with other tribal people around the world, I read the Exodus stories with Canaanite eyes. And, it is the Canaanite side of the story that has been overlooked by those seeking to articulate theologies of liberation. Especially ignored are those parts of the story that describe Yahweh's command to mercilessly annihilate the indigenous population.

Robert Allen Warrior, "A Native American Perspective: Canaanites, Cowboys, and Indians," in *Voices from the Margin: Interpreting the Bible in the Third World* (Maryknoll, NY: Orbis Books, 2006), 237.

> The central feature of the account for the tribes of Israel was the part played by Yahweh in their liberation. They did not read the exodus as a secular revolutionary movement. Yahweh was on their side and guided the movement through his prophet Moses. The fact that they succeeded in escaping from their enforced serfdom despite the powerful Egyptian army showed that God, who took the side of the poor in Egypt, was the true God.

George V. Pixley and Clodovis Boff, "A Latin American Perspective: The Option for the Poor in the Old Testament," in *Voices from the Margin*, 213.

> The Exodus released a totally different history of effects in so-called liberation theology, by attaining a new significance for the oppressed people of Latin America in their struggle for justice. . . . But how can a Palestinian read the book of Exodus? . . . If the Exodus of the Hebrews brought an end to foreign oppression and the attainment of a land of their own, then it meant exactly the opposite to the original inhabitants of Palestine, namely the invasion of their own soil and being dispossessed by foreign troops. After the Jews labeled their 'occupation' of Palestine in the 1930's and '40s an 'Exodus,' the Palestinians had even greater difficulty understanding the book of Exodus. The flip side of the rescue of persecuted Jews is that it spells tragedy for the Palestinian people.

Mitri Raheb, *I Am a Palestinian Christian* (Minneapolis: Fortress Press, 1995), 86–87.

> The book of Exodus tells of the emancipation only of the people Israel. . . . Gentile slaves in Egypt and elsewhere undergo no such change. And the emancipated people do not stay in Egypt but leave for the land of Canaan. There is no indication that the oppressive social system of Egypt would not go on as before. . . . If God's hearing the groaning, crying, and moaning of the afflicted slaves reflects "the preferential option for the poor," His remembering the covenant with Abraham, Isaac, and Jacob reflects the chosenness of Israel. Of the two concepts, chosenness is in this narrative the more important, for only it accounts for the identity of those freed in the exodus and for their leaving Egypt rather than staying: they are the descendents of Abraham, Isaac, and Jacob, and they leave in order to participate in God's fulfillment of his promise to give them the land of Canaan.

Jon Levenson, "Liberation Theology and the Exodus," in *Jews, Christians, and the Theology of the Hebrew Scriptures*, ed. Alice Ogden Bellis and Joel S. Kaminsky (Atlanta: Society of Biblical Literature, 2000), 223–24.

> ### these ideological readings
>
> Both the readings here assume that heterosexual relationships are normative. The difference between them is how they read the nature of the heterosexual relationships in the Song of Songs. These readings are open to challenge, not just from each other but also from readers who want to challenge the silent assumption of heterosexual "naturalness." Readers coming from LGBT (lesbian, gay, bisexual, and transgender) perspectives would necessarily be ideological—but no more ideological than any other readers.

There is no easy way to adjudicate between these ideological readings of the Song; there is no way to step out of ideology to make a decision. Some readings may make better historical or literary sense, but that decision on sensibility is hardly ever self-evident or easy. So reading this text involves reading ourselves as well, understanding why certain readings are appealing and asking why certain readings "make sense."

## The Book at the End of Modernity: Reading Conflict and Difference

In the period often called "modernity," western thinkers tended to elevate human reason, speaking fairly easily of truth secured by the exercise of reason and objectivity. Expressions of this modern "take" on human endeavors include historical readings that derive "facts" about ancient Israel and literary readings that seek an "objective" account of a text's operations. But the Hebrew Bible, like all other artifacts related to western culture, finds itself caught at the end of modernity. Confidence in human reason and certainty concerning a single "objective" viewpoint are no longer unwavering benchmarks of western culture.

There are ways forward past the various passions of modernity. Theological readings, especially those from premodern cultures, resist modernity's emphasis on a single, correct meaning. The rabbis and early Christian readers found all sorts of possible meanings in a text; texts are so crammed with meaning that they could not boil them down to a certain "point" or referent. Openness to this surfeit of meaning leads to conflict; these meanings do not always "get along," especially as these meanings are generated in and among interpretive communities.

Historical critics of the Hebrew Bible have begun raising questions beyond those of the politics (and political theology) of ancient Israel, looking to the Israelite family and to the ideological justification of Israelite and Judean statehood. In addition, some critics now consider historians as part of the process of interpretation, driven (or at least informed) by ideology. Thus, minimalists critique maximalist scholarship as part of both the broader western construction of the "Oriental" as mysterious "other" and the ideological project of Zionism. Minimalists' opponents charge them with ideological commitment to Palestinian statehood or ideological opposition to the modern state of Israel or to Judaism.

These are all postmodern gestures. This textbook is part of the project of reading the Hebrew Bible at the end of modernity. It will not develop a history of ancient Israel, nor will it provide a certain literary path to the "right" reading. Instead, it will disclose multiple meanings and demonstrate the contestation of ideology.

Such an approach to the Hebrew Bible does not mean that we, the authors, lack strongly held convictions, or that we think the Hebrew Bible need not be taken seriously. In our view, the Hebrew Bible forms or attempts to form the identities of its readers (ancient and modern), claiming (or projecting) the power to construct not only personal identities but also a whole world of meaning. The Hebrew Bible invites readers to inhabit a world of its own construction, a world strikingly different from that of today, not just historically but also ideologically. Our job is to expose the ways the Hebrew Bible constructs this world, not so you will embrace that world or reject it, but so you may understand it. To this project we now proceed.

| **Suggested Biblical Readings** | Genesis 28 |
| --- | --- |
| | Isaiah 7–8 |
| | Song of Songs |

**Discussion Questions**

1. Pick a story from the Hebrew Bible and read it in several translations. How do the translations differ? How do these differences affect how you understand the text?
2. Take the same story and compare your English translation (which translates the MT) to an English translation of the same passage in the LXX (a translation from 1851 is available online at http://www.ccel.org/bible/brenton and other places). What differences stand out? When there are differences, which text do you think is more likely original? Do you think the MT and the LXX tell the same story here?
3. Think of a movie that has a distinct historical setting. How do you think a historical critic would approach the movie? How do you think a literary critic would approach it?
4. Take a biblical story and make it into a screenplay. What assumptions do you have to make about the story in order to do this? What information do you have to provide that the story lacks? Does your screenplay end up having an ideological perspective?

**Suggestions for Further Reading**

Adam, A. K. M., ed., *Postmodern Interpretations of the Bible: A Reader*. St. Louis: Chalice Press, 2001.

Gunn, David M., and Danna Nolan Fewell. *Narrative in the Hebrew Bible*. New York: Oxford University Press, 1993.

Laughlin, John C. H. *Archaeology and the Bible*. New York: Routledge, 2000.

McKenzie, Steven L., and Stephen R. Haynes, eds. *To Each Its Own Meaning: An Introduction to Biblical Criticisms and Their Application*. Louisville, KY: Westminster John Knox Press, 1999.

Mulder, M. J., ed. *Mikra: Text, Translation, Reading, and Interpretation of the Hebrew Bible in Ancient Judaism and Early Christianity*. Minneapolis: Fortress Press, 1990. See especially the essays on biblical interpretation.

O'Keefe, John J., and R. R. Reno. *Sanctified Vision: An Introduction to Early Christian Interpretation of the Bible*. Baltimore: Johns Hopkins University Press, 2005.

Steck, Odil Hannes. *Old Testament Exegesis: A Guide to the Methodology*. 2nd ed. Translated by J. Nogalski. Atlanta: Scholars Press, 1998.

Sugirtharajah, R. S., ed. *Voices from the Margin: Interpreting the Bible in the Third World*. 3rd ed. Maryknoll, NY: Orbis Books, 2006.

# 3. *Introducing Identity*

Identities are complex and multiple and grow out of a history of changing responses to economic, political, and cultural forces, almost always in opposition to other identities.

—Kwame Anthony Appiah, *In My Father's House: Africa in the Philosophy of Culture*

How do people come to know who they are? Most initially identify themselves by their place in a family unit. Others turn to their profession—or, if in college, their major—to answer the question. Perhaps a hometown or a home state, province, or region serves to define its inhabitants, or, when out of their native country, their nationality may come to the fore. Identification by gender or age group as well as by a racial or ethnic designation places a person in broader categories. Sometimes religious affiliation provides key information. People highlight different aspects of themselves depending on who wants to know, in what context, and for what purpose. And when a person does things such as marry, accept a new position, or move, the labels for self vary. Moreover, claiming membership in one group generally excludes participation in others. Being Muslim means not being Hindu, for example, or being a citizen of Morocco means not being a citizen of China.

Throughout the biblical story, the identity of both "Israelite" and "non-Israelite" peoples proves impossible to express clearly or consistently. Families, clans, tribes, and nations suffer a variety of traumas that compromise the meaning of these traditional indicators. The mobility of populations—whether by choice, force of nature, or military conquest—frequently separates kin and removes any sense of connection with a particular locality. Marriages between families, clans, and tribal groups erase differences in what contemporary people call "race" or "ethnicity." Moreover, consistent interaction between peoples reshapes cultural, social, and religious norms and practices.

No one figure embodies all of the factors associated with identity discussed in this section of the textbook. But thanks to the complexities of his story, the character of Moses serves as an excellent starting point. The writers of the

## Race and Ethnicity

What "race" and "ethnicity" designate is complicated. Most people presume that "race" labels biological distinctions based on visible factors such as skin color and particular physical features. By the same token, typical use of "ethnicity" speaks broadly of common ancestry but also implies associated physical manifestations. Current genetic research helps demonstrate that categories based on ideas of color or certain bodily features arise as cultural and social constructs rather than rest on empirical data. As a result, many scholars claim that race does not truly exist. Ethnicity, on the other hand, still works as a descriptor when it designates linked ancestry in addition to elements such as shared history, stories, religion, language, geography, and cultural practices. More important, ethnicity in no way relates to any given set of typical bodily characteristics. See chapter 7 for further information.

biblical material imagine Moses, burdened with a complicated upbringing and living among foreigners, encountering God in a burning bush. There they depict him as unsure of his identity. When directed by this divine presence to deliver the people of Israel from their slavery in Egypt, the narrator presents Moses asking, "Who am I that I should go to Pharaoh and bring the Israelites out of Egypt?" (Exod 3:11). This simple question probes more than his qualifications for such a mission. A close reading of the text demonstrates how the first part of that question—"Who am I?"—haunts Moses virtually from the moment of his birth.

The way in which the narrative imagines Moses' struggle to find answers guides the study of identity in this chapter. Like the people of Israel throughout the biblical story, the Moses developed in the text strives to know who he is, to what people he belongs, and to what god he owes his allegiance. Also, like Israel, the text shows his view of himself and his place in the world varying in substantial ways over the course of his life. This instability of Moses' self mimics the shifting ideas of "Israel" and reveals the problems with assuming "Israel" ever designates one lasting and unaltered group or territory.

## Did Moses Exist?

Some scholars question the existence of a historical Moses, while others raise concerns about the accuracy of the stories told about his life. John van Seters, for example, writes, "The quest for the historical Moses is a futile exercise. He now only belongs to legend" (quoted in Dewey M. Beegle, "Moses," in *The Anchor Bible Dictionary*, vol. 4 [New York: Doubleday, 1992]). In other words, if a historical figure Moses existed, no one could know anything about him other than what the biblical text reveals. Treating the text in this manner places the focus on how the writers and editors of the book of Exodus generated a literary Moses, shaped his identity, and positioned him as an Israelite, a liberator, and a lawgiver. In this chapter, Moses functions solely as a character within the biblical story.

**Beginnings**

In ancient times, like today, many people defined themselves within a family unit—as a child, parent, spouse, sibling, or cousin, for example. (Chapter 4 takes a closer look at this practice in the Hebrew Bible.) But Moses' story, as narrated in Exodus, illustrates the often tenuous nature of kinship connections. Described as the son of **Levite** parents (Exod 2:1), Moses comes into the world as part of the familial line of Abraham, Isaac, and Jacob. Significantly, however, such an important character in the biblical story lacks a true genealogy; no name for either his father or mother appears here. This absence implies Moses' loss or lack of solid ties to the people of Israel.

He also faces the possibility of immediate death, as the text places the story of Moses' birth alongside Pharaoh's command to kill all the male **Hebrew** children under the age of two (1:22). The narrators credit the intervention of five women for saving the infant boy: Shiphrah and Puah, the Hebrew midwives who defy Pharaoh's order to kill male babies (1:15–20); his mother, who hides him for three months (2:2); his sister, who watches him until his recovery from a small basket in the Nile and intervenes to provide him care (2:4, 7–8); and Pharaoh's daughter, who pities him and takes him to raise as her own (2:5–6:10). As structured in the text, this story raises questions about Moses early on—for example, Will he come to know himself as Israelite or Egyptian?

### Israelite or Hebrew?

In Exodus, the terms "Hebrew" and "Israelite" assume the same group of people, but they function differently in the text. Exodus 1 mentions the "sons of Israel" (1:1) and reports that their growth into the "Israelites" feels threatening to Pharaoh (1:9, 12, 13). "Israelite" derives from the renaming of Jacob as "Israel" in Gen 32:27–28 and implies a shared family line.

"Hebrew" proves far more difficult to understand. Some scholars see a connection between the label *Habiru* (sometimes *Hapiru*)—a term appearing in over two hundred ancient Near Eastern texts from the eighteenth to the eleventh centuries B.C.E.—and the Hebrew people. The term *Habiru* routinely refers to small groups of people forced to move due to famine, war, disaster, debt, or other causes and who settled on the margins of society. They often organized around one leader and, eventually, became part of larger and more stable groups generally through military or other service. While any etymological link between *Habiru* and "Hebrew" has been widely dismissed, the lower socioeconomic status of these groups and their position as outsiders has led to the hypothesis that Israel (the Hebrew people), could have originated in a *Habiru*-like group.

Within Exodus, "Hebrew" appears solely where Egyptians identify the people except for one time in a legal text (Exod 21:2). In these chapters, Pharaoh and Pharaoh's daughter use it to refer to a group of people other than Egyptians (1:15–22; 2:6–7). Moses, raised as an Egyptian, employs it to express a sense of common identity with the "Hebrews" (2:11–13). The basis for the term, then, might be socioeconomic, although no one can know for certain.

Speculation about its use includes identifying the Israelites as representing a subgroup of the Hebrews or seeing "Hebrew" as a label placed by outsiders, while "Israelite" functions more as insider language. Exodus 3:18 might confirm this latter understanding when Moses receives instruction to identify this God to Pharaoh as "God of the Hebrews" (see also 5:3; 7:16; 9:1, 13; and 10:3).

## Reading Moses with Martin Luther King Jr.

Beginning on April 16, 1963, Martin Luther King Jr. penned his now-famous "Letter from Birmingham Jail" during eleven days in prison. Arrested in Birmingham, Alabama, for his campaign boycotting downtown merchants, King answers an April 12 statement by eight white clergy describing this action as "directed and led in part by outsiders" and "unwise and untimely." In this portion of the letter, King describes the relationship between oppression, identity formation, and the need for action:

> When you have seen vicious mobs lynch your mothers and fathers at will and drown your sisters and brothers at whim; when you have seen hate-filled policemen curse, kick and even kill your black brothers and sisters; when you see the vast majority of your twenty million Negro brothers smothering in an airtight cage of poverty in the midst of an affluent society; when you suddenly find your tongue twisted and your speech stammering as you seek to explain to your six-year-old daughter why she can't go to the public amusement park that has just been advertised on television, and see tears welling up in her eyes when she is told that Funtown is closed to colored children, and see ominous clouds of inferiority beginning to form in her little mental sky, and see her beginning to distort her personality by developing an unconscious bitterness toward white people; when you have to concoct an answer for a five-year-old son who is asking: "Daddy, why do white people treat colored people so mean?"; when you take a cross-country drive and find it necessary to sleep night after night in the uncomfortable corners of your automobile because no motel will accept you; when you are humiliated day in and day out by nagging signs reading "white" and "colored"; when your first name becomes "nigger," your middle name becomes "boy" (however old you are) and your last name becomes "John," and your wife and mother are never given the respected title "Mrs."; when you are harried by day and haunted by night by the fact that you are a Negro, living constantly at tiptoe stance, never quite knowing what to expect next, and are plagued with inner fears and outer resentments; when you are forever fighting a degenerating sense of "nobodiness" then you will understand why we find it difficult to wait. There comes a time when the cup of endurance runs over, and men are no longer willing to be plunged into the abyss of despair. I hope, sirs, you can understand our legitimate and unavoidable impatience.

King's words here both underscore and challenge the perspective of oppressed people as presented in the book of Exodus. Few Israelites rise up in any kind of rebellion in the story. But they do question a Moses who defends one among them, even to the point of death. Perhaps their complacence demonstrates the effects of "nobodiness." By contrast, the narrative shows Moses growing up in privilege and thus acting boldly, if somewhat foolishly, to forge ties to this people. In such situations of oppression, what might it take to overcome what King calls "nobodiness"?

The Martin Luther King Jr. Papers Project at Stanford University,
http://www.stanford.edu/group/King/frequentdocs/birmingham.pdf.

The writers of the text want to claim that Pharaoh's daughter's ability to raise Moses in her home shelters him but does not preclude him from knowing his true heritage. Exodus 2:11 reports that "one day, after Moses had grown up, he went out to his people and saw their forced labor. He saw an Egyptian beating a Hebrew, one of his kinsfolk." He responds to this sight by killing the Egyptian. The text shows Moses as deeply affected by blood ties and the situation of "his people." This act also exhibits a boldness that likely accompanied his formation as an Egyptian. Taking the life of a taskmaster exhibits a sense of entitlement not typical of an oppressed person who routinely suffers beatings and accepts them as a part of her or his reality.

The events unfolding in these opening chapters of Exodus prompt a question: What constitutes family identity? In the story, the character Moses defines himself by kinship connections; he defines himself as "Hebrew" presumably because of his Levite parents. Although only in the care of his biological family for a short time, the writers stress his actions as a grown man reveal an unshakeable identification with these people. This emphasis on "blood relations" denigrates the actions of Pharaoh's daughter, who "took him as her son" (Exod 2:10), and implies a possible host of negative associations with adoption as a mode of family formation. Do others call attention to his adoption? Does he appear distinctively different? Is he treated in some lesser manner? Does he resist their attempts to make him part of the family? The stressing of genetic ties privileges one kind of identity at the expense of another and attempts to draw a sharp line dividing things Israelite and things Egyptian—a line questioned continually by this same text. In fact, the name Moses itself expresses some of these contradictions.

As the story continues, a "Hebrew" character rejects Moses' identification with this group. The day after Moses commits murder in defense of one of his kin, the text describes a confrontation between Moses and two men fighting. He appeals to their common ancestry as a basis for peace, saying,

## the name Moses itself

According to the book of Exodus, Pharaoh's daughter chooses the name Moses (Exod 2:10). The text further claims that she, an Egyptian, selects a name derived from Hebrew: he becomes *Mosheh* because she draws him out (the Hebrew verb *mshh*) of the water. The authors of the text added this etymology to connect him more strongly with his birth family and with the Israelites.

More likely, however, she names him in her own language. The Egyptian verb *msy* means "to be born," and the noun derived from it, *ms*, is "child" or "son." So Rameses, the name of many pharaohs, is *Ra* plus *mss*, or "the child of Ra" (the sun god). *Moses*, then, simply means "child," and that choice makes sense since Pharaoh's daughter found the boy lacking parents.

His name, then, always bears a mark of disconnection: Whose child? What family? Which people? Unlike many other biblical names that carry meaning, the character of Moses receives an identity void of content. How he develops in the narrative provides whatever meaning the name will carry.

"Why do you strike your fellow Hebrew?" (2:13) His query meets with contempt as one of the men wonders why Moses assumes authority over the people and if he intends to kill again (2:14).

In considering what gives rise to this response, one reading might conclude that the man who is fighting questions the ease with which Moses assumes control. Perhaps the text prompts readers to think that growing up as part of an Egyptian family shaped Moses in ways he cannot recognize. Less privileged persons may immediately detect a difference in his readiness to act, to provide solutions, and to throw off the social order. They may reject him on that basis. Or perhaps this man knows Moses' story and resents that fate not only spared him from death but also lifted him out of slavery and suffering and into circles of luxury and power. For members of this enslaved group, identity might rest in shared experience as much as in blood, and Moses simply fails to qualify. Other interpreters might conclude that the two men see Moses as simply <u>another Egyptian</u>.

Moses' actions, as described, betray any real ties with his adoptive family, and that makes some readers question the characterization of Moses in this narrative. The willingness of Moses to commit murder on behalf of a slave might suggest his failure to assimilate into the culture of the people who raised him. The text then continues to picture Moses as afraid for his own security once he becomes aware of the public nature of his act. Indeed, he flees the country to preserve his life (Exod 2:14–15). Again, any kind of family relationship with the Egyptians is ignored here. Pharaoh fails to excuse Moses' behavior as he might the conduct of a grandchild and instead, without any investigation, seeks to kill him (2:15). The text leaves open a crucial point. If Moses did not kill an Egyptian, would he continue as a part of the Egyptian community? Marry an Egyptian woman? Work in the house or court of Pharaoh?

The text presents readers with other questions as well: Can Moses, knowing his family background, live comfortably among the Egyptians who oppress his people? Or, from a different angle, did or would the Egyptians ever fully embrace Moses? Yet another reading might hold that Moses' killing of an Egyptian assumes an authority only Pharaoh possesses and that the writers use this incident in his past to cast him as an outsider. The lengths the writers go to underscore his "foreignness" to the Egyptians reveals a great deal about their interests and certainly stresses the crucial nature of their making Moses an Israelite.

### another Egyptian

Could the resistance of these men to Moses mean that Moses was actually an Egyptian? Most famously, Sigmund Freud argues in *Moses and Monotheism* (1939) that an Egyptian Moses adopted the cause of the Israelites as his own.

**Next Steps**

As the story progresses, it describes Moses fleeing Egypt to the land of Midian, a region to the east of Egypt and on the other side of the Red Sea. Novelist Zora Neale Hurston describes this moment in her book *Moses, Man of the Mountain* with these words: "Moses had crossed over. He was not in Egypt. He had crossed over and now he was not an Egyptian. He had crossed over. . . . He felt as empty as a post hole for he was none of the things he once had been. He was a man sitting on a rock. He had crossed over" (San Francisco: HarperCollins, 1991). In this passage, she visualizes Moses as vacating his former self through geographic and emotional relocation. Similarly, the biblical writers present his time there, further complicating the question of his identity. But can a person truly void a self at will? Can one simply choose to inhabit a new identity? While Hurston creatively expresses Moses' desire to escape the bonds that tie him to Egypt, the biblical text imagines a Moses more conflicted in his own eyes and in the eyes of others.

According to Gen 25:1–6, the Midianites also descend from Abraham, but through his second wife, Keturah. If Moses indeed comes from a Levite line, the writers show him as sharing distant kinship with this people. Yet when Moses meets the seven daughters of a local priest and assists them with some problem shepherds while watering their flock (Exod 2:16–17), the story says the women report his aid to their father with these words: "An Egyptian helped us against the shepherds" (2:19). Perhaps Moses' dress, his speech, or an accent leads these women to label him Egyptian. Perhaps he tells them from where he came. Or maybe to these women in the middle of this remote country, all outsiders are labeled as "Egyptian."

Whatever the cause of the women's conclusion, Moses seems Egyptian to them, and their perception shows textually that his years in Pharaoh's daughter's house form him as much as his bloodline. No matter what differences the text presents between how Moses saw himself and other Egyptians, no matter how he feels about his adoption or his adoptive versus his biological families, no matter what other Egyptians might say to him about him, Moses comes across to these neighboring people as Egyptian. While the writers show him sharing common ancestry with these women

---

### Biblical Genealogies: Their Purpose and Function

Biblical genealogies commonly express idealized understandings of families, clans, tribes, and nations rather than presenting historically accurate information. The writers used genealogies as maps to articulate a community's feelings toward other groups and to offer rationales for the success of a relationship between peoples or explanations for enmity. The tone of these lists reads to most moderns like a formal record; the names also lend a certain definitive quality. While certainly rooted in family stories, genealogies frequently function not as history but as constructed memory. Attending less to their form and more to their function within the story helps modern readers understand their purpose.

### What Did Moses Look Like?

How did Moses appear? Was he similar to or different from Egyptians? The book of Exodus offers no details, but cinematic retellings make guesses, and they often reveal more about the interpreter than the text. In the classic 1956 film *The Ten Commandments*, Charlton Heston plays Moses. A long mane of hair and flowing beard and costuming provide the only attempts to vary his "typical" American appearance. By contrast, Yul Brynner's Pharaoh comes across as somewhat exotic. His Russian ancestry and bald head frequently led to his casting as a "foreigner." Elaborate headdresses and a bare chest contribute to his "otherness" in this film. In the 1998 animated motion picture *The Prince of Egypt*, the young Moses shares a common skin tone and facial features with Rameses, the next pharaoh. A variation in haircut distinguishes the sons of the ruler in Egyptian iconography and also in this film. The real distinction between the two in the movie comes through sound. American actor Val Kilmer voices Moses (and God!) while British actor Ralph Fiennes gives Pharaoh a more "imperial" tone.

via Abraham, the women see no feature in Moses' appearance that points to their relationship. The distinction between the Israelites and Egyptians thus might rest more on signs not easily recognizable in a casual encounter such as economic and political status. Or, perhaps even more radically, only the text draws a distinction between groups and does it solely to build the forthcoming narrative confrontation.

Moses ends up marrying one of the daughters—Zipporah (2:20–21)—and the birth of their son demonstrates his still unresolved struggle to understand himself. He calls the boy Gershom; the Hebrew word *ger* means "stranger" and *sham* designates "there." As the text explicates, the child's name evokes Moses' own sense of displacement: "I have been an alien residing in a foreign land" (2:22). The Hebrew perfect verb here might read it in at least two ways. Most commonly translated in the past tense, as above, the name speaks about Moses' discomfort as an Israelite in Egypt. Moses knows he did not, does not, and will not ever truly belong to that people. If, however, as the grammar allows, the translator chooses the present tense—"I am an alien residing in a foreign land"—the character of Moses says something about the temporary status of his home in Midian. This place belongs to his now father-in-law and wife, but it cannot provide a real home for him whether or not Moses proves to be an Israelite or Egyptian. In naming his son, Moses continues as a nonentity. The writers of the text claim he lacks ties to either his birth or adoptive families while also stressing his inability to locate a self-identity in marriage and fatherhood.

| More Complications | Moses shows up tending the sheep of his father-in-law in the far wilderness as chapter 3 of Exodus opens. In that remote place, away from other people and |

apart from any tribal or national territory, the story describes his encountering a deity. Here, this god offers Moses the opportunity to define himself as a part of the people in addition to becoming their deliverer and leader.

Initially, the narrative appears to present God firmly identifying Moses as an Israelite: "I am the God of *your father*, the God of Abraham, the God of Isaac, and the God of Jacob" (3:6). Note the use of the singular noun "father" instead of the standard "God of your fathers," denoting the entire ancestral line. God underscores that Moses' family of origin connects him to the Israelites no matter the circumstances of his rearing. The story might also picture God determining that Moses possesses unique qualifications to accomplish the task of liberating the Israelites. A member of the "family" and yet not himself enslaved, raised within the Egyptian royal house and yet not compromised by loyalties to it, no one better than Moses exists to mediate on behalf of the people. But if God attempts here to forge a not so readily evident connection to Moses, a reader might conclude that Moses knows nothing of this god and that this meeting serves as an introduction.

The task of searching for a sense of self often takes a person to external sources: "I am a parent" or "I am a daughter" defines one in relationship to family. "I am a lawyer" or "I am a teacher" relates self-understanding to what a person does professionally. "I am a Canadian" or "I am an American" relates one to others born or naturalized into citizenship in a particular country. In his encounter with a burning bush, Moses' character looks to the god within it for answers to questions that long have plagued him.

But even as the writers depict God forging a relationship between Moses and the Israelites and explaining what action Moses will, ideally, take on their behalf, two references to "my people" (3:7, 10) separate Moses from this group. Verse 10, in particular, stands out, with the text describing God as saying, "Come, I will send you to Pharaoh to bring my people, the Israelites, out of Egypt." Such language excludes Moses. Moses as an Israelite and any narrative links to the people disappear here. This distinction between Moses and the people leaves Moses, as the narrators picture it, quite rightly unmoved. The story shows him wondering aloud, "Who am I that I should go to Pharaoh, and bring the Israelites out of Egypt?" (3:11). A careful reader fires off a series of mental questions: Why should Moses place himself on the line? What would prompt his concern for these people or their god? Does Moses see himself as completely outside of the Israelite community after his experience in Egypt? Does Moses know this God at all?

The issue of what qualifies an individual for political and spiritual leadership looms large in this passage. As presented in the story, the presence of the deity provides the support required for effective service. The people must trust the God who sends Moses, and Moses must depend on God to empower him. But, even more significant, if Moses accepts this position to solidify his identity as an Israelite, the subsequent narrative yields only more confusion. As leader, Moses provides a visible presence to both the Israelites and Egyptians in the ensuing conflict. Although the text continues to maintain

**Fig. 3.1:** *Moses Striking the Rock,* **by Valerio Castello (1624–1659)** *This painting shows Moses producing water for the people of Israel to drink in the wilderness (Exod 17:1–7). The halo effect around his head indicates the power of God rests upon him. Although God promises to stand before Moses at the rock (17:6a), Moses receives the instructions to strike it, to bring forth water, and to allow the Israelites to drink (17:6b). The elders of Israel observe his action (17:6c). The people then ask, "Is the Lord among us or not?" (17:7). While the provision of water should convince them, they see only Moses and not God performing the work.*

*The text positions God as the force behind the spectacular events that unfold. But the stories tell how Pharaoh, the Egyptians, and the Israelites see Moses (and Aaron) acting before their eyes and often equate Moses with the God for whom he stands. Moses and Aaron (a peripheral figure at best) continually remind Pharaoh and the reader that they represent God and that the many signs performed come from God (7:17; 8:10; 9:3, 16). Sometimes God is credited by the recipients (8:8, 19; 9:27–28), while elsewhere Moses receives the recognition (10:7).*

that he merely channels the power of God, the writers also produce <u>a puzzling conflation</u> between Moses and God that complicates the reading of the story.

Differentiating where an invisible and unknown God begins from where a visible and known Moses ends proves problematic and makes it easy to understand how Moses takes on some of God's character and power for both the Egyptians and the Israelites. The confusion between Moses and God extends to God as well. Look, for example, at the narrative of the golden calf. When God and Moses, removed from the action, discover what the people have done, God claims that the disobedient Israelites belong to Moses (32:7). In this passage, God identifies Moses as the deliv-

### a puzzling conflation

This chart lays out how different characters often confuse Moses and God.

| TEXT | Characters Affected | Confusion of Moses and God |
|---|---|---|
| Exod 4:16 | Aaron | Moses "serves as God" to him |
| Exod 7:1 (see also 20:19, 21; 34:29–35) | Pharaoh and Aaron | Moses is "like God" to them |
| Exod 10:16 | Pharaoh | Sinned against God and Moses |
| Exod 14:10b–11 | People | Credit Moses with bringing them out of Egypt |
| Exod 17:2 | People | Argue with Moses, and he tells them that they are testing God |

erer of this people, forcing Moses to correct the record in verse 11: God delivers, not Moses.

This strange narrative blending of Moses and God raises some difficult questions about the identity of Moses. He appears as more than simply another Israelite. This blurring of boundaries between Moses and God could give him a unique status, placing him somewhere outside the community of Israel. Careful readers observe that once Moses agrees to take on God's mission to free Israel, God instructs him to tell Pharaoh the following: "Israel is my firstborn son. I said to you, 'Let my son go that he may worship me.' But you refused to let him go; now I will kill your firstborn son" (4:22–23).

If Israel stands as God's firstborn, Moses might stand with God as the parent of Israel, or with Israel as God's child, or somewhere between the two. The question of whom God intends to kill also looms large. An unusual narrative that follows both shocks and provides some clues for how to think about these questions.

Exodus 4:24 reads, "On the way, at a place where they spent the night, the LORD met him and tried to kill him." Without any referents, whose life God attempts to end remains ambiguous. Reading ahead shows that while Moses takes his family with him to Egypt, he (or maybe Gershom) comes under attack by God. Zipporah, Moses' Midianite wife, steps in decisively in the story by circumcising Gershom (identified in v. 25 as *her* son, so not precluding another child not fathered by Moses) and applying the bloody foreskin to "his" (Moses'?) penis (the text reads "feet," often a euphemism for "penis"). This action apparently wards off the divine attack (4:26), although again the pronouns make who acts and who gets spared ambiguous. Zipporah, according to the writers, declares that her ritual causes someone (Moses?) to become a bridegroom of blood to her.

No one knows what this story means; it puzzles scholars and other interested readers alike. Several interpretive possibilities present themselves. Moses, raised as an Egyptian, might seem to God a part of that people and thus an enemy. This line of thinking makes sense if Moses, although born a Levite, never received circumcision. After all, according to Gen 17:9–14, the covenant between Abraham and God requires circumcision of every male and the exclusion of any uncircumcised from among the people of God (Gen 17:14). (See chapters 6 and 7 for more information.) Readers interpreting this way conclude that Gershom's circumcision somehow "counts" for Moses as well.

Such a reading works, given the emphasis on identity and the attempts in Exodus to tie Moses directly to the Israelites. Unfortunately, it might fail on accurately reflecting Egyptian custom since the Egyptians also circumcised males, although typically at adolescence as opposed to on the eighth day following birth. Other interpreters account for this issue by claiming that an already-circumcised Moses needs a "reactivation" of the ceremony to bond him as part of God's covenant community, and thus the blood and foreskin of his son serve the purpose.

Then again, the text might present the attack as on Gershom as opposed to Moses. In this scenario, the child who represents alienation or otherness becomes the target perhaps not only of the deity but of Moses himself. For this interpretation, Moses' new identity depends on killing his self-understanding as separate or apart from the people of Israel, and the shedding of the blood of circumcision accomplishes this task. At this point, Moses' body (figuratively) and Gershom's flesh (literally) bear a distinguishing mark of belonging. Only after this harrowing ordeal can Moses reunite with Aaron, his Israelite brother, and complete the family unknown to him since his infancy. As a full member of the covenant community, Moses can now act on behalf of God and assume status as a deliverer.

No matter what kind of reading ultimately results, Moses certainly becomes emblematic of the struggle of Israel with God in this story. Tentative about his identity, his body demands the symbolic marks in order not to stand under the threat of God as "not Israel" and thus "not my people." Marked, he embodies belonging to God and becomes the paradigm of one consecrated to God, redeemed for service. While he now seems to possess all he needs to act as the ideal and idealized Israelite—leading the people from bondage to freedom, giving them the covenant and law, and emerging as one of the most central figures in the story of the people—he nonetheless continues to struggle for belonging. As the next section reveals, no one picture of Moses endures; to the end, who he is and to what people he belongs, if any, remains unresolved.

## Final Thoughts

Moses' life as narrated here illustrates the complications of identifying one's self in any kind of a stable or lasting way. The story of his birth, his childhood, and the making of his own family demonstrates how identities within such relational units shift regularly from childhood to adulthood, or through marriages, divorces, births, remarriages, and the deaths of various members of the group. Add to these factors the complexities of adoption, stepfamilies, or all of the modern technologies associated with childbirth—from sperm or egg donation to surrogacy—and the ways in which who gets drawn into the circle of family becomes even more difficult to determine. Moses also struggled with cross-cultural identifications and with the ways in which others reacted to him. Israelite? Egyptian? Midianite? In today's multicultural world, people of mixed ancestry still face the same feelings of not quite fitting in, of rejection, and of isolation (see Mitzi's Story, next page).

As the writers of the text demonstrate, Moses also changes depending on circumstance. When he marries and lives in Midian, he works as a shepherd; when he goes to Egypt and brings the people out, he takes the title of deliverer; when he communicates the covenant to the people, he becomes the lawgiver and their conduit to God. Each of these identities thus draws out

# Mitzi's Story

My mother has been the center of jokes and derogatory comments since my older sister was born. She was the one who took my sister by the hand and led her through the streets of Bangkok and Okinawa as eyes stared and people gathered to talk about the sambo baby. She was the one who took all my siblings to the grocery stores, the malls, the park, school, Burger King, hospitals, church. In each of these public arenas we were stared at either in fascination because we were a new "sight" or stared at with a look of disgust or both. Nigga-chink, Black-Jap, Black-Japanese mutt. The neighborhood kids, friends, and adults labeled my siblings and me with these terms especially after they recognized that my mother was completely intent on making us learn about Okinawan culture. On New Year's Day, we had black-eyed peas and mochi. We cleaned the house to start the year fresh and clean. "Don't laugh with your mouth too wide and show yo teeth too much," my mom would always tell us. "Be like a woman." I had not realized that I covered my mouth each time I laughed until someone pointed it out in my freshman year in college. When we disobeyed my mother's rule or screamed, we were being too "American." If I ever left the house with rollers in my hair, my mom would say I shouldn't do American things. "Agijibiyo . . . Where you learn this from? You are Okinawan too. Dame desuyo. Don't talk so much like Americans; listen first." There were several other cultural traits and values that I had inevitably inherited (and cherish) [while] being raised by a Japanese mother.

Growing up in an all-black neighborhood and attending predominately Black and Latino schools until college influenced my identity also. I was definitely not accepted in the Japanese circles as Japanese for several reasons, but that introduces another subject on acceptance into Japanese communities. Now this is not to say that the Black community I associated with embraced me as Blackanese, even though I think it is more accepting of multiracial people than probably any other group (because of the one-drop rule, etc.). There is still an exclusion for those who wish to encompass all parts of their heritage with equal weight, and there is also a subtle push to identify more with one's black heritage than the other part because "society won't see you as mixed or Japanese but BLACK." I can't count the number of times I have heard this argument. What I do know is that no society can tell me that I am more of one culture than another because of the way someone else defines me. I am Blackanese—a mixture of the two in ways that cannot be divided. My body and mentality is not split down the middle where half is black and the other half is Japanese. I have taken the aspects of both worlds to create my own worldview and identity. Like Anna Vale said in Itabari Njeri's article "Sushi and Grits," my mother raised me the best way she knew how, "to be a good Japanese daughter."

My father on the other hand never constantly sat down to "teach" us about being Black. We were surrounded by Blackness and lived it. He was always tired when he came home from work. He'd sit back in his sofa and blast his jazz. My mom would be in the kitchen with her little tape player listening to her Japanese and Okinawan tapes my aunt sent every other month from California. My siblings and I would stay at my grandmother's house once in a while (she cooked the best collard greens), and when my mom came to pick us up she'd teach her how to cook a southern meal for my father. Our meals were somewhat of an indicator of how much my mom held on to her traditions. My father would make his requests for chicken, steak or okra and my mom had learned to cook these things, but we always had Japanese rice on the side with nori and tofu and fishcake with these really noisome beans that are supposed to be good for you (according to my mom. I swear she knows what every Japanese magazine has to say about food and health). It was my mother who told us that we would be discriminated against because of our color, and it was my Japanese mother to whom we ran when we were called niggers at the public swimming pool in Houston. To say to this woman, "Mom, we are just black" would be a disrespectful slap in the face. The woman who raised us and cried for years from her family's coldness and rejection because of her decision to marry interracially, cried when my father's sister wouldn't let her be a part of the family picture because she was a "Jap." This woman who happens to be my mother will never hear "Mom, I'm just Black" from my mouth because I'm not and no person—society or government—will force me to do that and deny my reality and my being, no matter how offensive I am to their country or how much of a nuisance I am to their cause. I am Blackanese.

Mitzi Uehara-Carter, "On Being Blackanese," *Interracial Voice* (online journal), http://www.webcom.com/intvoice/mitzi.html. Used with permission.

**Fig. 3.2: Michelangelo's *Moses***
*Michelangelo's* Moses *(1516) sits in the Church of San Pietro di Vincoli in Rome at the tomb of Pope Julius II. Imagining Moses at an older age, Michelangelo presents him as confident and strong, with his hands on the law and the radiant power of God (symbolized by the horns) causing his face to shine. But the slight slump in his body demonstrates the weight of his responsibilities. Much like the portrayal in Deut 34, this marble Moses attempts to carry the myth of the character and so seems stable and unchanging even in the face of alternative images.*

different skills, shapes how others interact with Moses, and likely influences his view of himself.

The biblical text tries to afford him the status of one known in death. For the authors of Deut 34, Moses' life stands out as exemplary: "Never since has there arisen a prophet in Israel like Moses, whom the LORD knew face to face. He was unequaled for all the signs and wonders that the LORD sent him to perform in the land of Egypt against Pharaoh and all his servants and his entire land, and for all the mighty deeds and all the terrifying displays of power that Moses performed in the sight of all Israel" (34:10–12). Preserving his public life, these words capture only a fraction of the character encountered in the story and equate him solely with the heroic figure the Israelites claim to have revered in their experience of liberation from slavery. Elevated to great stature, he takes on a mythic quality, and whatever man might have existed gets lost within the persona.

If not for one detail mentioned twice earlier, the reader might miss Moses the human being altogether. In Deut 32:48–52 and 34:1–6, Moses gets only to see the promised land but not to cross into it, on account of disobeying God in an earlier incident. Although Deut 32:50 promises him a resting place with his family, Deut 34:6 reports that his burial takes place at an unknown site in Moab. The anonymity of his grave, apart from kin, in a strange land and not even among the people of Israel, reiterates important features of his life.

The character Moses dies with no lasting family connections, without a home in any country, and with no people who claim him completely as one of them. Unlike Jacob, whose bones Joseph and his brothers lovingly return to Canaan from Egypt (Gen 50:1–14), or Joseph, who asks for the same (Gen 50:24–26), Moses requests such treatment (Exod 13:19) and yet never makes it across the Jordan—never makes it "home." The liminal quality of his life finds expression in that unmarked grave: as a man without a family, a people, a country, Moses becomes fixed eternally in the unknown.

This textually complex Moses not only shows readers the convolutions involved in defining one's identity but also introduces the ways in which the people of Israel struggle with this same issue throughout the biblical story. The Hebrew Bible purports to relate the narrative of a people across almost two thousand years of history, but the picture of "Israel" in the biblical material never offers a stable or uncontested identity. Who belongs to this family or people or nation—and how—remains an open question. Further complicating the picture, no simple chronological or developmental line for Israel and no equation between Israel and some fixed geography in any one period exists. Where—or even if—borders appear to demarcate "Israel" in terms of territory, they change on a regular basis.

The biblical text offers a collection of snapshots of who Israel is, but like any photographs, they only capture one perspective on the subject at a single instant in time and often cannot communicate the rich series of people and events that have unfolded to create that moment. How the identity of this people develops through the stories of remarkable individuals—Israelite and non-Israelite—and through the ways this people interacts with others becomes one point of interest in exploring this material. Reading Moses here helps clarify these questions. As a figure existing "outside" of typical sources of identification, Moses the stranger and sojourner assumes and/or represents the shifting nature of "Israel" throughout much of the story of this people.

The next few chapters take some of the more common ways of defining identity in the biblical text and look more deeply at the cultural, societal, and historical factors that shaped these designations. These chapters also consider how "Israel" comes across to twenty-first-century readers in order to demonstrate identity as a process of definition that never ultimately concludes. New readers, after all, encounter Israel every day and bring it alive in new ways. From a person, to a family, to a group of people sharing a common faith, to nations with ever-changing geographical boundaries, the ideas conveyed and the content communicated in the single word "Israel" never remains set during the biblical period, and the term continues to take on new meanings as history unfolds.

The next chapters do not explain who Israel is, but rather they introduce some of the ways the biblical text and interpreters across time define Israel's identity. As with any relationship, when a reader makes the effort to see and learn more, new details appear for consideration.

## Suggested Biblical Readings

Exodus 1:1–4:31
Deuteronomy 34:1–8

## Discussion Questions

1. If you could somehow come face-to-face with Moses at the end of his life and ask him, "Who are you?" what do you think he would say?
2. Why do you think Moses identified so strongly with the Hebrews when he was a young man, especially when so many factors (environment, economic privilege) pushed him to identify with the Egyptians?
3. This reading of Moses suggests that his connection to a variety of peoples facilitated his commissioning by God. Consider other great leaders. Do you think a person's leadership might be enhanced by that person's interactions with different people, cultures, and life circumstances? Why or why not?
4. Think about the various identity markers discussed in this chapter (e.g., gender, vocation, class, ethnicity, geography, family). How would you rank these items in order of importance as they operate in your own life? How would those people who know you—family, friends, teachers—rank them as applied to you? What would be the similarities and differences?
5. If you had to choose one identity marker as being the most important in your life, which one would it be? Why?

## Suggestions for Further Reading

Walzer, Michael. *Exodus and Revolution.* New York: Basic Books, 1985.
Wildavsky, Aaron. *The Nursing Father: Moses as Political Leader.* Jerusalem: Shalem Press, 2005.

# 4. Family

The family is society in miniature, the place where we first and most deeply learn how to love and be loved, hate and be hated, help and be helped, abuse and be abused. It is not just a center of domestic serenity; since it involves power, it invites the abuse of power.

—John Dominic Crossan, *Jesus: A Revolutionary Biography*

Other things may change us, but we start and end with the family.

—Anthony Brandt, *Esquire*, September 1984

---

Who am I? To answer that question, most people need also to answer another question: Who is my family? Every individual comes into this world as part of some sort of familial unit, so the family frames some of the first, and longest, work of puzzling through identity. Yet such a process brings with it many challenges. For one, the form of the family to which a person belongs can vary dramatically from the forms of other families. For another, many people will belong to more than one family in a lifetime. Think, too, about how individuals take on multiple roles in a family at any one time (e.g., child, sibling, cousin). And they adopt new family roles and discard others, as time passes. All these factors can complicate attempts at figuring out "who I am" in a family context. Nonetheless, no one can afford to ignore the central role played by the family in forging identity. As the quotations above suggest, understanding ourselves requires understanding our families.

Family also functions centrally in constructing identities in the Hebrew Bible. When, for instance, Gen 12 begins to relate the story of the biblical Israelites, it does so in terms of a single family—the family of Abraham. Many other biblical narratives also hinge on family dynamics, and numerous laws in the Hebrew Bible also address family issues. The Hebrew Bible even projects the concept of family onto other social units such as tribes, peoples, and nations. But this centrality of family for the biblical Israelites should not surprise readers. Sociologists and anthropologists have learned that no matter where or when we look in the world, something akin to a family exists. The family is everywhere.

Yet the family also varies tremendously across time and space—in terms of structure, functions, meanings, dynamics, and relationships to other social units. Thus, reading the Hebrew Bible with "family" in mind requires caution. Otherwise, one runs the risk of imposing contemporary assumptions about what makes a family onto the biblical text. Such readings may prove especially difficult to avoid because of the Hebrew Bible's religious and cultural authority in the present time. But looking more closely at the varied ancient Israelite contexts in which "families" function demonstrates that modern and western understandings of family simply do not apply. Assuming direct linkages between the past and the present results in misunderstanding the experiences of ancient Israelites as well as misinterpreting the laws and customs described. Further, failing to comprehend fully what the biblical texts depict about aspects connected to the family such as gender roles and human sexuality may lead to imposing readings onto the text that do violence to people in the present day—especially those struggling to define themselves in new ways vis-à-vis family roles.

For help in thinking about the connections and comparisons between biblical and modern families, consider figure 4.1. It comes from a 1951 Motorola TV ad and portrays a Caucasian family of four inside their home. The picture depicts a father at his ease in the living room, with his two children—a son and a daughter—flanking him. All three have their attention held by the image on the TV screen. The mother, meanwhile, stands behind the others, her attention divided between the TV and her task of serving drinks to her husband and children. Although this portrayal is perhaps exaggerated, many people still today, even if only subconsciously, have this sort of image in mind when they think of the family. Yet it scarcely fits the reality of most families today. Factors such as divorce, remarriage, childlessness, stepfamilies, and gay couples produce myriad versions of the family. The picture thus promotes a very narrow and limited notion of what a

## Sociological and Anthropological Approaches

As we saw in chapter 2, many different ways of reading the Hebrew Bible exist. One of these, involving sociological and anthropological approaches, uses methods and theories from the social sciences to understand better the social world of biblical Israel. The approach bases itself on the recognition that humans, as social beings, order their societies in patterned ways. By comparing societies with similar social patterns, the approach offers further details and insights into the otherwise less well-known society. Take, for instance, the society portrayed in the Hebrew Bible. The text reveals it as based in small, rural villages. Its economic life centers on agriculture. And formal authority resides with adult males. Studying recent and current societies organized similarly (e.g., in Africa and the Mediterranean) helps us learn about other aspects of biblical society not always so clearly explained in the text itself. For example, in recent years this approach has shed more light on how biblical prophets, sages, and chiefs might have functioned. Other insights have provided more information about the dynamics of tribes, clans, and families. Because this chapter focuses on families in the Hebrew Bible, it relies heavily on the findings of sociology and anthropology.

**Fig. 4.1: A Typical Modern Family?**
*This picture depicts one very specific kind of family. But in the western world it also expresses a common ideal of the typical or normal family. As such, many imagine that all families should somehow conform to it, whether in terms of the number and identity of its members, their specific and respective roles, or how they relate to one another.*

family looks like. In fact, only 14 percent of all North American families today actually correspond to what it depicts.

Now look at figure 4.2. It presents a recent scholarly reconstruction of a "typical" biblical Israelite family. As we further detail the form and function of this so-called typical family in the following pages, we need to keep in mind that it, too, serves as an ideal. Like our own, biblical families also manifested much variety in their forms and functions.

**Fig. 4.2: A Typical Biblical Israelite Family?**
*The Hebrew Bible portrays families that vary considerably from one another in what they look like and how they function. Nevertheless, certain shared features also emerge. Biblical scholars use these features to help construct images of a typical biblical family. This picture presents one such image. It is based on a four-room house excavated by the Madaba Plains Project at Tall al-'Umayri, Jordan, and is typical of "four-room" or "pillared" domestic houses found in ancient Israel, Ammon, Moab, and Edom from the thirteenth through the sixth centuries B.C.E. Note in particular the age and gender of this family's various members, what they are doing, and how they relate to one another.*

---

**Family Structure**

In the Hebrew Bible the phrase ***bet av***, which literally means "house of the father," comes closest to contemporary words for "family." Both parts of this expression reveal distinct and important features of the social unit to which it refers. And both prove important in understanding the particular contours of the biblical "family."

Bet

Although translated above as "house," *bet* more accurately means "household." It refers not just to a specific structure in which people live but also

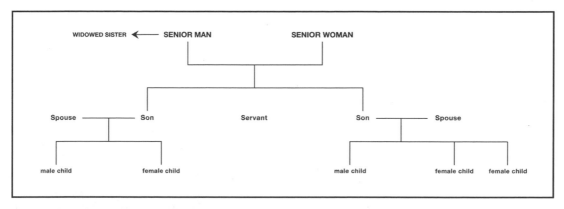

**Fig. 4.3: The Relationships in a Model** *Bet Av*
*This chart outlines the persons making up a sort of ideal biblical* bet av. *It identifies the various members according to their family roles, while also mapping their relationships to one another. But not only does this chart present only one possible ideal out of many; it also captures such a* bet av *at just one specific moment in time.*

encompasses everything associated with that structure, whether lands, animals, goods, or people. This kind of expansive meaning applies also to the human members of the *bet.* Unlike the nuclear model of the family so familiar in the modern western world, social anthropologists identify the form of the biblical family as extended in nature.

What does that mean? In terms of size, the typical *bet av* probably averaged about twelve to fifteen persons. It might have encompassed three generations: a senior man and woman, their children, and their grandchildren. In the middle generation it extended outward to take in all of the senior couple's male children, as well as their spouses. (The senior couple's female children moved out of the *bet av* when they married.) In addition, the *bet av* might also have included other relatives whose households had dissolved through death or other trauma. More prosperous households might have further numbered among their members slaves, servants, concubines, military captives, and/or resident aliens.

Of course, just like today's families, *bet avot* (pl. of *bet av*) might have varied considerably one from another in terms of their size. And, again like today's families, all *bet avot* experienced many changes in their size over time due to births, deaths, and other sorts of additions and leave takings.

Some of the various households in Genesis provide us with examples. Abraham's household initially consists of just Abraham and Sarah, his nephew Lot, and other unspecified possessions and persons. Later the text names two servants specifically—Eliezer and Hagar. Eventually the household expands with the births of Hagar's son, Ishmael, and Sarah's son, Isaac. When Sarah dies and Isaac matures, Abraham gets Isaac a wife, Rebekah. And after she joins the household, she gives birth to two sons, Esau and Jacob. At this point Isaac still remains part of his father's *bet av*, but later he will move on to establish his own (Gen 25:11). Overall, both Abraham's and Isaac's households appear rather modest in size, at least in terms of named members. (But note that Gen 14:14 has Abraham mustering for battle 318 men "born in his house.")

The household of Isaac's son, Jacob, on the other hand, assumes immense proportions. Besides Jacob himself, it includes two wives (Rachel and Leah), their two servant girls (Bilhah and Zilpah), twelve sons borne to these four women, at least one daughter (Dinah), as well as, eventually, all the various children borne to Jacob's sons. Exodus 1:1–5 claims that the total number of persons in Jacob's household came to seventy. Although this number stands out as suspiciously symbolic, it does point to the sort of huge size hoped for—and imagined as possible—for an Israelite *bet av*.

Interestingly, extended families actually prove rare among human societies. Their large size, coupled with the presence of several generations, raises the potential for strife within them. Why, then, do they appear in biblical Israel? One reason probably derives from the natural environment. Extended families increased the chances of survival for both the individual and the group in the face of rather harsh living conditions. Here readers come up against an irony. Biblical language sometimes effusively describes

### How We Read Genesis

Biblical texts do not provide straightforward accounts of what really happened. Instead, the texts express primarily the various ideas, thoughts, and claims of their writers; many of these wrote centuries after the time period they purportedly describe. Still, the texts do tell us about real social concerns. In Genesis, such concerns include: who qualifies as an appropriate spouse, how to distribute the family inheritance, what constitutes the roles and responsibilities of various family members, and how to approach and relate to outsiders. But, again, these concerns likely reveal more about the writers and their time period, not those of the depicted time period.

Another caution also pertains in reading the Genesis narratives. Legions of readers supposed that the texts depict a pastoral lifestyle. Thus, the ancestors as nomads wandered the desert margins with flocks of sheep and goats. Yet a closer reading of the text, bolstered by **comparative ethnography** (a subbranch of anthropology) suggests a somewhat different picture. In biblical times, people kept sheep and goats as a sort of reserve "bank account"; the meat and milk products served as a backup source of protein in case other food sources failed. But people risked disaster if they depended on just their flocks. What if a disease or water shortage decimated the herds? Hence, they spread the risk by also planting crops such as barley and wheat. Only certain family members, then, went out to pasture the flocks. Others stayed at a home base, caring for the field crops. Genesis texts allude to this strategy in a number of places—for example, "Isaac sowed seed in that land, and in the same year reaped a hundredfold" (Gen 26:12); "Listen to this dream that I dreamed. There we were, binding sheaves in the field" (37:6–7); and "Now his brothers went [away] to pasture their father's flock near Shechem" (37:12).

the Cisjordan as "a land flowing with milk and honey" (Deut 26:15). Yet maintaining oneself on the land actually posed many challenges. For one thing, producing enough food to sustain the population required cultivating not only the region's valleys but also its steep and rocky hillsides. And that called for the labor-intensive work of building and maintaining terraces on the hillside slopes. These terraces created the flat places necessary for planting crops, while also preventing soil erosion and slowing water runoff. A second challenge also confronted Israelite farmers: none of the four main soil types showed great promise for farming. Third, the chief water supply came from winter rainfall, not river irrigation as in both Egypt and Mesopotamia. But rainfall amounts in Israel tended to be both low and unpredictable. Some scholars estimate that drought occurred every three to four years out of ten. Finally, incredible diversity marked both the topography and the climate throughout the whole region, creating thousands of ecological microniches. To farm a certain plot of land effectively, one needed intimate knowledge of its distinct soils, terracing needs, rainfall patterns, prevailing winds, and so on.

These conditions gave rise to a particular social arrangement; in it, a small group of people became firmly tied to a particular plot of land (Heb.,

### Numbers in the Hebrew Bible

Sometimes in the Hebrew Bible numbers convey a literal meaning, such as the number of Abraham's men as 318 (although the rabbis interpreted this number in a nonliteral way; see chapter 2). Certain numbers, though, that appear over and over again often communicate instead a symbolic sense. Seven, for instance, means rest, fulfillment, and restoration: God rests on the seventh day of creation (Gen 2:2–3); the Sabbath day of rest occurs on the seventh day of the week (Exod 20:8–11); Pharaoh dreams of seven lean years and seven plentiful ones (Gen 41:1–36). Multiples of seven also occur: seventy elders go with Moses up the mountain (Exod 24:1, 9); the Babylonian exile lasts seventy years (Jer 25:12); the jubilee, when debts are canceled and slaves released, takes place every forty-nine years (Lev 25:8–55). Another symbolic number is ten, which indicates completion: the Egyptians suffer ten plagues (Exod 7:8–11:10); God gives Moses ten commandments (Exod 34:28); the law ordains a tithe of 10 percent (Deut 26:12). Meanwhile, the number twelve signifies order: Jacob's sons number twelve (Gen 35:22–26); so do the later Israelite tribes (Gen 49:28). And forty expresses the notion of a complete cycle: the flood rains fell for forty days and forty nights (Gen 7:12); it took Moses forty days and nights to receive instruction about the sanctuary (Exod 24:18); the Israelites wandered in the wilderness for forty years (Exod 16:35); David and Solomon both reigned for forty years (1 Kgs 2:11; 11:42).

Other numbers—such as three, four, and one thousand—also function symbolically. Such symbolic meanings of numbers can certainly frustrate literal readings of the text. But recognizing this practice as part of the cultural value system of biblical Israel assists readers in reckoning with a biblical code of meaning different from their own.

*nahalah*). This group, the *bet av*, needed sufficient members to work its land and produce enough to sustain its members, including both the able-bodied and those with physical limitations (the elderly, infirm, infants). But if the *bet av* grew too large, a separate set of problems arose. A smaller size helped limit and manage conflict among those in the group. It also better concentrated knowledge of the land's particular farming constraints among the group's members. Ideally the *bet av* grew large enough to support itself while remaining small enough to avoid discord and foster unity.

**Av**

Biblical Israel also used another strategy for managing group tension: putting the father in charge. *Av* means "father." Its explicit mention in the phrase *bet av* highlights both the centrality and the authority of the male head of the household. Having only one person at the center identifies the form of the *bet av* as **monadic**. Because this person is the senior male, further descriptors take hold. Specifically, social anthropologists refer to the biblical Israelite family as **patrilineal**: the tracing of group membership takes place through the father's line. They also label it **patrilocal**: the father determines where the group's members live. Finally, they call it **patriarchal**: the father has the final say over all the members of his household. The father's name also identifies the *nahalah* (land) for his particular *bet av*. And at the father's death, his male line (ideally his eldest son) inherits the property. Thus, the senior adult male not only defines the biblical *bet av*, but his male descendants also determine its continuation. In sum, then, everything and everyone in the biblical household circulated around and depended on the father.

The basic structure and functions of the biblical *bet av* serve as a backdrop for considering other topics, such as the Hebrew Bible's understanding of marriage, children, inheritance, sexual relations, religion, and education.

---

### Other Kinds of Biblical Families

Other biblical texts, however, construct different notions of the "family." Genesis 2:24 stands out as perhaps the most well-known: "a man leaves his father and his mother and clings to his wife, and they become one flesh." Social anthropologists call such a practice **matrilocality**. It names how the wife (and/or her family) determines where the couple lives. Other biblical texts support this family model in their use of the phrase *bet em* (mother's house). Although not explicitly describing a matrilocal residence, these texts do highlight women characters and their concerns. They thus view the household from a female perspective. So, for instance, Gen 24:28 refers to the *bet em* as part of a story negotiating daughter Rebekah's "marriage" to Isaac. Ruth 1:8 has Naomi urging her two daughters-in-law to return to their mother's house. And twice in the love poetry of Song of Songs the woman identifies her place of residence as a *bet em* (Song 3:4; 8:2). These texts reveal perspectives other than that of the dominant *bet av* about the shape of the biblical family. They suggest that the family was far from monolithic in form in biblical Israel.

These topics, and especially the distinctive laws, customs, and traditions attached to them, are taken up in the next sections.

## Marriage

Biblical Hebrew lacks a term equivalent to the English word "marriage." The most common expression used instead says that a certain man "takes" a certain woman "as/for a [his] woman" (Heb., *laqah le ishshah*). The phrase certainly implies inequality. It even suggests a kind of property arrangement in the male-female relationship. By presenting the man as the subject of the verb and the woman as the object, it conveys the notion that he owns her. Our understanding of the social world in biblical Israel confirms this picture. The coming together of a man and a woman functioned primarily as a social and economic exchange between groups. It did not foreground romantic feelings or commitments based on love. An Israelite "marriage" took place when a woman moved from her father's household to that of her new man's (i.e., husband's) household. That meant the joining of a woman to a man brought together not just two individuals but also two households. And even though the woman served as the medium for this new linkage, the senior males of each *bet av* governed its establishment.

An exchange of gifts helped cement the formal joining. Such exchanges did not, however, normally occur in the context of a festive celebration.

### The Meaning and Function of Marriage in the Recent Past

The economic aspect of "marriage" also comes to the fore when looking at its more recent history. Marriage generally signifies a legal institution governing two persons, their property, and their children. In theory, it holds for life and pertains to the vast majority of the population. However, for most of the last centuries the western world defined marriage rather in common-law terms. In this type of "marriage" two people lived together without the state's legal sanction. They instead bound themselves to one another through religious or family ceremonies having authority in local custom only. This informal arrangement worked because most people owned no property. Only the relatively small upper class needed legal arrangements to secure the control and transmission of property resulting from the joining together of two persons of wealth. "Marriage" thus functioned primarily as an economic concern: it regulated the movement of wealth and property throughout society and from one generation to the next. Marriages today, with their legal documents, religious ceremonies, and formal celebrations, echo the upper-class practices of the past. Situations where couples live together without marrying take after the common-law marriages of the past, although today's cohabiting couples may own significant property while those in the past did not.

Adapted from Jon L. Berquist, *Controlling Corporeality: The Body and the Household in Ancient Israel* (New Brunswick, NJ: Rutgers University Press, 2002), 61.

Indeed, biblical Hebrew lacks a term corresponding to "wedding." And wedding celebrations seem rather rare in the Hebrew Bible. But no matter how, when, where, or under what circumstances an exchange of gifts took place, the gifts themselves fell under two main headings: **bride-price** and **dowry**. Bride-price (Heb., *mohar*) indicates something of value given by the bridegroom (and/or the bridegroom's family) to the *bet av* of the bride, whose senior male often functioned as its representative. Biblical texts reveal a whole range of items serving as the bride-price. A law in Deut 22:29 sets the price at fifty shekels. In Gen 24 Abraham's servant, acting on behalf of Isaac, gives "costly ornaments" to both Rebekah's brother and mother. Jacob gives his labor—fourteen years total—to Laban in exchange for Laban's two daughters, Leah and Rachel (Gen 29). And in 1 Sam 18:20–29 David risks his life obtaining a hundred Philistine foreskins, which he then hands over to Saul for his daughter Michal.

A second kind of gift exchange, though not as clearly attested in the Hebrew Bible, involves the dowry. Bestowed on the bride by the *bet av* of her birth, it probably served as her share of the family inheritance. Since she was leaving her birth *bet av* for another, her inheritance needed to come in the form of movable goods. (As mentioned above, immovable goods—such as land—went to the male heirs; in a patrilineal system they stayed with the *bet av* of their birth and provided for its continuation.) In the Genesis narratives, a female servant often comprises the woman's dowry. Leah receives Zilpah; Rachel gets Bilhah (Gen 29:24, 29). Rebekah, when she leaves to join with Isaac, takes with her both her nurse and "her" maids (Gen 24:59, 61). Sarah, too, likely brought along Hagar, her Egyptian maidservant, when she

## The Economics of Modern Marriages

The haze of dreamy romanticism driving the design and planning of many of today's weddings seems a far cry from th e Hebrew Bible's understanding. Yet modern weddings do involve many practical social and economic elements. Consider that the average American wedding today costs at least $25,000. This kind of financial outlay benefits a whole array of businesses: jewelers, florists, caterers, photographers, dress designers, wedding planners, limousine rental agencies, and so forth. Think, too, of the economic exchange that operates, though often disguised, between the wedding party and their guests. When the bride, groom, and/or their families host an elaborate reception following the wedding ceremony, it often includes an expensive multicourse sit-down meal, unlimited drinks, and a dance continuing far into the night. But in return, the guests bring costly gifts for the couple. And this expense is on top of the cost of purchasing proper wedding attire, traveling to the wedding site, and providing oneself with overnight lodging. In terms of a wedding's social strictures, countless wedding manuals and bridal magazines detail the rituals and formalities governing modern weddings. They give out endless rules and guidelines for each aspect of the ceremony and everything related to it.

"married" Abraham, though the text does not make this claim explicitly (but see Gen 16:1–2). Elsewhere in the Hebrew Bible, Achsah's father gives her some springs of water (Josh 15:16–19; cf. Judg 1:12–15). And the Egyptian Pharaoh grants to his daughter the city of Gezer when she becomes Solomon's "wife" (1 Kgs 9:16). But whether dowry or bride-price or both, such economic exchanges confirmed the connections between two households now related to one another through the "marriage" of two of their members. The transactions also gave both households a financial stake in the well-being of the two persons in the new union.

Formal economic exchanges also eased anxieties provoked by the movement of women across *bet av* boundaries. These concerns come across in texts about identifying and choosing the "right" woman to marry. Social scientists speak here of **endogamy** (marrying insiders) and **exogamy** (marrying outsiders). Since women in biblical Israel always came into a *bet av* from elsewhere, all Israelite marriages were, in a certain sense, exogamous. But to smooth the tensions involved in bringing in outsiders, it made sense for households to ally with others close to them, whether in terms of culture, habits, traditions, and/or kin relations. Perhaps the ideal form occurred when first cousins joined: as kin, though not from the same household, they held much in common. Jacob contracts this type of marriage with Rachel and Leah (Gen 29). Yet notwithstanding the existence of such an ideal, many biblical texts undercut it. Any number of stories imagine alliances with women from far outside the *bet av*: Joseph marries the daughter of an Egyptian priest (Gen 41:45), Moses weds the Midianite Zipporah (Exod 2:21), David and Solomon both take non-Israelites (2 Sam 3:3; 1 Kgs 11:1), Boaz forms a union with Ruth, a Moabite (Ruth 4:13). Such unions might confer many benefits. They could forge new social and/or political connections, enhance economic interests, invigorate cultural practices and values, and renew the household's labor pool.

Besides having no term for "marriage," biblical Hebrew also lacks specific terms for "husband" and "wife." The word "husband" or "husbands" occurs eighty-three times in the NRSV translation of the Hebrew Bible. But each appearance results from a translator's decision to take the Hebrew word *ish*, or its plural *anashim* (meaning "man/men"), and render it as "husband/husbands." The translators presumably made this choice because the passages in which the words *ish* or *anashim* appear suggest or imply "marriage." The same thing is true with the English word "wife." It appears 289 times in the NRSV translation of the Hebrew Bible (along with 106 instances of the word "wives"). But, again, these appearances reflect a decision, based on the word's literary context, to translate the Hebrew word with the basic meaning "woman" (*ishshah*) as, instead, "wife."

The lack of Hebrew words equivalent to the English "husband" and "wife" also sounds a warning: do not assume commonalities between modern understandings of the roles of husband and wife and social practices in ancient Israel. The monadic structure of the Israelite *bet av* already hints at major differences. The Hebrew Bible does not display a paired husband-wife team as the foundation of a family. Rather, one dominant man takes and possesses a number of different women. One or more of these women may come from his kin relations and/or a closely allied household; as such, they perhaps come closest to modern notions of a wife. But other women of the household—slaves, servants, concubines, other household dependents—often also related to the senior male sexually and socially.

The diffuse meanings found with the terms *ish* and *ishshah* indicate something else too. Perhaps biblical Israel simply assumed that all men and all women would enter into an adult sexual relationship in the context of a *bet av*. Separate terms identifying "husbands" and "wives" became unnecessary. To be a "man" is to be a "husband"; to be a "woman" is to be a "wife." And even though no law appears in the Hebrew Bible's law codes directly commanding persons to marry, other laws presume such a charge (and see also Gen 1:28). And remaining single never receives attention as an option.

---

### Marriage Definitions in the United States

In 1996 the United States government approved as federal law the Defense of Marriage Act (DOMA). DOMA does two things. It gives states the authority not to recognize same-sex marriages performed in other states. And for the first time ever in American history, it creates federal definitions of "marriage" and "spouse": marriage is defined as an institution between one man and one woman; and a spouse can only be a person of the opposite sex in a marriage context. Since 1996 thirty-eight states have passed their own version of DOMA. Other states, meanwhile, have voted to legally recognize gay marriages and/or civil unions between two persons of the same sex.

In the ongoing discussions and debates surrounding these various legislative acts, some parties appeal to the Hebrew Bible and its supposed support for "family values." But questioning the validity of such appeals seems necessary given that "marriage" as such does not exist in the Hebrew Bible and that biblical "families" look and operate very differently from today's families.

In this light, consider how other communities have used the Bible to support their own ideologies of marriage and family. The nineteenth-century Oneida community in upstate New York practiced something known as "complex marriage." In it every man was married to every woman (and vice versa); the community allowed no exclusive attachments. John Noyes, the community's founder, had read the Bible and authored a text, *The Berean*, both of which, he claimed, supported such a practice. (He earlier called it "free love," the first person to coin that phrase.) At its height the Oneida community comprised over three hundred members before coming to an end in 1881. Another community founded in the nineteenth century, the Church of Jesus Christ of Latter-day Saints (the Mormons), held **polygyny** as a cornerstone practice of the community. The church's founder, Joseph Smith, justified it through his reading of the Bible along with the Book of Mormon. Although the central authorities for the Mormon community publicly distanced themselves from polygyny in 1890, some members, especially in fringe sects, still practice it.

## The Biblical *Av* and His Women

Examples abound in the Hebrew Bible of how other women besides the "wife" also related to the senior male. Abraham has sex with Hagar, an Egyptian slave girl in his household. According to Gen 16:1–4, he does so at Sarah's prompting in order to produce an heir. Jacob has sexual relations with the two female servants Bilhah and Zilpah for similar reasons. The sex happened more than once, since each woman gives birth to two boys (Gen 30:3–13). An unnamed Levite in Judg 19 takes for himself a concubine. Normally such a woman possessed a secondary status vis-à-vis a "first wife," and so was perhaps viewed as something between a servant and a "wife." But note that the Judg 19 text does not refer to any other women in the Levite's household. Elkanah acquires two women for his household: Hannah and Peninnah. Since the text mentions Hannah first, she might hold status as the senior woman/wife. Yet her childless state seems to demote her vis-à-vis Peninnah and her children (1 Sam 1:1–8). Gilead sleeps with a prostitute who bears him Jephthah (Judg 11:1). Later Jephthah's half brothers, sons of the legitimate or first "wife," drive him out of the family, clearly indicating his secondary status. Kings, of course, took for themselves numerous women, both "wives" and concubines. For the latter, note Rizpah, loyal concubine to Saul (2 Sam 3:7; 21:8–14), and the ten concubines of David (2 Sam 16:20–22; 20:3).

## Being Single Today

Today millions of persons live as singles. This situation has come about largely due to the economic freedoms gained by women in the last few decades. Finding that they no longer need to marry for their financial well-being, many women choose not to wed. But singleness manifests itself also among other population groups. That is, currently in the United States, 100 million people, almost equally divided between women and men, are unmarried and single; they comprise 44 percent of all U.S. residents age fifteen and over. Of these, 64 percent have never married, 22 percent are divorced, and 14 percent are widowed. Fifteen percent of all singles (14.9 million people) are age sixty-five and older. Further, studies show that even Americans who do marry will still live more of their adult years as single than married.

Further, no specific edicts regulate the behavior or duties of husbands or wives. The laws simply assume the existence of husbands, wives, marriage, and divorce. The societal expectations of taking one's appropriate place in a *bet av* carried such weight that no specific commands needed to be stated.

## Children (Sexuality, Inheritance)

The concept of a "traditional" family tends to include a husband, a wife, and their children. As seen above, though, biblical Hebrew provides no exact match to these notions of "husband" and "wife." However, terms do exist for father (*av*) and mother (*em*). The Hebrew Bible deems the having of children as something both necessary and good (Gen 1:28; 9:1–7; Ps 127:3–5).

Still, many stories also report parenthood as something frustrated or deferred (1 Sam 1–2). Or they indicate its perilous nature (1 Sam 4:19–22; 2 Sam 12:7–23). These themes extend throughout the Hebrew Bible, though they occur most regularly in Gen 12–35.

For instance, such a premium is placed on having children that the text claims a barren Sarah miraculously conceives at the age of ninety with the help of God (17:15–21; 21:1–7). Rebekah struggles to conceive and then, once pregnant, experiences difficulty with twins fighting in her womb (25:21–26). Rachel, too, feels discouraged over her inability to conceive, a feeling exacerbated by her sister Leah's giving birth to six sons and one daughter (29–30). Indeed, at one point Rachel cries out to her husband, "Give me children, or I shall die" (30:1). Ironically, she dies while giving birth to Benjamin (35:16–20). "Give me children, *and* I shall die" thus better voices her experience.

Recall one of God's main promises to Abraham: his descendants will number as many as "the stars of heaven and as the sand that is on the seashore" (22:17). Elsewhere the text states that Abraham will father a multitude of nations; kings, too, will come from him (17:5–6). This promise of many descendants lays down one of the two great cornerstones of the covenant between Abraham and YHWH (the other being possession of the land). Yet it all unfolds against the backdrop of the difficulties surrounding the birthing of children.

This fixation on having children stems from a basic quandary arising from the life conditions of ancient Israel: large families were necessary for the survival of all, but childbirth endangered women. Life in the biblical world was perilous. Onerous physical labor taxed bodies. Frequent accidents resulted in crippling injuries or death. The difficulties in producing enough food, given the marginality of the land and its climate, often led to a population suffering malnutrition (or at least severe undernutrition). And hunger made people more susceptible to disease and premature death. In this "pre-penicillin" world, a cut or a scrape, or even something as simple as a dental cavity, might produce a fatal infection. Moreover, the Hebrew Bible testifies to frequent warfare, and these military conflicts brought with them their own losses of life.

Given the constant threat of death, the population needed a high birthrate in order to maintain itself (to say nothing of increasing). Two problems emerge here. First, poor nutrition compromised women's health. They did not menstruate as frequently or conceive as readily, and the likelihood of both miscarriages and stillbirths increased. Second, women died in childbirth more than from any other cause, so female life expectancy fell below that of men. Estimates vary. Carol Meyers proposes thirty years as the average life expectancy for women, with forty years for men; Jon Berquist suggests twenty years for women, twenty-five years for men. Still another factor further exacerbated the situation: extremely high infant mortality rates meant that a woman needed on average nearly two successful births to produce one child who survived to the age of five.

These many and varied reproductive challenges help explain a number of practices and laws in the Hebrew Bible that secure and order sexuality to maximize pregnancies. For instance, as we have seen, the monadic structure of Israelite households gave <u>one senior male sexual access to many different women</u> in his domain. Such a system played a role in keeping as many women actively engaged in reproduction as possible. Laws also forbade sexual contact with women during menstruation, thus channeling sexual relations away from those times less likely to result in conception (Lev 18:19; 15:33; 20:18). Similarly, many of the incest laws proscribe sexual relations with older women in the household (mothers, stepmothers, aunts) who were likely no longer fertile (18:6–18). This desire and need to funnel all sexuality toward reproductive ends also helps explain laws prohibiting same-sex intercourse and intercourse with animals (18:22–23).

Fertility needs often limited the agency of women. A woman captured in war—if found desirable by her captor—became his sexual possession (Deut 21:10–14). No laws prohibiting rape existed; depending on the circumstance, a woman might have to marry her rapist (Deut 22:23–29; Exod 22:16–17). And the stories in Gen 19 and Judg 19 reveal the authority of the father in controlling sexual access to his daughters. In other words, women in biblical Israel possessed little, if any, control over their own sexuality. The high risk of death facing women due to complications of pregnancy and childbirth might have produced a certain reluctance on their part to engage in sexual intercourse. But society's need to reproduce itself trumped that reluctance. Human reproduction requires women's bodies. And so individual female desires gave way to collective demands.

Infertility also carried potentially different, and very unequal, meanings for women as compared to men. Certainly social pressure to produce offspring meant that the social and cultural worth of both men and women depended heavily on their having children. Yet the expectations of parenthood proved easier for men to meet than for women. Men could and did have multiple sexual partners. They could thus demonstrate their fertility by fathering children through any one of their women. But the culture

### one senior male sexual access to many different women

Anthropologists call this practice polygyny. It refers to a system in which one man possesses sexual rights over many women. It comes from the Greek roots *pol-* = many, and *gyn-* = *woman*. Another term, **polyandry**, from the Greek roots *pol-* = many and *andr-* = man, refers to the opposite system: one woman sexually controls many men. The latter does not appear very often among the world's societies, while the former predominates, as in biblical Israel. Israelite society's anxieties about reproduction help explain its adoption of polygyny. It fosters a higher number of pregnancies than other systems.

## Homosexuality in the Hebrew Bible

The Hebrew Bible's distinctive ideas about the family also matter in the modern social and religious debates about homosexuality. Consider first that the Hebrew Bible nowhere raises the issue of same-sex relations between women. This vacuum likely follows from the text's overall male orientation. With regard to same-sex relations involving men, a number of different texts present several different angles on the issue. First, the stories in Gen 19 and Judg 19 clearly condemn homosexual (male on male) rape. One male forcing sex on another male would presumably violate the integrity not only of the raped male but also his household. And since the household anchors society, such a rape threatens profound social chaos. (Raping a woman does not entail the same risk, since she does not own her own sexuality, nor does she define the *bet av*.)

Second, no text straightforwardly addresses the issue of homosexual orientation, for no text portrays consensual sexual relations between two men. Yet the story of David and Jonathan comes close. First Samuel 18:31 uses love and covenant language to describe Jonathan's relationship to David: "Then Jonathan made a covenant with David, because he loved him as his own soul." If such language referred instead to a man and woman, we would likely assume sexual intimacy as part of their relationship. And in biblical Israel, such a voluntary bonding between two male householders might actually work well to ally two households.

Third, Lev 20:13 states, "If a man lies with a male as with a woman, both of them have committed an abomination; they shall be put to death; their blood is upon them." This text seemingly proscribes all male same-sex behaviors (whether consensual or not). Yet the Hebrew is worded strangely: literally, it reads, "A man who sleeps with a male from the sleepings of a woman." And its context within a set of household incest laws suggests that this law functioned more narrowly to forbid only male sexual relations within the same household. In other words, biblical law leaves open the possibility of consensual sexual relationships between men belonging to two different households.

Adapted from Jon L. Berquist, *Controlling Corporeality: The Body and the Household in Ancient Israel* (New Brunswick, NJ: Rutgers University Press, 2002), 93–95.

## Rape in the Hebrew Bible

Biblical Hebrew has no word precisely equal to our word "rape." The term most often used in such contexts (*anah*) carries the primary meaning of "afflict, humiliate." But a wide array of situations comes under the province of this term. Certain texts, for instance, describe God as afflicting humans (e.g., Pss 90:15; 119:75) and Egyptians as afflicting the Israelites (Exod 1:11, 12). Consider, too, that our modern definitions of the term "rape" depend, if imperfectly, on the notion of consent—that is, the law defines rape as sex without a person's consent, however that consent is achieved or understood. But the Hebrew Bible does not, for the most part, consider women their own persons. Thus, gaining their consent makes no sense within the biblical worldview. The story of Tamar, daughter of David, provides an instructive example. When her half brother, Amnon, forces her to have sex with him, she protests only the timing and conditions under which it occurs, not the occurrence itself: she pleads with him to speak to their father and to arrange a "marriage" for them. After that, he can avail himself freely of her sexuality (2 Sam 13:1–14). Tamar's own desires, sexual or otherwise, are entirely beside the point.

required monogamy of women. So if and when infertility did occur, the stigma fell much more directly and narrowly upon them.

Begetting children did not end a woman's worry; begetting the "right" children was crucial. And in the absence of DNA testing, how do men guarantee the paternity of the children borne by women they supposedly possess? Such concerns stand out as central in a culture constructed patrilineally, where name, lineage, and inheritance all pass through the male line. In order

---

### Prostitution in the Hebrew Bible

Many states and countries today have made prostitution illegal. But nowhere in the law codes of the Hebrew Bible does any such prohibition appear. Nor do any of the biblical narratives suggest a legal ban on prostitution. At most some texts allude to its morally questionable nature. For instance, after Judah engages a prostitute—who turns out to be his own daughter-in-law in disguise!—he tries to cover it up by referring to the prostitute as a *qedeshah* (Gen 38:21). This Hebrew term carries religious overtones, for it stems from the root *qdsh* (holy, set apart). Earlier scholars argued that it referred to a cult or temple worker engaged in sexual acts with a sacred function. That is, a holy sex act was supposedly believed to stimulate the land into fertility through a sort of sympathetic magic. However, most scholars now recognize the ambiguity of the evidence for such an interpretation. In any case, the Hebrew Bible does not make prostitution against the law, though it does register a certain disapproval of it. Even the "harlot with a heart of gold" theme, known cross-culturally and found also in the Hebrew Bible, underscores this basic notion. Thus the texts employing this theme likely function as exceptions that prove the rule. See, for instance, the harlot Rahab in Josh 2 and 6 who saves the Israelite spies; note too the good mother/harlot in 1 Kgs 3:16–28 who is willing to give up her only child.

---

### Determining Lineage

A patrilineal system clearly functions in the Hebrew Bible. Ruth 4:18–22, for example, provides a short genealogy of David that names only the relevant men in his ancestry. The census recorded in Num 26 describes the clans solely by their male heads. However, by the first or second centuries C.E. this system had changed. In order to determine to whom one belonged, one made a reckoning through the female line. Thus, a person was Jewish if his or her mother was Jewish—a practice that continues in Orthodox Judaism today. The Mishnah (*Qidd.* 3:12; *Yebam.* 7:5), a set of Jewish writings dated to this time, provides the basis for this practice. Some scholars suggest it may have been patterned on Roman law concerning children born to parents not legally married or married to persons of different legal and social standing. Others argue that it functioned as an outreach strategy to claim as Jewish the children of Roman women who converted to Judaism while their husbands remained pagans. In any case, the change makes sense when methods for proving paternity lack, while maternity never comes into question. Moreover, this accounting helps a community more readily cope with a scarcity of men. And that could easily occur due to such factors as military service or death in battle.

to maintain social and economic structures, one needs to govern carefully the links made between male generations. Yet it all depends on female sexuality. Hence, male control of women's bodies almost naturally becomes rigid and intense. Biblical laws and traditions therefore place a high priority on female virginity and severely penalize adulterous relationships (Deut 22:13–22; Exod 20:14).

Still more problems loom. Transmitting property from one generation to the next can proceed in an orderly and secure manner in families with only one son, but what happens when there are multiple male heirs? Dividing the land and other holdings among many sons could jeopardize a *bet av*'s ability to maintain control over the property in question. But an unequal division of property would disadvantage (and anger) heirs receiving a lesser share or no share at all. Biblical Israel seemed to respond to this dilemma by favoring the property over the children. And it utilized the rules of **primogeniture** to do so. In this system, the eldest son normally receives a disproportionately large share of the inheritance (Gen 25:29–34), with a text in Deuteronomy specifically advocating a double portion (21:17).

Numerous biblical texts, though, betray the frustrations with and limitations of this arrangement. Often enough, biblical narratives rather gleefully upend this supposed norm by having a younger son end up as the "real" heir. Indeed, this reversal happens so often in the family narratives of Genesis that it actually becomes the new norm. For instance, Isaac, through the will and actions of both the deity and Abraham, garners favor over his

---

### The Hebrew Bible's Understanding of Adultery

The Hebrew Bible holds to a rather narrow definition of adultery. First and foremost, the Hebrew Bible understands adultery as a crime of property, not a sexual offense. The property is that of a woman's sexuality, particularly as used for procreative ends. Moreover, the woman herself does not own it but rather the man who has charge over her. (This is most commonly her father, husband, brother, or uncle.) Thus, adultery occurs when a man poaches upon, or steals, the sexual property of a woman owned by another man. Hence, in biblical law the crime of adultery takes place when a married or betrothed woman has sexual relations with a man other than her husband or betrothed. Or, from the acting male's perspective, it occurs when he has sexual relations with a woman "owned" by another man (Deut 22:22–24; Lev 18:20; 20:10). If no man owns the woman (e.g., she is an orphan, widow, or prostitute), no crime takes place—even if the man is married. A more ambiguous situation involves a man, whether married or unmarried, who has sex with an unbetrothed woman under the authority of some male, usually her father. In this case, the man must pay the woman's father a bride-price and take her into his household as his woman/wife, unless the father refuses (Exod 22:16–17; Deut 22:28–29).

Readers of the Hebrew Bible should thus avoid equating adultery with a practice such as **fornication**. Most often the latter term covers a whole range of sexual offenses: prostitution, pornography, consensual sex between unmarried persons, as well as adultery.

older brother, Ishmael (Gen 17:15–22; 21:8–14). Jacob, through both his own trickery and that of his mother, Rebekah, receives the blessing of his father and becomes the true heir instead of his older twin brother Esau (Gen 25:19–34; 27:1–46). And among the twelve sons of Jacob, Joseph (the second youngest) leads the next generation instead of Reuben, the eldest. As well, this tradition assigns fourth-born Judah a significant leadership role (Gen 37:2–4; 47:29–48:22). The phenomenon appears also elsewhere in the Hebrew Bible. For example, the narrative clearly prefers Moses over his older siblings, Aaron and Miriam (Exod 6:20; Num 12). Likewise, the prophet Samuel chooses David, the youngest of eight sons, as king (1 Sam 16:1–14). And Solomon, one of David's younger sons, inherits the throne from his father (1 Kgs 1:5–40). So while the rule of primogeniture expressed an ideal, the complexities of families often produced different outcomes. The orderly devolution of the family legacy to the next generation depended on circumstance as much as on law or custom.

But what if a family had only daughters, or no children at all? Regarding the former, daughters could serve as placeholders for the family holdings. However, they had to marry men from their close kin (technically, from their own **clan**). The resulting children, which ideally included sons, then became the "true" possessors of the inheritance (Num 27:1–11; 36:1–12). In the case of childlessness, the story of Abraham offers instruction. At various times before the birth of Isaac, Abraham contemplates several different strategies for securing an heir: adopting his nephew Lot into sonship, doing the same for his servant Eliezer, and begetting a child with the female servant Hagar.

## Primogeniture in Today's World

The following short story excerpt illustrates how more recent cultures continue to find primogeniture useful as a rule for determining inheritance:

"I think it's such a mistake to let the younger ones fancy that there is anything superior in being the eldest. My little nephews and nieces—"

"Yes," said Harriet. "But one's got to prepare people for life, hasn't one? The day is bound to come when they realise that all Peter's real property is entailed."

Miss Quirk said she so much preferred the French custom of dividing all property equally. "It's *so* much better for the children."

"Yes; but it's very bad for the property."

"But Peter wouldn't put his property before his children!"

Harriet smiled.

"My dear Miss Quirk! Peter's fifty-two, and he's reverting to type."

Dorothy L. Sayers, "Talboys," in *Lord Peter: A Collection of All the Lord Peter Wimsey Stories*. ed. James Sandoe (New York: Harper & Row, 1972), 447.

### The Inalienability of Land in the Hebrew Bible

This principle of the inalienability of land expresses itself insistently and profoundly in the story of Naboth's vineyard (1 Kgs 21:1–29). In it the king himself desires some land belonging to Naboth, even offering compensation for it. But the latter resolutely refuses to hand it over. And he turns to the deity for support in denying the monarch: "The LORD forbid that I should give you my ancestral inheritance" (1 Kgs 21:3). Social and cultural values likely explain Naboth's refusal. That is, Naboth does not really own the land. Rather, he serves as a placeholder for land that actually belongs to the whole *bet av*—past, present, and future. Parting with the land would mean betraying all the members of his *bet av*. Land's importance in sustaining the biblical household also comes up in prophetic texts. For instance, Mic 2:2 condemns those who "covet fields, and seize them; houses, and take them away; they oppress householder and house, people and their inheritance" (cf. Isa 5:8). Legal texts, too, reveal the significance of the land vis-à-vis the *bet av*. In fact, a number of laws present rather striking tactics for safeguarding a household's land otherwise at risk (Lev 25:23–28; Num 36:6–9; see also Deut 19:14; 27:17). See chapter 8 for additional discussion.

The sheer number of biblical stories pertaining to children and inheritance demonstrate the primacy of these issues for biblical Israelites. In turn, these emphases highlight again the centrality of the *bet av* in the social structure of biblical society. The smooth functioning of a household at any particular moment in time and its continuance through time—from generation to generation—received high priority. The narrative especially underscores the inalienability of the land attached to any particular household. According to the text, God promises Abraham not only a people (nation) but also a land; this foundational role of territory results in no stories in the Hebrew Bible of land sold outside of the family.

## Other Functions of the *Bet Av*

The *bet av* also determined many other aspects of Israelite society reflected in the Hebrew Bible. Among them are law, education, religion, and the care of the dead. In many societies today, these aspects of life operate in a variety of places outside the family household: courthouses, public schools, synagogues, churches, mosques, hospitals, and funeral homes. None of these institutions existed in ancient Israel; the family, at least in part, realized their functions instead.

### Law

In the legal realm, the male head of the *bet av* exercised certain judicial authority over his household. Slaves, of course, by virtue of their role, came under the total authority of the senior household male. However, biblical law did grant slaves protection from murder or other physical injury by their masters (Exod 21:20–21, 26–27). Children presented a more complex situation. Fathers "owned" their children according to several laws; as such, the text sometimes assigns them an economic value. Parents could thus sell children into bondage in order to pay off debts (2 Kgs 4:1–7; Neh 5:1–5), and biblical law explicitly allowed a father to sell his daughter for sexual use, that is, concubinage (Exod 21:7–11). Even more disturbing, the Hebrew Bible hints that household heads held the power of life and death over children and their spouses. For example, Judah sentences his daughter-in-law to death by burning (Gen 38:24). Further, several instances of child sacrifice in the Hebrew Bible illustrate the extreme authority of a father relative to his children (Gen 22:1–19; Judg 11:29–40; 2 Kgs 16:3; 17:17; 21:6).

In contrast to such cases, the law also establishes limits to parental authority. Specifically, Deut 21:18–21 presents the case of a son disobedient to his parents. Think not of a mischievous child, but rather of a mature son rebelling against his parents and threatening the well-being of the whole *bet av*. But instead of the father deciding privately on an appropriate penalty, both parents must bring the son before the whole community for judgment and punishment. Two things emerge in reading this text. First, the larger social group controls the conduct of its members; it resolves "family" conflicts. It thereby undercuts the authority of the father while favoring instead the authority of the collective. Second, the father and mother act together. Their joint responsibility brings to mind many other biblical texts demanding that children honor mother and father equally (Exod 20:12; 21:15, 17; Deut 5:16; 27:16; and Prov 20:20; 30:11, 17). Hence, whatever ultimate or final authority the male head might possess, at least in formal or public contexts, mothers also held considerable, if not precisely equal, power over household dependents, be they children, slaves, or servants.

## Education

The interdependent authority of both parents also manifested itself in the educative functions of the *bet av*. Take note, though, that education for ancient Israelites meant something different from modern ideas about learning. Current systems of schooling focus on reading, writing, math, science, and achieving competence in a number of academic fields. But most scholars agree that only a small minority of the population in ancient Israel could read. Fewer still could write. And only a tiny fraction, perhaps 1 to 2 percent, attained the sort of sophisticated writing skills needed to create literature.

Instead, for most Israelites education involved the learning of those life skills vital for subsistence. Rather than formal "schooling," this education was more like an apprenticeship. The older generation transmitted valuable information and skills to the younger generations, and they did so primarily along gender lines. In households dependent directly on the land, senior males trained the boys to care for crops and manage livestock. Basic lessons included how to plant, weed, prune, and harvest a variety of crops.

More specialized lessons came in learning the unique qualities of the *bet av*'s land in terms of soil type, terrain, and climate; this knowledge helped optimize land use and ensure high crop yields and the best care of herds. Younger males also learned from their elders helpful strategies for clearing land, digging cisterns and storage pits, building and maintaining agricultural terraces, and constructing and repairing domestic structures. All these came under the domain of males due to the demands for maximum physical strength.

Female responsibilities in the *bet av* revolved around food and textile production. For the former, older females instructed younger girls in how to plant and care for a "kitchen" garden. Its yield included such fruits, vegetables, and spices as melons, pomegranates, cucumbers, onions, leeks, cumin, and garlic. Further lessons centered on food processing, including the grinding of grain into flour, the making of cheese and yogurt, and the drying of grapes, olives, and other produce. Girls also learned how to prepare meals, receiving instruction in how to bake bread, prepare porridges and stews, and so on. Textile production, meanwhile, necessitated training in spinning wool fibers into thread, weaving thread into cloth, and sewing cloth into garments and other materials such as blankets and sleeping mats. Finally, of course, older women no doubt passed on to the younger generation the accumulated wisdom pertaining to childbirth and the care of children. (See figure 4.2 for an illustration of household members at their various tasks.)

Besides life's daily needs, Israelite society also needed to pass on its laws and history to subsequent generations. This education, too, occurred largely

### A Biblical Depiction of a "Woman/Wife of Worth"

Proverbs 31:10–31 comprises the well-known description of a "woman/wife of worth." In a number of ways her duties correspond well to those of a typical woman in the biblical *bet av*. For instance, several times the text mentions both that she provides food (vv. 14, 15, 16) and works in textiles (vv. 13, 19, 22). She also supervises others (v. 15), engages in business transactions (vv. 16, 18, 24), and acts charitably toward the poor (v. 20). In addition, though, her household includes servants (v. 15), she has surplus income to purchase land (v. 16), and her husband sits in honor (and leisure) at the city gate (v. 23). These latter indicate clearly that she comes from the upper classes. The text thus arises from, and speaks to, an elite. As such, it fits well its literary context, since the book of Proverbs overall addresses itself to wealthy urban males. But if Prov 31:10–31 speaks at least in part to the desires of a certain class of men, readers must use caution in viewing it as a straightforward description of women and their lives. Still, however much this text does or does not relate to a female reality, the array of social and economic functions taken on by this woman make her far more than "just a housewife." That phrase is used often in the western world where socioeconomic structures isolate, demean, and ignore household work. It has little meaningful relevance in the biblical context.

within the *bet av*. Regarding the law, for instance, several texts in Deuteronomy enjoin the people to teach the law to their children; the urgency of this charge is seen in the oft-attached motive clause "so that one's days may be long and prosperous in the land" (Deut 6:7; 11:19–21; 32:46–47). Regarding historical traditions, the Hebrew Bible preserves five formal question-and-answer texts. Each of them pinpoints one or more significant events of biblical history: the exodus, conquest, gift of land, and the receiving of the law (Exod 12:26–27; 13:14–15; Josh 4:6–7, 21–23; Deut 6:20–24). These question-and-answer texts perhaps modeled a learning dialogue between parent and child akin to that found in the Passover Seder, when a child asks an adult, "Why is this night different from all other nights?" But because these texts employ father-son language (in the Hebrew), questions arise about whether the women of the household also learned the fundamentals of their people's historical traditions in this manner. Could they have learned another set of traditions instead of, or in addition to, the ones recorded in the texts listed above? (See Judg 11:39–40 for one such possible "alternate" tradition.)

*Religion*

Besides law and history, the *bet av* also educated its members in the area of religion. In fact, the household not only nurtured and sustained its members' religious orientation and practices; it also determined them. "Personal" religion probably did not exist in ancient Israel. Instead of an individual's making a free and independent choice to worship according to his or her own dictates, a person's religion proceeded from that of the *bet av*. One's deities were simply the deities of one's family. The ancestor traditions, when naming God, repeatedly make reference to a person's family lineage: God is "the God of my father" (Gen 31:5; cf. 26:24; 28:13; 31:42, 53; 32:9; 46:1–3). The Song of Moses utilizes similar language: "This is my God and I will praise him, my father's God, and I will exalt him" (Exod 15:2). And when Ruth transfers into Naomi's family, she as a matter of course adopts Naomi's god as her own (Ruth 1:16, "Your people shall be my people, and your God my God").

Material finds as well as textual traces underscore the role of the *bet av* in carrying out religious rituals. Archaeologists have discovered numerous incense stands, small altars (see fig. 4.4), and miniature model sanctuaries in domestic contexts. These items suggest a ritual corner or shrine situated in some households. Did such places provide a locus for a family to venerate its ancestors? Textually, the mention of *teraphim* (household gods) in the stories of Rachel and Michal suggest that possibility—if these household gods modeled, or were otherwise connected to, familial ancestors (Gen 31:34–35; 1 Sam 19:13, 16; cf. Judg 17:4–5).

Or perhaps these domestic cult shrines fulfilled another function. Many material remains and biblical texts focus on cult practices related to female fertility. For instance, archaeologists have recovered, often in domestic contexts, hundreds of small clay figurines of nude females at sites in the Cisjordan; these statues probably represent fertility deities (see fig. 4.5). Numerous biblical texts indicate the involvement of many Israelites in the worship of fertility deities such as Baal and Asherah, demonstrating popular concerns with fertility in regard to children, animals, and the land (1 Kgs 18:17–40; 2 Kgs 21:1–9; Jer 44:15–19). Chapter 13 provides more detail about these deities and the worship practices associated with them. But given the consequences of fertility for biblical women discussed previously, women's prominence in these cultic fertility practices makes sense (see especially Jer 44:15–19). And even though the biblical writers often attack such practices, their vehemence testifies to the enduring nature of this kind of religious expression among the Israelites.

Periodically, members of the *bet av* made a pilgrimage to a cult center for worship. Presumably the household (or some subset of it) journeyed together, as the story of Elkanah and his family indicates (1 Sam 1; cf. Exod 10:9; 23:14–17). Sacral meals sometimes played a part in these pilgrimage festivities (1 Sam 1:4, 9; Deut 12:5–12). At other times the family consumed such meals within the home. For instance, David's brother, the presumed head of the household, requires him to attend an annual family sacrifice

---

### Religious Diversity in the Biblical World

The Hebrew Bible foregrounds a religious orthodoxy that calls for worshiping YHWH alone and doing so according to the guidelines of the Jerusalem priesthood. Yet many of its texts also indicate that the people actually engaged in a diversity of worship activities and beliefs about the sacred. The people not identified as the covenanted people of Israel certainly worshiped deities other than YHWH: the Philistines worshiped Dagon, the Moabites venerated Chemosh, the Ammonites revered Milcom (or Molech), and so on. But even those who saw themselves as among the descendants of Israel held to a variety of beliefs and practices. Some perhaps incorporated the worship of other deities along with YHWH. These deities might have included the ones referred to above or others, such as the Queen of Heaven. (Jeremiah 7:16–20 and 44:15–28 refer to her in a prophetic tirade against the people.) Further support for this latter comes from an inscription found at Kuntillet 'Ajrud, a site in southern Cisjordan. According to most scholars, it reads "YHWH and his Asherah." It thus implies that for some Israelite people, at least, YHWH had a wife (see also the discussion in chapter 13). Other Israelite peoples probably worshiped YHWH or held beliefs about YHWH that were more generally at odds with what the religious authorities in Jerusalem advocated. Here consider especially the biblical texts denouncing worship at "high places," probably some sort of localized outdoor shrines (see 2 Kgs 12:3; 14:4; 15:4, 35; Amos 7:9). This kind of diversity of religious thought and expression may also illustrate how yesterday's orthodoxy can so easily become today's heresy, and vice versa. In the case of ancient Israel, certain peoples at such and such a time and place may have affirmed ideas and rituals that people of later generations condemned.

**Fig. 4.4: Horned Altars from Megiddo**
*Archaeologists have uncovered numerous small stone incense altars at various sites throughout the Cisjordan. Most appear in domestic contexts, suggesting their use within the household. Used to burn incense, many probably functioned to honor a particular deity or deities. These six examples, all from Megiddo, typify such stands: carved from soft limestone, square in shape, and with horns projecting from each of the four corners.*

**Fig. 4.5: Fertility Figurines**
*These five clay figurines represent a small sample of the hundreds of such figurines found at sites in the southern Cisjordan. Archaeologists name them "pillar figurines" because their lower part looks like a solid pillar. Their upper torso and head depicts a naked female; note how the position of the figurines' hands and arms draws attention to the breasts. Most scholars conclude that such figurines symbolize a goddess of fertility, perhaps worshiped especially by women.*

held in Bethlehem, the family's dwelling place (1 Sam 20:5–6, 28–29). And Jer 16:5–9 refers to the "house of mourning" and the "house of feasting" (*bet marzeah, bet mishteh*); the text suggests a funerary meal shared periodically among family members to commemorate departed members of the family.

*Death and Burial*

Jeremiah 44:15–19 also points to how the *bet av* controlled death and burial practices. In most cases, in fact, family members interred their dead in a cave located on the *bet av*'s familial property; the entire household thus shared a final resting place. Whether naturally occurring or hewn out by human hands, the cave itself generally consisted of a central chamber lined with shelves cut out of the rock on which to place the bodies. After about a year, or once the flesh had decayed, family members gathered up the bones of the dead and stored them elsewhere. Most often the storage area was either a pit dug into the cave floor or a separate small chamber off to the side of the main chamber (see fig. 4.6). In any case, this practice of gathering up bones serves as the likely source of the biblical phrase "to be gathered to one's people" (Gen 49:29; cf. Gen 25:8, 17; 35:29; 49:33; Deut 32:50; Judg 2:10).

Not even death, then, severed the links between a person and his or her *bet av*. Just as during one's life a person experienced most aspects of human society through and among the living members of a certain *bet av*, so too after death a person's bones mixed with the bones of the other dead members of that *bet av*. Ruth's avowal to Naomi expresses it clearly: "Where you die, I will die—there will I be buried. May the LORD do thus and so to me, and more as well, if even death parts me from you!" (Ruth 1:17).

### Worshiping the Dead

The textual and archaeological evidence suggests further that Israelite families may have venerated their dead, attributing to them magical or semidivine powers. These powers either needed placating or could be called upon for special favors or blessings. The veneration in general relies on the notion that since the deceased now inhabit the netherworld, they have special access to otherworldly powers. A particularly vivid example of this notion at work occurs in 1 Sam 28. The story has King Saul employing a medium to call up the dead prophet Samuel. Saul hopes to find out from Samuel what the future holds in light of an impending battle with the Philistines. Elsewhere, though, the biblical text repeatedly proscribes practices associated with the veneration of ancestors. Yet the very existence of the proscriptions indicates that at least some (many?) people did, in fact, hold to them. The idea is further supported by the existence of a cult of the dead that operated in other places in the ancient Near East. The Egyptians designed the pyramids, for instance, as structures to secure the happiness and well-being of a dead pharaoh. They believed that a pharaoh's death elevated him to a divine status. From that position, if appeased, he would extend special blessings to the Egyptian people.

**Fig. 4.6: Line Drawing of the Ketef Hinnom Tomb, Jerusalem**

*This line drawing shows a particularly fine example of a cave tomb. It depicts the Ketef Hinnom tomb, located just south of Jerusalem, which dates to the last days of the monarchic period (and after). The main chamber contains a number of burial couches, complete with head rests, on which the dead were initially laid out. The tomb also includes a side chamber, below floor level, where bones were later deposited after the flesh had decayed off of them.*

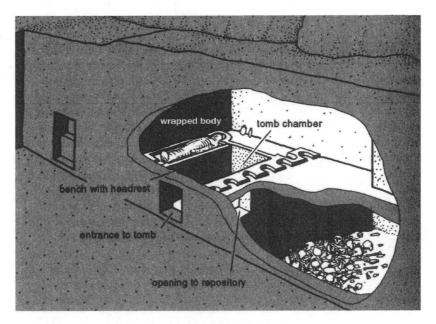

Mourning rituals further strengthened the connections between the living and the dead. These practices might have included lamenting, cutting oneself, and shaving off part of one's hair (see further chapter 6). Regarding lamenting, women took a leading role (Jer 9:17–22). And although the law codes forbade cutting and shaving (Deut 14:1–2; Lev 19:27–28; 21:5), the necessity of speaking against them suggests they were practiced—though how widely, we cannot definitively say. Archaeology reveals yet another practice associated with caring for the dead: burying them with at least a modest number of grave goods. Items most often found in excavations include jewelry, weapons, and a variety of pottery vessels; the latter perhaps held food for the dead. Presumably all such items carried some sort of special meaning or significance during the lifetime of those with whom they were now interred. Families also occasionally set up markers or monuments to honor and commemorate the dead. A pillar, for instance, marked the graves of Rachel (Gen 35:20) and that of an unnamed prophet (2 Kgs 23:17), respectively. In both these instances, though, burial occurred away from the family cave tomb.

The essential role of the *bet av* in caring for the dead made burial apart from it a profound tragedy. Hence, even though a prophet of Judah predicts that sad fate for the unnamed man of God, when it does happen, he works to mitigate its effects by burying him in his own tomb (1 Kgs 13:20–32). The *bet av*'s centrality in funerary practices also helps explain the importance of acquiring a familial cave tomb. The story of Abraham, for instance, contains an elaborate account of the purchase of a cave at Machpelah to serve as the burial site for his family. No doubt this act receives special emphasis because

Abraham and his lineage had not otherwise come into possession of their own land (Gen 23:1–20; cf. 25:8–10; 35:29; 49:33; 50:7–14). Securing a tomb in this circumstance gave them some sense of permanence; once acquired, it could not be lost. Moreover, it reveals another reason for the inalienability of a *bet av*'s landed property: to sell one's land to outsiders meant selling also the bones of one's family.

## Identity and the *Bet Av*

As outlined above, a wide and varied set of life activities and functions flowed around and within the *bet av*: work, education, religion, the law, caring for the dead. In ancient Israel, people did not atomize life in the same way as often occurs in today's world. Many people, for instance, can and will choose between marrying and not marrying, having a career or having children, leaving home for college or staying in one's hometown. But the ancient Israelites rarely had such life choices available to them. Nor in general did different aspects of life compete for them, so that they had to find some sort of balance among them all. Instead, practically everything—from the most mundane to the most extraordinary—operated very routinely within the context of the *bet av*. And all the different life functions commingled rather easily. However, work (the economic role of the family) did

### Rites of Passage

Analyzing familial roles brings to mind another aspect of identity formation: rites of passage. These practices chart the movement of time for an individual; they also mark a person's transition from one life stage to the next. In today's world all sorts of achievements function this way: experiencing a first kiss, earning a driver's license, getting a first job, graduating from school, having a child, getting married, and so on. But while rites of passage operate in all cultures, in no way do all cultures share the same set of rites. Or, if and when they do, the rites do not necessarily mean the same thing. Practically none of the experiences listed above as characteristic of modern culture find any place in the world of the Hebrew Bible. And those ceremonies that do, such as marriage, carry far different meanings.

Another example: birthdays. People in the western world tend to make much of them, celebrating with cards, gifts, and parties. But the Hebrew Bible evinces almost no awareness of birthdays; most Israelite people did not even know the day, perhaps even the year, of their birth. Why? First, the biblical world deflects attention away from the individual and toward the collective—whether family, clan, or people. Since birthdays highlight the individual, they would counteract this focus on the group. Second, given the high infant and child mortality rates, people probably resisted investing too much emotional weight in the annual passage of time for a young child. It was far too likely the child would not survive to the age of five. The resulting feelings of loss would simply place too much of an overall psychological burden on persons in that society.

likely receive a certain priority, simply because of the urgency of subsistence needs. This latter means the Israelite *bet av* functioned much more as a productive and reproductive unit than an emotional unit. Such a "property" model of the family still operates in many parts of the world today, especially in Asia and Africa. It also still holds in agrarian settings in North America and Europe—at least where the small, family-held farm preserves some sense of this mode of life.

In the Israelite world, this type of family functioning further meant that one could scarcely separate one's sense of self from one's place in a *bet av*. Who one was was largely equivalent to one's familial social role: father, mother, son, daughter, servant. What one did or achieved accorded with that role, and one did not so much act for oneself as for the benefit of the *bet av*. Further, all these social enactments, done in and through one's role in the household, shaped and determined one's inner life. Hence, one's familial role—and presumably how well or poorly one fulfilled the demands of that role—generated psychological processes and feeling states. Ancient Israelites would have found it difficult to conceive of their own thoughts, wills, agencies, and desires as distinct from those laid down for them by societal expectations.

Did this mean people in biblical Israel had no emotional lives? Of course not! The pathos of the lament psalms and the sexual passion in the Song of

### Love in an Arranged Marriage

To see how love can develop within the context of an arranged marriage, consider the autobiography of an upper-class Indian woman, Shudha Mazumdar, married in the early twentieth century (*Memoirs of an Indian Woman*, ed. Geraldine Forbes [Armonk, NY: M. E. Sharpe, 1989]). Shudha marries at thirteen years of age. She meets her husband, eleven years older than herself, for the first time on their wedding day. When her mother initially informs her about her marriage, Shudha bursts into tears, mostly because she does not want to give up her schooling. But the planning for the wedding soon fascinates and absorbs her. About her husband during the wedding ceremony, she writes, "Beside me walked my husband and though I did not know him then and had hardly seen his face I found comfort in his presence" (81). This quiet but auspicious beginning leads, in the following first days of their married life, to long talks between the two of them. And when after ten days she returns to her parents for a visit, she remarks, "The acquaintance with my husband had been forged into good friendship, and we promised to write each other till we met again" (89). Several years into the marriage, she describes the two of them as "extremely happy" together (106). Later still, when her husband's job requires their temporary separation, she writes that she "grew sick at the thought of leaving my husband" (111). And at yet another point she expresses her gratitude for the veil because it hid her doleful face; she did not want to be teased by her sister-in-law, for "in those times, it was highly improper to exhibit interest or affection for one's husband or wife" (118). In this instance, then, although love did not function as a pretext for their marriage, it certainly developed afterward and came to define fundamentally their relationship to one another.

Songs demonstrate otherwise. What becomes difficult to assess is the emotional content of lives lived so much within the constraints of assigned social roles. For example, when Rachel mourns her childless state, does she do so because, as an individual, she so desires to have a child (Gen 30:1)? Or does she grieve because her society's value system expects her to lament her barrenness? Similarly, how much, if any, emotional warmth and intimacy existed between spouses? After all, such "marriages" were arranged in nature, and driven mostly toward productive and reproductive ends. Moreover, the couples often experienced a significant lack of privacy, not least because they often lived with or near the husband's parents. Yet the experiences of spouses in arranged marriages today testify to how warmth and intimacy can develop between them; this may simply happen at different times in the history of the relationship.

Thinking that absolute freedom governs a person's choice of a life partner betrays a certain naiveté, since most people operate with significant, though often self-imposed, constraints on their choices. That is, most people will not seriously consider a partner different in, say, race, class, language, religion,

## Widows and Orphans in the Hebrew Bible

Because of the male monadic structure of the biblical household, the biblical terms "widow" and "orphan" do not mean precisely the same things as they do in contemporary culture. In the Hebrew Bible "widow" (Heb., *almanah*) signifies a woman who has lost both her husband and other males who might support her socially and economically, such as her father, father-in-law, or an adult son of economic means. Perhaps these other males are all dead too, perhaps they simply refuse their support, or perhaps (in the case of the son) no such person ever existed. In any case, a woman with no male kin able or willing to maintain her finds herself in an extremely precarious position (e.g., Ruth and Naomi). Similarly, "orphan" (Heb., *yaton*) in the Hebrew Bible refers to a child without a father or other male relative to care for him or her. The term applies even if the child's mother is still alive, since a woman on her own does not normally possess the means to support either herself or her children. Oftentimes the Hebrew Bible mentions the two categories together, as in the command "You shall not abuse any widow or orphan" (Exod 22:22). The text also repeatedly recognizes their legal, social, and economic marginality: "[The wicked] . . . kill the widow and the stranger, they murder the orphan" (Ps 94:6); "They drive away the donkey of the orphan; they take the widow's ox for a pledge" (Job 24:3); "that widows may be your spoil, and that you may make the orphans your prey!" (Isa 1:2). Yet the text also establishes some compensatory safety nets. For instance, a gleaning law allows widows and orphans to collect leftover scraps from the fields of harvest and so feed themselves (Deut 24:19–21). Interestingly, unlike all other women, a widow can make a vow or pledge free from the interference of any man. Presumably this is so because no man has committed himself to caring for her (Num 30:3–16). Finally, since the biblical definition of widows and orphans centers on their lack of ties to any adult male and how that deprives them socially and economically, no biblical term corresponding to the English word "widower" exists. Definitions of that term find no anchor in the conceptual world of the Hebrew Bible.

ethnicity, geography, education, and/or nationality. Or if some do cast their net of choice so wide, they may not readily acknowledge the challenges that come with such partnerships. In any case, even if emotional constraint did characterize the relationship between biblical spouses, both of them likely found compensation by maintaining closer relationships with their families of origin—possibly throughout the entirety of their married lives.

Because of the crucial role played by the *bet av* in determining so much about a person's life, those cut off from it—whether in life or death—existed, basically, as nonpersons. Without a place in a *bet av*, one lost a whole range of essential social connections. This fact explains why widows and orphans figure so largely in the biblical text as objects of pity and charity: their positions place them outside the security of any household. One's place and role in the Israelite family determined one's place in society, and so also one's sense of belonging, or lack thereof, in the world.

## Other Social Networks: Clans and Tribes

Although the *bet av* operated as the central kinship structure in biblical Israel, two others, the *mishpahah* and *shevet* (sometimes *matteh* is used instead), also functioned in significant ways. In the Hebrew Bible each *bet av* is part of a *mishpahah* (clan), and each *mishpahah* belongs to a *shevet* (**tribe**). Thus, a biblical Israelite stood within an interlocking network of three kinship units: *bet av, mishpahah, shevet*. So the text (in reverse order) identifies Achan when Joshua finds him guilty in the Israelite defeat at Ai: "So Joshua . . . brought Israel near tribe by tribe [*shevet*], and the tribe of Judah was taken. He brought near the clans [*mishpahot*, plural of *mishpahah*] of Judah, and the clan of the Zerahites was taken; and he brought near the clan of the Zerahites, family by family, and Zabdi was taken. And he brought near his household [*bet*] one by one, and Achan son of Carmi son of Zabdi son of Zerah, of the tribe of Judah was taken" (Josh 7:16–18). Other texts use a similar strategy of identification—as in the inheritance case of the daughters of Zelophehad (Num 27:1; 36:1, 10–12), when Saul is chosen as king (1 Sam 10:20–21), and in the self-deprecatory formulas of both Saul (1 Sam 9:21) and Gideon (Judg 6:15). Identity in the Hebrew Bible thus depended on a person's social location within a threefold web of kinship units.

Biblical scholars struggle to define and adequately explain the *mishpahah*. One problem centers on translation. In English *mishpahah* most often translates as "clan." However, social scientists point out that "clan" normally denotes kinship units characterized by exogamy (i.e., marrying outside of one's own "clan"); the biblical *mishpahah* featured endogamy (i.e., marrying within the "clan"). Thus, instead of "clan" many biblical scholars prefer to translate *mishpahah* as "protective association of families." Though awkward, the phrase does name a fundamental function of the *mishpahah*: safeguarding the integrity of each *bet av* within its orbit.

The *mishpahah* did so largely by relying on the **goel**, the kinsman-redeemer. This man (and the *goel* was invariably male) acted in a variety of ways, depending on the particular circumstances threatening a *bet av*. For instance, if someone murdered the head of a *bet av*, the *goel* avenged that murder. If the head of a *bet av* died childless, the *goel* had sexual relations with his widow in order to raise up a male heir for the deceased head. If the *bet av* fell into poverty and its head sold part of its land, the *goel* bought it back, either in advance or after it had been sold to someone else. And if, more generally, the head of a *bet av* fell into debt, the *goel* helped by providing interest-free loans, supporting him and his dependents within his own workforce, or buying them out of debt-servitude. Normally, the closest male relative to the male lineage of the particular *bet av* under attack functioned as *goel*: first brother, then uncle, then cousin, and then more generally any male relative.

The *mishpahah* also denoted a unit of territory. That is, just like *bet av*, *mishpahah* referred not only to all its human members but also to all its territory. At times a *mishpahah* likely accorded with a single village: every *bet av* in that village thus belonged to the same *mishpahah*. Likewise, the land owned by each village *bet av*, when considered collectively, comprised the total territory of that one *mishpahah*. At other times, especially when the population expanded and more densely inhabited settlements developed, two or more *mishpahot* might comprise a single village or town.

When biblical Israel made use of a people's militia, *mishpahot* also served as military units. The census lists of Num 1 and 26 clearly construct the functions of the *mishpahot* in this way (Num 1:2–3, 26:1–2). And when Gideon raises an army to battle the Midianites, he begins with persons of his own *mishpahah*, the Abiezrites, before summoning also members of the rest of the *mishpahot* of his tribe (Judg 6:34–35; 8:2).

## Levirate Marriage

Levirate marriage (from the Latin *levir*, "brother-in-law") appears cross-culturally. It derives from a society's felt need to preserve a lineage at risk of dissolution because no male heirs exist. In levirate marriage, if a married man dies childless, his nearest male relation marries the dead man's widow. Society then regards the first male child of their union as the dead man's heir. This son then acquires the dead man's property, memorializes him, and so continues the dead man's "name." The practice further gives the deceased's wife the economic security and social status that comes with having a son, thereby preventing her slide into the precarious state of widowhood. In the Hebrew Bible, a law in Deut 25:5–10 describes the conditions of levirate marriage most clearly and completely. Narrative examples appear in Ruth and Gen 38 (the story of Judah and Tamar). Note that the law in Deuteronomy limits the levirate obligation to a brother living within the same household as the dead man. The narratives presume that the obligation holds for any near kinsman. Further discussion of the economic dimensions of levirate marriage occurs in chapter 8.

The final kinship unit of significance in the Hebrew Bible is the *shevet* (tribe). Many readers might assume that this unit held pride of place. After all, even those only slightly acquainted with biblical material have heard about "the twelve tribes of Israel." Yet the tribe as a social unit likely impinged the least on the day-to-day life of the Israelites. Moreover, like the *mishpahah*, challenges abound in understanding the precise meaning and functions of the *shevet*. On the one hand, scholars more readily accept the English word "tribe" as a suitable translation for *shevet*. On the other hand, "tribe," according to anthropologists, has dubious utility as a social scientific category. At

### The Number of *Mishpahot* in Ancient Israel

How many *mishpahot* existed in Israel? The listing of clan names in Num 26 totals about sixty clans, or about five clans per tribe. (The listing is done according to the lineages of the twelve sons of Jacob.) But given the (admittedly limited) knowledge about ancient Israel's overall population size, this number seems rather small, unless extraordinarily large numbers are attributed to each clan. Besides, certain narrative texts mention clan names not appearing in Num 26. For instance, 1 Sam 10:21 says that Saul comes from the Matrite clan; 1 Sam 17:12 reports that David comes from the Ephrathite clan. Neither of these clan names shows up in Num 26. No doubt still other clans existed whose names have disappeared from the written records. Presumably both the number and names of clans fluctuated over time as a result of such events as war, famine, plague, a spike or decline in birthrates, and so forth.

### What Is a Tribe?

Over time the term "tribe" has named many different kinds of societies. In early Roman history *tribus* referred to "a third part" of the people, many use "tribe" for the various indigenous peoples of North America, and the term might also bring to mind nomadic peoples living in Africa, Asia, or elsewhere. But since these societies have little in common with one another, "tribe" as a reference to all of them becomes largely meaningless. However, anthropologists have more recently worked to refine that to which the term properly applies. One way of doing so turns on how a society may develop organizationally. Tribes can grow out of a preceding stage known as "band societies." While a band society normally sustains itself through hunting and gathering, a tribal society centers on agriculture. Size also matters: while a band society may number fewer than a hundred, a tribe normally consists of several thousand persons. In addition, tribes develop a number of cross-cutting groups (beyond the households or smaller living groups) that bind the people of a tribe together into a tighter and more coherent unity. Such cross-cutting groups might be military, religious, or economic in nature. For Israel these likely included a unit of militia drawn from tribal members, a periodic gathering of tribal members for worship at a shrine or high place, and perhaps also traders and craftspeople who traveled among a tribe's villages. In any case, a tribal society displays features clearly distinct from a band society. But it also differs from a state, a social form that can develop out of a tribal society (see chapter 10).

### How Many Tribes?

In a few places the Hebrew Bible actually gives the number of tribes as something other than twelve—for example, ten (or eleven) in Judg 5:14–18; eleven in 2 Sam 19:43 and 1 Kgs 11:31; thirteen in Gen 48:5. Most often, though, the texts maintain a twelve-tribe total. And they do so even while expressing variety regarding the specific constituent members making up that totality. Since the tribes supposedly all descended from the sons of Jacob, the different lists in the Hebrew Bible display this variety of membership most often according to which sons (and their tribal descendants) count and which do not. For instance, some lists include Simeon (Deut 27:12–13; 1 Chr 2:1–2), but others omit him (Deut 33:6–25 and Judg 5:14–18). Similarly, the priestly tribe of Levi sometimes gets counted in the twelve-tribe listing; other times it does not (Num 2–3; Ezek 48:1–7, 23–27). When the lists exclude either Simeon or Levi, they often make up the difference by expanding Joseph's lineage into two tribes. Each of these then is traced back to one of the two sons of Joseph: Ephraim and Manasseh. All in all, more than twenty variant tribal lists appear in the Hebrew Bible, some genealogical, others geographical. But most, if not all, are constructed according to some idealized scheme.

the least, though, we can say that for ancient Israel, as for many other peoples, the tribe (*shevet*) was its largest recognizable kinship unit.

Biblical tradition insistently fixes the number of Israelite tribes at twelve—though the participant members vary in the different lists. Still, each list always links every tribe by descent to one of the twelve sons of Jacob. But despite this textual celebration of twelve tribes, they seem to have functioned meaningfully in only two ways. In the military realm, *shevet* sometimes denoted the largest viable fighting unit (just as *mishpahah* could refer to a medium-sized fighting unit). Also, like the *mishpahah* (as well as a *bet av)* the *shevet* also specified territory; in this case *shevet* referred to the largest meaningful unit of geography in ancient Israel (e.g., the territory of Judah). Naming one's *shevet* thus served as one way of explaining where one was from, one's geographical address.

Although both the *mishpahah* and the *shevet* carried out certain useful social and cultural functions, the *bet av* far outstripped them in importance, especially in matters pertaining to daily life. Human life in ancient Israel rested on the foundation of the *bet av*.

## Conclusion

Perhaps because the *bet av* carried so much meaning and functioned so widely in Israel, it also found its way into thinking about the national political and religious life of the people. As such, it projected onto the people as a whole the *bet av* idea, and it further assigned the role of the *av*—the patriarchal father—to YHWH and/or the king. Psalm 89:26–36 provides a particularly apt illustration of this kind of thinking. Verse 26 has YHWH claiming that the Israelite king "shall cry to me 'You are my Father.'" YHWH promises to respond by making the king his firstborn son (v. 27). Here YHWH functions as the father while the king fulfills the role of firstborn son, presumably in a sort of cosmic or divine *bet av*. Later in the psalm, though, the king takes on the role of father while the people he rules becomes his children, in a sort of nationalistic *bet av*: "If his [i.e., the king's] children forsake my law and do not walk according to my ordinances . . ." (v. 30). Projecting the *bet av* onto the national political and religious realm presumably helped sustain the given nature of the *bet av*. It made it seem "natural," a taken-for-granted social structure. But it also likely reinforced the power of the *av*, the patriarch, on whatever level he operated. That is, even as father YHWH ruled over the cosmic household and the patriarchal king ruled over the national household, so too did every Israelite senior man rule over his own household, and not only as father but perhaps also, at least in the thinking of some, as king and deity. The *bet av* was powerful indeed, both as a lived reality in the social realm and as a cultural ideal.

This reckoning of the structure, function, and meaning of the biblical *bet av* demands inquiry into its effect on present-day readings of the Hebrew Bible, especially its teachings about the family. Much discussion currently circulates around family values issues, and some of the conversation partners appeal to the Hebrew Bible in order to legitimate their positions. But do those appeals always have integrity? Do they reflect a fair and correct understanding of the biblical *bet av*? Is it problematic if they do not? For instance, should a stance against abortion that appeals to the Hebrew Bible also contend with that textual world's demographic needs? Should a stance wanting to advocate the authority of parents vis-à-vis their children also make room for the text in Deuteronomy allowing for parents to condemn their children to death for disobedience? Or should a stance protesting gay marriage recognize that nothing in the Hebrew Bible prohibits lesbian unions? More generally, how does one take teachings about a familial social unit presupposing an agrarian and patriarchal society, one accepting of such practices as slavery, levirate marriage, and concubinage, and utilize it in the present day? If one does so by picking and choosing among different biblical texts, privileging some and ignoring others, who and what determines those choices? Down through the centuries of reading the Hebrew Bible, its explosive qualities have often been recognized; perhaps nothing illustrates that better than the intersection between the Hebrew Bible's teachings about the *bet av* and its potential application or misapplication to thinking about the family in other times and places.

**Suggested Biblical Readings**      Genesis 11:27–12:20; chapters 16; 20–21; 23–31; 35; 37–50

**Discussion Questions**

1. Consider the assumptions and purposes of marriage in your own culture. For instance, think about how you would answer the following questions: (1) Whom can you marry? (2) Why will you marry? (3) What is required before a marriage can take place? (4) What is the relationship between marriage and children? (5) What are the status and expectations of the husband and wife, respectively? (6) Where will you live? (7) Who has the power to make decisions about family property? Now think about how your answers compare to how the Hebrew Bible constructs the meaning and purposes of "marriage." What is similar? What is different? (Adapted from Ronald A. Simkins, "Kinship in Genesis 16 and 21 and Numbers 27 and 36," in *Teaching the Bible: Practical Strategies for Classroom Instruction*, ed. Mark Roncace and Patrick Gray [Atlanta: Society of Biblical Literature, 2005], 86–87.)

2. Make lists of what the various members of your family do. Think about how they spend their time, for instance, or where they locate themselves most often. Within the family context do they function primarily as producers (contributors) or consumers (takers)? How does each member's functioning compare to his or her counterpart in biblical Israel?

3. What, if anything, do you find appealing about the lifestyle of the biblical *bet av*? What strikes you as most distasteful or difficult about how life was carried out in the *bet av*?

4. Look for articles, editorials, or news accounts that argue about family values while also appealing in some way to the Hebrew Bible. Given what you have learned about the biblical *bet av* in this chapter, do you think the arguments in these sources reflect a correct understanding of the structure and function of the *bet av* in the Hebrew Bible? If not, how would you formulate a response to them?

**Suggestions for Further Reading**

Berquist, Jon L. *Controlling Corporeality: The Body and the Household in Ancient Israel*. New Brunswick, NJ: Rutgers University Press, 2002.

Borowski, Oded. "A Day in the Life of the Ahuzam Family." In *Daily Life in Biblical Times*, 109–26. Atlanta: Society of Biblical Literature, 2003.

King, Philip J., and Lawrence E. Stager. *Life in Biblical Israel*. Louisville, KY: Westminster John Knox Press, 2001.

Perdue, Leo G., Joseph Blenkinsopp, John J. Collins, and Carol Meyers. *Families in Ancient Israel*. Louisville, KY: Westminster John Knox Press, 1997.

# 5. Gender

There is no gender identity behind the expressions of gender. . . .
Identity is performatively constituted by the very "expressions" that are
said to be its results.
—Judith Butler, *Gender Trouble: Feminism and the Subversion of Identity*

"Is it a boy or a girl?" When parents expect a child, most of them will ask this question, or have it asked of them by others. And with ultrasound technology they can find out the answer even before the child's birth. Of course, the technology also brings with it a dilemma, since parents must then decide exactly how (and when) they want the question answered. Be that as it may, the question itself points to the tremendous significance of gender in shaping identity.

While other identity markers such as family origin, ethnic group, or class location entail a certain amount of fluidity, western culture tends to mark gender in binary terms. That is, class identity may range from upper class to middle class to lower class (to name only the most obvious categories). The ethnic choices offered in census polls present a wide variety of options—for example, Caucasian, African American, Hispanic. The roles taken on within a family (parent, child, partner) vary as time passes and circumstances change. But when it comes to gender, western culture expects one to be either wholly male or wholly female.

Yet such an expectation can bring with it a host of problems. Consider, for instance, those persons born with ambiguous genitalia. In approximately one out of every two thousand births, biological markers make it difficult to assign a person simplistically to one or the other gender. And deciding whether or not to alter surgically such children so that they "fit" can bring much physical and psychic pain.

Not only does western society expect persons to identify exclusively with one or the other gender; it also assigns specific meanings to each gender. An old nursery rhyme points to some of these meanings.

**131**

> What are little boys made of, made of?
> What are little boys made of?
> Snips and snails, and puppy-dogs' tails,
> That's what little boys are made of.
>
> What are little girls made of, made of?
> What are little girls made of?
> Sugar and spice, and everything nice,
> That's what little girls are made of.

More broadly, think about what comes to mind with the words "feminine" and "masculine." Traditional notions of **femininity**—at least in mainstream North American society—tend to include the following traits and qualities: soft, passive, domestic, nurturing, emotional, dependent, sensitive, and delicate. Traditional notions of **masculinity**, meanwhile, often call up these kinds of associations: strong, hard, tough, aggressive, rational, competent, in control, and independent.

Societies also differentially value the two genders. Many women find it easy to admit that they identified as tomboys while growing up. But few men willingly acknowledge that others perceived them as "sissies" when they were young. This example illustrates the privileging of the masculine over the feminine. Its meaning resonates because even with the many advances made toward gender equality, many people still commonly perceive those roles and traits associated with men and masculinity as superior to those associated with women and femininity. And that ranking, in turn, influences a huge range of social, political, economic, and legal policies and practices.

Gender ranking also exists in the Hebrew Bible. Depending on how one makes the calculations, only 5.5 to 8 percent of the total names found in the Hebrew Bible denote women; all the rest refer to men. And as Moses, David,

---

### Sex versus Gender

Scholars note a distinction between sex and gender. Put simply, sex refers to biology, the raw physiological facts that generally divide humans into the two categories of male and female. Gender, meanwhile, points to what a particular society makes of these sexual differences. That is, a society constructs meanings for sexual differences, such that different and specific traits, behaviors, expectations, and assumptions become assigned to the ideas of masculine and feminine. Note further that the meanings of gender can vary according to time and place—that is, femininity and masculinity can mean different things in different societies and in different time periods.

Recent scholarship, however, has raised certain challenges to this way of thinking about sex and gender. It argues that even biology already exists in a cultural system that gives it meaning. Thus, the supposedly fixed biological categories of male and female depend on already-gendered cultural expectations. Another complication also pertains: **intersex persons** do not easily or obviously fit within the binary of male/female. So both sex and gender exist along a continuum of possibilities instead of as exclusive binaries.

## masculinity as superior

Examples abound of how a gender hierarchy continues to operate today. In the economic realm, for instance, working women in the United States currently earn only about 76 cents for every dollar that men earn. Even within the same occupation women often make 20 to 35 percent less than men. A glass ceiling also still exists: less than 2 percent of the Fortune 500 companies have women CEOs or presidents. In other areas of life, too, pronounced disparities mark the lives of women (and men). Rape and other forms of sexual violence disproportionately affect women, even as a huge percentage of these crimes continue to go unreported and unpunished. Although some religions now affirm women's leadership in the highest echelons, the Roman Catholic Church (with 1.3 billion adherents worldwide) does not ordain women to the priesthood. In the world of politics, far fewer women than men receive appointments as judges, ambassadors, and cabinet ministers. In no country's legislature does the percentage of women representatives reach—let alone exceed—50 percent. In the Congress of the United States, women comprise only about 15 percent of the total.

Solomon and a host of others illustrate, men take on most of the positions of power and leadership. Biblical men also engage in a wide and diverse range of offices and occupations: judge, ruler, sage, prophet, merchant, trader, warrior. Biblical women receive attention primarily for their roles as wives and mothers. Moreover, only two biblical books bear the names of women as their title: Ruth and Esther.

This hierarchy of gender partly reflects the cultural world from which the Hebrew Bible springs. But it also derives more particularly from those persons primarily responsible for the writing and editing of the biblical text, namely, the male elites of the urban upper classes. This privileged minority group shaped the material found in the Hebrew Bible. Their work means that the text reveals relatively little about the lives of women, or, for that matter, the lives of those men (rural, poor) outside of their inner circle. Readers need to keep this narrow perspective in mind when reading for gender in the Hebrew Bible.

This chapter looks closely at some of the ways gender constructs the identity of biblical characters in a way comparable to class, ethnicity, and family roles. It opens with an examination of how the Hebrew Bible envisions masculinity and femininity. Samson serves as an exemplar of the **hypermasculine**—an exaggeration of the traits the Hebrew Bible tends to associate with masculinity—with Jacob as a potentially feminized contrast. Esther then models the **hyperfeminine**—an exaggeration of the traits the Hebrew Bible tends to associate with femininity—while the story of Jael works as a decided foil. The chapter then takes up places in the text that express a certain confusion or ambiguity about gender as a polarized entity. This gender "confusion" also comes into play in how the text does and does not imagine the deity as gendered. Finally, the chapter ends with a close reading of the story of Adam and Eve (Gen 2:4b–3:24). As the Hebrew Bible's prototypical humans, their portrayal both supports and undercuts the **gender binary** of exclusively masculine and exclusively feminine.

## Masculinity and Femininity in the Hebrew Bible

Given that the Hebrew Bible emerged over a long period and in various cultures, readers should expect a certain lack of coherence in these texts regarding what makes a person "masculine" or "feminine." Nevertheless, it is possible to isolate certain characteristics that tend to count as one or the other. Masculine figures in the Hebrew Bible typically exhibit strength, aggression, and control. "Strength" refers to physical ability to do work and to outdo one's colleagues, both through brute strength but also through other manifestations such as speed, agility, and technical skill. Think of David as he rose to the kingship. "Strength" also includes sexual activity; the strong sire children, such as Abraham producing sons even as an old man. "Strength" does not primarily refer to "strength of character" or "resolve," although such characteristics may also be part of the way the Hebrew Bible presents a strong figure.

"Aggression" refers to ways male characters in the Hebrew Bible satisfy their desires and secure advantage over others. More specifically, it often characterizes the public, physical, direct, and competitive manner through which men achieve those goals. Simeon and Levi acting to avenge the loss of their sister Dinah's honor in Gen 34 serves as one example. But aggression need not be limited to angry outbursts of rage against other people; it can also include more subtle attempts to gain advantage. A character such as Joseph who uses his favored status and his wiles to rise to prominence comes to mind. The Hebrew Bible presents masculine aggression differently depending on the focus of the male's desire, be it land, possessions, or women.

The writers of the Hebrew Bible expect male characters to project "control"—a mastery of the natural world or the wills of other people. Displays of control sometimes make use of strength and aggression. Sometimes, however, control relies on possession of knowledge, a special relationship to a powerful figure (especially YHWH), or the ability to channel energy toward a clear goal. Moses' unique, close standing to YHWH certainly qualifies here. "Controlling" masculine characters are dominant, decisive, and act independently of others.

Feminine figures in the Hebrew Bible typically exhibit nubility, deceptiveness, and acquiescence. Nubility as a category moves beyond the narrower term "beauty." Certainly the Hebrew Bible speaks of feminine figures as beautiful, on the occasions when it pauses to describe a character's appearance. But the Hebrew Bible, using the same words (*yafeh, tov mareh*), speaks of masculine figures' "good looks" (e.g., Joseph in Gen 39:6 and David in 1 Sam 16:12). Beauty, then, can cut both ways. When feminine characters are in view, the Hebrew Bible tends to add other attributes to beauty, such as sexual allure, fertility, and youth. This constellation of characteristics comprises "nubility." Readers might consider the young woman celebrated in Song of Songs as a clear example.

"Deceptiveness" describes trickery used to gain access to resources, justice, and other things not readily available to women. Deception may involve lying, use of beauty, promise of sexual access, ways of dress, and clever use of language. Negative examples abound, from Potiphar's wife attempting to seduce Joseph, to the personification of "folly" in the book of Proverbs standing prepared to lure young men to their death. But the Hebrew Bible does not necessarily present deceptiveness as a negative trait. Rather, it functions as a normal way for women in a patriarchal society to act; thus, the "wiles of women" are normative—such as Tamar's trickery to spur Judah to action in Gen 38.

"Acquiescence" captures a set of characteristics that place the feminine figure in a relationship of dependence upon another (usually masculine) figure. The acquiescent feminine figure may display passivity in certain situations, or she may actively demonstrate loyalty, obedience, or submissiveness. She may take certain action to please a masculine figure, or, as is often the case in descriptions of feminine figures as mothers, she may sacrifice herself, willingly or unwillingly, for others (again, usually masculine others). Sarah's willingness to pose as Abraham's sister or Hagar's compliance to go to Abraham's bed demonstrates this quality.

These traits certainly do not exhaust the characteristics associated with masculinity or femininity in the Hebrew Bible. Rather, they provide a useful framework for exploring how the writers of the biblical text construct gender. This chapter makes use of these heuristic categories to look at exemplary characters. Each section begins with an extreme example of masculine or feminine: Samson, the hypermasculine final judge in the book of Judges, and Esther, the hyperfeminine woman who becomes queen of Persia, show in their very extremity how these qualities work. But these characters do not simply present a pure or rigid ideal. Their gendered identities are always in process.

The malleability of gender identity will become clearer as each section presents characters with a tempered version of masculinity or femininity. Here Jacob, the progenitor of Israel, will serve as an example of the tempered masculine while Jael, the Kenite woman who slays a Canaanite general, provides insight into the tempered feminine. These less-certain constructions, alongside the "hyper" manifestations, demonstrate the anxiety circulating around gender identity in the Hebrew Bible. And the attempts of biblical writers to shut down these anxieties and normalize the status quo reveal some of the process developed to maintain gender identity.

*The Hypermasculine: Samson*

The narrative of Judges presents Samson as a hypermasculine figure renowned for his brute, physical strength, his aggressive behavior, and his assumption of control as a judge of Israel. His story begins with a full chapter devoted to his birth to a childless couple—a method used in the Hebrew Bible to mark him as a gift from God (Judg 13). Known for his sexual exploits, crude sense of humor, superhuman strength, and unabashed violence, he embodies characteristics that typify an exaggerated sense of masculinity. But even though his story ends with the note that he led Israel for twenty years (Judg 16:31), the text offers no indication that the Israelites ever gained real relief from their Philistine opponents by Samson's efforts.

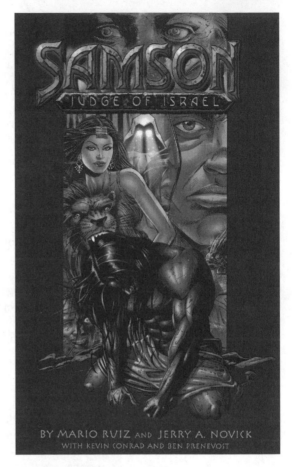

**Fig. 5.1: Cover of *Samson: Judge of Israel***
*The American Bible Society, through its Metron Press imprint, published* Samson: Judge of Israel *in 2004. In this first attempt of the Society to break into the graphic novel market, Samson, it seems, offered an obvious place to begin. Current popular culture, especially religiously oriented segments of popular culture, plays up the "superhero" edge in the Hebrew Bible's portrayal of Samson. And this use has implications for gender identity. In the summer of 2007, various news agencies covered the decision by Wal-Mart to stock toys from One2Believe, including their 13-inch-tall "Spirit Warrior," a buff Samson figurine that their Web site claims is a "big tough toy that boys will love to play with."*

This section explores how the biblical writers construct an almost comic book image to present this he-man from the tribe of Dan.

### Strength

According to the biblical story, Samson's strength provides an essential marker of his character and helps define him as masculine. Even people who know little of the Hebrew Bible probably know of Samson's strength. And the stories are clear on this point. Possessed by YHWH's spirit, Samson rips a lion apart with his bare hands (Judg 15:6). Again under divine influence, he dispatches a thousand Philistines using only a donkey's jawbone as a weapon (15:15). Even without YHWH's spirit, Samson manages to dislodge the city gate of Gath and carry it forty miles uphill to Hebron (16:3)! And in his conversations with Delilah, Samson intimates that his strength sets him apart. He claims that if Delilah tied him up in the correct manner, he would "become weak, and be like any person" (16:7, authors' translation; see vv. 11, 13, 17).

### Aggression

Samson's aggressive tendencies, while not as celebrated as his strength, receive prominent attention in these stories. Directed toward satisfying his desires, particularly his desire for revenge, Samson's aggression drives the plot of the narrative. He avenges his supposed mistreatment at the hands of the Philistine wedding party and his father-in-law by destroying their crops and orchards. Then when the Philistines kill his wife and father-in-law, the writers depict Samson as saying that he "will not stop until I have taken revenge" (Judg 15:7). A mass killing results from his behavior in this case (15:8). And the last word about Samson shows him again plotting more vengeful violence (16:28).

Samson also aggressively pursues various bodily appetites. When he wants to eat, he eats honey from the carcass of a lion, unconcerned with or contemptuous of the restriction that he eat only clean food. When Samson wants to drink, even YHWH experiences his forceful demands: "You [YHWH] have granted this great victory by the hand of your servant. Am I now to die of thirst, and fall into the hands of the uncircumcised?" (15:18).

But the writers celebrate Samson most for his sexual appetite, which he also pursues vigorously. Samson demands a Philistine wife, despite parental disapproval, simply because "she pleases me" (14:3). Later, Samson merely sees a prostitute in Gaza and immediately "enters" her (16:1). Samson sees; Samson takes. And while the NRSV may lead the reader to view Samson as head over heels in love with Delilah (16:4), "he lusted [*ye<sup>e</sup>hav*] after" her might be a better rendering (cf. 2 Sam 13:15 for the NRSV translating the verb *ahav* as "lust"). Samson's sexual desires hardly count as a "weakness" for women; rather, they demonstrate the way his masculine identity and his bent toward aggressive violence come together.

Sexual relations and aggression also connect when Samson publicly accuses the Philistine wedding party of violating his wife: "If you had not plowed with my heifer, you would not have found out my riddle" (Judg 14:18). Samson

---

## Plowed with My Heifer

Samson's claim that the Philistines had "plowed" with his bride sounds strange to modern readers. But other cultures sometimes use plowing imagery to speak of sexual intercourse. From about five thousand years ago in Mesopotamia comes this selection from "The Courtship of Inanna and Dumuzi":

> Inanna begins: "As for me, I, who will plow my vulva? Who will plow my high field? Who will plow my wet ground? As for me, the young woman, who will plow my vulva? Who will station the ox there? Who will plow my vulva?"

> Dumuzi replies: "Great Lady, the king will plow your vulva. I, Dumuzi the king, will plow your vulva."

> Inanna: "Then plow my vulva, man of my heart! Plow my vulva!"

*Inanna, Queen of Heaven and Earth: Her Stories and Hymns from Sumer*, trans. Diane Wolkstein and Samuel Noah Kramer (New York: Harper & Row, 1983), 37.

assumes that the Philistines behave belligerently, just as he would. For Samson, that aggression could only be expressed through sexual means.

### Control

One could conclude that the biblical text portrays Samson as controlled by his sexual passions or as someone dangerously "out of control," who takes actions without a thought to consequences. In both cases, Samson would count as "unmasculine" by the standards discussed. Yet in Samson's story, Samson actually asserts and displays control over others as expected from a hypermasculine figure.

For example, Samson controls his parents both by what he says (demands for a Philistine wife, Judg 14:2) and what he leaves unsaid (the origins of the honey, 14:6, 9). He then attempts to control the wedding party through his riddle, a riddle that is based on experiences that Samson keeps secret (14:14). Thus, Samson alone in the story knows how things are. And when Samson's wife gains the solution and uses this knowledge to betray him to her people, the threat to Samson's dominance produces aggressive outbursts of Samson's strength (14:19; 15:4).

The narrator also draws Samson as a masculine figure capable of "playing" with the notion of control. For example, the Judeans, *with Samson's permission* (15:12–13), bind him with two new ropes. And in Samson's game with Delilah, she ties him up three times, on each occasion in a manner of his own suggestion (16:7, 11, 13). Why does Samson allow himself to be bound these ways? Perhaps he allows others to secure him only to make clear that he cannot be constrained by anyone else. When Delilah shouts, "The Philistines are upon you, O Samson" (16:9, 12, 14), Samson sees this attack as a chance to demonstrate his power. He seems to enjoy toying with Delilah, all the while knowing the illusory nature of the ropes' (and Delilah's) control over him. Each time, ropes prove no match for this he-man (15:15; 16:9, 12, 14).

### Masculinity Reversed: The Rest of the Story

In the story, Samson loses the game with Delilah when he cedes control of secret knowledge. As a result, he loses each aspect of his masculine identity. Samson's strength vanishes with <u>the cutting of his hair</u> (16:17, 22). The

### the cutting of his hair

Hair in the Hebrew Bible signifies vitality (see chapter 6). Biblical texts such as Judg 5:2 associate long, loose hair especially with virility and military might. We can see a similar association in the present day. According to the Web site of the League of Bald Headed Men (http://www.bald.com.au), the hair restoration industry in the United States takes in almost 600 million dollars annually. Balding men, responding to American culture's connection between masculine identity and a full head of hair, naturally spend most of this money. But the cultural linkage between hair and masculinity has its limits. According to a 2005 study, American men now express more of a conflicted attitude toward the equation of body hair with masculinity, leading to greater acceptance of men having body hair removed (Michael Boroughs, Guy Cafri, and J. Kevin Thompson, "Male Body Depilation: Prevalence and Associated Features of Body Hair Removal," *Sex Roles: A Journal of Research*, May 1, 2005).

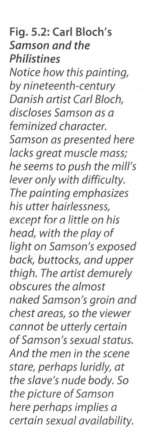

**Fig. 5.2: Carl Bloch's _Samson and the Philistines_**
_Notice how this painting, by nineteenth-century Danish artist Carl Bloch, discloses Samson as a feminized character. Samson as presented here lacks great muscle mass; he seems to push the mill's lever only with difficulty. The painting emphasizes his utter hairlessness, except for a little on his head, with the play of light on Samson's exposed back, buttocks, and upper thigh. The artist demurely obscures the almost naked Samson's groin and chest areas, so the viewer cannot be utterly certain of Samson's sexual status. And the men in the scene stare, perhaps luridly, at the slave's nude body. So the picture of Samson here perhaps implies a certain sexual availability._

Philistines bind Samson with bronze shackles, not ropes, curtailing his aggressive outbursts. They also gouge out his eyes, taking away his ability to see and effectively exert power (Judg 16:21). Samson must now passively comply with his masters' commands to entertain the crowds (16:25), being led about by a youth (16:26). In addition, the Philistines make Samson grind grain, traditionally women's work (see Eccl 12:3; Job 31:10). Samson now counts as more feminine than masculine.

At the end of Samson's story, something of his masculinity returns, again expressed through his hair (16:22). When his hair grows back, he displays aggressive violent strength by controlling the circumstances of his own

**Fig. 5.3: Gustave Doré's** *Samson Destroying the Temple*
*Samson's suicidal vengeance may also demonstrate the return of Samson's sexual aggression. Samson forces the "legs" of the Philistine temple apart, committing one last "sexual" act upon the Philistines.*

death and the deaths of three thousand Philistines (16:30). This partial restoration of Samson's masculinity shows its vitality as a category in the definition of his identity.

*The Tempered Masculine: Jacob*

Since the Hebrew Bible presents Jacob as the ancestor of all Israelites (he receives the name "Israel" as well as "Jacob") one might expect the stories to show him as an exemplar of masculinity. But Jacob is no Samson. The stories compare Jacob to other males, and he often emerges as less of a "man." Moreover, Jacob frequently lives not independently, but rather in other men's households. And even when he heads his own *bet av*, he fails to consistently appear as clearly in charge. Looking at the three characteristics associated with masculinity reveals Jacob's gender identity as gradually developing and changing, with no certain outcome.

### Strength

Jacob's story begins with constant comparisons to his twin brother and polar opposite, Esau. Esau is characterized as a hairy huntsman; Jacob is described as a "quiet man, living in tents" (Gen 25:27). Esau seems to possess "typical" masculine strength; his agility and bravery make him a natural at seeking game. And he possesses a familiar mark of strength, the bow (27:3; cf. 1 Sam 2:4). Jacob, however, commands a stewpot, not a bow. And he has "smooth skin" (27:11).

Isaac's blessing, which Jacob steals, promises him strength: his brother and others will serve him (27:29). But in the face of Esau's threat to kill him, he flees (27:43). Jacob's first display of physical strength comes only after he has left his father's household. Local (male) shepherds refused to move the rock that covered the mouth of <u>a well</u> until all the other local shepherds were present. Jacob does it himself (29:10). At this point Jacob may at least claim something of a masculine identity.

### Aggression

While Jacob's strength takes time to emerge, he possesses a form of aggression right from the outset of his story: he emerges from his mother's womb grasping his brother's heel (Gen 25:26). But his aggression actually appears rather passive. He gains Esau's birthright through an apparently unplanned encounter. Once Esau expresses his need for food, Jacob takes advantage (25:29–34). Further, Jacob, in his forties, requires instruction from his father on the time to marry (28:1) while Esau has already married twice (26:34). And Jacob steals his brother's blessing only after his mother, Rebekah, orders him to do so (27:8). This story provides a good contrast with that of Samson, who never needs cajoling to act and coerces his parents into action (Judg 14:1–4). In the opening stories, Esau's insistent pursuit of food and wives and Rebekah's assertive pursuit of Isaac's blessing for her favorite son overshadow the ambitions of Jacob the heel grabber.

---

#### <u>a well</u>

In the Hebrew Bible, wells serve as a traditional place for men to work out their masculine identities. Moses drives shepherds away from a well in the wilderness so that Jethro's daughters can water the flocks (Exod 2:16–17). This act of strength nicely matches Jacob's. In both these instances, wells disclose a kind of sexual energy. Both these stories of men, women, and wells end with marriage, as does the story of Eliezer's quest to find a wife for Isaac (Gen 24:10–31). Wells also function as sites for negotiation between males, showcasing aggression and control (Gen 21:25–34; 26:12–33).

Jacob's aggression, like his strength, only fully emerges after he leaves home. When Jacob sees Rachel, he knows what to do. He immediately performs his feat of strength by removing the stone from the mouth of the well, and then he greets her with a kiss (Gen 29:9–12). By the time a month passes, he loves her and agrees to serve Laban seven years in exchange for her. And those seven years "seemed to him but a few days because of the love he had for her" (29:20). When he departs from Isaac's *bet av* and must act on his own, Jacob emerges as masculine.

### Control

Jacob's ability to control other people first appears in the story of his securing the birthright. Here Jacob knows he has something Esau wants and recognizes Esau's openness to a trade. But while Jacob obviously gets the better of this deal, Jacob requires the willing participation of his brother. Jacob controls Esau to the extent that he controls access to the stew. He does not control Esau in any other way.

In the next story, Jacob obtains the blessing of his father Isaac by controlling both Esau and Isaac through deceit. Deceit often appears as a feminine category in the Hebrew Bible. So just as Jacob exhibits masculine control in the first story through the feminine act of food preparation, here Jacob secures masculine control through typically "feminine wiles." Close readers of the story will note that Rebekah actually functions as the active participant here: she projects authority in the household through deceit and through giving commands to Jacob (27:5–17).

This uncertainty marks almost all of Jacob's attempts to gain control of others, even after he leaves home. Following his vision at Bethel, he attempts to control God through a vow (28:20–22). He promises to serve God only if the deity guarantees him food, clothing, and security. No one can assess how much this pledge affects God. Jacob certainly receives care along the way, and he returns to the Cisjordan in peace, but the narrator never tells readers precisely how much such provision comes from God.

Jacob's fathering numerous children, an act that should be a strong demonstration of masculinity, ironically gives evidence of Jacob's subordinate position. Leah, Jacob's less-loved wife, makes a deal with Rachel, Jacob's more-loved wife. Rachel will get what she wants—some mandrakes (aids for conception) that Leah's son Reuben had dug up. Leah will get what she wants—sexual access to Jacob: "When Jacob came from the field in the evening, Leah went out to meet him, and said, 'You must come in to me; for I have hired you with my son's mandrakes.' So he lay with her that night" (30:16). Apparently Jacob shows up in whatever bed his wives determine.

The real battle for control comes in Jacob's relationship with Laban. At the start, Laban clearly rules his *bet av*, of which Jacob becomes a part. Laban decides which of his daughters (29:15–30) will marry Jacob first, without informing his future son-in-law. And so Laban gains a purported fourteen years of Jacob's labor for his two daughters. Later in the story,

Jacob testifies to Laban's abusive treatment (31:36–42). But the younger man finally begins to wrest control from Laban and establishes his own *bet av* (30:30). Cleverly using his knowledge of animal husbandry, Jacob amasses great wealth at Laban's expense (30:43). And he manages to get away from Laban without losing these flocks, leaving Laban powerless to control his daughters and animals any longer (31:43)

### Masculinity Developed

As Jacob returns to the land of his birth, more of his masculine identity comes to the fore. The most extreme instance of this development comes in the story of Jacob's wrestling with "a man" (32:24) who turns out to be divine. Jacob's strength allows him to control this divine being until it wrenches his hip out of its socket. Still, Jacob keeps wrestling. This being, whom Jacob later claims to be God, then changes Jacob's name to Israel as a token of Jacob's ability to "strive" victoriously with the divine and humanity (32:28). This new name emphasizes Jacob's masculine qualities. (Chapter 13 includes a more complete discussion of this name.)

Despite God's promise that Jacob will strive and succeed, Jacob's return to the Cisjordan means he must immediately deal with his brother, Esau. The text highlights Jacob's fear of his brother's superior strength (32:3–21). Both before their meeting and during it, Jacob calls himself Esau's servant and behaves in a subservient way (see 32:3–5, 13–21 and 33:5–14 for examples). The irony of this language stands out, given the promises earlier in the story that Esau and others would serve Jacob (25:23; 27:29).

But the text clearly highlights Jacob as his brother's equal. No more comparisons appear opposing Esau's looks and interests to Jacob's. The story shows this newfound similarity when Esau resists accepting Jacob's gift by claiming that he already has enough (33:9). Jacob responds by claiming he has all he needs as well (33:11). Both model masculinity as successful leaders of their respective *bet avot*.

Nonetheless, as head of his own *bet av*, Jacob's masculine identity, especially his ability to control others, gets put on display—but it also experiences limitations. For instance, Jacob assumes the power to name his son Benjamin, erasing Rachel's desire to call him Ben-oni (35:18). This act changes previous behavior; Leah and Rachel named all his sons born in Laban's household. And Jacob controls the blessings to his descendants. He rejects Joseph's insistence that he give a greater blessing to Joseph's firstborn son, Manasseh, choosing instead to give it to the younger son, Ephraim (48:17–20). The story also shows Jacob delivering a final speech, in which he blesses each of his sons. But these "blessings" certainly lack any desire to show equality to his children. Indeed, some do not seem to be blessings at all. Issachar gets slavery (49:15), Gad will be raided (49:19), and Dan "shall be a snake by the roadside" (49:17). At the end of his life, Jacob the patriarch reserves great fortune for some sons, while withholding his approval from others—a classic demonstration of his strength and control.

**Fig. 5.4: Eugene Delacroix's *Jacob Wrestling with the Angel* (Detail)**
*Eugene Delacroix, a French artist of the nineteenth century, paints a Jacob with obvious muscular strength. Jacob here aggressively takes the fight to his opponent. Jacob invades his space, even as the divine being moves to tear Jacob's hip. Interestingly, Delacroix chooses to image the divine being as an angel, rather than as God. And the divine being does not appear to struggle much with his clearly muscle-laden opponent—a view somewhat at odds with the account in Genesis.*

But Jacob's abilities still remain ambiguous. In the story of Dinah, Jacob rules *his* household (34:30). Yet he cedes aggression, and perhaps ability to control, to his sons. Simeon and Levi plot revenge against the local population for the violation of their sister. They initially manipulate the Shechemites (34:13–17) and ultimately murder the men and take the women and children as loot (34:25–29). The sons clearly show themselves as stronger, more aggressive, and more in control of events than their father.

In one brief instance, the firstborn son, Reuben, also threatens Jacob's ability to control the household. Reuben has intercourse with Bilhah, the maidservant of Rachel, to whom Jacob has had sexual access (35:22). But although Reuben's sexual aggressiveness threatens to upset the hierarchy of the *bet av*, the story does not show Jacob doing anything about it until Jacob removes Reuben's rights as firstborn in his last speech (49:4). In this speech, Jacob also finally "settles the score" with Simeon and Levi, who displeased Jacob with their violent aggression against the people of Shechem (34:30; 49:5–7).

The story of Joseph, too, places Jacob's control of the *bet av* at issue. Initially, he appears as an appropriate senior male. For example, he controls the destiny of his son Benjamin. The others sons argue, cajole, and even offer the lives of their own sons (42:37) in order to get Jacob to allow Benjamin to go with them to Egypt. Jacob also commands due deference and respect. Judah, for instance, begs to be imprisoned in place of Benjamin, admitting that he fears "to see the suffering that would come upon my father" (44:34). Judah subordinates himself to Jacob's needs here, offering his own body to spare his father pain.

Yet this story limits Jacob's control and hence his masculinity. His sons successfully deceive him into believing that Joseph dies (37:31–35). And they keep this cover-up in place for decades. The story remains silent about Jacob's reaction to his discovery of the deception, preferring to emphasize Jacob's joy at hearing the good news (45:25–28). This lack of any response on Jacob's part, even in his last speech, where he addresses other problems with his control of the *bet av*, underscores the passive nature of Jacob throughout this story.

In his story, Jacob becomes more of a "man" by learning to control women, his household, and even God. But his control is never complete. And he avoids, almost at all costs, forms of aggression that might endanger his household and his standing. This passivity makes Jacob seem less strong, less masculine, what one might expect from "a quiet man, living in tents" (25:27). Jacob defers his aggression, waiting until the end of life to settle scores. So Jacob's gender identity, while masculine, shows the kinds of nuances and shifts in identity possible for characters in the Hebrew Bible, even characters essential to the national identity.

*The Hyperfeminine: Esther*

In contrast to the masculinities of Samson and Jacob, the narrative of the book of Esther presents its title character as hyperfeminine. Esther first appears in the context of a quest for the perfect woman, and she indeed seems to meet the highlighted ideal criteria for women (Esth 2:2–4). The text clearly describes her as nubile: young, "fair and beautiful" (2:7). Her names also reflect her beauty and desirability: the Hebrew *Hadassah* means "myrtle," and the Persian *Esther* may be a reference to **Ishtar**, the Babylonian goddess of love and war, and/or to the Persian word for "star." Esther also immediately strikes the reader as submissive. Taken into the king's harem, she "pleases" and "wins the favor" of the king's eunuch (2:8–9). The text also starts hinting at her deceptiveness. She conceals the identity of her people and her kindred at the behest of her guardian Mordecai (2:10).

---

### myrtle

A common Mediterranean evergreen plant, myrtle enjoys a reputation for its pleasantly fragrant oil and its white, starlike flower. The ancient Greeks associated myrtle with Aphrodite, their goddess of love.

### Nubility

The text presents Esther as a beautiful woman. But apparently her natural beauty needs enhancing. Thus, the story narrates that the harem girls undergo a twelve-month regimen of treatments consisting of oil of myrrh, perfumes, and cosmetics (2:12). These procedures prepared the women for a night with the king. If the king "delighted" in a particular woman, she might receive a return summons (2:14). Esther thus further ensures her sexual allure by following the dictates of the harem's eunuch (2:15). As a result, the king more than delighted in Esther; he loved her "more than all other women," and she won his favor and devotion (2:17).

Her appearance stands her in good stead yet again when she must approach the king at a time when palace protocol forbade contact. After fasting and putting on her royal robes, the narrative describes how she stands in the inner court of the king's palace and waits for the king to notice her through the entrance doors to his throne room (5:1). As soon as he sees her, she wins his favor (5:2) just as she did before (2:17). Since she says nothing and clearly violates the king's command, the text seems to suggest her

---

### Vashti: The Other Woman

Before Esther even appears in the book that bears her name, the text tells the story of another woman, Vashti, wife of King Ahasuerus of Persia. Vashti possesses some ideal female characteristics: she is "beautiful" and "fair to behold" (Esth 1:11). But she does not act appropriately for a female. She disobeys the order of her husband and king, shaming her husband in the eyes of his male companions and arousing his rage (1:12). In fact, the biblical text imagines her disobedience as provoking the rebellion of *all* women against their husbands (1:17–18). Thus, Vashti functions as a negative contrast to Esther who, unlike Vashti, not only exhibits beauty but also is depicted as behaving in a proper, feminine manner.

---

### Ancient Cosmetic Treatments

The Hebrew Bible mentions or alludes to a variety of cosmetic treatments. While anointing with oil especially signifies consecration of objects or persons for holy use, it also serves for purely aesthetic purposes (e.g., Ps 133:2; Eccl 9:8). The Hebrew Bible also notes the use of aromatic substances or perfumes, such as myrrh, aloes, and cinnamon (Song 1:13; 5:5; Prov 7:17), and speaks of perfume boxes in Isa 3:20. Finally, the outlining of the eyes receives mention (Jer 4:30; Ezek 27:17; 2 Kgs 9:30)—the character Job even names one of his daughters *qeren happuk* (Job 42:14), literally, "horn of eye paint." Archaeological investigations have uncovered a multitude of cosmetic substances and tools such as dishes, palettes, tweezers, mirrors, combs, perfume containers, and tubes of kohl, a black eye paint.

---

### golden scepter

Kings utilize scepters as a sign of royal authority. In the context of Esther's story, the golden scepter may function as a phallic representation.

---

beauty as the reason for the king's favor. Further, the golden scepter that the king extends to her and that she touches intimates her appearance is sexually arousing (5:2).

### Deceptiveness

The narrative depicts Esther's deceptiveness primarily in the scenes in and around the banquets. Recall that Esther kept her ancestry a secret (2:10, 20). But as the story unfolds, the Judeans, her people, stand under the threat of annihilation by decree of the king (3:8–10). Her cousin Mordecai prevails upon her to plead the Judeans' case before her husband (4:8–14). She takes an indirect approach to achieve her goal. After using her beauty to get an audience with the king, she merely invites him to a banquet (5:4).

This invitation works on the principle that a way to a man's heart is through his stomach. In the Hebrew Bible, food preparation and provision often assist women in securing what they want (see, for example, 1 Sam 25:18–31; Gen 27:5–17). Moreover, these banquets also entail significant amounts of wine and thus weakened resistance (Esth 1:8; 5:6; 7:2). But when the king presents her an opportunity to make her request during the banquet, she demurs. Instead, the text heightens her deceptiveness by presenting her as coy and coquettish; she merely invites him to a second banquet (5:8). At this second event, she waits through another day and much more wine before petitioning her husband the king for the lives of her people (7:2–4).

The text describes her request as dependent upon her sexual allure. When she fingers the guilty party, the king's servant Haman, the king leaves the room in anger (7:7). Haman approaches Esther on her couch to beg for his life, and when the king returns, he assumes that he sees a sexual assault in progress (7:8). Instead of correcting this impression, the text depicts Esther as remaining silent and allowing for Haman's summary execution

---

### remaining silent

The story of Potiphar's wife in Gen 39:6–18 presents the inverse of this situation but still focuses on female deceptiveness. There the woman seeks a sexual liaison with Joseph, a male servant in the household, but he refuses. She grabs his garment as he flees and uses this "evidence" to accuse him of a crime he did not commit. Unlike Esther, who remains silent, Potiphar's wife voices a false accusation.

---

(7:10). Deceptiveness prevails. The narrator imbues the character Esther with the qualities of a "typical" woman. She never takes a direct approach, but rather plays on her husband's weaknesses.

### Acquiescence

Like many biblical women, Esther's identity depends on or derives from some male figure. In the story, two men stand out in this regard: her cousin Mordecai, who adopts her and serves as her guardian (2:5–7), and her husband, King Ahasuerus. The narrator continually presents Esther as obedient, loyal, and submissive to the various men in her life. For example, when she first goes to the king, she does only what the king's eunuch Hegai tells her to do (2:15). Likewise, when Mordecai instructs her to keep her ancestry secret, she follows his orders (2:20). But when Mordecai's orders bring her loyalty to the king into question, she lets the authority of another male trump Mordecai by following the established rules of her husband's home, the palace (4:11). And when she finally submits to Mordecai's request, she performs a typically feminine act of acquiescent self-sacrifice: "If I perish, I perish" (4:16).

### Femininity Reversed: The Rest of the Story

Just as Samson is not a pure example of the hypermasculine, neither does Esther completely embody the hyperfeminine. While the text generally emphasizes Esther's beauty and submissiveness, once Haman hatches his plot against her people, it also characterizes her as taking initiative and demonstrating bravery. For example, she assumes agency by ordering the eunuch Hathach on an errand (4:5). She also decides to disobey the king and approach him when not allowed contact (4:16). And she even gives orders to Mordecai regarding fasting with the Judeans (4:16), thus reversing the prior hierarchy of command. At this point in the story, Esther does not seem to fit the acquiescent or submissive role. She takes action by planning a series of banquets that unmask Haman and make clear to the king her people's plight. After Haman's execution, she sets Mordecai over the house of Haman (8:2), and she pleads again with the king on behalf of her people (8:3–6).

But then Mordecai takes over again. He orders the king's secretaries to write an edict (8:9), and he pens, seals, and sends off letters in the name of the king (8:10). Nonetheless, Esther remains present. She requests of the king a second day for the Judeans to avenge themselves against their enemies (9:13), and, either alone (9:32) or together with Mordecai (9:29, 31), commands the Judeans to celebrate the festival of Purim. The book ends, however, as it began, with the portrait of a powerful man: "For Mordecai the Judean was of second rank to the king Ahasuerus. And he was great among the Judeans. He was a favored one among the multitude of his brothers, one seeking good for his people and a spokesman for the security of all his seed" (10:3, authors' translation). Once Esther renders her womanly service, she recedes from view.

*The Tempered
Feminine: Jael*

The book of Esther presents its hyperfeminine heroine as defeating Haman, the enemy of her people. Likewise, a woman named Jael acts decisively to dispatch the Canaanite general Sisera, enemy of the Israelites (Judg 4–5). But when considered in light of the three characteristics of the feminine, she not only expresses these qualities quite differently but also demonstrates more traditionally masculine traits.

### Nubility

The narrative presentation of Jael never explicitly names her as beautiful, youthful, sexually appealing, or fertile. But she nonetheless indirectly reveals some of these key feminine traits. For example, the writers identify her wife as the woman of Heber, the Kenite (Judg 4:17). Additionally, she acts maternally by taking the tired warrior Sisera into her tent, covering him with a blanket, and feeding him milk (4:18–19). These acts of comfort, however, ultimately take a dangerous twist. Finally, her name means "mountain goat." Proverbs 5:19 associates this animal with the young wife in whom a husband is to take delight. (NRSV reads "a graceful doe"; see JPS for a more accurate rendering as "a graceful mountain goat.")

---

### Deborah: The Woman Warrior

The story of the Israelite judge Deborah intertwines with that of Jael. Like Jael, Deborah does not readily associate with features of nubility. While the NRSV translates Judg 4:4 as the "wife of Lappidoth" and she gets the label "mother in Israel" (5:7)—possibly implying connections with sexuality and fertility—these texts are complicated. The Hebrew in Judg 4:4 literally reads "woman of torches." A rather obscure phrase, it possibly connects to war. Nahum 2:4 describes the chariots rushing about in the defeat of Nineveh as "torches," using the same root word seen in Judg 4:4. And it also likens them to lightning; Barak, the general Deborah commands, means "lightning."

Moreover, with regard to Deborah, the image of "mother" also is set in a martial context. Her means of providing for her children, Israel, comes from the plundering of enemies (Judg 5:7). Consider, too, that her name, Deborah, means "bee." In other biblical texts, bees are associated with ravaging armies (Isa 7:18; Deut 1:44; Ps 118:12). Finally, even as the text labels her a woman prophet (*ishshah n$^e$viah*, Judg 4:4), she acts more like a military commander. She summons and gives orders to Barak, the commander of the Israelite forces (Judg 4:6–7). And Barak refuses to go into battle without Deborah present (4:8).

Nonetheless, the text also assigns a certain kind of femininity to Deborah. For example, she sings a victory song in Judg 5, while Barak takes care of the aftermath of the battle by leading away the captives (5:12). The biblical writers often associate such singing with women (see Exod 15:20–21; 1 Sam 18:6–7; Judg 11:34). But she still acts in most respects as a male military leader. By contrast, the biblical text portrays Jael in more ambiguous female terms.

### Deceptiveness and Acquiescence

Jael demonstrates a tempered femininity by presenting an exaggerated quality of deceptiveness paired with an absolute negation of any acquiescence. Her encounter with Sisera makes these traits clear. With regard to deceptiveness, she lures Sisera into her tent with false promises of safety and security (Judg 4:18–19). Given the peace treaty between Sisera's king, Jabin, and the *bet av* of Jael's husband (4:17), Jael's deceit stands out as even more pronounced.

The writers also play with a kind of sexual tension in the two versions of the story. In Judg 4, Jael invites Sisera to turn aside "to me" (4:18). Sisera enters into a private space, seeking refuge and water, and Jael instead offers him milk—the product of female bodies—and gets him into a prone position. In chapter 5, the text contrasts her inviting actions with the speculations of Sisera's mother. She imagines that his taking a girl or two as the spoil of war delays his arrival home (5:30), when in reality a woman pretending to provide him comfort has murdered him.

Not acquiescent in any manner, Jael stands in complete violation of the loyalty, submissiveness, self-sacrifice, and passivity expected of women. As already noted, her husband Heber struck a peace agreement with the Canaanite king. She fails to act in accordance with that treaty and thus shows disloyalty to her *bet av*. Indeed, she refuses to submit to the orders of any man. When Sisera asks for water, for instance, she gives him milk. The character Jael also rejects a path of self-sacrifice. If she had followed orders and remained loyal to her *bet av*, she likely would have been raped, kidnapped, or killed for providing aid and comfort to Israel's enemy. Instead, she herself kills. In sum, Jael refuses passivity but secures her ends directly by violently dispatching Sisera.

The biblical text complicates the manner of Sisera's death by providing two versions. In Judg 4, Jael sneaks up quietly on a resting Sisera and drives a tent peg through his head (4:21). This penetration of his body places Jael in the position of the victorious male after battle. Her figurative "rape" of the defeated Sisera feminizes him. Judges 5, however, pictures Sisera in a different, perhaps standing or kneeling, position. Jael kills him with hammer blow to the head that shatters his skull, causing him to slump to the floor (5:26–27). Here the text presents her as aggressive warrior striking down her enemy.

The writers do not tell any more of Jael's story. Instead, the song in Judg 5 concludes by evoking "normal" gender roles. A woman singing (Deborah) quotes a woman (Sisera's mother) acknowledging the typical aftermath of war for women. Men rape women (5:30) and steal their possessions to bring home to their female relatives (5:31). Thus, Jael's act of defiance does not serve as the last word in Judg 4–5. The usual fate of women as passive victims rises to that position.

## Gender Anxieties

So far, this chapter has demonstrated how some characters present a more stringent version of femininity or masculinity, while others present a more tempered or moderate account. Yet all conform more or less to the Hebrew Bible's expectations of gendered identity. In other words, the assignment of different gender roles for men and women remains clear. Some biblical narratives, however, confound the separation of male and female roles. These texts often reveal an anxiety about such a confusion of categories and work quickly to resolve them and return the characters to their proper places.

## *Women in Masculine Gender Roles: Ruth and Naomi*

Female characters do not always conform to the Hebrew Bible's typically feminine traits. The book of Ruth, for instance, narrates a story of women who, at least for part of the account, live and act independently of male characters. Although the book begins with a description of an Israelite *bet av* (Ruth 1:1–3), the man and his two sons die, leaving Naomi, the man's wife, and his sons' two Moabite wives, Orpah and Ruth, without male leadership (1:3–5). These women, left on their own, exhibit some of the more typically male traits of strength, aggressiveness, and control in order to survive.

Normally, Israelite widows fall under the control of some man—whether a surviving son, a brother, a father, an uncle, or any near male kinsman. In the book of Ruth, however, the location of these women in Moab removes the possibility of Elimelech's other kinsmen stepping in. Naomi thus plans to return home and encourages her daughters-in-law to return to their mothers' houses (1:8) in order to secure some hope of marrying again (1:12). Ruth refuses and instead returns to Israel with her mother-in-law (1:16–18). They form a social unit of their own.

Ruth demonstrates significant initiative in this text. She "clings" to her mother-in-law and departs from her homeland (1:14). The biblical text uses the same terminology of "clinging" in Gen 2:24: "Therefore a man leaves his father and mother and clings to his wife, and they become one flesh." This word suggests that the relationship between the daughter-in-law Ruth and her mother-in-law Naomi substitutes for the usual relationship of wife and husband. But the

### clings

The Hebrew verb translated as "clings" in Gen 2:24 and Ruth 1:14 (*dbq*) signifies an especially close relationship of faithfulness in which generally a subordinate's identity becomes closely bound up with the identity of a superior, such as between a man and a woman (e.g., Gen 2:24; 34:3; Josh 32:12; 1 Kgs 11:2), a king and his people (e.g., 2 Sam 20:2), or God and worshipers (e.g., Deut 10:20; 11:22; 13:5; Jer 13:11). This "clinging" relates in Gen 2:24 to the notion of becoming "one flesh," likely signifying a unit of reproduction.

**Fig. 5.5: A View of Ruth and Naomi's Relationship**
*The precise nature of the relationship between Ruth and Naomi remains ambiguous. In this lithograph from the late nineteenth century, oddly titled* The Parting of Ruth and Naomi, *an anonymous artist plays up the emotional attachment Ruth supposedly feels for Naomi, producing a romantic embrace.*

proposition that two women, without any man, could form "one flesh" makes a revolutionary claim against the patriarchal context of the biblical world.

Additionally, once in Bethlehem, Ruth sets out to provide food for the household by <u>gleaning</u> and becomes its economic mainstay (Ruth 2:2). She takes extraordinary initiative to survive without the support of any man. But the text reveals some discomfort with her independence and attempts to show her in a more typical role. For instance, the landowner, Boaz, expresses concern for her safety by voicing the potential for her to suffer abuse from male field hands (2:8–9). And Ruth shows Boaz due deference after he offers her access to his crops and water (2:10).

But Boaz does not reveal that he is related to Naomi's family and gives her little more than the remains of his field (2:14–16). So the women must seize control again by pushing Boaz into assuming his rightful position as their kinsman and thus to integrate themselves back into normal gender roles. At this point, Naomi finally acts. She reveals to Ruth that Boaz is a relative, a potential *goel*, or redeemer, and instructs Ruth to dress up and then approach Boaz as he lies sleeping on the <u>threshing floor</u> (3:3–4). These actions seem to set up a seduction or sexual entrapment—a risky strategy. At the threshing floor, a woman could easily be mistaken for, and treated as, a prostitute (see Hos 9:1).

Ruth bravely (or foolishly) performs Naomi's instructions—up to a point. After Boaz is "in a contented mood," she "uncovers his feet." "Feet" here represents a common euphemism for the genitals. She then lies down until Boaz awakens (Ruth 3:7–8). While Naomi told her to wait for Boaz's instructions (3:4), Ruth instead tells him what to do (3:9). The words "spread your cloak over your servant" function as a double entendre with sexual connotations. First, they echo Boaz's earlier speech, when he blesses Ruth by YHWH, the God of Israel, "under whose wings you have taken refuge" (2:12). The Hebrew word *kanaf* lies behind the English words "cloak" and "wings." Such a statement implies that Ruth now asks Boaz to spread the same protection over her. In the context, it surely means a proposal of marriage. Second, the phrase insinuates an invitation to sexual intercourse (see Ezek 16:8). The risky strategy works. Ruth motivates Boaz to act as the *goel* and take responsibility for Naomi and her family.

The female characters take initiative and, in doing so, express a more typically male role. But once they reach their goal, the narrator quickly and powerfully moves to foreclose on any anxiety over such mixing of gender roles by returning the characters to an unambiguous patriarchal environment. From this point, neither Ruth nor Naomi speak; the story turns to the public world of men, negotiating land and women at the city gate (4:1–11). This process of incorporation concludes when Boaz takes Ruth as his wife and she bears him a son (4:13). The text also depicts Naomi as a mother (4:17) and a nurse (4:16) with a grandson who will care for her in her old age (4:15). In this restored *bet av*, everyone again assumes their proper gender identities. Indeed, the final spoken words belong to the women in the community

## gleaning

Gleaners collect anything that remains of the crops after the harvesters reap the produce from the fields and orchards. Leviticus 19:9–10 and 23:22, as well as Deut 24:19–21, instruct the harvesters to leave some of the crop for the poor, resident aliens, widows, and orphans to gather.

## threshing floor

Men process grain on the threshing floor. During the harvest, at the end of a day of work, they also eat, drink (and likely get drunk), and then sleep there to protect the grain.

(4:14–15, 17) and underscore the gender ideology that sees the bearing of sons as the most potent source of women's power in a patriarchal world. And the last narrated words of the book offer a traditional genealogy listing only the fathers and sons (4:18–22). The patriarchal world, revolving around the centrality of the male, has closed in again.

*Other Examples of Gender Anxiety*

While the book of Ruth most obviously displays the text's anxiety over maintaining proper gender roles, many other stories demonstrate problems with women assuming more masculine attributes as well as men becoming feminized. For example, when Miriam challenges Moses along with her brother Aaron, she assumes a male prerogative to speak publicly (Num 12:1–2). As a result, while Aaron merely gets chastised, Miriam gets struck with leprosy and suffers separation from the camp (12:6–15). Likewise Ahab and Jezebel appear to switch gender identities. In the struggle to obtain Naboth's vineyard, Jezebel takes control and acquires the property by writing letters in Ahab's name as well as instructing her husband on what to do (1 Kgs 21:8–15). She acts while the king remains passive. By contrast, the writers report that when Naboth refuses Ahab's command, Ahab takes to his bed and refuses to eat (1 Kgs 21:4). Although both Ahab and Jezebel meet an inglorious end, Ahab dies as a "real man" on the battlefield (1 Kgs 22:34–37), while Jezebel's body gets crudely desecrated beyond recognition (2 Kgs 9:30–37).

Several legal texts also take up these concerns. Deuteronomy 25:11–12 describes a situation where a woman intervenes in a fight between two men. In this instance, the text forbids her from grabbing the testicles of her man's opponent. Such a brazen attack on masculinity receives no mercy; she would lose her hand as punishment. No similar stipulation against men grabbing each other's testicles in a fight appears. Maintaining intact male genitalia also gets attention in Deut 23:1. There, men with crushed testicles or a missing penis cannot take their place in the assembly of God. Their ambiguous gender identity threatens proper relationship to the divine. Additionally, the text forbids cross-dressing in Deut 22:5. In this case women cannot wear men's garments, nor can men put on the clothing of women. Such behavior is classified as abhorrent to God because it confuses male with female. Finally, the text speaks strongly in favor of men engaging in sexual relations with women only. Male sexual contact with other men means one male must take on a passive or a feminized role, and the law claims such as abomination (Lev 18:22 and 20:13).

Current debates about the status of same-sex relationships indicate that even today's world exhibits anxiety over gender identities. The confusion of male and female gender roles, whether in manner of dress or occupation or sexual behavior, threatens the stability of the male/female binary. As demonstrated, however, gender as a social construct is remarkably fluid. The stories of the Hebrew Bible illustrate some of this variability while simultaneously expressing great anxiety about it and attempting to rein it in.

**Fig. 5.6: Gustave Doré's** *Ineffable God*
*This Gustave Doré print, from* La divina commedia di Dante Alighieri, *demonstrates the common idea of a bodiless and thus a genderless deity.*

## God and Gender

We have looked to some of the literary representations of biblical persons to help access some of the assumptions operative regarding gender in the Hebrew Bible. But this discussion has left out the gender identity of the main character: God. Although chapter 13 provides a much fuller discussion about God, examining the divine character here will help underline the importance of, and problematic issues concerning, gender identity in the Hebrew Bible.

Many readers object to the notion of God as having a gender identity. To speak of God as "masculine" or "feminine" seems to say too much about the deity. And both Jewish and Christian traditions frequently attempt to place God beyond the physical realm. But the Hebrew Bible presents God as a character, and as a character God displays traits associated with both masculinity and femininity. Chapter 6 explores how the biblical texts conceptualize a body for God and use physical features to describe the divine. The present chapter, while acknowledging the reluctance to avoid direct description of the deity, examines texts that imagine the character of God with gendered language, categories, and ideas.

*God as Masculine*

The language used for the deity assumes God as masculine. The common noun for "god" in Hebrew (*el*) is masculine, and the name "YHWH" likely derives from a masculine form of a verb (see chapter 13 for more on the divine name YHWH). Additionally, when depicting God's actions or speech, the Hebrew Bible invariably uses <u>third-person masculine singular verbs</u>. Moreover, several ancient Israelite inscriptions envision YHWH as a male god with a female consort (see the examples in chapter 13). The language and cultural context of ancient Israel thus point to the Israelite god, YHWH, as a masculine figure.

The Hebrew Bible largely replicates this context by imagining God in a variety of masculine roles. God appears as a king surrounded by his divine council (1 Kgs 22:19; Isa 6:1–2; Ps 82:1), or as a dread warrior, coming forth to crush his would-be opponents (Exod 15:3; Judg 5:4–5; Mic 1:3–4; Hab 3:3–6), or as a patriarch, the head of a *bet av* and husband of Israel (Hos 2:16–20). In other words, when conjuring images to render the divine comprehensible, the writers of the Hebrew Bible most often picture God exhibiting the typically masculine characteristics of strength, aggression, and control. Masculinity thus becomes the default position in the Hebrew Bible's gender construction of the divine. References to God with the masculine pronoun "he" simply underscore this assumption.

*God as Feminine*

Despite dominance of masculine imagery for God in the Hebrew Bible, feminine imagery occasionally comes to the fore. Such images focus almost exclusively on activities and characteristics associated with mothering. The

### third-person masculine singular verbs

Like many languages, Hebrew divides the world into masculine and feminine. Verbs appear in either the first, second, or third persons. First-person forms denote "I" in the singular or "we" in the plural. Second person indicates the actions of "you" in both singular and plural numbers, and third person designates "he" in the masculine singular, "she" in the feminine singular, and "they" in the plural. First-person forms do not have assigned gender. But second- and third-person forms do. Hence, to make reference to one man and to describe that man as "he," the third-person masculine singular applies.

> ### nursing
>
> Nursing, of course, requires breasts. One of the common names for God in the Hebrew, El Shaddai, might mean "God of the breasts."

texts sometimes directly place God in this role (e.g., Deut 32:18; Isa 42:14; 49:15). More frequently, however, the linkage between God and birthing happens through the use of the Hebrew term for "womb" (*rekhem*), the supposed seat of compassion (*rakhamim*). This language generates a unique empathetic connection between a biological mother and child grounded in the physical acts of carrying a baby and giving birth. So when the text speaks of God as showing compassion, it alludes to a maternal womb-based way of relating. For example, in Jer 31:20, God claims Ephraim as a child, and the text shows God using this term for "womb" alongside a second term (*meah*), which likely also refers to the uterus:

> Is Ephraim my precious son?
>   Is he a child of delight?
> As often as my speech is against him,
>   I yet call him to mind.
> For this reason my womb [*meay*] moves for him;
>   I will surely have compassion [womb-feeling; *rakhem
>   arakhamenu*] on him, says the LORD. (authors' translation)

The Hebrew Bible also depicts God as <u>nursing</u> the infant Israel. In Num 11:12, the writers show Moses asserting that God conceived, gave birth, and nursed Israel and thus God (as opposed to Moses) should assume responsibility for them. The Hebrew Bible also portrays God as treating Israel as any Israelite mother treats her children: God feeds, carries, and teaches Israel to walk (Hos 11:3–4). Indeed, any time God gives Israel food, God fulfills a role usually assigned to women in Israelite society (e.g., Deut 32:13–14).

Other female images for God also appear in the Hebrew Bible. For example, when the authors of Proverbs think of wisdom as a significant attribute of God, they develop it as feminine. Female divine wisdom relates intimately to the divine creation of the cosmos (see Prov 8:22–31). (For more information on this surprising association of the feminine with God, see chapter 11.)

*God as Masculine and Feminine*

The Hebrew Bible images God predominantly as fulfilling masculine roles, but God occasionally demonstrates feminine characteristics as well. This mixture of the masculine and feminine places God as a character in the Hebrew Bible in a gender bind, not defined completely by the qualities of either gender.

> ## continuum
>
> The statement that God created them "male and female" should not be read as producing an exclusive binary. Like "good and evil" or "heaven and earth," the expression "male and female" functions to indicate the two ends of a continuum. For example, when God creates heaven and earth, God creates everything *from* heaven *to* earth. Likewise, when God creates male and female, God creates a continuum of everything *from* exclusively male *to* exclusively female.

Genesis 1:27 expresses this continuum of gender categories in the creation of humanity: "So God created humankind in his image, in the image of God he created him; male and female he created them" (authors' translation).

Here the text shows its anxiety about gender. It starts out by saying God created humankind *bᵉtsalmo* (in his image). The Hebrew here attaches a masculine-singular ending (his) to the noun (image) to indicate that the image reflects a masculine subject. And God creates what the text says is a "him." But then two genders emerge in the image of God, because God creates "them" male and female. Thus, even as the text attempts to assert God as masculine, it undercuts that idea immediately by claiming that God's image embraces both the masculine and feminine. Such a picture fits with the notion demonstrated in this chapter that the Hebrew Bible does not produce stable, "perfectly" masculine and feminine characters. Nowhere does this dynamic come across more clearly than in the story of Adam and Eve in the garden.

## Reading the Garden: An Exemplary Tale

When thinking about gender in the Hebrew Bible, many readers turn immediately to the narrative of Adam and Eve. As the story of the first man and woman, it presumably establishes a paradigm for gender identity. The religious and cultural fascination with this text demonstrates the pervasiveness of such an interpretive approach. Most readings see gender identities as binary opposites in this text and understand the female character as subordinate to the male. This section begins by looking at some of these traditional interpretations before rereading the text to question how it constructs gender.

When considering traditional religious readings of the garden story, a famous example appears in the New Testament book of 1 Timothy:

> Let a woman learn in silence with full submission. I permit no woman to teach or to have authority over a man; she is to keep silent. For Adam was formed first, then Eve; and Adam was not deceived, but the woman was deceived and became a transgressor. (1 Tim 2:11–14)

The writer here appears to place great weight on the order of the creation and its perceived production of a gender hierarchy. Additionally, the text places the woman in the role of the first to commit sin. And that supposed act generates incredible social consequences: women must remain silent and cannot occupy authoritative or dominant roles in either church or society.

This blaming of the woman also appears in an ancient text in the Jewish tradition. Sirach 25:24 says, "From a woman sin had its beginning, and because of her we all die." Here the woman assumes responsibility for the fate of humankind; she brings death into the world. Some later rabbinic writings continue this train of interpretation and justify various restrictions and obligations placed exclusively on women by reference to the supposed sin of the woman in Gen 2–3 (e.g., *Genesis Rabbah* 17.8; *b. Shabbat* 31b). Women, for example, must light Sabbath candles and observe purity regulations as the result of the actions of this first woman.

Culturally common images in the west also typically present Eve as a temptress leading the man to his downfall with the bite of an apple. Bruce Springsteen's song "Pink Cadillac" describes Eve as just such a seductress before the man in the song rejects the fruit and instead falls for a woman in an amazing car. The ABC television show *Desperate Housewives* not only uses highly sexualized images of women alongside a tree with a snake and an apple in its opening credits; it also portrays its five women stars in tight, low-cut, black gowns reclining on a bed of apples in its print ads. Any survey of western art would quickly multiply these examples.

These cultural representations of this story assume a clear binary between male and female. Such an emphasis on gender role exclusivity comes out in contemporary debates about gay rights. A common sign among protestors against such rights reads, "God created Adam and Eve, not Adam and Steve." This slogan expresses belief in a definitive biological distinction between the two sexes at the beginning and as a part of the divine plan. The argument does not acknowledge biology as part of a culturally constructed gender continuum or the existence of intersex persons.

As these examples illustrate, cultural ideas about gender roles tend to be read back into the text and to shape readers' understandings of what the text conveys. If one assumes an exclusive gender binary, readings common to the western cultural tradition result. But if one sees gender as a more complicated and destabilized continuum of possibilities, alternate readings emerge. A close reading of Gen 2:4b–3:24 opens up these new interpretive possibilities.

The text begins in a place similar to that articulated in Gen 1:27. According to the story, God molds an <u>adam from the adamah,</u> or a human

### adam from the adamah

The Hebrew word *adam*, besides being a pun on the word for "earth" or "ground" (*adamah*), can function in three ways: (1) as designating one person or human being, usually with no indication of gender; (2) as a collective term for all of humanity, again with no indication of gender; (3) as the proper name "Adam." Thus, the gender, if any, of *adam* can be determined only by context, and even then it might remain ambiguous.

from the ground (Gen 2:7). The only physical trait of the *adam* worthy of mention at this point—nostrils—certainly does not identify this creature as male or female. Pronouns alone suggest masculinity for this human (see Gen 2:15–17), and yet in Hebrew the masculine may also be read as neuter. For example, when God addresses the *adam* in the second-person masculine singular, the *adam* could also be understood as undifferentiated—neither male nor female. Again, nothing in the text definitively indicates biological maleness. Nor does the work assigned—tilling and keeping of a garden (Gen 2:15)—assume a man's duties (see chapter 4 for a description of the typical division of labor between men and women in the Israelite family).

Such an undifferentiated creature produces some anxiety about the stability of gender identity. How does one conceptualize this creature without the category of gender? The writers assert that God takes the initiative to resolve this issue by determining that the *adam* needs an *ezer kᵉnegdo* (Gen 2:18). Translations of what the deity envisions certainly reflect some of the translators' assumptions about gender:

|  |  |
|---|---|
| KJV | I will make him an help meet for him. |
| ASV | I will make him a help meet for him. |
| Darby | I will make him a helpmate, his like. |
| Douay-Rheims | Let us make him a help like unto himself. |
| NIV | I will make a helper suitable for him. |
| ESV | I will make him a helper fit for him. |
| NAS | I will make him a helper suitable for him. |
| NRSV | I will make him a helper as his partner. |
| NKJV | I will make him a helper comparable to him. |
| CEV | I need to make a suitable partner for him. |
| NAB | I will make a suitable partner for him. |

Typically most translators choose some form of the word "helper" alongside an expression of comparability or equality to render this phrase. Understanding the Hebrew, however, proves challenging.

The word *ezer*, or "helper," carries connotations of "assistant" or "subordinate" in English. But in Hebrew, it occurs most often in reference to God (see Deut 33:26–39 and Pss 33:20; 121:1–2; and 124:8 for examples). In these contexts, the word suggests strength and surety as well as the ability to perform duties appropriate to a divine being, such as rescue and protection. In Gen 2, the passage places God's expression about the *adam*'s need immediately following the assignment of tilling and keeping the garden—perhaps suggesting that two could accomplish more, and in a more satisfactory manner, than one.

The second term, *kᵉnegdo*, consists of three parts: the preposition (*kᵉ*) meaning "like," "as," or "according to," plus the word *neged* ("over" or "against") and a masculine pronoun denoting "him" or "it." A literal translation might read "like against it." This word simultaneously intimates similarity and difference. On the one hand, the preposition speaks to correspondence

**Fig. 5.7: Wiligelmo da Modena's *Portrayal of Man and Woman***
*Wiligelmo da Modena's early twelfth-century relief on the façade of the Duomo in Modena, Italy, suggests the continuum between the male and female. Both toil at the same labor, and any distinction between the two remains superficial at best.*

by evoking comparison or reflection. But *neged* places this new thing in a counter position to the *adam*.

This strange mixture of correspondence and contrast plays out in the way the text presents the generation of the new being. Initially, the writers show God returning to the *adamah* in order to produce something from the same substance as the *adam* (Gen 2:19). But nothing results as an *ezer kᵉnegdo* (2:20). Success comes only by withdrawing building material (a rib or a side) from the *adam* and constructing the new being (2:21). Then the *adam* declares the deity's work done: "This thing at last is bone of my bones and flesh of my flesh; this thing will be called Woman [*ishshah*], for out of Man [*ish*] this thing was taken" (2:23, authors' translation).

In a sense, the text here produces two new creatures. The *adam* claims identity as an *ish*, a word that denotes a biological male. The woman he labels *ishshah*, denoting a biological female and evoking both similarity to, and difference from, *ish*. Built from the same bone and flesh, and with a similar-sounding label, the woman appears like the man. But she is not an exact copy. The text presents this distinction as provoking some anxiety in the *adam* and a desire to remerge: "Therefore a man leaves his father and his mother and clings to his woman, and they become one flesh" (2:25, authors' translation).

The biblical story thus lacks a strict binary that opposes male and female. It also fails to generate any secondary characteristics associated with masculinity or femininity. No list of duties or responsibilities more appropriate to one gender as opposed to the other appears. The story rather presents a continuum connecting the man and woman that God produces. But the story goes on to say that this ambiguity cannot last. As it moves into Genesis 3, it forecloses on this connectedness and narrates stable, oppositional, and ranked gender identities for this man and woman.

When chapter 3 of Genesis opens, the writers hint at some degree of separation between the man and the woman by presenting the woman as engaged independently in a conversation with the serpent. However, a careful reading still indicates her connection with the man. In the Hebrew, every time the serpent speaks the word "you" (3:1, 4), the pronoun appears in the second-person masculine plural. That is, even though only the woman speaks, the grammar indicates that the man also stands there as a silent partner in the conversation. A small Hebrew prepositional phrase underscores his presence: verse 6 reports that the woman ate the fruit and gave some to the man, who was *immah*, or "with her."

According to the text, this action—the eating of the fruit—provokes more separation between the two. The narrator reports that their eyes open to a recognition of their nakedness or sexual difference (3:7). Further, when God appears to question the man about ingesting this fruit against God's command, the man articulates their division by blaming God for giving him this woman (3:12). The narrator then shows God laying out the consequences of the couple's actions, resulting in encoded gender roles. The woman now will <u>suffer pain in childbirth and subordination to her man</u> (3:16), and the man must labor with much difficulty to provide sustenance. He also will eventually die (3:18–19).

## suffer pain in childbirth and subordination to her man

Biblical scholar Carol Meyers provides an alternate reading for Gen 3:16: The word *itstsabon* (translated here as "pangs") also occurs in Gen 3:17, where it refers to the man's agricultural toil or work. More generally, then, it connotes work labor as opposed to the labor of childbirth. Similarly, the Hebrew word rendered "childbearing" better translates as "pregnancies." Instead of discussing the distress of women in giving birth, this verse more likely refers to the lives of women in the agricultural context of ancient Israel—more work and more pregnancies. Such an overwhelming number of responsibilities might certainly dissuade women from wanting to get pregnant. Desire for a man, however, ensures that the sexual act will occur and the *bet av* will continue.

Carol Meyers, *Discovering Eve: Ancient Israelite Women in Context* (Oxford: Oxford University Press, 1988), 95–121.

The separations persist. The writers associate the man with death (3:19), while the woman produces life (3:20). He names, and she gives birth (3:20). But a strange new kind of undifferentiation of the two figures also occurs. Even though the serpent tells the woman that both of their eyes will open and they will be like God (3:4), the narrator reports that this happens only to the man (3:22). Further, the text literally says that the man alone is expelled from the garden (3:23–24). In other words, at the close of this story, his identity appears to subsume that of the woman, and she disappears. This absence marks a loss of the continuum of gender possibilities linking male and female. Instead, the writers present the male as the norm and shut down any other constructions of gender identity and difference.

But it does not hold. Eve appears in the following story, in the very next verse (4:1). Thus, the story of the first humans serves as yet another demonstration of how stable gender identities never remain fixed. As shown throughout this chapter, every time the text attempts to define masculinity or femininity rigidly, complications arise. Competing constructions of what it means to be male or female remain constantly in play. To try to impose a binary of masculine and feminine invites failure. The cultural constructions of identities prove far too complex to allow for such simplistic categorizations.

| | |
|---|---|
| **Suggested Biblical Readings** | Genesis 1:27; 2:4b–3:24; 25:19–34; chapters 27–35; 49<br>Judges 4–5; 13–16<br>Ruth<br>Esther |

| | |
|---|---|
| **Discussion Questions** | 1. Together with your classmates, make lists of the characteristics typically associated with male or female in our society. Do these characteristics sometimes overlap? Are they the same for all members of society? Identify where a fluidity in gender roles generates anxiety.<br>2. Think of present-day examples of hypermasculinity and hyperfemininity. Look in advertising and forms of popular culture such as movies, video games, music, and art. Can you locate more tempered or moderate models of femininity and masculinity? Is it meaningful to speak of gender as a continuum rather than a binary?<br>3. Find examples of the Bible's being invoked to support certain gender roles in today's society. Do such uses of the Bible give any recognition to cases of gender ambiguity in the biblical texts? |

**Suggestions for
Further Reading**

Bellis, Alice Ogden. *Helpmates, Harlots, Heroes: Women's Stories in the Hebrew Bible*. Louisville, KY: Westminster John Knox Press, 1994.

Brod, Harry, and Michael Kaufman, eds. *Theorizing Masculinities*. Thousand Oaks, CA: Sage Publications, 1994.

Fewell, Danna Nolan, and David M. Gunn. *Gender, Power, and Promise: The Subject of the Bible's First Story*. Nashville: Abingdon Press, 1993.

Newsom, Carol A., and Sharon H. Ringe, eds. *The Women's Bible Commentary*. Expanded ed. Louisville, KY: Westminster John Knox Press, 1998.

# 6. The Body

The body, rather than being a naturally given datum, is a socially constructed artifact like other cultural products.

Bryan Turner, "The Body in Western Society: Social Theory and Its Perspectives"

Just as it is true that everything symbolizes the body, so it is equally true that the body symbolizes everything else.

Mary Douglas, *Natural Symbols: Explorations in Cosmology*

Like family and gender, the body shapes identity in the Hebrew Bible. Yet for most readers, the body probably receives little thought. After all, many come to the text seeking something "spiritual," something removed from or beyond the materiality of bodies and other aspects of physical existence. When the seventeenth-century philosopher René Descartes pronounced, "I think, therefore I am," he concisely expressed the tendency of western thought to separate nonmaterial aspects of life, such as the mind, from the

## Dualism of the Mind and Body

The **binary dualism** of mind and body dates back at least to the ancient Greek philosopher Plato. Plato argued that true reality consists of the immaterial universal forms or concepts that make the phenomenal world intelligible. He believed that access to these forms and concepts can only be gained through a nonphysical entity, the intellect, and that the body tends to get in the way of this knowledge. Christians generally took this concept further, positing a radical distinction between the immortal soul and the degrading physical body. Much later, the French philosopher Descartes reasoned that, since he could doubt that he had a body but not that he had a mind, the mind must be a nonphysical substance separate from the body. For Descartes, consciousness, which contains the essence of human identity, resides in the nonmaterial mind quite distinguished from the physical brain. Thus, both the religious and secular heritage of the western world have encouraged thinking of the body as separate from, and inferior to, the real essence of humanness in the mind or the soul. However, to assume that the Hebrew Bible also shares this view would be erroneous. The biblical text speaks of the body in very different terms.

physical existence of the body, and further, to value the mental over the physical. But bodies serve to identify people to one another and to themselves. Bodies also function as the medium of feeling, thinking, and actions. So locating true identity in a self that is conceptualized as separate from the body (although it inhabits a body) ignores physicality as shaping people's identities and how they experience the world.

Yet today, despite a legacy of mind-versus-body dualism, North American culture obsesses over the physical body. Magazine covers announce how to get thin quickly, what foods to eat, and promise <u>miraculous physical transformation</u>. Makeovers remain popular in print and on television, and people idolize celebrities with perfectly toned, tanned bodies and idealized features. Body modification practices ranging from piercing and tattooing to plastic surgery, as well as inordinate attention to clothing and cosmetics, take on an increasingly prevalent role in North American society. These practices seem to indicate a reversal of the old dualism that valued the soul or mind over the body by making bodily concerns primary.

However, today's obsession with the body deals less with actual bodies and more with the imagination or fantasy of the body. Modern society differs little from other societies across time and space in making the body not merely a physical fact but also a symbol that bears various meanings. What constitutes "the body" is highly influenced, if not entirely constructed, not by the physical fact of the body but by the worldviews we imbibe and inhabit as members of particular cultures. The same holds true for the societies behind the composition of the Hebrew Bible. This chapter investigates the way that the Hebrew Bible conceptualizes the body and various practices associated with it, and the importance of understanding the distinctions between its notions of the body and our own.

In this chapter, examining the descriptions of the body and its various parts in the Hebrew Bible will reveal how the biblical text imagines the normative body and the consequences for bodies that do not fit that norm. Next, examining various rules for sexual activity, diet, and body

---

### miraculous physical transformation

The domains of exercise and diet, and other ways of disciplining or modifying the body, have been embraced even by religious institutions and have entered into popular practices of religiosity. Witness the popularity of books with titles such as *Body by God: The Owner's Manual for Maximized Living,* or *Fit for God: The 8-Week Plan That Kicks the Devil OUT and Invites Health and Healing IN.* These titles are all the more ironic because studies have suggested that affiliation with more conservative forms of Protestant Christianity in the United States and the consumption of religious programming on television correlate with obesity (see the research of Kenneth Ferraro of the Center on Aging and the Life Course at Purdue University: http://www.purdue.edu/UNS/html4ever/2006/060824.Ferraro.obesity.html).

## The Body as a Symbolic Construction

Historically varying views of body weight or size, for example, demonstrate that the body is a symbol to which different cultures and societies attribute different meanings. Modern western societies see obesity, although increasingly prevalent, negatively as both unattractive and a health hazard. But many traditional societies viewed excessive weight more positively. Especially when experiencing irregular food supplies, such societies correlated fatness with higher social status, wealth, and fertility. Members of such societies perceived fat people as more sexually desirable and associated plumpness with health and good fortune; conversely, thinness indicated poor health and a low social position. Women's bodies in particular seemed to receive these perceptual evaluations; examples include the corpulent female fertility figurines commonly found in Paleolithic archaeological contexts (see fig. 6.1) and the voluptuous female nudes of the seventeenth-century painter Peter Paul Rubens (see fig. 6.2). (See also chapter 8 for a description of the fat "cows of Bashan" in the book of Amos.)

**Fig. 6.1:** *Venus of Willendorf*
*Paleolithic fertility figurine from Europe, (ca. 30,000–25,000 B.C.E.)*

Fig. 6.2: Peter Paul
Rubens' *Three Graces*
(1636–1638)

modification in the Hebrew Bible will show the relation of cultural practices
to the human body. Finally, the relationship between the human body
and the imaging of God in the text raises the issue of the body in relation to
the divine.

## The Human Body in the Hebrew Bible

References to the physical human body fill the Hebrew Bible, but translation
choices and interpretive presuppositions often obscure them. Psalm
16:7–10 serves as an excellent example when comparing the NRSV with a
more literal translation:

| Psalm 16:7–10<br>(NRSV) | Psalm 16:7–10<br>(authors' more literal translation) |
|---|---|
| I bless the LORD who gives me counsel; in the night also my *heart* instructs me.<br>I keep the LORD always before me; because he is at my *right hand*, I shall not be moved.<br>Therefore, my *heart* is glad, and my *soul* rejoices; my *body* also rests secure. | I bless YHWH, who advises me; also, nights, my *kidneys* chasten me.<br>I place YHWH before me continually; because he is at my *right hand*, I will not slip.<br>Therefore, my *heart* is glad, and my *liver* rejoices; also, my *flesh* [or "my *penis*" or "the issue of my *penis*"] dwells in security. |
| For you do not give me up to Sheol, or let your faithful one see the Pit. | For you do not abandon my *throat* [*nephesh*] to Sheol; you do not give your faithful one to see the Pit. |

The NRSV contains two references to the heart, and one each to the right hand, the body, and the soul. This translation encourages a reading that places no real emphasis on the physical body but is rather concerned with the spiritual realities of the heart and soul. It thus easily fits a Cartesian or Platonic body-soul distinction. In contrast, the <u>literal translation</u> embodies the speaker by mentioning a whole range of body parts and organs: kidneys, heart, liver, throat, right hand, and flesh (or penis).

The use of figurative associations between parts of the body and emotions or thoughts makes sense to readers of English accustomed to, for example, associating the emotion of love with the heart. But the biblical figurations might seem obscure or bizarre, especially when the liver expresses joy or the kidneys admonishment! Additionally, some of the biblical expressions read ambiguously—for instance, the word "flesh" might simply mean "flesh," but it also often serves as a **euphemism** for the penis, or it figuratively refers to the children resulting from the use of the procreative organ.

## literal translation

Interlinear translations and analytical concordances can assist readers who do not know Hebrew to see behind the translations to the Hebrew text. For example, the KJV (the basis of most analytical concordances) translates Ps 16:7b as "my *reins* also instruct me in the night seasons." An analytical concordance reveals that the Hebrew word behind "reins" (translated as "heart" in the NRSV) is *kilyot*, which basically means "kidneys," and then metaphorically signifies the site of emotion and affection.

Besides the problem of translations and interpretations that obscure the references to the physical body in the Hebrew Bible, the biblical text contains no word that simply translates to the modern English word "body." English translations variously render as "body" Hebrew words literally meaning "flesh," "bones," "bowels," "belly," "corpse," or "carcass." (A further complication is that two of these Hebrew terms, the ones for "flesh" and for "belly," also denote, in some cases, sexual organs). Problematic is not just translating the words but also negotiating two different conceptual frames of reference for the words. The only words in the Hebrew Bible close to a modern concept of the physical body (*geviyah, nevelah, peger*) most often refer to a lifeless corpse (e.g., Num 14:29; 1 Sam 31:10; Isa 34:3) or a person without self-determination (such as the body of a slave—see Gen 47:18–19; Neh 9:36–37). These Hebrew words rarely equate to a fully alive individual. Rather, when the biblical text imagines a live human being, it portrays not

## Euphemism

Euphemism substitutes an agreeable, indirect, or mild term for one that may be offensive or considered unpleasant. As such, euphemisms occur most often for words denoting sex, excretion, death, or religion. For example, in English, sexual intercourse is euphemistically labeled "hooking up," "getting it on," or "fooling around." Similarly, urination and defecation go by the terms "number 1" and "number 2," especially with children. A dead person "has passed on" or "departed." "Gosh," "darn," and "heck" in exclamations substitute for the religious terms "God," "damn," and "hell."

The Hebrew Bible also commonly uses euphemisms for sexual matters. The word "hand" (*yad*) stands for "penis" in Isa 57:8 and likely also in Song 5:4. The word "feet" (*raglayim*) can signify either the male or female genitals in passages such as Isa 7:20 and 2 Sam 11:8. Similarly, the word "flesh" or "meat" (*basar*) can mean the genitalia, as in Lev 15:2, 19 (in the latter verse, the NRSV has rendered *basar* as "body") and Ezek 23:20. Implements such as the staff, bow, and arrow are employed for the penis, as in Gen 49:10, while association of women with a well or a quiver also carries euphemistic sexual connotations, as in Prov 23:2. The Song of Songs particularly uses flora and fauna as sexual euphemisms or innuendos.

Instead of the Hebrew verb for sexual intercourse (*shagel*), the writers of the Hebrew Bible prefer to say "to lie with," "to enter into," or "to know." In fact, even where the biblical text uses *shagel*, the **Masoretic** editors prompt readers in a note to instead pronounce the verb *shakab*, "to lie with" (e.g., Deut 28:30; Isa 13:16). Apparently, the Masoretes considered the word *shagel* obscene. Other biblical euphemisms for sexual intercourse include seeing, covering or uncovering someone's "nakedness" (*erwa*; e.g., Lev 18), and likely also "spreading one's cloak" over a person (as in Ezek 16:8).

Biblical Hebrew also has terms for feces (*khere* or *khari*) and urine (*shayin* or *shen*), but the Masoretic scribes added a note to the biblical text in 2 Kgs 18:27 and Isa 36:12 for readers to use the euphemisms "what comes out" and "waters of the feet" instead. "To cover one's feet" means defecation (as in 1 Sam 24:3). The word for "idols" (*gillulim*) in passages such as Lev 26:30 and Jer 50:2 may disparagingly refer to excrement, since it relates to a word for "dung" (*galal*).

just a mere physical body but rather a **nephesh**, a combination of constituent parts animated by the breath.

The word *nephesh* relates etymologically to the throat. This concept makes sense when considering the throat as a channel; it functions to link the outer world—with its oxygen, water, and food—to our inner world, which demands all these elements to survive. Without the throat, or *nephesh*, no life exists. Or, as long as the breath continues to flow through a person's throat, a person lives. Additionally, the *nephesh* or throat serves as the channel of verbal communication, which is vital to the survival of human groups. Thus, *nephesh* indicates a physical body imbued with life.

The creation of the first human in Gen 2:7 clearly illustrates the status of the *nephesh*: "Then the LORD God formed man from the dust of the ground, and breathed into his nostrils the breath of life; and the man became a living being [*nephesh*]." Death reverses this process: as the breath returns to God and the body returns to dust, the *nephesh* disappears: "When you take away their breath, they die and return to their dust" (Ps 104:29; see also Job 34:14–15 and Eccl 12:7).

Some parts of the Hebrew Bible associate the *nephesh* not with the throat but with blood (e.g., Lev 17:11, 14; Deut 12:23). This connection appears first when Noah and his descendants receive permission to eat animal flesh: "Every moving thing that lives shall be food for you. . . . Only, you shall not eat flesh with its life [*nephesh*], that is, its blood" (Gen 9:3–4). The loss of blood in animal slaughter (or in the murder of human beings—see the story of the first murder in Gen 4) leads naturally to linking blood with the principle of life. The Israelite priests, in particular, equated the *nephesh* with blood and thus used blood extensively in various religious rituals. They poured blood on the altar (e.g., Lev 1:5) or sprinkled or smeared blood (e.g., Lev 16:15; Exod 12:7) as part of various sacrificial rituals. Exodus 4:25–26 portrays even circumcision as a sacrificial blood ritual.

Because Greek translators of the Hebrew Bible rendered the Hebrew word *nephesh* as *psyche*, a word that Greek philosophers came to equate with the divine essence of a person existing eternally and independently of the

## After Death

For most of the Hebrew Bible, there is no real life after death; the text describes dead persons as "gathered to their ancestors" (e.g., Gen 25:8), continuing at most to have only a radically diminished shadowy existence in an underworld place called Sheol. The Hebrew Bible depicts Sheol, also called the Pit, the grave, or Abaddon (place of destruction), as a dark, negative place—dry, dusty, and silent—where the dead lack memory, agency, or even consciousness (see Ps 88:3–12; Job 10:20–22; Isa 14:9–11; 38:18–19 for some particularly depressing depictions). Nonetheless, the general population of ancient Israelites likely believed that the dead in Sheol continued to play an active role in their lives (see the section on death and burial in chapter 4).

body, the Hebrew concept of *nephesh* transformed into the western concept of the "soul." However, this meaning makes no sense in the thought world of the Hebrew Bible, where the material and nonmaterial aspects of a person never separate or oppose one another in this way. When thinking of a human, the Hebrew Bible pictures not a soul *in* a body but rather the person as a *nephesh*—an animated or ensouled body.

While no word strictly equal to the English word "body" exists in the Hebrew Bible, the text still reveals an extensive vocabulary of words for different parts, both external and internal, of the human body. These words, however, rarely function in a visually descriptive way—that is, the text rarely describes the actual physical shape, size, or color of the body and its parts. Rather, various parts of the human body correlate with specific dynamic actions. This point comes across easily when working with external parts of the body: the eyes relate to the dynamism of the gaze, the ears to hearing and understanding, the arms to strength and action, and the feet to subjugation. But such connections also occur with the internal organs, where certain emotions or intellectual abilities tie to the heart, liver, or kidneys. Today people also make such associations with parts of the human body, such as love with the heart and rationality with the brain. Yet the Hebrew Bible makes links that often differ from those common today.

While the Hebrew Bible rarely provides full descriptions of the physical human body, the Song of Songs offers an exception when it depicts the lovers praising one another's attributes. (Chapter 2 portrayed these poetic descriptions as formally similar to *wasfs*, or Arabic wedding songs.) Two examples, first an amorous description of the man by the woman and then of the woman by the man, indicate that the dynamism associated with different parts of the body takes precedence over a description of purely physical attributes. The text in each case shows no concern that readers reproduce a mental likeness of the lovers; rather, it encourages readers to share in the emotional delight that the lovers have in each other.

The woman describes her lover in Song 5:10–15, beginning with the top of the body and proceeding downward. Most of the details she mentions metaphorically relate the dynamic quality of the attribute named. For example, "eyes like doves" (5:12) evokes the sacred animal messenger of the love goddesses in the ancient Near East; the phrase thus says less about the shape and color of the eyes than about the love communicated by the glance

### *nephesh* transformed

The KJV regularly translates *nephesh* as "soul"; thus, Gen 2:7 reads, "And the LORD God formed man of the dust of the ground, and breathed into his nostrils the breath of life; and man became a living soul." The NRSV more accurately translates *nephesh* in this text as "living being," but also retains the translation "soul" for *nephesh* in other instances, such as the phrase "all your heart and soul" (e.g., Deut 4:29; 6:5).

of the eyes. (Song 4:9 and 6:5 present other examples of the power of the eyes' gaze.) "Cheeks like beds of spices, yielding fragrance" and "lips like lilies, distilling liquid myrrh" (5:13) likewise say little about the actual appearance of the cheeks and lips; instead, they indicate the aromatic and moist sexual allure of the lover's mouth, primed for kissing. (Song 4:11 and 7:9 also mention the sensual liquid and olfactory allure of the mouth.)

As the lover proceeds downward, she describes the arms, genitals, and legs of her lover (5:14–15). Some readers find it shocking that the text mentions the genitalia, although the reference often is obscured both by the translation ("body") and by euphemism in the Hebrew. The Hebrew word used in 5:14 (*meim*) literally means "bowels" or "internal organs" but can also refer more specifically to the source of procreation. Biblical Hebrew lacks a simple word for "penis" and so instead uses words such as "feet," "loins," "hand," "belly," "bowels," or "flesh"; confusion arises in that each of these euphemisms, of course, also carries a literal meaning.

When the man describes his lover in Song 7:1–5, his descriptions also involve mainly the dynamic eroticism of the body parts. Beginning this time from the bottom of the body and proceeding to the top, the man admires the graceful steps and alluring thighs of the woman (v. 1) and praises her aromatic and moist genital area (v. 2). "Navel" here likely functions as a euphemism for "vulva," and the clause "Your belly is a heap of wheat, encircled with lilies" describes the stomach and pubic hair. The woman's breasts captivate his attention like two frolicking fawns (v. 3), while her neck, eyes, nose, head, and hair suggest royal splendor and opulence (vv. 4–5).

Ecclesiastes 12:1–7 presents a different kind of body cataloging. While scholars contest the interpretation of these enigmatic verses, one traditional possibility sees this passage as presenting images of the decrepitude of old age and the relentless approach of the body toward death. Although no parts

### Descriptions of Physical Characteristics in the Hebrew Bible

While the Hebrew Bible includes some references to skin and/or hair color, or to height, these serve less as strictly physical descriptions and function rather to emphasize certain underlying qualities. Reddish hair and skin (often translated as "ruddy")—characteristic of Esau (Gen 25:25), David (1 Sam 16:12; 17:42), and the lover in the Song of Songs (5:10)—signal health and vigor. Lamentations 4:7–8 and 5:10 contrast light and dark skin as a difference between prosperity and famine; conversely, the Song of Songs values dark skin (1:5–6) and hair (5:11) as sensuous. The exceptional tallness of Saul (1 Sam 9:2) and of some Philistine warriors (1 Sam 17:4; 2 Sam 21:15–22) emphasizes their military prowess; in contrast, David may have been somewhat short (1 Sam 16:6–7, 12) and therefore needing to prove his valor more directly. The biblical text often describes Israel's leaders as "handsome"; examples include Joseph (Gen 39:6), Moses (Exod 2:2), Saul (1 Sam 9:2), and David (1 Sam 16:12). In these cases, translators render the Hebrew word *tov*, which literally means "good" or "pleasing," but here likely indicates leadership and moral excellence beyond a merely stunning physical appearance.

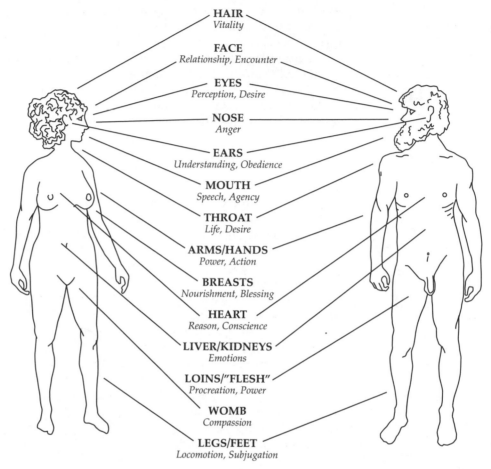

**HAIR**
*Vitality*

**FACE**
*Relationship, Encounter*

**EYES**
*Perception, Desire*

**NOSE**
*Anger*

**EARS**
*Understanding, Obedience*

**MOUTH**
*Speech, Agency*

**THROAT**
*Life, Desire*

**ARMS/HANDS**
*Power, Action*

**BREASTS**
*Nourishment, Blessing*

**HEART**
*Reason, Conscience*

**LIVER/KIDNEYS**
*Emotions*

**LOINS/"FLESH"**
*Procreation, Power*

**WOMB**
*Compassion*

**LEGS/FEET**
*Locomotion, Subjugation*

© Susan P. M. Cherland

**Fig. 6.3: Meaning of the Body's Parts in the Hebrew Bible**

of the body receive explicit mention, commentators find various figurative expressions for body parts. In verse 3, the "guards that tremble" may refer to shaky knees or legs on which the "bent strong men" totter, the "women who cease grinding because they are few" represent the molars lost over the course of time, and those "looking dimly through windows" conjures up failing eyes. The expressions in verse 4 offer figures of impaired mobility ("The doors on the street are shut"), dysfunctional appetite or digestion ("The sound of the grinding is low"), inability to sleep ("One rises up at the sound of a bird"), and deafness ("All the daughters of song are brought low"). The first half of verse 5 rounds out this description with imaginative references to white hair ("The almond tree blossoms"), stiff joints ("The grasshopper drags itself along"), and lack of sexual desire and vigor ("Desire fades"). These descriptions do not follow any particular order but seem to offer an impressionistic overview of the process of old age. The final and unavoidable consequence—death—comes with the breaking of various items such as bowls or cords and culminates in the return of the substance of the body to the earth and of the life-breath (*ruah*) to God (vv. 6–7).

The foregoing examples only begin to access the many ways in which the Hebrew Bible portrays the parts of the human body. The following boxes offer a more comprehensive tour of the body from the perspective of the biblical text.

### Hair Signifies *Vitality*

Since hair signifies vitality, one does not normally cut the hair of the head except in mourning. Forcibly cutting a man's hair is to emasculate him; enemies are treated in this degrading manner (e.g., 2 Sam 10:4). The Hebrew Bible especially regulates the hairstyles and beards of priests (Lev 19:27–28; Ezek 44:20) and forbids Nazirites to cut their hair at all (Num 6). Hairstyles could mark ethnic identity (Jer 9:26). While the Hebrew Bible generally regards hair positively, the story of Samson, biblical Israel's long-haired hero (Judg 13–16), associates long hair with a dangerous wildness and overtones of eroticism.

### Face Signifies *Relationship, Encounter*

The body presents the face to the world as its main communicative aspect. The Hebrew Bible mentions the face more often than any other part of the body. To face someone connotes contact and relationship, while turning one's back connotes a breaking of communication and relationship. So also in human relations with the divine: God's face is a source of blessing (e.g., Num 6:22–27), while God's back is a sign of rejection (e.g., Deut 31:17). That God speaks to Moses "face to face as one speaks to a friend" (Exod 33:11) signifies the special intimate relationship between Moses and God.

### Eyes Signify *Perception, Desire*

The Hebrew Bible mentions the eyes four times as often as the ears, indicating its dominant visual orientation. Even the ancient creedal statement of the Israelites, the Shema, which begins, "Hear, O Israel" (Deut 6:4–9), contains provisions for the inscription of the words in visual form on the hands, forehead, and doorposts. As in ancient Near Eastern cultures generally, the Hebrew Bible emphasizes the importance of seeking a vision of God (e.g., Ps 17:15; Job 42:5) and imagines God overwhelmingly in anthropomorphic form. The gaze of the eyes expresses desire, whether good, as in the gaze that seeks God or the gaze of the lovers in the Song of Songs (e.g., Ps 121:1; Song 4:9), or bad, as in the envious gaze or the evil eye (e.g., Prov 23:3–5; Deut 15:9).

## Nose Signifies *Anger*

The dynamic function the Hebrew Bible assigns to the nose perhaps differs most from modern conceptions. The snorting of the nose expresses anger. Thus, Rebekah warns her son Jacob to flee from his brother, Esau, "until your brother's anger [literally, "nose"] against you turns away" (Gen 27:45). Even God's nose becomes inflamed and snorts with anger, as in YHWH's warning to Moses, "Let me alone so that my wrath [literally, "my nose"] may burn hot against them" (Exod 32:10). Thus, burnt offerings and incense present fragrant smells to appease God's irritated nose (e.g., Gen 8:21).

## Ears Signify *Understanding, Obedience*

The ears signify hearing—more precisely, hearing that pays attention and internalizes what is heard (e.g., Prov 15:31; 22:17; Isa 50:5). In this sense, ears stand for obedience, and so it is fitting that wearing certain earrings in the ancient Near East could mark one's allegiance to a particular deity (Gen 35:4 and Exod 32:2–4 evocatively associate earrings with deities). Similarly, a slave who submits to ritual ear piercing demonstrates a free decision to stay with his or her master (Exod 21:6; Deut 15:17). Apart from obedience, ears also connote attention. The Hebrew Bible depicts even God as having ears to be attentive to the cries of those who suffer (e.g., 2 Sam 22:7; Ps 130:1–2).

## Mouth Signifies *Speech, Agency*

The Hebrew Bible emphasizes the mouth and tongue as the organs of speech, and it highlights the power of speech to initiate action and to work for good or evil, for truth or deception: "Death and life are in the power of the tongue" (Prov 18:21). Two of the commandments of the Decalogue warn against the wrongful use of spoken words (Exod 20:7, 16; Deut 5:11, 20), and the book of Proverbs abounds with admonitions to proper speech (e.g., Prov 12:18; 29:20). The book of Psalms most highly esteems speech in praise of the deity (e.g., Ps 51:15). The Hebrew Bible assigns the ultimate creative power of speech to God, who can create by merely speaking the world into being (Gen 1).

## Throat Signifies *Life, Desire*

The term *nephesh* in the Hebrew Bible, often translated as "soul," "living being," "person," or "life," literally means "throat." The throat is the part of the body through which breath, food, and speech pass, and therefore it signifies the animating energy of life: "The human being became a living *nephesh*" (Gen 2:7). The throat is not passive, however, but always actively desires satisfaction of its needs: "For he satisfies the thirsty [literally, "the thirsting throat"], and the hungry [literally, "the hungering throat"] he fills with good things" (Ps 107:9). The throat also expresses primal emotions of joy and adoration: "Bless the Lord, O my soul [literally, "my throat"]!" (Ps 103:1).

## Arms and Hands Signify *Power, Action*

The Hebrew Bible commonly uses the arm or hand as a metaphor for power: "The LORD your God brought you out from there with a mighty hand and an out-stretched arm" (Deut 5:15). Ancient Near Eastern iconography depicts the out-stretched arm and hand of the king as representing the king's power over his enemies. Furthermore, as a symbol of potency, the hand also euphemistically refers to the penis and, by extension, to a man's progeny: "I will give, in my house and within my walls, a monument [literally, a "hand"] and a name better than sons and daughters" (Isa. 56:5).

## Breasts Signify *Nourishment, Blessing*

The Hebrew Bible associates the dynamism of nourishment and blessing with the female breasts. The book of Isaiah, for example, pictures Jerusalem as a nurs-ing mother dispensing consolation and delight from her breasts (66:11). One of the names of God in the Hebrew Bible, *shaddai* or *el shaddai* (usually translated as "the Almighty" or "God Almighty"), may relate to the Hebrew word for breasts and thus portray God as a fertility deity.

## Heart Signifies *Reason, Conscience*

Contrary to modern associations of the heart with the emotions, the Hebrew Bible sees the heart as the site of reason, intelligence, planning, and conscience. One desires "a mind [literally, "a heart"] to understand" (Deut 29:4) and prays, "Create in me a clean heart" (i.e., a clear conscience; Ps 51:10). Thus, in biblical parlance, in order to find out how someone thinks, one would not try to get into that person's head but rather into the person's heart.

## Liver and Kidneys Signify *Emotions*

The Hebrew Bible associates the emotions with internal organs other than the heart, such as the kidneys and the liver, or with the "inward parts" in general. Internal organs express the pairing of emotion and intelligence, as in Ps 26:2: "Test my heart [literally, "my kidneys"] and mind [literally, "my heart"]." They describe emotional upheaval, as in Lam 2:11: "My eyes are spent with weeping; my stomach [literally, "my inward parts"] churns; my bile [literally, "my liver"] is poured out on the ground." (Interestingly, the lungs are not mentioned in the Hebrew Bible). In biblical parlance one would not tug at someone's heartstrings but rather at his or her "kidneystrings"!

## Loins and Flesh Signify *Procreation, Power*

The Hebrew Bible associates the loins, the area of the body defined by the two thighs or the two sides of the hips, with procreation: "The total number of people born to Jacob [literally, "emerging from the loins of Jacob"] was seventy" (Exod 1:5). A soldier wears a belt and a sword at the loins, signifying readiness for battle. Thus, the procreative power of the loins is readily conflated with aggressive masculine power: "Gird your sword on your thigh, O mighty one [literally, "on your loin, O warrior"]" (Ps 45:3).

## Womb Signifies *Compassion*

The Hebrew Bible associates compassion with the womb or uterus: "Compassion [literally, "womb-feeling"] for her son burned within her" (1 Kgs 3:26). Compassion thus connects particularly with women (e.g., Isa 49:15), although the Hebrew Bible also portrays men as expressing it (e.g., Ps 103:13; Jer 42:12). Hosea 11:8 describes God as having "womb-feeling"—"my compassion grows warm and tender"—but only in the ancient Syriac and Targumic versions of the book of Hosea. The Masoretic Text reads *nekhum*, a word meaning "comfort or compassion" but unrelated to *rekhem*, the word for "womb." Scholars speculate that the ancient versions preserve an older reading that the Masoretic Text, either by accident or design, obscured.

## Legs and Feet Signify *Locomotion, Subjugation*

Like the arms and hands, the Hebrew Bible associates the feet and legs with power, but more particularly with the power of subjugation and domination (e.g., Isa 63:3). Subjects fall in obeisance on their faces at the feet of their sovereign, and dominion means to have all things under one's feet (e.g., Ps 8:6). The Hebrew Bible associates the trampling of the feet with the violence of military subjugation (e.g., Isa 63:3, 6). As with the hand, however, the feet can also euphemistically refer to the genitals. The Masoretic scribes, for instance, recommended reading "waters of the feet" for the word "urine" in 2 Kgs 18:27.

As should be obvious by now, the human body and its various parts represent more than a simple anatomical reality in the Hebrew Bible. In fact, the biblical text seems more interested in associating the body and its parts with diverse dynamic actions and states of human experience. The human body, in effect, becomes a page or canvas on which the biblical writers express their particular sentiments, understandings, and ideologies. That the writers conscript the human body in this fashion is clearly evident upon examining the Hebrew Bible's notions of the normative or ideal body.

**The Normative Body in the Hebrew Bible**

When the Hebrew Bible imagines the human body, it also expresses assumptions about the normative body, the type of human body the Hebrew Bible implicitly considers as a standard or ideal against which to measure all actual bodies. Such an ideal is not surprising in that most cultures tend to project norms of perfection. In North America, the ideal or normative body might suggest a relatively youthful image embodied by a popular celebrity or pictured in a fashion magazine (see figs. 6.4 and 6.5). The cultures coming to expression in the Hebrew Bible imagine an ideal body that differs in important respects from these modern notions.

The Hebrew Bible understands the human body as an expression of the vitality of its various parts. The ideal or normative body is thus, first of all, dynamically alive and not a dead carcass (whether literally or figuratively). Second, this body remains whole, meaning it contains all its proper parts and functions in the right number and order. Third, the ideal body maintains strict, fixed boundaries between itself and the environment—it does not ooze or leak, and it avoids contact with dead bodies or bodies not whole in some way.

The depiction of the priests in Lev 21 gives an example of those persons in biblical Israel who needed, as nearly as possible, ideal bodies in order to serve. Verses 1–4 and 11 restrict contact with the dead, while verses 7 and 13–14 prohibit interaction with the bodies of women prostitutes, divorcees, or widows. (Note that the Hebrew Bible here assumes that the normative body is male.) Further, prohibitions prevent priests from modifying their bodily appearance by shaving their heads or beards in certain ways or making gashes in their flesh (vv. 5, 10). Some scholars understand these last items as part of mourning or funeral rituals, which priests are to avoid as part of the requirement that they distance themselves from the dead (vv. 1–4 and 11).

To this point, the ideal body seems achievable, since any male could attempt to avoid the foregoing practices. But the normative priestly body also excludes persons involuntarily afflicted by a variety of "blemishes" or physical defects:

> For no one who has a blemish shall draw near, one who is blind, or lame, or one who has a mutilated face or a limb too long, or one who has a broken foot or a broken hand, or a hunchback, or a dwarf, or a man with a blemish in his eyes or an itching disease or scabs or crushed testicles. (Lev 21:18–20)

The biblical text here disqualifies persons with diseases or impairments from officiating at the altar. The book of Deuteronomy extends this disqualification to the entire population of male Israelites. It bars, for example, all those with crushed testicles or lacking a penis from the Israelite worship assembly (Deut 23:1). The Hebrew Bible here excludes **eunuchs** and other

**Fig. 6.4: The "Ideal" Modern Female Body**
*An example of what might pass as an ideal female body today.*

**Fig. 6.5: The "Ideal" Modern Male Body**
*An example of what might pass as an ideal male body today.*

males unable to procreate from being Israelites. Ability to procreate is part of the normative body.

Other texts, however, undermine such strictures. The legal codes of the Hebrew Bible, for example, prohibit the exploitation of the blind or the deaf (Lev 19:14; Deut 27:18). Genesis 32:31 portrays Jacob, the ancestor of the Israelites, walking with a limp after encountering God. According to 2 Sam 9, King David protects the <u>crippled son of Jonathan</u>, the only surviving descendant of his predecessor, Saul. Finally, messages of future hope in the Hebrew Bible sometimes proclaim the removal of impairments: "Then the eyes of the blind shall be opened, and the ears of the deaf unstopped; then the lame shall leap like a deer, and the tongue of the speechless sing for joy" (Isa 35:5–6). Even castrated men or eunuchs are promised their place in the worshiping community (Isa 56:4–5).

These counterexamples notwithstanding, certain visible blemishes of the body mean ostracism not only from religious participation but also from society in general. Various skin conditions, which modern translations often erroneously label as "<u>leprosy</u>," present the most difficulty. As outlined in Lev 13:1–46, various lesions, boils, and discolorations of the skin lead to a period of quarantine; the afflicted persons must dishevel their heads, tear their clothes (exactly the opposite of the requirements for priests in Lev 21:10), and live away from other people. The character Job, when stricken with some sort of skin disease, laments his exclusion from society (Job 19:13–22).

Skin afflictions compromise the integrity or wholeness of the body by breaching the proper boundary of the body that the skin represents. Likewise, other breaches in the boundary of the body, which allow substances to ooze or leak out of the body, prove problematic. Leviticus 15 calls special attention to male and female sexual discharges, both normal (ejaculation and menstruation: vv. 16–24) and abnormal (gonorrhea, urethral infection, and prolonged or abnormal menstrual flow: vv. 2–5, 25–30). These discharges result in a period of uncleanness. Normal female menstruation results in a period of uncleanness twice the length of that which normal male seminal emission causes, indicating again that the ideal body in the Hebrew Bible is preeminently male. Periods of uncleanness affect a person's eligibility to participate in worship (see the analysis of worship practices in chapter 12).

Sickness and disease in general compromise the integrity and wholeness of the normative body and disrupt a person's ability to function in society. The Hebrew Bible views illness not just as a physical problem but primarily

### crippled son of Jonathan

David likely protects Mephibosheth, Saul's crippled heir, not for compassionate reasons but to guard himself politically against being usurped by a descendant of Saul. Elsewhere the Hebrew Bible describes hatred between the lame and blind, and David (2 Sam 5:8). In fact, the biblical text seems to deliberately contrast the agile David, who leaps and dances (2 Sam 6:16; see also 2 Sam 22:34, 37), with the lame Mephibosheth (2 Sam 4:4; 9:3, 13) as a way to emphasize the ending of one dynasty and the beginning of another. Likewise, the Hebrew Bible marks the eventual end of the Davidic dynasty with disability: the last Davidic king, Zedekiah, is blinded by the Babylonians (2 Kgs 25:7). Disability in these cases becomes a symbol of political downfall.

### leprosy

Most scholars agree that the Hebrew term *tsaraat*, traditionally translated as "leprosy," does not indicate true leprosy or Hansen's disease. Rather, the term points to a variety of conditions discoloring and affecting the human skin as well as fabrics and walls of houses (Lev 13–14). The biblical text likely refers to various lesions, boils, and burns in the skin. In fabrics and walls, the text may have various molds, fungi, or mildews in mind.

also as impairing a person's expected social role. Infertility provides a good example. While not an illness in that it does not usually cause physical sickness or threaten death, infertility prevents a woman from fulfilling her expected role as a mother. The numerous biblical accounts of women having difficulty conceiving (e.g., Sarah in Gen 11:30; Rebekah in Gen 25:21; Rachel in Gen 29:31; Hannah in 1 Sam 1:2) indicate that infertility presented a significant problem in the society of the biblical writers (see the section on children in chapter 4). Inadequate nutrition likely caused infertility in many cases, but the biblical text insists that the real cause is God, who inexplicably "closes the wombs" of certain women (the texts do not consider that the male partner might be infertile). The Hebrew Bible assigns the same cause, that is, God, to any sickness or impairment. In this, the biblical texts share the ancient Near Eastern view that illness is an instrument of the deity. And just as God causes illness, so also only God can cure illness (e.g., Job 5:18; Exod 15:26).

The normative body is thus alive, whole, male, and not characterized by any abnormalities or illnesses. In addition, the Hebrew Bible favors certain body attributes, such as right-handedness. Judges 3:15–29 portrays left-handedness as a treacherous (although useful) anomaly when the Israelite

## Sickness and Health Care

The Hebrew Bible is generally not interested in a specific diagnosis for any illness but rather focuses on whether or not the sufferer will recover (e.g., 1 Kgs 14:3; 2 Kgs 1:2; 8:8). Neither does it usually detail healing rituals or therapies except for prayer, which appears as the most common therapeutic strategy. For example, King Hezekiah, after receiving the news that his illness is fatal, prays and then recovers (2 Kgs 20:1–5; Isa 38:1–5). The application of a fig poultice to his boil appears as an afterthought (2 Kgs 20:7; Isa 38:21).

Psalm 38 presents a more extensive example of a prayer for healing. The sufferer acknowledges that YHWH caused illness because of sin (38:1–5) and complains not only of pain and exhaustion but also of social ostracism and suspicion (38:11–12). A confession of sin is an integral part of the prayer (38:18).

Although the biblical text presents God as the healer (Exod 15:26), various human intermediaries appear as part of the healing process. Prophets in particular convey YHWH's message as to whether the patient will recover or not, but they may also pray for the patient and occasionally perform or prescribe various healing actions. The prophet Elijah, for example, prays and stretches himself upon a sick child three times (1 Kgs 17:17–24), and the prophet Elisha advises the leprous foreign army commander Naaman to wash seven times in the Jordan River (2 Kgs 5:8–14). Other individuals and means also appear at times as part of the healing process. First Samuel 16:14–23 depicts a young David providing music therapy for King Saul, who is tormented by an evil spirit sent by God. A bronze serpent manufactured by Moses provides healing from snakebite (Num 21:4–9) and appears as an object of worship, likely for healing, in the Jerusalem Temple (2 Kgs 18:4). But the Hebrew Bible as a rule disparages depending upon human or medicinal help for illness without appealing to YHWH (2 Chron 16:12; Jer 46:11; 51:8–9).

Ehud strikes the enemy king Eglon with a sword wielded unexpectedly in the left hand. At the least, the Hebrew Bible associates the left hand with lesser rank. Genesis 48:13–20 describes Jacob as blessing his younger grandson Ephraim with his right hand to signify his superior status over his older brother, Manasseh, whom he blesses with his left hand. Similarly, rites of ordination for priests include anointing with sacrificial blood on the right ear lobe, right thumb, and right big toe (Lev 8:23–24). The Hebrew Bible frequently mentions God's right hand (e.g., Exod 15:6; Pss 16:11; 118:15; Isa 41:10; Lam 2:3) but never God's left hand. As in many traditional Middle Eastern cultures to this day, the left hand carries dishonor often connected to its use for toilet activities. Thus, the biblical text perceives being unable to distinguish between one's right and left hands as a serious flaw (Jonah 4:11).

One might inquire as to the ideal age of the normative body in the Hebrew Bible. Modern western societies idealize a youthful appearance and lifestyle while often discounting or shunning older people and signs of age. At first glance, the Hebrew Bible seems exactly the opposite. The Hebrew Bible's frequent mention of authoritative and honored persons called "elders" seems to venerate old age. The biblical text depicts elders serving variously as representatives of the people (e.g., Exod 3:18; 19:7–8; Judg 11:4–11), as part of the governing authorities (e.g., 2 Kgs 10:5; Ezra 6:7–8), as judges (e.g., Deut 21:18–21), or as advisors (e.g., 1 Kgs 20:7–8). Leaders such as Abraham and Moses become influential only once they attain an older age, and the sayings of Proverbs show older and wiser parental figures instructing the young.

However, average life expectancy in the ancient world was only a fraction of life expectancy in today's North American society. Whereas a Canadian, American, or European today can reasonably expect to live eighty years or more, archaeologists estimate the average life span of an Israelite peasant to have been as low as twenty-five years. Due to the dangers inherent in childbirth, women peasants on average lived even fewer years. Only a minority of the Cisjordanian population who lived in cities such as Jerusalem, with their concentrations of wealth, luxury, a wider range of food, and less dangerous occupations, could expect life spans perhaps two to three times as long as the average peasant. Still, even if the term "elder" refers primarily to age, for the majority of Israelite peasants, it would hardly conjure up images of seniors in their seventies or eighties.

Rather, the term "elder" in the Hebrew Bible refers primarily to social superiority and authority and only relatively to age. In fact, the Hebrew term for "elder" (*zaqen*) relates to the Hebrew word for "beard" (*zakan*). "Elders" are thus mature (i.e., bearded) adult males who rightfully exercise patriarchal authority. In this respect, the normative body emerges as that of a bearded adult male exhibiting neither the immaturity and inferiority of the young, nor the decrepitude and impotence of the few who have survived to old age (e.g., 2 Sam 19:32–35; 1 Kgs 1:1–4).

## The Hebrew Bible and Disability

The Hebrew Bible considers a variety of conditions as disabling a person's participation in society and religion, some of which, such as skin conditions or body irregularities, no longer qualify as particularly disabling today. Such changes in perception demonstrate disability as a social construct. That is, although biological conditions may cause definite impairments, whether or not societies in different historical contexts perceive such impairments as disabilities varies.

Today, various groups and agencies are making concerted efforts to remove unnecessary obstructions to the ability of people with various impairments to be fully functioning members of society. Yet disabled people report that some religious people question or resist such efforts. (See "Keeping the Faith," by Josie Byzek, in the December 2002 issue of *New Mobility*, the magazine for wheelchair users, for stories behind the following description. The article can be accessed online at http://www.newmobility.com/articleView.cfm?id=627& action=browse). In line with the portrayal of the normative body in the Hebrew Bible, such people consider disabilities as blemishes or impurities that should prevent full integration into "normal" society. At their worst, proponents of this view accuse the disabled of justly suffering the punishment of some sort of sin. Or they promise the end of disabilities in the afterlife, which sounds to the disabled as if they have no worth until they are dead. Even those who consider it their religious obligation to welcome and accommodate disabled people will often draw the line when it comes to accepting disabled religious leaders, unwittingly replicating the requirements that the Hebrew Bible lays down for priests.

The biblical authors empower or disempower the disabled by the way that they depict persons who do not measure up to the standards of the normative body. Persons who do not measure up to these standards constitute a large population: women, the young and the decrepit old, the diseased, those with irregular bodies, and so on. Cultural notions of the normative body and its opposite, such as the disabled body, are powerful means of inclusion and exclusion.

## The Normative Social Body

The Hebrew Bible imagines not only an ideal or normative physical human body; it also projects an ideal of the normative human society, often in ways similar to its portrayal of the normative physical body. Just as the text imagines the ideal human body as male, complete with all its functioning parts, and with intact boundaries, so also it conceives of social institutions such as the family, the people, or the nation as similarly headed by a male, complete with a functioning hierarchy of different parts, and with carefully policed boundaries. The Hebrew Bible portrays these social institutions as bodies on a larger scale; hence the term "social body" describes them.

The leakage of sexual fluids breaks through the boundary of the individual physical body and so requires careful management. The same sexual fluids also connect different bodies in the act of sexual intercourse and so contribute to the creation and maintenance of the larger social body of the family. This procedure also requires proper negotiation. Leviticus 18:6–23 and 20:10–21 present a catalogue of proscribed sexual behaviors that restrict a male's legitimate sexual partners. These texts ban incest, intercourse during menstruation, adultery, male same-sex intercourse, and bestiality, but for pragmatic rather than moral reasons. These measures restrict sexual activity and the resulting birth of offspring to members within the same household, which in turn protects the lineage of the dominant male of the household. They also maximize successful pregnancies in a subsistence economy (see the section on children in chapter 4). In other words, they protect the boundaries and integrity of the normative social body of the Israelite household, or *bet av*.

Yet many stories in the Hebrew Bible portray the breaking of these sanctions, often without censure. Abraham produced a child with his half-sister Sarah (Gen 21). Lot's daughters' sexual intercourse with their father produced the ancestors of the Moabites and Ammonites (Gen 19). Tamar disguised herself as a prostitute, seduced her father-in-law Judah, and gave birth to an ancestor of King David (Gen 38). And even King David's adultery with Bathsheba (2 Sam 11)—while roundly condemned—resulted in the incorporation of the mother of his future heir, Solomon, into the royal harem. These examples demonstrate the actual permeability of the sexual boundaries of the family's social body. The description of these practices in narrative biblical texts often does not conform to the ideals or norms in legal biblical texts.

The maintenance of proper boundaries also operates on the level of the social body of the people or nation. Here, intermarriage, the transfer of females across the ethnic boundary, threatens a problematic breaching of boundaries between different peoples. The story of the botched attempt at intermarriage between Jacob's family and the Shechemites in Gen 34 illustrates the potential danger. The books of Ezra (see 9:1–10) and Nehemiah (see 13:23–31) express similar concerns, reporting attempts to dissolve existing intermarriages by ejecting non-Israelite women and their children from Israelite households.

At the same time, examples of the violation of these norms also abound in the Hebrew Bible. The book of Ruth narrates the incorporation of a

## Incest

The incest prohibitions in Lev 18 and 20 describe a rather comprehensive set of family relationships from which sexual activity is excluded. A man is not to have sex with his mother, his sister, his granddaughter, his aunt, his daughter-in-law, or his brother's wife. Neither is a man to be in a simultaneous sexual relationship with two sisters, or with a woman and her daughter (the text assumes the possibility of polygyny). Missing in all this is an explicit prohibition of a man's having sexual relations with his daughter. Many commentators insist that father-daughter incest is implicitly prohibited in Leviticus. Given the patriarchal assumption of the father's ownership of his daughter until she marries and comes under the guardianship of another man, perhaps the writers of the text did not imagine the need for an explicit prohibition.

Moabite woman into an Israelite household. The book of Esther does not seem to express any anxiety about the intermarriage of the Jewish Esther with the Persian king. Joseph marries the daughter of an Egyptian priest (Gen 41). Again, these examples demonstrate the actual permeability of the ethnic boundaries of the social body of the people or nation as opposed to the ideal or norm.

The concept of the whole body with proper boundaries remains an ideal for the individual body, the familial body, and the body of the ethnic group or the state. While the Hebrew Bible records strict regulations of movement across the boundaries of both physical and social bodies so as to maintain a particular sense of bodily integrity, it also reports violations of the regulations. This tension between ideal norms and actual practice indicates that the normative sense of the body functions as an ideal social-cultural construction and requires some flexibility to account for the actual contingencies of human existence.

## Body Practices

Besides imagining the body, both individual and social, as a means of conceptualizing identity, the Hebrew Bible also discusses what one does with the body: how one uses, maintains, modifies, and reproduces the body. Four issues emerge here: eating, clothing, body modifications, and sexual reproduction. Since eating involves the movement of items across the boundary of the body, the Hebrew Bible contains dietary regulations. Clothing functions to cover the body, throwing into relief how the Hebrew Bible considers the disclosure of the physical human body to the eyes of others and especially the status of nakedness. Body modification receives an ambivalent evaluation in the Hebrew Bible, which prohibits trimming hair or scarification but requires circumcision. And finally, since sexual reproduction produces new bodies, the Hebrew Bible presents detailed regulations of sexual behaviors.

### Eating and Food

Cultures develop food choices and preferences based on a number of factors, including objective realities such as environmental constraints, and more subjective constructions such as the cultural value of food. In modern western cultures, while diets to some extent reflect factors such as seasonal availability and nutritional value, food more frequently is conceptualized on a symbolic level. The fast-food industry appeals to our busyness with promises of convenience, "fat free" and other labels evoke a concern with weight management, and gourmet items reveal a desire to say something about class or status.

In an analogous fashion, the Hebrew Bible lays out dietary rules that form a symbolically coherent system based on the notion of the whole body.

Specific environmental constraints certainly contributed to the origin of these practices, since the production of food depends largely on conditions such as climate and soil. But in their present form, these guidelines express a desire to maintain the ideal body of the individual and the analogous social bodies of the family and people or nation through appropriately regulated food. A detailed list of these rules appears in Lev 11; Deut 14 contains a somewhat shorter and revised list.

The classificatory logic behind these lists of permitted and prohibited foods rests on the categorization of creatures into those that live on land, those that fly in the air, those that live in the water, and those that "swarm." Within each category, a set of interlocking characteristics comprises the ideal. Creatures that demonstrate these characteristics are acceptable sources of food, while those that do not are forbidden. Distinctions among land and water animals generate the clearest examples. Regulations permit eating land animals with divided hoofs that also chew their cud (Lev 11:2–8). Therefore, the Hebrew Bible accepts the cow and the sheep as legitimate food sources but forbids pigs. Even though a pig possesses the required divided hoof, it does not chew its cud. In the case of water creatures, the Hebrew Bible allows only fish that possess scales *and* fins, and prohibits any other aquatic creatures (Lev 11:9–12). Shrimp, then, fail to make the cut. The rationale in the other categories of flying and swarming creatures lacks clarity and involves a certain amount of abstract systemization. However, the overall division of foods into prohibited and permitted categories replicates and supports similar binary categories of clean/unclean, holy/profane, and whole/blemished expressed in other cultural practices related to the body (e.g., childbirth, skin diseases, and sexual discharges; see Lev 12–15).

If these rules regarding food construct and maintain a particular version of the ideal body, which must consume only "clean" food, how much more so do the regulations for the sacrificial food offered to God. Here the animals sacrificed must not only conform to the categories of permitted food, but they must also be male and without blemish, according to Lev 22:17–25. This stipulation mirrors the requirement that priests possess the ideal bodies of men without physical flaws. Furthermore, according to the Hebrew Bible, God possesses a prodigious appetite requiring at minimum two lambs sacrificed each day accompanied by flour, oil, and wine (e.g., Exod 29:38–41). In addition, the various other sacrifices detailed in Lev 1–7 and Num 28–29 increase considerably the amount of food, especially red meat, offered to God. First Kings 8:63 details that, on the occasion of the dedication of Solomon's Temple, God received up to 22,000 oxen and 120,000 sheep! While the amounts indicated represent significantly larger portions than humans typically consume, two considerations emerge. First, sacrifice meant burning only part of the animal; the priests and sometimes the worshipers ate the remainder of the meat (see chapter 12 for a detailed

### the feeding of God

Readers may find strange the notion that God eats. Yet the Hebrew Bible explicitly describes sacrifices as God's food (e.g., Lev 3:11; 21:6; 22:25; Ezek 44:7), and the altar on which they are offered it sometimes calls a table (Mal 1:7, 12). Furthermore, the burned offerings produce a "pleasing odor" for God (e.g., Gen 8:21; Lev 3:16; Num 28:2). To be sure, other parts of the Hebrew Bible play down or reject such anthropomorphic depictions of the deity (e.g., Ps 50:12–13; Mic 6:6–8). The Hebrew Bible seems to say both that sacrifices serve as God's food and that God requires no food (see chapter 12 for further analysis of sacrifices).

description of different sacrifices). Second, the feeding of God in ways befitting the stature of the deity illustrates the same logic of the choices available to humanity. Feeding the divine requires whole and perfect food.

*Clothing and Nakedness*

The normative body in the Hebrew Bible requires proper clothing. Nakedness does not receive a positive evaluation. The first human beings, as depicted in the Genesis story, become aware that they are naked after eating of the tree of the knowledge of good and evil, and they immediately proceed to cover themselves (Gen 2:25; 3:6–7). Thereafter, the writers of the biblical text associate public nakedness with shame and humiliation. For example, Noah curses the one who sees him naked in a drunken stupor, but blesses those who cover his nakedness (Gen 9:20–27). David's wife Michal chastises him for exposing himself while dancing in a religious procession (2 Sam 5:14, 20). Several biblical texts vividly express the humiliation of defeat in war by depicting the public stripping and exposure of the losers (e.g., Isa 20:1–5; Lam 1:8).

As implied in these examples, the Hebrew Bible is especially concerned that the body's sexual organs be covered. The instructions for priests further demonstrate this concern. Exodus 20:26 warns against priests climbing up to the high altar on steps, lest they expose their nakedness (i.e., genitals). As well, the special vestments for priests include underpants specifically meant to cover their genitalia (Exod 28:42–43; Lev 16:4). The ideal bodies of the priests, especially their private parts, are to remain unseen.

The same biblical laws empower priests to examine the exposed bodies of others to determine the severity of skin ailments (Lev 13:1–16). Generally, however, in the Hebrew Bible only one's legitimate sexual partner can view one's nakedness. In fact, the expression "to uncover the nakedness of someone" euphemistically indicates sexual intercourse. This expression appears in the list of sexual taboos in Lev 18 and 20. The prohibitions against incestuous relations, for example, begin, "None of you shall approach anyone near of kin to uncover nakedness" (18:6). Further, "uncovering nakedness" can also connote sexual violence and rape (see the discussion in chapter 13 of Hos 2 and Ezek 16). The normative body in the

Hebrew Bible thus overall avoids nakedness, with its strong connotations of exposure, shame, and illegitimacy.

Avoidance of nakedness implies the need for clothing. The Hebrew Bible frequently refers to articles of clothing, but usually in general terms without specifying a particular garment. In biblical stories, putting on clothing signals advancement in status (e.g., Gen 41:42), while stripping or tearing clothing signals a loss of status (e.g., Gen 37:23) or sorrow over death (e.g., 2 Sam 1:11–12). The most essential (and sometimes only) article of clothing a person owned was the outer cloak, worn during the day and slept in at night (Exod 22:26–27). Wool and linen were the most common textiles, but Deut 22:11 prohibits mixing them in the same garment. Deuteronomy 22:12 mandates adding tassels to the corners of one's cloak. These distinctive clothing styles become an important component of identity, especially ethnic identity.

Clothing can also signal one's specific role within society. The Hebrew Bible details a set of ornate garments for the priests (Exod 28) as a sort of uniform but also to protect them from divine anger when they are working (28:43). Occasionally other garments are associated with particular roles, such as distinctive clothing that widows (Gen 38:14) or virgin daughters of the king (2 Sam 13:18) wear. A special robe marked Joseph's favored status in his family (Gen 37:3). Deuteronomy 22:5 prohibits cross-dressing so that there would be no confusion between the normative male body and the female body. Clothing thus functions in the Hebrew Bible not only to cover nakedness but also to establish and maintain specific social identities.

*Body Modifications*

In Lev 19:27–28 and Deut 14:1, the Hebrew Bible presents explicit injunctions against two sets of practices resulting in body modification. First, these texts prohibit certain hairstyles involving trimming of the hair of the head or beard, or shaving the head. Second, they prohibit lacerating, gashing, or otherwise inscribing one's flesh (technically this refers to scarification, not tattooing, since the texts do not mention any application of color). Again, the biblical text singles out priests as required to conform to these taboos. Elsewhere the Hebrew Bible associates cutting or shaving hair and scarification, along with the tearing of one's clothes, with mourning and lamentation, particularly for the dead (e.g., Isa 22:12; Jer 7:29; 16:6; 41:4–5; 47:5; Amos 8:10; Mic 1:16). Since the text characterizes the normative body as full of life, it must distance itself from practices that are associated with death.

In light of the prohibition of gashing and laceration, the requirement of **circumcision**, or the cutting away of the foreskin of the penis, presents somewhat of a contradiction to the picture of the normative body in the Hebrew Bible. Given that the ideal body is male and is thus biologically defined in part by possession of a penis, it seems strange to require a ritual that intentionally alters the penis. Clearly, for the biblical writers, the penis is deficient in its natural state and requires modification to serve its purpose

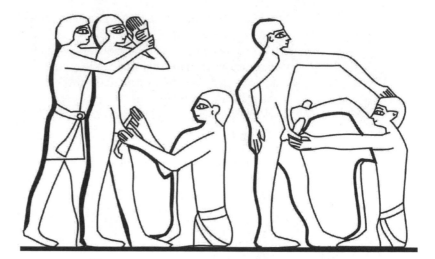

**Fig. 6.6: Circumcision in Ancient Egypt**
*Tomb drawing, ca. 2350–2000 B.C.E. illustrates the practice of circumcision in ancient Egypt.*

as a mark of identity. But why modify the male reproductive organ since, by the cultural codes regulating nakedness, this sign of identity generally remained hidden?

The involvement of the penis suggests an explanation relating to fertility. In the Hebrew Bible, penises generate the seeds that constitute the next generation. In fact, in Hebrew, the same word, *zera*, functions to designate both semen and a person's descendants. Therefore, the practice of circumcision might ensure or enhance fertility, analogous to the pruning of fruit trees to enhance productivity. Leviticus 19:23–25 suggests this comparison with its enigmatic prohibition of eating fruit from newly planted fruit trees until the fifth year. Before that time, the text labels the fruit "uncircumcised" (translated as "forbidden" in the NRSV). However, this comparison fails to account for the necessary role of the female partner in procreation.

A second explanation focuses on an analogous relationship between the male penis and the female reproductive organs. Unlike the irregular seminal emissions of the penis, the vagina produces a monthly issue of blood. The Hebrew Bible considers blood important, frequently associating it with the animating force of life, or the *nephesh*. The blood produced by the cut of circumcision may thus ritually emulate menstrual blood. While some texts view menstrual blood as polluting (e.g., Lev 15:19–24), it also signals the fertility and life-giving power of the female body. The rite of circumcision thus symbolically transfers that power to the male. In this way, the normative male body is imbued with even more power in that it shares or usurps the unique female ability to produce new life.

The repeated emphasis on blood in the enigmatic circumcision story of Exod 4:24–26 hints at a third interpretive possibility. When YHWH attempts to kill Moses, Zipporah wards off the attack with the ritual of circumcision. The ritual thus functions analogously to blood sacrifice. Just as the priest spills the blood of the sacrificial victim by the altar to avert God's anger and punishment (e.g., Lev 4), so also circumcision functions to avert divine retribution. The normative body thus symbolically carries a mark connected to the unblemished sacrificial victim that is acceptable to the deity.

The normative body is not to be modified except through circumcision. Whatever the explanation for this exception might be, the Hebrew Bible clearly insists on it.

*Sexual Intercourse*    Finally, the Hebrew Bible contains material aiming to regulate the sexual activity of the human body. As we have seen, the biblical texts generally use euphemisms for the sexual act: "to lie with," "to go into," "to uncover the nakedness of," and sometimes "to know." Unlike the others, the last euphemism does not seem to involve a physical act but rather a mental operation. What is it that one knows in the sexual act? Genesis points to two concepts. First, after YHWH creates the first woman (*ishshah*) from the first man (*ish*), the second creation account concludes, "Therefore a man leaves his father and his mother and clings to his wife [literally, "his woman"], and they become one flesh" (Gen 2:24). In other words, the text imagines the sexual act as the creation of a new reality. The man leaves his parents and creates a new social body with the woman.

Second, following sexual intercourse with the first man, the first woman conceives and gives birth to a son. The biblical text then puts these words into her mouth: "I have produced a man with the help of the LORD" (Gen 4:1). This phrase could be translated, "I have created a man just like YHWH [did]." The text thus intrinsically links the sex act with procreation; through sexual intercourse human beings take on godlike qualities and create new life. In fact, Gen 19:31–32 calls the function of sex to produce offspring "the manner of all the world."

The Hebrew Bible thus overlays the simple physical act of sexual intercourse with normative cultural expectations: sex creates a new social body, and it results in offspring. And the biblical text proscribes sexual acts that do not fit these cultural expectations. Not that the Hebrew Bible totally ignores the pleasurable aspects of sex—the text advises a man to "rejoice in the wife of your youth. . . . May her breasts satisfy you at all times" (Prov 5:18–19), and the Song of Songs revels in pure erotic pleasure. However, the Hebrew Bible tends to emphasize instead the idealized function of sex in creating families and children.

Since the Hebrew Bible constructs the normative body as male, it also presents the sex act almost exclusively from a male point of view. The rape legislation of Deut 22:28–29 supplies an extreme example. Punishment for the male rapist requires him to pay a fine to the female victim's father (since the act violates the father's property) and to marry his victim, with no possibility of divorce. The legislation channels the sexual act from an illegal context into a legal context where it conforms to the cultural norms

> ## Gendering the Body
>
> The Hebrew Bible generally seems to assume that, beginning with creation (Gen 1:27), humans divide neatly into male and female. While anatomically most people possess either male or female genitalia, the social meanings that society assigns to this difference have varied widely throughout history. During the medieval period, for example, Europeans firmly believed that the female vagina was actually an inverted penis and that the ovaries were actually internal testicles. In other words, people used to believe that females were really poor copies of males. Today people operate with different assumptions about the meaning of sexual differences. While many tend to think of male and female as polar opposites, increasing recognition of the role of society in assigning gender roles has opened up a space for people to place themselves at various points between the male and female poles.
>
> The Hebrew Bible presents the belief that the normative body is male, making its division of humans into male and female asymmetrical. That is, the biblical texts understand femaleness as having lesser social status than normative maleness. In fact, the second creation story in Genesis makes femaleness a derivation of maleness (Gen 2:21–22; see the analysis of the Adam and Eve story in chapter 5).

of family and procreation. But the text totally ignores the position of the female victim.

The Hebrew Bible also includes one-sided expectations of women in marriage. Deuteronomy 22:13–19 demands proof of the bride's virginity but no corresponding proof for the bridegroom. And the ordeal for a woman suspected by her husband of adultery (Num 5:11–31) finds no corresponding ritual for a husband suspected by his wife. Further, the Hebrew Bible locates the inability to have children exclusively in the barrenness of the female sexual partner, allowing the male in this situation to procure another sexual partner (e.g., Gen 16, 30).

According to the Hebrew Bible, sexual intercourse, when properly controlled and regulated, reinforces the social order. However, by its very nature sexual intercourse dangerously crosses body boundaries. Even legitimate sex acts lead to daylong uncleanness and the necessity of a ritual bath (Lev 15:18). Sexual acts are to be kept separate from contact with the holy (e.g., Exod 19:14–15; 1 Sam 21:4–5). For the normative male body, sex is problematic, since it is absolutely necessary but simultaneously disruptive.

## God's Body

This chapter has focused on the human body as a core component of identity. To examine how the Hebrew Bible imagines the body of God as a component of identity may at first glance seem ridiculous. Traditional religious readers insist on defining God as a spiritual being and therefore lacking a

**Fig. 6.7: William Blake's** *The Ancient of Days*
*William Blake's depiction of God in human form.*
*(Lessing J. Rosenwald Collection, Library of Congress. © 2008 The William Blake Archive. Used with permission.)*

body. Deuteronomy lends support to this position: "You once stood before the LORD your God at Horeb. . . . The LORD spoke to you out of the fire. You heard the sound of words but saw no form; there was only a voice. . . . You saw no form when the LORD spoke to you at Horeb out of the fire" (Deut 4:10, 12, 15).

But compared to other parts of the Hebrew Bible, this passage from Deuteronomy looks more like the exception than the rule. The Hebrew Bible frequently describes God with physical human characteristics or forms. God strolls in the garden of Eden (Gen 3:8), helpfully closes the door of the ark before the flood (Gen 7:16), inhales the fragrance of Noah's sacrifice after the flood (Gen 8:21), and curiously descends to see what the builders of the tower of Babel want to accomplish (Gen 11:5). Copious descriptions picture God with eyes to see (e.g., Ps 11:4) and ears to hear (e.g., Ps 31:2), as sitting on a throne (e.g., Ps 47:8), and as possessing a heart (e.g., Gen 8:21) and a mighty upraised right hand and arm (e.g., Deut 5:15). Even God's finger appears (Exod 31:18). Likewise, artists have not shied from depicting God with a human form.

Most suggestively, in the first creation story God "created humanity in his image, in the image of God he created him, male and female he created them" (Gen 1:27). Scholars have spilled gallons of ink trying to explain the meaning of humanity's having been created in God's image. Most interpretations favor answers in which the image of God indicates some sort of non-material resemblance between human beings and the deity—for example, that God's image means humanity has a share in God's spiritual reality, or that humans are empowered to make moral decisions or to create analogously to God, or that humans are to serve as God's vice-regents, exercising God's dominion over creation.

All these explanations avoid the most straightforward and simple reading—that "image" implies physical resemblance. The Hebrew words *tselem* (image) and *d\u1ebdmut* (likeness) normally indicate a bodily copy. For example, Gen 5:3 describes Adam as becoming the father of "a son in his likeness, according to his image." Similarly, in the opening vision of the book of Ezekiel, "God's image" takes on human form:

> And above the dome over their heads there was something like a throne, in appearance like sapphire; and seated above the likeness of a throne was something that seemed like a human form. Upward from what appeared like the loins I saw something like gleaming amber, something that looked like fire enclosed all around; and downward from what looked like the loins I saw something that looked like fire, and there was a splendor all around. (Ezek 1:26–27)

Obviously, the body of God described in this passage differs from normal human bodies, as the references to fire and splendor indicate (see the analysis of God's depiction in Ezekiel in chapter 13). So while the concept of the "image of God" may not only or primarily concern physical likeness, it nonetheless suggests some material form or visual likeness. God's "body" relates in some way to a human one even if God lacks the perishable flesh and bones of humanity.

Unlike the description of the bodies of the lovers in the Song of Songs, the Hebrew Bible offers no comprehensive description of God's appearance. Although it depicts plenty of humans, ranging from Abraham to Daniel, as explicitly seeing God, the Hebrew Bible remains reticent, ambiguous, and partial about the details of their visions. The book of Daniel describes an "Ancient of Days" with white clothes and white hair (Dan 7:9). Jacob wrestles with a "strange man" at night that he ultimately identifies as God after the encounter (Gen 32:24–30). The scroll of Isaiah pictures God sitting on a throne, with the hem of his robe filling the Temple (Isa 6:1). At the least, these portrayals suggest that, according to the Hebrew Bible, God is, or can be, perceptible to the physical senses.

God's image as male and female in Gen 1:27 suggests further that the deity may have sexual characteristics. Yet again, the Hebrew Bible remains demure on this point. On the one hand, Ezek 1:27, in its vision of God, mentions the likeness of "loins," the pubic area associated especially with the procreative power of males. The hem of God's robe in Isa 6:1 may suggest the private parts, given the use of the same Hebrew terminology (*shul*) in passages that associate the hem or skirt with exposure of the genitalia (Jer 13:22, 26; Lam 1:9; Nah 3:5). On the other hand, God's name *shaddai* or *el shaddai* (translated as "the Almighty" or "God Almighty") seems to include a shortened form of the Hebrew term for the female breasts, and Gen. 49:25 associates "the Almighty" with "blessings of the breasts and of the womb." And as we have seen, the Hebrew Bible attributes "womb-feeling," or compassion, to God.

Nonetheless, the Hebrew Bible exhibits tensions about the visible form or body of God. While depicting Moses conversing with God face-to-face (Exod 33:11), the text also reports that YHWH turns down Moses' request for a vision of the deity: "You cannot see my face; for no one shall see me and live" (Exod 33:20). Moses only fleetingly glimpses YHWH's back (Exod 33:23) as the deity recedes from his view.

Indeed, the Hebrew Bible gradually pulls the deity out of direct view. The early books of the Hebrew Bible, especially Genesis, describe God as visibly and directly present. However, successive books replace God's visible form more and more with dreams or visions of God and with the words of prophets and mediators who speak in God's name. Toward the end, the Hebrew Bible quotes less of God's direct speech, and God's miraculous interventions in the human world are missing. The book of Esther does not even mention God. In the end, God's body recedes from view in the Hebrew Bible.

---

## Conclusion

The Hebrew Bible clearly expresses concern about the body and, by extension, about the material world. Yet interpreters influenced by the Cartesian dualism that privileges the mind over the body tend to read the Hebrew Bible primarily as a collection of traditions about purely "spiritual" matters. The result is contempt for the body that justifies its exploitation and, by extension, the exploitation of anything material. If the body and soul are separate, then bodies need to be disciplined so that they do not obstruct the soul, or bodies can be safely abused—even killed—since they are only temporary. The Hebrew Bible's stress on the body and materiality offers a strong rebuttal of these tendencies.

At the same time, the Hebrew Bible, as part of its work of constructing identities, puts forward an ideal of the normative body that excludes some bodies entirely and establishes a hierarchy of varying acceptability among those that remain. In addition, the Hebrew Bible mandates various bodily disciplines to attain and maintain its ideal norm. Yet the biblical text also recognizes that these ideals are continually compromised by the vagaries of life. In this, the Hebrew Bible illustrates the cultural processes that go into the construction of body ideals in all societies, modern society included, and the tension between such ideals and people's actual bodily experience.

| | |
|---|---|
| **Suggested Biblical Readings** | Psalms 16, 38, 88<br>Ecclesiastes 12<br>Song of Songs 4–7<br>Leviticus 11, 13, 15, 18, 20, 21<br>Exodus 4:24–26; chapter 33<br>Isaiah 56<br>Genesis 1:26–27 |
| **Discussion Questions** | 1. How much time do you spend daily on your body? Include time spent applying makeup, grooming, working out, and so forth. How much money do you spend on bodily covering and adornment? Do these concerns with the body today contradict the Cartesian privileging of the mind over the body?<br>2. What associations do the different parts of the body carry in contemporary culture? For example, what do the heart and the head symbolize? How do contemporary associations compare with those that the Hebrew Bible makes?<br>3. How do magazines, television, and popular movies depict a normative body in contemporary culture? Compare these depictions with the Hebrew Bible's image of the normative human body.<br>4. How does a social body such as a college or university today include or exclude certain bodies and bodily behaviors?<br>5. Draw a picture of God. Compare the drawings produced by various students. How do they relate to the discussion in this chapter about God's |

"body"? What are the cultural backgrounds of all these various depictions of the divine?

**Suggestions for Further Reading**

Berquist, Jon L. *Controlling Corporeality: The Body and the Household in Ancient Israel.* New Brunswick, NJ: Rutgers University Press, 2002.

Staubli, Thomas, and Silvia Schroer. *Body Symbolism in the Bible.* Translated by Linda M. Maloney. Collegeville, MN: Liturgical Press, 2001.

# 7. Ethnicity

But who am I, and what is my people?
          —King David, 1 Chronicles 29:14

The night is beautiful,
So the faces of my people.

The stars are beautiful,
So the eyes of my people.

Beautiful, also, the sun,
Beautiful, also, the souls of my people.
          —Langston Hughes, "My People"

---

The sense of being part of a particular people is a core component of identity. Langston Hughes, famous African American poet and writer, penned his poem "My People" to evoke and celebrate the beautiful identity of black Americans. Chief Seattle is said to have claimed in 1854 that "every part of this soil is sacred in the estimation of my people," thus indicating the special connection with the land that was part of the identity of native people. Contemporary students in North America and Europe might similarly identify themselves as members of a particular people. Perhaps they see themselves as descendants of certain immigrant groups, such as Bavarians from Germany or Punjabis from Pakistan and India. Many might identify themselves more generally with the people of their nation or their geographic area of origin. At any rate, all these notions of peoplehood share in common two dynamics: a sense of commonality with a particular people, and a sense of difference from other peoples.

The Hebrew Bible is also deeply concerned with a sense of peoplehood, especially with the identity of a particular people called the Israelites or Israel. It details this people's common characteristics: their origins and ancestors, the norms that are to define their way of life, the stories of their heroes, and various expressions of their hopes and dreams. At the same time, the Hebrew Bible contrasts the identity of the Israelites with other peoples from whom the Israelites are to differ, peoples such as the **Egyptians**, the **Philistines**, and the **Canaanites**. This chapter will explore some of the ways in which the Hebrew Bible constructs peoplehood. It will focus on the Israelites but will also examine some of the other peoples mentioned in the

Hebrew Bible, peoples with whom the Israelites interact and from whom they are often called to be different.

## Ethnicity

While peoplehood might include notions of **race** and **nation**, this chapter will use a more specific social scientific concept of peoplehood called **ethnicity**. Human groups build a sense of ethnic identity on their belief that the members of the group share some sort of common origin (descent), and on their practice of certain social behaviors believed to be unique to the group (culture). Stories and rituals that speak of and commemorate a common origin and history indicate descent, while specific marriage, dietary, linguistic, religious, and other practices provide the content of culture. Insofar as the Hebrew Bible portrays the Israelites as descendants of a common triad of ancestors—Abraham, Isaac, and Jacob—and ascribes to them certain unique cultural practices, such as the observance of the **Sabbath**, the Israelites are an ethnic group.

Common origin traditions and treasured cultural traits define the *internal* content of ethnicity. Ethnic groups also have an *external* aspect consisting of their relationships to outsiders. They tend to portray certain outsiders as especially different so as to highlight the unique identity of the ethnic group, in effect allowing their members to say, "We are who we are because we are *not* like them." The external differentiation between "us" and "them," or insider and outsider, creates a boundary that defines the ethnic group. Ethnic groups tend to be very attentive to this boundary, and to whom it

### Ethnicity, Race, and Nationality

While the concept of ethnicity overlaps with the concepts of race and nation, they can be differentiated. The concept of race makes universal divisions between humans based largely on physically visible characteristics, such as skin color or facial features. In contrast, ethnicity makes distinctions based on culture and stories of origin; consequently, people classified as being part of the same racial group may define themselves as part of different ethnic groups. For example, American Indians or First Nations peoples may be classified by the government as part of the same race, but they may identify themselves with different tribes having different origin stories and cultures.

The concept of nation is used to construct a sense of peoplehood associated with a statelike political institution. In contrast, ethnic groups do not necessarily require a political structure, and they can constitute subgroups within a nation-state or can cross national boundaries. For example, Japanese-Americans may distinguish themselves as a group within the United States, and Kurds constitute an ethnic group found in the different nation-states of Iraq, Iran, and Turkey.

Ethnic groups, races, and nations all share in the fact that they are socially constructed categorizations.

includes and excludes. The degree to which the boundary can be crossed, and by whom, is often variable and contested. The Hebrew Bible often evokes the ethnic boundary surrounding the Israelites, such as in these two examples from Leviticus in which God demands that the Israelites be different (the word "you" in the Hebrew text is in the plural form here): "You shall not do as they do in the land of Egypt, where you lived, and you shall not do as they do in the land of Canaan, to which I am bringing you" (Lev 18:3). "You shall be holy to me; for I the LORD am holy, and I have separated you from the other peoples to be mine" (20:26).

Actual people in concrete times and places construct ethnicity, and so one can most easily observe ethnic identity in contemporary groups. However, if the ethnic group in question existed in the past, as did the Israelites of the Hebrew Bible, people today no longer have direct access to them and their work of ethnic identification. All that survives may be the stories that the ethnic group created, including myths of common ancestry, a name by which the group identifies itself, shared memories of a common past, means of commemorating significant events and heroes, and material outlining differences with other groups. If the society in the past was at least partially literate, some of these stories may have been written down, and perhaps strung together in a grand narrative (like Genesis through 2 Kings in the Hebrew Bible). It is through those stories that have survived to the present that one can today try to reconstruct or imagine the ethnic dynamics of peoples in the past.

Therefore, although direct access to the ancient peoples with which the Hebrew Bible is concerned is not possible, a collection of written documents has survived from the past—that is, the Hebrew Bible. Many of these documents are concerned with the identity of a particular people in the past called Israel. This collection is selective in that it does not include all available written sources or various other stories and traditions that may have existed in oral form and were not written down. But looking at the documents of the Hebrew Bible through the lens of ethnicity enables readers today to sense how these writings portray the formation of, and struggle with, ethnic identities, both of the Israelites and of the other peoples with whom the Israelites interacted.

The Hebrew Bible has a diversity of terms for the ethnic notion of peoplehood, as well as a variety of approaches to different ethnicities. This chapter will outline these various approaches, which range from the idealization of human differences, to an ambiguous sort of coexistence between different ethnic groups, to a complete and violent rejection and exclusion of different groups. These various approaches are all illustrated in the main narrative of the Hebrew Bible as it begins in Genesis. Then the chapter will examine how ethnic groups other than the Israelites occupy an important place in providing various contrasts to Israelite ethnic identity. Finally, the chapter will describe the way the Hebrew Bible deals with the interesting problem of the **"inside-outsiders,"** or the non-Israelite minorities within Israelite society.

---

### Terms for "Ethnicity" in the Hebrew Bible

The English term "ethnicity" comes from the Greek word *ethnos*, a word that generally means "people" but, interestingly, also came to be used to denote "foreigners"—that is, peoples who are not part of one's own ethnic group. In the ancient Greek translation of the Hebrew Bible known as the Septuagint, the Greek word *ethnos* is used most often to translate the Hebrew word *goy*, but it also frequently translates the Hebrew word *am*. Both *goy* and *am* can mean "people"; the difference between them is often not clear. (The two words occur together, for example, in passages such as Exod 33:13 and Deut 4:6 without any apparent distinction in meaning.)

*Goy*, used over 300 times in the Hebrew Bible, seems to more precisely connote a people associated with a particular territory or governing system and so is often translated into English as "nation." The Hebrew Bible generally pictures the Israelites as a *goy* among other *goyim* (e.g., Deut 7:7; 9:14). But the word also begins to take on a more negative reference to the non-Israelite nations that are seen in some way to threaten the identity of the Israelites (e.g., Deut 7:11ff.; Ezek 20:32). This tendency parallels the secondary meaning of the Greek word *ethnos* as "foreigner."

The Hebrew Bible prefers to refer to the Israelites as an *am*, a word appearing more than 1,800 times in the Hebrew Bible. The word *am* focuses more on the connotation of common origins and kinship relations, and is therefore closest in meaning to the modern term "ethnic group."

---

## Idealization of Differences: Ethnic Diversity

The Hebrew Bible begins by portraying all humans as originating from common ancestors, namely, Adam and Eve. While various differences among people arise, often resulting in violence, such as in the stories of Cain and Abel (Gen 4) and the procreation of the Nephilim giants (Gen 6:1–4), the narrative stresses the common heritage of all humanity. It is only in Gen 10, after the flood (Gen 6–9), that one finds a sense of ethnic division.

Genesis 10 is often entitled the "Table of Nations" by biblical commentators, but the word "nations" is misleading, since it is too easily confused with a modern notion of territorially and politically bound nation-states. In fact, Gen 10 refers not just to nations (*goyim* in Hebrew) but also to a mishmash of categories based on territory (land), cultural traits (language), and kinship ties (family; see Gen 10:5, 20, 31). The picture of the world that Gen 10 paints is thus very diverse, variously differentiating many ethnic groups by geographical location, pattern of descent, and cultural attributes. Notably, Gen 10 attaches no value judgment to the differences between these groups, but merely describes them. The differences do not obscure the common origins and primordial unity of the diverse human race, but are a natural part of attempting to give expression to the <u>totality of human peoples</u>.

The story immediately following Gen 10, however, portrays differences as divisive. Commentators traditionally interpret the story of the tower of Babel in Gen 11:1–9 as depicting an idyllic Eden-like human community, with a single language (and culture?), ruined by human pride and punished by forced dispersal and differentiation. However, such an interpretation does not take into account the portrayal in the previous chapter (Gen 10) of the development of multiple ethnic groups and languages as natural and unproblematic.

The Babylonian setting of the story in Gen 11 suggests a different interpretation. **Babylonia** was an ancient empire, and in an empire, the use of one language and the enterprise of building a city and a tower describe not some idyllic time but rather harsh imperial policies meant to impose unity, to subjugate, and to assimilate conquered peoples. The Mesopotamian-based empires of Babylonia and **Assyria** both engaged in monumental building projects, and evidence shows that at least Assyria imposed the Akkadian language to facilitate an imperial propaganda of unity.

In contrast to this coerced imperial unity, God charges humanity in Gen 1:28 to "multiply and fill the earth." Genesis 10, with its description or ethnic map of the various peoples, with all their differences, spread throughout the known world, indicates that humanity has fulfilled this charge. The

## The World according to Genesis 10

The names listed in Gen 10 are a mixture of proper names, gentilics (names indicating a people originating from a common ancestor), and toponyms (place names), often indicating overlapping categories. For example, verse 4—"The descendants of Javan: Elishah, Tarshish, Kittim, and Rodanim"—presents five names. Of these, Javan, Elishah, and Tarshish are proper names of persons, but they are also toponyms: Javan designates Greece or a territory in Asia Minor, Elishah likely refers to the island of Cyprus, and Tarshish seems to refer to a seaport along either the Mediterranean coast or the southern coast of Arabia. The name "Kittim" is a plural in Hebrew and functions as a toponym for the islands of the Aegean Sea or as a gentilic designating a particular people (in later texts it designates the Greeks or perhaps the Romans). The last name, "Rodanim," again a plural gentilic form, likely refers to the inhabitants of the island of Rhodes. The Masoretic Text reads "Dodanim" here, but this is probably a scribal mistake for "Rodanim" since the Hebrew letters *d* (ד) and *r* (ר) are easily confused. "Rodanim" is the way the name appears in the Septuagint and some other ancient manuscripts, and in 1 Chr 1:7.

## totality of human peoples

The impression of unity in Gen 10 is further supported numerically. Noah's sons are the ancestors of seventy peoples, the number seventy signifying totality in the biblical world. Japhet is the progenitor of fourteen peoples, Ham of thirty (not counting the material about the mighty warrior Nimrod in verses 8 to 12, which seems to be an addition that interrupts the flow of the list), and Shem of twenty-six. The same numbers appear in 1 Chr 1:4–23. In Gen 46:8–27, the total number of the members of Jacob's family, the ancestors of the Israelites, also adds up to seventy. Thus, the totality of the people Israel mirrors the totality of the seventy peoples of the human race.

immediately following story of Babel thus describes a step backward, toward an imperially sanctioned homogeneity, or erasure of difference, that is not part of the deity's original intention. The confusion of languages (Gen 11:7) is therefore not a punishment but a <u>restorative move</u> to reactivate the dispersal of the peoples (Gen 11:8) as originally intended, and to defend diversity against homogenizing efforts.

From the perspective of ethnicity, the early chapters of Genesis seem to accept and even celebrate ethnic diversity. But beginning with Gen 12, the narrative shifts its focus from all of humanity to a particular ethnic group. Genesis now presents stories of the ancestors of the Israelites. It presents as well stories of the origins of a variety of ethnic groups related to the Israelites, not to acknowledge diversity, but rather to highlight the distinctiveness of the Israelites. In fact, the main plot now revolves around the question of who will inherit the special promises of God made to Abraham and thus be included as an Israelite. Instead of supporting the ethnic inclusiveness of Gen 10, the plot now relentlessly prunes Abraham's family tree, excluding various branches of the family and leaving only one line that leads to the ancestor Jacob, also called Israel, from whom the Israelites take their name.

### restorative move

One could, of course, read Gen 10 and 11 as two variants on the theme of human diversity, the former seeing it as positive, natural, or neutral, with the latter viewing it negatively, as a punishment. Biblical scholars tend toward this sort of interpretation by assigning each chapter to a different source: Gen 10, they say, comes from a priestly source, while Gen 11:1–9 comes from a non–priestly source called the Yahwist. However, if one reads the present biblical text sequentially, then the interpretation of the story of Babel as a restoration of ethnic diversity seems more persuasive.

### Defending Diversity against Homogenization

Read as affirming difference and condemning attempts to impose similarity, the story of Babel resonates strongly with the struggles of many ethnic groups today to maintain their identity, as embodied in their culture and especially their language, against the global assault of western culture and the linguistic dominance of English. For example, many indigenous or aboriginal groups place great priority on the preservation of their particular languages as the key to their cultural survival as distinct ethnic groups. The United Nations Educational, Scientific, and Cultural Organization (UNESCO) documents the desire of various ethnic groups worldwide to preserve their intangible cultural heritage, which includes oral traditions and expressions, performing arts, rituals and festivals, and traditional knowledge and craftsmanship. All of these depend to some extent on the preservation of distinct languages. As of November 15, 2006, some sixty-eight member states of the United Nations had indicated acceptance of a Convention for the Safeguarding of the Intangible Cultural Heritage.

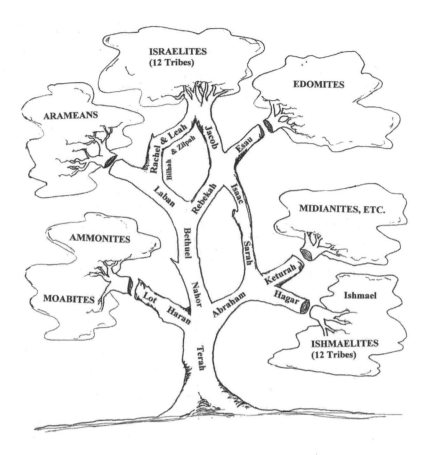

**Fig. 7.1: Pruning the Family Tree of Genesis**

© Susan P.M. Cherland

## Ambiguous Coexistence: Israelite Ethnicity

Israelite peoplehood in the Hebrew Bible begins with Abraham, to whom God gives a set of promises:

> I will make of you a great nation [*goy*], and I will bless you, and make your name great so that you will be a blessing. I will bless those who bless you, and the one who curses you I will curse; and in you all the families of the earth shall be blessed. . . . To your offspring I will give this land. (Gen 12:2–3, 7)

These divine promises, reiterated several times in the stories of Abraham and his descendants Isaac and Jacob (see Gen 13:14–17; 15:5, 7, 18–19; 17:4–8; 22:17–18), set the process of ethnic differentiation into motion. Gradually, a distinct ethnic identity coalesces around Abraham, marked by the notion of **covenant**, a ritual of **circumcision**, a name change, and a territorial association.

Covenants are treaties, alliances, or pacts between two or more peoples, or between a deity and a person or people. After the flood, God "establishes"

(Heb., *heqim*) a universal covenant with Noah, and through him with all humans and "every living creature of all flesh that is on the earth" (Gen 9:16). In contrast, in Gen 15 God "cuts" (Heb., *karat*) a covenant with Abram (later called Abraham) that applies only to him and his descendants and thus functions to differentiate Abram's family from others. The peculiar expression in biblical Hebrew that now appears for establishing a covenant—literally, "to cut a covenant" (*karat berit*)—reinforces this ethnic differentiation. Abram literally enacts this expression in the ritual of covenant making by cutting three animals in half and placing them opposite each other (15:9–10).

A further covenant ritual in Gen 17 continues the process of differentiation by introducing a different sort of "cutting" to mark off those who are included in this particular covenant—the ritual of circumcision. God commands Abraham to circumcise himself and all his male offspring (17:9–12), a command that Abraham obeys (17:23–27). Circumcision thus functions ethnically as a cultural practice that both characterizes the descendants of Abraham internally and marks them as different from other groups externally. Those of the group who are not circumcised are to be "cut" in another way: "Any uncircumcised male who is not circumcised in the flesh of his foreskin shall be cut off [Heb., *karat*] from his people; he has broken my covenant" (17:14). Circumcision thus cuts a boundary around the ethnic group claiming common descent from Abraham. In fact, claiming common descent from Abraham is not enough; in order to be an Israelite male, one must be circumcised.

The covenant in Gen 17 displays three other characteristics. First, it is ancient, an "everlasting covenant" (17:7, 13, 19). This description corresponds with the subjective **primordial** feeling that often accompanies ethnic identification—namely, the conviction that one's ethnic group and its characteristics have existed virtually unchanged from "time immemorial." In reality, however, ethnicity is not a fixed category. Specific ethnicities have histories of origin, development, and change. Ethnic boundaries often shift, and groups mobilize ethnicity often only selectively to meet a specific need or crisis, such as forced migration, economic inequality, or a breakdown in other identities.

Second, a name change signals the inauguration of the covenant. Abram becomes Abraham (17:5), and his wife, Sarai, becomes Sarah (17:15; see also

### name change

Both versions of Abraham's name mean something like "exalted father (ancestor)," and both versions of Sarah's name mean "princess." The changes are therefore insignificant in form or content and likely reflect different dialects of Hebrew. However, even small differences can be significant in the Hebrew Bible: the biblical text plays on the similarity in sound between Abraham's longer name *Avraham* and the phrase *av-hamon*, "father of a multitude" (Gen 17:5).

the later change of the name Jacob to Israel in 32:27–28 and 35:10). A change of name typically signals a new identity, and distinctive names are often important markers of membership in an ethnic group.

Finally, this covenant includes the promise of land, a promise that Abraham has already previously heard (12:7; 13:14–17; 15:18–21). Ethnic identification for many ethnic groups often includes an association with a homeland, whether that homeland is real or mythic, and whether they actually occupy it or only hope for it or nostalgically remember it.

The distinction between those inside and those outside of this new ethnic group does not work perfectly. Complications appear. Circumcision, first of all, is not unique to the Israelites but is shared by other ethnic groups in the ancient Near East. The Hebrew Bible itself, in Jer 9:24, attests to circumcision among the Egyptians, **Edomites**, **Ammonites**, and **Moabites** (in contrast, Assyrians, Babylonians, and Philistines did not practice circumcision). The boundary that circumcision "cuts" is thus ambiguous; a cultural practice that the Hebrew Bible highlights as a sign of Israelite distinctiveness actually signifies dissimilarity with only some groups and similarity with others.

Second, the boundary "cut" by circumcision is not impenetrable: outsiders can gain access. The circumcision that God commands Abraham to perform includes "the slave born into your house and the one bought with your money from any foreigner who is not of your offspring" (17:12, 27). In other words, not all members of the covenant people marked by circumcision are literally offspring of Abraham. While ethnic identification is often based on a belief in descent from primordial ancestors, such descent is often fictive. Ethnic groups add and drop members as they develop and change

### Reversing Circumcision

During the Hellenistic period following the conquests of Alexander the Great, Greek culture spread among the Jewish communities living in the Near East. Hellenized Jewish men adopted, among other Greek practices, public nudity in the baths and gymnasia. Since the Greeks regarded circumcision as an indecent, even barbaric, mutilation of the genitals, these men attempted to hide or reverse their circumcisions. Some wore a sheath over the penis, or pulled the skin around the penis forward and secured it with a pin or fibula. Others submitted to a surgical procedure called epispasm, which reconstructed the foreskin. A variety of sources mention these attempts, which continued into the Roman period, including Josephus (*Antiquities* 12.5); 1 Macc 1:15; *Jubilees* 15:26–27; 1 Cor 7:18; and various rabbinic texts.

Circumcision could be more than a social liability. After the Jewish revolt against Rome in 66–70 C.E., circumcision enabled the Romans to identify Jews for punishment. The Roman emperor Hadrian (117–138 C.E.) outlawed circumcision entirely. More recently, under the Nazi regime of terror in the 1930s and 1940s, circumcision became a matter of life and death for European Jews, causing some again to seek to hide their identity through surgical attempts to reverse their circumcisions.

throughout their history. Just as insiders can be "cut off" from their people and become outsiders (17:14), so also outsiders can "cut in" and cross the boundary to become insiders (17:12).

A third complication is that circumcision is a mark of identity not normally visible since it is covered by clothing. It has more value, therefore, as a characteristic internal to the group than as a characteristic marking distinctiveness externally to outsiders (see the discussion of circumcision in chapter 6). However, after the biblical period, some descendants of the Israelites, finding circumcision a liability in their relationships with outsiders, made attempts to reverse it.

All these complications show that circumcision only ambiguously establishes a boundary between Israelites and outsiders. Such ambiguity underlines the largely subjective nature of ethnic identity: it does not occur naturally, but is socially imagined and thus often contains a mixture of fact and fiction. But even within the boundary of Israel, circumcision marks an ambiguous identity. Most strikingly, circumcision only applies to males and so structurally places women in the position of outsiders; only by virtue of their relationship to males (fathers or husbands) are they members of the ethnic group. Yet, ironically, only through women is the ethnic group able to perpetuate itself and grow. Sarah, for instance, is necessary for Abraham to become the ancestor of the Israelites, and the biblical text designates her, like Abraham, as the ancestor of nations and kings (compare Gen 17:6 with 17:16).

The line of exclusion inside the boundaries of Israel can also run through the males, however. God commands Abraham to circumcise *all* his male offspring (17:9–13) as sign of the everlasting covenant. However, the text then has God intending to establish the covenant exclusively with Abraham's son Isaac, whom Sarah will bear in the future (17:18–21). The latter move effectively excludes Abraham's older son, Ishmael, even though Ishmael is circumcised (17:23–27). So, on the one hand, the biblical narrative prunes Ishmael from the family tree and makes him an outsider. Abraham even sends Ishmael and his mother Hagar away (21:14—the Hebrew term trans-

## Interpreting the Ishmaelites

Genesis excludes Ishmael from the chosen people. Ironically, the apostle Paul does the exact opposite. He transforms Ishmael typologically into a symbol of the chosen people, the Jews, who adhere to the Mosaic law (Gal 4:21–28). Isaac, Abraham's other son, Paul typologically transforms into a symbol of the Christians. Unfortunately, Christians have far too often historicized Paul's typology to justify **anti-Semitism**. Interestingly, Muslims, the other member of the family of western monotheists, claim that their prophet Muhammad descended from Abraham through Ishmael. All three faiths thus lay claim to Abraham as their spiritual ancestor, a claim that has led less to familial harmony and more to vicious family feuding.

lated "to send away" can also mean "to divorce"). Ishmael consequently marries an Egyptian woman (21:21) and generates his own ethnic group, the **Ishmaelites** (25:12–18). On the other hand, Ishmael bears the covenantal mark of circumcision, is called the "seed of Abraham" (21:13), and receives the divine promise of becoming a great nation (17:20; see also 16:10 and 21:18) just like Abraham (12:2). By including elements that seem to both include and exclude Ishmael, the biblical narrative undercuts the notion that the divine covenant is unambiguously exclusive. The Ishmaelites are both Abraham's descendants like the Israelites, and an ethnic group separate from the Israelites; they are both ethnic insiders and outsiders.

Nonetheless, Ishmael represents the beginning of a series of exclusions among Abraham's descendants. Excluded next are Abraham's children by another wife, Keturah; like Ishmael, Abraham also sends them away (25:1–6). These children become the ancestors of various ethnic groups, including the **Midianites**. Then Isaac, Abraham's favored son, disinherits his firstborn, Esau, in favor of the second-born Jacob (Gen 25 and 27). Esau becomes the ancestor of the Edomites. Only with Jacob do the exclusions stop: the covenant includes all of Jacob's sons, who all became ancestors of Israelite tribes.

Besides this series of exclusions of near relatives, Genesis also contains stories of other ethnic groups to which the Israelites are related in other ways. The Ammonites and Moabites descend from Abraham's nephew Lot (Gen 13, 18) and so are cousins of the Israelites. The Israelite ancestors associate and even intermarry with Egyptians, Philistines, and **Aramaeans**. The Egyptian Pharaoh almost incorporates Sarah into his household (Gen 12); also Egyptian is Hagar, the handmaiden by which Abraham has his first son (Gen 16). The Philistine king of Gerar, Abimelech, twice almost marries into Abraham's family (Gen 20, 26). The Aramaeans supply wives for Isaac (Rebekah—Gen 24) and Jacob (Leah and Rachel, Zilpah and Bilhah—Gen 29–30). But in all these cases, the association is cut short. Pharaoh returns Sarah to Abraham, and Abraham expels Hagar. The deity prevents the king of Gerar from marrying Sarah, although the king maintains cordial relations with Abraham's descendants and cuts a covenant with Isaac (26:26–33). The Aramaeans cut a covenant with Jacob to divide their territory from that of the Israelites (31:43–54). These stories all try to clarify the ambiguous boundaries of the developing ethnic group of the Israelites vis-à-vis other peoples.

## Violent Rejection and Exclusion: Genocide

A third approach in the Hebrew Bible to different ethnicities is the attempt to resolve the ambiguities of ethnic boundaries through violence, as, for example, in Gen 34. The story begins rather inauspiciously when Shechem, the local Hivite prince (Hivites were one of the tribes of Canaanites indigenous to the Cisjordan), crosses ethnic boundaries by <u>assaulting Dinah</u>, Jacob's daughter. The two families involved negotiate a marriage. As a condition, the outsider Hivites must undergo circumcision so as to become ethnically integrated with the Israelites, who promise, "Then we will give our daughters to you, and we will take your daughters for ourselves, and we will live

---

### <u>assaulting Dinah</u>

Does Shechem sexually assault Dinah? The ambiguity of the Hebrew makes it difficult to determine. The text uses four verbs in Gen 34:2: he sees [*raah*] her, takes her [*laqakh*], lies with her [*shakkav*], and humiliates her [*anah*]. His "taking" can connote either forcible seizure, or taking her as his woman (the usual way the Hebrew Bible describes marriage). And while "lie with her" certainly means sex, what exactly happens in their encounter remains ambiguous. The verb *anah* often occurs in describing scenes of sexual assault (e.g., 2 Sam 13; Judg 20), but it might simply mean that her liaison with Shechem shames her by changing her status to nonvirginal while she is still officially unmarried. At any rate, the biblical text does not consider Dinah's viewpoint or whether she had given consent.

---

### Genocide

The term "genocide" was coined in the 1900s to describe acts aimed at destroying a defined human group, whether national, ethnic, racial, or religious. According to the United Nations' Convention on the Prevention and Punishment of the Crime of Genocide, promulgated in 1948, genocidal acts can include killing or causing serious bodily or mental harm to members of the group, forcing onto the group conditions deliberately intended to destroy it, instituting measures to prevent births within the group, and forcibly transferring children of the group to another group. While genocide is most overt in the form of one-sided mass killing, it can also take place more subtly via measures meant to gradually erase the existence of a particular human group.

Nazi perpetrators of the Holocaust were tried for genocide against the Jewish people in the Nuremberg Trials of 1945–1946. More recently, the world has witnessed attempts at genocide in the former Yugoslavia (the attempt of Serbs in Bosnia to "cleanse" their territory of Bosnian Muslims), in Rwanda (the attempt of Hutus to annihilate the Tutsis), and in the Darfur region of Sudan (the attempt of Arab militias to destroy indigenous African peoples). The treatment of native peoples in the Americas by the European colonizers has also been described as genocidal. Various attempts at genocide are also part of the story of the Hebrew Bible. For example, Pharaoh's policies against the Hebrew people in Exod 1–2 are genocidal, as are also the divine command for the Israelites to annihilate the Amalekites (1 Sam 15:3) or the indigenous inhabitants of the Cisjordan (Deut 7:1–2) and genocide of the Jews as proposed in Esther.

Genocide involves the radical intensification of the normal division between "us" and "them" to the extent that those who are "other" are totally dehumanized; no longer considered human, these "others" can be exterminated. Perpetrators of genocide typically deny that they are doing anything wrong and may even interpret their actions as an altruistic sacrifice for the benefit and survival of their own group.

among you, and become one people [*am*]" (Gen 34:16; contrast 24:3 and 28:1, which devalue intermarriage with Canaanites).

However, the planned ethnic integration of Hivites and Israelites does not succeed. While the Hivites are recuperating from the effects of circumcision, Dinah's full brothers, Simeon and Levi, attack them, killing the males and taking the women, children, and livestock as plunder (34:25–29). From an ethnic perspective, Simeon and Levi are attempting to preserve the ethnic homogeneity of their group by a genocidal attack on outsiders who seem to threaten this homogeneity. For them, the only alternative to incorporating the foreign Hivites is to annihilate them. The story shows that an increasing emphasis on differentiations that cut between people can ultimately culminate in ethnic violence. The extreme form of this violence is **genocide**, the attempt to exterminate an entire people.

However, differentiation from others does not inevitably lead to violence. At the same time as exclusive ethnic differentiation increases in the narrative of the Hebrew Bible, reminders of a larger human unity and the possibility of harmonious relationships across lines of difference also appear. Genesis portrays Abraham as in most respects living a life of cooperation and interchange with other peoples: he has Amorite allies (14:13), prays for the Sodomites (18:16–33), and has good relations with the foreign peoples of Salem (14:18–20) and Gerar (20:14–17). He only reluctantly expels Ishmael (21:9–14) and, if anything, expresses his ethnocentrism only in his desire that his son Isaac marry not one of the local Canaanites, but someone from the "old country" of Mesopotamia, from which he himself originally came (24:3–4).

The dynamic of ethnicity proves to be a helpful lens through which to read the biblical narrative of Israel's beginnings. It prevents readers from too quickly deflecting the narrative into theological or metaphysical concerns and keeps the story rooted in the very earthly processes by which a people—in this case, the Israelites—develop an identity and engage in a dialectic of exclusion and inclusion. The same dynamic operates today in the aspirations of various groups to have their particular identities validated, and in the danger that an overzealous concern with difference cuts boundaries marked by the shedding of blood.

## Ethnic Others

Ethnic identity depends not only on characteristics internal to the ethnic group but also on a sense of being different from other groups. Thus, the biblical story defines the Israelites not only internally but also by contrast to a variety of other peoples. The biblical writers seem to be eager to differentiate the Israelites from three peoples in particular: the Egyptians, the Canaanites, and the Philistines. Their eagerness is likely based on a couple of possibilities: (1) that the Israelites interacted with members of these other groups so closely that, in the view of the biblical writers, the Israelites were in danger of being unable to construct and maintain a sufficiently unique identity; and/or (2) that at least some Israelites originated from these other groups and, in the view of the biblical writers, maintained their connection to their original group to a degree that threatened their unique Israelite identity.

The following material examines some of the ways the Hebrew Bible portrays the Egyptians, Canaanites, and Philistines, as well as the Edomites and Moabites, over against the Israelites. Additional ethnic "others" in the Hebrew Bible that cannot be explored here include the Assyrians, Babylonians, Amorites, Midianites, and Ammonites.

*Egyptians*

The Egyptians loom large in the Hebrew Bible as a people over against the Israelites. The biblical text presents the exodus of the Israelites from the land of Egypt as the foundational event of Israelite identity (e.g., 1 Sam 12:8; 1 Kgs 8:53; Jer 11:4). Already before the story of the exodus, the book of Genesis presents Egypt as a land of plenty and a refuge in times of famine, but also as a place that threatens Israelite identity. When Abram and Sarai go down to Egypt to escape famine (12:10–20), Abram passes Sarai off as his sister, and the Pharaoh takes her into his harem. God sends a plague to prevent this ethnic assimilation of the Israelite ancestress into Egypt, and eventually the Pharaoh sends Abram and Sarai off with extravagant gifts. This story anticipates the later and much longer narrative of how another Pharaoh endangers the Israelites in Egypt until, forced by a series of plagues, he sends them off also, again with extravagant gifts (Exod 3:21–22; 11:2; 12:35–36). The ideological lesson taught by both stories is that the Israelites, while they might spend time in Egypt temporarily for purposes of survival (and enrichment), are not to assimilate with the Egyptians or consider Egypt as their origin or home. Nor are Egyptians to be allowed into the Israelite ancestral bloodline. When an Egyptian woman, Hagar, bears Abraham's firstborn son, Ishmael, he is excluded in favor of Isaac, Abraham's second son through Sarah (Gen 16, 21).

In contrast, the story of Joseph in Egypt (Gen 37–50) suggests assimilation between Israelites and Egyptians. When Joseph rises to prominence in Egypt (41:37–45), he marries an Egyptian—the daughter of an Egyptian priest, no less—and the Pharaoh gives him the Egyptian name "Zaphenath-paneah" (a name that includes a reference to an Egyptian deity). His Egyptian wife gives birth to two sons, Manasseh and Ephraim (41:50–52), who are fully included in the kinship group of the Israelites, becoming the ancestors of two of the tribes of Israel. The story of Joseph contains no evidence that the Israelites found the religion of the Egyptians strange, threatening, or unacceptable. In fact, when Joseph's father, Jacob, dies in Egypt, Egyptians accompany his body back to his burial place in the Cisjordan with a great mourning procession (50:1–14), and when Joseph dies, he is embalmed in the Egyptian manner and placed in a coffin in Egypt (50:26). The only dissonant note is that Egyptians find associating with shepherds and eating with Hebrews (a term of contempt for low-class outsiders) an abomination (43:32; 46:34); in other words, the farming Egyptians made an ethnic and class distinction between themselves and what they perceived as rather unruly and unsophisticated sheep- and goat-herding foreigners. Notwithstanding such prejudices, the book of Genesis ends with the Israelites comfortably settled and at home in Egypt. Perhaps they even thought of themselves as Egyptians.

The picture changes drastically in the book of Exodus. A change in the ruling dynasty brings to the throne a Pharaoh who does not remember or appreciate the benefits Joseph brought to Egypt (Exod 1:8). The drastic increase in Egyptian royal state power that, according to Gen 47:13–26, Joseph made possible, enables this Pharaoh to enslave the Israelites, forcing them to work on state building projects. The story continues with the appearance, from the ruling Egyptian household itself, of a liberator named Moses, but he has a very difficult time persuading the Israelites that they are not at home in Egypt and that they need to leave. Even when they have left, the narrative portrays the Israelites as continuing to identify with Egypt; they miss Egypt and <u>complain</u> so much about their new circumstances that God eventually decrees that they must all die in the wilderness so that a completely new generation, without Egyptian roots, can enter the promised land as bona fide Israelites (Num 14:22–23; see also 26:64–65).

These stories show the Egyptians as ethnically "**near neighbors**" to the Israelites—that is, peoples with whom the Israelites identify and live, and who thus threaten to blur the boundaries of ethnic identification. Therefore, God sends the ten plagues (Exod 7–12) "so that you may know that the LORD makes a distinction between Egypt and Israel" (11:7; see also 8:23 and 9:4). That God needs to assert this distinction with such vigor suggests that it was not self-evident to the first audience of the story.

Other parts of the Hebrew Bible show evidence of an Israelite origin tradition that places Israel's beginnings in Egypt (with Moses) instead of originally in Mesopotamia (with Abraham). For example, the prophet Amos knows Israel's beginnings in Egypt—"I brought you up out of the land of

---

### complain

As the Israelites move through the wilderness on their way from Egypt to the land promised to them by God, they frequently murmur and complain about their circumstances and long nostalgically for their past lives in Egypt (see, for example, Exod 14:10–14; 16:2–3; Num 11:4–6, 18; 14:2–4; 16:13–14; 20:3–5). These vignettes present Israelite nostalgic identification with Egyptians as the voice of rebellion against YHWH, the god of the Israelites. Exodus 12 institutes the ritual of the Passover in part to counter such nostalgia. Passover is a perpetual ritualized reminder of the exodus, and thus of the ethnic difference between Israelites and Egyptians.

Egypt" (Amos 2:10; see also 3:1 and 9:7)—but makes no mention at all of the ancestor stories of Genesis. Likewise, Pss 78, 106, and 136 rehearse the story of the deliverance of the Israelites from Egypt without any reference to the ancestor stories of Genesis. The book of Ezekiel speaks of God revealed for seemingly the first time to the Israelites when they were idol worshipers in Egypt:

> Thus says the Lord GOD: On the day when I chose Israel, I swore to the offspring of the house of Jacob—making myself known to them in the land of Egypt—I swore to them, saying, I am the LORD your God. . . . And I said to them, Cast away the detestable things your eyes feast on, every one of you, and do not defile yourselves with the idols of Egypt; I am the LORD your God. (Ezek 20: 5, 7)

The Hebrew Bible seems to contain several origin traditions for the Israelites, sometimes asserting that they were originally Egyptians, but more frequently insisting that they were originally from Mesopotamia. (Archaeologists provide a third option: based on the similarity of Israelite and Canaanite material culture, they suggest that the Israelites were originally Canaanite.)

According to Exodus, the Egyptian Pharaoh is the first to distinguish the "people of the sons of Israel" as "them" in opposition to the Egyptian "us" (Exod 1:9–10). In typically propagandistic fashion, Pharaoh inflates the numbers and strengths of the Israelites and insists that they are conspiring with Egypt's enemies and planning to leave the land. Pharaoh's ethnic invective functions to legitimate the securing of a new source of royal labor. Once

---

### Traditions of Israelite Origins

The prophetic writings of Hosea know two origin traditions—Israelite origins in Mesopotamia according to the patriarchal accounts of Genesis (Hos 12:2–4, 12) and Israelite origins according to the exodus from Egypt in Exodus (Hos 11:1; 12:9, 13; 13:4)—but it is unclear whether they present these traditions as complementary or competing. Joshua combines both traditions: "Now therefore revere the LORD, and serve him in sincerity and in faithfulness; put away the gods that your ancestors served beyond the River [i.e., beyond the Euphrates, in Mesopotamia, from which Abraham came] and in Egypt, and serve the LORD" (Josh 24:14).

Greek literature dating from about 300 B.C.E. to the first century C.E. most frequently depicts the Israelites as originating in Egypt; examples include the works of writers such as Hecataeus of Abdera, Manetho, Diodorus Siculus, Strabo of Amaseia, Aprion, and Chaeremon (see Menachem Stern, *Greek and Latin Authors on Jews and Judaism*, vol. 1, *From Herodotus to Plutarch* [Jerusalem: Israel Academy of Sciences and Humanities, 1976]). While some of these accounts may be intentionally defamatory, not all of them are. At any rate, these accounts possibly reflect traces of a genuine origin tradition held by various Jewish groups. The alignment of these origin stories in Greek literature with hints of an Egyptian origin for the Israelites in the Hebrew Bible is itself suggestive.

he has set the machinery of ethnic differentiation into motion, it does not take long for one ethnic group to feel revulsion toward the other (1:12); revulsion soon escalates to genocidal policies (1:15–22). Noteworthy is that the Egyptian royal elite initiates ethnic differentiation as an economic strategy to aggrandize more power to itself. From the perspective of this elite, the Israelites are "Hebrews," an outsider term of opprobrium connoting foreignness, threat, and especially low socioeconomic standing. Ethnic difference here is not the result of covenants and kinship relations, as in Genesis, but of state policies.

The story of the midwives (1:15–21) shows resistance to such state policies of ethnic differentiation. The two midwives themselves are either Egyptian or Hebrew—"Hebrew midwives" can be understood either as "midwives who are Hebrews" or as "midwives to the Hebrews"—already introducing a note of ambiguity into the ethnic differentiation of the narrative. Accused of disobeying orders by allowing male babies born to Hebrew women to live, they give Pharaoh an ambiguous double response. Playing on Pharaoh's language differentiating Hebrews from Egyptians, they cleverly describe this difference in words that can be understood in two ways: either "because they [the Hebrew women] are *vigorous* and give birth before the midwife comes to them" (as in the NRSV), or "because they are [*wild*] *animals* and give birth before the midwife comes to them" (1:19). The first possibility presents an ethnic stereotype complimentary to Hebrew women and implicitly derogatory to Egyptian women. The second possibility does the reverse by presenting an ethnic stereotype derogatory to Hebrew women (they are barbarians who breed and give birth like wild animals) and implicitly complimentary to Egyptian women. The midwives cleverly allow Pharaoh to hear what he already believes (the second possibility) while at the same time allowing the oppressed Hebrews to salvage a sense of worth in the face of their devaluation by the state (the first possibility). Communication across ethnic boundaries when a power differential is involved often involves such double entendres. The state may create and

## Resistance and Survival

Marginalized groups can appropriate the derogatory labels and discourses directed against them and turn them into a source of solidarity and resistance against the dominating group. Michel Foucault calls this process "reverse discourse," using the example of the term "homosexual," a negative term that was appropriated by the gay community as a means of self-organization and awareness (Michel Foucault, *The History of Sexuality*, vol. 1, *An Introduction*, trans. Robert Hurley [New York: Vintage, 1980]). More recently, the word "queer" has been appropriated in a similar fashion. Henry Gates notes the same process in the appropriation of the racial slur "nigger" as "nigga" by some African Americans, a process he calls "Signifyin(g)" (Henry Louis Gates Jr., *The Signifying Monkey: A Theory of African-American Literary Criticism* [New York: Oxford University Press, 1988]).

use ethnic differences to divide and rule, but oppressed or undervalued groups can also employ them to resist and survive.

Most of the Hebrew Bible maintains the status of the Egyptians as threatening ethnic "others" over against Israel. Examples include the prophetic oracles condemning the Egyptians (Isa 19; Jer 46; Ezek 29–32). But a reversal occurs in Isa 19. The chapter begins with the usual invectives and condemnations: God brings judgment upon Egypt in the form of military defeat and ecological disaster, and sarcastically demotes the vaunted wisdom of the Egyptians. But the tone of the chapter changes drastically in verse 18. Suddenly, the prophetic text mentions Egyptian cities that swear allegiance to the god of the Israelites and of places of worship to the god of the Israelites within Egypt. God is even pictured as healing Egypt. The chapter ends with a remarkable universalistic vision of the Egyptians and Assyrians worshiping together with the Israelites and being blessed by God: "Blessed be Egypt my people, and Assyria the work of my hands, and Israel my heritage" (Isa 19:25). That God should call the Egyptians "my people" is astounding compared to God's concern in Exodus and elsewhere to differentiate the Israelites as his people from the Egyptians. The biblical boundary of exclusion and inclusion between Israelites and Egyptians is not stable but shifts, marking Israel's ethnic identity as one of ambiguous coexistence with Egypt.

*Canaanites*

The Hebrew Bible portrays Canaanites, a term describing peoples indigenous to the Cisjordan, as stereotypical ethnic outsiders. They appear in a negative light from the beginning due to the actions of their ancestor in Gen 9. They threaten Israelite identity, especially in the stories in the books of Joshua and Judges where the Israelites take possession of Canaanite territory, and various laws scattered through the Pentateuch severely censure them. The Hebrew Bible often presents the Canaanites as one people among several others inhabiting the Cisjordan: "the country of the Canaanites, the

### Punishing *Canaan* in Genesis 9?

After the flood, Ham, one of Noah's sons, sees Noah lying naked in a drunken stupor; he informs his brothers, who carefully cover their father without looking at his nakedness. When Noah awakes, he curses Ham's son, Canaan, to a position of slavery (vv. 20–27). It is puzzling that Canaan is condemned for his father's indiscretion; perhaps an earlier story in which Ham was cursed has been edited to direct attention to Canaan, since his descendants, the Canaanites, are so strongly disavowed later in the Bible.

If Ham was originally the object of Noah's curse, not only his Canaanite descendants (10:6, 15–19) would be cursed but also Ham's other descendants, the Egyptians (10:13–14) and the Philistines (10:14), thus prefiguring the negative depiction of Canaanites, Egyptians, and Philistines vis-à-vis Israelites in the Hebrew Bible.

Hittites, the Amorites, the Perizzites, the Hivites, and the Jebusites" (Exod 3:8; see also Gen 15:19; Exod 13:15; Deut 7:1; Josh 3:10; and Judg 3:5). However, in passages such as Judg 1:1–10, the Canaanites begin to stand for all the nations whom the Israelites are to dispossess, as is also the case in later passages such as Neh 9:24.

Legal passages in the Hebrew Bible construct a boundary between Israelites and Canaanites and then proceed to enforce it in a variety of ways. Exodus 23:23–33 mandates the expulsion of Canaanites for religious reasons: "They shall not live in your land, or they will make you sin against me; for if you worship their gods, it will surely be a snare to you" (23:33). Therefore, Canaanite religious sites are also to be destroyed: "You shall utterly demolish them and break their pillars in pieces" (23:24; see also Num 33:51–56). Exodus 34:11–16 also mandates the destruction of Canaanite altars, pillars, and sacred poles but says nothing about expulsion. Instead, this passage prohibits intermarriage and covenants with the Canaanites, obviously presupposing that Canaanites and Israelites continue to live in close enough proximity for social interactions between them.

Deuteronomy 7:1–5 and 20:16–18 also prohibit intermarriage with Canaanites and command the destruction of their religious objects. But here the Israelites are not just to shun the Canaanites and prevent them from practicing their religion (as in Exod 34), or expel them (as in Exod 23 and Num 33), but they are to *annihilate* them: "You must utterly destroy them" (Deut 7:2). "You must not let anything that breathes remain alive. You shall annihilate them" (20:16–17). These texts mandate a holy war of extermination against Canaanites because of the threat they pose to Israelite identity.

These divine commands for genocide are problematic, to say the least. They would be troubling enough if they were confined only to a far distant

## "Utterly Destroying" the Canaanites

The Hebrew verb used for the annihilation of Canaanite tribes in Deut 7:2 and 20:17 is *kharam*, often translated as "utterly destroy." The objects of destruction are called **herem** (*kherem*), often translated as "devoted thing" or "ban"; it is under the latter term that information on the subject can usually be found in Bible dictionaries. *Kharam* connotes being set apart for the divine, either in the sense of being consecrated for cultic use, or, more usually, of being cursed for destruction. *Herem* can include material objects, livestock, men, women, and children.

In Deuteronomy, God commands the utter destruction of the inhabitants of Cisjordan by the invading Israelites; such destruction characterizes the stories of military conquest in the book of Joshua. The notion also appears later, most vividly in the story of King Saul's military campaign against the Amalekites in 1 Sam 15, where God commands Saul, "Now go and attack Amalek, and utterly destroy all that they have; do not spare them, but kill both man and woman, child and infant, ox and sheep, camel and donkey" (15:3). Such holy wars of genocide were not unique to the Israelites but were pursued by other peoples of the ancient Near East.

past. However, genocidal attempts by peoples or ethnic groups against others are all too familiar in the contemporary world. Sometimes perpetrators of ethnic violence use these particular biblical directives against the Canaanites to legitimize their aggression against those whose religious practices and beliefs they see as wrong. For example, the indigenous inhabitants or first nations of the Americas experienced such aggression at the hands of the European colonizers. Some Christian colonists saw their migration to the Americas as replicating the exodus of the Israelites to a new promised land and so tended to see the indigenous peoples they encountered as Canaanites—alien peoples with dangerous religious practices that were to be dispossessed or even exterminated. A good example is Robert Gray's widely circulated sermon tract, *A Good Speed to Virginia* (1609), which likens the English colonists to Israelites who will "drive out the Canaanites" (Josh 17:18). Ethnic solidarity defined over against other peoples has this ugly side.

On the other hand, historical evidence indicates that the genocidal directives of the Hebrew Bible are largely ethnic wish-fulfillments that were rarely carried out in practice. Much of the biblical narrative in fact *does not* depict the Israelites as actively seeking to exterminate other peoples. Although the book of Joshua attempts to show the conquest of Canaan proceeding via the annihilation of its inhabitants, this portrayal is contradicted by the summary of the conquest in Judg 1, which indicates that the Canaanites persisted in the land: "When Israel grew strong, they put the Canaanites to forced labor, but did not in fact drive them out" (Judg 1:28).

## First Nations of the Americas and Canaanites

Robert Allen Warrior, a member of the Osage nation, recognizes the negative legacy of the Puritan preachers who referred to Native Americans as Canaanites, thus justifying coercive conversion of them to Christianity, the appropriation of their lands, and their assimilation or annihilation.

Turning the negative identification of the conquerors on its head, Warrior decides to identify with the Canaanites and to read the biblical narrative of the conquest of the land divinely promised to the Israelites with "Canaanite eyes":

> The Canaanites should be at the center of Christian theological reflection and political action. The conquest stories, with all their violence and injustice, must be taken seriously by those who believe in the god of the Old Testament. Commentaries and critical works rarely mention these texts. When they do, they express little concern for the status of the indigenes and their rights as human beings and nations. The same blindness is evident in theologies that use the Exodus motif as their basis for political action. The leading into the land becomes just one more redemptive movement rather than a violation of innocent peoples' rights to land and self-determination.

Robert Allen Warrior, "A Native American Perspective: Canaanites, Cowboys, and Indians," in *Voices from the Margin: Interpreting the Bible in the Third World*, ed. R. S. Sugirtharajah (Maryknoll, NY: Orbis Books, 1991), 293.

King Saul is the only Israelite king the Hebrew Bible portrays as attempting to annihilate entire populations (the Amalekites in 1 Sam 15, and Nob, the city of priests, in 1 Sam 22). King David, in fact, avenges the Gibeonites, another people whom Saul had tried to exterminate, by allowing them to impale seven sons of Saul (2 Sam 21:1–14). The usual practice in the ancient world, and in the Hebrew Bible, was the subjugation of other peoples, not their annihilation (e.g., 1 Kgs 9:20–21).

Why does the Hebrew Bible express so much anxiety over the "Canaanite threat"? Perhaps it is because Israelites and Canaanites enjoyed close contacts and overlapping cultures and populations, thus confusing ethnic boundaries. Especially telling is that a supposedly Canaanite religious practice such as setting up a stone pillar—proscribed in Deut 16:22—is done without censure by Jacob (Gen 35:14) and Moses (Exod 24:4). Even in the passages mandating the extermination of the Canaanites, it is recognized that Israelites live with or among Canaanites. The laws against intermarriage with Canaanites (as in Deut 7:3–4), for example, would not be necessary if the Canaanites had actually been utterly destroyed. The books of Joshua (see 15:63; 16:10; and 17:12–13) and Judges (see 1:21, 27–36 and 3:1–6) picture the Canaanites and Israelites living in close proximity. Since near neighbors threaten to blur the boundaries of ethnic identification, it is understandable that Israelite narratives and laws would preserve attempts to neutralize this threat. No wonder the Hebrew Bible expends so much effort rejecting Canaanites so as to distinguish a unique Israelite ethnic identity.

The Hebrew Bible does not consistently portray the Canaanites in a negative light. The story of Rahab (Josh 2, 6), for example, contains a more positive picture, illustrating that ethnic boundaries can be undermined by extenuating circumstances. Rahab is a woman, and a prostitute at that. It seems that the crossing of ethnic boundaries takes place on the margins, among people—such as this unattached yet sexually active woman—who live on the edges of proper society. Furthermore, in a patriarchal society (and one in which a major ethnic marker—circumcision—is restricted to males), women can more easily cross ethnic boundaries.

### enjoyed close contacts

Archaeologists have discovered that the material culture of the early Iron Age villages in the highlands of the Cisjordan where the Israelites first emerged exhibits strong continuity with the Canaanite culture of the Late Bronze Age, especially in pottery. This suggests that Israelites shared a common culture with Canaanites and that most early Israelites were probably originally Canaanites who had adapted to the specific environmental demands of the highlands. Most scholars now recognize innovations such as the four-room courtyard house or the collar-rimmed storage jar as having existed before the Israelites emerged and as appearing also in non-Israelite areas and thus not useful as indicators of a unique Israelite ethnicity.

Joshua 2 portrays Rahab as a Canaanite woman running a brothel in Jericho. Surprisingly, she hides Israelites, who have come to spy out Jericho's defenses, from the authorities. Furthermore, she makes an astonishing <u>confession of faith</u> in the god of the Israelites and bargains for the life of her family. The mission of the Israelite spies would have failed without her intervention. Consequently, the Israelites spare her and her family when they attack Jericho, and her lineage lived among the Israelite people from that time on (Josh 6:22–25). Not only does Rahab guarantee the success of the Israelite mission against Jericho, but also the acceptance of her family among the Israelite people contravenes the negative treatment mandated for the Canaanites elsewhere. The story shows ethnic identity to be contingent and situational, invoked when necessary to assert a particular identity but subverted by the vagaries of social life.

## confession of faith

Rahab's confession that YHWH, the god of the Israelites, is "God in heaven above and on earth below" is exactly replicated only twice in the Hebrew Bible: by Moses in Deut 4:39 and by Solomon in 1 Kgs 8:23. Her religious identification with the god of the Israelites is unusual in that it crosses the boundaries between different peoples, each of whom was believed in the ancient world to have its own deity. While Rahab is not mentioned in the Hebrew Bible outside of the book of Joshua, a woman named Rahab appears as an ancestor of King David in the Christian genealogy of Jesus in Matt 1:5. The Jewish exegetical tradition also elaborated on the character Rahab, portraying her as a pious convert to the religion of the Israelites and, according to *Sifré to Numbers* 78, as the ancestor of eight Israelite priests and prophets.

## Tamar

Another more positive depiction of a Canaanite, also a woman, may appear in Gen 38. In this chapter, Judah, the **eponymous ancestor** of the most important Israelite tribe, not only fraternizes with Canaanites (his friend is Hirah the Adullamite) but also marries a Canaanite woman (the daughter of Shua the Canaanite). Given this context, it is likely that Tamar, chosen by Judah as the wife for his son, is also Canaanite, although the text does not explicitly mention her ethnicity. According to the biblical story, Tamar's first two husbands die and she is promised to Judah's youngest son. When it becomes clear that Judah does not intend to honor his promise, Tamar takes matters into her own hands: posing as a prostitute, she is impregnated by Judah himself. The narrative portrays Judah as condemning her to death for prostitution when he finds out that she is pregnant; she exposes his double standard by identifying him as the "john" who impregnated her. The tables are turned. The supposedly wicked outsider Canaanite is more right than the insider Israelite, as Judah freely admits (Gen 38:26). The children that Tamar bears to her father-in-law become legitimate descendants in the tribe of Judah, and one of them becomes the direct ancestor of King David (Ruth 4:18–22). The action of the Canaanite outsider has actually secured the future of Judah's insider lineage.

*Philistines*

In the main, the Hebrew Bible portrays the Philistines as incontrovertibly different from the Israelites. It especially contrasts the circumcised Israelites with the uncircumcised Philistines and presents them as enemy "others" over against which Israelite identity needs to be asserted. But when the Philistines first appear in Genesis, they seem relatively benign. Both Abraham and Isaac live for a time in Gerar, ruled by King Abimelech, a Philistine (Gen 26:1, 8). In spite of conflicts with Abimelech over the marital status of their wives, and over wells and grazing grounds, they eventually resolve these conflicts through negotiation and treaties or covenants (Gen 20; 21:22–34; 26:1–33). In fact, the biblical story pictures King Abimelech as more righteous than the deceitful patriarch. The patriarchs anxiously pass their wives off as their sisters in order to save their own skins (12:10–16; 20:1–18; 26:6–11), while Abimelech is respectful of the god of Abraham and Isaac, recognizes the special status of the Israelite ancestors, and makes covenants with them (21:22–32; 26:26–31).

This benign portrayal changes radically in the book of Judges, a text that clearly portrays the Philistines as threatening outsiders who oppress the Israelites. Philistine oppression provides the context for the story of the Israelite ethnic hero Samson, who indiscriminately attacks and kills numerous Philistines (14:19; 15:8, 14–16), burns their grain, olive trees, and vineyards (15:4–5), breaches the security of their cities by making off with the city gate of Gaza (16:1–3), and in a final <u>suicidal effort</u> pulls down the religious and symbolic center of the Philistine world, their temple, upon them (16:23–30). (See the analysis of Samson as a hypermasculine figure in chapter 5.)

---

### suicidal effort

Samson is arguably the original suicide bomber. Political philosopher Shadia Drury writes:

> There is an uncanny resemblance between Samson's attack on the temple of the Philistines as described in the Bible (Judges 16:26–31) and the terrorist attack on the World Trade Center in New York on September 11, 2001. The Bible tells us that on a busy holiday when about three thousand Philistines were celebrating in the temple, Samson decided to use his superhuman strength to push away the pillars that held up the temple so that the whole edifice came crumbling down, crushing him and hundreds of innocent people in the rubble.
>
> On September 11, 2001, Mohamed Atta hijacked a plane and crashed it into one of the towers of the World Trade Center. Atta's crime was more technologically sophisticated, but morally speaking the two crimes were identical. In both cases innocent victims were buried alive in the rubble—innocent people met a gruesome death that they could not have anticipated or deserved. It is difficult not to conclude that Samson was as much of a terrorist as Atta. Yet we regard Atta as a criminal—the incarnation of evil—but we go along with the Bible in portraying Samson as a hero. Is there any difference between them that would justify such radically different ascriptions?
>
> It may be argued that Samson was merely an instrument of God's will. And God wished to punish the Philistines for their idolatry and their iniquity. They deserved what they got. Besides, Samson sacrificed his own life in order to carry out the justice of God. But if we accept this excuse for Samson, we must also accept it for Atta.

Shadia B. Drury, *Terror and Civilization: Christianity, Politics, and the Western Psyche* (New York: Palgrave Macmillan, 2004), 148–49.

At the same time, however, the text portrays Samson as blurring the ethnic boundary between Israelites and Philistines: he marries Philistine women and consorts with Delilah, likely a Philistine prostitute (14:1–4; 16:1, 4). In the end, he does not succeed in delivering the Israelites from Philistine oppression at all. Judges portrays Samson as an ineffectual hero in order to illustrate the shortcomings of a purely charismatically led and politically unorganized ethnicity (the Israelites) against a more powerful competitor (the Philistines). The message is that Israelite ethnicity must be organized by a central state in order to be effective against threats such as the Philistines.

Thus, in 1 Samuel, the Philistine threat forms the backdrop of the organization of Israel's first monarchy (1 Sam 4–8). Israel's first king, Saul, who is resolutely anti-Philistine, dies in defeat on the battlefield against the Philistines (1 Sam 31). The biblical story continues by portraying Saul's successor, King David, as finally turning the tide against the Philistines; however, at the same time David has suspicious Philistine connections. Before becoming king, David worked as the bodyguard of King Achish of Gath and was given the Philistine town of Ziklag as a residence (1 Sam 27). When David becomes king, he retains a private army of Gittites, according to 2 Sam 15:18–22 and 18:2 (the name "Gittite" refers to persons who come from the Philistine city of Gath) and the Israelite ark temporarily rests in the house of a Gittite on its way to Jerusalem (2 Sam 6:10–11). (See the analysis of David's Philistine connections in chapter 9.) The biblical text thus presents the ethnic boundary between David and the Philistines, as previously with Samson, as ambiguous and porous. Like Moses, a hybrid leader exhibiting both Israelite and Egyptian identity (e.g., Exod 2:19; chapters 13–14), Samson and David straddle the boundary between Israelite and Philistine.

At the same time, the Hebrew Bible ridicules the Philistines, focusing especially on debunking their warrior masculinity and deriding their uncircumcised status. David achieves victory as a lightly armed and untrained youth against the huge, heavily armed, and armored professional Philistine warrior and hero Goliath (1 Sam 17). He follows up this feat by procuring a hundred Philistine foreskins as a marriage present in order to become King Saul's son-in-law (1 Sam 18). Earlier, when the Philistines capture the main religious artifact of the Israelites, the ark (1 Sam 4–6), the image of their god Dagon keeps falling over in the presence of the ark no matter how much it is propped up (1 Sam 5:1–5), and they are afflicted with "tumors" (perhaps <u>hemorrhoids</u>; 1 Sam 5:6–12). Ethnic groups characteristically use humor and mockery of this sort to construct the boundary between themselves and others. Other biblical examples include the story of the Israelite Ehud and the Moabite king Eglon in Judg 3, while modern examples include jokes about ethnic groups, usually now considered offensive.

### hemorrhoids

The Hebrew word *ofelim* in 1 Sam 5:6–12 means "swellings" or "mounds," likely tumors of some sort. The cognate Arabic word refers to tumors or swellings in the anus, which seems to be the way the Masoretic editors of the Hebrew Bible understood the word: a note in the margin of the Hebrew text indicates that the Masoretic scribes thought the word should be pronounced *tehorim*, which means "hemorrhoids." (For a humorous take on the Philistines and their hemorrhoids, see Christopher Fisher's "The Fellowship of the Golden Emerod," from the April 2006 issue of *The Wittenburg Door* and accessible online at http://archives.witten burgdoor.com/archives/emerods.html.)

*Edomites*

The Hebrew Bible's portrait of the Edomites contains a radical reversal in ethnic sentiments. Genesis depicts the Edomites as a people descended from Isaac's firstborn son, Esau. When Esau loses his privileges as the eldest brother and heir to his younger brother Jacob (Gen 25:29–34; chapter 27), readers are tempted to associate positive characteristics with Jacob and negative ones with Esau in order to justify the choice of Jacob as heir. However, the text portrays both Esau and Jacob in a morally questionable light: Esau seems to value his belly over his birthright (25:29–34), and Jacob is a deceitful trickster (27:1–46; 30:25–43). Furthermore, Jacob actually blesses both Jacob and Esau in similar terms (Gen 27:28–29, 39–40), although this similarity is obscured by some English translations that seem to want to portray Jacob and Esau as polar opposites.

Other texts in Genesis and Deuteronomy give positive evaluations of Esau and his descendants, the Edomites. When Esau and Jacob meet after being estranged for many years, Esau receives Jacob back with open arms (Gen 34:4). Genesis 36 ends the Jacob saga with an extensive genealogy not of the Israelites but of the Edomites, who become an extensive people with kings long before the Israelites. Deuteronomy continues this generally positive portrayal by prohibiting the Israelites from hating their brothers, the

### English translations

The NRSV translation of Gen 27:39 ("See, away from the fatness of the earth shall your home be, and away from the dew of heaven on high") makes the first part of Isaac's blessing of Esau negative, whereas the JPS translation of the same verse ("See, your abode shall enjoy the fat of the earth and the dew of heaven above") makes it positive and parallel to the first part of Isaac's blessing of Jacob in 27:28. The Hebrew text here is ambiguous, and therefore both translations are possible. However, the NRSV emphasizes a more negative portrayal of Esau by translating Isaac's blessing of him as a curse.

Edomites (Deut 23:7), and from dispossessing them when the Israelites inherit the promised land (2:5, 12, 22).

However, the prophetic literature of the Hebrew Bible transforms the Edomites into the archetypal enemies of the Israelites, expressed most harshly by God's declaration in Mal 1:2–3: "I have loved Jacob but I have hated Esau." Jeremiah 49:7–22; Ezek 25:12–14; and Obadiah present other examples of prophetic denunciations of Edom. Notably, these prophetic texts all address the aftermath of the disastrous destruction of Jerusalem and the Judean state by the Babylonian Empire in 587/586 B.C.E. The Hebrew Bible accuses the Edomites not only of standing by and watching the demise of their near neighbors and relatives but also of gloating over the destruction and taking advantage of it by occupying Judah's southern territories (see Ezek 35). The prophetic book of Obadiah most explicitly expresses the sense of sibling betrayal that these actions engendered (see especially vv. 10–14).

Near neighbors prove problematic in the construction and maintenance of ethnic identities. The Hebrew Bible portrays Edomites and Israelites as "brothers" as long as they remain in separate territories (as in Genesis) or as long as Israelites dominate Edom (as they largely did under King David and his successors, the kings of Judah; see 2 Sam 8:13–14 and 2 Kgs 14:7). But when the Hebrew Bible describes the Edomites attempting to shake off the yoke of the Israelites (2 Kgs 8:20–22) and eventually becoming independent and taking advantage of the defeat and exile of their Israelite "brothers," the ethnic boundary between the two groups becomes one not of affiliation but of <u>exclusionary hatred</u>. Again, clearly ethnic identity and ethnic sentiments vary and can shift radically with changes in circumstance and context.

*Moabites*

The Hebrew Bible narrates Israelite stories and so generally does not give expression to the subjective impressions and feelings of the other peoples who are mentioned in relation to the Israelites. One wonders what the Egyptians, Canaanites, Philistines, Edomites, and other peoples might have said had they been given a voice to tell the stories from their perspective. While it is usually impossible to reconstruct the ethnic voices of these "others," sometimes documents recovered from the ancient Near East can help to give these peoples their say. One example is a Moabite inscription dating to the ninth century B.C.E., which gives access to Moabite constructions of ethnicity (see fig. 7.2).

Before examining this inscription, note that the Hebrew Bible generally portrays the Moabites in negative terms. Although distant relatives of the Israelites, they are tainted by their sexually taboo origins in the incestuous union of Abraham's nephew Lot with his daughters after the destruction of Sodom and Gemorrah (Gen 19:30–38). Deuteronomy mandates that the Moabites are to be perpetually excluded from the assembly of Israel (Deut 23:3). Judges details how the Israelite hero Ehud managed to assassinate the Moabite king Eglon, in a story replete with scatological ethnic humor that associates the Moabites with human excrement (Judg 3:12–30). Although the book of Ruth presents a Moabite as part of King David's ancestry (4:22), elsewhere David subdues the Moabites and makes them vassals (2 Sam 8:2). The Hebrew Bible describes King Jehoram of the northern kingdom of Israel mounting an expedition against the Moabites to subdue them after they have rebelled (2 Kgs 3). According to the story, the Israelites experience victory on this military campaign until King Mesha of Moab sacrifices his firstborn son; then "a great wrath came upon Israel, so they withdrew from him and returned to their own land" (2 Kgs 3:27).

The Moabite inscription concerns this same time period; in fact, it was commissioned by King Mesha on the occasion of the construction of a new temple for the Moabite god Chemosh (or Kemosh). The inscription displays a striking similarity to the Hebrew Bible's Israelite ideology. Changing the name "Moab" in the inscription to "Israel" and the name of "Chemosh" to "YHWH" would yield a text not out of place in the Hebrew Bible. Just as the Israelites in the Hebrew Bible attribute their defeats and victories to YHWH, so also the Moabite king in this inscription attributes Israelite oppression of the Moabites and Israelite gains in Moabite territory to the anger of his god

## Child Sacrifice

The Hebrew Bible mentions child sacrifice, usually condemning it. Often describing it as making one's child "pass through the fire," the Hebrew Bible attributes child sacrifice to the Canaanites (Deut 12:31) and associates it frequently with Canaanite deities such as Molech or Baal (e.g., Lev 18:21; 20:2–5; Jer 19:5–6). However, in the Hebrew Bible the Israelites also practice child sacrifice. The Israelite ancestor Abraham does not appear to be surprised by God's request that he sacrifice his son, although the actual sacrifice is averted at the last minute (Gen 22). Israelites described as actually sacrificing their children include the hero Jephthah (Judg 11:29–40), Hiel, the rebuilder of Jericho (1 Kgs 16:34; see also Josh 6:26), and Kings Ahaz (2 Kgs 16:3) and Manasseh (2 Kgs 21:6). In fact, the Hebrew Bible describes a particular site for human sacrifice in Jerusalem itself, called Topheth (e.g., 2 Kgs 23:10). The biblical text illustrates belief in the efficacious power of child sacrifice in 2 Kgs 3:27, where Moabite child sacrifice causes the victorious Israelite forces to withdraw.

**Fig. 7.2: The Mesha Inscription**

Chemosh, and Moabite victories over Israel to the favor of Chemosh. Just like an Israelite king, King Mesha is pictured as following the orders of his god— "And Chemosh said to me, 'Go, take Nebo from Israel'"—and as conducting war as a religious ritual (a holy war) by hauling the plunder into the temple of Chemosh and by slaughtering all the Israelites as a sacrifice to Chemosh.

This inscription presents Moabite ethnic identity in categories virtually identical to some of those used by the Hebrew Bible to construct Israelite identity. The subjective nature of ethnicity comes through here: Israelites and Moabites seem to share much the same culture and ideology but nonetheless see themselves as radically different ethnicities. Like the Moabites,

## The Inscription Commissioned by King Mesha of Moab

Translations appear in various collections of ancient Near Eastern texts.

I am Mesha, the son of Kemosh[-yatti], the king of Moab, the Dibonite. My father was king over Moab for thirty years, and I was king after my father.

And I made this high-place for Kemosh in Qarcho . . . because he has delivered me from all kings, and because he has made me look down on all my enemies.

Omri was the king of Israel, and he oppressed Moab for many days, for Kemosh was angry with his land. And his son succeeded him, and he said—he too—I will oppress Moab! In my days did he say [so], but I looked down on him and on his house, and Israel has gone to ruin, yes, it has gone to ruin for ever!

And Omri had taken possession of the whole la[n]d of Medeba, and he lived there [in] his days and half the days of his son, forty years, but Kemosh [resto]red it in my days. And I built Baal Meon, and I made in it a water reservoir, and I built Qiryaten.

And the men of Gad lived in the land of Atarot from ancient times, and the king of Israel built Atarot for himself, and I fought against the city and captured it, and I killed all the people [from] the city as a sacrifice for Kemosh and for Moab, and I brought back the fire-hearth of his uncle from there, and I hauled it before the face of Kemosh in Qeriot, and I made the men of Sharon live there, as well as the men of Maharit.

And Kemosh said to me: Go, take Nebo from Israel. And I went in the night and I fought against it from the break of dawn until noon, and I took it and I killed [its] whole population, seven thousand male citizens and aliens, and female citizens and aliens, and servant girls; for I had put it to the ban for Ashtar Kemosh. And from there I took th[e ves]sels of YHWH, and I hauled them before the face of Kemosh.

Excerpt from Klaas A. D. Smelik, *Writings from Ancient Israel*, trans. G. I. Davies (Louisville, KY: Westminster John Knox Press, 1991), 33.

the other peoples whom the Hebrew Bible mentions also had their own ethnic narratives, through which they validated certain cultural practices and boundaries as definitive of their group. It is all too easy to simply assume that the picture that the Hebrew Bible paints of these peoples from an Israelite perspective is accurate; one needs to remember that in the Hebrew Bible these peoples do not have their own voice.

## The Problem of the "Inside-Outsider"

The examination of Egyptians, Canaanites, Philistines, Edomites, and Moabites in this chapter has focused primarily on how the Hebrew Bible presents these peoples as a contrast to Israelite identity. This examination revealed that the ethnic boundary between Israelites and these other peoples is far more ambiguous, permeable, and unstable than one might first imagine. Nonetheless, the Hebrew Bible portrays these "others," even if often near neighbors, as definitely outside of where the Israelites generally live as the dominant group. Yet "others" or "outsiders" can also be located *within* the place where the Israelites live. The Hebrew Bible preserves the story of how the Egyptian Pharaoh defined the Israelites themselves as outsiders within Egyptian society. As that story illustrates, the dominant ethnic group considers such "inside-outsiders" as dangerous threats. This section will examine how the Hebrew Bible approaches the problem of the inside-outsider in relation to Israelite ethnicity.

The law codes of the Pentateuch frequently refer to a class of persons known as "aliens" or "**resident aliens**" (called "sojourners" or "strangers" in some translations), often in a binary pairing with native Israelites—for example, "There shall be one law for the native and for the alien who resides among you" (Exod 12:49). The Hebrew word *ger*, translated as "alien," refers to a long-term resident within Israelite territory who is, however, not part of the local Israelite kinship and landownership system and therefore is likely dependent to some degree on an Israelite patron for protection and support. Resident aliens could include entire households and were usually of foreign origin, but they may have lived within Israelite society for generations. Their status contrasted with the Israelite "native," a translation of the Hebrew *ezrakh* (sometimes translated as "citizen"), referring to those rooted in the local community via kinship and landownership. Resident aliens pose a problem for ethnic boundaries since they are located on the inside instead of the outside; the biblical law codes propose a variety of strategies to deal with this contradiction.

One strategy integrates resident aliens into the cultural and religious practices and norms of the Israelite natives, while still maintaining a distinction between the two groups. This option appears in laws that include resident aliens along with natives in celebrations of religious festivals (Exod 12:19, 48–49; Lev 16:29; Num 9:14; Deut 16:11, 14) and in various rituals of sacrifice, offering, and purification (Lev 17:8; 22:18–19; Num 15; 19:10; Deut 26:11). In some of these instances, resident aliens seem to have the option of

---

### "Inside-Outsiders" as Dangerous Threats

A modern example of the fear of the "inside-outsider" is anti-immigrant sentiment. Anti-immigrant rhetoric depends on a contrast between "us" and "them" and typically argues that immigrants refuse to assimilate to the dominant culture and threaten to overwhelm and replace the way of life of the native citizens. Such sentiment against the inside-outsider becomes more prevalent in times of crises; during World War II, descendants of German and Japanese immigrants in Canada and the United States were accused of disloyalty, and the Japanese were interned in camps. Recent anti-immigrant sentiment in the United States is especially directed at Hispanics. And, since the terrorist attacks of September 11, 2001, Muslims are often portrayed as dangerous inside-outsiders within western societies.

freely participating in these Israelite religious acts, and only Exod 12 demands that they be circumcised if they wish to participate; in other instances, they participate as part of their dependency on an Israelite patron. Resident aliens must also observe certain dietary and sexual taboos (Lev 17:10–16; 18:26), keep the Sabbath (Deut 5:14), and avoid child sacrifice (Lev 20:2). In the judicial sphere, they have access to equal justice (Deut 1:16) and cities of refuge (Josh 20:9). In fact, Deuteronomy admonishes the Israelites to love the alien, remembering that they once experienced the vulnerability of being aliens in the land of Egypt (Deut 10:19). These stipulations all integrate resident aliens sufficiently into Israelite life so that Israelite norms are not disrupted, but they still preserve the distinction between resident aliens and Israelites.

Another strategy absorbs or assimilates resident aliens completely into Israelite society by providing them with a patrimonial share of Israelite land (which probably also involved becoming part of an Israelite genealogy). This option does not appear in any of the legal material in the Pentateuch but forms part of the idealized plan for the restoration of the temple and the Israelite community in Ezek 40–48. After outlining a new allotment of territory to the Israelite tribes in chapter 47, the text concludes:

> So you shall divide this land among you according to the tribes of Israel. You shall allot it as an inheritance for yourselves and for the aliens who reside among you and have begotten children among you. They shall be to you as citizens of Israel; with you they shall be allotted an inheritance among the tribes of Israel. In whatever tribe aliens reside, there you shall assign them their inheritance, says the Lord God. (Ezek 47:21–23)

This process, while radicalizing the equal treatment of aliens and natives to the extent that the difference between them will virtually disappear, is actually similar to the process, according to the Hebrew Bible, by which the various Israelite tribes, early in their formation, absorbed various groups. For example, Caleb, a Kenizzite (one of the Canaanite tribes according to Gen 15:19 but an Edomite group according to Gen 36:11, 15 and 1 Chron 1:36), is given Hebron within the tribe of Judah as an inheritance (Josh 14:13–14; 15:13). In 1 Sam 30:29, the towns of the non-Israelite Jerahmeelites and

---

### keep the Sabbath

The Hebrew Bible mentions Sabbath observance as a distinct practice of the Israelites and thus as a distinguishing ethnic characteristic. Exodus 20:8–11 and Deut 5:12–15 mandate abstinence from work on the seventh day of the week as the main form of Sabbath observance. The penalty for noncompliance is death (Exod 31:14; 35:2; Num 15:32–36), but the Hebrew Bible nonetheless indicates problems with Israelite compliance (e.g., Jer 17:19–23; Neh 13:15–18). In Isa 56:2–8, faithful Sabbath observance enables even eunuchs and foreigners, usually excluded from the Israelite community, to gain access.

Kenites are included as locations of the "elders of Judah." And Hepher, Tirzah, and Shechem, listed as clans within the Israelite tribe of Manasseh (Josh 17:2–3), are elsewhere Canaanite cities (Josh 12:17, 24; Gen 34). More generally, the Israelites preserved a tradition that they were not all pure descendants of Jacob but rather a mixed group (Exod 12:38; Num 11:4).

A third strategy marginalizes the resident alien from participation in Israelite life by clearly differentiating the behavior expected of the Israelite from that expected of the resident alien. In this way the ethnic boundary is kept intact. Thus, Lev 23:42 requires only the native Israelite to live in booths during the festival of Sukkot. Deuteronomy 14:21 allows the resident alien to eat carrion while such meat is taboo for native Israelites (this directly contradicts Lev 17:15–16). Deuteronomy 28:43–44 reflects the fear that Israelites could become dependent on the aliens residing among them.

In these various strategies, resident aliens from particular ethnic groups could be treated differently, as the following text from Deuteronomy indicates:

> No Ammonite or Moabite shall be admitted to the assembly of the LORD. Even to the tenth generation, none of their descendants shall be admitted to the assembly of the LORD. . . . You shall never promote their welfare or their prosperity as long as you live. You shall not abhor any of the Edomites, for they are your kin. You shall not abhor any of the Egyptians, because you were an alien residing in their land. The children of the third generation that are born to them may be admitted to the assembly of the LORD. (Deut 23:3, 6–8)

One final strategy requires the expulsion of the resident alien. The books of Ezra and Nehemiah powerfully present this option but use somewhat different terminology. Instead of the binary differentiation of resident alien from native Israelite, they portray oppositions such as the following:

| | | | |
|---|---|---|---|
| People of Israel | vs. | Peoples of the lands | Ezra 9:1 |
| Holy seed | vs. | Peoples of the lands | Ezra 9:2 |
| Those of Israelite descent | vs. | Foreigners | Neh 9:2 |
| Israel | vs. | Those of foreign descent (literally, "mixture") | Neh 13:3 |

Ezra and Nehemiah, considered as one book in the Hebrew tradition, narrate the story of colonists in the Persian Empire who, by the authority of Persian imperial decree (2 Chron 36:23; Ezra 1:2–4), settled in the Persian province of Yehud (Judah), centered around the city of Jerusalem. These colonists claimed to be the descendants of Israelites taken captive and exiled to Babylon several generations earlier; thus, they called their community "the exiles" (*Golah* in Hebrew; see, for example, Ezra 1:11; 2:1) or "the assembly of the exiles" (Ezra 10:8).

This community settled a land that was not empty but occupied by peoples whom these books refer to as "peoples of the lands." Ezra-Nehemiah does not specify who exactly these peoples of the lands were. However, since not all the Israelites were exiled or killed in the earlier Babylonian attacks against Judah and Jerusalem, it is likely that the peoples of the lands included descendants of these Israelite survivors. Nonetheless, the text portrays these peoples of the lands as a threat. Not only do they resist the various projects of the community of the exiles (e.g., Ezra 4), but they are also characterized as unclean and practicing abominations (Ezra 9:11). In fact, Ezra explicitly compares the peoples of the lands to "the Canaanites, the Hittites, the Perizzites, the Jebusites, the Ammonites, the Moabites, the Egyptians, and the Amorites" (Ezra 9:1), all foreign peoples listed in the Pentateuch, from whom the Israelites were to distinguish themselves. However, the text in Ezra intensifies the distinction to such an extent that even outsider women married to Israelite men, and their children, are <u>excluded and expelled</u>:

> We have broken faith with our God and have married foreign women from the peoples of the land, but even now there is hope for Israel in spite of this. So now let us make a covenant with our God to send away all these wives and their children, according to the counsel of my lord and of those who tremble at the commandment of our God; and let it be done according to the law. (Ezra 10:2–3)

Ezra-Nehemiah justifies the innovative expulsion of foreign wives and their children through a creative interpretation of several texts from the law codes of the Pentateuch. Ezra's prayer in Ezra 9:10–12 combines the ban on intermarriage with Canaanites in Deut 7:3 with a quotation from Deut 23:6 commanding the Israelites not to seek the welfare of the Ammonites and Moabites. However, Ezra expands these prohibitions beyond the original peoples mentioned in Deuteronomy so that they apply to the peoples of the lands, who are equated with the Canaanites, Ammonites, Moabites, and

---

### excluded and expelled

The divorce and expulsion of foreign wives and their children represents a radical departure from the practice attested in most other parts of the Hebrew Bible. Since the ancestry of a child is traced through the father, children born to an Israelite father and a non-Israelite mother normally would be considered Israelite. Famous examples of this principle include Manasseh and Ephraim, children of Joseph by an Egyptian wife (Gen 46:20), and Obed, the grandfather of King David, child of Boaz by his Moabite wife, Ruth (Ruth 4:13–17). Not that the Hebrew Bible favors intermarriage of Israelite men with foreign women—marriage within the kin group is the norm, and intermarriage is condemned in some passages such as Deut 7:3–4, which sees marriage with Canaanites as an incitement to idolatry (precisely the reason why 1 Kgs 11:1–8 censures King Solomon for his many foreign wives). However, the patrilineal method of reckoning descent would still give insider Israelite status to the children of such unions. Not so in Ezra-Nehemiah, where the Exile community is to expel not only foreign wives but also their children.

others (Ezra 9:1). Similarly, Neh 13:1–3 generalizes the specific exclusion of the Ammonites and Moabites in Deut 23:3–6 to justify the separation from Israel "of all those of foreign descent" (literally, "of all mixture").

These new interpretations reveal an intense fear of losing the identity of the group due to "foreign" incursions through intermarriage. However, the biblical text leaves us uncertain about whether these plans to divorce foreign wives and send them away with their children were ever carried out. The Hebrew text of Ezra 10:44 ends the chapter enigmatically: "All of these had married foreign women, and some had wives with whom they had sons." The NRSV attempts to resolve the ambiguity by quoting from 1 Esdras 9:36, a later interpretive retelling of Ezra, thus adding the additional phrase "and they sent them away with their children."

Other voices in the postexilic writings of the Hebrew Bible contest the exclusive approach of Ezra-Nehemiah to intermarriage and the treatment of inside-outsiders. The book of Ruth, for example, narrates the gradual acceptance of a Moabite woman as an ancestor within the Israelite ethnic group. The book of Jonah contrasts the rebellious Israelite prophet with the pious foreigners to satirize Israelite ethnic exclusiveness. A further extraordinary example comes from the third section of the prophetic book of Isaiah. Many scholars date Isa 56–66 to the early postexilic period, since it seems to reflect the same struggle over the identity of the restored Israelite community in Yehud as found in many other postexilic texts. Given the

## Ezra's Prayer and Deuteronomy

The following chart shows how the text in Ezra combines and interprets two different texts from Deuteronomy:

### Ezra 9:10–12

And now, our God, what shall we say after this? For we have forsaken your commandments, which you commanded by your servants the prophets, saying, "The land that you are entering to possess is a land unclean with the pollutions of the peoples of the lands, with their abominations. They have filled it from end to end with their uncleanness. Therefore, *do not give your daughters to their sons, neither take their daughters for your sons*, and *never seek their peace or prosperity*, so that you may be strong and eat the good of the land and leave it for an inheritance to your children forever."

### Deut 7:1–4

When the LORD your God brings you into the land that you are about to enter and occupy, and he clears away many nations before you—the Hittites, the Girgashites, the Amorites, the Canaanites, the Perizzites, the Hivites, and the Jebusites, seven nations mightier and more numerous than you—and when the LORD your God gives them over to you and you defeat them, then you must utterly destroy them. Make no covenant with them and show them no mercy. *Do not intermarry with them, giving your daughters to their sons or taking their daughters for your sons*, for that would turn away your children from following me, to serve other gods.

### Deut 23:3, 6

No Ammonite or Moabite shall be admitted to the assembly of the LORD. Even to the tenth generation, none of their descendants shall be admitted to the assembly of the LORD. . . . *You shall never promote their welfare or their prosperity as long as you live.*

attempts of the community of exiles in Ezra-Nehemiah to separate themselves from the peoples of the lands and to exclude and expel foreigners, the
following passage is striking in contrast:

> Do not let the foreigner joined to the LORD say,
>     "The LORD will surely separate me from his people";
> and do not let the eunuch say,
>     "I am just a dry tree."
> For thus says the LORD:
> To the eunuchs who keep my sabbaths,
>     who choose the things that please me
>     and hold fast my covenant,
> I will give, in my house and within my walls,
>     a monument and a name
>     better than sons and daughters;
> I will give them an everlasting name
>     that shall not be cut off.
>
> And the foreigners who join themselves to the LORD,
>     to minister to him, to love the name of the LORD,
>     and to be his servants,
> all who keep the sabbath, and do not profane it,
>     and hold fast to my covenant—
> these I will bring to my holy mountain,
>     and make them joyful in my house of prayer;
> their burnt offerings and their sacrifices
>     will be accepted on my altar;
> for my house shall be called a house of prayer
>     for all peoples.                              (Isa 56:3–7)

This passage also interprets a legal text in Deut 23:1–8, but instead of
expanding and generalizing Deuteronomy's prohibitions as Ezra-Nehemiah
does, this text from Isaiah challenges and overturns them. While Deut 23:1
bans a man with damaged genitalia, that is, a man incapable of procreating,
from entering the assembly of YHWH, the text from Isaiah welcomes

### eunuchs

While the English word "eunuch" signifies a castrated male, the Hebrew word behind the translation (*saris*)
refers to an official in the royal court, without necessarily referring to his physical condition. However, in many
societies of the past, servants or officials with close access to the ruler were castrated in order to lessen the likelihood that such officials would try to usurp the ruler and establish their own dynasty. Patriarchal societies often
stigmatized eunuchs as shameful or effeminate males, making it easier for rulers to execute and replace them
with impunity. The Hebrew Bible mentions eunuchs in relation to the royal court of the Israelite kings (e.g.,
1 Kgs 22:9; 2 Kgs 8:6; 9:32; 23:11; 24:15—the NRSV often translates the term "officials") but tends to associate
them more often with a foreign context. Thus, one finds mention of eunuchs (again translated simply as "officials" or "officers") in Egypt (Gen 37:36; 39:1; 40:2, 7) and in the Babylonian and Persian courts (Dan 1; Esther).
Therefore, parts of the Hebrew Bible present these officials in contexts where they appear doubly stigmatized
as both sexually lacking and foreign.

eunuchs, that is, castrated men, into the temple. Likewise, while Deut 23:3–8 bans Ammonites and Moabites from the assembly of YHWH forever, and Edomites and Egyptians for two generations, the text from Isaiah welcomes foreigners in general into the temple. The Isaiah text seems explicitly to be countering the language of separation of foreigners found in Ezra-Nehemiah (Ezra 9:1; 10:11; Neh 9:2; 10:28; 13:3). In Isa 56, not blood kinship but rather Sabbath and covenant observance qualify a person for inclusion in the Israelite community.

The various ways the Hebrew Bible portrays the treatment of inside-outsiders illustrates again that the ethnic boundary between insiders and outsiders is variously constructed. Sometimes the boundary is not important, but at other times it becomes so crucial that ethnic groups consider expulsion or even annihilation of ethnic "others." Between these two extremes are many other strategies. Even within the same ethnic group, different ethnic strategies and sentiments may be evident, leading to radically different interpretations of the same foundational texts.

## The Scandal of Particularity and Anti-Semitism

A key notion of Israelite peoplehood is that of a special covenant that God makes, first with Abraham, the Israelite ancestor (Gen 15, 17), and then through Moses with the Israelites themselves (Exod 24). This covenant, by definition, excludes other peoples. The idea of the Israelites as God's chosen people (Deut 4:32–40; 7:6; see also Amos 3:2), and the corollary that other peoples therefore do not enjoy this special relationship, does not sit well with modern notions of inclusiveness and multiculturalism. In the past, outsiders criticized the Jewish descendants of the Israelites for believing that they were God's chosen people. The two religious traditions descended from Judaism, Christianity and Islam, each in its own way critiqued what it saw as Jewish theological exclusiveness, while subtly transferring notions of chosenness to its own exclusive community.

But as we have seen, the particularity and exclusiveness of the covenant underlying Israelite ethnicity, and the boundaries with other peoples constructed around it, are not as clear in the Hebrew Bible as one might expect

### Christianity and Islam

Christian theology, basing itself on the arguments of Paul in Gal 3:28, formally calls into question distinctions based on ethnicity, class, or gender, but in practice it has disinherited the Jews and arrogated to Christians the exclusive right to be "Israel." The Islamic tradition likewise questions the notion that God would exclusively choose one people, seeing this as contradictory to the universality of God (see Qur'an 5:18), while in practice subordinating the Jewish and Christian religious traditions by portraying them as deficient and corrupt.

or desire. God's particular choice of the Israelites takes place against the more **universalistic** backdrop of the primordial story of the entire human race in Gen 1–11. And outsiders do in fact cross the boundary to become Israelites or, at the least, seem to have ready access to the god of the Israelites. At the same time, however, the Hebrew Bible consistently affirms the election or choice of the Israelites as God's special people. Therefore, tensions between universalistic and **particularistic** ideologies, and over the inclusiveness or exclusiveness of the covenant, are not just later reactions to the biblical tradition but are already part of those Israelite traditions preserved in the Hebrew Bible.

The Hebrew Bible sometimes gives God's particular choice of the Israelites a larger universalistic purpose: God chooses them to be a divine source of blessing for the rest of the world (Gen 12:3; 18:18) or to attest to the truth of monotheism (Isa 45). However, even when the Israelites fail at these purposes, God does not revoke their status as God's chosen people even though harsh judgment may fall upon them. God does not choose the Israelites because of their superiority over any of the other peoples in the world (Deut 7:7; 9:6). The stories of the dysfunctional families in Genesis, the complaints of the Israelites in the wilderness in Exodus and Numbers, the various shortcomings of the Israelites listed in the prophetic books, the defeat of the Israelites at the hands of the Babylonians in 2 Kings, and the continuing disputes over identity in the postexilic community in Ezra-Nehemiah—these actually demonstrate that the Hebrew Bible portrays the Israelites as flawed. It depicts God as choosing to create the Israelites as a special people, not out of rational calculation but out of love and loyalty (Deut 7:7–8).

The oscillation between universalistic and particularistic notions in the Hebrew Bible puts into perspective its construction of Israelite ethnicity. On the one hand, a particularistic demarcation between insiders and outsiders is absolutely necessary for the construction of group or ethnic identity; those who would deny this dynamic are engaged in an <u>implicit gesture of exclusion</u> whereby they have (unconsciously) universalized the characteristics of their own (often unacknowledged) group and marginalized other perspectives. On the other hand, the polarity between insiders and outsiders, as the Hebrew

## implicit gesture of exclusion

Dominant groups such as white people in North America do not need to think very much about their ethnic or racial identity because in North American society their identity is taken for granted and rarely challenged. Such groups often unknowingly engage in implicit gestures of exclusion precisely when they are trying to be inclusive. For instance, white students might dismiss their differences with ethnic minorities with an offhand phrase like "We all bleed the same color of blood." What they do not realize is that, by asserting a universal identity with which they are comfortable, they have obscured their own position of privilege and erased the right of the minority group to its distinctive identity.

Bible shows, is never simple and clear but rather complicated, shifting, and ambiguous. When groups apply the boundaries rigidly, usually in a situation of perceived threat, then they become bloody.

Therein lies the irony of religious-based anti-Semitism or Jew-hatred. In effect, Jew-hatred simplistically and selectively solidifies the fluid and complicated biblical boundaries of the chosen people and then turns them as an accusation against Jews. However, the traditions of the Hebrew Bible do not allow for such perverse and distorted generalizations. Instead, as the analysis in this chapter on ethnic identity in the Hebrew Bible has attempted to demonstrate, the biblical texts present a grand meditation on the interrelated dynamics of universalism and particularism, of inclusiveness and exclusiveness.

## Conclusion

The Hebrew Bible frequently expresses concerns over ethnic identity. The biblical text declares the Israelites as God's chosen people and contrasts their identity over against other peoples or ethnicities. But the difference between peoples is not a simple demarcation. Rather, the ethnic boundary between peoples shifts with circumstance and develops and changes over time. Human beings construct ethnicity as part of their shifting identities. The content of ethnicity thus varies, and the ethnic boundary is rarely as impermeable as it is portrayed. Ethnic identity can facilitate peaceful coexistence but, especially in times of crisis, it can also be an excuse for violent attempts to exclude or even annihilate those who are defined as outsiders. So also today, ethnicity continues to play an important role in the construction of identities.

## Suggested Biblical Readings

Genesis 9–12, 15, 17–20, 25–27, 29–31, 34, 38, 41, 50
Exodus 1
Deuteronomy 4–7, 23–24
Judges 1–3, 14–16
1 Samuel 15
2 Kings 3
Ezra 9
Nehemiah 9, 13
Isaiah 19, 56
Obadiah

## Discussion Questions

1. Does your own identity include a sense of ethnic belonging? Is there an ethnic group whose origin traditions you share? Do you follow certain

cultural practices identified with a particular ethnic group? Were you born into an ethnic group with which you perhaps no longer identify, or find yourself identified ethnically by others even though you yourself may not share a strong sense of ethnic belonging? Or do you share in the identity of more than one ethnic group, finding yourself to be a sort of hybrid straddling two or more identities, like Moses or David?

2. The Hebrew Bible variously idealizes ethnic differences, depicts an ambiguous coexistence of different ethnicities, or mandates the rejection and even annihilation of ethnic "others." Can you think of other possibilities for dealing with ethnic differences? How does the Hebrew Bible relate to modern concerns with cultural and religious pluralism and with the modern notion of multiculturalism?

3. For which identity is it worth fighting for to the death? Conversely, should certain identities be discouraged or even exterminated? How should those who follow the Hebrew Bible deal with its genocidal directives?

4. Are there parallels between the homogenizing policies of the ancient Babylonian Empire as depicted in the Hebrew Bible, or the genocidal policies of the ancient Egyptian Empire, and the policies of modern world powers?

## Suggestions For Further Reading

Barth, Frederik. Introduction to *Ethnic Groups and Boundaries: The Social Organization of Culture Difference*, edited by F. Barth, 9–38. London: Allen & Unwin, 1969.

Brett, Mark G., ed. *Ethnicity and the Bible*. Leiden: Brill Academic Publishers, 1997.

———. *Genesis: Procreation and the Politics of Identity*. London: Routledge, 2000.

Fenton, Steve. *Ethnicity*. Cambridge: Polity Press, 2003.

Greifenhagen, F. V. *Egypt on the Pentateuch's Ideological Map: Constructing Biblical Israel's Identity*. Sheffield: Sheffield Academic Press, 2002.

Olyan, Saul M. *Rites and Rank: Hierarchy in Biblical Representations of Cult.* Princeton, NJ: Princeton University Press, 2000.

Smith, J. Z. "What a Difference a Difference Makes." In *"To See Ourselves as Others See Us": Christians, Jews, "Others" in Late Antiquity*, edited by J. Neusner and E. S. Frerichs, 3–48. Chico, CA: Scholars Press, 1985.

Spina, Frank Anthony. *The Faith of the Outsider: Exclusion and Inclusion in the Biblical Story*. Grand Rapids: Wm. B. Eerdmans Publishing Co., 2005.

# 8. Class

Some men worship rank, some worship heroes, some worship power, some worship God, and over these ideals they dispute and cannot unite—but they all worship money.

—Mark Twain, "In Vienna"

Money matters. Indeed, some might argue that money carries more significance than any and all other factors in forming identity. Just note what Mark Twain's statement above asserts: that people can and do disagree about all sorts of key issues—but about the importance of money they all agree. Certainly money informs many crucial aspects of life: where and how one lives, how a community sees a person, the opportunities available in education and employment, and so forth. Even fascination with the lives of the rich and famous acknowledges money's importance. The different lives lived by those with money—especially those with lots of money—sells magazines and serves as fodder for many television shows. Perhaps F. Scott Fitzgerald said it best in his story "The Rich Boy": "Let me tell you about the very rich. They are different from you and me."

Money—that is, coin or paper currency—serves as a common barometer in the world for measuring wealth. But societies without a money system also develop ways of reckoning wealth. They do so most often in terms of various kinds of property: land, structures, animals, material goods. This system held sway in the world from which the Hebrew Bible sprang. In fact, material wealth, or the lack thereof, stands forth as a major theme in the biblical text. The Hebrew Bible refers to wealth more often than it refers to faith, praying, and love combined. And biblical texts of widely different genres and time periods concern themselves with what it means to either possess or not possess material goods. A particular focus turns on the situation of the poor and on God's response to the social and economic injustices that led to their plight. This emphasis also manifests itself linguistically: biblical

Hebrew employs no less than seven different words for "poor," allowing for many nuances in the text's description of, and attention to, those in poverty.

The biblical material also displays a diversity of viewpoints on both the causes and consequences of wealth and poverty. Many of these viewpoints resonate with commonly held notions today, whether by individuals or by governments, financial institutions, corporations, or charitable organizations. In general, some of these notions coalesce around the idea of individual responsibility, in which the choices and actions of individuals play the largest role in determining their economic standing. Others center on the role of more impersonal and collective forces that account for people's relative levels of wealth or poverty in terms of social, political, and economic practices and policies, whether enacted locally or globally.

As a marker of identity, wealth or the lack thereof translates into one's membership in a certain class. But proceed cautiously here: class means different things to different people. When used in everyday discourse, "class" often serves as a shorthand way of identifying—rightly or wrongly—aspects of a person's life that may or may not relate directly to his or her relative wealth. For instance, it calls up ideas about a person's level of education and the nature of his or her work, as well as that person's leisure activities, preferred foods, and tastes in books, music, and other forms of entertainment. Hence, those who enjoy opera, read literary classics, attend the symphony, listen to public radio, and/or have a college education get assigned to one class. Those who listen to country music, chew tobacco, watch NASCAR, go bowling, and do not have a high school diploma belong to another class. None of these activities necessarily depends on the amount in a person's bank account.

When used in scholarly circles, the term "class" often means something rather different. It frequently hearkens back to the work of **Karl Marx**. This nineteenth-century thinker analyzed the changes wrought by the industrial revolution and the capitalist structure on which it depended. He further postulated the development of a two-tier class system. One class, which he referred to as the bourgeoisie, owned the means of production—that is, they held title to factories, production companies, investment firms, and so on. The other class, the proletariat, labored for wages in the factories, companies, and firms owned by the bourgeoisie. Marx believed conflict between these two classes was unavoidable, with the violent overthrow of the bourgeoisie by the proletariat as the inevitable outcome. Historical events have not on the whole verified Marx's belief; however, his analyses of the dynamics of wage labor and surplus capital still have great explanatory power today in understanding the workings of our global economy.

However, Marxist analyses work less well in understanding the specifics of the economic and social dynamics of the world depicted in the Hebrew Bible. After all, the text knows nothing of investment bankers, commodity traders, and factory owners; nor does it depict assembly-line workers punching time clocks or service industry personnel dependent on hourly wages. More generally, the economy analyzed by Marx revolved centrally around the use of surplus capital for investment. But the economy depicted in the Hebrew Bible turns, rather, on the control of land. That is, in the world of the text a person's relative class standing links less to how much financial capital that person controls; rather, it depends primarily on how much land and its produce he or she either directly or indirectly oversees.

Notwithstanding these distinct differences between Marx and the Hebrew Bible, his notion of the term "class" still functions meaningfully as a general category for analyzing the Hebrew Bible's various takes on the economic dimensions of life and how that shapes identity. After all, just like Marx and modern readers, the Hebrew Bible recognizes general distinctions between the rich and the poor, the haves and the have-nots, the wealthy and the oppressed. It too constructs various meanings around obtaining, possessing, and/or losing material wealth. In tracing out some of these meanings in the Hebrew Bible, readers discern some of the many ways in which, according to the biblical text, class shapes identity.

Although the text overall contains much diversity in its treatment of the rich and the poor, it also agrees on a few basic presuppositions. These presuppositions generate a general shared ideology about wealth and poverty in the Hebrew Bible. Two in particular stand out.

First, the Hebrew Bible values the material world highly. Not only did God create it, but an intrinsic goodness also adheres to it: "God saw everything that he had made, and indeed, it was very good" (Gen 1:31). The biblical text further asserts that God wants people to enjoy this material world—all of it—in all its physicality and earthiness: "He will love you, bless you, and multiply you; he will bless the fruit of your womb and the fruit of your ground, your grain and your wine and your oil, the increase of your cattle and the issue of your flock" (Deut 7:13). Benefiting from the earth and its yield thus falls in line with the deity's will for humans. As a consequence, the text rarely equates the lack of material goods—poverty—with being pious or faithful toward God. Certainly the text never idealizes poverty, nor does it evaluate it positively. And the Hebrew Bible rarely encourages persons to deliberately impoverish themselves. At the same time, possessing much wealth does not

## When Poverty Equates with Piety

By way of contrast, consider such practices as renunciation and asceticism. People carry out these forms of self-denial in a number of ways—for example, by refraining from food, drink, sleep, and/or sex. Such practices also get incorporated into monasticism, a religious movement that centers on withdrawing from the world and living simply. Among the religions that have monastic movements are Hinduism, Buddhism, Taoism, and Christianity. In general, such movements stem from the belief that various sorts of physical discipline can develop or strengthen one's spiritual life. Thus, distancing oneself from the possession of earthly goods is perceived as bringing about enhanced piety.

necessarily threaten the wholeheartedness of one's righteous standing before God. The text imagines many persons as both immensely rich and as religious role models—for example, Abraham, Isaac, Jacob, David, Solomon, Job. In sum, in the Hebrew Bible being poor does not automatically make one good, just as being rich does not automatically make one wicked.

Second, the Hebrew Bible knows little about "money." Modern economic transactions generally make use of coins and paper bills, along with their electronic equivalents (credit cards, bank cards), guaranteed by some state authority. But coinage functioning in this way originated only in the seventh century B.C.E. in western Asia Minor (present-day Turkey), from which place it spread only slowly through the rest of the Near East. Indeed, the Hebrew Bible first mentions coinage in Ezra 2:69, a postexilic text. Prior to that time, economic transactions took place through **barter**, wherein people traded surplus or unwanted goods for those wanted or needed. Barter also worked for the payment of taxes, tribute, or duties. Here one paid "in kind"—that is, a set amount of some object or good. Since Israel's economy based itself on agriculture, most people bartered with such items as cattle, sheep, or goats, or measured amounts of grain, wine, or olive oil.

But barter can be cumbersome and inconvenient. Imagine, for instance, the many challenges facing a person transporting a goat for trade, especially over long distances. While in transit its value might fluctuate radically, especially if it sickens or dies, or its destination point experiences a surplus or shortfall of goats. So people eventually used certain metals—first copper, then silver and gold—as a more convenient medium of exchange. They normally shaped the metal into certain forms—ingots, bars, bracelets, earrings—and then traded them for whatever they needed. Of course, people still needed to calculate the exact value of the metal; they did so by weighing it on a balance. But weighing failed to guarantee the metal's purity or quality. Moreover, the weighing might well occur outside the purview of any official authority or be done by those untrained in the use of weights and balances; as a result, a certain amount of slipshod weighing and/or cheating no doubt took place. The invention of coinage alleviated these problems. Issued by both imperial and local (city) governments, the coins' symbols or marks stamped into them signaled the political order's guarantee of the coins' absolute worth.

But since land, not coinage, served as the cornerstone of the economy depicted in the Hebrew Bible, the text's structuring of classes rests on who controls the land and how. Three main classes come into view. One class forms around each individual *bet av*'s controlling just enough land to support the members belonging to it. As such, it functions, and can be named, as a class of small landholders. A second group consists of those persons with the means to bring under their control increasingly large swaths of land into ever more sizable landed estates. They function as an elite class in the Hebrew Bible. A third class comprises people without land and thus existing on society's margins. As landless persons they serve as an underclass

**Fig. 8.1: Ancient Coins**
*Silver drachmas in front of the small terra-cotta jug in which they were found. The drachma was one of the world's earliest coins and became common in the Hellenistic era.*

## YHWH as Ultimate Owner of the Land

Although class structure in the Hebrew Bible centers on human ownership of the land, this basic principle stands in some tension with another textual understanding claiming that YHWH owns the land. This latter idea finds succinct expression in Ps 24:1: "The earth is the LORD's and the fullness thereof" (cf. Lev 25:23; Josh 22:19; Pss 39:12; 119:19; Jer 2:7; 16:18). To manage the tension between these two perspectives, one strategy situated human landowners as simply the stewards or caretakers of the land on behalf of YHWH, the ultimate owner.

in the Hebrew Bible. The remainder of this chapter takes up in turn each of these three classes, analyzing the Hebrew Bible's assertions about how their members acquire, maintain, and/or lose (landed) wealth. As well, it looks at how various texts construe the effects of wealth and its lack on individuals, these various classes, and the society as a whole.

## The Small Landholding Class: The *Bet Av* Ideal

"They shall all sit under their own vines and under their own
fig trees,
and no one shall make them afraid.                    (Mic 4:4)

This quotation from Micah expresses a particular biblical ideal for ordering ancient Israel's society and economy. At base it envisions every *bet av* holding its own plot of land and farming it. Note the emphasis on grapevines and fig trees. From the first planting of a grapevine or fig tree to its initial harvest of fruit can take as long as ten years. So the ideal intimates the further hope that each *bet av* will live on, and work, its land for a long time—long enough, perhaps, to feel truly safe and secure. Moreover, the sort of peace and prosperity imagined for each and every *bet av*, and all the individuals within it, presumably extends outward also to society as a whole. Without a doubt this ideal captured the minds and imaginations of many: besides Mic 4:4 the Hebrew Bible includes statements of it, with some variation, in no less than three other places (1 Kgs 4:25; Isa 36:16; Zech 3:10).

Chapter 4 detailed the structure and many of the functions of the *bet av*. Recall in particular its explanation of the male head, or *av* (father), functioning as its center. As such, he also held the final say in most, if not all, matters pertaining to the family economy. Thus, the economic determinants of the vast majority of the population received authorization and depended primarily on the senior male of the household to which they belonged. A prominent example of this dynamic comes through in the Decalogue law dealing with covetousness: "You shall not **covet** your neighbor's house; you shall not covet your neighbor's wife, or male or female slave, or ox, or donkey, or anything that belongs to your neighbor" (Exod 20:17; cf. Deut 5:21). This law states that "you" should not covet any of "your neighbor's" property. In the Hebrew, both "you" and "your neighbor" occur in the masculine singular. That is, the command directs itself solely to male household heads: they must avoid desire for the property of other senior males. And note how the law further specifies "property": it includes the (male) neighbor's wife as well as his servants, house, field, and animals.

Other texts elaborate further on the economic power held by the male head over his household property. Several laws depict him as possessing near absolute control of the household, even over the persons belonging to it. For instance, the male head could (1) sell his daughter into slavery (Exod

21:7), (2) strike his slave (though not to the death; Exod 21:20–21), and (3) override vows made by his wife and daughter (Num 30:1–15). Several narratives present fathers with the power even to take their children's lives: Abraham comes close to sacrificing his son (Gen 22), Jephthah kills his daughter (Judg 11:29–40), and the king of Moab offers up his eldest son as a sacrificial burnt offering (2 Kgs 3:27).

Still, the male head lacked life-and-death powers over many of his other male relatives: grandsons, brothers, father, grandfathers, or uncles. Nor do the texts construe him as having the absolute freedom to dispose of the family's landholdings. The Hebrew Bible never portrays any father, or anyone else for that matter, voluntarily parting with the *bet av*'s landed property. The land sustained the family throughout all its many generations; preserving it took priority over the needs or wants of any one person or even any single generation.

Moreover, with power often comes responsibility. A father's social and economic obligations toward his householders—at least as these found expression in several laws—effectively tempered his power. For instance, the law demanded that he provide a **Sabbath** (Heb., "rest") every seventh day for <u>those</u>, whether human or animal, <u>who labored within his household</u> (Exod 20:8–10; 23:12; Deut 5:12–14).

He was also financially liable for any damages caused by the household's animals (Exod 21:28–36; 22:5). And when freeing an Israelite who had labored as a **debt slave** in his household, he was obligated to provide supplies to enable the Israelite to make a new life for himself (Deut 15:12–15). The law even required the male head to ensure rest for the land itself: "For six years you [masculine singular] shall sow your land and gather in its

### those who labored within his household

Curiously, in the several enumerations of those who deserve a Sabbath rest, the wife never receives mention. The various texts specify a rest day for the male householder's children, his servants (and even their children; cf. Exod 23:12), the animals, and the household guests (i.e., "resident aliens")—as well as the senior male himself. Why no reference to the senior woman of the household? Readers must decide if this oversight is intentional or accidental.

### debt slave

In ancient Israel (as elsewhere in the ancient Near East) persons who defaulted on a loan still needed somehow to make good on what they had borrowed. (Bankruptcy was not an option.) Hence, a creditor had the right to appropriate the personal property of the borrower (house, animals, farming tools) in an amount equal to that owed. If these holdings did not suffice, both law and custom allowed for the selling of the debtor and/or his dependents into slavery. The sum received from their sale served as credit against the outstanding loan amount.

yield; but the seventh year you shall let it rest and lie fallow. . . . You shall do likewise with your vineyard, and with your olive orchard" (Exod 23:10–11).

The household head's economic responsibilities also come out in certain narratives. Two duties stand out as primary: arranging marriages for his children and formally transmitting the inheritance to his son(s). Examples of the former include Abraham's dispatching his servant Eliezer to the land of Aram to find a wife for his son Isaac (Gen 24); Jacob's negotiating with Hamor over the marriage of his daughter, Dinah, to Hamor's son, Shechem (Gen 34:4–17); and Saul's devising a union between his daughter Merab and David. (And when that plan falls flat, Saul marries another daughter, Michal, to David; 1 Sam 18:17–28.) Accounts of a father's bestowing the family inheritance to his sons occur in Gen 27 (Isaac and his two sons, Jacob and Esau) and Gen 48–49 (Jacob and his twelve sons). An important exception concerns Zelophehad, a man with no sons. Here a law allowed his five daughters to inherit. However, they had to take husbands from within their clan so that the family property ultimately would remain within it (Num 27:1–11; 36:2–12; Josh 17:3–6).

Of course, fathers did not operate entirely on their own in the *bet av*. Chapter 4 pointed to some of the inner dynamics of a household's social economy, outlining the probable tasks, duties, and responsibilities held by other household members (women, children, servants). Nevertheless, the Hebrew Bible grants clear primacy to the father and the land: they comprise the two centers around which everything and everyone else pivots. So what happens if either or both are lost or destroyed? Presumably even the possibility of their loss would undermine that which depends on them: the ideal of every household economically secure and independent on its own plot of land.

The Hebrew Bible, clearly anxious about such possibilities, presents a number of stratagems for dealing with threats to—or outright losses of—either the land or the father. Take first the loss of land. Most often this threat arose because a household fell into debt. And any number of factors, either alone or in combination, might lead to the gradual or sudden accumulation of such debt: (1) inept management of the land and its resources; (2) a loss of household members, preventing the effective working of the land; (3) a series of poor harvests, brought on by drought, crop diseases, insect infestations, or some other cause; (4) natural disasters, such as earthquakes and storms, that might wreak havoc on an entire area; (5) a tax burden imposed by political authorities either local or more distant; and (6) wars.

One way to get out of debt involved selling property. Biblical law sets out several strategies by which a property sale might resolve a debt without ultimately compromising the affected *bet av*. One involves the **goel** (redeemer), a close male relation of the household head. In chapter 4 the discussion of the *goel* turned on his role in preserving the family lineage; here the focus centers on his role in saving the *bet av*'s land. So, for instance, if a *bet av* did sell part or all of its land, a law of redemption expected the *goel* to buy it. Presumably he then would return it to the household immediately. Or, alternatively, he would hold it until such time as the household head could himself purchase it back (Lev 25:25–28). But a land sale might arise only as a last resort: other laws allow for a father to sell one or more household members into slavery, the resulting profits being used to pay off the debt (see Lev 25:39; Exod 21:7–11; cf. Deut 15:12–18; Exod 21:1–6). Moreover, if the household head never managed to buy back the land (from either the *goel* or another purchaser), the legal materials provide for yet another form of redress. The law of **jubilee** calls for all land to return to its original owners every fifty years (Lev 25:10–17). This law thus imagines that acquiring land through purchase did not grant the purchaser perpetual ownership of the land. Rather, it gave him only the right to a certain number of harvests of that land until the next jubilee. In effect, the financial transaction allowed for something more akin to renting than to buying.

And what about the loss of a male household head? If no male heir exists to replace him, the lineage risks dying out. Here again biblical law envisions a way to countermand the loss. The practice of **levirate marriage** directs a *goel* to engage in sexual intercourse with the dead man's wife. If and when the sex act results in a male child, that boy receives identification as the heir of the dead man and not of the *goel*. He thus inherits all the rights and responsibilities of the deceased household head (Deut 25:5–10; cf. Gen 38; Ruth 4). As such, his lineage would then also preserve and sustain the *bet av* from that point onward.

As a whole, the biblical ideal that keys itself to a small landholding class imagines a static socioeconomic system. Rather than expanding the economy, it hopes simply to maintain the status quo. That makes it unlike modern market economies, where businesses seek out new markets, companies measure their accomplishments by how much they expand, and investors hope for bullish stock markets (i.e., markets in which investment prices rise faster than their historical average). In the uncertain world of ancient Israel, where plague, drought, famine, and/or warfare could quickly decimate the society and its economy, one scarcely dreamed of growth. The most to aspire to was simply hanging on to what one already had. The ideal was basically conservative.

The ideal also presupposes, and aims for, an egalitarian social and economic system. It imagines every household and its landholdings as precisely equal to every other household in both size and quality. But it simply defies the imagination to suppose that any society can rigidly create and maintain such a system. In the Hebrew Bible, for instance, any number of texts freely acknowledge that some families consisted of more members, and more talented and skilled members, than others. No doubt, too, some landholdings possessed finer soils, received better amounts of rain, and fortuitously avoided drought and pest damage more than others. Over time these kinds of differences inevitably resulted in a situation of markedly unequal households.

Of course, the laws outlined above aim to correct such imbalances. But many of them seem rather unrealistic and impractical. A man with the *goel* role thrust upon him might not want to pay off the debt of a near kinsman (even supposing he has the means to do so). He might also want to avoid sexual relations with a kinsman's widow, for in this socioeconomic system it might well lead to financial responsibilities that would drain his own resources. And how workable is a system that expects the return of all property to "original" owners once every fifty years?

Consider that none of these laws carry with them any penalties, whether physical or financial, if and when someone breaks them. Whatever enforcement power they have comes instead from more general inducements, whether positive (God will bless you) or negative (God will curse you). Only the levirate marriage law brings with it a specific type of consequence: refusing the role of *levir* could result in a public shaming (Deut 25:9–10).

In addition, the fullest source for many of these laws, the book of Leviticus, derives from relatively late in the biblical period. Further, outside of the legal codes these laws—whether directed toward restoring the *bet av*'s land or its senior male—receive scarcely any mention. In particular, narrative materials scarcely ever record their implementation. Only the prophetic book of Jeremiah and the novella of Ruth have such accounts (Jer 32:6–15; 34:8–16; Ruth 4). And in Ruth what occurs varies somewhat from what the legal materials prescribe, especially with regard to how the *goel* functions.

It is likely then that biblical Israel had laws "on the books," so to speak, that never received effective enforcement. At most, perhaps only a few of these laws ever found their way into actual practice—and even then on only

## The Homestead Act: A Similar Ideal?

In 1862 the United States Congress passed the Homestead Act. Its purpose was to encourage the settlement of undeveloped lands. Any citizen or head of a family at least twenty-one years of age could lay claim to 160 acres of land. If that person then successfully resided on it and cultivated it for five years, he or she gained free and clear title to it. Proponents viewed this act through a utopian lens: they saw the poor being able to grab for themselves a bit of the American Dream. But the reality fell far short of the ideal. The act provided no "seed money" for acquiring the tools, seed, and livestock required to establish oneself; it also simply assumed that all would possess the necessary farming skills to make a go of it. Those persons who did settle faced huge adversities arising from the physical conditions of the frontier: drought, blizzards, locust plagues, and an oftentimes crippling isolation. Further challenges arose from cattle ranchers, unscrupulous speculators, and poor oversight by the General Land Office. In the end, of some 500 million acres given out between 1862 and 1904, homesteaders successfully settled less than one-sixth (about eighty million acres). Most of the rest came under the control of speculators, cattlemen, miners, lumbermen, and railroads.

In 1872 Canada passed the Dominion Lands Act, closely based on the U.S. Homestead Act. It too aimed to open up western lands to settlement, and it too had only questionable success. Railroad companies controlled much of the most favorable land, and a protracted economic recession discouraged many from initially acting on it.

a very limited, ad hoc basis. Viewed collectively, these laws likely functioned much more to express and support a utopian ideal that remained far from the actual realities of ancient Israel's society and economy. But that scarcely means dismissing either the laws or the ideal to which they point as unimportant or irrelevant. An ideal can act powerfully on both individuals and societies—firing imaginations, inspiring actions, providing explanations for past and present events. The next sections show how a whole array of other biblical texts, from a wide diversity of contexts, continue to call upon, struggle with, and sometimes resist this ideal. They speak to the central ways in which the notion of a small landholding class functioned as the base reference point for the Hebrew Bible's imagining of the economic order and the construction of class identity.

## The Elite Class

In addition to a small landholding class, the Hebrew Bible also recognizes and concerns itself with a so-called elite class. This class, like that of the small landholders, depended on land to define itself economically. However, the types of connections forged between the elites and the land differed markedly from those of the small landholding class—especially in terms of exactly who controlled the land and how, what benefits ensued from it, and who profited from those benefits. As such, a very different system of production and distribution came into play.

Members of the elite class controlled much larger swaths of land than those of the small landholding class. These plots of land were much too big for the elites to work themselves; instead, they hired others to work the land for them. And rather than living on the land they owned, most often the elites dwelled in urban locales. They were thus doubly alienated from the land: they neither worked it nor lived on it. That they did not labor on it also typifies their more general exemption from physical labor, the backbone of most other peoples' lives.

The landed estates of the elites also differed from the small landholdings in the kinds of crops grown. In the small landholding class each *bet av* worked its own land with an eye to producing practically everything it needed to support itself. A typical *bet av* thus cultivated a wide array of crops, including different grains, fruits, and vegetables. It also cared for a variety of livestock: sheep, goats, donkeys, cattle. And it further processed both the crops and animal products in a variety of ways so as to adequately feed and clothe all its members and otherwise maintain them.

The elites, however, did not consume directly or solely the products of their own land. Rather, they engaged in **monoculture**: cultivating a single cash crop to the exclusion of other uses of their land. In ancient Israel the main cash crops were grapes and olives. These fruits were transformed into high quality wine and olive oil and then often exported, with the elites receiving a high rate of return on their investments. From the profits, they then purchased whatever they needed to support themselves—and not only what they needed but also what they wanted. The great surpluses produced by their estates allowed them to acquire any number of luxury goods. Hence, along with little or no physical labor and living mostly in cities, the elites carried on a lifestyle marked by conspicuous consumption.

How, though, did elites come by their wealth? In particular, how did they come into possession of large swaths of land, especially when social and legal forces supporting the *bet av* ideal ran counter to it? The next section takes up that question, detailing some of the ways in which the Hebrew Bible renders the emergence of an elite class.

## The Emergence of Elites

The Hebrew Bible alludes to four main mechanisms for acquiring wealth. Three of them turn directly on the land's significance for wealth—and so they each involve ways for getting hold of (more) land. These three ways are (1) simply seizing it, done most often by kings; (2) receiving it as a gift, most often from a king; and (3) taking it over when a borrower uses it as collateral and then defaults on the loan. A fourth mechanism does not depend on land, though it does connect once again to the king: in it the requirements of a king's administration and the economic policies he institutes call forth a variety of skilled positions that bring with them both wealth and status.

Either directly or indirectly, all four of these mechanisms depend on actions and policies of the monarch. Hence, establishing the monarchy as a political system in biblical Israel also impacted the economy, not least by creating—or at least intensifying the emergence of—an elite class. So analyzing how elites emerged means highlighting biblical depictions of royal activities, particularly those that have an economic dimension to them.

The first mechanism has kings simply seizing land, an action facilitated by the power of the state—particularly the army—behind them. The Hebrew Bible names three specific expressions of such land seizures, according to the kind and size of territory seized and the means for doing so. The first centers on the military conquest of significant territories outside the otherwise understood bounds of Israel. For instance, 2 Sam 8 has David conquering a number of non-Israelite peoples. They include the Philistines, Moabites, Aramaeans, Edomites, and Amalekites (2 Sam 8:12). By subduing these peoples, David also takes control of the territories they inhabit. Other biblical passages, too, tell of biblical kings campaigning, with more or less success, against foreign rulers and the domains they govern—for example, Ahab of Israel and Jehoshaphat of Judah against Aram (1 Kgs 22:1–4, 29–36); Jehoram of Israel and Jehoshaphat of Judah, together with Edom, against Moab (2 Kgs 3).

The text's description of a second kind of land seizure by kings involves more localized territories, especially those more or less within the bounds of Israel proper. The most obvious example again concerns David. At a point in the story when he is still consolidating his control, 2 Sam 5:6–10 describes him and his forces marching on Jerusalem. Various texts (2 Sam 5:7; Judg 1:21) understand this city, along with the land immediately surrounding it, existing as a politically independent enclave within territory otherwise dominated by the Israelite tribe of Judah. David's success in taking it allows him to incorporate it into his holdings—and eventually to make it his capital. This kind of royal land seizure does not receive elaborate textual attention elsewhere; the David story may have served as an exemplar for what otherwise can only be inferred. For instance, Judg 1:27–28 asserts that a number of cities in the Jezreel Valley lay outside of Israelite control, even though the region all around it was held by various Israelite tribes. But in other texts reflecting the later monarchical period, these cities are identified as Israelite domains (e.g., 1 Kgs 4:12). Presumably some sort of action was imagined as taking place that led to Israelite control of these lands, whether by conquest, treaty, or something else.

A third kind of royal land seizure appears in 1 Kgs 21. It concerns Ahab, ruler of the northern kingdom of Israel. The text depicts him as coveting a small plot of land next to his palace that is currently owned by Naboth and used as a vineyard. Ahab wants to convert it into a vegetable garden for himself. Here the king concerns himself with a small and very restricted piece of land. The tale eventually has Ahab ending up with this property, though only after some rather complicated machinations on the part of his queen, Jezebel. In any case, other instances of this kind of land seizure do not appear in the Hebrew Bible; the Ahab story seems to be an isolated example.

In the Ahab story, the king intends a very private and personal use of the land he desires. But the situation proved otherwise in the larger territories that kings came to hold. Various texts suggest that kings employed several different strategies through which they could exploit and so profit from the larger land areas under their control. Three emerged as central: imposing a tax on the land's yield, setting some apart as estates under the king's direct control, and granting certain tracts of land as gifts to others.

With regard to taxation, the Hebrew Bible actually describes the workings of several different systems—employed at different times, under various circumstances, and using an array of payment methods. One of the most commonly used involved **tribute** (Heb., *mas*). Tribute was frequently the mode of taxation employed against outside lands and the people who inhabited them. In such situations the preexisting systems of production and ownership may well have continued largely unchanged. The conquering king simply added on the obligation of collecting and turning over to him (or more likely his agents) whatever was demanded as the tribute.

Normally the Hebrew Bible speaks in terms of a tribute handed over annually. But the payment itself could take on several different forms. At times the people may have paid simply "in kind." That is, the levy imposed upon them had them simply turning over a certain percentage of their annual yields. First Samuel, for instance, specifies the amount as 10 percent:

"He [the king] will take one-tenth of your grain and of your vineyards. . . . He will take one-tenth of your flocks" (1 Sam 8:15, 17). This kind of tribute rather directly and straightforwardly exploits the land and its produce. But in other instances a more indirect exploitation of the land occurred, especially when the imposed tribute involved more distant lands. Concerns about spoilage and a desire for more overall efficiency might lead to converting goods in kind into items of comparable worth. Even without a coinage system, this worth often enough translated into some other form of precious metals.

For instance, 2 Samuel 8 states in a general way that the conquered Moabites and Syrians were "servants of David" who "brought tribute" (2 Sam 8:2, 6). But the text also positions David as specifically commandeering various artifacts of silver, gold, and bronze from the nations he subdued:

> David took the gold shields that were carried by the servants of Hadadezer, and brought them to Jerusalem. From Betah and from Berothai, towns of Hadadezer, King David took a great amount of bronze. . . . Joram brought with him articles of silver, gold, and bronze; these also King David dedicated to the LORD, together with the silver and gold that he dedicated from all the nations he subdued. (2 Sam 8:7–8, 10b–11)

In addition to in-kind and precious metal payments, tribute also took on a third form: forced labor, or **corvée**. A number of biblical texts specifically associate King Solomon with this practice (1 Kgs 5:13–18; 9:15–23; for other kings' use of such labor, see 1 Sam 8:11–13). Some passages further see Solomon imposing such labor not just on foreigners but also on Israelites. For instance, 1 Kgs 5:13 reads, "King Solomon conscripted forced labor out of all Israel; the levy numbered thirty thousand men." The text specifies that for Solomon's reign most of this corvée directed itself toward the king's many and various building projects: his palace, the Jerusalem Temple, stor-

### A Modern Analogy to Forced Labor?

Forced labor no doubt strikes many readers as abhorrent. But something analogous to forced labor actually exists in the open in many countries. These countries currently require from all their young people some period of time (usually a year) in service. Most often this service takes place in the military. Israel, for instance, mandates military service for both men and women (while allowing some exemptions). Other countries, including Germany, Norway, and Switzerland, require military service of men, while providing women with the opportunity to volunteer for such service. In Egypt military service is decreed for men, while comparable civilian service is demanded of women. In recent years discussions have also occasionally surfaced in the United States about establishing such a mandated year of service, not only or primarily in the military but also in social service agencies or other kinds of volunteer programs. As yet, though, no serious policies have been set in motion in order to institute such a practice.

age cities, and military garrisons. But some of it may have gone also toward work on landed estates owned directly by Solomon.

This latter supposition identifies another use for the land seized by monarchs: royal estates, the profits from which went more or less directly into the king's own coffers. No biblical text directly connects any specific king with this practice. Rather, a passage in 1 Sam 8 alludes to it in a more general way as part of the overall economic dynamic of biblical kings: "These will be the ways of the king who will reign over you. . . . He will appoint . . . some to plow his ground and to reap his harvest" (1 Sam 8:11–12). Note the reference here to forced labor: the king appoints (conscripts?) people into certain kinds of labor. But note further the particular kind of work they do, and where. The text's mention of "*his* ground" and "*his* harvest" implies land owned directly by the king and so reserved for his special use and benefit.

A few verses later, 1 Sam 8 identifies an additional way by which kings made use of the land they had obtained—they gifted it to others: "He [the king] will take the best of your fields and vineyards and olive orchards and give them to his courtiers" (1 Sam 8:14). No doubt such gifts of land functioned often as rewards or payment for those who had loyally served the king. Perhaps they also bound the recipients more closely to the ruler; in essence, then, the king was buying their continued loyalty to him and his policies.

These land gifts point to the second major mechanism by which persons acquired wealth: having it bestowed on them in the form of parcels of land from the king. So far this section has focused primarily on just the king, but an elite class cannot just begin and end with the monarch. A "class" presupposes a group of people, even if they comprise only a tiny minority of the whole and even if they primarily associate with, and/or depend on, the king as the source of their wealth. A number of biblical texts recognize the existence of such persons in lists that name various personnel in the direct employ of the king (see chapter 10). They include high-ranking military officers, palace bureaucrats, and temple priests (2 Sam 8:16–18; 20:23–26; 1 Kgs 4:1–6; cf. 2 Kgs 18:18). No doubt these persons derived their social and economic status, and so their class standing, more or less directly from the king himself. And, at least in part, land served as the mode for expressing and securing their enhanced socioeconomic status.

A third mechanism for creating an elite class also depended on the monarch, though in a more indirect fashion. It connected to the various trade initiatives put forth by the king. That is, a monarchy's centralizing power allowed for more control of the movement of goods both within and beyond a country's borders. Managing that control required a variety of skilled personnel: merchants, traders, moneylenders, tax collectors, and overseers of forced labor. Presumably the persons who took on such roles possessed the sort of management skills and economic savvy needed to ensure that they carried out their duties in an orderly, efficient, and systematic fashion. Or perhaps that is too idealistic. Maybe political cronyism determined who got these jobs. In any case, such positions no doubt provided many social and economic benefits, and so they operated as a source of wealth for another group of persons, who then also constituted part of the elite class. Although biblical texts do not, in the main, speak directly of such persons, they do describe various trade networks and systems of forced labor and tax collection. These logically presume the existence of personnel to support them (see especially 1 Kgs 4:7–19, 22–28; 5:8–16; 9:10–28; 10:11, 14–29).

A fourth mechanism facilitating the development of an elite class finds expression in two maxims: "wealth begets wealth" and "the rich get richer, the poor get poorer." That is, however they had obtained their wealth, once the elites had it, they were in a position to create more wealth. They did so especially by making loans to others. If and when borrowers defaulted on their loans, lenders claimed the **collateral** as their own. And such collateral—whether in the form of land, buildings, or material goods—would then further enrich the lending elites. Such defaults likely happened with some frequency: loan transactions in the ancient world often involved extremely high interest rates. Evidence from fifth-century B.C.E. Elephantine, a Judean colony in Egypt, shows that borrowers paid 5 percent per month in interest; lenders added unpaid interest to the principal, leading to an annual interest rate of at least 60 percent.

Since land often comprised a person's most significant economic asset and one kept in reserve until all other options for raising funds had failed, land often also ended up as defaulted collateral. Such defaults led to an increase in elite landholdings, such that the rich would "add field to field" (Isa 5:8). Social scientists term this process **latifundialization** (from the Latin *latifundia*, meaning "large estates"); it denotes situations where land accumulates into the hands of a few wealthy landowners to the deprivation of the peasantry. This process, repeated and intensified over time, came to alter the whole rural landscape of ancient Israel.

In sum, a reading of a wide array of biblical texts brings out four main mechanisms for obtaining wealth: seizing land, receiving land as a gift, working for the king to implement his various trading initiatives, and taking over land (or other property) serving as collateral on a loan that goes into default. Again, three of them center on the further acquisition of land;

## The Rich-Get-Richer Dynamic Today

Many economic policies today also operate on the principle that if one already has wealth, it is easier and faster to come by more wealth. For instance, one earns a higher rate of interest on a CD (certificate of deposit) with a greater dollar amount: a $10,000 CD benefits from an interest rate higher than that for a $2,000 CD. Another example involves the estate tax, a "death duty" imposed on the transfer of property from a deceased to his or her heirs. In the United States, the estate tax has recently been challenged. If repealed, it would disproportionately advantage those people (and their heirs) in control of considerable assets, not those with little or nothing to pass on.

all of them more or less turn on the monarchy. Also, these four mechanisms did not operate in isolation from one another. For instance, a merchant or overseer of forced labor might find such favor with the king that he receives some land as a gift. With the profits accrued from the land's yield, he can lend to others. And if he then forecloses on their land, he would experience a further increase in the size of his estates, giving him yet more riches. Or take another example: a small landowner experiences a number of years with extremely good crop yields. He uses the profits to win favor with the king such that he attains a significant position in the administration, or perhaps for his son. The benefits from that position allow for the purchase of even more land and so even more wealth for its owner. In any case, however these various mechanisms might have intertwined and reinforced one another, they led, ultimately, to the making of an elite class.

*The Prophetic Perspective on the Elites*

Most of the biblical texts that evoke the ways in which elites acquire wealth come from the narrative extending from Joshua through 2 Kings. But other biblical materials also address issues surrounding the elites and their wealth. Yet they do so in a different way, especially by more centrally assessing the effects of such wealth. Their evaluative stances give voice to more explicit moral judgments about the elites and how they use their wealth. Two main positions come into view: (1) condemning the elites, declaimed most emphatically in the prophetic materials; and (2) defending or at least benignly accepting the elites, expressed most often in the wisdom tradition. The present section proceeds with a focus on the condemnatory arguments made in prophetic texts; a following section then analyzes the messages about the elites found in the wisdom material.

By way of introduction, consider the following:

> They shall all sit under their own vines and under their own fig trees,
>     and no one shall make them afraid.          (Mic 4:4)

> On that day, says the LORD of hosts, you shall invite each other to
>     come under your vine and fig tree.          (Zech 3:10)

The first verse appeared earlier in this chapter, introducing the section on the small landholding class and the socioeconomic ideal affirming it. The statement itself comes from a biblical book based on the words and deeds of the Judean prophet Micah. The second verse, an almost exact parallel to the Micah text, also derives from a prophetic book. It is no accident that similar statements, both based on the ideal, occur in two different prophetic books. The prophetic materials overall give ample evidence for their support of the ideal that envisions land and all its social and economic benefits distributed evenly among, and so benefiting equally, each and every biblical household.

However, as a way of expressing support for this ideal, prophetic texts devote considerable attention to condemning the elites. A frequently used strategy turns on highlighting the extremes of wealth characteristic of elite lifestyles. A number of texts focus particularly on the luxurious housing enjoyed by the wealthy:

> Ah, you who join house to house,
>     who add field to field,
> until there is room for no one but you,
>     and you are left to live alone
>     in the midst of the land!
> . . . . . . . . . . . . . . . . . . . . . . .
> Surely many houses shall be desolate,
>     large and beautiful houses, without inhabitant.          (Isa 5:8–9)
>
> You have built houses of hewn stone,
>     but you shall not live in them;
> you have planted pleasant vineyards,
>     but you shall not drink their wine.          (Amos 5:11; cf. Zeph 1:13)
>
> I will tear down the winter house as well as the summer house;
>     and the houses of ivory shall perish,
> and the great houses shall come to an end,
>         says the LORD.          (Amos 3:15)

These passages identify a number of specific housing practices pursued by the elites. For one, they strive to build ever larger houses for themselves, situating them within expanding tracts of property. For another, they do not use the more common and cheaper mudbrick in their construction; instead, they invest their riches in paying for the more expensive cut and shaped

## The Prophets and Prophetic Literature

Prophecy appears as a widespread phenomenon throughout the ancient Near East, including ancient Israel. In the Hebrew Bible no less than fifteen books carry the names of persons identified as prophets. But herein lies also a dilemma. Careful study of these books indicates that many of them came about only as the end result of rather long and complicated compositional processes. These processes presumably had their beginning with the words and deeds of the prophets themselves. What then ensued likely involved the work of scribes who collected and further composed material related to the prophets. As the materials passed on through many hands and many generations, further editing occurred, even in the final stages of revising that led to the form in which these books appear today. Thus, from our present-day vantage point, it becomes difficult, if not sometimes impossible, to distinguish between the words of the "original" prophets and the later scribes and editors. Readers should not assume that any particular statement found in a prophetic book necessarily derives directly from the prophet himself. Instead, this material conveys ideas valued generally by prophetic circles such that they worked to preserve and promulgate them.

**Fig. 8.2: Samarian Ivory Plaque**
*An ivory plaque from eighth-century-B.C.E. Samaria*

stones for both the houses' foundations and the walls. In addition, their wealth further affords them the ability to own both a winter house and a summer house. From a prophetic standpoint grounded in the small land-holding ideal, these practices are an outrage—especially if simultaneously keeping in mind others who live homeless, in substandard shacks, or as renters in dwellings owned by others.

Still another affront occurs in the phrase "houses of ivory," which alludes to the houses' interiors. Archaeological excavations at the royal city of Samaria have uncovered hundreds of ivory plaques (see fig. 8.2). Many have small drill holes, suggesting they were attached as decorative elements to house furnishings, such as wooden beds and chairs. They may also have decorated the houses' walls. Ivory was a luxury item in the ancient world, and so another reason arises for prophetic condemnation of the elite: whereas the poor can scarcely afford any furniture at all, the elite adorn theirs with expensive carvings made from imported elephant tusks.

A passage in Isaiah highlights another way in which the rich engage in ostentatious displays of wealth. Here the text focuses specifically on the behavior of elite women and how they spend lavishly on clothing, jewelry, and perfume, thereby flaunting both themselves and their affluence:

> In that day the Lord will take away the finery of the anklets, the head-bands, and the crescents; the pendants, the bracelets, and the scarfs; the headdresses, the armlets, the sashes, the perfume boxes, and the amulets; the signet rings and nose rings; the festal robes, the mantles, the cloaks, and the handbags; the garments of gauze, the linen garments, the turbans, and the veils. (Isa 3:18–23)

But merely possessing and displaying wealth scarcely constituted the only problem. Prophetic texts also criticize the elites for taking advantage of their wealth to carry on with a lazy and idle lifestyle: "Alas for those who are at ease in Zion, and for those who feel secure on Mount Samaria" (Amos 6:1; cf. Isa 3:16). Their wealth also allowed them to indulge in lavish and profligate partying:

> Hear this word, you cows of Bashan
>     who are on Mount Samaria,
>     . . . . . . . . . . . . . . . . . . . . . .
> who say to their husbands, "Bring something to drink!"    (Amos 4:1)

> Ah, you who are heroes in drinking wine
>     and valiant at mixing drink . . .                      (Isa 5:22)

> Ah, you who rise early in the morning
>     in pursuit of strong drink,
> who linger in the evening
>     to be inflamed by wine,
> whose feasts consist of lyre and harp,
>     tambourine and flute and wine . . .                    (Isa 5:11–12)

> When their drinking is ended, they indulge in sexual orgies;
>     they love lewdness more than their glory.              (Hos 4:18)

According to Amos, these parties took place both in private homes (Amos 6:4) and in the sanctuary (2:8). Not surprisingly, these parties involved music and (presumably) copious amounts of alcohol. Lavish food (5:22; 6:4) and even sexual orgies seem also to have had their place.

Prophetic texts not only decry the elites for their lifestyle of conspicuous consumption and rank idleness. They also berate the elites for the many

## cows of Bashan

When Amos refers to the rich women of Samaria as "cows of Bashan," the writer may intend an insult directed toward their class standing. But the women themselves might well have taken it as a compliment. Bashan, a territory in the northern Transjordan, possessed especially fertile soil. In ancient times this fertility yielded much cattle, timber, and field crops. By comparing the Samarian women to the well-fed cows of Bashan, the text indirectly calls them fat, which seems impolite from a contemporary perspective. But the beauty ideals of the ancient Near East, rather than aiming for physical slenderness, might well have oriented themselves more toward fleshiness. Fat likely signaled one's membership among the elites: it meant one could afford copious amounts of food and drink while also not being subject to the sorts of arduous physical labor that would quickly burn off those calories. For Amos, the women's fatness demonstrates their greed and selfishness in the face of the extreme neediness of others. But for the women themselves, it likely announces their beauty and prosperity. (See also the discussion in chapter 6 of the Hebrew Bible's normative or ideal body, and the implied comparison to western cultural ideals about the body.)

ways in which they oppress the poor and powerless. Here the texts speak especially of how the elites manipulate a variety of legal, economic, and religious systems so as to advantage themselves and further grind down the weak and vulnerable. It all adds up, according to the prophetic material, to a situation in which injustice is everywhere on display.

In the legal-juridical realm, the elites took bribes; indeed, they went even further than that by actively soliciting them: "Everyone loves a bribe and runs after gifts" (Isa 1:23; cf. 5:23; Amos 5:12; Mic 3:11; 7:3). They also composed unjust laws: "Ah, you who make iniquitous decrees, who write oppressive statutes" (Isa 10:1). They loathed those who actually tried to play fair, and act justly, in the courts: "They hate the one who reproves in the gate, and they abhor the one who speaks the truth" (Amos 5:10).

And the elites actively shunned, as well as passively ignored, the powerless people who sought redress in the courts: "to turn aside the needy from justice and to rob the poor of my people of their right, that widows may be your spoil, and that you may make the orphans your prey!" (Isa 10:2; cf. 1:23; 5:23; Jer 5:28; Amos 5:12). In sum, those responsible for upholding the law instead perverted it: "The officials within it are roaring lions; its judges are evening wolves that leave nothing until the morning. . . . They have done violence to the law" (Zeph 3:3–4; cf. Hab 1:4).

Concerning the economic realm, the prophets focus on marketplace activities; they specifically zero in on the cheating that took place around the buying and selling of goods: "We will make the ephah small and the shekel great,

### the gate

Archaeological excavations have uncovered gate complexes that include (besides towers, the remnants of doors, and angled approaches) two to four rooms flanking either side of the passage into the city. Sometimes lined with stone benches, these rooms would have served ideally as places to hear legal cases. (Imagine, perhaps, the city elders seated on the benches and the litigants standing before them.) The Hebrew Bible contains numerous references to city gates functioning as the site of judicial decision making (see, for instance, Deut 21:19; Josh 20:4; Ruth 4:1). In addition, at and around the city gate, merchants plied their trade, travelers camped out, kings interacted with their subjects, prophets delivered their messages, and elders administered justice.

### the ephah small and the shekel great

Ancient Israel made use of various sorts of weights and measures. The ephah was the most common unit of dry measure. Equaling about three-fifths of a U.S. bushel, it measured the amount of grain (or any sort of dry commodity) being sold. The shekel was the standard unit of weight: calculated at slightly over eleven grams, it weighed the metal (whether in the form of ingots, jewelry, or something else) being used to purchase goods (see http://www.ibs.org/niv/table_measures.php).

and practice deceit with false balances" (Amos 8:5b; cf. Hos 12:7 and Mic 6:10–11). By making their ephah smaller than the standard, dishonest merchants cheated buyers out of the full value of their purchases. For instance, buyers might suppose they had received a full ephah of grain, when they had actually walked away with only seven-eighths of that measure. And when a merchant used a heavier than normal shekel, he demanded, and presumably collected, more than the just amount of the purchase price (metal amount) of a market item. In either case, such merchants were falsifying their weights and measures, a ridiculously easy thing to do in the absence of absolute, external controls. Perhaps even more outrageous is this observation from the book of Amos: "buying the poor for silver and the needy for a pair of sandals, and selling the sweepings of the wheat" (Amos 8:6; cf. 2:6). For paltry sums—no more than the price of a pair of shoes—prosperous elites buy, and so come to own, human beings who have fallen into debt. At the same time, these elites put on the market, and sell for a handsome price, even the waste products of wheat.

In the religious sphere, the prophets see the abuse of the poor occurring in a more indirect fashion. That is, they charge the elites with blindly and carelessly ignoring the plight of the poor even while continuing on with their worship activities. Some sense of the prophetic indignation about this thoughtlessness comes through in the exhaustive listing of the various acts of worship in which the privileged engage: praying, burning incense, bringing offerings, observing holy days, and gathering together in a congregation. For example, Isa 1:12–13 declares, "Trample my courts no more; bringing offerings is futile; incense is an abomination to me. New moon and sabbath and calling of convocation—I cannot endure solemn assemblies with iniquity." The text goes on to urge the elites instead to "cease to do evil, learn to do good; seek justice, rescue the oppressed, defend the orphan, plead for the widow" (Isa 1:16–17; cf. Amos 5:21–24).

For the prophets, such worship is making an empty show of fealty to God. It is full of hypocrisy, especially when people are actually impatient for it to be done with so they can get back to the "real business" of buying, selling, and getting rich: "Hear this, you that trample on the needy, and bring to ruin the poor of the land, saying, 'When will the new moon be over so that we may sell grain; and the sabbath, so that we may offer wheat for sale?'" (Amos 8:4–5).

By specifying elite abuses along so many fronts—legal, economic, and religious—the prophets adjudged the entire social and cultural system as riddled with corruption. With injustice so pervasive, the poor and powerless have few avenues for redress; they are caught up in and trapped by a system that wreaks profound and devastating havoc on their lives. Micah 3:1–3 puts it in perhaps the most extreme and graphic terms. It claims nothing less than that the elites were cannibals, consuming the very flesh of those they victimized: "Listen, you heads of Jacob and rulers of the house of Israel! . . . who tear the skin off my people, and the flesh off their bones; who eat the flesh of my people, flay their skin off them, break their bones in pieces, and chop them up like meat in a kettle, like flesh in a caldron." The relentlessness of this imagery and its gruesomeness bears witness to the passion that the prophets brought to bear on their condemnation of the elites.

Gauging both the motivations and the effects of this prophetic stance toward the elites remains difficult. What drove those responsible for these condemnatory statements? The texts themselves often provide only fragmentary clues about their life circumstances. With regard specifically to class identity, some references actually put the prophets among the elites. The prophet Isaiah, for example, has regular audiences with the king and other leaders of the people; he may also serve as a priest in the Jerusalem Temple (Isa 6:1–4; 7:1–4; 37:1–2; 38:1–6). For Jeremiah, the material depicts a more mixed situation. He belongs to a priestly family, but one exiled to the village of Anathoth (Jer 1:1; cf. 1 Kgs 2:26–27). But Jeremiah himself prophesies mostly in Jerusalem, where his oracles periodically land him in prison and threaten him with death (Jer 20:1–2; 26:10–11; 32:2–3; 33:1; 37:11–21). Yet he also has powerful advocates among the elites who regularly bail him out (Jer 26:16, 24; 36:9–19; 38:7–13). The situation pertaining to Amos and Micah is even trickier to discern. Both these prophets come from villages in the rural hinterlands of Judah: Amos from Tekoa, Micah from Moresheth (Amos 1:1; Mic 1:1). Amos 1:1 and 7:14 further identify this prophet as a herdsman and dresser of sycamore trees. But whether that implies he was solidly a member of the small landholding class or someone more economically marginal, working on land held by others, is unclear.

Questions also emerge about the impact on others of this prophetic stance toward the elites. In the first place, who exactly listened to these words? The texts do not always identify a particular intended audience—whether the king, all urban elites, the rural poor, other constituencies, or the people in their entirety. Perhaps such vagueness was deliberate. And even when a text does target a certain audience, it certainly does not preclude others from "listening in." Another challenge rests in measuring the reception given to the prophetic word; again, the biblical text itself does not always provide such a report. But presumably a whole range of responses ensued—all the way from wholehearted embrace, through cool indifference, to outright rejection. Much probably depended on the stakes a particular person or community had in the ideas (and ideal) being promulgated. A further related difficulty derives from evaluating the supposed truth claims made by the prophets. Their message comes to us in stylized form, their words and phrases shaped for maximum rhetorical effect.

*The Wisdom Perspective on the Elites*

Did other societal sectors agree with how the prophetic materials assessed the elites? The answer is no, at least in light of the Hebrew Bible's wisdom texts. The wisdom perspective evaluates the elites much more positively, although it often does so more subtly and more indirectly than do the prophets. Consider, for instance, the following summation of the rule of King Solomon, who, according to certain biblical texts and traditions, was the wisest king who ever lived: "During Solomon's lifetime Judah and Israel lived in safety, from Dan even to Beer-sheba, all of them under their vines and fig trees" (1 Kgs 4:25). This verse redeploys the ideal of a small landholding society to advance a positive view of the monarchy and, by extension, the entire elite class. It insists, unlike the prophets, that rather than compromising the well-being of the small landholders, the elites actually support and sustain them. This positive assessment of the elites receives perhaps its fullest expression in the Hebrew Bible's three wisdom books; in them several positive themes circulate about wealth and those who possess it.

A first theme views wealth as a sign of God's blessing. One reaps material benefits as a consequence of one's righteousness before God. Proverbs 13:21 states it perhaps most bluntly: "Prosperity rewards the righteous." Similarly, Prov 10:22 asserts, "The blessing of the LORD makes rich" (cf. 3:9–10; 10:3; 13:25; 15:6; 28:20, 25). This equation between wealth and righteousness also operates indirectly in the wisdom tale of Job. The story starts by describing Job as "blameless and upright, one who feared God and turned away from

---

### Wisdom in the Hebrew Bible

As conventionally understood, three books constitute the wisdom literature of the Hebrew Bible: Job, Proverbs, and Ecclesiastes (also called Qoheleth). "Wisdom," of course, can call forth a variety of definitions. At minimum, biblical wisdom deals not just with knowledge per se but also with what we do with that knowledge. That is, wisdom aims to make use of what a person knows in order to discern meaning and make sound judgments, both about oneself and about the world, in both its natural and social aspects. There is thus a moral and ethical dimension to it. In the Hebrew Bible, wisdom depends on making close observations about the world in both its micro and macro expressions. It thus presupposes a fundamental order to the universe that, ideally, humans can access. Indeed, for wisdom, the way for humans to succeed lies in coming to know at least some of that order and aligning themselves with it.

Some biblical wisdom materials come in the form of short, pithy sayings that likely originated in rural village settings—for example, "A soft answer turns away wrath" (Prov 15:1). These sayings attest to the common and widespread roots of the wisdom tradition. They likely got passed on orally before eventually being captured in written form. But they actually comprise only a part of what we find in Job, Proverbs, and Ecclesiastes. Each of these books in its present form presupposes, generally, a more formal situation of instruction, one in which a young urban elite man receives training on how to succeed: in life, in a variety of social settings, and more particularly in the administrative circles of the royal and priestly courts (see, for instance, Prov 25:1; see also 22:17; 24:23). This specific context arguably shapes the attitudes toward the rich and the poor, and the conditions of wealth and poverty, expressed in the wisdom books. And besides these three wisdom books per se, wisdom themes also make an appearance in certain psalms (e.g., Pss 1, 19, 49, 112), folktales (e.g., that of Joseph in Gen 37, 39–46), and historical narrations (especially concerning Solomon's reign in 1 Kgs 3–11).

evil" (Job 1:1). And it immediately continues with a delineation of the many possessions that make Job so wealthy (1:2–3). A psalm text with wisdom connotations also elaborates on this notion that riches indicate God's favor: "Happy are those who fear the Lord, who greatly delight in his commandments. . . . Wealth and riches are in their houses, and their righteousness endures forever" (Ps 112:1, 3). But perhaps the most grandiose claims of all about the outcomes for honoring God come from Prov 22:4: "The reward for humility and fear of the Lord is riches and honor and life."

A second rather prominent theme emerging from wisdom texts advocates an ethic of work. In doing so it claims that wealth will follow naturally and inevitably if one simply works hard: "In all toil there is profit" (Prov 14:23). "The hand of the diligent makes rich" (Prov 10:4). "The diligent obtain precious wealth" (Prov 12:27). Several proverbs attend particularly to the work of farming, not surprising given the centrality of agriculture in ancient Israel. Some further target specifically the labor involved in tilling the soil—for example, "Those who till their land will have plenty of food" (Prov 12:11; cf. 10:5; 28:19). Again, the sentiment expressed conveys every confidence that <u>wealth is within reach</u> of any and all persons who apply themselves to their labors.

A third theme displayed by the wisdom materials stresses that wealth enables generosity toward the poor, thereby indirectly defending the elites who have such wealth. Several proverbs convey this idea, but in quite terse statements—for example, "Those who are generous are blessed, for they share their bread with the poor" (Prov 22:9; cf. 11:24–25; 14:21; 19:17). However, several longer narrations elaborate more fully on this theme. For instance, Prov 31:10–31, a poem praising a woman/wife of worth, includes the statement that "she opens her hand to the poor, and reaches out her

### wealth is within reach

The positive assessment of wealth that comes in the Hebrew Bible's wisdom literature finds echoes in a teaching espoused by a number of Christian churches today. Referred to sometimes as the "gospel of prosperity," it asserts that God not only wants to save people from their sins and lead them to heaven, but also that God wants to bless them materially in the here and now. Those persons who hold to this teaching are unabashed about describing the immense wealth that God wants for God's followers and how they should dream big, aspiring to six-figure incomes, assets in the millions, and so on. And, of course, they have scripture to back them up—not only wisdom texts but also a whole range of materials in both the Old and New Testaments. Propounded especially in Pentecostal and conservative evangelical traditions, this gospel receives perhaps its most notable press in and through a number of megachurches and television ministries. Two prominent examples of persons preaching this prosperity gospel are Joel Osteen, through both his Lakewood Church in Houston and its associated television programming, and Joyce Meyer, by means of her books and television preaching.

hands to the needy" (31:20). Since the context makes clear her wealth, this depiction of the elites understands charity work as part of what they do and how they live their lives. Similarly, Job's recollections of his life before disaster struck him lays stress on the good works he did toward those in need (Job 29:12–13, 15–17; 30:25; 31:13, 16–22, 32, 39).

Although overall the wisdom material sees wealth as a good thing, it occasionally sounds a more restrained and cautionary note. This more cautious attitude receives perhaps its most extensive and elaborate expression in Eccl 5:10–6:9. The passage starts by asserting that the desire for wealth can never be fully satisfied: the more one has, the more one wants. Often enough this never-ending spiral can lead only to immense frustration (5:10; 6:7, 9). The text further points out the capricious and unreliable nature of wealth; a bad business venture, a risky investment gone wrong, a natural or human disaster—any of these occurrences can quickly do away with all of one's fortune (5:13–14). Moreover, the having of wealth does not necessarily bring with it the capacity to enjoy that wealth; often enough the poor enjoy life just as much, if not more, than do the rich (5:12, 17). Finally, however much wealth one gains in one's life, sooner or later death brings it to an end. Not only can you not take it with you, but all that wealth will now go into the hands of others who did not work for it (5:15–16; 6:1–3).

## The Imperial Context and Its Shaping of the Elites

The book of Ecclesiastes' skepticism about wealth likely follows from the context within which its author lived and wrote. In the postexilic era huge empires variously held sway over much of the Near East. In the face of such immense power, Ecclesiastes recognizes that not even wealth can fully protect or insulate. The caprices of distant emperors and their political and economic policies made it impossible to attain any sort of lasting stability or security (see chapter 11). Even more, the elites often found themselves squeezed between their imperial overlords and the local population, over which they still had responsibility. Expected to satisfy the empire's demands for the required tax and tribute payments, they naturally enough met resistance and experienced resentment from the lower classes when trying to collect it.

Passages from Nehemiah, another postexilic biblical text, testify to this squeeze on the elites. Nehemiah 9:32–37 expresses some sense of the economic burden inflicted by the empire, especially on the elites. Note the specification of various elite groups in the following passage (the addressee is God):

> . . . all the hardship that has come upon us, upon our kings, our officials, our priests, our prophets, our ancestors, and all your people, since the time of the kings of Assyria until today . . . Here we are, slaves to this day—slaves in the land that you gave to our ancestors to enjoy its fruit and its good gifts. Its rich yield goes to the kings whom you have set over us. . . . They have power also over our bodies and over our livestock at their pleasure, and we are in great distress. (Neh 9:32, 36–37)

Nehemiah 5 views the situation from another perspective. It presupposes that the elites have shifted what is perceived as an unfair portion of the imperial tax demands onto the rest of the population. As a result, the people suffer enormous economic want. In order to survive they are forced to borrow, but the interest charges lead to debt foreclosure on their properties and the selling of their children into slavery (5:1–5). Their complaints prompt Nehemiah, the governor currently ruling the Judeans on behalf of the Persian overlords, to take action. The text here places Nehemiah in an interesting position. By virtue of his role he is himself in the elite class; the text nevertheless works hard to distance him from the other elites. In the first place, he brings charges against these elites, condemning them for taking interest and demanding that they return the people's foreclosed properties (5:6–13). Second, the text insists that Nehemiah did not act like the other elites, since he did not contribute to the people's economic oppression; specifically, he "did not demand the food allowance of the governor, because of the heavy burden of labor on the people" (5:18; cf. 5:14–19).

A very different word about imperial power comes through elsewhere, one that views such power in a positive light. Placed in the mouth of one of its representatives, the Rabshakeh, chief steward of the Assyrians, the message comes at a time when the Assyrian war machine threatens to overwhelm Judah. In a speech given before the walls of Jerusalem, the Rabshakeh urges the Judeans to submit to rather than resist the Assyrian Empire. He promises that if the Judeans make peace with him, then "every one of you will eat from your own vine and your own fig tree" (Isa 36:16; cf. 2 Kgs 18:31). In effect, the Rabshakeh is claiming that the ideal of a small landholding class depends on imperial rule. This use of the ideal radically subverts its intent as compared to its use elsewhere in the Hebrew Bible. Yet its appropriation testifies also to the real allure and benefits of empire.

Wealth fascinates, and the Hebrew Bible, like so many other texts and contexts, partakes of this fascination. But also like other texts and contexts, it cannot settle on any one viewpoint about it. Some biblical texts, like the

## benefits of empire

A scene from Monty Python's *Life of Brian* plays off this notion that imperial rule benefits those so ruled. It depicts a small band of Judean revolutionaries in 33 C.E. meeting to plan their next move against the Roman occupying forces. Their leader, Reg, attempts to stir them into action and so defiantly asks, "And what have they [the Romans] ever given us?" At first his question is met with silence. But then, one by one, his followers propose, among other things, "Aqueducts?" "Sanitation?" "Roads?" "Irrigation?" "Medicine?" "Education?" "Public order?" "Peace?" Recognizing the truth in their suggestions, and how these many benefits can and will deflate the fervor fueling their revolutionary zeal, Reg can only respond haphazardly by sputtering a repetition of his first question: "But what have the Romans ever done for us?"

prophets, claim that wealth is gained unjustly and that those who possess such wealth contribute to much suffering in the world. Other texts, like the wisdom materials, maintain a diametrically opposite position: wealth is good, and those in possession of it bring great blessings onto others. Besides these two collections of materials, the Hebrew Bible also contains any number of other statements that opine on wealth's relative worth and value, its dangers, and its meaning and functions for individuals and society as a whole. In that sense the Hebrew Bible resonates well with contemporary times, where wealth also fascinates—and unsettles.

## The Poor

Since in ancient Israel wealth depended on land, it follows that in the Hebrew Bible the poor are those either without land or with only a tenuous hold on it. The latter includes those persons whose plots of land are too small or marginal to effectively support them. But it might also include persons without the wherewithal to work the land they do hold. For instance, Ruth 4:3 refers to a parcel of land belonging to Elimelech and now, by extension, his widow, Naomi. Yet the story also depicts both Naomi and her daughter-in-law Ruth as destitute. Naomi's land, on its own, does not seem to enable an end to their economic deprivation.

Those people without any land at all fall into three major categories in the Hebrew Bible. One category consists of people who never at any time had any land because either they or their ancestors were not linked to ancestral holdings. The Hebrew Bible identifies this group as consisting of, in the main, Levites and **resident aliens**. The Levites, according to various biblical texts, descend from Levi, one of Jacob's sons. As such, they number among the tribes of Israel. But unlike the other tribes, the text prohibits them from holding land. They are not to work as farmers; instead, they are to minister to the Lord in priestly capacities (Deut 10:8–9; Exod 32:25–29; Num 8:5–26). Texts further speak of their subsistence deriving from donations or tithes given by the other Israelites in recognition of their cultic services (Deut 14:22–29; 26:12–15)—hence their landless state. Resident aliens (Heb., *gerim*), meanwhile, includes foreigners, outsiders, and/or strangers in Israelite society. The origins of such people derive from elsewhere than any of the lineages of the Israelite tribes (see chapter 7). As such, they too are excluded from any apportionment of land.

Another category of landless persons includes people who once possessed land but then lost it. Most often these persons originated as small landholders who got buried under such a crushing debt load that they had no recourse except to sell off their land. Any number of adverse circumstances—working either singly or in combination with one another—might eventuate in a debt impossible to overcome except through a land sell-off: an outsize tax burden, inept land management, a series of poor harvests, unwise borrowing decisions, and so forth. Interestingly, the Hebrew Bible has no set term for such persons, nor do they function as a highlighted category of the poor—unlike the Levites, resident aliens, widows, and orphans.

That brings forward the last biblical category of the landless: widows and orphans. Their landless state comes about in a more indirect fashion than the other groups. Women and children did not normally have the right to hold land in ancient Israel. Any connections they had to the land came through men to whom they were linked, that is, husband and fathers. Women and children thus looked to these male landholders for their social and economic well-being. But if these men died and no other male relative stepped in to take their place, the women and children were set adrift. As widows and orphans, they had no secure positioning within the male-centered social structures. And they also lost all firm linkages to the land that served as the economic mainstay of their society.

Widows, orphans, Levites, resident aliens, and debtors who had lost their land—in the main, these groups comprised the poor in the Hebrew Bible. They all fell through the cracks of a system intended to embody the biblical ideal of the social economy, one in which everyone belonged to a household supporting itself on its own plot of land. The cracks existed even though any number of biblical laws aimed to function as a safety net for those most vulnerable, striving either to prevent them from falling through the cracks at

## The American Farm Crisis of the 1980s

In the biblical world the scenario outlined for small landholders losing their land finds analogies in many different times and places. As one example, consider the 1980s farm crisis in the United States, a crisis in which huge numbers of farmers lost their lands due to debt foreclosure. In the early 1970s lowered trade barriers coupled with huge Soviet demands for American grain led to a sharp upswing in crop prices. Land values also rose. These increases, coupled with low interest rates, persuaded many farmers to borrow heavily in order to expand their productive potential and reap even more profits.

But the boom was followed by a bust. A number of factors played into it: rising interest rates, a drop in the value of farmland (in some areas by as much as 60 percent), record harvests leading to overproduction and a glutted market, the imposition of a grain embargo by President Carter on the Soviet Union to punish them for invading Afghanistan, the drying up of other foreign markets for American grain. And so between 1980 and 1988 profits for middle-level American farmers declined by 36 percent. Farm indebtedness rose to $215 billion, double what it had been in 1978. Unable to make good on loans taken out during the boom years, many farmers found themselves facing foreclosure on properties that had been in their families for generations.

The crisis also provoked other kinds of costs: divorce rates and alcohol abuse spiked, cases of child abuse and neglect greatly increased, and dramatic murder-suicides occasionally rocked small rural communities. By the late 1980s the farming landscape in the United States had markedly altered: while the overall acreage farmed remained about the same, the total number of farms in existence declined as the average farm size doubled. So-called superfarms also emerged, such that the top 4 percent of farm operations came to produce one-half of the food. This situation continues to the present day.

all or, once fallen, to alleviate their plight (see the section earlier in this chapter on "The Small Landholding Class: The *Bet Av* Ideal"). But as the prophets continually remind the reader, the safety nets either did not function at all or fell far short for those in need of them.

Without either land or a secure place in a social network connected to the land, the poor struggled to survive in whatever ways were open to them. Women on their own (i.e., widows) had fewer options than men. If in an urban area, they might try to sustain themselves by begging and/or working as prostitutes. In a more rural locale they could turn their hand to **gleaning** (the gathering up of the leftovers of the harvest), a practice enshrined in the traditions and laws of the people (Ruth 2; Lev 19:9–10; 23:22; Deut 24:21). But any of these strategies allowed at best only a precarious existence.

Men, either alone or with dependents, might find work on land owned by others. In such situations they likely functioned as seasonal laborers, employed at times of intense labor demands (e.g., the harvest) but otherwise left jobless. Similarly, they might find employment in the cities, as a hired hand to an artisan or merchant. Here too the work might expand or contract according to the needs of those who hired them and so not guarantee any long-term economic security. Men also could enter into military service: this option likely proved especially attractive to younger sons, who stood less chance of inheriting land by which to support themselves. And men, like women, could engage in begging, prostitution, and/or the gleaning of field crops. Finally, men might turn to banditry, especially as part of outlaw gangs roaming the fringes of society: both Jephthah and David, for instance, do so at various times in their lives (Judg 11:3; 1 Sam 22:2).

The Hebrew Bible rarely gives voice directly to the poor themselves. Instead, their voices are mediated through others, namely, the male urban elites responsible for the text. These elites manifest a variety of standpoints toward the poor: some sympathize and defend them; others blame and condemn them. Interestingly, these elite writers also often use widows, orphans, and resident aliens as symbols for the poor in general (Exod 22:21–22; Deut 10:18; Ps 146:9; Jer 7:6; 22:3). This move allows the writers to distance themselves personally from the poor; after all, as male adult Israelites they will never themselves fall into any of these three categories. And so, by extension, they will never presumably be among the poor themselves.

*Prophetic Sympathizers and Defenders of the Poor*

Most often the Hebrew Bible depicts the prophets as those who sympathize with and defend the poor. They do so both directly and indirectly. Indirectly, the prophets attack and condemn the elites, whom they hold responsible for the situation of the poor. Directly, the prophets urge care for the poor (Isa 58:6–9; Ezek 16:49) and warn against exploiting and oppressing them (Amos 2:6; 8:6; Isa 3:14–15; Ezek 22:29; Zech 7:10).

An even more direct advocacy of the poor by the prophets appears in two prophetic tales found in 1 and 2 Kings. In one, a widow appeals to the prophet Elisha for help. Her situation is dire: having already lost her husband, she now faces the loss of her two children, who are to be sold into slavery to pay her debts. When Elisha learns that all she has left is one jar of oil, he orders her to collect empty vessels from her neighbors, go into her house and shut the door, and begin pouring oil into them. Enough oil flows forth to fill all the vessels; once sold, the profits enable her to pay off her debts and also support both herself and her children (2 Kgs 4:1–7). So the prophet succeeds in lifting this woman out of her poverty. But it takes nothing less than supernatural intervention to make it happen.

Perhaps an even more poignant narrative appears in 1 Kgs 17:8–16. Set during a time of severe drought, it involves the prophet Elijah. The tale begins with God instructing the prophet to journey to Zarephath; there he will find a widow to care for him. But the widow seemingly knows nothing about this plan! When Elijah arrives and sees her at the city gate, he asks for some food. But she replies, "As the LORD your God lives, I have nothing baked, only a handful of meal in a jar, and a little oil in a jug; I am now gathering a couple of sticks, so that I may go home and prepare it for myself and my son, that we may eat it, and die" (1 Kgs 17:12). Her words testify to the extreme destitution faced by the biblical poor. As well, they voice the desperation and hopelessness that resulted. But in this story Elijah saves the day, for as long as he stays with this widow and her son, the oil never gives out, nor does the jar of meal—a miracle similar to Elisha's.

But the salvation granted this widow is the exception, not the rule. Even in the Hebrew Bible miraculous interventions are far from an everyday occurrence. And once again the tale involves a poor widow, a figure far removed from those who determined so much of the shaping of the biblical text. Moreover, this particular widow comes from Zarephath, which belongs to Sidon, a leading city in Phoenicia. That is, this widow lives in non-Israelite territory, and she herself is also most likely a non-Israelite (note her words to Elijah in 1 Kgs 17:12: "As the LORD *your* God lives . . ."). The narrative here thus features a character far removed from the Israelite, male, urban, elite standpoint that otherwise governs the biblical text. This story thus in effect constructs an extreme "othering" of the poor.

Yet overall, the prophetic materials maintain a generally sympathetic stance toward the poor—indeed, they defend the poor. As part of this defense, they hold the poor blameless for their situations. Instead, they imagine poverty as largely the outcome of systemic forces—social, political, economic—put in motion by the elites and sustained by them.

*Wisdom's Blame and Condemnation of the Poor*

While the prophets imagine the situation of the poor coming about through circumstances far beyond their control, the wisdom perspective holds otherwise. It proposes a much more individualistic explanation of the causes and consequences of poverty, and those mired in it.

Perhaps the most dominant wisdom attitude centers on blaming the poor themselves for their hapless condition. In support of this attitude, wisdom texts put forward a number of different factors that they assert can lead to poverty. One especially prominent cause singles out a person's own laziness: "A little sleep, a little slumber, a little folding of the hands to rest, and poverty will come upon you like a robber, and want, like an armed warrior" (Prov 6:10–11 and 24:33–34; cf. 10:4; 14:23; 21:5). Another cause points to foolish or stubborn behaviors on the part of a person: "Poverty and disgrace are for the one who ignores instruction" (13:18). "One who follows worthless pursuits will have plenty of poverty" (28:19). A third cause focuses on those who engage in riotous or overly sumptuous living: "Whoever loves pleasure will suffer want; whoever loves wine and oil will not be rich" (21:17). But although the causes themselves vary, these texts all agree that somehow the poor themselves are responsible for their own lowly circum-

### Holding the Victims of Poverty Responsible for Their Situation

Examples are not hard to find of similar sentiments propounded elsewhere. Consider first a dialogue from Charles Dickens' *A Christmas Carol*. In it two unnamed gentlemen call on Scrooge, asking him to make a donation on behalf of the poor and destitute. But Scrooge responds, "The Union workhouses? . . . Are they still operating? . . . [And] the Treadmill and the Poor Law?" The gentlemen admit that these welfare agencies are still quite busy. However, one of them explains, because "they scarcely furnish Christian cheer of mind or body, . . . a few of us are endeavoring to raise a fund to buy the Poor some meat and drink, and means of warmth." When they ask Scrooge how much he is willing to give, he replies, "Nothing . . . I wish to be left alone. . . . I help to support the establishments I have mentioned—they cost enough: and those who are badly off must go there." And even when the gentlemen identify those places as truly horrible, Scrooge does not waver, sending the men off without contributing anything at all, even though he is a prosperous businessman (Charles Dickens, *A Christmas Carol* [Mount Vernon, NY: Peter Pauper Press, 1943], 13–15).

Another famous instance of unfeeling disdain for the poor is attributed to Marie Antoinette. After being informed that the poor and dispossessed were complaining about their extreme destitution, she supposedly said, "If they have no bread, let them eat cake." She seemingly had no comprehension that lacking bread indicated that they lacked anything at all to eat.

A final example dates from much more recent times. Barbara Bush, ex-first lady of the United States, was touring a shelter set up in the Houston Astrodome for victims of Hurricane Katrina. In a question-and-answer session aired on National Public Radio, she observed, "What I'm hearing, which is sort of scary, is they all want to stay in Texas. Everyone is so overwhelmed by the hospitality. And so many of the people in the arena here were underprivileged anyway, so this is working very well for them." Her perception that the refugee shelter was working out "very well" sidesteps consideration of the many adverse factors that brought them to this place: many had lost their homes, their social networks, and, in some cases, family members and friends.

stances. It is entirely because of their own choices and behaviors—poor and unwise as they have been—that they find themselves destitute. This blame-the-victim strategy entirely sidesteps any systemic considerations for the causes of poverty. It makes poverty an entirely personal issue. And it encourages a distant and moralizing tone on the part of those who are not poor toward those who are.

Such an attitude in the wisdom literature likely results, at least in part, from instructors concerned for the future well-being of their students. Teachers hope to convince those they instruct to refrain from lazy, foolish, stubborn, and/or feckless behaviors, and so they set out as a warning what such behaviors lead to: social and economic ruin for those who engage in them.

Interestingly, even though the wisdom perspective holds that the poor have only themselves to blame for their situation, it also stresses that others should not make fun of them. They still belong to God's creation and they still come under God's care: "Those who mock the poor insult their Maker" (Prov 17:5). "The rich and the poor have this in common: The Lord is the maker of them all" (22:2; cf. 28:27; 29:13).

Nevertheless, the wisdom material, on the whole, is far from sympathetic to the poor and oppressed. Largely ignoring the systemic causes of poverty, the wisdom texts make the situation of the poor into a very private and individualized matter—and one explained always and only by recourse to what individuals have done themselves. As such, this material is a far cry from the prophetic perspective on the poor.

## Conclusion

> They shall all sit under their own vines and under their own fig trees,
> and no one shall make them afraid.    (Mic 4:4)

The Hebrew Bible holds to a specific ideal for ancient Israel's social and economic order. It finds its clearest and most succinct expression perhaps in the above verse from Micah (as well as the verse's several parallels in 1 Kgs 4:25; Isa 36:16; Zech 3:10). But many other texts also insist on this ideal by way of how they specifically and variously promote it. Hence, law codes aim to maintain it, prophetic materials support it, and various narratives presuppose it. The cumulative effect works as a sort of relentless prodding toward a very particular class vision—one rather egalitarian in character, perhaps even one gesturing toward a classless society.

However, other biblical passages present different understandings of class issues. These passages, especially in the wisdom materials, value wealth and poverty differently, such that wealth gets assigned a positive value whereas those without wealth are slighted, ignored, or made entirely responsible for their plight. In other words, rather than urging a vision of relative social and economic equals, these materials accept and even embrace a hierarchy of classes. They present very different imaginings about the social and economic structure of ancient Israelite society.

The ways in which the ideal permeates so many different texts in the Hebrew Bible, as well as the various understandings that push back against the ideal, testify to the importance of class as a marker of identity in the Hebrew Bible. But the push and pull of these different texts—with their different attitudes about wealth and poverty—also gesture toward something else: the ways in which power dynamics become implicated in questions concerning class and class identity. This allusion to the workings of power leans toward the next section of the textbook, which takes up and focuses on the many ways in which power, like identity, serves as a significant paradigm for reading the Hebrew Bible. After a chapter introducing the concept of power, the next chapters will detail some of power's operations in such various modalities as the state, ideology, media, and understandings of the deity.

|  |  |
|---|---|
| **Suggested Biblical Readings** | Exodus 21:1–23:19 |
| | Leviticus 25 |
| | Deuteronomy 15–16; 23:19–25; 24:6–22; 25:13–16 |
| | 1 Samuel 8 |
| | 1 Kings 4–5; 9:10–10:29; 17:8–16 |
| | 2 Kings 4:1–7 |
| | Amos 1–6 |
| | Isaiah 1–5 |
| | Proverbs 31:10–31 |
| | Ecclesiastes 5:10–6:9 |
| | Nehemiah 5, 9 |

**Discussion Questions**

1. Read through the biblical legal materials supporting the ideal of a small landholding class (i.e., the materials listed above in Exodus, Leviticus, and Deuteronomy). What laws do you deem most admirable? What laws seem most strange, harmful, or impractical? What would be some of the consequences if our society lived according to these laws?

2. Construct a debate in which one side voices the prophetic perspective toward the elites and the other side voices the wisdom perspective.

3. Assess your own economic identity. Consider your annual income as well as your assets. In terms of class, where do you place yourself? Do you envision it changing? If so, what factors will contribute to that change?

**Suggestions for Further Reading**

Hoppe, Leslie J. *There Shall Be No Poor among You: Poverty in the Bible.* Nashville: Abingdon Press, 2004.

Lang, Bernhard. "The Social Organization of Peasant Poverty in Biblical Israel." In *Anthropological Approaches to the Old Testament,* edited by Bernhard Lang, 83–99. Philadelphia: Fortress Press; London: SPCK Press, 1985.

Premnath, D. N. "Latifundialization and Isaiah 5.8–10." In *Social-Scientific Old Testament Criticism,* edited by David J. Chalcraft, 301–12. Sheffield: Sheffield Academic Press, 1997.

Soares-Prabhu, George M. "Class in the Bible: The Biblical Poor a Social Class?" In *Voices from the Margin: Interpreting the Bible in the Third World,* edited by R. S. Sugirtharajah, 147–71. Maryknoll, NY: Orbis Books, 1991.

# 9. Introducing Power

Power is not an institution, and not a structure; neither is it a certain strength we are endowed with; it is the name that one attributes to the complex strategical situation in a particular society.
—Michel Foucault, *The History of Sexuality*, vol. 1

When some people hear the word "power," the concept of strength comes to mind. Perhaps images of a muscular individual capture the idea, or maybe thoughts of soldiers, tanks, and guns. Others might equate power with office or influence, as with a political leader such as the president of the United States or the prime minister of Canada or the United Kingdom. Or perhaps a business executive like the CEO of Nike or Coca-Cola makes the point. Another person could favor defining power as a particular kind of relationship and envision a parent disciplining a child, a teacher instructing students, or a boss assigning an employee a task.

As Foucault indicates above, what defines power often defies articulation in any stable or lasting manner. Think back to how chapter 3 showed that numerous factors constituted Moses' self-understanding and determined the way others saw him. And those factors shifted depending on circumstances. Likewise, what makes up "power" also varies. Although most people refer to power as if an individual, a group, a government, a country, a religious shrine, or even a deity possesses it, to do so misunderstands how power operates. Power, like identity, constantly moves—arising in specific situations and generating varied effects.

The image of a web helps clarify this idea. Interchanges between persons, families, governments, and other interests produce connections. Strands of a web symbolize those exchanges. A complex pattern forms over time, and strategic positions—places that stand at or near the most action—certainly emerge. Becoming entrenched in a specific location, however, often equates to missing out on developing links in other places. Power, then, rests not with one player or in one locale. Rather, power emerges in interactions, and successfully using power requires both sensitivity to its evolution and the flexibility to move so as to keep current on where the most important transactions occur.

A closer look at one of the biblical characters whom the writers depict as expressing power demonstrates the concept. The stories told stress David as exemplary leader, symbol of the nation, and hope of future generations. Looming large in the biblical imagination as a slayer of giants, composer of psalms, founder of a dynastic line, and prototype for future kings, David embodies, according to these stories, a mythic status. Although also recounting his adultery, inability to parent his children effectively, and lack of control over his closest associates, the biblical writers present David as rising above these shortcomings, and he continues to garner their admiration and praise. Indeed, they claim that any defeats he suffers come only by human hands and that he retains eternal divine support (2 Sam 7:14–15).

Therefore, to most readers the character of David embodies power as king, as the ideal of Israel, and as a mythic figure. In this framework, however, David stands not as a possessor of power but rather as a site or a location where power expresses itself. The difference in perspective shows how power constantly shifts and demands that those persons seeking to use it move and change with its dynamics. While limitations of space and time prevent a thorough examination of all the ways in which the biblical writers show David situated in power relations, this chapter will look at some images of him as king in order to think about how he demonstrates the functions of power.

## An Image of the King

Travelers to Firenze (Florence), Italy, flock to the Galeria dell'Accademia to glimpse one of the most famous statues in the world: Michelangelo's *David*. At 17 feet (5.1 meters) tall, the marble work dominates the room in which it stands. The impressive form captures an idealized male beauty. Chiseled between 1501 and 1504, this piece originally stood in the Piazza della Signoria at the entrance of the Palazzo Vecchio, or town hall. A replica still stands in that location today.

This familiar image of David shows how the king of an ancient fledgling state becomes a mythic commodity for other cultures to use. Like many other artists, Michelangelo chose to represent David at the time of his purported battle with the famed Philistine giant Goliath. The biblical tale cer-

### purported battle

Although the biblical story in 1 Sam 17 celebrates the defeat of Goliath at the hand of the boy David, 2 Sam 21:19 credits Elhanan son of Jaare-oregim, a man from Bethlehem, with the victory.

**Fig. 9.1: Michelangelo's** *David*

tainly possesses many dramatic elements that inspire the artist. A young shepherd faces an experienced and able warrior with nothing more than a slingshot in hand, and fells him almost effortlessly. But while most renderings present David in victory, Michelangelo focused on a different moment. He sculpted the future king calm, deliberate, and unafraid immediately prior to battle. In this pose, and with the placement of the statue at the town hall (instead of the cathedral as originally planned), the statue becomes a political act of power. Following the expulsion of the influential Medici family in 1494, this *David*—placed outdoors in 1504—symbolized the new republican rule. The moment of a young and inexperienced boy preparing

### independent Florentine state imagined itself

At the conclusion of the fourteenth century, a small group of merchant families governed the city of Florence under the leadership of the Medici. This family acquired its wealth through banking and commerce. Many of the leaders became patrons of art, literature, and humanist thinking. The best-known among them, Lorenzo the Magnificent, ruled from 1449 to 1492. His son Piero, however, lacked his father's political sense and ruled for only two years before being forced out of the city of Florence by the people.

The newly established republican rule that resulted lasted little more than a decade before the Medici reestablished control. In the tumultuous interim, the new leaders made Michelangelo's *David* a symbol of their government. Less affluent and established than the Medici, the republicans saw themselves in the young but bold boy who defeated the powerful and favored giant.

to take on the great warrior echoed across time and place and stood as a representation of how an <u>independent Florentine state imagined itself</u>.

Michelangelo imbues his work—among the most well-known pieces of art in the world—with David's mythic grandeur. The beauty of his face, the elegance of his physical body, the relaxation of his demeanor, and the assurance conveyed in his nudity express the boldness, courage, confidence, and theological uprightness indicated as marking the character of David in the text. It celebrates not the king but rather the ideal of a young, brave, and overmatched shepherd claiming victory before going on to forge a young, bold, and uncertain nation. This statue demonstrates the resonance of David's story across generations. This youthful man became both one of the primary expressions of real and idealized power for the people of Israel and a legendary figure enduring across times and cultures to evoke the same.

## Entering the Power Web

According to the biblical text, David enters into Israel's story at a time of political conflict. The system of governance in place—the judges—fails when Samuel attempts to pass on leadership to his sons, but none rules honorably (1 Sam 8:3). As a result, the biblical writers depict the people of Israel as demanding a king (8:5) and Samuel reluctantly complying with this request by anointing the Benjaminite Saul (10:1; see also 10:9 and 10:22–24). But, at least as the writers tell it, Saul falls short of God's demands. So God then instructs Samuel to anoint a new king even as Saul sits on the throne (1 Sam 16).

Whatever rationale the text offers, David—the second man anointed—challenges the sitting royal family and then eventually becomes king. Such an action requires political acumen as well as the ability to manipulate and deploy resources to advantage. How then does David come off as such a glowingly positive figure? The first exercise of power demonstrates. The

## Saul's Loss of the Divine Favor

For many readers, the stories about Saul and David seem a bit odd. According to the narrative, Saul fails as king in the eyes of God, but not in the estimation of the people. This failure necessitates the selection of a replacement. Two stories explain his supposed decline; Saul performs a ritual burnt offering in 1 Sam 13 to entreat the favor of God in an upcoming battle and, in 1 Sam 15, saves spoil from a defeated city.

To a modern student of the biblical text, Saul's performing a ritual offering to God when Samuel fails to show up at the appointed time (10:8–14) hardly qualifies as open defiance of God or serves as cause for the loss of divine support of his monarchy. Similarly, Saul's sparing of the Amalekite king and the most valuable animals in 1 Sam 15:3 feels forced as a rationale for the withdrawal of God's approval. An obvious editorial bias against Saul shapes any reading of the material.

writers work hard to legitimize David's position and the assault he makes on the Saulide king and his family by becoming masters of what contemporary media term "spin." Creating a compelling backstory for this contender for the throne and casting every event in a light favorable to David, they generate a convincing case for his place as ruler.

*The Mythic Life*

Think of elections for high office today. Voters often look not only at a candidate's qualifications for the job but also at what the candidate claims about himself or herself as a person. And a gripping biographical narrative can seal a nomination or a vote.

The biblical text shapes David's background to fit the image of an ideal king. In fact, careful reading of the material might suggest that the writers went so far as to forge an Israelite ancestry for the future monarch. They report

## Shaping a Biography

In the modern political process, conscious shaping of a person's history plays an important role. Bill Clinton's first nomination as president in 1992 at the Democratic National Convention in New York City included an introductory video biography, *Bill Clinton: A Man from Hope*. (See the highlights in narrative form at http://clinton1.nara.gov/White_House/EOP/OP/html/Hope.html or watch the video on the Clinton Foundation Web site: http://www.clintonfoundation.org/video.htm?title=Bill%20clinton:%20The%20Man%20from%20Hope.)

This video effectively brings viewers from Clinton's birth to a poor, single mother in the small town of Hope, Arkansas, through his life and political rise. A type of rags-to-riches American story, the film presents Clinton as the ultimate underdog made good.

One of the best features illustrating the conjuring of image comes in a photograph. A high-school-aged Clinton visits John F. Kennedy's White House in 1962 and shakes the president's hand. Clinton and his advisors wisely used this photo to link the young presidential hopeful (Clinton was 45 at the convention) to the youthful and popular Kennedy (age 46 at his death in 1963), intentionally playing on the magical lore that permeates the story of the assassinated JFK. The handshake connects Clinton with a leader valorized in the public memory and thus boosted his appeal to voters still making judgments about an unknown governor of Arkansas running against a sitting president.

that the youngest son of Jesse came from the Ephrathite clan in Bethlehem of Judah. Strong association of David with the city of Bethlehem certainly appears throughout the stories about him (1 Sam 16:1, 18; 17:12, 58; 20:28). But for readers, this assertion comes across as slightly troubling. Why not name David by tribe as the writers introduced Saul as a Benjaminite in 1 Sam 9? His designation by clan and location alone might suggest that David descends from neither Jacob nor Judah.

Other texts reveal the character of David as a bit apologetic about his family of origin. Discussions of a possible marriage to Saul's eldest daughter, Merab, prompt the writers to show David asking, "Who am I and who are my kinsfolk, my father's family in Israel, that I should be son-in-law to the king?" (1 Sam 18:18). One way to read this line pictures David acknowledging his lack of familial ties to the people of Israel. Later, after marrying and abandoning Saul's younger daughter Michal, he demands her back when seeking Israel's throne (2 Sam 3:12–16). While an easy interpretation assumes that he requires Michal to claim the office of king as a member of the house of Saul, a more nuanced evaluation might also see her as his only firm link to the people of Israel.

David's ancestry matters to the biblical writers because in making him the paradigmatic king for the people, they need a strong character grounded through a firm connection to the larger body they call "Israel." If an outsider or a foreigner assumes the role, the myth of Israelite identity residing in blood ties dissipates. But, as with the character of Moses, the narrative's David reveals mysterious and unsettled origins. Two postexilic texts attempt to clarify the matter. The book of Ruth presents his great-grandmother as a Moabite

## David's Ancestry

In his book *David's Secret Demons: Messiah, Murderer, Traitor, King*, author Baruch Halpern summarizes some of the problems with David's background succinctly: "David bears a name without a basis in Israelite nomenclature. His father is of indeterminate origin, and opponents invoke the father's name when heaping scorn on David. His genealogy is suspect. The status of his ancestral home town is in some doubt. In fact, even the text of 1 Samuel maintains that he sought refuge for his family in Moab, a tradition that programs the peculiar tradition of Ruth that he had a distant connection to a Moabite ancestor" (Baruch Halpern, *David's Secret Demons: Messiah, Murderer, Traitor, King* [Grand Rapids: Wm. B. Eerdmans Publishing Co., 2004], 275). When combined with his close association to a Jebusite city as a young man, his connection to the Philistines as a mercenary, and the fact that he lacks a credible tribal association, the question of David's relationship to the people of Israel looms large. As Halpern indicates, no one can know for certain David's background and its putative connections to Israel. But "the indications are that the connections were at best tentative, temporary, fragile, from the start. David's opponents may well have claimed he was a foreigner" (p. 275).

Halpern's thinking serves to prompt a closer look at the biblical traditions about David and different consideration of the story as presented.

> ## The Tribe of Judah
>
> According to the Hebrew Bible, Israel began as a conglomerate of twelve tribes. Twelve stable entities, however, strikes many students of the biblical material as forced. Recall the section in chapter 4 demonstrating how the names for the groups vary and any sense of tribal unity looks regional at best. Moreover, the emergence of the tribe of Judah as a power came late—most likely in the time from Hezekiah to Josiah (727–609 B.C.E.). So even if David legitimately belonged in the genealogical tree of Jacob, he likely emerged from a grouping rather loosely associated to the more powerful core tribes of the period.

(Ruth 4:17–18), thus acknowledging some mixed blood in his past, while still claiming that he descends directly from Jacob's fourth son, Judah. Likewise, 1 Chr 2:9–15 ties him to Judah without any equivocation. Given the importance of kinship connection in the postexilic period, the need to generate absolute certainty of David's connections to the house of Jacob in the story does not surprise. But note the lack of such assurance in earlier materials.

These stories of David reveal power in action. Legitimizing the man who took the throne away from the Benjaminite house of Saul requires considerable savvy. Instead of lauding an outsider and mercenary who wrests the kingdom from its first monarch in an uprising followed by a civil war, the biblical material recasts David. Careful shading of his familial heritage stands at the root of his reinvention and makes him a strong center for the national mythos.

*The Anointings*

Public proclamation of rule serves as a marker of legitimacy. Coronations often formalize monarchies by gathering concerned parties and investing the king or queen with symbols of their position, such as a crown. In modern democracies, leaders receive inauguration in like fashion by formally reciting an oath and engaging in appropriate celebratory events. Performing such rituals attempts to assign power and encourages others to recognize and support the leader.

In ancient Israel, the pouring of oil on the head, or **anointing**, ceremonially marked the selection of an individual for specific office—in this case, as the monarch. The text presents David as the recipient of such a practice on three different occasions. In 1 Sam 16:1–13, the prophet Samuel singles him out as a young boy. The people anoint him to serve as king of the tribe of Judah in 2 Sam 2:4 and again to symbolize his ascension as king of the tribes of Israel in 2 Sam 5:3.

Understanding of these latter two occasions comes readily. When becoming the head of state for Judah and then for Israel, public ceremonies formalize a process. But the anointing of David as a young man proves far more challenging to understand. Readers must ask what function such an introduction to the character of David serves.

The account reports that Samuel sets out on a mission to find God's replacement for the disobedient Saul. After Samuel arrives at the house of Jesse, Jesse shows him his seven older sons, but the prophet rejects each. Only the youngest, described as quite handsome (1 Sam 16:12), reportedly earns the favor of God. Several details in the story stand out. For example, its location seems odd. In this private home, David emerges in the narrative secretly—at the behest of God and from relative obscurity. Only subsequently do stories about his service in the court of Saul as a musician (16:14–23) and his saving of the Israelites from the Philistine warrior Goliath (1 Sam 17) give him a more public face.

The placement of the initial anointing serves to indicate that David arrives in the king's orbit only after his selection as his successor. By putting the story first, the writers disrupt any interpretation of David as executing machinations within the household of Saul to further his ambitions. Such suspicion might exist given the narration about his subsequent friendship with Saul's son Jonathan (18:1–5; 19:1–7; 20:1–42), his marriage to Saul's daughter Michal (18:17–29; 19:8–17), and his success in winning over the people (18:6–9, 12–15, 30). Instead, the writers blunt criticism of David by placing his rise under the direction of God from an early age.

Second, this anointing serves a legitimizing function when David assumes the throne in Israel. The text says the people see David as a leader because "the LORD said to you: It is you who shall be shepherd of my people Israel, you who shall be ruler over Israel" (2 Sam 5:2). Notice how the speakers indicate that God communicated to David—and David alone—his selection to serve as king. The people of Israel could know of this choice only if David, some member of his family, or Samuel repeated it. And, given Saul's position as king, to make such a claim invited charges of treason.

The need for caution from the reader comes across clearly here. Whether the anointing by Samuel actually occurred remains questionable. Given that the text presents Samuel as a respected prophet and that he anoints Saul, his legitimation of David would carry authority. Since Samuel dies before Saul and cannot choose David as Saul's successor in a proper time frame, the earlier, secret selection confers Samuel's seal of approval. And it cannot come under subsequent scrutiny. The two later anointings of David come from the people instead of God or God's agents—and they can face challenges. From a literary perspective, then, it makes sense to affirm David as a divine choice and thus close down potential disputes over his authority.

The repetition of anointings calls to mind the politically charged situation and reiterates why David as a rightful ruler proves crucial to the story. The monarchy exists in a fledgling state. With the death of Saul and his heir Jonathan, succession questions materialize. Add to this picture the story of the death of Abner, Saul's military commander, at the hand of David's military commander, Joab (2 Sam 3:26–30), and the assassination of Saul's son Ishbaal by his own captains (4:5–8), who then come to David with his head. Everything seems to turn to the advantage of David, and questions of his complicity in these events naturally arise. What did he know and when did he know it?

The biblical writers work hard to remove any possibility of David's involvement in the demise of these leaders. He grieves for Saul and Jonathan (2 Sam 1), kills the messenger who assisted in Saul's death (1:15), and rewards the people of the city who cared for their bodies (2:4–7). With his public mourning for Abner, the writers declare that he wins the hearts of the people (3:31–38). And the execution of Ishbaal's assassins along with the public display of their severed bodies (4:12) demonstrates his regard for the fallen king. Again, the narrative piles on the positives and raises the question: Does David simply benefit from a fortuitous series of events,

## Napoleon Crowns Himself

Tradition reports that in 1804 as Napoleon prepared his coronation as emperor of France in the Cathedral of Notre Dame, he summoned Pope Pius VII to crown him in the tradition of Charlemagne. When the moment came for the pope to place the crown on Napoleon's head, he refused to kneel because to do so would acknowledge that authority came from God and from Rome—and did not ultimately rest with him. So he grabbed the crown and stood before the altar and placed it on his own head.

A careful biblical reader might wonder if the writers of David's story pull a reverse "Napoleon." Instead of resisting the authority of the divine, they embrace a divine anointing to legitimate their man. Then again, other readers might conclude that the writers blunt David's ambition. Ready to take the crown and place it on his head, the story serves to circumvent his hunger for the role by placing him in the midst of a divine saga.

## Images of a Conflict

The 2000 presidential election in the United States ended in conflict and dispute. With Al Gore holding 255 electoral votes and George W. Bush 246, neither man accumulated the 270 needed to win, and three states remained too close to call. Mathematically, only the state of Florida mattered.

Disputes over vote totals, access to the polls, and miscast ballots held up final counts for weeks. Only the intervention of the United States Supreme Court, in a five-to-four decision, stopped the recounts and declared Bush the winner. He subsequently became the forty-third president of the United States.

Bumper stickers (and other forms of pop art) challenged his right to office. A few samples demonstrate the anger of many citizens over what they understood to be a stolen election and an illegitimate presidency: "Hail to the Thief." "Don't Blame Me: My Vote Didn't Count." "Bush Will *Never* Be My President."

In a stable democracy such as the United States, protest feels comfortable and appropriate because legitimization comes from established institutions like the Supreme Court and the Congress (which certified the vote under the leadership of Al Gore). A more fragile government, however, might have toppled under the weight of such a divided populace.

or might he stand as the one shaping their course—whether directly or indirectly?

No matter what the case, since David wins the throne and the biblical writers build the rationalization for a monarchy around him, justifying his occupation of that position becomes necessary. As an expression of power, the literary choice to include a divine anointing at the outset offers the appearance of stability to a new state struggling for recognition and suffering the pangs of a civil conflict raging between rival contenders for the throne. And it generates a legend around David that sustains his personal reputation in spite of many subsequent questionable actions in the story of his life.

| | |
|---|---|
| **Surfing the Power Web** | The trappings of rule communicate a king's rightful place to his subjects as well as to other regional states. As the narrative presents it, once David assumes the kingship of Israel, he acts quickly to establish his place. By choosing a city and establishing his capital there, he constructs a site from which he can operate as monarch. Bringing the ark of the covenant into the city authorizes it as a location where the deity dwells and oversees his rule. And expanding his family ensures his legacy into the future. |
| *Jerusalem, the Capital* | A king needs a place to seat his government. As seen in chapter 1, at the founding moments of a nation, sometimes the right locale can prove elusive. The site must draw people together as well as fit into the history and story of the larger nation. And, of course, practical concerns also impinge upon a decision. Israel, for example, faced a number of external threats (not to mention neighboring enemies within unclear borders) that necessitated a defensible space. |

When the monarchy began, no capital existed. First Samuel 10:26 reports that shortly after his public proclamation as king, "Saul also went to his home at Gibeah, and with him went warriors whose hearts God had touched." A member of the tribe of Benjamin, Saul remained in his family home and worked from there. Without a defined city to locate the institutions of his reign, people traveled to his residence when they needed to find him (14:2; 21:6; 23:19; 26:1). First Samuel 11 serves as an interesting example of how this process worked. In this story, the harassment of two tribes by the Ammonites leads them to send messengers to secure the help of the king and his warriors. When they arrive, verse 5 pictures Saul out behind his oxen. Rather than holding court or engaging in high-level administrative business, the king works the land.

Here he appears more like the head of a *bet av* than of a nation. No national story or ideology supports his rule from an administrative center. And, clearly, he does not possess the apparatus of a state. First Samuel 11:7

records that to call together a fighting force, "he took a yoke of oxen, and cut them in pieces and sent them throughout all the territory of Israel by the hand of messengers, saying, 'Whoever does not come out after Saul and Samuel, so shall it be done to his oxen!' Then the dread of the LORD fell upon the people, and they came out as one man." With only a few warriors around him and no standing military, he must wait for troops to respond. Likewise, no evidence of his seeking advice from a court or other advisors appears.

By contrast, the text presents David as following his anointing with the selection of a capital city. The story reports, however, that he chooses neither a city under Israelite control nor one associated with any of the tribes. Rather, he marches on Jerusalem, a Jebusite stronghold nestled high in the hills, with fortifications and a good water supply. If, as described by the writers earlier, his family lived in Bethlehem, David would know this location well given that it sits less than ten miles (sixteen kilometers) from the purported home of his youth. Moreover, the text shows him wandering extensively in the region as a fugitive. Situated between Hebron—his home in Judah—and the area occupied by the more dominant northern tribes, the city pulls together Judah and Israel. Taking advantage of this familiarity assumes the strategic advantage expected of a man with military and political prowess.

This story also invites an alternative reading. The biblical account reports that David knew no permanent home after coming into Saul's service as a young man. Further, when David fled Saul, the writers say that his brothers and other members of his father's household followed him (1 Sam 22:1). This movement meant no family remained for Saul to attack. But it also hints at the potential loss of a family home or land. As a new king, then, and possibly as an outsider to Israel, he likely saw problems in simply appropriating land from a tribal group. Needing support from the tribes, such a move ran the risk of antagonizing his detractors. If, indeed, he lacked blood connection to the people, annexing property could have undermined him from the outset. So seeking a good locale under the control of the Jebusites—a people not associated with whatever existed of "Israel"—made sense. It removed the threat of any tribal politics, demonstrated David's military acumen, and offered him a neutral site from which to build his base of operations.

*Moving the Ark*    But the text shows David going even further to establish this city as central to the state. For a king in this region at this time, effective reign rested on the support of a patron deity. Given all the questions about David's connections to the people of Israel, readers must also consider with what god his allegiance rested. Certainly, the overwhelming textual evidence presents him as a worshiper of the God of Israel. A closer look at the textual traditions raises a few questions about this association.

One of the more famous stories about David involves his demonstrating the fitness of Jerusalem as a capital and the rightness of his rule by bringing the **ark of the covenant** into the city. <u>A symbol of the divine presence</u>, it affirms the deity's defense of this place as well as protection of and favor toward its human administrative structure. According to the biblical narrative, the ark's story stretches back to the days of the exodus; it traveled with the people in the wilderness (Exod 25:10–22; cf. Deut 10:1–5). Joshua 3 presents the ark as preceding the people as they come into the land, and Josh 6 describes it as instrumental in the defeat of the city of Jericho. First Samuel 4 relates how the Philistines capture it in battle but then seek its return after it causes significant problems in their community. When David comes on the scene, the returned ark remains in quarantine in the city of Kiriath-jearim (1 Sam 7:2; or Baale-judah in 2 Sam 6:2).

The text describes showy public displays by David in two attempts to bring the ark into the city. Dancing and music (2 Sam 6:5, 14–15) come first and, in the second instance, extensive sacrifice (6:13, 18). For people living in cultures inundated by various media available 24/7, such ceremony might not seem like a big deal. But in the ancient world, the associated activities represented a unique occasion. The text also claims that David gave away foods such as bread, meat, and sweet raisin cakes to all of the people (6:19). Whether that food came from the offerings or from another source remains ambiguous. But the sharing of the substance of a meal with the people certainly encouraged the residents to accept David and this god as capable of making provision for them.

In the story Michal, the daughter of Saul and first wife of David, shows disdain for the entire process. This representation of her, typically interpreted as marking the closure of any connection between the house of David and the house of Saul, makes sense. If the ark represents traditions held by Saul and his family, then the appropriation of their god by David comes across as offensive to this daughter. The affront multiplies if David comes from a people other than Israel. As the text continues, Michal and David spar over his actions, and he demonstrates his control over her by never sleeping with her again. Although long estranged, Michal holds the position of the first wife. And as daughter of Saul and thus a princess of

---

### A symbol of the divine presence

Popular films such as *Raiders of the Lost Ark* confirm the biblical impression of the ark as the mediator of the presence of God. Readers of the text, however, need to proceed with caution. When the ark emerged as a symbol, and when it became important to the people, remains in question. Most of the stories about it come late in the tradition. And as biblical accounts like the stories of the golden calf (Exod 32) and Jeroboam I's establishment of sanctuaries at Dan and Bethel with their golden bulls (1 Kgs 12) demonstrate, association of YHWH with such animals remained powerful for many people. How large a role the ark actually played in the history of Israel and what it meant to the average person is impossible to know.

Israel, any child born to her would, in spite of birth order, hold some sway with partisans of Saul who still held political clout. By reporting that "Michal, the daughter of Saul, had no child to the day of her death" (2 Sam 6:23), the writers reveal the complete mastery of David over the house of Saul. His kingdom has risen, and he celebrates the public installation of the patron god, while Saul's house definitively dies out.

*A Dynastic Legacy*

The near eradication of Saul's house presents David the opportunity to construct his own family rule, and the writers affirm a Davidic dynasty within the divine plan. They claim that when David reveals his desire to construct a temple for God, he receives a refusal from the prophet Nathan. Instead, the writers highlight God making a promise to the king: "Moreover, the LORD declared to you that the LORD will make you a house" (2 Sam 7:11) Further, they assert the deity promises David that "your house and your kingdom shall be made sure forever before me; your throne shall be established forever" (7:16).

To ensure the fulfillment of this prophecy and his lasting rule, David needs a successor. Not coincidentally, notices about his family show up in close proximity to his anointings. After David becomes king of Judah, 2 Sam 3:2–5 reports an expansion not only in terms of children but also <u>wives</u>. Not surprisingly, 2 Sam 5 reports that on coming into Jerusalem, David takes on even more wives and concubines and increases the size of his family. Thirteen additional sons receive notice by name, although the text also mentions the birth of daughters.

Modern readers might wonder why David needs such an extensive family and not "<u>the heir and the spare</u>" more common in contemporary monar-

### wives

The reports of increases in a king's number of wives, particularly the notation of Maacah's status as a princess (daughter of King Talmai of Geshur), reveal how kings made political marriages to build bonds with other nations. Similar to the ways women served as currency between *bet avot*, they also served to link peoples and nations. Thus, according to the writers, David begins to express his power regionally by making an alliance with the kingdom of Geshur. Such marriage alliances, combined with the increase in children, solidify the position of David's family to continue to reign after his death.

### the heir and the spare

This terminology refers to the obligation of a crown prince to produce at least two sons, ensuring the continuity of the family line and reign. If something happens to the eldest son, another stands in line to the throne.

chies. Much as in a *bet av*, a large number of children in a royal family demonstrated a king's virility and his fitness to oversee a household and thus to oversee a state. Moreover, as in the *bet av*, each child took on specific roles to serve the whole. Duties of state likely occupied the members of the king's household, including military and civil service functions.

## Conclusions

The textual support for David and his rule knows few qualifications. The writers show him as constructing an apparatus to support his reign. In his selection of a capital city, in the installation of a patron deity, and in the establishing of a house of heirs capable of extending the rule he initiates, David generates for himself a position from which he can express power as a king. But each activity also points up potential weakness. A Jebusite city as the choice of a capital can signal "outsider." Bringing in the ark might hint at a similarly unfamiliar deity. Or perhaps it indicates appropriation of a god not his own. And the family he builds, as the story unfolds, threatens David as king. The murder of David's heir Amnon by his half brother Absalom demonstrates the discord (2 Sam 13), and Absalom's nearly successful coup d'état undermines the rule of his father (2 Sam 15–18).

In these texts, power stays in constant motion, shifting as relationships and circumstances vary. So describing David as "Surfing the Power Web" rather than "holding power" makes sense. A surfer requires both incredible focus and balance. As the water moves and generates tremendous energy, the one attempting to harness it and ride the wave must constantly react appropriately. Missteps result in wipeouts. Even the most ideal run ends. Power works in the same manner. The conditions David faces never stay the same. Sometimes his efforts prove successful, and at other times he fails. But he emerges in and from the text overall as an amazing champion.

## Webmaster

The David standing in Firenze stands poised to make history. Assuming the "facts" of the story told, the stone will leave his slingshot in mere moments and he will claim an improbable victory over an enemy of greater stature and experience. The biblical writers claim Goliath mocks David when he sees him: "Am I a dog that you come at me with sticks?" he asks (1 Sam 16:43). But the young man stands resolute, and in the end he walks away with the head of the warrior.

Carving a legend in stone does not limit its interpretive possibilities. As the people of Firenze demonstrated, *David* assumed a specific political meaning based in large part on the statue's placement near government buildings. What if it stood in a church as originally planned? And what does it say today, standing as one of the great icons of art in a museum crowded with tourists? A fixed image still can undergo manipulation.

The biblical David illustrates the point. In the brief history of the monarchy, the kingdoms split quickly, and both often survived only as vassals under the control of much larger entities. The state frequently skirmished with smaller countries such as its northern neighbor Aram; what hope could they maintain to match up against large empires such as the Assyrians, Babylonians, Egyptians, Persians, Greeks, or Romans? But even after many defeats, the idea of David stood. Jeremiah 33:17 says, for example, "David shall never lack a man to sit on the throne of the house of Israel." Indeed, the biblical writers might have created the ideal of David to encourage the people in difficult historical moments.

This supposition certainly helps explain how David becomes the model for the **messiah**, or anointed one, in both Judaism and Christianity. Jewish notions of this figure often conform to the criteria set out in Ezek 37:24–28:

> My servant David shall be king over them; and they shall all have one shepherd. They shall follow my ordinances and be careful to observe my statutes. They shall live in the land that I gave to my servant Jacob, in which your ancestors lived; they and their children and their children's children shall live there forever; and my servant David shall be their prince forever. I will make a covenant of peace with them; it shall be an everlasting covenant with them; and I will bless them and multiply them, and will set my sanctuary among them forevermore. My dwelling place shall be with them; and I will be their God, and they shall be my people. Then the nations shall know that I the LORD sanctify Israel, when my sanctuary is among them forevermore.

The great medieval Jewish writer Maimonides builds on this idea: "In future time, the King Mashiach [Hebrew for "messiah"] will arise and renew the Davidic dynasty, restoring it to its initial sovereignty."

Christianity, by contrast, identifies Jesus Christ as this Davidic figure. The Gospel of Matthew, for example, opens with a genealogy identifying Jesus as both a son of David and a son of Abraham. Likewise, the apostle Paul spoke of Christ as—at least in terms of the flesh—descended from David (Rom 1:3). The book of Revelation names Christ as the Lion of the tribe of Judah and the Root of David (Rev 5:5).

Each tradition, then, molds this "David" into what its community needs. A young warrior on the brink of greatness for the people of Firenze, a righteous king for Jews seeking a messiah, a conquering cosmic hero to the writer of Revelation, David takes on many guises. And as in the presentation of many public leaders, readers can discern nothing other than the myth surrounding him. Larger than life, like Michelangelo's work, he serves diverse agendas for peoples far removed from those who first told his story and demonstrates how an image can embody many different dreams. In this way, David functions as a location of power both in the biblical text and beyond.

**Suggested Biblical Readings**

1 Samuel 16–1 Kings 1, especially 1 Samuel 16–17 and 2 Samuel 1–7

**Discussion Questions**

1. Can you identify mythic political figures in your own nation's history that have come to embody particular ideals that the state wants to advance? What purposes do such figures serve?
2. How does the idea of power circulating and an individual seeking to move with it differ from the concept of power residing in a person or in an office or position? Can you think of situations in your own experience where you could see power moving among people? How did people act so as to tap into and express that power?
3. In the story of the struggle between Saul and David, identify how the writers present Saul as ineffectual. Did they make good choices in order to persuade readers that Saul was unfit to serve as king?

**Suggestions for Further Reading**

Alter, Robert. *The David Story: A Translation with Commentary on 1 and 2 Samuel.* New York: W. W. Norton & Co., 1999.

Halpern, Baruch. *David's Secret Demons: Messiah, Murderer, Traitor, King.* Grand Rapids: Wm. B. Eerdmans Publishing Co., 2004.

Pinsky, Robert. *The Life of David.* New York: Random House, 2005.

# 10. The State

Rome wasn't built in a day.
—Anonymous

Living securely within the boundaries of nation-states such as Canada, the United States, or the United Kingdom frequently means taking for granted the complicated structures that produce the life most residents enjoy. Call 911, and police, fire, or emergency medical responders come. Children receive an education in public schools. Street maintenance crews take care of potholes or snow removal. Court systems adjudicate criminal and civil matters. Public utilities produce drinkable water from the tap, and city or county sewers eliminate waste from toilets. And an equipped military stands ready to defend a country's interests.

## Nation and State

The use of language for governmental systems requires some precision. In general, "**nation**" designates an entity that might draw from common ethnic, cultural, or social heritage to bind a people. Chapter 7 demonstrates that the biblical writers constructed such a unity where diversity actually existed. The "Israelites," for example, certainly included people from multiple ethnic groups. And the story the Hebrew Bible presents about the evolving nation stresses "all Israel" even as various political factions jockeyed—often violently—for position.

By contrast, "**state**" makes reference to a politically organized series of institutions exercising authority over a defined territory and population. States possess the power to compel compliance to their norms and standards and typically exercise some degree of autonomy from surrounding entities.

The term "nation-state" joins these two ideas, describing entities from seventeenth-century Europe to the present.

This web of services makes the state visible to its residents and demonstrates how such entities use their resources to benefit the communities they create. But states do more than simply provide services. States also enact power. A government, for instance, structures a society through a myriad of regulations and laws and then enforces these codes to promote its notion of public order. A police officer writing a ticket for speeding serves as one example. Or think of the stringent security measures required to board a plane. And states can and do compel their citizens to perform a variety of functions—from paying taxes, to obtaining licenses to perform particular tasks, to serving in the military. People comply with the laws of the state in order to avoid <u>penalties</u> such as prison or fines.

The image of a web works to illustrate how states express power. Complex bureaucracies organize regulatory and legal authority in a diffuse manner. As a result, citizens experience the control a state asserts in myriad locations. And with a variety of officials working within this apparatus to enforce its control, a state's power remains fluid. Power rests in no one place or agency and resides with no one official.

To make the situation even more problematic, many kinds of states exist. The United States functions as a constitutionally based federal republic, while Canada features a national government that combines a constitutional monarchy, a parliamentary democracy, and a federation. Other forms of government—from monarchies to dictatorships to single-party totalitarian rule to theocracies—also organize a common life among people. And each system functions according to its own rules and permits its officials different levels of authority, control, or, on the other side, citizen participation.

Such a multiplicity of forms also demonstrates the arbitrary nature of the state as an institution. In other words, nothing compels the choice of any particular governmental model or even of constructing a state apparatus at all. In fact, the state explored in this section, Israel, challenges readers from the outset. The conditions that prompted the rise of the monarchy and the development of its institutions remain obscured by biblical writers

## penalties

To populations afforded fewer rights, the power expressed by the state often results in oppression and/or discrimination. The enforcement of Jim Crow laws in the American South from the late nineteenth century to the middle of the twentieth century, for instance, meant separate facilities for black and white citizens. Different water fountains, public restrooms, or seating on buses all became the norm. Women lacked the right to vote in the United States, Canada, and the United Kingdom until the early twentieth century and thus possessed no voice in government. In many places around the globe today, persons disagreeing with the state face long prison sentences for their opposition to official policies. Think of Nelson Mandela imprisoned in South Africa from 1962 to 1990, or Aung San Suu Kyi often under house arrest in Burma for most of the period from 1989.

## promoting a Davidic kingship

The biblical record clearly presents a biased account of the two states of Israel and Judah. From the perspective of the writers, only the Davidic kingship stands as legitimate in the eyes of YHWH (2 Sam 7:1–17; 1 Kgs 2:24; 9:5; 15:11; 2 Kgs 22:2). The northern kingdom not only seceded, but its rulers also violated the will of the deity simply by serving as kings. Although some of Judah's monarchs receive negative assessments, the entire group does not receive the absolute condemnation reserved for the northern rulers. Almost the exact words recur to evaluate every leader of Israel, as in the notice on Azariah: "He did what was evil in the sight of the Lord, as his ancestors had done. He did not depart from the sins of Jeroboam son of Nebat, which he caused Israel to sin" (2 Kgs 15:9; see also 1 Kgs 15:34; 16:19; 22:15; 2 Kgs 13:2, 6, 11; 14:24; 15:18, 24, 28).

interested solely in <u>promoting a Davidic kingship</u> seated in Jerusalem. This textual glorification of the Davidic line features the presentation of Solomon as the ruler who consolidates monarchical authority and reigns in glory from a magnificent Jerusalem. Most scholars see here an exaggeration of the record. Archaeological exploration supports the city and its environs as undergoing significant development only in the eighth century B.C.E. In generating this image of a previous golden era, then, the writers cast the early monarchy as far more successful than the evidence likely corroborates and thereby grant these first kings greater legitimacy at the outset.

Despite its overhyped support of the monarchy, the Hebrew Bible nonetheless reveals a great deal about the functioning of power within a state structure. This chapter explores how the biblical writers imagine Israel's negotiations of state power from the rise of the monarchy, through the split into two states, and into domination by a succession of empires. Taking the picture of Solomon's administrative cabinet as a starting point, this idealized vision reveals how the biblical writers constructed monarchic power and provides a point of departure to explore how power moved between and among various interests. The chapter then examines alternative locations of power, including some consideration of the place of the prophets. Finally, it closes with a brief look at the ways the power dynamic shifts following the dissolution of the states. The relationship between "Israel" and empire receives attention.

## Solomon and the Conjuring of the State

According to the biblical writers, the kingship in Israel faced a succession crisis as David neared death. With no positive pattern established for transition of rule, questions as to the identity of the next ruler arose. The biblical text portrays Adonijah as enjoying the rights of the oldest son in addition to the support of key players such as Joab, the military commander, and Abiathar, the priest (1 Kgs 1:7). But the text also reports some division among the persons surrounding David: Zadok, Benaiah, Nathan, Shimei, and Rei all support the younger Solomon (and thus oppose Adonijah) for unspecified reasons (1 Kgs 1:8).

Clearly, this succession reveals a complicated circulation of power. These stories describe a group of officials or a king's court who work for the monarch and conduct the business of the state surrounding the throne. With David weak and dying, the sons must jockey for position, and seeking the backing of key officials proves necessary to ensure their success. The exact nature of the machinations that determine Solomon's success in ascending to the throne <u>remains unknown</u>, but the writers show him ban-

### remains unknown

First Kings 1 depicts the prophet Nathan soliciting the aid of Bathsheba to approach an ill and diminished David. According to the story, they plot together so that she informs the king of Adonijah's plans to secure the crown and reminds him of a "promise" to make Solomon his successor. Nathan confirms her words, and David complies by elevating his younger son. Ascertaining the accuracy of such a story proves impossible.

### The Costs of Constructing a State

Kings and the apparatus they build to support their reign—the state—express power locally, nationally, and internationally. For the people of Israel, living in a region marked by frequent conflict and contested for its valuable military and trade routes, establishing a structure designed to secure borders, foster respect, and effectively utilize its resources seemed logical. Constructing and maintaining such, however, demanded a significant outlay of resources. The Hebrew Bible outlines some of these demands and their drawbacks.

The writers of 1 Samuel show God warning the people about what choosing a king might mean for their way of life (see chapter 8 for more detail). Impressing sons into the military and craft services, demanding daughters for work in his household, and levying steep taxes on crops and other holdings all receive mention (1 Sam 8:11–17). The problems emerge readily. Subsistence in the land proved difficult enough, but taxation burdened every *bet av* in terms of its overall production. The departure of sons and daughters in order to serve the state decreased the workforce, amplifying the reduction in living standards. Moreover, the loss of children altered not only the family dynamics within the *bet av* but also the social structure of entire communities. Problems presumably developed over who would inherit, how heads of household built their authority and made reasonable commitments to other members, and what methods of exchange bound different units together in alliances.

The economic and social changes accompanying the establishment of a monarchy raised opposition to the king. Although the biblical writers typically dismiss resistance (see 1 Sam 10:27, for example), the struggles of the early rulers and the breaking apart of Israel after only three kings demonstrate some of the internal pressures on this new form of governance.

ishing or killing his opponents in order to consolidate his hold on the crown (2 Kgs 2:13–46). The story goes on to report that he takes the rudimentary governing apparatus built by his father David and transforms it into a full-fledged state bureaucracy. In this manner, his reign comes to symbolize the apex of biblical Israel on the world stage and models the right organization of royal power.

*Solomon's Court*

This organization is specified in a list purporting to name Solomon's coterie of officials. Such a listing, like the ones naming David's inner circle (2 Sam 8:15–18; 20:23–26), depicts a power ideal. Such a developed royal bureaucracy likely emerged much later than Solomon. So while not historical documents, these rosters still offer a notion of how court life functioned. Thus, when read for how power moved around the king, they offer some interesting insights into not only the position and duties of these most important officials but also into how they operated in relationship to one another.

## Solomon's Administrative Officials

First Kings 4:1–19 names various high officials of Solomon and their duties:

| | |
|---|---|
| Azariah son of Zadok | Priest |
| Elihoreph and Ahijah sons of Shisha | Secretaries |
| Jehoshaphat son of Ahilud | Recorder |
| Benaiah son of Jehoiada | Commander of the army |
| Zadok and Abiathar | Priests |
| Azariah son of Nathan | Over the officials |
| Zabud son of Nathan | Priest and king's friend |
| Ahishar | In charge of the palace |
| Adoniram son of Abda | In charge of the forced labor |

These twelve officials over Israel provided food for the king and his household:

| | |
|---|---|
| Ben-hur | Hill Country of Ephraim |
| Ben-deker | Makaz, Shaalbim, Beth-shemesh, and Elon-beth-hanan |
| Ben-hesed | Arruboth |
| Ben-abinadab | Naphath-dor |
| Baana son of Ahilud | Taanach, Megiddo, Beth-shean to Abel-meholah |
| Ben-geber | Ramoth-gilead |
| Ahinadab | Mahanaim |
| Ahimaaz | Naphtali |
| Baana son of Hushai | Asher, Bealoth |
| Jehoshaphat | Issachar |
| Geber | Gilead, country of King Sihon of the Amorites and King Og of Bashan |
| One unnamed official | Judah |

### Priests

Many readers might find the location of the priests at the top of this roster (as well as in several other places on the list) obvious. The linking of the Hebrew Bible to holiness in much of western culture often means that contemporary audiences tend to understand biblical peoples as far more "religious" than moderns. If this premise holds, certainly a king would want to foster a close relationship with priests as divine conduits in order to comprehend God's will for him and for the nation. Such a reading, however, dramatically misunderstands the priesthood and its function in the monarchy.

Priests serve God, but under the direction of the king. For example, when the text describes David's bringing the ark of the covenant into the city (2 Sam 6), the writers assert that he establishes the presence of a patron deity and thus legitimizes his reign. A deity in this role requires the appropriate officials to manage the divine presence by engaging in the prescribed rituals. Even as these priests appear to function in the service of God, however, they work for the state, and their loyalty rests with the king as their actual patron. The story of David's flight from Jerusalem during Absalom's coup d'état illustrates the complexities of this king-deity-priest relationship.

According to 2 Sam 17, as all of the partisans for David depart the city, the priests come along, transporting the ark. Their allegiance goes to the man. The biblical writers try to alter that focus by reporting that David sends them back, claiming that priests should remain with the king whom God selects to rule (15:25–26). While apparently inserting the will of God into this process, the David presented by the writers also attempts to fix the deity's presence within the city and thus with the state situated in it. In this ideal, God remains with the established institutions, and whoever sits as king retains authority over the priests who serve this deity.

Solomon appears, according to the narrative, to fix firmly this relationship between God and the king by constructing a temple for the deity in Jerusalem followed by a palace adjacent to it (see chapter 12 for a full discussion of the Jerusalem Temple). A group of priests serves in this complex and assumes multiple responsibilities. As representatives of the patron deity, they maintain the shrine that authorizes the king as divinely selected and sanctioned. These duties serve both political and religious purposes. For example, the priest Uriah follows the orders of King Ahaz with regard to the construction of an altar and the offerings made in 2 Kgs 16:10–16.

This altar replicates one Ahaz sees in Damascus and displaces the bronze altar dedicated to YHWH. Ahaz makes an offering on "his" new shrine and instructs the priests to use this altar for the morning burnt offerings, the evening grain offerings, the burnt and grain offerings of the king and the people, the people's drink offerings, and to dash it with the blood of the offerings and sacrifices. The story reports that the priest Uriah complies with the king's directions in this regard. Meanwhile, the original altar of God gets relocated and used as more of a private conduit between the king and the deity. The precedence of the altar modeled on the one Ahaz sees in Damascus demonstrates how the temple functions as a political space and responds to the needs of the king. Apparently Ahaz wants the trappings common to other such sites in order to show his similarity to other rulers. Further, he clearly controls the actions that occur within the temple precinct as the priests respond to his directives.

Additionally, once Jerusalem exists as both a cult center and a royal city, the temple and the palace draw people to it. This flow of traffic serves as an economic engine for the king. It generates revenue through the trade within and around its environs as well as through tax collection. Priestly employment, then, also involves securing and administering funds.

Second Kings 12:4–5 illustrates this point in its description of the actions of King Jehoash and his priests. Here the king orders the priests to use all donations to the temple for necessary repairs. This funding includes both income from offerings, voluntary gifts, and required taxes. The priests, however, fail to observe this mandate. As a result, the writers show the king setting up a new financial system administered through the king's secretary and the high priest for temple maintenance. This passage clearly indicates the monetary flow the temple generates. And while the priests ignore the king's wishes, the text certainly does not appear to show them acting autonomously or outside of his purview. Rather, they simply expect him to perform upkeep of the temple building. Such an assumption likely reflects the common view that the shrine functions as a state building and thus the state must administer it. The priests take a role in this collection and distribution of funds (see also 2 Kgs 22:4), but in cooperation with a member of the king's cabinet.

### Secretaries

The word "secretary" carries many connotations for a modern reader, from an administrative assistant who coordinates a schedule and handles routine correspondence, to a cabinet secretary running a government department or agency. Little material in the text assists readers in understanding this role in the monarchy as presented by the Hebrew Bible. But the high placement of these officials on both Solomon's and David's lists of administrative personnel (2 Sam 9:17; 20:25) indicate that they likely functioned as principal aides to the king. In this capacity, they managed how power circulated around the king by controlling who got access to him and when.

Shaphan, the secretary during Josiah's reign, illustrates a part of the secretarial function. According to the text, he serves as a communication link between the king and the high priest (2 Kgs 22:3–10). Further, he receives mention as a member of the delegation sent out to authenticate a book of law found in the temple (22:11–20). These duties demonstrate the close relationship between the king and secretary. Such a position of trust and confidence perhaps suggests a role that modern readers would label "chief of staff."

### Recorder

Keepers of the official archives, the recorders exercised the power to shape the information about a king and his actions. Mentions within the biblical material of the Books of the Annals of the Kings of Israel and Judah likely illustrate the work of these officials (see 1 Kgs 14:19 for an initial reference). This standard formula recurs throughout 1 and 2 Kings, typically appearing immediately prior to a sovereign's death notice (see 1 Kgs 14:29; 15:7, 23, 31; 16:5, 14, 20, 27 for examples).

A recorder possibly served also as a herald. As a court official, this person took charge of making royal proclamations and also oversaw the diplomatic communications between kings. Proclamations and/or edicts appear rarely in earlier biblical materials. Their frequency in Chronicles, Ezra, and Esther—all postexilic texts—suggests the influence of the Persian imperial system on this form of communication (see Ezra 1:1; 6:11; 2 Chr 36:22; Esth 2:8; 3:12; 8:8–9, 17; 9:1, 13).

### Military Commander

The commander of the troops stands out as a person around whom significant power circulates. States need military forces to protect their interests, but kings require loyal servants in this role given the ability of an army to unseat a ruler. For example, Abner, the military commander of King Saul and then of his son King Ishbaal, attempts to defect to David (2 Sam 3:12) and deliver Israel to him. Likewise, Zimri, a commander over half of King Jehu's chariots, assassinates the king and rules in his place (1 Kgs 16:9–10). The text tells the same story of duplicity about Pekah, a captain of Israel's king Pekahiah (2 Kgs 15:25).

The primacy of military rule stands out on David's list of officials (2 Sam 8:15; 20:23) but receives less emphasis in the cabinet of Solomon. An examination of the figures named suggests some of the reasons for the variation. When considering David's reign, both the list of officials and the stories related depict Joab as a powerful and dominant character. Similarly, the

### Joab

Son of David's sister Zeruiah, Joab first appears in the struggle between the houses of Saul and David and likely holds David's trust because of his familial connection. A ruthless right-hand man, he kills enemies such as Saul's military commander Abner (2 Sam 3:27), takes care of problems such as Bathsheba's husband, Uriah (11:14–27), and rids David of his rebellious son Absalom (18:14), all in service of his king. The book of Chronicles credits him with earning his place by leading the attack that secures Jerusalem (1 Chr 11:6), a tale not recounted in Samuel.

The stories indicate closeness between David and Joab. For example, in both 2 Sam 4:24–25 and 19:5–7 the writers depict Joab as speaking to the king in a direct, even scolding, manner. But 1 Kgs 2:5–6 includes David's warning Solomon about Joab's treachery. According to the narrative, Joab sides with Solomon's older brother Adonijah in their competition for the throne. Solomon neutralizes Joab's influence by ordering his death in a bloody purge against all those persons who opposed his reign (1 Kgs 2:28–35). This order shows the importance of Joab's position and the danger he represents to the new king.

## The Cherethites and the Pelethites

Many scholars associate these warriors with the Philistines. Given David's pitched battles with this people (see 1 Sam 18:6–7, 27–29), readers might wonder why he would surround himself with "enemy" warriors. But the narrative also reports that David worked for the king of Gath, a Philistine ruler, while a fugitive from Saul (1 Sam 27–30). While understanding his service here as that of a mercenary proves the most common interpretation, the possibility that David—perhaps not an Israelite—connects deeply with this people also exists.

Numerous examples illustrate the long-term loyalty of these warriors to David and to David alone. They support him during Absalom's coup (2 Sam 15:18) and help him resist the rebellion of Sheba (20:7). And they ensure the installation of Solomon as king by placing him on David's mule and parading him about the city (1 Kgs 1:38, 44).

Cherethites and the Pelethites, David's personal bodyguards under the command of Benaiah (2 Sam 8:18; 20:23), receive mention. Their role demonstrates how power focuses on the person of the king. The death of a monarch potentially damages or destroys the whole state (see 1 Sam 31:8–13; 2 Sam 1:11–16; 4:5–12, for examples). His protection, then, not only assures the continuation of his life but also secures the stability of the throne.

As a point of comparison, the roster of Solomon's "cabinet" in 1 Kgs 4 places his military commander fourth. The biblical writers indicate no significant armed engagements during Solomon's reign and thus assume the military took on a smaller role. Command in his reign shifted to Benaiah, and Benaiah's previous association with the Cherethites and the Pelethites disappears from the text. This omission may indicate they became part of the regular forces or, more likely, that their loyalty extended only to David and ended at his death.

### Solomon's Other Officials

The Hebrew Bible also imagines Solomon's state as including persons overseeing work in the palace and a corps of forced labor. Understanding the functions of these officials requires some background information.

The text describes how Solomon divides the land, with the exception of Judah, into twelve smaller units to govern more effectively. Given the number twelve, many readers might conclude that Solomon's division of the kingdom somewhat approximates the old tribal lines. But the writers offer a different layout (1 Kgs 4:7–19), which deliberately erases these borders, especially

## a different layout

This division of the land puzzles many scholars. The place names vary. Some identify regions, some name cities, and some lack any certainty regarding their referent. Overlaps also appear. What kind of administrative units this list constructs remains unclear.

within close proximity to Jerusalem. This state structure undercuts any potential lingering political allegiances that might threaten monarchic rule. But the narrative also presents the arrangement as dramatically favoring Judah and the south by putting in place a system that defends the core by exploiting the periphery. The text moreover suggests that the resulting inequalities serve as a primary cause of the kingdom's division after Solomon's death.

A district ruler oversaw each region. According to 1 Kgs 4:7, each functioned primarily to provide food for Solomon and his household one month out of every year. One month of supplies for the king might seem a reasonable demand on the surface. But 1 Kgs 4:22–28 presents a picture of what each *day* supposedly entailed in terms of supplies for Solomon's kingdom:

> 30 cors (1 cor = 46.5 gallons) choice flour
> 60 cors meal
> 10 fat oxen
> 20 pasture-fed cattle
> 100 sheep
> various deer, gazelles, roebucks, fatted fowl
> barley and straw for the horses

While certainly an exaggerated list in terms of quantity, it nonetheless makes an important point. The production of goods that went to the king imposed an enormous burden on the population of a region. Growing and harvesting crops, manufacturing flour, oil, or meal, and raising animals all demanded significant resources in terms of land, time, and personnel.

## The causes of the Division of the Kingdom

While 1 Kgs 9:20–22 claims that Solomon enslaved no Israelites, 1 Kgs 5:13–18 questions this supposition. It reports that Solomon forced some 30,000 Israelite men to work in shifts that rotated one month in Lebanon and two months at home. The writers use the stresses of this work as a likely contribution to the events described in 1 Kgs 11:26–40. There they show Jeroboam, one of Solomon's administrators, leading a revolt against Solomon. Some scholars postulate that Jeroboam, charged with maintaining the forced labor over the "house of Joseph" (1 Kgs 11:28), recruited his workforce from the northern tribes. This text indicates that their service exceeded that of peoples in regions closer to Jerusalem. The enormous obligations placed on this populace serves as one explanation for their revolt. Similarly, Solomon's selling of twenty cities to Hiram of Tyre (1 Kgs 9:10–14) functions for the biblical writers as a source of anger for the people of the region and perhaps a contribution to their dissatisfaction with his rule. Finally, a persistent north-south split never really dissipated and so fueled this rebellion. No matter what the cause or series of causes, the text indicates that Jeroboam failed to defeat a powerful Solomon. However, following the king's death, the writers show him challenging Solomon's son and successor, Rehoboam, and forcing the kingdom to divide.

Relinquishing precious foodstuffs to a monarch diminished the resources of rural citizens in favor of fueling the state apparatus. Although not made clear in the text, a logical assumption holds that the overseer of the officials made certain that the local governors performed their function and delivered the necessary supplies.

In addition to procuring foodstuffs, a king also needed to erect monumental structures and to establish and maintain protected sites as demonstrations of his wealth, the firmness of his control over a region, and the favor of the patron deity. According to the text, Solomon built not only an elaborate temple-palace complex but also fortified locations such as Hazor, Megiddo, and Gezer against military threat (1 Kgs 9:15–17) and constructed multiple store cities to supply the troops (9:19). In this drought-prone region, food constituted a precious commodity. The ideal ruler of a state needed to maintain adequate supplies to feed his officials and workers even in times of want.

To accomplish all of these projects, the writers report that Solomon imposed a heavy tax burden and impressed a labor force. Another official, the chief of forced labor, functioned to staff these efforts and ensure the success of these enterprises. According to the text, the pressure of establishing such monumental structures drained Solomon's resources and forced him to adopt measures that contributed to the division of the kingdom shortly after his death.

Solomon's list of officials also includes Zabud, a priest and "king's friend" (1 Kgs 4:5). The friend almost certainly served as a counselor or advisor. Abishar "was in charge of the palace" (4:6). This role likely involved maintaining the complex and overseeing the persons working within it. The administrative roster concludes with the names of the regional officials whom the writers posit as overseeing the production of goods and services for the crown in a given area.

The Hebrew Bible indicates a variety of others also moved within the power web surrounding the king. Zabud, a priest and the king's friend, and his brother Azariah, who oversaw the officials, both receive mention as sons of Nathan. Likely sons of the **prophet** Nathan, who advised David (2 Sam 7, 12) and assisted in the palace intrigues to get Solomon on the throne (1 Kgs 1), their mention demonstrates the power of family connections in gaining access to the king. Additionally, it suggests the possibility of hereditary office. Finally, it places prophets in the administrative circle of the monarch.

Although not mentioned in the roster of officials of either Solomon or David, prophets certainly functioned in service of the king. Indeed, the text

### in service of the king

Texts from the eighteenth century B.C.E. city of Mari also reveal the words of prophets directed toward the king. Giving advice on everything from how to rule to discerning good times for battle, they demonstrate links between monarchs and a corps of prophets.

presents multiple scenarios where prophets act in support of the monarchy. For example, Samuel anoints the first king, Saul (1 Sam 10:1), as well as his successor, David (16:11–13). The division of the kingdom into Israel and Judah also features the prophetic selection of Jeroboam to lead Israel (1 Kgs 11:29–32). Prophets participate in the preparations for battle via consultation (see 1 Kgs 22:6, for example) and offer advice on political issues (2 Kgs 19:7; Isa 7). Prophets of deities other than YHWH also work within the courts of some kings (2 Kgs 3:13). Most of the material in the Hebrew Bible, however, preserves prophetic opposition to the sitting monarch. An examination of the prophet in this role appears in the next section of this chapter.

While receiving no notice in the list of officials connected to Solomon, the queen mother, Bathsheba, nonetheless takes on a significant role. The writers show Nathan approaching her with a plan to move a feeble David toward supporting Solomon as his successor (1 Kgs 1:11–14). Clearly, the narrative assumes that court officials know her well and count on her access to David in order to achieve success. Moreover, when the displaced older brother Adonijah makes his last move toward the throne by attempting to acquire David's concubine Abishag (1 Kgs 2:13–18), he also comes to Bathsheba. Adonijah's approaching the queen mother assumes her position of influence over Solomon. Although not a formal advisor, she clearly maintains open lines of communication both with David and her son, as well as the perceived ability to sway their thinking. She thus occupies a pivotal role in the court.

Other stories confirm the role of the queen mother in this power web. First Kings 15:13 makes reference to the position as an office in the bureaucracy of the state rather than simply as a biological relationship. Note how Maacah receives mention as mother of both Abijam (1 Kgs 15:2) and Asa (15:10)—even as the text lists them as father and son (15:8). Her removal from the role comes about as a result of violating the king's policies; she no

---

### Isaiah in the Royal House?

Some speculation exists in scholarly circles connecting the prophet Isaiah to the royal house. This "Isaiah of Jerusalem" most often gets credited with material found in chapters 1–39 of the book of Isaiah. The writers describe his call to prophesy in language that suggests knowledge of and/or presence in the temple (Isa 6:1–6). Further, as the text presents the material, he enjoys remarkable access to kings Ahaz (see Isa 7:1–17, for example) and Hezekiah (Isa 36–39), as well as to other royal officials (22:15–16). And words attributed to him include much material favorable to the Davidic kingship (16:5), including two royal poems (9:2–7 and 11:1–9). But Isa 36–39 appears to indicate some separation from the everyday realities of the royal court. When King Hezekiah requires counsel, he sends some of his closest advisors to Isaiah (37:2, 5). Whether employed directly by the king as part of the administrative bureaucracy or simply local to Jerusalem, Isaiah stands out as a prophet generally in support of the Davidic line seated in the royal city.

longer fits the right administrative profile. Athaliah, mother of Ahaziah (2 Kgs 8:26), also wields significant influence. After her son's death, she sets out to destroy the remainder of the royal family to consolidate her own rule (11:1–3). Likewise, the book of Jeremiah speaks of the queen mother as holding a regal role (Jer 13:18; 29:2).

*Conclusions*

At least as recorded in the text, Solomon establishes the material signs of a state apparatus. A court filled with bureaucrats relates the complexity of his role and shows his adeptness at managing the responsibilities of the monarchy, just as the palace, the temple, and all of the fortified cities and other structures demonstrate his ability to garner resources for his government. In other words, kings enact power by creating administrative bureaucracies and building visible signs of their rule.

But the biblical material reports that Solomon displays power in a myriad of other forms as well. He uses manipulation, or accepts the benefits of the machinations of others, in order to take the throne from his brother (1 Kgs 1:1–53). The writers recount how he banishes or kills all his possible enemies at court to consolidate his rule (2:13–46). Marrying foreign women, he builds diplomatic alliances (3:1; 11:1–13). He engages in relationships with other countries through land deals (9:10–14), commercial trade (9:26–28), and through his sponsorship of and reputation for wisdom (3:16–28; 4:29–34; and 10:1–39).

But even this idealized picture of power comes with a cost for him. The writers indicate that promoting his interests through the apparatus of the state has generated opposition both at home and abroad. First Kings 11:14–40 offers details about some of his adversaries. The writers' description of the rebellion of Jeroboam and the almost immediate division of the kingdom following Solomon's death indicate the depth of the resistance to his rule. The next section examines some of the people and structures who contested the power of the state as well as their place in its dissolution.

## Opposition to Monarchy and the Dissolution of the State

The attempt to create an Israelite state looks fairly successful to many readers. It should. The Hebrew Bible strives to depict state formation as a natural progression: after coming into the land (Josh 1–12), the people of Israel settle by tribes in various regions (Josh 13–21) and work together to struggle against their enemies under the leadership of charismatic figures (Judg 2–16). When that system of leadership begins to falter, the people determine to become a monarchic state—all, of course, under the watchful eye of a supportive YHWH (1 Sam 8–13). Given the fervor with which the biblical writers idealize and promote Davidic rule from Jerusalem, this assessment of stability does not surprise. Indeed, even after the division into two states, the northern kingdom, or Israel, manages to survive for around 200 years, and the southern kingdom, or Judah, lasts approximately 335 years. These histories, especially for North Americans, feel long. But length of time in existence fails to account for the internal strife, the external pressures, and the almost constant level of political struggle marking these histories.

The Hebrew Bible itself, however, includes many stories that point to the instability of these states from their inception. For example, the first king, Saul, competes with David for control of the throne (1 Sam 18:7, 12–16; 19:17; 20:31; 23:17). Following Saul's death, a civil war between the house of David and the house of Saul's son Ishbaal ensues (2 Sam 3:1). David's eldest son and heir Amnon dies at the hands of his younger brother Absalom (13:28–29). This same son executes an almost successful coup d'état to unseat his father from the throne (2 Sam 15–18). Another rival, Sheba, revolts soon after (2 Sam 19–20) and demonstrates remaining tensions between David and some persons within the tribe of Benjamin. At the time of David's death, his sons Adonijah and Solomon engage in competition to rule, with Solomon ultimately killing his brother (1 Kgs 1–2). Jeroboam

### Organizational Structures in Israel Prior to the Monarchy

When considering who acted to enforce social order, local rule—through the *bet av* and clan—dominated for much of the biblical period. The stories told in the text, however, describe a coherent group of tribes that, when combined, formed an entity called "Israel." Further, this "Israel" enjoys a rather stable and successive leadership from Moses to Joshua to various judges. However, scholars see little external, nonbiblical evidence to support such a picture.

Think instead of a people living on the land but without fixed boundaries that define a nation. A *bet av* possessed property, but demonstrating ownership often depended on its ability to control and defend those holdings or an associated village or a city. Particularly powerful families, clans, or tribes frequently held sway in a given area and sometimes joined with others to expand territory or ward off enemies. But as local and regional conditions changed, familial arrangements and clan alliances shifted in response.

Different systems of organization also existed in the region. Urbanization in Cisjordan stretches back to at least the fourth millennium B.C.E. and included both walled cities as well as smaller villages. City-states, ruled by local elites, often allied with one another for survival through trade and defense. By the Late Bronze Age, however, approximately the time when the Hebrew Bible claims Israelites came into the land, Egypt ruled administratively over most of the region and disallowed significant fortifications. But both external pressures in the region and internal problems at home forced Egyptian rule to collapse, and profound changes resonated throughout the area.

Small village life became more common. New peoples—including the Philistines—arrived from around the Mediterranean basin. Without pressure from a large external presence such as the Egyptians, more opportunities existed for new political entities to emerge. The level of political coordination of the Israelites during their emergence in Cisjordan, however, remains unknowable.

leads a rebellion against Solomon (11:26–40). And, at Solomon's death, the kingdom divides (1 Kgs 12).

These two states also saw their share of difficulties. Jerusalem, the capital city in the south, sat a mere ten miles (16 km) from the border with Israel. Geographic proximity often precipitated conflict (see 1 Kgs 14:30 and 2 Kgs 14:11–14 for two examples). Skirmishes with other neighbors, particularly Aram, Assyria, and Babylonia from the north, and Egypt in the south, frequently meant that kings paid tribute to stronger nations to serve as their vassals (see 2 Kgs 10:32–33; 17:3; 18:14 for a few instances). Conflict continued to rage internally as well. Judah's commitment to the Davidic house resulted in slightly more stability with regard to leadership. As a state that lasted 135 years longer than its northern neighbor, Judah seated twenty rulers, while Israel saw nineteen men on the throne. The north, by contrast, <u>never managed a dynasty of any length</u> and suffered through ten coup d'états to determine who led the country.

Moreover, the construction of a state represents a political choice that often displaces previous forms of governance and favors certain subsets of the populace over others. In the case of the people of Israel, local decision making by elders—whether at the level of the *bet av*, the clan, or the tribe—erodes as a central authority begins to emerge. This process shifts locations of power, often dramatically, and results in significant social and cultural upheaval. But the allegiance of people tends to remain with traditional institutions. A modern example helps to demonstrate the point. Lt. Col.

---

### <u>never managed a dynasty of any length</u>

In spite of a larger territory with richer resources, the northern kingdom clearly suffered far more political instability than the south. Trying to govern a vast region with far greater diversity of traditions certainly contributed to the problems, as did possession of land desirable to neighbors. But the lack of a stable ideology supporting the dynastic aspirations of a particular line also made it difficult for rulers to establish legitimacy.

Two examples of the struggle for control of the kingship demonstrate the point. Jeroboam's son Nadab succeeds him but within two years suffers assassination at the hands of Baasha (1 Kgs 15:25–32). Likewise, Baasha enjoys a longer rule, followed by the rise to power of his son Elah. After only two years, Elah's assassination leaves the throne in the hands of his killer, Zimri (16:8–14). Then Zimri rules for a mere seven days before his death at the hands of Omri (16:15–20).

Compare another similarly troubled time from near the end of the northern kingdom to see the persistence of this instability. After the long and prosperous reign of Jeroboam II (785–745 B.C.E.), his son Zechariah rules for only a few months before losing his life to the assassin Shallum. Shallum functions as king for one month before his death at the hands of Menahem. After a nine-year rule, he dies naturally and his son Pekahiah succeeds him. Less than a year passes before Pekah assassinates him. A short reign ensues before his death at the hands of Hoshea, who begins his reign as a vassal of Assyria. His revolt and the subsequent attack by the ruler of Assyria, Shalmaneser V, brings Israel to an end in 722/721 B.C.E.

Mark Meadows, a member of the U.S. Army's Tenth Mountain Division, summed up a similar situation in Iraq during 2006: "If you were to say to any Iraqi, what is your No. 1 loyalty, it will always be to their family, and then you can ask what's your No. 2 loyalty, and it will always be to their tribe, and their No. 3 loyalty would be to their sect, No. 4 will be to their nation" (quoted in Kevin Whitelaw, "Friends, Family, and Foes: In Iraq, Shiites and Sunnis Fight, But Sometimes, They Marry," *U.S. News and World Report* online, posted April 26, 2006, http://www.usnews.com/usnews/news/articles/060501/1iraq-2.htm.) His comment highlights the staying power of established social structures within a society and pinpoints the source of much of the opposition to the state, both in Iraq and in the biblical material about Israel.

Thus, in spite of the extolling of the state seen in the Hebrew Bible, other centers of power clearly existed and functioned to challenge reigning monarchs. The next section looks at some of these alternate or rival positions that express a power different from and in opposition to the state. Examining the role of the elders offers insight into the ongoing sway of the *bet av* in the daily life of most people. The organization of households into clan and tribal groupings that dealt with issues such as defense and justice offered familiar, reasonable alternatives to the state. The place of local sanctuaries enters in here as well. Deities connected with specific shrines captured the devotion of the people and provided alternatives to the worship of the patron deity in Jerusalem.

Perhaps most familiar to biblical readers, prophets give voice opposing the decisions of various kings, the institutions and bureaucracies they generate, and the social inequities that result from the new order. But their position within Israelite culture and tradition varies significantly. Some prophets appear to be associated with local shrines. Others work in groups or guilds and wander within specific regions. Still more seem directly tied to the king and work within his administrative apparatus. Prophets also, at times, reveal connections to significant families opposing a sitting ruler. An exploration of their work in this section reveals ways in which they attempt to block expressions of monarchic power.

### Bet Av *and Local Rule*

The impulse for establishing a monarchical state emerged in the central highlands of the Cisjordan. According to the book of Judges, the territory of Ephraim became a locus of activity in association with the lands designated to Manasseh, Gilead, and Benjamin. Power circulates around the possession of land, and the stories told demonstrate how organizing *bet av* landholders into extended groups governed by elders maintained order. Judges 11, for example, shows the elders of Gilead approaching Jephthah to serve as their military commander (Judg 11:4–6) in a time of conflict. Jephthah reminds them of how they participated in dispossessing him of his father's holdings (11:7–8), thus revealing something of the range of responsibilities they assumed. Likewise, Judg 21:16–24 pictures community elders determining a strategy to get wives for the Benjaminites. Leadership of larger organizational units (or what the biblical text calls "Israel") initially comes from these regions (see Gideon in Judg 6–8, Abimelech in Judg 9: 6, and Jephthah in Judg 11:11 for examples) at the behest or with the authorization of these senior landowners. Saul, from a prominent Benjaminite household (1 Sam 9:1–2), apparently forges his control by working within these channels.

Saul earns his reputation by opposing a Philistine threat to the region (1 Sam 13), but like Abimelech before him, who sought the office of king (see Judg 9), he maintains his base at home with family and a small garrison of men. And he works his land between battles! His son Jonathan fights alongside him (1 Sam 13:16; 31:1–2) and his uncle Abner commands his army (14:50; 26:5). Like any good male head of household, he marries his daughters off for strategic purpose (18:17–29; 25:44; 2 Sam 21:7–9). And he makes allies with important leaders in the region. For instance, the text presents Saul associating with priests from the line of Eli at Shiloh (1 Sam 14:3). Most of the loyalty he earns, however, comes from his ability to proffer military protection (14:47–48) and his willingness to buy a following by providing leading figures with land and higher standing (22:7–8).

The lack of any unified "Israel" bringing together these regional groups becomes clear when the writers present David's challenge to Saul. With a sphere of influence centered in the south, David demonstrates how an ambitious man can leverage the support of key householders into a kingship. See, for example, how when David battles with the Amalekites and gains spoil in 1 Sam 30, he divides it between his friends and the elders of Judah (30:26–31). These rewards purchased him some sway. The story of David and Nabal in 1 Sam 25:1–42 further illustrates the point. David asks for supplies in exchange for his "protection" of Nabal's property. As presented, David's pitch reveals that he did nothing except not take from Nabal, and so he basically extorts resources. Although Nabal shows himself as less than enthusiastic (25:10), his wife complies (25:18). Eventually through such actions, he gains enough favors to assume the position of king.

Thus when Saul dies, these elders crown David first in Hebron (2 Sam 2:4), and then eventually he earns the same position over Israel (5:3). But their attention can shift quickly. A similar grouping of elders betrays him. As Absalom attempts to take the throne, he sends word to these local rulers of his intent and expects their support (15:10). The text then reports that upon Absalom's death, David must dispatch emissaries to the elders of Judah to reconstitute his claim as king (19:11–15). Note that he turns to those households in the south where Absalom found sympathy. But he also lost the favor of northern families, who return to his service slowly and with some apparent reluctance. The text shows them late to the scene after David crosses the Jordan River (19:16–20). Shimei's public repudiation of David as he leaves Jerusalem (16:5–8) and Mephibosheth's absence from the group departing the city with David (19:24–30) also indicate a residual opposition to David from groups in the north. Moreover, the biblical writers present Sheba, a Benjaminite, as attempting to rally Israel to a revolt before David

> ### people of the land
>
> The Hebrew term *am ha-arez* means "people of the land" and occurs seventy-three times in the Hebrew Bible. What the term means remains unclear, and it appears to vary depending on the historical period. While some scholars argue that it can make reference to the people as a whole, others see it specifying a specific class of citizens—most likely landholders.

reconsolidates his kingdom (20:1–2). To squelch this effort, David must call on troops from Judah and his personal bodyguard (20:4–22).

The model of state that results depends, then, largely on the coalitions a leader builds among the *bet av* landholders, clans, and tribes with the resources to mount a challenge should such action prove necessary or desirable. And the participation of the <u>people of the land</u> in the revolt against Athaliah (2 Kgs 11:13–16) illustrates the ongoing importance of a ruler's earning the loyalty of such groups (whether or not the "people of the land" equates precisely to the "elders") to stay on the throne. Similar mentions of these people of the land flexing political muscle as kingmakers comes in the enthronements of Josiah (21:23–24) and Jehoahaz (23:30).

The constantly shifting circulation of power requires readers to look closely at how the biblical writers depict groups outside of the royal court in a variety of stories. Even though they sometimes force kings to bend to their will, in the story of Jehu's coup things unfold a bit differently. There the "elders" become a location of refuge for Ahab's descendants. Jehu demands that they—along with former leaders who had supported the Omride dynasty (2 Kgs 10:1–8)—publicly dump the heads of Ahab's sons as a sign of their support for him as their ruler. Even though they comply out of fear of Jehu, he goes on to kill all of them (10:9–11). When destroying potential enemies, Jehu leaves no stone unturned. The text implies that these elders might foment opposition to Jehu's rule; mass extermination solves the problem.

This story also features another group of key players in the formation and continuation of the state—the prophets. Jehu comes to the throne at the instigation of the prophet Elisha (9:1–13). Although Jehu's companions call the representative who comes from Elisha to anoint Jehu king a "madman" (9:11), the authority of his pronouncement touches off an immediate response (9:12–13). The next section looks at the often-difficult relationship between the prophets and the state.

*Prophets*

Most readers associate biblical prophecy solely with the fifteen named books in the Hebrew Bible. Limiting their consideration to these texts vastly misunderstands how these figures function in the biblical material. Joshua, Judges, Samuel, and Kings all received designation as *Neviim*, or "prophets," in addition to books such as Isaiah, Jeremiah, Ezekiel, Hosea, Joel, and Micah. Such labeling most likely reflects the inclusion in these stories of named prophets such as Deborah, Samuel, Elijah, Elisha, Micaiah, and others, as well as the mention of prophetic bands that worked around the countryside. Of even more significance, these texts describe the purported arrival of the people of Israel into the land, their settlements, and the rise (as well as the decline) of monarchic states as a form of governance. While prophets appeared prior to the formation of the state and following its dissolution, the close association between prophets and kings certainly stands out in the Hebrew Bible.

Prophets sometimes worked as part of the state system. When functioning within the king's household and bureaucratic apparatus, their basic loyalty to the state remained intact even though they occasionally voiced strong words against a king or a king's policies. Nathan's rebuke of an adulterous David (2 Sam 11:27–12:15) and Isaiah's stern words to Ahaz when he refuses to ask for a sign (Isa 7:13) offer ready examples.

But prophets also regularly appear as functioning apart from the structures of the state. The stories of the prophets Elijah and his successor Elisha, for instance, describe a <u>prophetic company</u> working in the Cisjordan (1 Kgs 20:35; 2 Kgs 2:3, 5, 7, 15; 4:1, 38; 5:22; 6:1; 9:1). Although scholars know little about these groupings, the text offers a few scattered hints. They appear, for example, to live a rather simple and spartan lifestyle. Second Kings 1:8 presents Elijah unshaven and in plain garb. And although 1 Kgs 19:19 shows Elisha as working the land prior to his call, his killing of his oxen demonstrates his loss of livelihood in order to take on the prophetic task (19:21). At least for a short period of time, Elijah lived by the Wadi Cherith and, as legend states it, depended on ravens to bring him food (17:5–6).

Prophecy in such groups also is associated with ecstasy or <u>possession</u> by a charismatic spirit. Saul, for example, meets a band of prophets following

### prophetic company

Anthropologists note that in many cultures and times, prophets work together in groups. A group of followers accredits a prophet as a valid mediator between the spiritual and mundane realms. Working in social isolation, then, would mean ceasing to function effectively as a prophet. While the Hebrew Bible most often focuses on prophets' interactions with the king, court, and public at large, a few texts mention prophetic companies (see 1 Sam 19:20; 1 Kgs 20:35; 2 Kgs 2:3, 5, 7, 15; and 4:1, 38 for examples).

### possession

Prophetic figures (including prophets, mediums, and shamans) frequently display behaviors associated with possession by a spirit. These actions include trances, catatonic states, manic fits, self-abuse, and various forms of ecstasy. Some figures likely encouraged such experiences through actions such as the ingestion of psychotropic substances, use of musical instruments (1 Sam 10:5), fasting, controlled diets, or blood loss (see the prophets of Baal in 1 Kgs 18:28).

his anointing as king and joins in their "prophetic frenzy" (1 Sam 10:10). This connection between Saul and spiritual possession recurs throughout his life (see 1 Sam 11:6; 16:14–23; and 18:10–11 for examples). The text here attributes Saul's success and failure as a monarch directly to the deity and implies that in order to lead Israel effectively, such close ties to the divine prove necessary. This model of charismatic leadership relates directly to the stories told in the book of Numbers, where God's spirit rests upon the seventy elders (Num 11:25–30), as well as in Judges, where God raises up and empowers people for particular times and purposes (see Judg 2:18; 3:9–10; 6:11–18). But the construction of the prophet as a charismatic leader disappears as an inherited kingship takes hold in both the north and the south. Indeed, by 1 Sam 19:18–24 the image of the prophetic frenzy appears more of a liability than an asset. Here, groups of Saul's messengers get caught up in a whirl of agitation that even overtakes the king. As a result, he strips off his clothes and lies naked, looking far more like a madman than a ruler.

But no consistent picture of how the prophets communicate comes across in the biblical material. Numbers 12:6–8, for example, presents Miriam and Aaron challenging Moses' special status by putting forward their own connections to the divine. The text shows God responding that most prophets receive revelation in visions or dreams but that Moses encounters God face-to-face. The unique closeness of Moses to God distinguishes him as a superior (and unquestioned) leader. Prophecy takes on a different cast in Judg 4, which names Deborah a prophet. Her role centers on delivering judgments for the people (4:5) and rousing the troops for war at the behest of God (4:6–7). By contrast, Judges 6:8–10 demonstrates a pattern that becomes familiar in the named prophets. Here the prophet brings a word or oracle from the deity. First Kings 22:19 explicates how at least one prophet receives such a message by showing Micaiah standing in the throne room of God and watching a revelation of Ahab's downfall unfold. And Elijah and Elisha earn their notoriety and following not only with their words but also through their ability to perform miracles (1 Kgs 17:8–16; 2 Kgs 4:1–7).

Prophets in the Hebrew Bible clearly gain the most attention, however, in their confrontations with reigning monarchs and their officials. And these stories say something about their social location. Although typically outside of the state apparatus, in many cases prophets still appear enormously well connected and influential. Three prophets serve as illustration. Take Jeremiah, for instance, who came from a priestly family. Some possibility exists that his father, Hilkiah, worked as the high priest under King Josiah (Jer 1:1 and 2 Kgs 22:4, 8). Hilkiah discovers a book of the law and sends it out for authentication to Huldah, a prophet (2 Kgs 22:14–20). She in turn is named as the wife of Shallum (22:14), a keeper of the royal wardrobe. Shallum, uncle of Jeremiah according to Jer 32:7, heads a family with strong links to the royal court. Shallum's son Maaseiah serves as keeper of the royal threshold (Jer 35:4), and Maaseiah's son Zephaniah functions as a priest who carries messages to Jeremiah (21:1; 37:3).

Jeremiah's critiques of the state, then, come not from an "average" resident of Judah, but rather from a man deeply connected to the bureaucratic apparatus of the state and likely holding some <u>influence with important players</u>. From this place, he speaks out forcefully against kings he sees as acting outside of the interests of Judah. For example, the text of Jeremiah indicates the prophet's extraordinary disdain for both Jehoiakim's and Zedekiah's policies (see Jer 21:1–10; 22:13–19; and 27:1–28:17 for examples).

According to the book of Jeremiah, the prophet goes to the Temple at the outset of Jehoiakim's reign and delivers his Temple sermon (Jer 26:1). Here he directly attacks the legitimacy of the kingship by claiming that failure to

### influence with important players

Jeremiah appears to possess more than family ties to the royal court. When in trouble over his Temple sermon (Jer 7 and 26), a man named Ahikam son of Shaphan (26:24) assists him. Shaphan served as the secretary of the king (2 Kgs 22:3), and Ahikam also works in the court (22:11, 14). Shaphan's other sons also aid Jeremiah. Elasah carries Jeremiah's letter to the exiled community in Babylon (Jer 29:3), and Gemariah allows a reading of Jeremiah's scroll in his home (36:10). In turn, Gemariah's son Micaiah brings a report of this scroll's words to a whole cadre of officials (36:11–13) who ultimately act to protect Jeremiah from the angry king (36:19).

### The Kingship during the Time of Jeremiah

The leadership of the state during the time of Jeremiah proves immensely complicated. According to the Hebrew Bible, following the assassination of Amon (2 Kgs 21:23–24) by persons within his court, "the people of the land" killed the conspirators and placed an eight-year-old Josiah on the throne. While a "people of the land" receive mention in 2 Kgs 11:18 as associated with the destruction of an altar to Baal in Jerusalem, the identity or the motivations of this group remain uncertain. Jeremiah 1:1 reports his call to prophetic service as occurring during the reign of Josiah.

Josiah later engaged, according to the biblical material, in a massive reform of cultic practice before his death at the hands of Pharaoh Neco of Egypt (2 Kgs 23:29). "The people of the land" then place his son Jehoahaz on the throne (23:30–31) over his older brother Eliakim. This situation lasts for three months, until Pharaoh Neco returns from his northern military campaign. At that point, he takes Jehoahaz into custody and puts Eliakim on the throne under the name Jehoakim (23:31–35). Jehoakim reigns for eleven years. Initially a vassal of the Egyptians, he turns to the Babylonians after the international situation warrants change. When he subsequently rebels against the Babylonians, they march against him. He dies, perhaps luckily, and his eighteen-year-old son Jehoiachin rules for three months before the Babylonians accept his surrender and take him into exile with leading officials in 597 B.C.E. The Babylonians place his uncle Zedekiah on the throne. He remains loyal for several years before rebelling. Nebuchadnezzar subsequently marches on him, laying siege to and ultimately destroying the city in 587/586 B.C.E.

follow the law of God and heed the words of the prophets will result in the destruction of the Temple and the fall of Jerusalem (26:4–7). In other words, he pronounces that YHWH as patron deity will not protect the Temple or the city if the king fails to behave properly (see chapter 11 for more detail). This declaration directly attacks the legitimacy of Jehoiakim's reign and comes close to treason. Indeed, the text reports that Jehoiakim himself kills the prophet Uriah for speaking a similar message (26:20–23). Jeremiah's words result in his seizure, trial, and the narrow avoidance of a death sentence.

This close brush with execution fails to temper Jeremiah's criticisms. When Jehoiakim begins construction on an elaborate new house using forced labor (22:13–17), Jeremiah not only condemns the action but also speaks of the king's coming death in inglorious terms (22:18–19). Perhaps most controversial, when declaring the divine displeasure with the people of Judah—and thus also against the king—for their lack of fidelity (25:1–7), he claims that God says, "I am going to send for all of the tribes to the north, says the LORD, even for King Nebuchadnezzar of Babylon, my servant, and I will bring them against this land and its inhabitants, and against all these nations all around: I will utterly destroy them, and make them an object of disgrace" (Jer 25:9). Asserting that YHWH sides with an opposing national leader threatening the annihilation of Jerusalem and Judah certainly presents Jeremiah as an enemy of the state. And he continues these attacks once Zedekiah becomes the king and threatens to break his ties to Babylon (Jer 21:2–7; 27:1–28:17). At best, Jeremiah represents a contingent of the population that sees Babylon as a superior choice over Egypt in terms of its ability to influence the international scene. At worst, Jeremiah advocates a treasonous stance with regard to the established monarch in Jerusalem.

Claiming that YHWH sides with an enemy certainly riled not only the king but also other prophets who supported the idea of the Davidic monarchy and assured the stability of Jerusalem. In this instance, while Jeremiah labels all competing prophets liars (Jer 27:9–10, 14–18), the text reports that Hananiah speaks a word of the Lord directly to Jeremiah, promising swift deliverance of the people (28:1–4, 10–11). The question of who speaks with authority and in whom to place one's trust certainly arises.

But even more, the level of political debate stands out. Jeremiah's denunciations of the king and the state look remarkably similar to what today might get labeled as from the opposition party or the party out of power in a modern political system. While Jeremiah laments his status as derided and outcast (for examples, see 11:19; 15:15–18; 18:18–23; 20:7, 10), he manages to survive not only the political tumult of Jerusalem in this period but also the invasion and overthrow of the nation.

While Jeremiah provides the clearest case of a well-connected prophet's using his influence to oppose the state and its rulers, other persons of influence certainly take on the sitting king and bureaucracy as well. Amos, for example, travels from Judah to Israel and confronts the policies of Jeroboam II at the <u>Bethel sanctuary</u>. The priest Amaziah reports his activities to the king and tells the prophet to earn his living in Judah (Amos 7:10–13) because the sanctuary belongs to the king and does not allow such words against the reigning monarch and his policies. Amos's angry retort showcases a disdain for prophetic communities and paid prophets; he claims not to come from a family of prophets and to earn his living as a herdsman and dresser of sycamore trees (7:14). The question of Amos's identity and profession remains unclear. An outsider in terms of any connection to prophetic circles and a Judean in the northern kingdom, he appears to hold no vested interest either in speaking the word of God or in the state of Israel. But his words showcase a well-developed understanding of the international scene (1:3–2:16), a deep knowledge of the cult and ritual (2:5, 3:9, 14; 4:1, 4; 5:5–6; 6:1; 7:13; 8:14), and a strong sense of social justice (2:6–8; 4:1–3; 5:10–15, 21–24; 6:1–7; 8:4–6). Perhaps a wealthy landowner, he might be prominent among the so-called people of the land—not an insider with regard to the royal court, but nonetheless somewhat influential.

Another prophet about whom scant biographical data exists also seems rather comfortably placed within the social system. Ezekiel receives identification as a priest and as the son of Buzi (Ezek 1:2–3). Presented as speaking from Babylon, the writers place him in the first group of citizens taken into exile around 597 B.C.E. Within this community, he maintains a position of some status, as evidenced by the elders or rulers of the group in exile coming to visit him on multiple occasions (8:1; 14:1–3; 20:1; 33:30–31). Contemporaneous with Jeremiah, he also criticizes the rule of Zedekiah and envisions the loss of state power to Babylon (12:1–5; 17:1–22; 21:18–32). And he indicts members of the royal entourage by name (11:1–4). But given his location apart from the city, his condemnation of an Israel polluted by false worship

## Bethel sanctuary

Following the division of the kingdom into Israel and Judah, the writers report that Jeroboam I feared an erosion of his authority because the Temple sat in Jerusalem for pilgrimage and worship as well as for legitimation of Judah and the Davidic dynasty in the eyes of the people. Consequently, he established cult sites at Bethel in the south and Dan in the north to control the religious life of the people in the newly established Israel (1 Kgs 12:25–33).

## Micah and the Rural Landowners

The biblical text also apparently links the prophet Micah to rural life and landowners. While the writers rarely identify a prophet's hometown, Micah is connected to the village of Moresheth (Mic 1:1)—likely a small village southwest of Jerusalem. Oracles attributed to him critique the loss of traditional family lands (2:2, 4) and condemn persons who plot against "my people" (2:8–9; 3:1–3). And he and Jeremiah alone predict the destruction of the urban center of Jerusalem (3:12).

(see 8:1–9:11, for example) and visions of the departure of the divine presence from the city (10:1–22; 11:22–25) take on a different tone. Blame can reside in a corrupt Jerusalem, while the exiles hope to take part in a reconstitution of a proper state. In his images of a new and restored city (Ezek 40–48), the kings no longer hold charge over the Temple and its precincts (43:7–9). Rather, the priests assume leadership to ensure right relationship to the divine (43:18–27), but not just any priests. The text indicates a lingering but unspecified resentment toward the Levites, and they are demoted (44:10–14), while the Zadokites ascend to a place of honor (44:15–16). The prophet does not lose confidence in the Davidic line (27:24–28) but envisions a ruler who, by establishing proper worship, ensures YHWH's fidelity to the reestablished and unified nation (Ezek 46).

These three prophets all represent a lively political opposition and demonstrate that kings, their policies, and their administrative personnel faced serious and concerted challenges. The stress frequently surfaced during periods of strong external pressure from rival nations and pitted groups with considerable influence but different perspectives against one another. This identification of named prophets as persons with clout stems from what few biographical details the text provides about men such as Isaiah, Jeremiah, Ezekiel, and Amos. Most of the prophetic voices in the biblical material, however, remain shrouded in anonymity. Only a handful of books named for prophets appear in the Hebrew Bible, and outside of brief mentions of their names, the texts reveal little if anything about their lives. But given the similarity of their messages, the assumption of a comparable status for other prophets makes sense.

As in much political discourse, prophetic commentary often took on an urgent and biting tone. Micah directs vitriol toward rulers of the southern kingdom by likening royal officials to cannibals (Mic 3:1–3). He further accuses the leaders of perverting justice, the judges of accepting bribes, the priests of teaching for a price, and the prophets of delivering oracles for money (3:9–11). Hosea likewise indicts both priest and prophet (Hos 4:4–6) for rejecting knowledge, and priests for earning a profit from engaging in false religious rituals (4:7–14). Shockingly direct language about Israel's whoredom dominates his rhetoric (see chapter 13 for a more detailed discussion). Further, he accuses the king of supporting Baal worship (5:1–7). In Zephaniah, no one escapes blame for the destruction of the land. Priests who worship falsely stand under condemnation (Zeph 1:4–6) alongside the king's sons and officials (1:8–9) and the traders who made themselves rich by false means (1:10–13). All of them, he says, will come to a violent and painful end.

The existence of such dissent makes the movement of power obvious. State authority and its resources clearly struggled at times to quell opposition. But the biblical material that survives indicates that the state lost some of the more harshly confrontational battles between prophets, the king, and the bureaucracy (see 1 Kgs 18:20–40; Jer 28:1–17; and Amos 7:10–17 for examples). For modern readers steeped in democratic systems, open airing of divergent viewpoints indicates a healthy governmental system. But a monarchy functioned differently. Kings, particularly those threatened by internal and external instability, depended on an ability to impose their will and their policies to maintain order. So the text presents biblical rulers as working to stifle dissent. Ahab and Jezebel, for example, set out on a systematic campaign to kill the prophets of the Lord (1 Kgs 18:3–4; 19:1–3). And Jehoiakim burns the words of Jeremiah (Jer 36:20–26) to stop their spread. Absent such control, prophets could stir up forces capable of threatening the king and his policies as well as the existence of the state itself. Ahijah's word from the Lord encourages Jeroboam's continued rebellion against the house of Solomon (1 Kgs 11:26–40). Likewise, Elisha's support of Jehu (2 Kgs 9:1–13) undergirds Jehu's violent rise. And some might argue that Jeremiah's support of Babylon not only contributed to Judah's ultimate fall, but that his favorable treatment of the rival state illustrated his complicity with the enemy ruler (Jer 39:1–40:6).

## Local Shrines

Alternative sites for worship of both YHWH and other deities challenged the authority of a king. Local shrines drew in people regionally and offered an option for the maintenance of religious obligation away from Jerusalem and the king's Temple, a site sanctioned by the king and one that added to his coffers. The biblical writers fashion a number of these local shrines as precursor locations to the Temple. The writers of Josh 18, for example, talk about Shiloh as the site of the tent of meeting. This tent served as a mobile space for the ark of the covenant. First Samuel 1–3 further depicts Shiloh as the place where Samuel comes to serve YHWH and associates it with the priestly family of Eli. The city of Shechem receives a more mixed treatment. Although Josh 24 depicts this place as the site of a covenant ceremony marked by a stone under an oak pillar (Josh 24:26), Judg 9 mentions it as a more complicated location. A shrine there facilitates worship at a temple named both Baal-berith and El-berith (Judg 9:46) (see further discussion in chapter 13). But although the narratives only occasionally mention these sites after the erection of the Temple, readers must imagine that they continued to function.

According to the Hebrew Bible, sacred spaces filled the Cisjordan. The books of Isaiah, Jeremiah, and Ezekiel all describe false worship "under every green tree" (Isa 57:3; Jer 2:20; 3:6, 13; 17:2; Ezek 6:13; 20:47). And the book of Deuteronomy reveals considerable concern with eradication of these locations. Deuteronomy 12 stresses the need to demolish completely all altars not dedicated to God and to present offerings only at an appropriately authorized location (understood as Jerusalem). Indeed, concern with the preeminence of Jerusalem as a shrine dominates much of the historical material in the Hebrew Bible. The condemnation of Jeroboam (and most of the northern kings in his name) focuses on his establishment of altars rival to the Temple (1 Kgs 14:9–10; all subsequent kings are connected to this act with the phrase "walking in the ways of his ancestor [Jeroboam] and in the sin that he caused Israel to commit" ([1 Kgs 15:26] or some variation thereof [15:34; 16:2, 19, 26; 22:52]).

**Israel after the State: The Politics of Empire**

The complex international scene put tremendous pressure on both Israel and Judah and ultimately resulted in the downfall of each state as an independent entity. The Assyrians decimated the northern kingdom in 722/721 B.C.E., and the Babylonians did the same to the southern kingdom in 587/586 B.C.E. Given the tenuous nature of the monarchy from the outset, these failures hardly surprise biblical readers. During the period after the exile and beyond, the remaining Israelites found themselves governed by a succession of world empires. These empires exercised political authority in dramatically different ways than the people had experienced under local monarchies. Their imperial politics left their marks on the Hebrew Bible, as demonstrated in more detail in chapters 8, 11, and 12. In this context, it is sufficient to discuss briefly how the empires, in particular the Persian Empire, organized political power in what had been Judah, now called Yehud.

The rise of the Persian Empire in the middle of the sixth century B.C.E. swept away Babylonian control of the Cisjordan. Cyrus, the Persian emperor, and Darius, his successor, brought in a new system of governance. Unfortunately, little textual evidence exists to explain the precise organization of political power after the exile. But the elite that likely wrote and certainly edited most of the books of the Hebrew Bible collaborated with the Persians. And they left behind a number of texts imagining the political functioning of Israel in this new setting that provide readers hints of how the idea of Israel as a state survived under empire.

*Yehud as a Colony*

Best understood as a <u>colony</u>, the province of Yehud existed as a political entity only to serve the basic needs of the Persian Empire. The Persians required a stable region close to Egypt, its economically powerful but politically restive <u>satrapy</u>. Moreover, the empire sought to extract as much eco-

### colony

North Americans likely associate the notion of Yehud as a colony with the colonization of their own continent by the Spanish, French, English, and others. Such a linkage might lead to an erroneous understanding of the dynamics at work in Yehud. In the colonization of North America, the European powers sent out representatives to a new land, where they subjugated, to varying degrees, the native population. In the establishment of Yehud as a colony, the Persians never attempted to settle their own people in the Cisjordan. Rather, they used Judeans emigrating home from exile in Babylon to establish a relationship with the population of the Cisjordan. These two groups supposedly shared a common ethnic heritage. So to call Yehud a colony should not conjure up images of the "settling" of Jamestown, Quebec, Saint Augustine, or New Amsterdam by a nonnative group. Rather, it should evoke comparisons with the economic function of these cities: to serve the seats of their respective empires in Europe by appropriating and developing the resources of North America.

nomic surplus as possible from regions it controlled. So Yehud as a colonial government functioned to facilitate the transfer of tribute, usually precious metals, to the Persian court.

The Persian province of Yehud lacked the developed court of officials described as functioning in service of the monarchs of Israel and Judah. Instead, the Persians appointed a governor for the province—sometimes a native Persian, sometimes a person from the area. When required, these governors oversaw a military garrison. They always managed a small coterie of scribes. Provincial authorities communicated constantly with other imperial officials by means of an empirewide postal service, often sending along information from a network of spies and informers—the "king's ears." The scribes facilitated these interactions. They also played a vital role in keeping economic and political records and securing compliance with imperial edicts, especially those dealing with taxation.

The Persians also made careful investments in local building projects. According to the writers of Nehemiah, they supported the construction of a new wall around Jerusalem (2:1–10). This wall functioned to protect the residents against raids by local gangs of bandits and thus allowed more people to live securely in the city. Indeed, after the wall was completed, it appears efforts were made to repopulate Jerusalem (Neh 7:4–5; 11:1–2). Persian interest in such a venture centered on concentrating a larger population and its attendant wealth in the city. By using the residents of the city to draw in resources and surplus goods from the hinterlands, these goods became more accessible to the empire.

According to the Hebrew Bible, the most important of these building projects replaced the Temple destroyed by the Babylonians. Workers completed it in 515 B.C.E., early in the reign of Darius I. The biblical material tends to focus on the new Temple's connection to YHWH: it signals divine blessing, it helps secure the people's relationship to YHWH, and it responds

## satrapy

A system of political management generally associated with Cyrus the Great and his successors, a satrapy effectively functioned as a large province governed by a representative of the emperor.

## keeping economic and political records

Tablets discovered at Persepolis, one of the many capitals of the Persian Empire, reveal a Persian passion for record keeping. Made of fired clay incised with cuneiform writing, these tablets record various administrative details but focus especially on the transfers of payments "in kind" (amounts of foodstuffs and the like) into the royal coffers and payments out as salary. Around 30,000 of these tablets exist. While the Persians undoubtedly maintained archives like this one elsewhere, the archives at Persepolis stand out as some of the few to survive.

### Temples as a Risky Imperial Strategy

The Persians supported local shrines for good reasons, but the policy of sponsoring their construction entailed risks. First, subsidizing these shrines proved expensive. While the book of Ezra exaggerates the amounts involved (Ezra 7:11–26), temples did require sacrificial animals and other foodstuffs, in addition to maintenance. The emperor Xerxes (486–465 B.C.E.), in fact, responded to this concern by ceasing imperial financial backing altogether during his reign.

Second, a shrine could rouse contention among factions of the local elite, nullifying the imperial desire for orderly administration. The book of Malachi, for instance, expresses tensions among the elite in Jerusalem fostered, in part, by Xerxes' removal of financial support for the Temple. Likewise, Josephus reports that intrigue over the office of high priest led to a murder in the Temple precincts and oppressive intervention by the Persians (*Antiquities* 11.297–303).

Finally, by creating and supporting a local institution, the empire manufactured a central symbol for the people. Thus, a temple could serve as an ethnic rallying point for the local populace against imperial rule. So, for example, when the Seleucid ruler Antiochus Epiphanes (175–164 B.C.E.) desecrated the Temple (see 1 Macc 1:20–28 [in the Apocrypha]), some Judeans perceived his rule as a threat to a basic constituent of their ethnoreligious identity. As a result, an open revolt ensued.

to YHWH's desire for a Temple (see, for example, Hag 2:8). The Persians, naturally, acted not out of any theological motivation; rather, for them, the Temple served as a place to deposit and hold large amounts of precious metals and other materials. Additionally, it provided an institutional base for the local elite, whose support they needed.

*The Elite as a Collaborator Class*

Readers might assume that the most affluent among the residents of Jerusalem would uniformly oppose Persian imperial authority and seek a return to some sort of political independence. But the Persians actively courted these elites to ensure their loyalty and thus promote stability in the region. The rebuilding of the Temple serves as one example of this effort. Many people in Jerusalem, such as the priests and the scribes who kept temple records, owed their livelihoods to the Temple and thus looked with favor on the empire that built and supported it. Other elites, such as merchants, traders, and lenders, also benefited by the Temple's ability to concentrate capital. Its regular program of activities in addition to the pilgrimage feasts ensured a constant supply of "tourists" with whom they could conduct business.

Further, the Persians also employed the elite to help administer the province. Allowing this group some semblance of authority assured their cooperation with the empire. But it also put pressure on those persons occupying imperially sponsored roles to balance the needs of the local populace with the demands of the empire. The biblical writers provide a few images of the ways in which the elites assumed such positions and handled these issues. Zechariah, for example, imagines political power as divided between the Persian governor and the high priest (Zech 4:1–14, 6:9–14). And Nehemiah, a Yehudite serving as Persian governor, expresses concern that his enemies not hold high-level priestly offices (Neh 13:4–9, 28–29). Neither text details how such shared authority worked, but the presentation of Nehemiah's apprehension hints at the complexity in the relationship between Temple administration and political authority.

Further, throughout the period, the biblical writers intimate that the Persians allowed the local elite to control matters not of imperial interest. For example, while scholars express skepticism about the efficacy of Ezra and Nehemiah's campaigns against intermarriage (Ezra 9:1–10:44; Neh 13:23–27), the texts certainly assume that the Persians allowed these efforts. Likewise, the Persians expressed no concern over matters such as Nehemiah's enforcement of Sabbath restrictions (Neh 13:19–22).

As time passed, the high priest came to serve as leader of the local elite and held a great deal of administrative power in his own right. The gradual decline of the Persian Empire, as it spent itself in constant warfare with the Greek city-states, encouraged such a shift in power. Again, the elite acted on matters over which they had some control, and the Hebrew Bible records traces of conflict among them from that period. The later chapters of the book of Isaiah (Isa 56–66), for example, exhibit differences of opinion about the value of the Temple. And, although they are difficult to understand, various oracles in the later chapters of Zechariah vociferously attack "shepherds," apparently a figure for some members of the local leadership (Zech 10:2–3; 11:4–17; 13:7–9).

So while the elite in Jerusalem lacked the kind of authority their predecessors exercised during the period of the monarchic state, a form of political power still remained within their reach. Collaboration with the Persians provided enough benefit to accept the loss of political autonomy, although the occasional text hints at some hope for the restoration of the state. The book of Haggai, for example, presents the governor Zerubbabel as the grandson of Jehoiachin, one of the last kings of Judah and thus a Davidic leader, and describes him as YHWH's signet ring. And the writers of Zechariah imagine the restoration of the Davidic house and its victory over all the nations of the earth (Zech 12:7–10) in addition to praising YHWH as the ultimate king (Zech 14). The idea of the state, then, however idealized, continues even in a time of empire. (Chapter 11 explores the various ways the image of a king persists and functions in the biblical material.)

## Conclusions

The success of any state rests on the right alignment of internal and external factors. A government must secure for its people a comfortable existence in terms of food, clothing, and shelter—the things people need from day to day. Citizens need to recognize fairness in systems such as taxation, conscription, and the application of justice. Protection from threats also looms large, as does stability in rule from one generation to the next.

The geographic location of Israel and Judah and the mixed nature of their populations set the stage for difficulties in state formation and longevity from the outset. Only rare rulers like an Omri managed to exert authority effectively over their own territories and across the region. Too frequently, more powerful neighbors demanded concessions in order to keep a king on the throne, and compliance became the only option. The difficult demands of the land in terms of its agricultural production could also have a dramatic impact on a king. A severe drought, for example, might provoke political unrest as people grew hungry. And the uniting of a populace across regional divides also meant adjusting to ethnic, cultural, and social differences. Where might a leader find a common cause to draw a citizenry together?

Moreover, the shifts from local to national rule fundamentally altered the ways people lived. The resultant changes in basic social institutions met with resistance in many quarters and, without stable leadership, new systems failed to evolve to assist persons displaced and disenfranchised by these changing norms. Rulers needed to adapt their institutions as conditions warranted. And they suffered consequences when they could not offer the people a way of life that met their needs.

Planting lasting institutions in such an unstable environment meant that the experiment in state power would enjoy only limited success. Even without the extraordinary external pressures on this land, the massive internal variance challenged the earliest rulers and never let up. While the biblical writers stress the great mythos of a nation, the practical realities shaped the outcome. And the outcome was a systemwide failure.

| **Suggested Biblical Readings** | 1 Samuel 8–13 |
| --- | --- |
| | 1 Kings 1:1–4; chapters 11–14 |
| | 1 Kings 17–2 Kings 9 |
| | Jeremiah 21:1–10; 22:24–30; 26:1–29:32 |

**Discussion Questions**

1. Think about the people surrounding political leaders today. Who wields significant influence? What are the most powerful administrative positions and why? When are new positions created and for what purposes?
2. Make a list of the pressures that you see impinging upon Israel and Judah. Then consider how those pressures contributed to the ultimate decline of each state.

3. What kinds of issues arouse dissatisfaction with a state? Can you name various ways in which you see different responses to such issues in places around the world? When and for what causes does violence most often break out?

4. How does opposition to the state express itself in governmental systems with which you are familiar? Are there modern equivalents to the prophets? If so, who might they be? Or do you see something like the people of the land? Where?

**Suggestions for Further Reading**

Fox, Nili Sacher. *In Service of the King: Officialdom in Ancient Israel and Judah*. Detroit: Hebrew Union College Press, 2000.

Ishida, Tomoo. "Solomon." In *The Anchor Bible Dictionary*, Vol. 6. Garden City, NY: Doubleday, 1992.

Miller, J. Maxwell. "History or Legend? Digging into Israel's Origins." *Christian Century*, February 24, 2004, 42–47.

Petersen, David L. *The Role of Israel's Prophets*. JSOT Supplement Series 17. Sheffield: JSOT Press, 1981.

Wilson, Robert R. *Prophecy and Society in Ancient Israel*. Philadelphia: Fortress Press, 1980.

# 11. Ideology

A society is possible in the last analysis because the individuals carry around in their heads some sort of picture of that society.
—Louis Wirth, preface to *Ideology and Utopia: An Introduction to the Sociology of Knowledge,* by Karl Mannheim

This observation [the Louis Wirth quotation above], with the important addition of "and their place in it," might serve as a fair introduction to current ideology theory.
—James Kavanagh, "Ideology"

Our discussion of power in the Hebrew Bible began by looking at an obvious place: the state. The next step, **ideology**, may seem more obscure. Today people use this term negatively. To have an ideology is to be "biased" or "unfair." If people cannot see things the "right" way, they are blinded by ideology. And those persons accused of being "ideological" are usually either on the "far left" or "far right." There are no ideologues in the middle of the political spectrum, where "reasonable" people live.

By contrast, recent work in social and literary theory has developed "ideology" as a useful term in investigating texts. **Karl Marx**, while he did not invent the term "ideology," certainly made it into a vital term in social (and, eventually, literary) analysis. For Marx, the dominant classes of a society (if they are to remain dominant) must develop ways to dissuade the nondominant classes from disturbance and revolt. Ideology serves this purpose. Putting an armed soldier on every street corner may effectively discourage disturbance and revolt, but it is expensive and, ultimately, inefficient. No king of Judah had such a force, yet the Davidic monarchy stayed in power for over four centuries. How? Ideology.

But was the Davidic ideology powerful because it was "right"? Some Marxists would argue all ideologies are false and that social analysis will reveal an ideology's falsehood. The question of whether an ideology is true or false, however, is irrelevant. An ideology is a basic set of assumptions that describe the way reality operates, "the way things are." It is the picture of society that people have in their heads. Holding these assumptions determines how people interpret the world and how they understand themselves and their place in the world.

But what does this have to do with power? Ideology is more powerful even than a society's more obvious places of power (governments, religious communities, families). Ideology undergirds those places of power by making their exercise of power seem natural. As a set of covert assumptions, it is not up for debate; it structures the debate. So ideologies make certain social structures seem obvious and irrefutable.

For example, consider recent disputes concerning the United States' participation in torture and extrajudicial confinement. Both the Bush administration and its critics spoke of violations (and nonviolations) of "human rights." The belief that all humans have certain rights, such as the right to avoid indefinite detention without trial, would have struck the authors of the Hebrew Bible as peculiar. "Human rights" is an ideological project of a particular place (North America and Europe) and a particular time (post-Enlightenment). But despite this historical origin, western discourse views these rights as part of "the way things are." And to accept these "human rights" as a given supports the universal validity of governing authorities that are said to gain their power through the exercise of, and respect for, human rights. The ideological construct "human rights" thus makes liberal democracy seem "natural."

This chapter explores four major ideological "projects" visible in the Hebrew Bible: the King-Zion complex, the Sinai-Nation complex, the Sage-Order complex, and the Empire-Colony complex. They are not mutually exclusive; they could either support each other or undermine each other at a given time. They also develop and change over time. Investigating each one provides an introduction to the ways they structured the world and related to dominant forms of political power.

## The King-Zion Complex

The Davidic dynasty would have been hard-pressed to force the loyalty of Judah through coercive means. Rather, the dynasty relied on ideology, in particular an ideological understanding of kingship in relation to YHWH, the national god, and his shrine on <u>Zion</u>. This ideological complex may be

### Zion

In the Hebrew Bible, **Zion** primarily refers to the hill on which the Temple stood. It can also apply to the whole city of Jerusalem (Isa 2:3) or its residents (51:16). Later, the term "Zion" was transferred to a different hill in Jerusalem, the supposed location of David's tomb and the place of Jesus' last supper with his disciples. So if you go to Jerusalem today, you can see the Temple Mount / Harem al-Sharif (the Zion of the Hebrew Bible) as well as a different place now called Mount Zion.

The ideological understanding of Zion in ancient Israel should not be confused with Zionism. Zionism is a modern movement concerned with the establishment, preservation, and prosperity of a Jewish state in the Cisjordan.

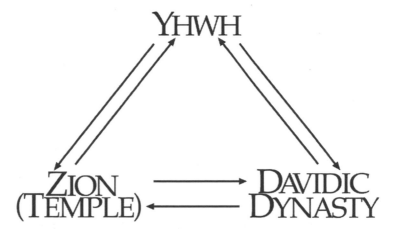

**Fig. 11.1: The King-Zion Complex**

represented as a triangular relation (see fig. 11.1). Each "player" in this system buttresses the other two. While looking closely at each relationship in this complex, it will be helpful to keep the system's end result in mind: it makes the dynasty's power appear obvious and irrefutable.

*Relating the King and Zion: 1 Kings 5 and 8*

In 2 Sam 7, YHWH proclaims his support for David and his dynasty. But YHWH also assigns the dynasty the duty of building a temple: David's son will build YHWH's house on Zion (7:13). This brief mention intimates that the **Temple** will be a dynastic project: YHWH's house will be a dynastic achievement.

This intimation becomes abundantly clear in the account of the Temple's construction in 1 Kings 5, which describes the political conditions necessary for this project to succeed. The Temple project gives evidence of the dynasty's military and economic success. Solomon proceeds only because God provides him with "rest on every side," that is, protection from foreign armies and agricultural catastrophe (1 Kgs 5:4). So Solomon has immense resources—in both foodstuffs (5:11) and forced labor (5:13–17)—to invest, as well as the diplomatic savvy to negotiate deals (5:12). The focus in this chapter is firmly on the dynasty's power and Solomon's own abilities, grounded in the firm backing of the kingmaker YHWH (5:5).

One might wonder why the Davidic dynasty was so keen to expend this amount of capital. The account of the Temple's dedication in 1 Kgs 8 provides some answers. Notice the way the authors here have Solomon cleverly merge dynasty and Zion: "Now the LORD has upheld the promise that he made; for I have risen in the place of my father David; I sit on the throne of Israel, as the LORD promised, and have built the house for the name of the LORD, the God of Israel" (8:20). And at the Temple's dedication, the authors have Solomon pointedly mention YHWH's open-ended dynastic support: "Therefore, O LORD, God of Israel, keep for your servant my father David that which you promised him, saying, 'There shall never fail you a successor before me to sit on the throne of Israel, if only your children look to their way, to walk before me as you have walked before me'" (8:25). So the Temple's functioning and the dynasty's permanence are, in essence, the same thing.

The linkage of dynasty and Zion, here expressed literarily, was also expressed in ancient Israelite society. The dynasty provided the Temple with resources for offerings (e.g., 1 Kgs 8:62–64). The Temple, standing close to the palace, attracted gifts from the populace and encouraged economic activity in Jerusalem. So court and Temple were hardly separate institutions. The rhetoric of Solomon's prayer is remarkably apt: the fates of Zion and the dynasty cannot be separated.

*Relating the King and YHWH: Psalm 89*

Second Samuel 7 and 1 Kings 5 and 8 picture the origin of the relationship between dynasty, deity, and shrine. They also provide some hints as to the effects of the relationship between king and shrine. But they do not give a full picture of the ideological development of this relationship. Regarding the relationship between the king and the deity, these texts simply assert that they both have houses on the same mountain (see fig. 12.1) and seem to share long-term goals and strategies. The Psalms, in particular Ps 89, provide a fuller description of how this ideology of the king and Zion plays out.

In this psalm the agreement between David and YHWH goes beyond the relationship described in 2 Sam 7. The psalm begins with YHWH speaking about the covenant with the Davidic dynasty (Ps 89:3–4). But then it moves directly to lengthy praise of YHWH as the securer of cosmic order (89:5–18). In this section of the psalm, YHWH is the one who

- rules all heavenly beings (89:6–8);
- controls the chaos of the sea (89:9);
- ensures order by destroying the chaos dragon, Rahab (89:10);
- owns the cosmos (89:11); and
- works through the king to defend the people (89:18).

The psalmist then elaborates on YHWH's relation with David as if it were YHWH's final act in securing the cosmic order. For example, while YHWH has secured order by ruling the sea, the king now has those powers (89:25). And the psalm clearly equates the created order and the Davidic monarchy: it will be as constant as the sun and the moon in the sky (89:36–37). The ideological assumption here is clear: YHWH and the king together control the order of the cosmos through their joint rule in the Temple (the location at which the psalm is sung). To deny that relationship is to risk stepping outside of ordered "reality" into chaos.

But this ideology seems to be threatened by events in the "real" world: the monarch has failed in battle, an event interpreted as rejection by YHWH (89:38–39). Is the ideological assumption of unity of king and YHWH now dead? Not for the psalmist. The psalmist does not abandon the basic ideology of king and Zion. Instead he reasserts that YHWH is still in control and continues to sponsor order. On the basis of that assumption, the psalmist has readers assume the persona of the monarch and implicitly appeal to YHWH to make the world better correspond with the ideology:

> Remember, O Lord, how your servant [the Davidic king] is taunted;
>> how I bear in my bosom the insults of the peoples,
> with which your enemies taunt, O LORD,
>> with which they taunted the footsteps of your anointed. (89:50–51)

## Chaos and Monsters

Chaos appears in many guises in ancient mythological texts. In Ugaritic mythology (from the late second millennium B.C.E. in an area now part of Syria), the god representing the sea (Yamm) serves as a figure for chaos. Yamm eventually loses his battle with Baal, the fertility god. In the Hebrew Bible, YHWH defeats the sea at creation (e.g., Ps 93:3–4). For both Ugaritic and Israelite mythology, the sea itself is home to a variety of beasts, usually conceived of as dragons or sea serpents, that represented chaos: Leviathan, Tannin (with seven heads), and Rahab. YHWH (like Baal in other texts) is said to have defeated Leviathan (Ps 74:13–14). Finally, the force of death, understood in Ugaritic myths as the god Mot, also indicates cosmic disorder. Mot captures and kills Baal, causing the dry season, but Baal eventually returns to life and gains the upper hand. Order (and rain) is restored. Likewise, the Hebrew Bible sees death as a numinous, destabilizing force (Jer 9:21), and YHWH will, at some point in the future, swallow it up (Isa 25:8).

## Kings as Divine?

The king ruling on Zion and the God ruling on Zion enjoy a close relationship. They serve similar cosmic functions and exercise similar mundane powers. But Ps 89 hints at something a bit more than that. After God grants the Davidic king control over the chaotic forces of sea and river, the king cries out that God is his father (89:26). God responds that he will make the king the firstborn (89:27). The language of birth and family implies adoption. More evidence for this divine adoption appears in Ps 2, where YHWH says to the king, "You are my son; today I have begotten you" (2:7). This text, perhaps recited at a coronation, gives the king a status above all other people. According to these psalms, the kings of Israel and Judah were sacral figures; they joined with the divine in ways ordinary mortals could not. Unfortunately, the Hebrew Bible gives little information about how ancient Israelites practiced this notion of sacral kingship.

Israel's neighbors present more options. The Mesopotamian kingdoms held views in many ways similar to those in ancient Israel: the king's status was elevated or "near divine." There is, of course, much room for nuance here, and it is difficult to say with certainty how an ancient Assyrian would have answered if asked, "Is your king a god?" It is somewhat clearer in Egypt. The pharaoh was taken to be the incarnation of any number of gods while also being the child of the god Re. So this king actually was considered to be a god.

The ideological regime can thus account for the monarch's occasional losses.

Of course, the Davidic line eventually comes to an end. And this dissolution of the Davidic line will force later writers to alter the King-Zion complex radically, but that time is not yet for this psalmist.

*Relating YHWH and Zion: Psalm 48*

Psalm 48 provides more information on the relationship between YHWH and Zion, exemplifying the King-Zion ideology by stressing YHWH's defense of Zion:

> Great is the LORD and greatly to be praised
>   in the city of our God.
> His holy mountain, beautiful in elevation,
>   is the joy of all the earth,
> Mount Zion, in the far north,
>   the city of the great King.                          (48:1–2)

This "Mount Zion" truly existed in Jerusalem, but the psalmist describes it in "unreal" terms: a high place in a city that is off the beaten path in the ancient world is *really* the "joy of all the earth." And this hill, which is not even the highest mountain in the neighborhood, is *really* "beautiful in elevation." Moreover, this site in the southern half of the Cisjordan is *really* located in the far north.

---

### The Uniqueness of Zion

Biblical scholar Jon Levenson examines how ancient Israelites described Zion's fundamental role in the cosmos through the image of the "cosmic mountain." This idea was common in the ancient Near East: a cosmic mountain is supposed to have a unique, universal power. Levenson elaborates several characteristics that point to Zion's unique status:

1. Zion is cosmically central. It lies at the center of the world (Ezek 5:5; cf. 38:12).

2. Zion is located on the **axis mundi**. This axis connects heaven, earth, and the underworld. So when Isaiah has his vision in the Temple (Isa 6:1–8), he really sees a meeting taking place in heaven. This axis is thus the major (if not only) communication relay between the gods and the people. When the exiles in Babylon pray, they are to pray toward Jerusalem and the Temple, and if they do so YHWH will hear in heaven (1 Kgs 8:48–49).

3. At Zion, time is not ordinary; indeed, on Zion it is as if time does not pass at all. All things are "unblemished," as if newly created; the place is a paradise. Thus, the authors of Ezekiel can parallel the garden of Eden and the mountain of God (Ezek 28:13–14; cf. Isa 51:3).

Jon Levenson, *Sinai and Zion: An Entry into the Jewish Bible* (San Francisco: Harper & Row, 1985), 111–37.

**Fig. 11.2: The Temple Mount / Harem al-Sharif as Seen from the Mount of Olives**
*This picture looks down on the site of the Jerusalem Temple, now the location of the Dome of the Rock (the domed building in the center left of the picture). The view is from the Mount of Olives and shows that that mountain is somewhat taller than Mount Zion.*

The psalmist makes extravagant and incorrect claims. Why should the Israelites, who after all could see the hyperbole here, pay attention to these descriptions? Because the psalm expresses an ideological understanding of Zion, not a geographic one. The ideology explains the geographical "blunders" here. The psalmist understands Zion as the very dwelling of YHWH but does so by making a correspondence between Zion and Zaphon, the traditional abode of the god Baal, located in the far north. The psalmist claims here that YHWH, as a more powerful god than Baal, possesses Baal's northern mountain, having "transferred" its status to Zion. And as YHWH's own mountain, Zion is understood as the place where the heavenly world and the mundane world come into contact. Heaven and earth somehow touch there, and only there. So the hill of Zion has a cosmic function, allowing hyperbolic descriptions ("joy of all the earth," "beautiful in elevation"). This ordinary mountain is in fact no ordinary mountain. In this psalm, the psalmist invites the reader to see Zion as a vital, essential place.

The psalm concludes by describing Zion once again, this time focusing on the city's various fortifications:

> Walk about Zion, go all around it,
>     count its towers,
> consider well its ramparts;
>     go through its citadels,
> that you may tell the next generation
>     that this is God,
> our God forever and ever.
>     He will be our guide forever.          (48:12–14)

Notice here how YHWH and Zion are inseparable. The physical manifestations of Zion's power that serve to protect it are equated with YHWH ("*this* is God"). Zechariah elaborates this image, having YHWH become "a wall of fire all around [Zion]" and "the glory within [Zion]" (Zech 2:5). Both this passage and Ps 48 effectively blur the line separating YHWH and Zion, as either the actual battlements of the wall or an insuperable "wall of fire" ensures Zion's perpetual existence. And they ground the claim that YHWH will be Israel's god <u>forever</u>.

*Living with the King-Zion Complex: Hezekiah*

The King-Zion ideology made the king's power as obvious as the sun rising in the morning. But what effects would such an ideology have on the practice of politics? King Hezekiah provides an example of the ways the King-Zion ideology operated politically. The Hebrew Bible presents Hezekiah as gaining support from the King-Zion ideology yet also experiencing the problems ideology can create for a leader.

In Isa 9, Isaiah anticipates a new monarch, probably Hezekiah, who will set things right. This Davidic ruler will relieve the burden imposed by the Assyrians and will abolish warfare (9:4–5). Isaiah moves on to celebrate the "birth" of this ruler; such language could refer either to Hezekiah's birth or his symbolic birth when crowned king:

> For a child has been born for us,
>     a son given to us;
> authority rests upon his shoulders;
>     and he is named Wonderful Counselor, Mighty God,
>         Everlasting Father, Prince of Peace.
> His authority shall grow continually,
>     and there shall be endless peace
> for the throne of David and his kingdom.
>     He will establish and uphold it
> with justice and with righteousness
>     from this time onward and forevermore.
> The zeal of the LORD of hosts will do this.                    (9:6–7)

Here Isaiah extols Hezekiah in terms familiar to the King-Zion complex. And Isaiah links the ruler's identity to YHWH, describing this king as a mighty god, a father whose rule does not end, a leader who will bring secu-

---

### forever

In modern English, "forever" conjures up "eternity," something with no beginning or end, a space outside time. This idea of eternity has been a vital part of western philosophical and theological inquiry. But in the Hebrew Bible, the word frequently translated as "forever" (*olam*) really indicates something like "most remote time," either past (from the most remote time) or future (to the most remote time). Thus, *olam* functions ideologically to indicate the assured continuous existence of a feature *within* time. So in Ps 48, YHWH's role as guard (linked to the fortifications of Zion) has been and will be a part of "the way things are."

rity. Granted, Hezekiah is not a god here. YHWH's zeal is the active principle, for YHWH acts to "establish" and "uphold" the Davidic ruler. But the Davidic monarch is YHWH's chosen vessel; the monarch is not like the rest of us.

The expectations in Isa 9 are high—one might call them irrationally high. Perhaps Hezekiah will be able to improve on his father Ahaz's record, but establishing "endless peace" and ruling with "justice and righteousness from this time onward" (9:7) seem like tall orders for anybody, even one styled a "mighty god" (9:6). Yet the King-Zion ideology in a sense requires these expectations: the king and the Temple are supposed to guarantee cosmic order, with YHWH's support. And these ideological guarantees could inspire not only false hopes but unwise political moves as well. In other words, the monarch's security could be jeopardized by the very ideology that secures his position.

Apparently, Hezekiah believed in the hopes that Isaiah laid out for him. Later in his reign, he sensed an opportunity to revolt against Assyria (2 Kgs 18:7). It should be said, of course, that Hezekiah may also have based his revolt on pragmatic considerations (indications of Assyrian weakness, a desire to keep Assyrian tax money in Judah, a need to grant some relief to the people to buttress his own position). But the dynasty's ideological base would have anchored a revolt in YHWH's own will and his constant residence at Zion.

But, in this instance, the ideology proved more of a trap. The revolt in 701 B.C.E. went poorly; the Assyrians destroyed most towns in Judah and besieged Jerusalem. Yet Hezekiah continued to get advice that Zion would not fall: "I [YHWH] will defend this city to save it, for my own sake and for the sake of my servant David" (Isa 37:35 and 2 Kgs 19:34). What happened next is a matter of dispute. According to Isa 37:36–38 (and a parallel passage in 2 Kgs 19:35–37), the angel of YHWH struck down 185,000 Assyrian soldiers and the Assyrian king withdrew, then was swiftly assassinated. However, 2 Kgs 18:13–16 reports that Hezekiah capitulated to the Assyrian

### Reading Prophetic Oracles

Prophetic oracles only rarely indicate clearly who spoke them and to what precise figures and conditions they refer. Isaiah 9 is thus typically vague. Scholars differ over whether Isaiah ever said these words and to whom they refer. This passage could be, for example, a later oracle written to extol another king, perhaps Josiah. These judgments are difficult to make, and certainty is impossible. Identifying the speaker here as Isaiah and the subject as Hezekiah is at least defensible. While reading prophetic oracles for their historical referents is never certain, reading them for their ideological stance can be somewhat easier. To whomever this text refers, it clearly promotes the King-Zion ideology. YHWH intends to work through a new king to secure benefits for the people.

king, giving him all the silver and gold from the Temple. <u>Assyrian records</u> support this latter version; it is more likely that Hezekiah bought his way out of trouble. Consider what difficulties the King-Zion ideology would have placed in the way of such a pragmatic solution. Isaiah's statement above is not just theological speechifying; it powerfully argues against any negotiation with the Assyrians. Why should Hezekiah give the Assyrians silver and gold when YHWH will rise to defend city, temple, and dynasty?

Hezekiah apparently overcame the obstacle of the King-Zion ideology and made peace. Yet surrender to the Assyrians did not mean surrendering the ideology. The story of the miraculous deliverance of Jerusalem supported the ideology quite nicely, whatever its relation to actual events. And even Hezekiah's pragmatic survival could be styled a miraculous interven-

## Assyrian records

Here is a report on the events in Jerusalem from the annals of Sennacherib:

> He [Hezekiah] did not submit to my yoke, I laid siege to 46 of his strong cities, walled forts and to the countless small villages in their vicinity, and conquered (them) by means of well-stamped (earth-)ramps, and battering-rams brought (thus) near (to the walls) (combined with) the attack by foot soldiers, (using) mines, breeches as well as sapper work. I drove out (of them) 200,150 people, young and old, male and female, horses, mules, donkeys, camels, big and small cattle beyond counting, and considered (them) booty. Himself I made a prisoner in Jerusalem, his royal residence, like a bird in a cage. I surrounded him with earthwork in order to molest those who were leaving his city's gate. His towns which I had plundered, I took away from his country and gave them (over) to Mitinti, king of Ashdod, Padi, king of Ekron, and Sillibel, king of Gaza. Thus I reduced his country, but I still increased the tribute and the *katru*-presents (due) to me (as his) overlord which I imposed (later) upon him beyond the former tribute, to be delivered annually. Hezekiah himself, whom the terror-inspiring splendor of my lordship had overwhelmed and whose irregular and elite troops which he had brought into Jerusalem, his royal residence, in order to strengthen (it), had deserted him, did send me, later, to Nineveh, my lordly city, together with 30 talents of gold, 800 talents of silver, precious stones, antimony, large cuts of red stone, couches (inlaid) with ivory, *nimedu*-chairs (inlaid) with ivory, elephant-hides, ebony-wood, boxwood (and) all kinds of valuable treasures, his (own) daughters, concubines, male and female musicians. In order to deliver the tribute and to do obeisance as a slave he sent his (personal) messenger.

This account is hardly objective; these annals exist to promote Sennacherib's authority and to persuade the reader of Sennacherib's political and military acumen. He obviously inflates the numbers here for propaganda purposes. And he will not come out and say he let Hezekiah buy his way out of trouble, though the extensive list of tribute hints in that direction.

James B. Pritchard, ed., *Ancient Near Eastern Texts Related to the Old Testament*, 3rd ed. (Princeton, NJ: Princeton University Press, 1969), 288.

tion by YHWH. However Hezekiah managed it, Zion did not fall. And this deliverance gave ample evidence that the King-Zion ideology "worked": the power of Assyria was no match for YHWH, the Davidic dynasty, and the divine abode on Zion.

*The King-Zion Complex after the Monarchy*

The end of the Davidic monarchy and the destruction of the Temple in 587/586 B.C.E. should have given the lie to the King-Zion ideology. Even the rebuilding of the Temple in 520–515 B.C.E. should not have been able to "rebuild" the King-Zion complex, for a very basic reason: How can one speak of YHWH's continuing relationship with a dynasty that is no longer operative? One leg of the King-Zion tripod is gone; collapse is certain. But habits of the mind die hard. And "failed" ideologies often provide the raw materials for new ideological formulations. So it was that the King-Zion ideology survived in altered form in the exile and afterward. Judeans after 587/586 B.C.E. reformulated the King-Zion complex in three ways to account for the missing Davidic monarch.

### Response 1: Replace the Dynasty with Cyrus (Second Isaiah)

The writers of Second Isaiah relied on the thought patterns of the King-Zion ideology to make a case for maintaining Judean identity in Babylon. While exhibiting an almost cloying passion for the future of Zion, these writers claim that Cyrus, the emperor of Persia, was God's anointed one, or messiah (Isa 45:1). At this time, Cyrus was threatening Babylon from the north and east. Babylon's defeat was only a matter of time. There were, of course, a whole host of geopolitical reasons for Persian ascendancy. But the writers prefer to see YHWH as sponsoring Cyrus's conquest of Babylon. And the Persian ruler would fill, in some way, a position analogous to that filled by the Davidides: the text has YHWH link him to the cosmic order and to YHWH's plans to secure Zion's essential place in the cosmos (45:12–13).

### Zion as a Character in Second Isaiah

Second Isaiah almost always connects Zion to anticipated joy and/or salvation. And, like much ancient Near Eastern poetry, it describes the city as a female figure. This descriptive move allows the use of the figure of the forsaken woman to speak of Zion's present state ("But Zion said, 'The LORD has forsaken me, my Lord has forgotten me'" [49:14]) as well as the figure of the abused female slave (52:1–3). And, using a common motif in the Hebrew Bible, the writers have YHWH claim Zion as "daughter" (52:2; also see 1:8; 10:32; 16:1; 37:22; 62:11; Mic 4:8, 10, 13; Lam 2:1, 4, 8, 10, 13, 18). The writers also at times identify their audience, Judean exiles in Babylon, as Zion, forcing the exiles to identify with that distant place that the writers claim will yet be their destiny (51:15–16).

**Response 2: Replace the Dynasty with a Future Hope (Haggai/Zechariah)**

After Cyrus conquered Babylon in 539 B.C.E., some elite Judean exiles gradually returned to the area around Jerusalem, the now-Persian province of Yehud. The prophets Haggai and Zechariah came early in the reign of Darius I (ca. 520 B.C.E.), along with others determined to rebuild the Temple. But support for the Temple project was not unanimous. Many residents in Yehud (especially those who had not been exiled) would have questioned the necessity and the expense of the Temple, as well as wondered about its leadership. So Haggai and Zechariah used their rhetorical gifts to move their audience to support the new institution. And they appealed to what they assumed would have been a shared set of values: the King-Zion ideology.

On the basis of that ideology, the writers record Haggai as making extravagant claims for this new Temple. Building a new Temple will restore crop yields (Hag 2:18–19). Further, a pilgrimage of the nations to Zion will occur, filling the new Temple with treasure exceeding that of Solomon's edifice (2:7–9). In the text of Haggai, Zion continues as the world's center, and as such, will inevitably require a grand Temple.

But what of the Davidic dynasty that was to rule from Zion? The writers asserted that YHWH would soon establish Zerubbabel, presumably a Davidide (but one with a Babylonian name) serving as the Persian governor of Yehud, as a chosen figure, a "signet ring": "On that day, says the LORD of hosts, I will take you, O Zerubbabel my servant, son of Shealtiel, says the LORD, and make you like a signet ring; for I have chosen you, says the LORD of hosts" (Hag 2:23). While not using the term "messiah," this text seems to be part of that thought world: YHWH would soon cast down the other kingdoms and raise up a good king, an anointed one of the line of David, to rule from Zion.

The text of Zechariah also makes large claims for Zerubbabel's authority in line with the King-Zion ideology, but stresses his role in rebuilding the Temple. Zerubbabel would see the project through, from its inception (bringing out the "top stone" [Zech 4:7]) to its completion (4:9). But the book of Zechariah also demonstrates the difficulties in using the King-Zion ideology under Persian rule. Zerubbabel disappears from view after this point. Some scholars thus suggest that the Persians removed Zerubbabel to blunt such extravagent (and destabilizing) claims for Zerubbabel's role. The Persians could not abide any extra "signet rings" running about!

---

### signet ring

Kings used signet rings to mark documents as having royal authority; thus, the ring itself could be used as a symbol of that authority. In Hag 2:23 the king in question is YHWH, and Zerubbabel represents YHWH's ruling power. In addition, Haggai probably has in mind a tradition that the Davidic monarch served as YHWH's signet, as seen in Jer 22:24. By calling Zerubbabel YHWH's signet ring, Haggai was at least hinting that Zerubbabel would be (or deserved to be) the king of Judah, not just the Persian governor of the region.

While these claims of a Persian removal of Zerubbabel are speculative, it is fairly clear that the book of Zechariah extols the high priest, Joshua, as much if not more than the Davidide Zerubbabel. Joshua, not Zerubbabel, appears wearing a crown (6:11). Indeed, Zechariah imagines both the governor and the high priest functioning as "anointed ones" in his vision of the two olive trees (4:11–14). The book of Zechariah channels the royal imagery of the King-Zion ideology onto the priesthood. Although it does not use the term "messiah" here, this text represents a first step on the road to what would become "<u>dual messianism</u>," the idea that both a priestly and a royal messiah would appear at the end of days. Such a view reflects both long-standing hopes for renewal of the Davidic dynasty and the knowledge that, for much of the Second Temple period, the high priest held a great deal of authority in the province of Yehud. The ideology adjusted the hopes it conjured to fit a new political reality.

### Response 3: Replace the Dynasty with Priests (Chronicles)

The book of Zechariah alters the expectations for the *future* inherent in the ideology: a Davidic ruler and a priest would share authority. The books of Chronicles, however, offer an alternative view of the *past*. The Chronicler, in retelling the story of the monarchy from 1 and 2 Kings, emphasizes the role of the Davidic kings in establishing and maintaining the Temple and gives

---

### dual messianism

The Essenes, the group of Jews in the late Second Temple period who authored many of the Dead Sea Scrolls, developed the notion of dual messianism, claiming that, at the end of the age, two messiahs would come and preside over a "messianic banquet." Since this scroll is not complete, the translator made judgments as to what words best fill in the various holes in the text. The added material appears in brackets.

> When God engenders (the Priest-) Messiah, he shall come with them [at] the head of the whole congregation of Israel with all [his brethren, the sons] of Aaron the Priests, [those called] to the assembly, the men of renown; and they shall sit [before him, each man] in the order of his dignity. And then [the Mess]iah of Israel shall [come], and the chiefs of the [clans of Israel] shall sit before him, [each] in the order of his dignity, according to [his place] in their camps and marches.... And [when] they shall gather for the common [tab]le, to eat and [to drink] new wine, when the common table shall be set for eating and the new wine [poured] for drinking, let no man extend his hand over the first-fruits of bread and wine before the Priest; for [it is he] who shall bless the first-fruits of bread and wine, and shall be the first [to extend] his hand over the bread. Thereafter, the Messiah of Israel shall extend his hand over the bread, [and] all the congregation of the Community [shall utter a] blessing, [each man in the order] of his dignity.

"The Messianic Rule," in *The Complete Dead Sea Scrolls in English*, trans. and ed. Geza Vermes (New York: Penguin, 1997), 159–60.

them, especially David, <u>a more priestly appearance</u>. In Chronicles, David establishes the priestly bureaucracy (1 Chr 16:4–7, 37–42), selects the site for the Temple (22:1), and prepares for its actual construction (22:2–5; 29:2–5). The Chronicler also cleans up the characters of the Temple's founders, David and Solomon, distancing the holy Temple from any taint. David's affair with Bathsheba and his murder of Uriah vanish. Solomon's passion for foreign women and their gods likewise disappears.

The Chronicler sees the establishment and maintenance of the Temple as the key, lasting accomplishment of the Davidic dynasty. Thus, Chronicles ends its account of the history of the Israelites with the Persian order to restore the Temple (2 Chr 36:22–23), while its main source, Kings, ends with a focus on the future of the Davidic line (2 Kgs 25:27–30). The Chronicler effectively collapses the triangular King-Zion ideology into a bipolar YHWH-Zion relationship by blurring or combining dynasty and Temple.

The royal King-Zion ideology survived the end of the dynasty in altered forms. Its strength testifies to the ability of ideologies to maintain a hold on the imagination. The priests who operated the rebuilt Temple reconfigured the King-Zion ideology to avoid revolutionary action against imperial authorities. While it always bore within it the seeds of rebellion (e.g., Zerubbabel), it tended to produce good imperial subjects.

## The Sinai-Nation Complex

The King-Zion ideology focused on a triangular relation among YHWH, the Davidic dynasty, and the Temple on Zion as the key to maintaining cosmic order. While this ideology appears frequently in the Psalms and some of the prophetic literature, it hardly covers the whole of the Hebrew Bible. The Torah, for example, does not focus on the royalty's place in the cosmos. In fact, the story of Israel's meeting with its god at Mount Sinai, the center of the Torah, presents a different ideological perspective from the King-Zion complex. Here the emphasis falls on the people's identity and existence in relation to their ruling national god, YHWH. This relationship, or **covenant**, is basic to this ideology.

*Ancient Treaties, Covenants, and Ideology*

Israelites derived their idea of covenant from ancient **suzerainty treaties** or loyalty oaths between kings. A more powerful king, or suzerain, made these agreements with a vassal, a king who was, for the present, no match for the suzerain. These treaties and oaths bear an often-striking relationship with the contents of the Torah. And these texts perform ideological work, endeavoring to create a "natural" relationship between the two parties, a relationship that will become a part of the way both parties understand "the way things are."

The suzerainty treaties and oaths from the ancient Near East claim unquestionable power for the suzerain. All initiative rests with him. He does not need to make this agreement with a weaker power but does so out of his magnanimity. Frequently the suzerain, in the treaty's historical prologue, points to historical events as evidence of both his grace and his initiative.

In response, the vassal king swears loyalty to the suzerain, and he does so in the presence of deities, who serve as witnesses to the treaty. The treaty assures the vassal that continued loyalty will bring blessings. And the treaty contains a set of graphic potential punishments, expressed as curses to be enforced by the gods, helping ensure the vassal's obedience. Some of the curses cover items that a king, even a suzerain, cannot directly control (e.g., famine, disease). Others clearly imply that the suzerain will be the real enforcer (e.g., destruction in war). In either case, the suzerain and vassal are in an obviously asymmetrical relationship: the suzerain (and the gods who act on his behalf) hold all the cards. The vassal's only real choice is submission.

But these treaties do not necessarily reflect the actual relations between kings. Rather, they imagine these relationships in ways that may obscure the actual power dynamics of the situation. So in the treaties, the suzerain has no need of the vassal. Any action the suzerain takes is purely unmotivated grace for the vassal. In "real" politics, however, a suzerain might easily need a vassal relationship with a weaker power. It may be in the suzerain's best interest not to occupy a vassal state with his army; better to let the vassal run his own affairs, pay tribute, and let the suzerain's army fight elsewhere. The potential vassal king surely knows of these political exigencies. The utter asymmetry of power in the treaties thus covers for a more complex situation. The treaties invite their audience to live in (and to internalize) a simpler world of hyperpowerful suzerains and useless, weak vassals.

The treaties also imagine that the status quo is the will of the gods, who will act to support the current power structure. Thus, the treaties style any change in the power structure as violation. But it is abundantly clear that, curses or no, things change. The relative strengths of the kingdoms will vary

# Israel's Covenant and Ancient Near Eastern Treaties

Numerous parallels exist between the covenant ideas in the Torah and the suzerainty treaties of the ancient Near East.

## Preamble: The suzerain identifies himself

These are the words of the Sun Mursulis, the great king, the king of the Hatti land, the valiant, the favorite of the Storm-god, the son of Suppiluliumas, the great king, the king of the Hatti land, the valiant. (From the treaty between the Hittite king Mursulis and Duppi-tessub of Amurru; ca. fourteenth century B.C.E.)

I am the LORD, your God. (Exod 20:2)

## Historical Prologue: The suzerain elaborates his actions that led to the treaty

When your father died, in accordance with your father's word I did not drop you. Since your father had mentioned to me your name with great praise, I sought after you. To be sure, you were sick and ailing, but although you were ailing, I, the Sun, put you in place of your father and took your brothers (and) sisters and the Amurru land in oath for you. (From the Treaty of Mursulis and Duppi-Tessub)

Then Moses went up to God; the LORD called to him from the mountain, saying, "Thus you shall say to the house of Jacob, and tell the Israelites: You have seen what I did to the Egyptians, and how I bore you on eagles' wings and brought you to myself." (Exod 19:3–4)

## Stipulations: The terms of the treaty (which demand loyalty)

If any (of you) hears some wrong, evil, unseemly plan which is improper or detrimental to the crown prince designate Ashurbanipal, son of your lord Esarhaddon, whether they be spoken by his enemy or his ally, by his brothers, by his sons, by his daughters, by his brothers, his father's brothers, his cousins, or any other member of his father's lineage, or by your own brothers, sons or daughters, or by a prophet, an ecstatic, a dream-interpreter, or by any human being whatsoever, and conceals it, does not come and report it to the crown prince designate Ashurbanipal . . . (Treaty between Esarhaddon of Assyria and Ramataya of Urakazabanu, ca. 670 B.C.E.)

If anyone secretly entices you—even if it is your brother, your father's son or your mother's son, or your own son or daughter, or the wife you embrace, or your most intimate friend—saying, "Let us go worship other gods," whom neither you nor your ancestors have known, any of the gods of the peoples that are around you, whether near you or far away from you, from one end of the earth to the other, you must not yield to or heed any such persons. Show them no pity or compassion and do not shield them. (Deut 13:6–8)

## Deposit of Treaty: The treaty will be stored at a temple and read at certain occasions

A duplicate of this tablet has been deposited before the Sun-goddess of Arinna, because the Sun-goddess of Arinna regulates kingship and queenship. In the Mitanni land (a duplicate) has been deposited before Tessub, the lord of the *kurinnu* of Kahat. At regular intervals shall they read it in the presence of the king of the Mitanni land and in the presence of the sons of the Hurri country. (From a treaty between the Hittite king Suppiluliumas and Kurtiwaza of Mitanni, fourteenth century B.C.E.)

When Moses had finished writing down in a book the words of this law to the very end, Moses commanded the Levites who carried the ark of the covenant of the LORD, saying, "Take this book of the law and put it beside the ark of the covenant of the LORD your God; let it remain there as a witness against you. . . . Assemble to me all the elders of your tribes and your officials, so that I may recite these words in their hearing." (Deut 31:24–26, 28)

### List of Witnesses: The gods before whom the treaty oath is sworn

(The treaty) which he has made binding with you before Jupiter, Venus, Saturn, Mercury, Mars and Sirius; before Ashur, Anu, Enlil, and Ea, Sin, Shamash, Adad, and Marduk . . . (Treaty of Esarhaddon and Ramataya)

I [Moses] call heaven and earth to witness against you today that I have set before you life and death, blessings and curses. Choose life so that you and your descendants may live. (Deut 30:19)

### Curses and Blessings: The consequences of keeping or breaking the treaty

Just as rain does not fall from a copper sky, so may there come neither rain nor dew upon your fields and meadows, but let it rain burning coals in your land instead of dew. . . . Just as this ewe is cut open and the flesh of its young placed in its mouth, so may he (Shamash?) make you eat in your hunger the flesh of your brothers, your sons, and your daughters. (Treaty of Esarhaddon and Ramataya)

The sky over your head shall be bronze, and the earth under you iron. The LORD will change the rain of your land into powder, and only dust shall come down upon you from the sky until you are destroyed. . . . In the desperate straits to which the enemy siege reduces you, you will eat the fruit of your womb, the flesh of your own sons and daughters whom the LORD your God has given you. (Deut 28:23–24, 53)

Source for treaties: James B. Pritchard, ed. *Ancient Near Eastern Texts Related to the Old Testament*, 3rd ed. (Princeton, NJ: Princeton University Press, 1969), 203–5, 534–39.

### stable

The treaties' concern for stability appears in their frequent demand that they are not to be altered or effaced:

> [Whoever will] give orders to efface [th]ese inscriptions from the bethels [i.e., the pillars in the shrine], where they are [wr]itten and [will] say, "I shall destroy the inscrip[tion]s and with impunity(?) shall I destroy KTK and its king," should that (man) be frightened from effacing the inscriptions from the bethels and say to someone who does not understand, "I shall engage (you) indeed(?)," and (then) order (him), "Efface these inscriptions from the bethels," may [he] and his son die in oppressive torment.

Treaty between Bir-Ga'yah king of KTK and the king of Arpad, ca. 750 B.C.E., from *The Context of Scripture*, vol. 2, ed. W. W. Hallo (Leiden: Brill, 2000), 216.

over time; a vassal, sensing this, could cease paying tribute or act disloyally in other ways. So the treaties dream up a world in which power is <u>stable</u>, residing in unchanging gods and kings.

*The Sinai-Nation Complex: Rewriting the Treaties*

The Sinai covenant, the centerpiece of the Sinai-Nation ideological complex, uses the suzerainty treaties as a model. Yet it changes them in several ways, transforming their ideology. First, the Sinai covenant places YHWH in the role of the powerful suzerain. Second, the Sinai covenant places the people Israel in the role of the vassal king. And third, since the Sinai covenant eliminates human kings from the treaties, it need not automatically support the treaty ideology's assumption of the "status quo" power of monarchs. We will examine these three aspects of the Sinai-Nation complex in the stories of founding the covenant in Exodus, especially Exod 19–24 and 32–34.

### YHWH as Suzerain

In similar fashion to the King-Zion ideology, the Sinai-Nation ideology understands YHWH as king. But YHWH's royal authority is not simply assumed as it was in the King-Zion ideology. The Sinai-Nation ideology, based as it is in ancient Near Eastern treaty thought, develops its picture of YHWH's royal power as a gracious initiative. In Exod 19, for example, YHWH broaches the possibility of a relationship with Israel only after claiming to have performed a gracious initiative on Israel's behalf: the destruction of the Egyptians and the bearing of Israel out of Egypt "on eagles' wings" (Exod 19:4). YHWH sought out Israel, this potential vassal people, and acted on their behalf. If the people obey YHWH's voice and keep YHWH's covenant, they will continue to ratify their relationship with YHWH. YHWH fails to mention what will occur if the people reject this relationship either now (by saying no) or later (by violating its terms).

In the treaty tradition, the suzerain reserves the right to punish the disloyal vassal, while claiming that the gods themselves also enforce the agreement. But for Israel no other gods serve as enforcers, because YHWH is the only god with whom Israel is supposed to have contact. So there are no gods to share the suzerain's authority. YHWH as suzerain possesses all the power and will punish the disloyalty of the vassal through whatever means are available, including the outright erasure of the vassal from the earth.

This dynamic becomes clear in the story of the golden calf (Exod 32). While Moses sojourns on Sinai, receiving from YHWH more stipulations of the covenant, the people almost immediately show disloyalty. They request that "gods" be made, suggesting that they will worship other deities than YHWH, the equivalent of a vassal's rejecting a suzerain and allying with a hostile power. Making matters worse, the people contradict YHWH's claim to have brought the people out of Egypt by claiming that Moses delivered them from Egypt (32:1). The Israelites ("the people") utterly deny the suzerain's gracious initiative that is central to covenant ideology.

Vassals in the ancient Near East could and did successfully reject their suzerains. But in this story, as in the treaties, the suzerain will not allow such an action to proceed. YHWH immediately backs out of the relationship, asserting that the people came out of Egypt on *Moses'* initiative: "The LORD said to Moses, 'Go down at once! *Your* people, whom *you* brought up out of the land of Egypt, have acted perversely" (32:7). Since YHWH has all the power, YHWH's voiding the treaty is the same thing as threatening to erase Israel (32:9–10).

Although Moses manages to persuade YHWH not to destroy Israel, YHWH's power remains beyond question. YHWH has, for some reason, decided not to do what was both possible and expected. Thus, the relationship with YHWH (and therefore the people's continued existence) always stays under threat. YHWH will keep a healthy distance from the people, lest he kill them for disobedience (33:3).

### Israel as Vassal

In the Sinai-Nation ideology, the nation (or people) takes the place of a vassal king. The stories in Exodus clearly represent the people in this manner by presenting them as one character, having one voice. And that voice accepts vassal status: "The people all answered as one: 'Everything that the LORD has spoken we will do'" (Exod 19:7–8; cf. 24:3, 7).

When YHWH appears on the mountain, the people as a body (Moses included) receive the basic stipulations of the covenant—the Ten Commandments, or ten "words." They represent the requirements of a distinct relationship between a god, YHWH, and that god's vassal community, Israel; they define what it will mean for this vassal to remain loyal. Thus, these commandments are not, in this context, a form of universal law that all humans should obey. They are for this vassal and only this vassal.

On the basis of the gracious initiative shown by YHWH in the exodus, the people must not worship other gods. They must not worship YHWH through images, nor are they to use YHWH's powerful name in wrong ways.

---

### The Ten Commandments

While the Hebrew Bible insists on ten "words" vital to the Sinai covenant (Exod 34:28; Deut 4:13; 10:4), their content and numbering are not certain. Exodus 20 and Deut 5 offer two versions of the Ten Commandments, also known as the Decalogue, and differing versions of some commandments. For example, in the Exodus version, the Sabbath recalls God's acts of creation, while in Deuteronomy it recalls Israel's experience of slavery in Egypt. Some early translations have the commandments in different orders as well: one important Septuagint manuscript (Codex Vaticanus) lists adultery, theft, and murder in Exod 20 but adultery, murder, and theft in Deut 5.

Different faith traditions also number these commandments differently. Jews take the prologue, YHWH's claim to have brought Israel out of Egypt (Exod 20:2), as the first commandment, then combine the next two commandments—"no other gods" and "no idols"—into the second commandment. Catholics and Lutherans also combine the "no other gods" and "no idols" commandments, but as their first commandment. To keep the number at ten, they divide the "Do not covet" commandment in two ("Do not covet your neighbor's wife" is a separate commandment). Orthodox Christians, Anglicans, and most Protestants take the "no other gods" and "no idols" commandments as numbers 1 and 2, respectively, and put all the anticoveting material in the tenth commandment.

## The Audience of the Ten Commandments

While the stories in Exodus speak of the whole people here, and clearly intend all Israel to be bound by the agreement, the commandments themselves reveal a narrower audience. The commandment not to desire a neighbor's wife clearly assumes an all-male audience. And that same commandment implies that the neighbor is certainly not poor: he owns land and other things worth coveting. Further, not everyone has the ability to rest on the Sabbath. Despite the idealized picture of the commandment, Sabbath rest may have been a luxury that the "sharecroppers" of the ancient Cisjordan could not afford. So while the text says "people," it hints that "people" really means "male landowners."

## The Ten Commandments and Penalties

The Decalogue provides no explicit penalty for violating its commandments. So it differs from much of the legal material in the Torah, which is couched in if—then language. If you do X, then certain punishments follow, although extenuating circumstances may alter the penalty. In other words, the laws present certain cases. Exodus 21:12, for example, mandates that anyone who kills another person should be killed. But then the text presents a case (lack of premeditation) in which the penalty can be avoided (21:13–14). This kind of law is "case" or "casuistic" law.

By contrast, the legal material in the Ten Commandments shows no interest in the particular circumstances of a murder or in the punishments that might be applied. It simply prohibits a crime and demands acceptance. This kind of law is "apodictic" law and occurs occasionally in the Torah.

They must demonstrate their relationship to YHWH by resting from labor on the seventh day, marking themselves off from other nations. And they must refrain from practices that destroy the life of the community (dishonoring parents, murder, adultery, theft, perjury, and greed).

If the Israelites obey these stipulations, they confirm their role as YHWH's vassal, his "treasured possession," with a distinct role in the political structure of the world (Exod 19:5–6). In comparison to other nations, the Israelites would be seen not as a vassal "loser," but as the privileged nation (the "priestly kingdom," Exod 19:6) chosen to be loyal to YHWH. The analogy is clear: Israel is to other nations as the priesthood is to common folk. But Israel, of course, may choose to disobey the stipulations, to be a disloyal vassal. In that event, would YHWH find another treasured possession and destroy Israel? Or would Israel continue to exist, but as a "nonspecial" nation?

### The Uncertainties of Human Leadership

If this open-ended relationship is to continue, it will require some form of human leadership. Where the treaty tradition clearly indicates kings as responsible parties, Israel, through altering the structure away from human kings, leaves the question of leadership open. Because of this omission, the

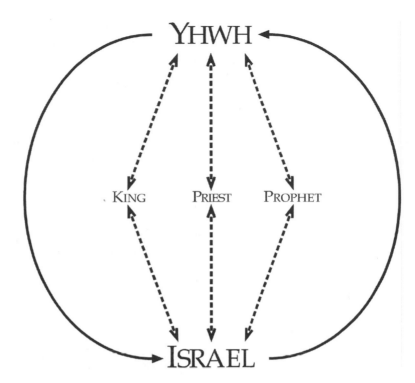

Fig. 11.3: The Sinai-Nation Complex

Sinai-Nation ideological complex is not as easy to visualize as the King-Zion complex. Here the relationship between YHWH and the people may be mediated by a number of human leaders. Or YHWH may relate to the people as a whole either through speech (as at Sinai) or through action (fulfilling certain blessings or curses). In short, this diagram (see fig. 11.3) could work in any number of ways for ancient Israelites, depending on the precise context and how the current political powers understood their roles.

In the founding stories of the Sinai-Nation complex, Moses helps YHWH and Israel establish and maintain their relationship. But Moses' leadership functions in nonstandard ways. The text does not describe Moses as a king or as the ancestor of monarchs. Moses does not serve <u>as a priest</u>,

### as a priest

A covenant ratification in Exod 24 presents Moses in priestly terms: he constructs a place for worship and dashes the blood of the sacrifice on the altar, a duty reserved to priests (24:6). He also throws blood on the people, sealing the treaty between them and YHWH (24:8). Yet Moses does not himself perform the sacrifice, assigning that task to others. And his reading of the covenant to the people reprises his role as go-between, as a messenger between YHWH and the people (24:7). Moses' role does not quite fit that of "priest."

nor do <u>his children</u>; his only relation to the priests is through his brother Aaron. Neither priests nor kings find affirmation of their particular political roles in the figure of Moses.

We may see something of the prophet here in Moses; he serves as an intermediary. The people elevate Moses as their negotiator in all further talks with YHWH, since YHWH's unmediated presence seems dangerous (Exod 20:18–21). But Moses, if he <u>appears to be a prophet</u> here, is a prophet unattached to any royal court or any clear support group. In short, as a prophet, Moses is not quite standard issue. So while the stories here do not imagine a nation without hierarchy, neither do they imagine a royal, priestly, or prophetic bureaucracy. Moses' leadership could be taken to affirm powerful human leadership, a leadership vitally in touch with the will of the deity and thus supportive of a strong monarchy and/or priesthood. But Moses could also show a way of organizing power that disregards the inherited structures of monarch and priesthood. Mount Sinai could be a rival to Mount Zion or a potential ally.

### his children

In an intriguing story in the book of Judges, an opportunistic cultic functionary accepts a post as priest to the household of a certain Micah, who had built a shrine featuring a silver idol (Judg 17). Somewhat later, the Israelite tribe of Dan migrates through the area and takes this priest, along with the idol and the rest of Micah's cultic equipment, to serve at their shrine. The story then identifies the priest, who presides over idol worship, as a grandson of Moses (18:30).

Some scholars claim that this story, along with other hints in the priestly genealogies in the Hebrew Bible, indicates that, at some point in Israel's history, there existed a line of priests who traced their ancestry to Moses. That assertion remains highly speculative. In any case, the story in Judges strongly implies that any priesthood descended from Moses is improper: it sponsors idolatry, benefits by theft, and attempts to worship YHWH outside Jerusalem. In that way, it fits well with the Torah, which claims that only descendants of Aaron can serve as priests.

### appears to be a prophet

Deuteronomy explicitly states that Moses served as a prophet and that valid prophets serve after the fashion of Moses (Deut 18:15–19). Later, Deuteronomy goes even further, claiming that Moses is not only a standard but also an unreachable standard. Moses was a uniquely effective prophet: "Never since has there arisen a prophet in Israel like Moses, whom the Lord knew face to face" (Deut 34:10).

*Sinai versus Zion: Jeremiah and Revolutionary Impulses*

The Sinai covenant grounds Israel's very existence in the initiative of a god portrayed as a treaty-making suzerain. But beyond that affirmation of monarchy, little else in the stories in Exodus directly justifies royal power. In fact, their negative portrayal of the Pharaoh may undermine royal pretensions and power. So perhaps "Sinai values" do at times contradict the robust view of royal power held in the King-Zion ideology.

Such a contradiction appears in the work of the prophet Jeremiah. In Jeremiah's time, Babylon threatened the kingdom of Judah. Jeremiah believed that Judah should surrender to Babylon, a belief that stemmed from both a political calculation (Babylon would eventually control the region) and a theological perspective (YHWH was using Babylon to punish Judah for various sins). Such a stance faced heavy ideological opposition from the King-Zion complex. Enemies could not destroy Zion; foreigners could not extinguish the Davidic dynasty. The psalms claimed as much, and the deliverance (miraculous or not) under Hezekiah affirmed this stance. There should be no reason to fear the coming of the Babylonians; Judah could not lose.

But from where does Jeremiah get the authority (and the chutzpah) to challenge this ideology? The book of Jeremiah provides a couple of hints. First, Jeremiah had political support from families at court, especially the family of Shaphan (Jer 26:24) and "the elders of the land" (26:17–19). Second, Jeremiah's language echoes the Decalogue (7:9–10), a central feature of the covenant at Sinai. Jeremiah uses the Sinai-Nation ideology to challenge his audience's acceptance of the King-Zion ideology.

Jeremiah, also in line with the Sinai-Nation complex, claims that YHWH's initiative is not completely controlled by royal processes or the cult apparatus. For Jeremiah, the existence of Zion is not a bad thing, but it must not diminish YHWH's ability to act. YHWH can abandon Zion, and thus the people, if he wishes (7:3–4).

Thus, Jeremiah's ideological response claims YHWH the suzerain's initiative as central. Jeremiah asserts that the people of Judah have rejected the divine initiative (as did the people of the northern kingdom) and hence deserve a similar erasure:

> And now, because you have done all these things, says the LORD, and when I spoke to you persistently, you did not listen, and when I called you, you did not answer, therefore I will do to the house that is called by my name, in which you trust, and to the place that I gave to you and to your ancestors, just what I did to Shiloh. And I will cast you out of my sight, just as I cast out all your kinsfolk, all the offspring of Ephraim. (Jer 7:13–15)

For Jeremiah, YHWH will act to punish disloyalty to the covenant. And this punishment will threaten the continued existence of the current political-cultic establishment (the status quo). So YHWH can be, in defense of his own complete power over Israel, a kind of revolutionary.

The book of Deuteronomy restates the establishment of the Sinai covenant. The basic material in Deuteronomy dates from the rule of King Josiah, who attempted to expand Judah's influence through a national renewal program. His program included a healthy respect for Zion, centralizing all cultic observances there (Deut 12:5–28; 2 Kgs 23:4–20). But Josiah included an idea also expressed by prophets such as Amos and Jeremiah: the people must keep certain stipulations in order to assure themselves of continued existence. Deuteronomy thus represents a careful ideological balancing act between binding YHWH in close relationship to king and Zion and proclaiming YHWH's free divine initiative.

Unlike the stories of Sinai in Exodus, in Deuteronomy YHWH specifically approves the monarchy. There will be a king, but the king will not behave like typical monarchs. He must not acquire a large cavalry force, too much money, or a large harem, nor may he claim to be above the people. And the only duty incumbent upon the monarch is to read the book of Deuteronomy (Deut 17:16–20)! One might wonder why anyone would want to be king. But through this description of the monarchy, Deuteronomy makes clear that, in its view, monarchs must respect the Sinai covenant.

Along with supporting at least the existence of the monarchy, Deuteronomy supports Zion. For example, all worship of YHWH must take place in Jerusalem (Deut 12:2–4). Deuteronomy also demands that the people move the celebration of Passover, which rehearses the exodus, from local communi-

---

### Deuteronomy and the Monarchy: An Idealized Picture

Deuteronomy's picture of the king, a man with little wealth, no harem, but an obligation to read Deuteronomy daily, is hardly realistic. Instead, Deuteronomy conjures an idealized picture of the monarch. This act of imagination also appears in the evaluation of various monarchs in the books of Kings. These books are part of a larger historical work (Joshua, Judges, Samuel, and Kings) written from the perspective of the authors of Deuteronomy. The Deuteronomistic authors of Kings comment on the reign of each king of Israel and Judah. But each king is judged not on standards such as economic growth or geopolitical security, but on whether he fulfills Deuteronomy's idealized expectations.

For the Deuteronomistic historians, no kings of Israel did any good, for all of them supported the cult sites outside of Jerusalem founded by the first king of Israel, Jeroboam I. Even the Israelite king Omri, who made Israel into a major regional power, counts as a failure (1 Kgs 16:25–26). Kings of Judah can earn passing grades, but only if they support the Deuteronomists' program of cult centralization and the elimination of certain religious practices. So Amaziah earns a positive assessment, though he could have done better had he gotten rid of worship sites outside Jerusalem (2 Kgs 14:3–4). The authors say nothing of the political accomplishments during Manasseh's lengthy reign, but they do mention that he sinned against YHWH, following the "abominable practices" of other nations (2 Kgs 21:2). The idealized picture of the monarch in Deuteronomy thus determines in large part the way the authors of Deuteronomy and Joshua-Kings present the history of Israel and Judah.

ties to Zion (16:1–8). The motives here are not simply theological. Concentrating all sacrifice at the Temple ensures it income, supports its bureaucracy, and gives the monarchy more economic power to conduct its affairs.

But while Deuteronomy mandates centralized worship, it does not support Zion without qualification. The choice of a place of worship must be, in good vassal treaty form, a matter of divine initiative. Thus, Deuteronomy does not mention Jerusalem or Zion; it simply speaks of worshiping at the place YHWH will select "as a dwelling for his name" (12:11). In other words, Deuteronomy asserts that YHWH will not identify totally with Zion. Rather, only YHWH's "name" will dwell there. YHWH, who still holds initiative, is larger than the particular space of Zion.

The mediating position of Deuteronomy modifies the possible revolutionary impact of the Sinai covenant. Various leaders, including kings, priests, and prophets, aid the people in fulfilling the nation's oath to be loyal to YHWH. And Deuteronomy also presents YHWH as less willing to play the revolutionary by allowing a place for dynasty and Temple and ensuring a future for his vassal people.

The editors of the book of Deuteronomy knew of the destruction of the Temple and the exile to Babylon. They mention the exile as a grave punishment, alluding to it in their lists of curses—the actions the aggrieved suzerain, YHWH would take (28:63–65). Yet these editors also claim that YHWH's gracious initiative will not end. The threat of exile shows YHWH's power and enforces loyalty, but it will not necessarily erase the people from the earth. If they will only recall the covenant's stipulations, YHWH will return them from exile (30:1–4). YHWH, while still suzerain, will not utterly destroy the wayward vassal.

The Sinai covenant encouraged the community as a whole to see its own conduct as evidence of its relationship to YHWH. Keeping certain stipulations ensured the community's continued existence, then, not the power of the king, his army, or his bureaucracy. Thus, the Sinai covenant attempted to form the community's "social self" in ways that did not always cohere well with the King-Zion ideology. The book of Deuteronomy, as well as the historical books written from its ideological perspective, provide at least a glimpse of the kind of ideological conflict that may have marked Israelite and Judahite culture.

## The Sage-Order Complex

The Sinai-Nation ideology demonstrated little interest in the cosmos. Its field of vision centered on Israel. As long as the YHWH-Israel relation was secure, Israel was secure. One may assume (although this is not explicitly stated) that, no matter what Israel did, YHWH would still be YHWH and the cosmos would keep functioning. In contrast, the King-Zion ideology assumed that the king held an essential place in the production of cosmic order. And the very

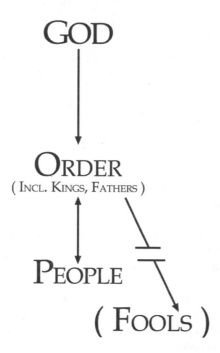

**Fig. 11.4: The Sage-Order Complex**

existence of Zion, the point of intersection between the divine and human realms, also secured cosmic order. Ancient Israelites, however, spoke about the cosmos in ways less linked to king and Zion or YHWH's suzerainty. The authors of Israel's wisdom literature claimed that God had created an ordered cosmos, and they associated that order with various figures (e.g., nation, father, king, emperor). This ideological project (see fig. 11.4) defined those who would not act in accord with this order as "fools," while those who internalized their place in God's order were "wise." In this way, this project made certain kinds of social power seem obvious and irrefutable.

> ### the authors of Israel's wisdom literature
>
> These authors are usually called "sages," even though it is unlikely that "sage" was an actual position in society. Members of the elite who possessed enough leisure time to study and collect various forms of **wisdom**, they served as scribes, local government officials, and priests.

*Creation as Ideology: Genesis 1*

Present-day conflicts over claims regarding human origins show the ideological nature of any statement about creation (and an orderly universe). Notions of creation inform a community's idea of who it is and for what purposes it exists. For example, according to the *Enuma Elish*, a Babylonian text, conflict between gods generated the world. One god, Marduk, slew the chaotic sea goddess, Tiamat, and built the cosmos from her watery body. Humans, made from blood leftover from the conflict, were fashioned to serve the gods. Marduk then founded his temple in Babylon.

This text has an obvious ideological point: the temple of Marduk and the political and cultic arrangements in Babylon were part of the order of the universe. The *Enuma Elish* was not simply a text that, when read, would persuade the Babylonian audience of the absolute centrality of the king in the cosmos. The text was read every year at the new year's celebration, at which the king of Babylon "took the hand of Marduk" and was confirmed in his role as leader for the coming year. So the festival linked Marduk's subduing chaos with Marduk's role in supporting the orderly rule of the Babylonian monarch.

The creation narrative in Gen 1:1–2:4a advances its own ideological claims while contesting those in the *Enuma Elish*. Unlike the *Enuma Elish*, Genesis reveals no cosmic conflict; nothing fights against God. God is in serene control, manufacturing everything by command ("And God said X, and there was X"). Israel's god, always in charge, thus appears more powerful than Marduk, who had to fight to rule.

The authors of Gen 1:1–2:4a also make the Sabbath the crown of creation. Resting on the Sabbath, which marks Israel off from other nations, is an essential part of the way "the world really is." Israelites are thus in tune with cosmic reality, while the Babylonians are not. This difference between the Sabbath-observing Israelites and the Sabbath-ignoring Babylonians and Persians is "baked into" reality. Cultural differences are not cultural; they are natural. The natural order supports Israel's distinct social existence. So the authors of this Israelite creation text had an ideological purpose: to show their fellow Israelites that they were a distinct part of the cosmic order built by their powerful God.

## Wisdom as Ideology: Proverbs

Notions of created order not only appear in stories of creation; they also inform the wisdom literature written by ancient sages in Israel and its neighbors. These sages assumed that the gods had created an orderly world, so they sought to discern the order of things through careful observation. One can learn much from watching ants, badgers, locusts, and lizards (Prov 30:24–28). Moreover, sages in various lands could come up with similar materials (ants are industrious and thus "wise" no matter what nation they reside in). And because these sages were frequently government officials who (unlike almost everyone else) could travel, they shared this information across national and religious boundaries.

Those highly trained few at the court of the king were not the only people examining the world. Members of the older generation commonly passed down observations about how things "really are." Thus, some material in the book of Proverbs derives from this "folk" or "family" wisdom. Proverbs claims at points to be father-son (or occasionally mother-son) instruction (Prov 1:8). But although some proverbs originated at home, the book of Proverbs as it now stands attempts to instruct young men for jobs in the court of the king. The sages advise that these men control their tongues (10:31), avoid drunkenness (23:29–35), refrain from gossip about court politics (11:13), accept discipline (10:17), and attempt to match a deed to its proper time (26:4–5). This court-based system of ethics was not just "wise"; it also reflected the order of the cosmos. And if this code of conduct were violated, it would bring disorder upon court and world.

While the order discerned by observation tends to be stable, Israelite sages did not view it as inactive. The personification of wisdom/order,

## Wisdom as an International Phenomenon

Wisdom in the ancient Near East was international, with sages sharing common insights between nations with different kings and gods. The best example of such sharing in the Hebrew Bible are the parallels between Prov 22:17–24:32 and the Egyptian wisdom text *The Instruction of Amenemope* (ca. 1100 B.C.E.). Both claim thirty sections, while delivering similar advice, as this small sample indicates:

| Proverbs | The Instruction of Amenemope |
|---|---|
| Have I not written for you thirty sayings of admonition and knowledge, to show you what is right and true, so that you may give a true answer to those who sent you? (22:20–21) | Mark for yourself these thirty chapters: they please, they instruct, they are the foremost of all books. (27.7–9) |
| Make no friends with those given to anger, and do not associate with hotheads. (22:24) | Do not fraternize with the hot-tempered man, nor approach him to converse. (11.12–13) |
| Do not remove the ancient landmark that your ancestors set up. (22:28) | Do not displace the surveyor's marker on the boundaries of the arable land. (7.11) |
| Do not wear yourself out to get rich; be wise enough to desist. When your eyes light upon it, it is gone; for suddenly it takes wings to itself, flying like an eagle toward heaven. (23:4–5) | Do not exert yourself to seek out excess and your allotment will prosper for you; if riches come to you by thievery they will not spend the night with you; as soon as day breaks they will not be in your household; although their places can be seen, they are not there. (9.14–19) |

The number of these parallels indicates that the compilers of Proverbs probably borrowed material from *Amenemope.* Israelite sages apparently did not have a problem with using wisdom material from other cultures.

*The Instruction of Amenemope,* in *The Literature of Ancient Egypt,* ed. William Kelly Simpson, 3rd ed. (New Haven, CT: Yale University Press, 2003), 224–43.

## *Hokmah* and YHWH

*Hokmah* is not only wisdom personified, but she also enjoys a special relationship with YHWH: "The LORD created me [*Hokmah*] at the beginning of his work, the first of his acts of long ago" (Prov 8:22). The word translated "created" here could also be rendered as "acquired" or "conceived." So *Hokmah* may be YHWH's first creation, or something acquired or birthed by YHWH at the start of creation.

    *Hokmah*'s precise role with YHWH in creating the cosmos likewise features a difficult translation: "I [*Hokmah*] was beside him [YHWH], like a master worker; and I was daily his delight, rejoicing before him always, rejoicing in his inhabited world and delighting in the human race" (8:30–31). The term "master worker" could also be "little child." So *Hokmah* could have been a divine architect working alongside YHWH or a child applauding each created thing. In either case, the relationship is close.

    It is not easy to make sense of this seemingly divine female figure. She cannot be another god, given the development of monotheism, but she is clearly not a kind of angel. *Hokmah* is thus best understood as a hypostasis, a divine attribute personified. She is YHWH's own wisdom, shown in creation. The writers here develop this attribute as if it had independent existence in order to examine this particular feature of YHWH and help explain how YHWH relates to the created order.

*Hokmah* (Hebrew for "wisdom"), displays the active nature of the divine ordering of the world. *Hokmah*, though a female figure, behaves in ways unlike typical Israelite women. She publicly cries out, begging her (male) audience to abandon folly and <u>embrace understanding</u> (Prov 1:20–33; 8:1–36; 9:1–6). She also supports kings in their duties (8:15–16). A young man who ignores *Hokmah*, the ordering principle of the world, courts destruction (1:23–32). But one who aligns his life with *Hokmah* guarantees a blessed life (1:33).

In Proverbs, persons aligning themselves with God's order gain life, while those ignoring God's order die. Notice the similarity, on the surface, to the Sinai-Nation ideology: those who do right are blessed, and those who do wrong are cursed. But here no special relationship between a god and a people exists; an automatically functioning order in the universe blesses or curses. The sages hold that God's will appears not in a covenant with the people but in a universal order displayed in creation.

This universal order supported any number of other hierarchical arrangements. The young man reading Proverbs thus found himself inscribed into two unquestionable hierarchies: father-son and king-courtier. The text holds that this young man should be grateful for the beatings administered by his father; they saved his life from **Sheol** (Prov 23:13–14). And he should always strive to keep the king happy. An angry king means death could be close at hand (16:14–15). Accepting these arrangements, part of the "way things are," guarantees life. So the ideology of the sages at court is not politically neutral.

---

### <u>embrace understanding</u>

Male sages personified wisdom as female, giving erotic overtones to their embrace of knowledge (and *Hokmah*'s pursuit of them). A passage from a collection of psalms found at Qumran demonstrates the parallel between gaining knowledge and gaining sexual intimacy:

> I was a young man before I had erred, when I looked for her.
> She came to me in her beauty when finally I sought her out.
> Even (as) a blossom drops in the ripening of grapes, making glad the heart,
> (So) my foot trod in uprightness, for from my young manhood have I
>     known her.
> I inclined my ear but a little and great was the persuasion I found.
> And she became for me a nurse; to my teacher I give my ardor.
> I purposed to make sport; I was zealous for pleasure, without pause.
> I kindled my desire for her without distraction.
> I bestirred my desire for her, and on her heights I do not waver.
> I spread my hand(s) and perceive her unseen parts.

The allusions to sexual contact are magnified if one understands several words here as double entendres. The verb "know" can refer to a mental act or the act of sexual intercourse; the "hand" and "foot" can serve as euphemisms for the phallus.

James A. Sanders, ed., *The Dead Sea Psalms Scroll* (Ithaca, NY: Cornell University Press, 1967), 115.

It demands submission to God's order, manifested in kings, fathers, and other authority figures.

*Wisdom, Ideology, and the Empire: Qoheleth's Dissent*

The God of Proverbs is less involved in the world than the YHWH of Exodus. *Hokmah* helps to close this gap, displaying divine interest in human society, but she is still not nearly as "hands on" as YHWH at Sinai. This sense of distance from the regal king of the universe fits well with the period of imperial rule, in which Yehud found itself as a small province governed from far away. The author of the book of Ecclesiastes, Qoheleth, demonstrates the ways wisdom interacted with imperial authority.

Qoheleth agrees with the authors of Proverbs that observation of the world is essential to understanding. But while those sages looked at the world and saw clear evidence of an order blessing the good and punishing the bad, Qoheleth disagrees. Qoheleth looks around and sees a world of monotonous cycles (Eccl 1:3–9), a world of grotesque injustice (5:13–17), a world of random rewards and punishments (9:11–12), a world in which the overwhelming power of death negates all accomplishments (2:15–17).

At this point, one might see Qoheleth as something of a revolutionary, puncturing the hierarchy-loving sages of ancient Israel, demonstrating that their hierarchies do not bring their promised benefits. But Qoheleth does not joyfully reject all things ordered, making a meaningful life in a lawless universe. Rather, Qoheleth believes that there is an order, but that human observation can never comprehend that order well enough.

Qoheleth makes this claim in his famous meditation on "for everything there is a season" (3:1–8). This poem is a marvelous assurance that there is an order, a proper time for everything. But this order is arbitrary, and people "cannot find out what God has done from the beginning to the end" (3:11). Discerning the proper time to do a particular act proves impossible. One does not know whether one's actions support this arbitrary order or resist it. The proper response, then, to this unknowable order (and its partner, arbitrary imperial politics) is to enjoy life as much as possible, avoiding excess (8:15; cf. 7:16–18).

Qoheleth's picture of cosmic order strikingly resembles the kind of political order seen under imperial rule. Yehud during the time of the Persians and

---

### Qoheleth

The beginning of Ecclesiastes indicates that the author is "*qoheleth*, the son of David, king in Jerusalem" (Eccl 1:1). The image of the king vanishes after the middle of the second chapter. For this reason, as well as for linguistic ones, the author is almost certainly not Solomon. The Hebrew word *qoheleth* may be translated as "teacher," or even better, as "gatherer," since this sage collected both the wisdom of other sages as well as students to hear his teaching.

> ## Discerning the proper time
>
> The Byrds, a folk-rock group, sang an adaptation of Eccl 3:1–8 by Pete Seeger in their 1965 number one hit song, "Turn, Turn, Turn." Seeger and the Byrds put an ideological spin on the text that runs headlong into Qoheleth's own perspective. The song ends with "A time to love, a time to hate / A time for peace, I swear it's not too late." So the song suggests that Qoheleth's vision of a proper time for everything supports the claim that it is "not too late" to stop war, alluding to the Vietnam War. But Seeger and the Byrds failed to note that, for Qoheleth, it was utterly impossible to know whether a particular action was appropriate. No one knows when war is fitting or when peace is fitting. There are simply times when each is an appropriate part of the cosmic order. The song's ending line deftly takes the quietistic Qoheleth and makes him into an activist!

the Greeks rarely possessed a vibrant economy; severe taxation, drought, and famine were frequent. But Qoheleth does not suggest a revolution. Rather, even while Qoheleth protests against the arbitrary nature of life, against its routine injustices, he does not focus his anger on God, God's priests, the imperial governors, or the emperor. In fact, he does not seem to address any of these figures. He simply whispers his complaint in the ears of his students and moves on, with no suggestion that the complaint could be answered:

> Again I saw all the oppressions that are practiced under the sun. Look, the tears of the oppressed—with no one to comfort them! On the side of their oppressors there was power—with no one to comfort them. And I thought the dead, who have already died, more fortunate than the living, who are still alive; but better than both is the one who has not yet been, and has not seen the evil deeds that are done under the sun. (4:1–2)

Qoheleth knows of oppression, of abuse of power. But his ways of thinking do not support action against oppressors on behalf of the suffering. Rather, they allow him and his hearers to accept an arbitrary, inscrutable, oppressive order. In this, his advice is similar to the other sages: accept the status quo, for it represents the order intended by God.

## The Empire-Colony Complex

Qoheleth's thought provides a valuable introduction to the last set of ideologies, the Empire-Colony complex. Much of the Hebrew Bible came together during Persian and Greek rule. During this period, the elite of Yehud struggled to understand their place in the larger world of imperial politics. As a result, they developed diverse understandings of what empires meant and what their place was in the empire. And these understandings interacted with the larger ideological complexes we have discussed. The King-Zion complex, or at least its remnants, supported royal rule and the unquestioned importance of the Temple, though its emphasis on the Davidic dynasty could have

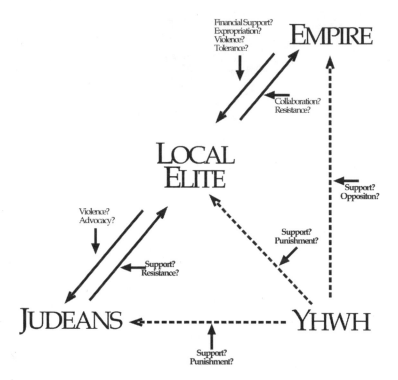

**Fig. 11.5: The Empire-Colony Complex**

opened the door to a local "nationalism" unwanted by foreign emperors. The Sinai-Nation complex, supportive of many models of human leadership, focused on Judean national identity as devotion to a god, not a dynasty. This way of thinking also tended to identify the people's suffering not with imperial policies but with divine displeasure. The Sage-Order complex fit well with the "global" politics of the empire and helped people understand God as the distant imperial ruler of a world order.

Two ideological approaches to imperial power in the Hebrew Bible serve as examples of the kind of discoveries that await the ideologically interested reader of the text. The Hebrew Bible texts from the period of imperial domination come from the elite in Jerusalem. These leaders, caught between the emperor, who supported their control over the Temple, and the rest of the Judeans, with whom they shared ethnic and cultural identity, faced a choice. Depending on the circumstances, this elite could attempt to resist imperial authority on behalf of Judeans or could impose imperial authority upon Judeans, with innumerable mediating positions between those two opposing strategies. They would bring YHWH in as a support for the chosen strategy. YHWH could support the emperor or seek to destroy the emperor. Thus, the diagram (see fig. 11.5) focuses on this elite, noting the variety of possible ideological solutions to the problems of living in the colony of a world empire.

*Esther: Playing with Power*

The book of Esther, a fictional account of the Persian court, says much about the way its authors imagined imperial power. At first glance, this text appears thoroughly to undermine any notion of imperial authority. The emperor, Ahasuerus, is a fool. In the very first chapter, his queen, Vashti, refuses to follow his orders, which he has given while under the influence of several days of drinking (Esth 1:10). So the king, in a fit of anger, issues a ridiculous (but immutable) order mandating that males rule their households (1:22). It is only to be expected that advisors would control this royal idiot, and, sure enough, he gives his power to them with little thought (3:10; 8:2).

Although pictured in an unflattering light, Ahasuerus possesses great authority. He can depose queens at will (1:19), information Esther surely keeps in mind. His word becomes immutable law, no matter if he proclaims it when inebriated (1:21). And he possesses unquestioned ability to visit violence on whomever he wishes. If he decrees that the Judeans are to be killed, so be it (3:12–15). If he decrees that the Judeans can defend themselves, so be it (8:8–14). And if it seems good to him to impale the dead bodies of Haman's sons in a grotesque public display, he orders it to be done (9:13–14). The book of Esther, while making the emperor into a buffoon, never questions or limits his ability to exercise power. Indeed, his very stupidity points to the arbitrary nature of imperial rule, but the book leaves it essentially unquestioned.

The book of Esther, then, using highly entertaining means, advises readers to accept imperial power while realizing its dangers. The best course of action is to be exceedingly careful in matters of state. Esther displays great courage, but it is courage thoroughly laced with caution. Imperial power may, if carefully approached, bring great benefits to the people. In its typically hyperbolic way, the book represents this by having Mordecai gain the second-ranking position in the empire and possess the emperor's signet ring, all to the acclaim of the crowds (8:15). The fantasy in Esther is not removing an idiot king, but using an idiot king to the community's own advantage.

*The End(s) of Power: Daniel and Apocalyptic Thought*

The book of Daniel includes a collection of stories (chapters 1–6) written and collected at various points during Persian and Greek rule of Yehud. Like Esther, they are fiction that imagines imperial power. The first section of the book of Daniel affirms imperial power in some ways, while tending to restrict its pretensions. The second half of Daniel (chapters 7–12) consists of a set of apocalyptic visions, most of which date from the depths of the crisis in Judean life in the Cisjordan under the Seleucid emperor Antiochus Epiphanes (167–164 B.C.E.). It models divine behavior on imperial authority, making the readers "subjects" of God's empire, while questioning (though not revolting against) imperial power.

## Introducing Apocalyptic

"Apocalyptic" is difficult to define, and so there are many competing definitions. Biblical scholar Greg Carey provides a helpful list of qualities that apocalyptic discourse tends to possess:

1. An interest in alternative worlds of space (e.g., heavenly realms) and time (e.g., the age to come)
2. Visions and/or auditions from God
3. Heavenly intermediaries who interpret visions and auditions
4. Intense symbolism, with images often from earlier cultural tradition
5. Pseudonymity (the works are written in the name of some ancient figure)
6. Cosmic catastrophe, which comes before deliverance
7. Dualism (either/or thinking—e.g., everyone is either righteous or wicked)
8. Determinism (God has determined the course of history)
9. Judgment and the afterlife
10. *Ex eventu* prophecy (prophecy after the fact; the author writes an accurate account of his past as if it were the future seen by the ancient visionary)
11. Cosmic speculation (interest both in astronomical phenomena and in heavenly beings such as angels)

Greg Carey, *Ultimate Things: An Introduction to Jewish and Christian Apocalyptic Literature* (St. Louis: Chalice Press, 2005), 6–10.

### Daniel 1–6

In these stories, Daniel and his friends operate at the upper levels of imperial administration. While there is little historical evidence that Judeans served in such roles, these texts imagine a world in which such service is possible. The stories thus represent an ideological "thought experiment," raising the question of the proper relations between Judeans and imperial power.

Nebuchadnezzar, the king of Babylon, is the imperial protagonist in the first four stories. The narrator insists that his power comes from God (Dan 1:1–2), and the stories give at least tacit approval to the extreme power of the imperial ruler. Indeed, Daniel himself considers Nebuchadnezzar to be an ideal monarch, due to his exercise of sometimes deadly power: "He killed those he wanted to kill, kept alive those he wanted to keep alive, honored those he wanted to honor, and degraded those he wanted to degrade" (5:19).

While these stories legitimate royal power, they also at least potentially subvert it. Daniel and his friends serve in the royal bureaucracy but on occasion contradict the empire's totalizing claims. Thus, Daniel's three friends submit to the royal power to kill, but deny its ability to force them to worship the king's statue: "If our God whom we serve is able to deliver us from the furnace of blazing fire and out of your hand, O king, let him deliver us. But if not, be it known to you, O king, that we will not serve your gods and we will not worship the golden statue that you have set up" (3:16–18).

Nebuchadnezzar himself later testifies that God took away his ability to rule after he bragged about his (not God's) power in building Babylon (4:30). When Nebuchadnezzar realizes that all power is derived from God, God restores his reason and his rule (4:36–37). The ideological perspective is clear: God grants power to empires, and thus they deserve respect. But imperial power becomes dangerous when it does not realize its origin in the will of the God of the Judeans.

These stories do not limit the exercise of imperial power or counsel revolt against it. Nebuchadnezzar learns the correct lesson about power: power comes from God. The stories in Daniel invite their readers to imagine themselves as servants of an imperial power whose existence represents the divine will. Yet when the imperial power contradicts the divine will, they counsel surrender to the empire's power to kill. Miraculous deliverance, from fiery furnace (Dan 3) or lions' den (Dan 6), will prove where power really lies.

### Daniel 7–12

In the "real" world, furnaces burn the faithful to death and lions eat whomever they please. A choice between faith and death appeared during the rule of Antiochus Epiphanes. The visions in Dan 7–12, written mostly in that period, attempted to sustain people during a crisis erupting from the exercise of imperial power. The visions reveal a god of extreme power, modeled on the emperor's power. But the visions also present imperial rule as utterly deficient, contrary to the divine will.

The vision in Dan 7 provides an excellent example of these themes. Daniel dreams of four beasts, amalgamations of features of various animals, arising from the sea. The sea, reprising its function in Gen 1 as chaos-needing-order, births these chaotic animals. They then exercise "dominion" (7:6). The vision presents God (here in the guise of the "Ancient One") asserting power as a rival emperor, using imagery drawn from the imperial court: thrones, throngs of attendants, books of records, and a death sentence.

The interpreting angel links these four beasts to particular empires, probably Babylon, Media, Persia, and Greece (7:17). The arrogant horn, identified as Antiochus Epiphanes, will use his power to attack God and God's "holy ones," the community around the author of the vision, for three and a half years ("a time, two times, and half a time," 7:25). God will then destroy Antiochus's empire, and the "holy ones" will rule an everlasting empire: "The kingship and dominion and the greatness of the kingdoms under the whole heaven shall be given to the people of the holy ones of the Most High; their kingdom shall be an everlasting kingdom, and all dominions shall serve and obey them" (7:27). The empire is a dangerous place for God's holy ones, until God establishes their own dominion.

YHWH's empire, not Antiochus's, is "the way things are." The visions in Daniel train their readers to be subjects of YHWH's empire. This empire calls into question the authority of human rule, especially that of Antiochus. But because of YHWH's extreme authority, the visions do not encourage readers to revolt. YHWH will, in YHWH's own time, defeat the enemy. YHWH is the sovereign emperor. YHWH is the only actor on the stage; all events are planned and directed by him. Thus, the visions counsel resistance only in the form of martyrdom.

This kind of resistance places all the initiative in the hands of the deity. God has determined when the story will end; human initiative that tries to change the timing is doomed to fail. The visions provide comfort: the reign of Antiochus will end soon. If one dies holding fast to traditional practice, there will be a reward of new life. If one leaves the tradition, joining the forces of the

---

### to revolt

Other literature from the period did encourage (or at least imagine) active resistance against imperial authorities. For example, the book of Judith (part of the Apocrypha) tells the story of the beheading of the Assyrian general Holofernes and the subsequent defeat of the Assyrian army through Judith's clever plotting. The literature from the latter part of the Second Temple period discloses a variety of possible stances for Judeans to take regarding their overlords, yet all these positions define the people in relation to imperial authority.

---

### Martyrdom and the Writers of Daniel 7–12

Current western discourse associates martyrdom with the September 11, 2001, attacks in the United States and with other forms of "suicide bombing." It has become commonplace to hear the claim that those who kill themselves do so because they will be guaranteed a certain number of virgins in heaven. It is more likely, however, that suicide bombers see this act of martyrdom as socially symbolic, as a way of resisting the western (and Israeli) occupation of Islamic areas as well as western cultural influences understood to be hostile to Islam. In other words, martyrdom in this instance is an act of political rhetoric; it is an argument for a particular political position.

In the visions of Daniel, there is the element of "eternal reward": "many" will rise to everlasting life (12:2). But to focus on that is to miss the rhetorical function of martyrdom. The authors of the visions characterize the would-be martyrs as the "wise" (Heb., *maskilim*). Indeed, the authors are probably part of this "wise" group. These *maskilim* are not military leaders, who provide little assistance (11:34), but leaders who have knowledge and understanding, which is "in reality" helpful (11:33). So the potential martyrdom of the *maskilim* argues for the validity of their knowledge. The interpreting angel explicitly links the purification of the martyrs with their understanding. If you do not accept that understanding, you are, by definition, wicked (12:10). So the visions in Daniel do not necessarily argue that all should be martyrs, but that the wise, many of whom are seemingly destined to be martyrs, deserve to lead the community.

### human initiative doomed to fail

"The apocalypse" as presented in popular culture typically clashes with the view presented here in Daniel. For example, the movie *Armageddon* (1998) concerns the imminent destruction of the earth by an asteroid. The title of the movie, drawn from the New Testament book of Revelation's account of the final battle between God and God's enemies, places the viewer in an apocalyptic context.

But the movie is no apocalypse, and its resolution is not like Armageddon at all. In the film, the human (Bruce Willis) is the hero; what he does will determine the survival of the world. In apocalypses like Daniel and Revelation there is no room for Bruce Willis. No human action can determine the outcome. People can only choose how to react to the events unfolding around them. For the book of Daniel, the correct human response is to wait for divine intervention and persevere in faith.

empire, a new life of contempt is in the offing (12:1–2). One's decision to hold fast to tradition and suffer will not speed the day of Antiochus's defeat but will instead show one's citizenship in the "real" empire, the empire of YHWH, destined to reveal its full power soon.

**Conclusion**

Israelite society was possible because the Israelites carried around in their heads a picture of that society and their particular place in it. These pictures varied over time and were not universally held; thus, there were ideological conflicts in Israelite society. The Hebrew Bible bears witness to those conflicts. But even with that diversity, the Israelites (even among the elite) did not spend time mulling over ideological assumptions. They simply accepted a picture of society and their place in it. They lived their lives while various forms of power played throughout society, forms made as natural as the winter rains, thanks to particular ideologies.

**Suggested Biblical Readings**

Genesis 1:1–2:4a
Exodus 19–24, 32–34
Deuteronomy 12; 16:1–17; 17:14–20; chapters 28, 30
2 Samuel 7
1 Kings 8:12–61
Esther
Psalms 2, 15, 24, 46, 48, 89
Proverbs 1, 8–9
Ecclesiastes 1–4
Isaiah 8:23–9:6; chapter 37; 45:1–8
Jeremiah 7, 26

Daniel 1–7, 12
Haggai
Zechariah 4; 6:9–15

---

**Discussion Questions**

1. Which of the ideological complexes do you think is least "reasonable"? Why?
2. How might your answer to question 1 be rooted in a contemporary ideological complex?
3. We have seen that the King-Zion complex was greatly altered by the events of 587/586 B.C.E. and following. Can you imagine other possible events that would force great alterations in the other complexes?

---

**Suggestions for Further Reading**

Berquist, Jon L. "The Dialectics of Colonial Society." In *Judaism in Persia's Shadow: A Social and Historical Approach*, 131–240. Minneapolis: Fortress Press, 1995.

Carey, Greg. *Ultimate Things: An Introduction to Jewish and Christian Apocalyptic Literature*. St. Louis: Chalice Press, 2005.

Crenshaw, James L. *Old Testament Wisdom: An Introduction*. 2nd ed. Louisville, KY: Westminster John Knox Press, 1998.

Grabbe, Lester. "The King" and "The Wise." In *Priests, Prophets, Diviners, Sages: A Socio-Historical Study of Religious Specialists in Ancient Israel*, 20–40, 152–80. Valley Forge, PA: Trinity Press International, 1995.

Kavanaugh, James H. "Ideology." In *Critical Terms for Literary Study*, edited by Frank Lentricchia and Thomas McLaughlin, 306–20. Chicago: University of Chicago Press, 1990.

Levenson, Jon D. *Sinai and Zion: An Entry into the Jewish Bible*. San Francisco: Harper & Row, 1985.

Whitelam, K. W. "Israelite Kingship: The Royal Ideology and Its Opponents." In *The World of Ancient Israel: Sociological, Anthropological, and Political Perspectives*, edited by R. E. Clements, 119–39. Cambridge: Cambridge University Press, 1989.

# 12. *Media*

| | |
|---|---|
| Arthur: | I am your king! |
| Woman: | Well, I didn't vote for you. |
| Arthur: | You don't vote for kings. |
| Woman: | Well, how did you become king, then? |
| Arthur: | The Lady of the Lake, her arm clad in the purest shimmering samite, held aloft Excalibur from the bosom of the water signifying by Divine Providence that I, Arthur, was to carry Excalibur. That is why I am your king! |
| Dennis: | Listen. Strange women lying in ponds distributing swords is no basis for a system of government. Supreme executive power derives from a mandate from the masses, not from some farcical aquatic ceremony. |

—*Monty Python and the Holy Grail*

"Ideology" refers to the idea of a society that people carry around in their heads. For instance, a certain set of ideas, "the King-Zion ideology," exercised a powerful control over how ancient Israelites viewed the world and themselves. But looking at ideas in and of themselves does not fully disclose the workings of ideology in a society. Ideologies also exist in a culture's practices, rituals, institutions, symbols, art, architecture, and images. "**Media**" designates these ways a society communicates and visualizes ideology. And while Dennis remains unconvinced, media are important. A "farcical aquatic ceremony" is a ritual that could, in the right set of circumstances, be a highly effective medium for expressing an ideological justification of "supreme executive power," at least as effective as the rituals of voting.

Previous chapters have already discussed media in some ways. For example, one could consider the ancient Israelite *bet av* as an institution (a medium) that transmitted certain ideological stances on gender and property. The very architecture of the *bet av* structured daily life in keeping with certain ideological assumptions concerning who was to perform what tasks. Family rituals surrounding marriage, such as the exchange of the bride price, also communicated these stances. Or one could view the monarchy as sponsoring a collection of media designed to justify its power: institutions (the bureaucracy), architecture (the palaces), rituals (coronations), and practices (record keeping). This chapter features two examples of media seen in the Hebrew Bible. First, it explores the **Temple** as an institution intimately related to the King-Zion ideology. Second, it looks at writing as a practice that both produced the Hebrew Bible and had definite social and ideological results.

## Zion and Temple

Chapter 11 demonstrated that Zion had an ideological function. Zion is a focal point, guaranteeing cosmic order. Texts from the Hebrew Bible describe it in mysterious and excessive ways: it is the cosmic mountain, it is a kind of paradise, it is the abode of the deity in the far north (Ps 48). Such a place seems unreal. Yet Zion was also an actual hill, with an actual temple built upon it. So while the King-Zion ideology made great claims for the imaginary significance of the place, the ancient Israelites had to do their imagining in the context of real buildings and practices. This section will describe the material existence of the Temple and its practices, with an eye to disclosing its ideological effects.

### A Tour of the Temple

What did visitors to Jerusalem during the monarchy see? Since there were few cities of any size in the region, the walls and gates that protected Jerusalem would have impressed them. But even more notable was the complex of buildings located at the city's highest point (see fig. 12.1). Among these buildings was the Temple of YHWH.

This Temple, along with the other buildings, sat on a hill with steep sides to the east, south, and west—a prominent and easily defended position. The Temple itself measured about 165 feet (50 meters) by 85 feet (26 meters), with the roof over its central section about 50 feet (15 meters) high. It faced east in a large courtyard; during the Second Temple period these courtyards were expanded and divided into various sections.

Those approaching the Temple first noticed in the courtyard on their right an immense bronze altar on which **sacrifices** were made. The altar was over 30 feet (9 meters) square and was tall enough (17 feet; 5 meters) to require a ramp for the priests to climb in order to put the sacrifices on top of the altar's fire. The massive altar itself displayed the power of the deity requiring the sacrifices, while the altar and the sacrifices also displayed the

---

### The Three Temples on Zion

The Temple in use during the monarchic period, often called Solomon's Temple or the First Temple, is the Temple whose dimensions are recorded in 1 Kings. These dimensions and other descriptions may come from late in the monarchy. And the Temple's precise appearance depended on a variety of factors: the security of the monarch, the vitality of the economy, and trends in architecture. The Babylonians destroyed this Temple in 587/586 B.C.E. The Second Temple, built with Persian imperial sponsorship in 520–515 B.C.E., had dimensions approximately the same as the First Temple. King Herod replaced this Temple in the last few decades B.C.E. with a building of the same dimensions but with much finer materials and with a vastly expanded courtyard. The Romans razed this Temple in 70 C.E. The First Temple serves as the example for the tour, although the Temple built by Herod was probably the most impressive of the three. All three would have had similar effects on the viewer.

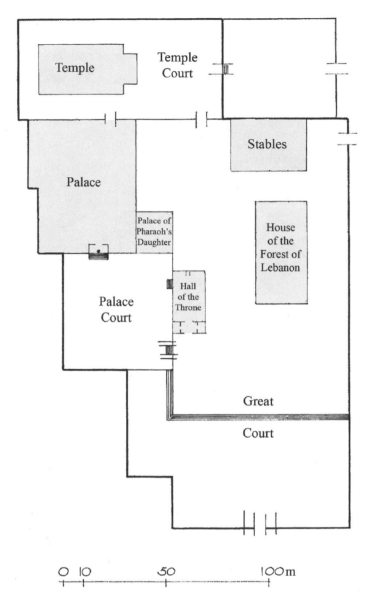

**Fig. 12.1: The Temple-Palace Complex**
*During the monarchy, the Temple shared space with a variety of buildings used by the king and his court. Some of these buildings were larger than the Temple, although the Temple was probably located at the top of the hill of Zion. The precise size and arrangement of the buildings eludes modern scholars. Notice that this map does not include the Hall of Justice and Hall of Pillars mentioned in 1 Kgs 7. The scholar who developed this map understood "hall of pillars" and "hall of justice" to describe the Hall of the Throne, not to represent separate buildings.*

power of the king and the court. The king provided many of the daily sacrifices and also financial support for the Temple (e.g., 1 Kgs 8:62–66).

On the left was an immense bronze basin (often called the "sea") about 8 feet (2.5 meters) tall and 18 feet (5.5 meters) across, sitting on top of statues of oxen facing north, south, east, and west (see fig. 12.3). This large "sea" echoed the subduing of water in creation (e.g., Ps 74:12–15), thus representing the cosmic order secured by the king and Zion. The frequent use of bull imagery picked up powerful elements of worship common to people in the

**Fig. 12.2: Artist's Representation of the First Temple**
*Here is a plausible view of the First Temple. This picture, rather like the Hebrew Bible, focuses on the Temple itself, ignoring the buildings and landscaping surrounding it.*

Cisjordan. The courtyard itself included other smaller basins on stands covered with designs featuring plants and animals. Groves of trees close at hand echoed these representations of plants, pointing to the fecundity guaranteed at this paradise, the cosmic mountain.

From the east front, one would enter a vestibule or forecourt area (Heb., *ulam*) through an entry marked by two freestanding 30-foot (9-meter) bronze pillars, which had elaborately decorated 9-foot (3-meter) tops. Two immense doors led to an interior room. Gold covered these doors, which featured carvings of various creatures, palm trees, and flowers (in later times, curtains, including one featuring the signs of the Zodiac, replaced the interior doors).

Behind these doors was the largest room of the temple (Heb., *hekal*), about 70 feet by 35 feet, with a 50-foot high roof. Light entered through windows high on the walls. Numerous candles added to the effect. Gold coated the wooden floor as well as the large doors, magnifying the light. The

### The Temple as Storage Place

From either the north or south sides of the Temple, visitors could see entrances to various storage chambers built into its sides. These chambers held more than supplies for worship. They would have contained at least part of the state treasury. And the priests would have stored any surplus from sacrifices there as well. So the Temple served as a kind of national bank, a place to hold a significant amount of resources, a place that concentrated capital. This economic function was likely a major reason the Persian Empire funded the reconstruction of the Temple: a concentration of capital made the empire's extraction of surplus via taxation that much easier.

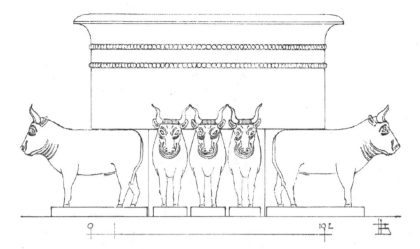

**Fig. 12.3: Artist's Representation of the Bronze Sea**
*The bronze sea provides an especially good example of the use of the bull motif in and around the Temple.*

candlesticks were also gold (the large seven-branched candelabrum, the menorah, was not original to Solomon's Temple but, once created, would have stood in this room). A small golden altar sat in this room, on which the priests burned incense. There was a golden table for the bread of presence, loaves of bread offered each week as an offering to YHWH.

Behind a set of doors like the ones between the vestibule and the main room lay the inner sanctum of the Temple (Heb., *debir*), the "Holy of Holies." This area was a 35-foot (10.5-meter) cube, featuring two immense golden cherubim that almost filled the space themselves (they each had an 18-foot [5.5-meter] wingspan). The cherubim guarded the ark, a box that

### The Temple and Gold

According to the books of 1 and 2 Kings, the golden fixtures of the Temple, as well as the gold stored in its chambers, attracted attention from foreign kings. The Temple was looted by the Pharaoh of Egypt (1 Kgs 14:16) and by Jehoash, the king of Israel (2 Kgs 14:14). They both took gold and other precious metals from the Temple treasury. Pharaoh took golden shields; Jehoash took golden vessels. The kings of Judah themselves used the gold and other material stored at the Temple to buy their way into alliances with foreign powers (1 Kgs 15:8; 2 Kgs 16:8) or buy their way out of attacks by foreign powers (2 Kgs 12:18). Hezekiah went so far as to remove the gold from the Temple's doors to pay off the king of Assyria (2 Kgs 18:16).

The books of Kings present the Temple as having a seemingly inexhaustible supply of gold and other treasures. While one king may lose the Temple's golden vessels, a later king can lose golden vessels again. This detail may represent an ideological commitment to the Temple's glory on the part of the writers, but it may also be based in historical reality: the king would have continually amassed as much precious metal as possible, storing it as decoration and vessels in the Temple.

**Fig. 12.4: Detail from the Sarcophagus of King Ahiram of Byblos (ca. 1250 B.C.E.)**

served as the footstool of YHWH, understood to be seated on the <u>cherubim</u>. As with the main room, gold coated the interior of this room.

Few Israelites would have seen all this; <u>only priests had access</u> to the interior of the Temple. But that does not diminish the ideological effect of seeing such a building, even from a distance. The Temple was, for its time and place, an amazing piece of architecture, a building that, by its very size and solidity, testified to the power of the Davidic dynasty and its patron deity, YHWH. As a visual medium, the Temple persuaded Israelites of the singularity of this place and of the utter stability of the power relationships suggested there.

The elite in ancient Israel certainly understood this effect. The immigrants leading the construction of the Second Temple, including the prophets Haggai and Zechariah, responded to claims that their new project

---

### <u>cherubim</u>

The cherubim were not cherubs, the round, infantlike creatures that appear on valentines and baby blankets. Rather, they were composite beasts, combining features of humans, eagles, lions, and bulls. They tended to have multiple faces and wings. YHWH rested on these creatures who, using their wings, could transport YHWH's presence (Ps 18:10; cf. Ezek 1). It is fitting, then, that they appear as part of YHWH's throne in the Temple. See fig. 12.4 for a parallel to YHWH's throne. Here the king, facing an offering table, is seated on a cherub throne while using a box as a footstool.

did not measure up to the great edifice Solomon had built. Some residents of Yehud derided the founding of the Second Temple as a "day of small things" (Zech 4:10). So Haggai issued a divine promise to those who may still have had visions of the First Temple dancing in their heads:

> I [YHWH] will shake all the nations, so that the treasure of all nations shall come, and I will fill this house [the Second Temple] with splendor, says the LORD of hosts. . . . The latter splendor of this house shall be greater than the former, says the LORD of hosts; and in this place I will give prosperity, says the LORD of hosts. (Hag 2:7, 9)

The writers of Haggai show sensitivity to the importance of appearances in both the execution and maintenance of such a large economic and ideological project as the Temple. This new Temple simply *had* to be visually imposing.

This concern for the visual may seem out of place in a discussion of ancient Israelites, who supposedly opposed visual representations of beings earthly and divine. The Sinai covenant strongly opposed the use of images (Exod 20:4–5; cf. Deut 5:8–9). But the King-Zion ideology reveled in the visual: opulent golden representations of trees, animals and flowers, bronze bulls, and the like. Not only did different ideologies exist in ancient Israel, but different material practices working in league with these ideologies existed as well.

These practices might seem to be in conflict. For example, Israelites accepted an image of a snake (Nehushtan) as part of the Temple cult, supported by a story about Moses using the object to cure snakebites (Num 21:8–9). Despite this story, later innovators under King Josiah (perhaps enforcing a stricter anti-image view) destroyed it (2 Kgs 18:4).

But the ark and the golden cherubim represent something of a compromise between the King-Zion ideology and the Sinai-Nation ideology. The ark and cherubim join two opposing functions: a visual representation of God's elaborate throne and a place for the deposit of the image-hating Sinai covenant (Deut 31:26). Proponents of the King-Zion ideology could point to the throne as evidence of perpetual divine favor secured through the Temple. Reformers such as the authors of Deuteronomy could point to the treaty deposited at the throne as limiting the Temple's ability to secure that

### only priests had access

The interior of the Temple was a medium that expressed (and undergirded) the priests' view of themselves. Working on a regular basis in gold-covered rooms in an impressive building while wearing special garments was bound to persuade the priests of their importance. It reminded them that their labor differed from that of the rest of the people. This identity maintenance was vital, given the difficult work done by **priests** (and by their assistants, the Levites): butchering animals, moving carcasses around, keeping drains clear for blood and water, and managing large crowds.

perpetual divine favor. One could "read" the meaning of the ark's presence in the center of the Temple in different ways, depending on one's ideological predilections.

*A View of the Temple in Action*

Typical Israelites saw the Temple in action only on **pilgrimages**, when they journeyed to Jerusalem for certain feasts. These feasts, Pesach (Passover), Shavuot (Weeks), and Sukkot (Booths), originated in family and clan celebrations of important moments in the agricultural year. Later, cults at local shrines, and then Jerusalem, took these feasts as their own.

Pilgrimage had definite economic benefits for Jerusalem, effects the elite there surely recognized. Large crowds spent large amounts of money for room and board. Deuteronomy, in fact, requires pilgrims to save a tenth of their produce in order to spend the proceeds in Jerusalem on "whatever you wish—oxen, sheep, wine, and strong drink, or whatever you desire" (Deut 14:26).

For the pilgrim, going to Jerusalem provided more than a chance to party or to support the local economy. The act of pilgrimage invited a <u>sense of dislocation</u>, a move away from the settled rhythms of agrarian life. This sense began with all the advanced planning needed for travel. The travel itself, usually undertaken by groups of pilgrims, would have featured discussing the coming events and singing various songs about Zion. By the time the pilgrims saw Jerusalem and its monumental architecture, they were ready for an experience of the "different," no matter how many times they had made pilgrimage.

Once the pilgrims reached Jerusalem they would, of course, experience many things not ordinarily encountered in rural Palestine; pilgrims "lived it up" at these feasts. They consumed wine and "strong drink" in larger quantities than normal (Deut 14:26; see also 1 Sam 1:14, in which Eli makes a quick assumption that Hannah was drunk while attending a pilgrimage feast). They also ate meat from quadrupeds (sheep or goats, usually), which

---

### sense of dislocation

In *The Sacred and the Profane* ([New York: Harper & Row, 1961], 68–113), Mircea Eliade explains this sense as the pilgrim's moving from mundane time to sacred time. The ancient religious festivals in some sense reenacted events from the time of origins, so participating in a festival meant being transported to that time, what Eliade calls *illud tempus*. Since *illud tempus* always recurs at the festivals, and the festivals occur on a regular basis, sacred time is circular. It is of a different quality than the mundane linear time typically experienced by ancients and always, for Eliade, experienced by modern people.

Eliade also treats the nature of sacred space (20–65). In Eliade's view, ancient people understood such places as the center of the universe, locations that secured the order of the world against chaos. The pilgrim, when present near this **axis mundi**, would experience a sense of dislocation more than that implied by simply relocating his or her body from the village to Jerusalem.

## Feasts in the Hebrew Bible

Here are the main feasts and other celebrations noted in the Hebrew Bible. This list represents feasts that Judeans would have celebrated in the mid–Second Temple period (ca. 250 B.C.E.), by which time the Hebrew Bible was largely complete.

| Feast (Hebrew) | Feast (English) | Occurrence | Pilgrimage? | Original Function | Eventual Function |
|---|---|---|---|---|---|
| Shabbat | Sabbath | Every seventh day | No | Mark moon phases? | Linked to creation, linked to slavery in Egypt |
| Chodesh | New Moon | Monthly | No, perhaps local shrines | Mark new lunar cycle | |
| Pesach | Passover | 14 Nisan (March/April) | Yes | Mark move to summer pastures? Celebrate lambing? | Combined together; as one feast they celebrate the exodus from Egypt |
| Massot | Unleavened Bread | 15–21 Nisan (March/April) | Yes | Mark the barley harvest | |
| Pesach Sheni (term not used in the Hebrew Bible) | Second Passover | 14 Iyyar (April/May) | Yes | Allow those unclean or away during Pesach to celebrate it | |
| Shavuot | Weeks/ Pentecost | A day in Sivan, fifty days after the sheaf of the elevation offering is presented (May/June) | Yes | Mark the wheat harvest, firstfruits of other crops | Associated with the giving of the Torah |
| Rosh Hashanah (term not used in the Hebrew Bible) | New Year | 1 Tishri (September/ October) | No | Unclear; involved enforced rest and trumpet blasts | Celebrate beginning of New Year |
| Yom Kippur | Day of Atonement | 10 Tishri (September/ October) | No | Purge sanctuary and people | |
| Sukkot | Booths/ Tabernacles | 15–21 Tishri (September/ October) | Yes | Mark the fall harvest | Recall wilderness wanderings, renew covenant |
| Purim | Purim | 12–13 Adar (February/ March) | No | Unclear | Celebrate defeat of enemies |

## How Many People Made Pilgrimage?

Estimating the size of crowds, even today, is far from an exact science. So data from the ancient world is difficult to use with certainty. Little information is available on the numbers attending feasts at the Temple in the Second Temple period. The most concrete numbers come from Josephus, who claims that three million pilgrims came to Jerusalem in 65 C.E. (*War* 2.280). This number is surely an exaggeration. Scholar E. P. Sanders (*Judaism: Practice and Belief, 63 B.C.E.–66 C.E.* [Philadelphia: Trinity Press International, 1992], 125–28) has evaluated Josephus and other pieces of ancient (and modern) evidence on pilgrimage and suggests that between 300,000 and 500,000 pilgrims would have attended Pesach (the most popular festival) in the latter part of the Second Temple period. In the time described in the Hebrew Bible, the numbers would have been smaller, but by what degree is not clear. But whether hundreds of thousands or "merely" tens of thousands attended festivals, managing such crowds would have been a logistical nightmare. Even so, these throngs of people also provided a huge, consistent economic boost to the region.

did not typically appear on the rural menu, since these animals were much too valuable for their milk and hair.

Animal sacrifice, a key part of the pilgrims' worship at the Temple, provided the meat for the feast. The Temple was a very efficient slaughterhouse, especially at festival times. Organized chaos ruled the day. A visitor would see bowls of blood thrown on the altar, priests rushing carcasses to butchering areas, pieces of fresh meat distributed to the offerer and <u>to the priests</u>, and would hear doomed sheep and goats bleating. The sight (and smell) would have been amazing. Pilgrims experienced the slaughter of an animal as numinous, not disgusting as modern western people might.

The Temple stayed open for business on days other than festivals. Times of national crisis demanded certain forms of worship (e.g., Joel 1–2). And "routine" daily sacrifice and worship, while not as well attended

## <u>to the priests</u>

Priests in ancient Israel could own land (1 Kgs 2:26; Amos 7:17) and by the Second Temple period (if not earlier) did not have to live in Jerusalem year round. Nevertheless, it seems that they relied heavily on sacrifices and offerings for their livelihood. The priests collected firstfruits and the firstborn of animals, claimed almost all of the grain products offered as sacrifices, and ate sizable portions of some offerings. The Temple also received monetary gifts, sometimes in lieu of actual produce or animals. Levites, the lower-level Temple personnel, were entitled to a tenth (the tithe) of all produce, though they had to pass along a tenth of that amount to the priests.

## Sacrifices in the Hebrew Bible

Worshipers at the Temple offered a variety of sacrifices for many reasons. These sacrifices differed as to the fate of the offering. This is a simplified chart based on sections of Leviticus and Numbers that explain the system, which, it should be noted, is not perfectly clear or consistent. In addition, actual practice in the Temple probably changed over time. Thus, there is more (and differing) information on the sacrifices provided in other sources, such as the works of the Jewish historian Josephus, the Mishnah, and the Talmuds.

| Sacrifice | Object | Result | Purpose | Biblical Texts |
|---|---|---|---|---|
| olah ("whole burnt"; "holocaust") | Quadruped, with grain and wine | Totally consumed on the altar | Thanksgiving; invocation of presence of deity | Lev 1; 6:8–13 |
| zebakh sh<sup>e</sup>lamim ("well-being"; "peace"; "shared sacrifice") | Quadruped, cakes, wafers | Altar: blood and fat Priests: a portion to take home and eat with family Offerer: a portion to take home and eat with family | Thanksgiving; joyous celebration at festival | Lev 3:1–17; 7:11–38 |
| asham ("guilt"; "reparation") | Quadruped (ram) | Altar: blood and fat Priests: the rest to eat that day at the temple | Making reparation for offenses against holy things | Lev 5:14–6:7; 7:1–10 |
| khatat ("sin"; "purification"; "purgation") | Quadruped, but often two doves; sometimes flour | Altar: blood and fat if quadruped Priests: in some cases, boil and eat in temple that day | Purification from "sin" (uncleanness or moral fault) | Lev 4:1–5:13; 6:24–30 |

## What Did Sacrifice Mean?

No one knows for certain what the average Israelite thought his or her sacrifice accomplished. There are a number of possibilities, and an Israelite may have thought several of these at the same time. Here are some options suggested by scholars:

1. Encouraging the deity to respond to the offerer with some kind of blessing. Scholars often call this understanding *Do ut des*, "I give so you may give."
2. Supplying the deity with sustenance, blood and fat being particularly sustaining of life in ancient Near Eastern thinking.
3. Providing a means by which to commune with the deity, with the sacrificial victim as the "bridge" between the spiritual and the mundane.
4. Purging sins and/or uncleanness from a deity's shrine or from a person, which allows the deity to continue to be present in the shrine or the person to be in the deity's presence.

(and featuring a much smaller number of sacrifices) was necessary. Any interruption of the *tamid*, the whole burnt offering offered at dawn and dusk (Num 28:1–8), would sever the linkage between YHWH and the people and threaten to destabilize the cosmic order (Dan 8:11–14).

The pilgrims could not help but notice the essential role of the priests and Levites in supervising and conducting the various rituals. The book of Leviticus indicates how complex the practice of sacrifice could be. Getting matters right (and it was essential to get matters right when in the presence of the deity) required extensive education in priestly traditions (e.g., Samuel's apprenticeship with Eli in 1 Sam 2). Only the priests could do certain things, only the priests knew how to do certain things properly, only the priests could wear certain <u>special vestments</u>. Watching sacrifices reinforced the notion that the priests were "special" and filled an essential social role.

This ideological affirmation of the priestly role could be expressed in an aesthetic understanding of their actions. The few eyewitness accounts of the rituals do not focus explicitly on priestly power but on the overwhelming beauty of the action. An observer in the second century B.C.E. described the high priest Simon ben Onias (ca. 200 B.C.E.) as follows:

> How glorious he was, surrounded by the people,
> as he came out of the house of the curtain [the Temple, now with
> a curtain at its entrance].

## Sacrifice: The Process

The offerer was responsible for getting the animal to the sanctuary and claiming the animal by laying hands on it. The offerer was also probably the one who dispatched the animal by slitting its throat. The Temple personnel, priests or Levites, collected the animal's blood, likely by holding a vessel under the wound, and threw it against the altar. They also butchered the carcass, placed the proper portions on the altar, made correct distribution of the other pieces, and disposed of any other remains.

## special vestments

Exodus 28 provides more information on the priests' clothing, especially that of the high priest. It emphasizes fine materials and careful workmanship, with the resulting "glorious adornment" (Exod 28:2, 40). By contrast, the typical Israelite did not possess many clothes, and these were basic. So the outfit worn by the priests, featuring linen underwear, a tunic, a sash, and a turban (Exod 28:40–43), would have been a much finer wardrobe than pilgrims would ever have expected to wear. By wearing the clothes, the priests would remind themselves of their status. They (and probably no one else) wore underwear, since they had to avoid exposure before YHWH. And they were privileged to see the high priest's costume up close, helping them remember that, while priests, they were in a definite hierarchy.

> Like the morning star among the clouds,
>   like the full moon at the festal season
> . . . . . . . . . . . . . . . . . . . . . . . . . . . . . . . .
> When he put on his glorious robe
>   and clothed himself in perfect splendor,
> when he went up to the holy altar,
>   he made the court of the sanctuary glorious.
> When he received the portions from the hands of the priests,
>   as he stood by the hearth of the altar
> with a garland of brothers around him,
>   he was like a young cedar on Lebanon
>   surrounded by the trunks of palm trees.
> All the sons of Aaron in their splendor
>   held the Lord's offering in their hands
>   before the whole congregation of Israel.     (Sirach 50:5–6, 11–13)

Another account from the late Second Temple period provides an apt summary of the dazzling effects:

> The total effect of the whole arouses awe and emotional excitement, so that one would think he had passed to some other sphere outside the world. I venture to affirm positively that any man who witnesses the spectacle I have recounted will experience amazement and astonishment indescribable, and his mind will be deeply moved at the sanctity attaching to every detail. (*Letter of Aristeas* 99)

Something utterly "out of this world" occurred in the Temple. Indeed, one could not speak of it without using highly poetic language.

---

### Priests, Levites, and Genealogy

Service as a priest in ancient Israel (or a Levite, a lower-level servant in the Temple) was not a possibility for most Israelites. One had to be a male from the right set of families. Thus, the priests were concerned about genealogy, and pieces of this genealogical material appear in the Hebrew Bible (e.g., Ezra 2:36–63; 1 Chr 6:1–81). Making all this varied and contradictory information fit together, and agree with various stories about the origins of priestly families (e.g., Num 16), is difficult. The following can be said with reasonable confidence: First, there is evidence in the Hebrew Bible for a variety of priestly families at a variety of shrines tracing their origins to particular founding figures (Levi, Aaron, Moses, Eli, Zadok). Second, competition among these priesthoods produced a number of varying and not always clear genealogical and historical claims. Third, by the Second Temple period, a consensus had emerged, reflected in large part in the Torah, that (1) all Temple personnel (priests and Levites) trace their ancestry to Levi; (2) those functionaries serving as priests trace their ancestry to Aaron, a descendant of Levi; and (3) those priests serving as high priests trace their ancestry to Zadok, a descendant of Aaron. Basically, the various competing priestly groups were forced together into one giant family tree.

> ## A Downside to Priestly Service
>
> To speak of the services at the Temple as having a kind of entertainment value may seem a sacrilege, but one of the effects of the service was to impress and transfix the viewer. It is also apparent that this mandatory public appearance by high-ranking officials could lead to problems. The Jewish historian Josephus reports that Alexander Janneus, high priest from 103 to 76 B.C.E., ran into difficulties:
>
>> As for Alexander, his own people revolted against him—for the nation was aroused against him—at the celebration of the festival [of Booths], and as he stood beside the altar and was about to sacrifice, they pelted him with citrons, it being a custom among the Jews that at the festival . . . everyone holds wands made of palm branches and citrons. . . . And they added insult to injury by saying he was descended from captives and was unfit to hold office and to sacrifice; and being enraged at this, he killed some six thousand of them. (*Antiquities* 13.372–73)

*Holiness: The Temple's Way of Working*

The Temple, through its monumental architecture and solemn sacrifices, educated the average Israelite on the power of YHWH and YHWH's priests and kings. But the Temple had more lessons to teach both priests and people, lessons that also pointed to the Temple as a "different" or special space. "**Holiness**" often expresses the Temple's unique status. The Temple is holy, just as YHWH is holy. Holiness here refers to separation: YHWH's holiness means that YHWH is separated from the mundane world in which mortals move. The Temple, while obviously a mundane institution, possesses a holy existence beyond the mundane. Humans in its vicinity are in close proximity to the "otherness" of YHWH and should understand themselves in the light of the divine presence.

Holiness is not just an idea about the Temple but is also expressed both in the mandating and banning of certain practices. The case of the man with an emission (Heb., *zav*) found in Lev 15 provides an example. In the thinking of the ancient Israelite priests, YHWH was highly interested in whether a man's penis was functioning appropriately. If not, the man was unclean, unfit to be in YHWH's presence (Lev 15:1–3). And not only that: the *zav*'s "**uncleanness**" spread by contact, like a contagion. So any chair the *zav* sat on or any bed he lay on was unclean, and if anyone touched those pieces of furniture, he or she would be unclean (vv. 5–6). Uncleanness also spread through fluids. If the *zav* spat on a person, that person was unclean (v. 8). And if the *zav* touched a pitcher, it would spread uncleanness, so it had to be broken (v. 12).

Emissions were just one thing that caused uncleanness. Of the causes of uncleanness, most are perfectly natural and should even be encouraged. After all, the future of the people depended on menstruation, emissions of semen, and childbirth.

So the priests do not wish the people to avoid such things completely. What the priests wish to avoid is the traces of these acts coming into con-

## Causes of Uncleanness

These causes of uncleanness are drawn from Leviticus and Numbers. The list is not exhaustive; Jewish tradition continues to develop understandings of these texts.

contact with a human carcass (Num 19:11, 16)
contact with a grave (Num 19:16)
entering a tent in which someone has died in the previous week (Num 19:14)
contact with a kosher animal's carcass, if the animal dies of itself (Lev 11:39)
eating the meat of a kosher animal, if the animal dies of itself (Lev 11:40)
contact with a nonkosher animal's carcass (Lev 11:24–28)
eating what dies of itself or is killed by wild animals (Lev 17:15)
contact with the scapegoat or sacrificed animals on Yom Kippur (Lev 16:26, 28)
conducting the ritual of the red heifer (Num 19:7, 21)
burning and collecting the ashes of the red heifer (Num 19:8, 10)
sexual intercourse (Lev 15:18)
menstruation (Lev 15:19–24)
hypermenorrhea (Lev 15:25–30)
childbirth (with a longer time of purification if a girl is born) (Lev 12:2–8)
ejaculation (Lev 15:16–17)
atypical discharge from the penis (Lev 15:2–15)
inability to discharge from the penis (Lev 15:3)
various skin diseases (Lev 13:2–46)
mold (on cloth or on a house) (Lev 13:47–59)

tact with the deity. Being a *zav* is not bad, but being a *zav* is "disorderly." The acts that cause uncleanness, while natural, in some way display either human changeability (dead bodies) or human bodies' lack of stable boundaries (menstruation, ejaculation, skin diseases). Even certain animals (nonkosher) violate the priests' notions of order: all quadrupeds simply *ought* to chew their cud, so pigs are "disordered." To be fit to be close to the divine presence, all traces of such disorder must be erased. Bringing disorder into the highly ordered space of the highly ordered deity courts disaster.

At first glance, the holiness regulations appear draconian; they demand close self-inspection and cast aspersions on typical human activities. But the priests were concerned only about the effects of such actions when in the presence of the deity. Imagine an average resident of Yehud. Since his last trip to the Temple, he has touched a weasel carcass, has had occasional sexual intercourse, and has helped prepare his cousin's body for burial. He must resolve this buildup of uncleanness before his next trip, usually through the passage of time (Lev 12:4–5; 15:13), immersion in water (15:13), and/or providing certain sacrifices (12:6–8; 15:14). But he does not obsess over his state of uncleanness. After a certain amount of time,

## Yom Kippur as "Disorder Management"

The rituals associated with Yom Kippur in Lev 16 present an annual erasure of the traces of disorder. The high priest first "makes atonement" for himself and his family (vv. 6–7) through sacrifice; in other words, he removes all traces of instability in order to survive being close to YHWH. Then he "makes atonement" for the sanctuary and the altar (vv. 15–19). The uncleanness of the people from the previous year, in addition to both their inadvertent and intentional violations of the requirements of the covenant, will build up on the sanctuary and altar if left untreated. The high priest ensures the stability of the sanctuary in two ways. First, he uses the sacrificial blood of a bull and a goat, sprinkling it on YHWH's throne in the Holy of Holies and on the horns of the altar. Second, he transfers the instability onto a goat, the "scapegoat," which is set free in the wilderness. In this way, the high priest ensures the continued efficacy of the priesthood and the sanctuary, as well as the ongoing relationship of the people and YHWH.

## Holiness in Architecture

In the course of its lifetime, the Second Temple included numerous courts and courtyards. These courtyards represented in architecture an ideological hierarchy of holiness, from the high priest (who could enter even the Holy of Holies) all the way down to non-Judeans (who were supposed to stay in the court of the Gentiles). The diagram of Herod's Temple in figure 12.5 shows these various courtyards, together with who was allowed where.

everyone in the village is unclean in some way, and life goes on well until the next pilgrimage.

The priests, who were regularly called to serve in the Temple, had to be more careful. Most priests were not in the Temple constantly but served in "shifts" for part of the year (working overtime at pilgrimage feasts). They still needed, however, to be keenly aware of the various causes of uncleanness and their "cure." The priests who penned Leviticus attempted to inculcate in their audience (probably fellow priests) the absolute importance of holiness. They even broke out of their typical listing of rules to tell the cautionary tale of Aaron's sons, Nadab and Abihu. When they offered unholy fire before YHWH, fire burst forth from YHWH's presence and burned them to cinders (Lev 10:1–2).

One place, the Temple, demanded certain controls on human bodies and behavior. At the Temple, Israelites could not allow their bodies to do the things they would do at home. Their bodies "meant" something different the closer they got to Zion. Zion was a place where life was construed differently, where normal blessings became extraordinary dangers, a place where for a brief time, people lived in a strikingly altered way. Visiting the Temple meant subjecting oneself to the power of God and priest.

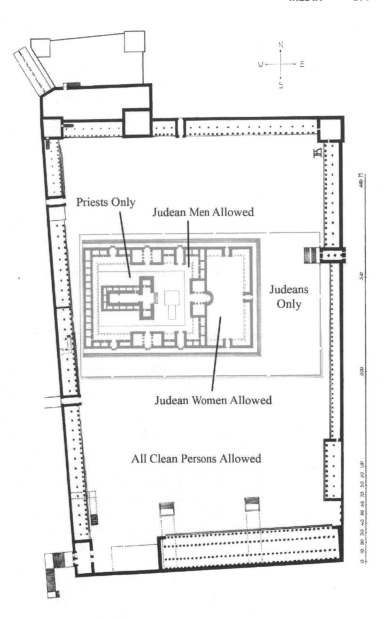

N
W ← → E
S

Priests Only

Judean Men Allowed

Judeans
Only

Judean Women Allowed

All Clean Persons Allowed

**Fig. 12.5: Plan of the Courtyards of Herod's Temple**
*The mapping of ideology onto the Temple's architecture had its limits. The hill on which the Temple sat would not allow a perfect square set of courts that would represent an even "flow" of holiness in all directions. The prophet Ezekiel, not hampered by the concerns of engineering, imagined just such an impossible building in his plans for a rebuilt sanctuary (Ezek 40–43). In fact, Ezekiel imagined that the whole city of Jerusalem, as a holy place, would also be a perfect square (48:30–35).*

*Conclusion*

So the Temple functioned as a medium for the King-Zion ideology. It was an institution that, by its architecture, economic centrality, personnel, and rituals, underlined its own centrality to the continued existence of the people. It taught Israelites to respect the priesthood, to honor the king whose largesse supported the Temple's operation, and to link their own experiences of joy and well-being with Zion's special status.

## Writing as a Material Practice

The Temple was, in many ways, an ideal example of the way institutions present ideology. Our other example, writing, is in some ways less obvious. First, writing in ancient Israel did not necessarily represent one ideological perspective. While the Temple served largely to communicate the King-Zion ideology, writing served as a medium for all of the ideological complexes discussed in chapter 11. The written psalms express the King-Zion ideology; the written stories of the exodus undergird the Sinai-Nation complex. So with writing there will not be the clear relationship of ideology to medium as there was with the Temple.

Second, modern people may be tempted to feel that the act of writing meant the same things for ancient Israel as it does in modern western cultures. But the way <u>writing functions</u> in a society varies greatly. How writing functioned in ancient Israelite society thus demands close attention. The "power questions" even intensify, since (by the end of the Second Temple period), a particular set of written materials (i.e., the Hebrew Bible) held a kind of authority for Jews.

### Writing in the Ancient Near East and Israel

Writing began around 4000 B.C.E. in Mesopotamia, chiefly to keep track of agricultural products and other goods. Writing developed in multiple ways. Egyptians relied upon hieroglyphics, which represent objects and ideas pictographically. Mesopotamians used wedge-shaped marks representing syllables (cuneiform). And residents of the areas along the eastern coast of the Mediterranean created sets of characters that came to represent the phonetic qualities of the spoken language: alphabets.

The alphabet removed the need to memorize a large number of pictograms. But despite this newfound simplicity, literacy did not become common. There were, undoubtedly, many different levels of literacy in the ancient world. Some people could recognize the stamp on a container (see fig. 12.9) well enough to tell its contents or its owner. Others may also have been able to write their name. But very few people could draw up a sales contract or record tax receipts; these duties were not widespread enough for

---

### writing functions

Writing has certain ideological functions in modern western culture, a fact not lost on a clever spider:

> "But Charlotte," said Wilbur, "I'm *not* terrific."
> "That doesn't make a particle of difference," replied Charlotte. "Not a particle. People believe almost anything they see in print. Does anybody here know how to spell 'terrific'?"

E. B. White, *Charlotte's Web* (New York: Harper & Brothers, 1952), 89.

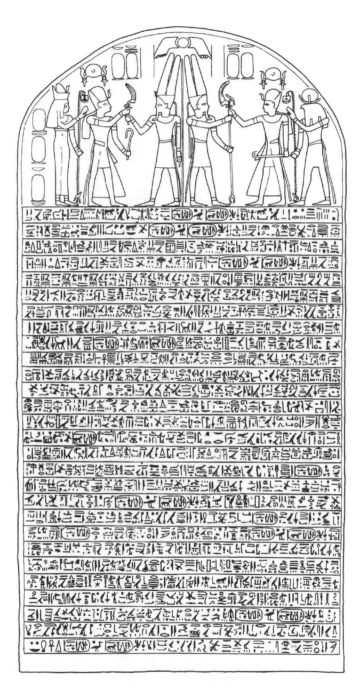

**Fig. 12.6: Line Drawing of the Merneptah Stele and "Israel"**
*Hieroglyphics from the Merneptah Stele, written in Egypt around 1208 B.C.E. The word set apart is "Israel." The stele contains the earliest mention of the people of Israel.*

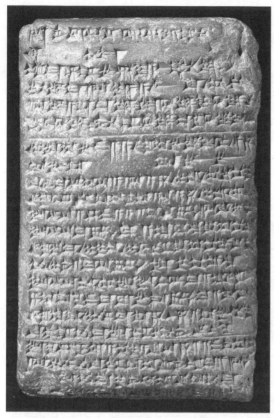

**Fig. 12.7: Amarna Letter 68**
*Letter from Burnaburiash of the Kassite Dynasty in Mesopotamia to Pharaoh Amenhotep IV (Akhenaten) of Egypt, ca. 1340 B.C.E. This tablet is part of the diplomatic archive found at Tell el-Amarna in Egypt. These Amarna tablets represent some of the most important sources on the history of the ancient Near East; many originated from the Cisjordan.*

**Fig. 12.8: The Gezer Calendar**
*Early Hebrew alphabetic script from the Gezer calendar, from the city of Gezer in the Judean highlands, ca. 925 B.C.E.*
*(http://www.holylandphotos.org; reproduced by permission.)*

## Early Ways of Writing

Writing could be done on stone with a chisel, on wet clay with a stylus or a stamp, on metal with an engraving tool, or on sheets of papyrus or pottery fragments (ostraca) in ink with a reed brush or pen. Occasionally, writing was done on a previously used (and incompletely erased) surface, producing what is called a palimpsest. In short, writing was part of any number of technological processes, and the use of a particular writing surface was in many ways an economic decision. The written works that became the Hebrew Bible eventually were written on scrolls of animal skin (vellum or parchment)—a significant economic investment. In addition, a scroll of animal skin would, in the climate of the central highlands, eventually rot. So to preserve scrolls of the Hebrew Bible texts, scribes had to copy them over on a continuing basis—also quite an economic investment.

most people to justify learning to read and write. These jobs fell to formally trained **scribes**.

A major purpose of writing in modern western culture—communication of content to a mass audience—was much less prominent in ancient Israel. For a text to communicate to most people, a literate person would need to read it aloud. But though not many people were literate, writing still could communicate a message. For example, rulers in the ancient Near East placed inscriptions in prominent locations. These inscriptions, often on pillars called stelae, frequently celebrated a king's victory or solemnized an agreement between two governments. Most people passing these monuments would have been oblivious to the precise content but probably would have associated the inscription with the authority of those who erected the pillar. Or perhaps oral traditions existed that explained the meaning of the writing. In either case, writing held a <u>mysterious power</u> that supported the power of the ruler who directed the inscription.

Writing greatly aided the maintenance of political authority in other ways. Letters could easily be sent throughout a realm, promoting a higher degree of central control. Local and national archives catalogued official statements and policies and could be consulted to determine the will of the government. Temples, as repositories of goods and treasure, were centers

## Becoming a Scribe

Scribes functioned in government settings as record keepers and administrators; the Israelite and Judean monarchies, as well as the later imperial governments, all employed scribes. Scribes could also be found in towns or villages, preparing wills and contracts. Perhaps Israel had scribal schools like those in Egypt and Mesopotamia, which used curricula focused on copying and reciting various texts and exercises. The Gezer calendar (see fig. 12.8), incised on a small limestone tablet, could easily be an Israelite example of such an exercise. And the book of Proverbs may have been collected not only for its messages to the reader but as a text on which a would-be scribe would practice. But little evidence exists for how Israelite scribes received training. It is ironic that the Hebrew Bible, a text that would not exist without the work of the scribes and often reflects their interests, is silent on such a basic point.

## mysterious power

Notice in figure 12.10 how difficult it is to make out even that there is an inscription, much less what that inscription says. Perhaps Darius I was not concerned with having the material read as much as with the impression merely seeing such an exercise would leave on the viewer. Writing was visible, which showed its importance to the empire, yet not legible, since the "meaning" of the entire display did not strictly depend on the inscription's content. Classicist Rosalind Thomas notes a parallel to this in ancient Greece: Ancient Greek inscriptions did not always attempt to transmit a certain piece of text to a reader. Many inscriptions were laid out with the letters in a grid, forcing odd divisions within words, creating an inscription that made little sense. The act of writing itself was the important matter. In short, these instances of writing magically displayed a power beyond what their contents would disclose (Rosalind Thomas, *Literacy and Orality in Ancient Greece* [Cambridge: Cambridge University Press, 1992], 74–88).

**Fig. 12.9:** *Lmlk* **Seal Impression**
*Many of the examples we have of writing in ancient Israel are stamps on clay jar handles. This stamp, from a jar dating to the time of Hezekiah (ca. 710 B.C.E.) contains only two words: lmlk (belonging to the king) above the representation of wings and a place name (Hebron) beneath them.*

of writing. The writings collected, if not commissioned, by these temples included local religious traditions held to be authoritative. By the time of the Persian Empire (if not earlier), it would be hard to imagine effective political power without scribes.

Writing as a practice in Israel and Judah was therefore closely allied with royal power and its ideological pretensions. More particularly, writing had a definite social location: the scribal bureaucracy around the king and, later, imperial representatives. Writing served as a medium for the ideological positions of this bureaucracy. But what were these ideological positions? First and foremost, scribes held an ideological commitment to the power and efficacy of writing. Their picture of society featured their own skill, their own technology, <u>at its very center</u>. The texts they wrote, both official records for the king and unofficial poems and stories, expressed their writing-centered view of the world.

---

### at its very center

Egyptian scribes expressed this writing-centered view in a memorable way in *The Satire on the Trades: The Instruction of Dua-Khety*, written in the early second millennium B.C.E. In this work a father tells his son how much better off he is by becoming a scribe:

> I do not see a stoneworker on an (important) errand or a goldsmith in a place to which he has been sent, but I have seen a coppersmith at his work at the mouth of his furnace. His fingers were like the claws of the crocodile, and he stank more than fish eggs. . . . The weaver inside the weaving house is more wretched than a woman. His knees are drawn up against his belly. He cannot breathe the air. If he wastes a (single) day without weaving, he is beaten with fifty whip lashes. He has to give food to the doorkeeper to allow him to come out to the daylight. . . . I mention to you also the fisherman. He is more miserable than (one of) any (other) profession, one who is at his work in a river infested with crocodiles. When the totaling of his account is subtracted for him, then he will lament. One did not tell him that a crocodile was standing there, and fear has (now) blinded him. When he comes to the flowing water, so he falls (as) through the might of God. See, there is no office free of supervisors, except the scribe's. He is the supervisor!

A Judean version of these sentiments may be found in Sirach 38:24–34.

William Kelly Simpson, ed., *The Literature of Ancient Egypt*, 3rd ed. (New Haven, CT: Yale University Press, 2003), 433–35.

**Fig. 12.10: The Behistun Inscription**
*Found in what is now western Iran, the Behistun Inscription provides a fine example of a monumental inscription. Around 520 B.C.E., Darius I of the Persian Empire directed the construction of this inscription and its accompanying pictoral representation on a mountain overlooking a major trade route. The inscription narrates Darius's rise to power (in three languages), while the pictures show him crushing a pretender to the throne and accepting tribute from subject peoples.*

The actual politics of this assumption of the vitality of writing could vary. Scribes generally supported the kings of Israel and Judah. At least scribes functioned in the court apparatus (e.g., 2 Sam 8:17; 20:25). Jeremiah complained that scribes misled the people through their support of the king and Zion: "How can you say, 'We are wise, and the law of the LORD is with us,' when, in fact, the false pen of the scribes has made it into a lie?" (Jer 8:8). But Jeremiah himself relied on a scribe, Baruch, to record his messages (36:4); so not all scribes, it seems, supported royal authority. The political position of scribes could therefore vary a great deal.

After the fall of Judah, the elite in Jerusalem, including the scribes, largely depended on foreign empires for their position. These empires used local priests and scribes to do vital administrative work. But the scribes also relied upon the economic and social resources of the province of Yehud and were, by and large, Judeans themselves. Tracing the development of writing as a medium for scribal ideology shows scribes negotiating their relationship with the king, the Temple, the emperor, and the people of the area. In this process, scribes often adopted ideological positions similar to the ideological complexes discussed in chapter 11. And as this medium of writing developed social power, a particular set of authoritative writings, the **canon** of the Hebrew Bible, emerged.

*Early Steps: The Prophets and Durable Writing*

The prophetic literature attests to some of the earliest traditions about the value of writing in ancient Israel. In this literature, writing matters for the most part because it is durable. Writing a prophet's words allowed those words to continue to exist. For example, Isaiah wanted certain of his prophecies recorded so they could be vindicated later, treating his work as a sealed official record. He sealed this work (and thus preserved it) until such time as it was needed for consultation (Isa 8:16–17; cf. 30:8–9). Writing did not give authority to his prophecies, but it allowed their ongoing vitality.

The prophet Habakkuk provides another example. YHWH instructs Habakkuk to write, again focusing on writing's permanence:

> Then the Lord answered me and said:
> Write the vision;
>> make it plain on tablets,
>> so that a runner may read it.
> For there is still a vision for the appointed time;
>> it speaks of the end, and does not lie.
> If it seems to tarry, wait for it;
>> it will surely come, it will not delay.          (Hab 2:2–3)

In order for the vision to survive until its fulfillment, Habakkuk must inscribe it on tablets. The metaphorical use of writing here differs somewhat from that of Isaiah. Isaiah envisions a document such as a deed, a writing sealed until the appropriate time. Habakkuk has a more public focus in mind; someone (a courier it seems) will be able to read this document, conceived as a letter or missive. But in both cases, writing is a technological means to preserve the vision.

|  |  |
|---|---|
| *Beyond Durability: Jeremiah's Scroll* | The book of Jeremiah features writing more prominently than any other prophetic text in the Hebrew Bible. It gives evidence of its own composition, referring to various scrolls (Jer 25:13; 30:2; 36:32; 45:1). Alone among the prophetic works, it mentions the scribe (Baruch) who wrote down the prophet's spoken words. And Jeremiah himself, caught as he was in court politics, provides an interesting case study in the ideological construal of writing. |

Jeremiah 36 presents a conflict between king and prophet over a particular scroll. This story demonstrates three claims for writing as a medium. First, as with Isaiah and Habakkuk, writing is valuable for its permanence. But here the permanence of writing is under threat. The king cuts Jeremiah's scroll into pieces and burns them, despite the strenuous objections of his scribes (36:22–25). The scribes see in this burning a direct attack not just on the author of the words but also on the permanence and validity of writing itself. The king can cavalierly destroy documents, a chief product of the bureaucracy, placing the scribes at court in a difficult position.

While the burning of the scroll raises questions concerning the scribes' efficacy, Jehoiakim's act will not prevent the fulfillment of the first scroll's threats of disaster. YHWH commissions another scroll, with additional material castigating Jehoiakim. Jehoiakim and the Davidic dynasty will pay for the destruction of the first scroll:

Thus says the LORD, You have dared to burn this scroll, saying, Why have you written in it that the king of Babylon will certainly come and destroy this land, and will cut off from it human beings and animals? Therefore thus says the LORD concerning King Jehoiakim of Judah: He shall have no one to sit upon the throne of David, and his dead body shall be cast out to the heat by day and the frost by night. (36:29–30)

YHWH intervenes to render the effects of writing enduring, in the face of writing's obvious susceptibility to destruction.

Second, writing is valuable for its ability to represent its author. Here writing is a strategy to allow Jeremiah's message to reach the people. Since Jeremiah has been banned from the Temple precincts, he sends Baruch there with a scroll of his words to be read to the crowd (36:5–7). When the scribes at court hear it, they ask if Jeremiah dictated its contents (36:15–18). After they are certain of this point, they take the matter to the king. Jeremiah, though in hiding, speaks to the people and obtains an audience with Jehoiakim. In this passage, writing does more than ensure permanence; it acts to replace the speaking voice of the prophet. It can accomplish things the prophet cannot. Writing, in a mysterious way, has the power to represent the divine will in ways that speaking cannot. But for the most part, its authority is always yoked to the prophet. The scroll represents Jeremiah's dictation.

Finally, writing is valuable because it can be edited. And because it can be edited, writing can exist outside the control of any one author. While the scroll basically represents Jeremiah's dictation, perhaps it represents a little more: "Then Jeremiah took another scroll and gave it to the secretary Baruch son of Neriah, who wrote on it at Jeremiah's dictation all the words of the scroll that King Jehoiakim of Judah had burned in the fire; and many similar words were added to them" (36:32). Here writing becomes, in a sense, self-authorizing. The editor of the text cleverly obscures the origin of the "similar words." The identity of the author is not of interest and does not validate the words; the fact that they are written in the scroll seems to be the editor's essential point.

*Birth of a Canon? Josiah and Deuteronomy*

The story of Jehoiakim and the scroll finds a close parallel in a narrative about Jehoiakim's father, Josiah, and the scroll found in the Temple (2 Kgs 22). In fact, the story in Jeremiah may be designed to play off the story of Josiah, showing Jehoiakim's departure from the standards set by his father. But the Josiah narrative raises different issues regarding texts, especially the issue of how texts gain social power.

First, the story pictures Josiah as initially interested only in Temple repairs (2 Kgs 22:3–7). But when the scroll appears, it drives the action. It becomes a major character in the story. The scroll, while functioning in this role, possesses a great deal of mysterious power, first revealed in its uncertain origin.

It is <u>simply found</u> in the Temple (22:8). Josiah orders an investigation; the prophet Huldah assures him the scroll is from YHWH (22:16). But the authors are utterly uninterested in precisely how the scroll got from YHWH to the Temple. It just appears as an already-powerful object.

Second, Josiah's reaction demonstrates the scroll's power. The scroll indicates where the people of Judah have failed to obey YHWH. As a result of this disobedience, Judah is doomed; Josiah's only advantage will be that he will die before YHWH brings destruction on the nation (22:18–20). Given that grim fate, one might expect Josiah to give up; the scroll has authoritatively announced an inevitable defeat. But the story's understanding of the efficacy of writing does not stop there. The king now begins a reform campaign to enforce obedience to YHWH's commands, although according to the text, God has already made up God's mind. In a sense, the text overpowers the king; Josiah simply must act on its dictates. Writing has power; it has moved a king to act and now shapes the lives of the people.

*Ezra: Another Scroll Appears*

The accounts of the missions of Ezra and Nehemiah, written more than a century after the story of Josiah, expand the presumed authority of written texts. Ezra serves as the key figure for understanding this shift in power dynamics. The narrator introduces Ezra as a priest of the line of Aaron, a "scribe skilled in the law of Moses" (Ezra 7:6) and "a scholar of the text of the commandments" (7:11). The narrator then asserts that Ezra came to Jerusalem, bearing a letter from the Persian king Artaxerxes (7:12–26). This letter commissions Ezra to support the cult of YHWH at the Temple with a massive infusion of imperial silver and gold, as well as to investigate the residents of Yehud and Jerusalem according to God's law (7:14). The letter also states that Ezra is to enforce this law on all people of the region between the river Euphrates and land of Egypt, granting him authority to enforce the imperial law as well (7:25–26).

The contents of this letter strike many scholars as improbable; the king grants far too much authority and money to Ezra. According to the calculations of historian Lester Grabbe (*A History of the Jews and Judaism in the Second Temple Period*, vol. 1 [New York: T&T Clark, 2004], 327), this letter grants Ezra and his party about twenty-seven-and-a-half *tons* (25,000 kilograms) of silver and gold. This would represent approximately 15 percent of the empire's annual receipts, all lavished on the cultic center of a tiny, out-of-the-way province!

This letter is more about the author's imagination than about actual imperial legal and economic policies. But the letter can still demonstrate how the scribes who wrote the book of Ezra envisaged their relationship to imperial power and to the power of texts. According to the letter, Ezra the scribe is worthy to exercise imperial authority. And the letter binds the authority of the Torah and the authority of royal writing together inextricably: "All who will not obey the law of your God and the law of the king, let judgment be strictly executed on them" (Ezra 7:26). Here writing as a medium supports a particular view of the world, a view that accepts the power of both emperor and God and, indeed, sees them in remarkably similar terms.

Ezra later appears presiding over a public reading of the Torah, just as Josiah had supposedly done (2 Kgs 23:1–2). Ezra's story, however, provides much more detail, giving greater insight into the ways that scribes understood their texts to operate socially. First, the scribal authors of Ezra and Nehemiah insist that the people have a vital interest in the contents of Ezra's written scroll. The people ask for the Torah to be read, actively imposing its regulations upon themselves (Neh 8:1). A group of scribes then helps the people understand the text, either by translating it into Aramaic or by

### The Power of Reading Aloud

The actual reading of a text aloud may display a magical power, as perhaps in Neh 8. Here is an account from a slave narrative of a slave's initial encounters with public reading. Notice how the act of reading the text assigns the slave a place in society and engenders his self-identification as the hated "other":

> [My master] used to read prayers in public to the ship's crew every Sabbath day; and when I first saw him read, I was never so surprised in my life, as when I saw the book talk to my master, for I thought it did, as I observed him to look upon it, and move his lips. I wished it would do so with me. As soon as my master had done reading, I followed him to the place where he put the book, being mightily delighted with it, and when nobody saw me, I opened it, and put my ear down close upon it, in great hopes that it would say something to me; but I was very sorry, and greatly disappointed, when I found it would not speak. This thought immediately presented itself to me, that every body and every thing despised me because I was black.

James Gronniosaw, *A Narrative of the Most Remarkable Particulars in the Life of James Albert Ukawsaw Gronniosaw, An African Prince, as Related by Himself* (Bath: W. Gye, 1772).

providing a running "color commentary" (8:7–8). All the people listen to the reading carefully, from early morning to midday. And the people respond emotionally to it, first weeping (8:8) and then rejoicing because of their newfound understanding (8:12).

But the content of the text is not the only thing that matters. The text, in and of itself, possesses power: "And Ezra opened the book in the sight of all the people, for he was standing above all the people; and when he opened it, all the people stood up" (8:5). The scroll of the Torah moves the people to action, before Ezra discloses a single word of it. They know it is God's law, here displayed as a material artifact; it demands their respect and attention.

Texts have now clearly entered the "power economy" in Yehud; they command assent, direct behavior, and demand interpretation. And they buttress the authority of the empire and its servants, Ezra and Nehemiah. Ezra, quoting the scroll, embarks on a major social reform campaign. Ezra wants the men of Yehud to divorce their non-Yehudite wives. Ezra's reasons could mix ethnic, economic, theological, and political concerns. For example, Ezra might believe that the province would be more stable and secure if land in Yehud stayed in Yehudite families. Or perhaps he thinks his position in the province would be aided by a move that bolsters the power of the returnees from exile over against the descendants of those who remained in the land. But the authors of Ezra have Ezra express his demand for the divorces

## The Torah and Imperial Authority

Some scholars have suggested that the Persian Empire itself "authorized" the Torah. That is, the empire wished to codify local laws and customs to assist with local administration. These laws would then possess implicit imperial backing. There is some evidence that Darius I (522–486 B.C.E.) had Egyptian law collected, but little evidence for how the imperial administration would have used the results. And it is doubtful that the empire would have expended such efforts on a small, relatively insignificant province such as Yehud.

## Nehemiah and the Torah

The book of Nehemiah implies that Nehemiah relied on the Torah in the course of his duties as governor of Yehud. After the people read the requirement that "no Ammonite or Moabite should ever enter the assembly of God" (Neh 13:1; cf. Deut 23:3), Nehemiah has Tobiah the Ammonite evicted from the Temple precincts. It is not clear that this represents Nehemiah's actual rationale. He had plenty of other reasons to expel Tobiah from Jerusalem other than honoring Deuteronomy; after all, he believed Tobiah was plotting against him (Neh 6:17–19). And Nehemiah, it seems, would have been able to rely on imperial support to realize his aims. But again, Nehemiah's actual reasoning is not as important as how the authors of the book of Nehemiah make Nehemiah appear to be primarily interested in enforcing Deuteronomy.

through the "words of the prophets," apparently a paraphrase of Lev 18:24–30 and Deut 7:3–4 (Ezra 9:10–12). Ezra, who supposedly travels to Yehud under the king's written authority, relies upon the authority of written texts when developing local policies. The two authorities, empire and text, coalesce in Ezra's mission.

*Writing and Empire: Esther and Daniel*

Ezra and Nehemiah indicate that something like canonical texts have emerged in Yehud. The Torah, or at least an early edition of the Torah, determined the community's behavior and granted it a distinctive identity. But canonization did not take place in a vacuum. Under the influence of imperial uses of writing, the discourse of Israelite culture shifted in favor of the authority of written texts. Additionally, texts of this period demonstrate the ideological complexity of writing, as the scribal elite attempted to negotiate their position between their fellow Yehudites and imperial power. So writing need not always be a medium for imperial ideology.

### Esther on Writing

In the book of Esther, the Persian king, Ahasuerus, issues all kinds of written edicts, sends letters throughout the kingdom translated into the proper languages (Esth 1:22), and creates written law. And the laws the king makes <u>cannot be changed</u>: their authority cannot be blunted: "If it pleases the king, let a royal order go out from him, and let it be written among the laws of the Persians and the Medes so that it may not be altered" (1:19).

Chapter 11 discusses how the book of Esther does not resist imperial power but recommends its careful use. The book's approach to writing fits with this strategy. Esther and Mordecai's success comes when they gain the ability to write (Esth 8:1–2). Using this power, Mordecai writes an edict in the king's name allowing the Judeans to defend themselves. The narrator carefully describes the process of penning the letters, sealing them with the

---

### cannot be changed

It is unlikely that the Persian Empire had a policy that laws, once written, could not be altered. The only slim evidence for such a policy, outside of Esther and Daniel, comes from the Greek historian Diodorus Siculus, who reports that the Persian emperor Darius III sentenced a man to death, then regretted the sentence, "but all his royal power was not able to undo what was done" (*Library of History* 17.30.6). This text may refer to the king's inability to reverse a death sentence once carried out and so would have nothing to do with laws being generally immutable.

It is best to see this claim of immutability as the authors of Esther and Daniel making imaginative claims for the power of imperial writing. Once a text is written, it can even overpower a king. It also allows the scribal authors to talk about their own power to write in relation to imperial power.

---

### Greek version

The book of Esther exists in two versions, Hebrew (MT) and Greek (LXX), which are both versions of an original Hebrew edition that is no longer extant. The Greek version contains six major blocks of material absent in the MT version, including lengthy prayers by both Esther and Mordecai. It also provides more than fifty mentions of God, who is not mentioned at all in the MT.

---

king's ring, and sending them to all provinces by "couriers, mounted on their swift royal steeds" (8:10–14).

Then Mordecai composes a letter, on his own account, adjuring all Judeans to celebrate the feast of Purim (9:20–23). Esther then writes a letter confirming the previous document (9:29). Finally, the narrator claims that the imperial archives contain a written record of the whole business (10:2). This burst of powerful writing at the end of Esther demonstrates that Esther and Mordecai cleverly coopted imperial power. The scroll of Esther not only advances two Judeans to royal authority; it also in a sense makes them scribes—holders of the power to write.

The book of Esther assumes the power of writing. In fact, the whole book of Esther, which justifies the celebration of Purim, sounds like one more royal edict. Early readers of the text thought so. The Greek version of Esther ends with this note:

> In the fourth year of the reign of Ptolemy and Cleopatra, Dositheus, who said he was a priest and a Levite, and his son Ptolemy brought to Egypt the preceding Letter about Purim [i.e., the scroll of Esther], which they said was authentic and had been translated by Lysimachus son of Ptolemy, one of the residents of Jerusalem. (11:1)

The Greek version claims the whole scroll of Esther is a "letter," echoing the burst of letters sent by Esther and Mordecai. And the end of the Greek version testifies to the craft and power of the scribes who translated and authenticated the letter.

In Esther, writing represents power. The scroll of Esther affirms the Judean pursuit of writing as a technology that defends against imperially sponsored ethnic violence.

### Daniel in the Lions' Den: A Conflict of Laws

The "immutable" law of the Persian king also appears in the story of Daniel in the lions' den. This tale takes a different approach to the power dynamic of imperial writing, introducing an explicit conflict between two laws: Judean and Persian. Scribes in the administration of Emperor Darius, jealous of Daniel's authority, use writing as the key weapon at their disposal to destroy him. They draft a law banning prayer to any being but Darius for a month. The scribes realize that this will create a conflict between Persian law and "the law of his [Daniel's] god" (Dan 6:5).

The narrator reports that Daniel resists the Persian edict, praying openly to God even though he knows that Darius has signed the document (6:10). God thwarts the enforcement of this law by rescuing Daniel from the den of lions, suggesting that God's writing has triumphed over the king's writing. But the story quickly reasserts the king's ability to exercise power through writing. The text shows Daniel claiming that he was rescued not only because he was blameless before God but also because his conduct did not injure the king's authority (6:22). Although he clearly violated the king's edict, <u>Daniel the resister</u> claims that his conduct has not diminished the king's abilities.

And Daniel's statement is true. The narrator presents Darius quickly commanding that the scribal plotters and their families be cast to the lions. He still controls matters of life and death. And then Darius writes. Just as in Esther, the king cannot revoke an immutable law, but he can supersede it by yet more authoritative writing. In his new text, Darius admits that God's dominion is endless, but he also claims that the Persian Empire is still a vital dominion, able to enforce the worship of Daniel's deity:

> I [Darius] make a decree, that in all my royal dominion people should tremble and fear before the God of Daniel:
> For he is the living God,
>> enduring forever.
> His kingdom shall never be destroyed,
>> and his dominion has no end.
> He delivers and rescues,
>> he works signs and wonders in heaven and on earth;
> for he has saved Daniel
>> from the power of the lions. (6:26–27)

---

### Daniel the resister

Mahatma Gandhi used the story of Daniel and the lions' den as an example of *satyagraha* (truth force), drawing a parallel to the life of Socrates:

> Satyagraha differs from passive resistance as the North Pole from the South. The latter has been conceived as a weapon of the weak and does not exclude the use of physical force or violence for the purpose of gaining one's end; whereas the former has been conceived as a weapon of the strongest, and excludes the use of violence in any shape or form.
>
> When Daniel disregarded the laws of the Medes and Persians which offended his conscience, and meekly suffered the punishment for his disobedience, he offered satyagraha in its purest form. Socrates would not refrain from preaching what he knew to be the truth to the Athenian youth, and bravely suffered the punishment of death. . . . It must be remembered that neither Daniel nor Socrates . . . had any ill will towards their persecutors. Daniel and Socrates are regarded as having been model citizens of the States to which they belonged.

M. K. Gandhi, "Congress Report on the Punjab Disorders, March 25, 1920," in *The Collected Works of Mahatma Gandhi* (Delhi: Ministry of Information and Broadcasting, 1965), 17:152–53.

The scribal authors of this story depend too much on imperial power to describe writing as meaningless or ineffectual. But they also know that conflicts may arise between the requirements of being Judean and the policies of the empire. And they realize that bureaucrats with hostile agendas may abuse writing. So this story presents not a revolution against extravagant imperial demands, but a complex negotiation of relationships in and among king, God, scribe, and text.

### Writing the End: Apocalyptic Visions

The apocalyptic visions that form the last half of the book of Daniel present YHWH as an emperor while contesting human imperial rule. Here YHWH keeps written records showing a predetermined plan for the course of events at the end of the age. These books determine the judgment on the wicked, chaotic empires (Dan 7:10). There is yet another book that includes the names of those who will be delivered at the end (12:1). Moreover, Daniel has his own book, which is destined to be unsealed at the time of the end (12:4). This book, with its odd images and cryptic numbers, calls for a <u>skilled interpreter</u>—a scribe schooled in the reading of such texts.

In the apocalyptic visions, YHWH is the true emperor. His extensive imperial archive, including the books of YHWH (12:1) and Daniel (12:4, 9), determines everyone's fate. His own scribal elite, including angels, Daniel, and those who are writing in Daniel's name, ensure the correct interpretation of information from that archive. The end of the age will not remove the need for writing and for those qualified to read written texts correctly. The way the visions develop writing reveals their authors' ideological stance regarding imperial power and regarding the vital social role of the scribe.

In apocalyptic writings, the scribal elite expands the authority of texts to include the fate of all things. And writing overpowers the worldly power of

---

### skilled interpreter

Reading the texts of the Hebrew Bible involved more than being able to vocalize the written text. The scribes who wrote the visions of Daniel understood themselves, through the image of Daniel, as capable of interpreting authoritative texts correctly. Such interpretations were vital, as Dan 9 shows. In that chapter, Daniel puzzles over Jer 25:11–12, which indicates that the people's suffering would end after seventy years. Daniel asks for clarification, and the angel Gabriel informs him that when the book of Jeremiah says seventy, it really means 490 years (Dan 9:24). Having recalculated Jeremiah's number, Gabriel goes on to show that the present time of the authors of Daniel is the time of restoration that Jeremiah really intended. The scribal authors of Daniel have, in effect, "saved" the Jeremiah text. What looked to be a prophecy either fulfilled with the first restoration of Jerusalem or left unfulfilled by Jerusalem's difficulties throughout the Second Temple period, when read correctly, is really a word for the authors' own age, a word of comfort. Jeremiah 25:11–12 can still be a meaningful and authoritative text—but only through the interpretive skill of the scribal author of Dan 9.

the emperor, disclosing the blessed future of those who refuse to go along with the imperial program. Writing and reading are vital to the management of conflict with the empire as well as the management of the emerging Judean identity.

Thus, many places in the Hebrew Bible reveal scribes at work, using the medium of writing to express a variety of ideological perspectives. In all of these articulations, however, the scribes make the basic ideological assumption that writing is vital to life. If the scribes had not assumed that writing is an essential cultural practice, the Hebrew Bible would not exist.

| **Suggested Biblical Readings** | Exodus 28–29 |
| --- | --- |
| | Leviticus 1–10, 12–16, 21–23 |
| | Numbers 15, 18–19 |
| | Deuteronomy 16 |
| | 1 Kings 5–7 |
| | 2 Kings 22–23 |
| | Ezra 7 |
| | Nehemiah 8 |
| | Esther 1, 8–10 |
| | Jeremiah 36 |
| | Ezekiel 40–43 |
| | Daniel 6, 9, 12 |

**Discussion Questions**

1. Walk around your campus. How does the architecture make certain assumptions about your place in society (and at the college or university) appear obvious?
2. Pay attention to the way your classes start. Does the opening of a class express a certain ideology?
3. What do you see in your culture that might be analogous to the way temples functioned in the ancient world?
4. Is writing still a medium that encodes power in our society? Do we have people who fill the role of scribes? What ideologies do they support?

**Suggestions for Further Reading**

Berquist, Jon L. "Postcolonialism and Imperial Motives for Canonization." *Semeia* 75 (1996): 15–35.

Davies, Philip R. *Scribes and Schools: The Canonization of the Hebrew Scriptures.* Louisville, KY: Westminster John Knox Press, 1998.

Douglas, Mary. "The Abominations of Leviticus." In *Purity and Danger: An Analysis of the Concepts of Pollution and Taboo*, 41–57. London: Routledge & Kegan Paul, 1966.

Grabbe, Lester. "Priests." In *Priests, Prophets, Diviners, Sages: A Socio-Historical Study of Religious Specialists in Ancient Israel*, 41–65. Valley Forge, PA: Trinity Press International, 1995.

Meyers, Carol. "Temple, Jerusalem." In *The Anchor Bible Dictionary*, 6:350–69. New York: Doubleday, 1992.

Milgrom, Jacob. "Israel's Sanctuary: 'The Priestly Picture of Dorian Gray.'" *Revue biblique* 83 (1976): 390–99.

# 13. Deity

How do you define God? Like this. A God I could understand, at least potentially, was infinitely more interesting and relevant than one that defied comprehension.

—Robert J. Sawyer, *Calculating God*

Many people with religious investment in the Hebrew Bible equate power with God. Without a doubt, the character of the divine proves the most enduring, complex, forceful, and authoritative figure revealed over the course of the Hebrew Bible. Creator, destroyer, deliverer, forger of covenants—the narratives depict the deity as driving much of the action in the stories and as shaping the destinies of all the other characters. Moreover, even as the texts generate multiple images of God and demonstrate how factors such as time, cultural influences, and geographic locale influenced writers' presentations of the divine, the biblical writers nonetheless attempt to maintain an overall impression of this deity as controlling and masterful.

Given the centrality of God to the biblical material and the claims about divine ability to shape the events described, some readers might wonder why this textbook delays discussion of this character until close to its conclusion. A simple explanation suffices: Most readers—believers and nonbelievers alike—bring to the biblical text preconceived notions about God. More important, many of these ideas understand the deity as ultimately powerful, the primary force not only of the stories presented in the Hebrew Bible but also of "real" events such as the creation of the world. The biblical authors often strive to produce and sustain such beliefs. Words that the writer of Isaiah attributes to the deity illustrate this impulse succinctly: "I am God, and also henceforth I am He; there is no one who can deliver from my hand; I work and who can hinder it?" (Isa 43:13)

Readers seeing the divine both as a location of power and as its ultimate source certainly influence the interpretive process. While reimagining a character like Moses or David might challenge ideas about what the Hebrew

Bible says, reassessing the deity raises the stakes significantly because it can feel taboo. And herein rests the dilemma. To excuse the biblical presentation of the deity from critical consideration situates the literary character of God as beyond inquiry. This special treatment of the deity also frequently leaves readers' assumptions about God unexamined. Such divine immunity from interrogation implicitly asserts that God somehow transcends the text and supersedes human comprehension. And as Robert Sawyer asserts in the quotation at the start of the chapter, a deity beyond understanding proves rather uninteresting, since nothing remains to ponder.

To approach the images of and ideas about the deity that the biblical writers communicate requires recognizing distinctions between ancient and modern conceptions of the divine. Further, readers must allow for multiple, nonunified, or even contradicting pictures of God—thus the late arrival of the deity in this textbook. While not meaning to privilege or set God apart, interpretation of the divine demands a firm grasp of critical reading skills for productive analysis. Knowing something about the history, culture, and social world of the text assists in seeing how all the stories emerge from specific settings. Looking behind the surface of the text and recognizing the complex nuances embedded there teases out new interpretive possibilities. And reflecting on one's location as a reader, acknowledging personal boundaries, and understanding how the questions posed determine an interpretation proves essential to understanding the deity produced.

The exploration of the deity in this chapter begins with identity—specifically, looking at the various names for God that the writers employ and what these names say about the connection of Israel's deity to other local

## What Shapes Understandings of God

A 2006 study conducted at Baylor University, *American Piety in the 21st Century* (available online at http://www.baylor.edu/content/services/document.php/33304.pdf), provides insight on how people in the United States approach the idea of God. Researchers found that only 10.8 percent of Americans were not affiliated with a denomination or a religious group of some kind and fewer than 5 percent who claimed a faith other than Judaism or Christianity. The 2001 census saw only slightly less religiosity among Canadians, with 7 out of 10 affiliated as either Protestant or Roman Catholic.

What proved most interesting about the Baylor study, however, came in questions regarding the beliefs of persons identified as religiously unaffiliated. Among that group, 62.9 percent claimed to believe in God or in some higher power, and 31.6 percent prayed occasionally.

These data reveal deep cultural ties to religion in both countries and demonstrate how the majority of the population possesses some idea of God—even if not currently practicing a particular faith. Such remarkable affirmation of the divine also means that recognizing what shapes concepts about God proves difficult to determine. Common agreement among a majority lends the impression of "naturalness" of beliefs and complicates critical inquiry by asking people to analyze matters that they accept without question.

gods and goddesses. Names given to the deity also reveal something about the conception of the character of the divine. Such consideration requires thinking about how the biblical material negotiates the relationship between the people and the deity. Here the question of one God among many or one God alone receives emphasis. Then, the issue of how the deity expresses power comes to the forefront. In this section, metaphors for the divine communicate God in power relations as a head of household, as a king, and as an emperor. How the writers use God to generate authority for different social and political interests emerges as a key consideration.

## Divine Identities

Most English readers of the Hebrew Bible miss the fact that the biblical writers use multiple names for the character God. Even when simple variations— "God" as opposed to "LORD," for example—stand out, the complexity of each name and its history often is lost to a casual observer. Add in an abundance of other appellations, such as "God Most High," "the LORD of hosts," or "God Almighty," and the situation becomes even more complicated.

All of this nomenclature reflects different places, times, and social and cultural settings. No one identity of the deity held sway for the people of the Cisjordan, and the stories told articulate the variations. Understanding these distinctions at the outset becomes essential to making sense of the material. Only in exploring the terminology used for the divine do readers begin a process of figuring out how the Hebrew Bible represents this most complex character.

But another, related issue also emerges strongly. In the process of editing, compiling, and canonizing the text, those persons responsible for this work amalgamated many divine figures into one God. By presenting this God as absorbing different characteristics of various celestial beings, they have elevated this character above location, time period, and cultural influence. Instead of a deity located within the strategic webs of power a particular culture generates and uses, the text manufactures a character who frequently appears to transcend the mundane or the ordinary. And a new kind of power relationship emerges. The God portrayed in the text not only occupies locations within the biblical material from which great power can be expressed, but this God also swallows up other gods in order to be realized.

### Elohim and El

English translations of the Hebrew word *elohim* commonly render it "God." The word itself actually reads as a plural and more accurately means "gods." Determining whether to think of a noun as singular or plural often depends on verb choice. For example, Gen 1:1 describes *elohim* creating the heavens and the earth. A third-person masculine singular form of the verb "to create" (he created) links to the noun (*elohim*) and directs readers toward taking the subject as singular: "God created." "In the beginning, God created" fits; no other good option exists because of what the grammar dictates.

In other instances, context functions as a guide. Exodus 20:3 pictures the deity as commanding the people to have no other gods (*elohim*) "before me." Here the lack of a verb connected to the noun *elohim* means translators must look for other clues in the text. Reading a singular proper noun here would require concluding that the writers establish the possibility of one, rival God competing with the deity who brought the people out of Egypt: "You shall have no other God before me." Such a choice fails to reflect the ancient Near Eastern context with its comfort in acknowledging the existence of multiple deities. In this case, then, reading a plural and nonspecific noun ("gods") makes more sense.

The language here also reveals a similarity between *elohim* and El, the supreme god of the Cisjordanian pantheon. <u>Myths about El</u> claim that this creator figure finished working in the past and now sits in the heavens presiding over the business of the other gods. Indeed, the writers of Ps 82 describe such a scene in the first verse: "*Elohim* (singular) takes his place in the congregation of El; in the midst of the *elohim* (plural), he holds judgment" (authors' translation). The God of Israel apparently comes to sit in this divine council among the other gods.

The close connection between the Israelites and El as depicted in the Hebrew Bible truly stands out in the name of the people: Isra-*el*. Genesis 32, the story where the name Israel first appears, describes Jacob as struggling with a "strange man" all night and then requesting a blessing (Gen 32:24–26). The figure renames Jacob as "Israel" and explains its meaning as one who has striven with *elohim* (32:28). The name "El" thus appears as part of a new identity bestowed (Isra-*el*), followed by the more familiar plural noun (*elohim*), indicating the divinity with whom Jacob wrestled. The word *elohim* here equates God with El. The writers use El again in Jacob's naming

---

### Myths about El

Texts discovered at the site known as Ugarit (today called Ras Shamra, on the northern coast of Syria) reveal that the god El served as the chief deity in the pantheon of gods in the area of the Cisjordan. He not only created the earth but also produced the other gods. The goddess Athirat functioned as his consort or female companion. Symbolized by a wooden pole or tree called an asherah, Athirat regularly appears within the Hebrew Bible as "Asherah." The union of Asherah and El produced Shahar and Shalem—dawn and dusk.

The myths sometimes name El as the father of Baal; likewise, Asherah occasionally gets mentioned as his mother. Biblical writers depict Baal as the most active Cisjordanian deity. This god of the storm (also known as Hadad) secures fertility through the provision of necessary rains. Baal frequently associates with the goddess Anat. Anat, in turn, receives credit for the defeat of Mot, or death, while Baal conquers Yamm, or the sea.

Although the Hebrew Bible associates these gods and goddesses with peoples from the Cisjordan, texts from Syria and Egypt mention their worship as well.

> ## Derivation of the Name "Israel"
>
> Most linguists see the name "Israel" as coming from the Hebrew verb *srh*, "to persist or persevere," plus the name of El. A formal translation might look like "El persists," a third-person imperfect form of the Hebrew verb, or "Let El persist," a jussive. This derivation differs from the story of Jacob's renaming in Gen 32, where Jacob stands as the subject and El serves as the object of the verb.

of the location for this encounter as Peni-*el* or "face of El" (32:30) and conclude that Jacob's seeing of God (*elohim*) motivated this choice. Readers might wonder whom Jacob worships or whose name the people carry forward. The use of El here alongside *elohim* indicates that the God of Jacob and the chief of the Cisjordanian pantheon likely denote the same deity.

In these texts and many others, the writers of the biblical stories reveal a deep familiarity with the god El; indeed, the name appears more than two hundred times in the Hebrew Bible. Moreover, in developing the character of the God of Israel, the writers frequently make use of El's identity. Look, for example, to the many variations on "El" occurring as names for the God of Israel. "El Shaddai," or "God Almighty," appears multiple times, most often in Genesis and, via the shorthand "Shaddai" alone, in Job (Gen 17:1; 28:3; 35:11; 43:14; 48:3; and Job 5:17; 6:4; 8:3, 5; 23:16; 33:4). Another popular designation, "El Elyon," or "God Most High" (Gen 14:19–20, 22; Pss 57:2; 78:35, 56) indicates the dwelling of God in the mountains or heavens—another common association with El. Also note "El Olam," or "Everlasting God" (Gen 21:33; Pss 90:1–3; 93:2; Isa 26:4), and "El Roi," or "the God who sees" (Gen 16:13).

*Baal*

Baal literally means "lord" or "master," and the term can refer to a number of different manifestations of the divine. Typically identified with the god of storms and fertility—Hadad—Baal controls some of the most intimidating forces of nature. Baal serves in this role to provide crucial rains, and thus crops, for a people living in a minimally arable land. Ugaritic texts from Ras Shamra offer the most complete picture about this god and his principal consorts, Anat and Astarte.

Baal often appears in opposition to the God of the Hebrew Bible. Many texts warn the people against worship of this supposedly rival god (e.g., Judg 2:13; 1 Kgs 18:21; Jer 23:27). The events depicted in Judg 9 challenge this view. In describing the attempt of Abimelech to establish a monarchy and rule over Israel, a temple in Shechem plays a key role as a place of refuge for his opponents. According to Judg 9:46, the holy site belongs to El Berith, or "God of the covenant." But Judg 9:4 earlier assigned this place of worship to Baal-berith, or "Baal of the covenant." Recall that Josh 24 presents Shechem as the location for the covenant renewal between YHWH and the people of Israel (see 1 Kgs 12:1, 25). These texts raise the question of what god the people worship in this place. El? Baal? YHWH? All three? One might wonder if the people worshiping at Shechem even recognized differences between these divine figures.

Readers of the Hebrew Bible continuously encounter the popularity of the worship of Baal. The majority of material about Baal comes from the seventh century B.C.E. prophets and the editors who produced the books of Joshua, Judges, Samuel, and Kings. They primarily pictured conflict between YHWH and other or "foreign" gods and goddesses. First Kings 18, for example, presents the prophet Elijah in a contest with the prophets of Baal and Asherah. There, the writers show Elijah asking the people to make a choice between YHWH and Baal rather than try to worship both (1 Kgs 18:21). Likewise, Jer 11:13 presents worship of Baal as a problem by describing the number of different gods the people worship and the altars to Baal in the streets of Jerusalem.

Further, important people took on the name of Baal: the judge Gideon receives mention as Jerubbaal (Judg 6:32), King Saul names his son and eventual successor Ishbaal (2 Sam 2:8), and his son Jonathan's child goes by Merib-baal (1 Chr 8:34 and 9:40; 2 Sam 9:6 substitutes "Mephibosheth"). These **theophoric names** raise questions about what god claims the allegiance of the people.

*Asherah*

The picture of the deity becomes even more complex when considering the associations of God with Asherah (a.k.a. Athirat). This female consort of El and sometimes mother of Baal appears in both biblical and nonbiblical materials. The word "asherah" or some form of it occurs around forty times in the Hebrew Bible. Approximately half of these occurrences come in a plural form and make reference to wooden poles that function in a cultic setting. When condemning the religious activities of the people of Judah, 1 Kgs 14:23 expresses this use clearly: "For they also built for themselves high places, pillars, and sacred poles [*asherim*] on every high hill and under every green tree." Deuteronomy 16:21 might indicate that these poles functioned as a representation of a tree. In the remainder of its appearances, "asherah" seems to function as a name for a goddess. The writers say that King Asa of Judah, for example, acts against his mother when she worships this goddess (1 Kgs 15:33). However, they show another king, Manasseh, promoting Asherah worship alongside that of YHWH (2 Kgs 21:7).

Extrabiblical material confirms Asherah worship in biblical Israel. Inscriptions at both Khirbet el-Qôm and Kuntillit ʿAjrud make reference to YHWH and "his Asherah."

*YHWH*

Into this mix of deities, the writers of the Hebrew Bible present a different name for the divine. The writers of Exodus show God identifying God's self to Moses at the burning bush, first through claiming a connection to Moses' biological father, then to Moses' ancestors, Abraham, Isaac, and Jacob (6:9). The story continues, with Moses demanding more detailed information

**Fig. 13.1: The Tanaach Cult Stand**

about the identity of this deity, especially the deity's name. The request articulates a desire to probe the character of this divine being, to know how the name captures the essence of this god. An enigmatic reply, "I am who I am" (Exod 3:14), leaves readers to ponder exactly what the writers present God attempting to reveal and what they let God leave unanswered.

In Hebrew this response reads *'ehyeh asher 'ehyeh* and relates loosely to the Hebrew name for God—יהוה, or YHWH. These four letters, known formally as the tetragrammaton, confuse scholars, who struggle to determine their meaning. The most common explanation in Jewish tradition centers on etymology or linguistic extraction. The triliteral Hebrew root היה, or *hyh*, means "to be" and can function in one of two different states used in Hebrew for verbal activity. The first state, the perfect, expresses completed action, most often in the past. The second, the imperfect, denotes incomplete, past, present, or future action. In this text, God speaks to Moses from the flame of fire using a first-person common imperfect form

## Khirbet el-Qôm and Kuntillit 'Ajrud

Evidence from Khirbet el-Qôm, an archaeological site near the city of Hebron in the south, comes from the eigth century B.C.E. Similar inscriptions from Kuntillit 'Ajrud in the Sinai date between the ninth and seventh centuries.

## The Tanaach cult stand

The Tanaach cult stand (see fig. 13.1), dated to the tenth century B.C.E., comes from Tanaach, an ancient site just south of Megiddo. The bottom layer of the four layers depicts two lions flanking a woman figure, the goddess Asherah. The lion serves as her sacred animal, thus aiding her identification. On the next level, two cherubim or similar winged figures surround an empty space. This absence might represent the entry to the Holy of Holies or the dwelling place of YHWH, or it could designate the lack of any one specific image for YHWH (as well as the prohibition against images). On the third level, Asherah recurs as a pole flanked by two ibex and then surrounded by two lions. Finally, the top panel shows a bull, an animal frequently associated with the God of Israel.

The function of the two deities together comes across on this stand. As the foundational figure, the goddess demonstrates her power. Given her location at the bottom, she represents the root of all things and shows her control of the underworld and the things of death. The open space above functions as a doorway on earth into this mysterious realm—a place where only deities dwell. As a pole, Asherah exhibits fertility; grounded in the earth and yet reaching to heaven, she feeds the life around her. Finally, the bull stands for the storm god, who brings the rain to ensure that this fertility continues.

of the verb היה (*'ehyeh*)—"I am" or "I will be." The name YHWH, what the people call God, possibly relates to a third-person masculine singular imperfect form of the verb "to be," meaning "he is" or "he will be." While the biblical story stresses the unique quality of this name, scholars speculate on connections to the names of other Cisjordanian deities. The text itself suggests that the term YHWH might come from other places. Stories in Exodus show Moses encountering this deity while tending the flock of his father-in-law, Jethro (also known as Reuel and Hobab), a priest of Midian (Exod 3:1). Similarly, an ancient song attributed to Deborah begins, "LORD, when you

## Names and Their Meaning

Naming bestows upon a person a distinguishing mark that differentiates him or her from all others. The writers of the Hebrew Bible frequently associate names with specific events in a story. Isaac's name, for example, comes from the verb *tskhk*, "to laugh," and describes his mother's response to the possibility of bearing a child at an old age (Gen 18:13; 21:5–7). Likewise, Ben-oni designates "son of my sorrow" (Gen 35:18) as Rachel was dying at his birth. But sometimes, as with the case of Moses in Exod 3, namings force meaning. In other circumstances, character comes to the fore. The name Jacob connects to the verb *aqav*, "to follow at the heel" or "to overreach." Since his birth immediately follows his twin, Esau, whom he subsequently supplants (Gen 25:26; Gen 27), this picture of him grabbing at the heel makes sense.

Names, then, frequently carry something of the story of a person with them. They reveal details about origin or character. The names of deities function in much the same manner. They often suggest something of the nature and character of the divine being in question.

## Traditions for Pronouncing the Name

The Jewish community understands that the holiness of the divine requires people to exercise caution in saying the name of God. It became custom not to speak the name of the deity out loud, even though no specific prohibition against this practice existed. Speakers thus say "*Adonai*" ([my] Lord) or "*Ha-Shem*" (the name) instead of the name YHWH in the biblical text or in a prayer.

When the consonantal text of the Hebrew Bible received vowel markings, the Masoretes reminded readers not to say the divine name by blending the vowels for *Adonai* with the four consonants in "YHWH." Creating an unpronounceable word gave readers a visual cue not to say it aloud. Naturally, however, people attempt to say it. In 1520 c.e., the confessor of Pope Leo X, a man named Peter Galatin, popularized a combination of the two in a now-famous form. The "Y" of YHWH when rendered in Latin became a "J," and the first vowel sound from *Adonai* is a short "a." Then comes an "h" with a long "o." The "W" goes to a "V" in Latin and combines with a longer "a" followed by the last "H." Together, "Ja-ho-vah" or "Jehovah" results. Although it is a word made up of mismatched consonants and vowels, some traditions now use it as a name for God.

Scholars consider "Yahweh" the most likely way one would articulate "YHWH." No definitive evidence exists to support this pronunciation.

went out from Seir, when you marched from the region of Edom . . ." (Judg 5:4). This connection might suggest close ties between YHWH and Edom. Midian, Seir, and Edom all locate places to the south of the Cisjordan but represent near neighbors (see Deut 32–33 and Hab 3). The precise origins of the name, however, remain unknown and likely unknowable.

What the writers meant to convey with this name also remains elusive. "I am" might evoke a stable, secure, and powerful god. This line of thinking takes "I am" (or "I will be") as connoting existence and understands God here to declare ongoing and everlasting presence. So when the writers of Lev 19 present the deity as repeatedly declaring "I am YHWH" (Lev 19:12, 14, 16, 18, 28, 30, 32, 37) or "I am YHWH your God" (Lev 19:4, 9, 25, 31, 34, 36), they could suggest God's presence in the community and the authority in the commands put forward to its members.

Alternatively, "I am" might communicate nothing: I am . . . The name in this case remains self-referential ("I am who I am") and devoid of any content. Further, even though offering it up in response to Moses' request so that he could identify this deity specifically to the people of Israel, God claims that the ancestors did not know this name (Exod 3:15, 16)—references earlier in Genesis notwithstanding. Again, the origins of this name, as well as its meaning, remain mysterious.

In spite of the questions about the name, the biblical text undoubtedly depicts YHWH as functioning much like El and Baal. For example, the prominent Cisjordanian deity, Hadad or Baal-Hadad, the god of the storm, the "rider of the clouds," appears in Ugaritic myths with lightning bolt in hand and a voice of thunder, prepared to water the grounds and assure fertility. Psalm 68:4 speaks of YHWH in a like manner, describing songs to God who rides in the clouds (see the section on Ps 89 in chapter 11). Psalm 29 reveals a similar storm God in language likely borrowed from Ugaritic hymns to this Baal; the voice of God thunders (29:3) and flashes in fire (29:7). Other psalms, particularly 77 and 114, also use such words to depict the action of the deity.

One of the most striking parallels comes between Ugaritic myths and Judg 5:4b–5. The following table illustrates the connections.

| | |
|---|---|
| The earth trembled, and the heavens poured, the clouds indeed poured water. The mountains quaked before the Lord, the One of Sinai, before the Lord, the God of Israel. (Judg 5:4b–5) | Baal opened a rift in the clouds; his holy voice Baal gave forth. Baal repeated the is[sue] of his lips. At his h[oly] voice the earth quaked; at the issue of his [lips] the mountains were afr[aid]. (the Baal Cycle [KTU 1.4 vii 28–32], translated in N. Wyatt, *Religious Texts from Ugarit*, 2nd ed. [Sheffield: Sheffield Academic Press, 2002]) |

The commonality of language here and in other texts reveals how the biblical writers looked to familiar images and texts about known deities in order to shape their presentation of YHWH. The divine reality they sought to convey required language that evoked ideas of deity for the people. And the Cisjordanian gods and goddesses filled that order.

*Conclusions about the Identity of This Deity*

The interchange of divine names and characteristics of these gods indicates that a common vocabulary for deity prevailed across the Cisjordan. The book of Hosea offers one last example. There the people attribute provisions required for worship of Baal—such as grain, wine, oil, silver, and gold—to Baal, while the prophet holds they come from YHWH (Hos 2:8). The confusion of YHWH with Baal, or even multiple baals, becomes clear later in the same chapter. The writers show YHWH saying that the people will use a new name to make reference to God—"My man," instead of the previously used "My Baal" (Hos 2:16–17).

Apparently, the commonality in understandings of the divine meant that the people saw the actions that the writers of Hosea purport to come from YHWH as consistent with what Baal accomplished. Identifying the actor seems important only to the prophet. For western readers, the amalgamation of divine names and functions can come across as confusing. Who is God? Is there more than one divine being? If so, in what relationship do these celestial figures stand? To think through these questions, a few theoretical issues require attention.

## Identity to Power: How Many Gods? Whose Gods? And What Does It Matter?

Typical, straightforward readings of the Hebrew Bible seem to present a God of Israel standing over against a series of rival gods from other nations. But the Hebrew Bible accepts the idea of an Israelite God answering to many names and exhibiting a range of characteristics associated with various divine beings. Nahum 1:2–8 demonstrates how the biblical writers intermingle characteristics of El, Baal, Asherah, and others to describe the God of Israel. Diverse terms for the divine function synonymously. For example, Nah 1:2 reads, "A jealous and avenging El is YHWH, YHWH is avenging and a Baal of wrath" (authors' translation). The text then continues to describe the actions of this deity in images common for Baal: the god of the storm (1:3), controller of the waters (1:4), and one who shakes the earth (1:5). No criteria exist to distinguish the God of Israel from El or Baal. These divine figures and their stories provided the language for deity within the Cisjordanian milieu, including for the Israelites. No other language existed.

But the biblical writers also push to distinguish the God of Israel from all other gods. The opening of the Ten Commandments provides a good illustration: "I am YHWH your *elohim* who brought you out from the land of Egypt, from the house of slavery; you shall have no other *elohim* before me" (Exod 20:2–3, authors' translation). "No other *elohim*" indicates that while YHWH, this God, demands priority, additional deities exist. Similarly, after the successful crossing of the sea, the writers of Exodus present the people singing a song to YHWH that asserts YHWH's superiority over these gods (Exod 15:11). And 2 Sam 7:23 speaks of the Israelites' God acting on their behalf by driving out other peoples and their gods. None of these passages expresses any doubt about the presence of multiple deities, although each offers some reason for preferring the God of Israel.

Biblical scholars once used the term **henotheism** to describe this phenomenon. It means declaring allegiance to one god without denying the existence of others. Today, academics prefer the word **monolatry**. Some questions arise about different nuances in meaning between the two terms. "Henotheism" asserts that while one god demands or deserves devotion, nothing prohibits other people from worshiping other gods. "Monolatry," by contrast, might suggest that even while recognizing other gods, only one god stands as worthy of worship.

Neither term arises within the text itself. Rather, they come mostly from nineteenth-, twentieth-, and twenty-first-century scholars attempting to classify and analyze the biblical material. Therein rests the problem. This language may actually fail to characterize accurately what the Hebrew Bible itself attempts to depict. Further, the biblical material may not reflect what happened in the worship life of most of the people.

A few texts help clarify this issue. The Israelites, at least for most of their history, lived in an environment accepting of many gods. Recall the story of Rachel stealing her father's household gods when departing with Jacob to return to his family home (Gen 31:19). Or look to how the writers of Exodus show the Israelites encouraging Aaron to fashion a golden calf to bring into focus the gods that rescued them from Egypt (Exod 32:4). Aaron builds this calf and then erects an altar before it to celebrate a festival to YHWH (32:5). This equation of YHWH to a calf and to the gods of the people shows openness to multiple deities. Even the common refrain enjoining the Israelites not to worship other gods, "Do not follow other gods, any of the gods of the people who are all around you" (Deut 6:14, for example; see also Exod 23:13; Deut 8:19; 11:16, 28; Josh 23:16; Judg 10:13; 2 Kgs 17:35), affirms the presence of many divine entities. And its frequent repetition likely indicates that the Israelites often exhibited devotion to these other gods and thus required reminders and rebukes to remain loyal to YHWH alone.

Given that local deities functioned to secure necessities and protection, the average Israelite likely acknowledged a variety of gods. Jeremiah 44 demonstrates the point. The writers portray the prophet condemning false worship, probably of Asherah, in the Egyptian exilic community. The text details the people's reply:

> Then all the men who were aware that their wives had been making offerings to other gods, and all the women who stood by, a great assembly, all the people who lived in Pathros in the land of Egypt, answered Jeremiah: "As for the word that you have spoken to us in the name of the Lord, we are not going to listen to you. Instead, we will do everything that we have vowed, make offerings to the queen of heaven and pour out libations to her just as we and our ancestors, our kings and our officials, used to do in the towns of Judah and the streets of Jerusalem. We used to have plenty of food, and prospered, and saw no misfortune. But from the time we stopped making offerings to the queen of heaven and pouring out libations to her, we have lacked everything and have perished by the sword and by famine." And the women said, "Indeed we will go on making offerings to the queen of heaven and pouring out libations to her; do you think that we made cakes for her, marked with her image, and poured out libations to her without our husbands' being involved?" (Jer 44:15–19)

As the biblical writers present it, the people believe that routine dedication to a goddess guarantees adequate provision of life's necessities. By contrast, following the urging of Jeremiah to worship YHWH alone brings on suffering. Note also how the text ascribes the worship of this queen of heaven to their ancestors as well as to their kings and officials. It admits the longevity of the practice and its official support from the state.

Ezekiel 20:27–28 characterizes the worship of the Israelites in a similar manner with its claim that the Israelites frequently made offerings upon various hills or near leafy trees. While not naming a deity or deities to whom these worshipers showed devotion, the text certainly leaves the impression that the Israelites worshiped a variety of gods. What the biblical writers condemn here and what others elsewhere label as "false" worship might be read as worship of other gods that, in the people's view, detracts nothing from any relationship to the God of Israel. Or perhaps the people understand their actions in these settings as devotion to YHWH—but with practices not acceptable to this prophet.

These passages indicate that "monolatry" might not work well as a designation for the devotional activities of the Israelites as described in the Hebrew Bible. Even if the writers encourage dedication to one god exclusively, the Israelites appear uninterested in complying with such directives. Rather, what appears in the text looks more like an attempt to negotiate between the general traditions common to the people of the Cisjordan and the emergent interests of Israel.

The drive to privilege a single deity comes across clearly in Ps 86. Stressing the uniqueness of the god receiving praise, the writers nonetheless offer no language specifically identifying YHWH as the deity in question:

> There is none like you among the gods [elohim], O Lord [adonai],
>    nor are there any works like yours.

> All the nations you have made shall come
>   and bow down before you, O Lord [*adonai*],
>   and shall glorify your name.
> For you are great and do wondrous things;
>   you alone are God [*elohim*]. (86:8–10)

This passage again acknowledges the reality of other gods while simultaneously declaring that only one matters. A better reading of this text might stress that even as other gods exist, this god stands out in both the divine and human realms. The point becomes even more urgent in the words of Isa 45:6b–7: "I am YHWH and there is not another; forming light and creating darkness; making good and creating evil; I, YHWH, am doing all of these things" (authors' translation). In this instance, the claim comes that no other deities exist. Scholars label that idea **monotheism**.

To understand this momentum toward allegiance to one God alone, or the confession that only one God exists, means to think about power. Without doubt, an "official" cult of the monarchy comes into play here. Recall from chapter 10 how an entire apparatus of prophets and priests receives mention as working in service of the deity—but at the behest of the king. The state cult comes under pressure to separate from "other" gods in order to facilitate the interests of the king. Gods and worship practices outside of the royally legitimized cult undermine the centralization of power the kings attempt to achieve.

But the writers of the text often voice strident opposition to cultic figures. Micah 3:11, for instance, speaks of the state and its cult in Jerusalem as functioning for monetary gain alone. Similarly, Jer 5:30–31 condemns prophets for false prophecy and priests for following their lead. Moreover, the leaders of this "official cult" often are accused of allowing rather permeable borders between the worship of their patron God YHWH and that of other gods. Ezekiel, for instance, catalogs a variety of false worship practices within the temple and its courts in Ezek 8.

Kings nonetheless need and use the deity to forge a national story. The narrative undergirding the state stresses YHWH's role in the history of the Israelites. From the time of the ancestors, to the exodus from Egypt, to the conquest and settlement of the land, and then to the establishment of the state under the leadership of a chosen king, YHWH's presence remains a constant. And this story stresses that the deity favors Israel above all other nations (see Gen 12:2–3; Exod 19:4–5; Josh 24:11–13; and 2 Sam 7:10–11, for examples). Even though the king's "spin" cannot erase the shared qualities between the deity the Israelites worship and other gods of this Cisjordanian pantheon, it nonetheless asserts a patron deity whose long history with them should evoke their loyalty—to YHWH and to the king.

This ideological division, a story of "us" versus "them," accomplishes several strategic purposes as well. Given that the final editorial shape of this story took place after the defeat of Jerusalem by the Babylonians in 587/586 B.C.E., the writers and editors needed to explain the collapse of the nation. "False" worship, or refusal to acknowledge YHWH to the exclusion of other deities, provided a strong rationale for the destruction of the divinely sanctioned state. This theological justification for geopolitical weakness removed any blame for failure of the national experiment from YHWH and placed it firmly on a wayward people (see Jer 21:8–9 for one clear instance of this thinking). A system that promoted one God above all others served this agenda.

The Israelites also needed a deity that existed outside the interests of the now defunct states of Israel and Judah. No local patron deity sufficed, primarily because no geographic locale contained the people any longer. This deity needed to possess the capability of reaching Israelites displaced and living throughout the ancient Near East. Additionally, as a defeated nation with little hope for autonomous political expression in a region of successive empires, only a deity who transcended all states or empires would do. Moving toward a position of one god, then, allowed the writers to position the Israelites in a position to express power even as the states suffered dissolution. Exclusivity in the divine realm meant that they stood in relationship to the only deity and thus connected to a force that could rival mighty empires and their purported gods. The words recorded in Isaiah express this idea succinctly: "I am the first and I am the last; beside me there is no god" (Isa 44:6, authors' translation).

These ways of characterizing the divine all construct complicated power relationships. Utilizing familiar ideas for the divine positions the deity to function within an existing web of social and cultural relations present in the Cisjordan. The realization of divine power happens within those structures. El Shaddai works within the *bet av* of Abraham (Gen 17:1) and Jacob (35:11) to produce a people, for example. Creating a contrast between this deity and other gods generates a different power dynamic. The exclusion of other peoples and their gods allows for the expression of divine preference. The presentation of the exodus, the conquest narratives, and the rise of the state each depend on the favor of this patron deity. Finally, a confession of one God alone carves out a space of divine prerogative that stands as unquestionable. A deity who creates the universe and runs it renders challenge useless. As creator and preserver of the universe, no earthly ruler can hold a position to move against God and, as stated, no other deity exists as a rival.

## Metaphorical Identities of the Deity: Embodied and Enacted Power

The biblical account, of course, does not communicate the idea of deity only in names or in categories such as henotheism, monolatry, and monotheism. In striving to reveal the nature and character of the Israelites' God, the writers frequently use metaphors. Drawn from the social and cultural worlds of the Israelites, metaphors embody the divine in familiar roles and thus show in a more comprehensible manner how divine power operates.

The selection of metaphors explored in this section in no way comes close to the totality of metaphors used for the deity in the Hebrew Bible. Rather, the images chosen come out of familiar social world settings: family, national politics, and international relations. The organization of this material does not imply a sequence. These conceptions of the deity often overlap and follow no chronological order.

*God, Jealousy, and the* Bet Av

Much of the Hebrew Bible stresses the idea that God relates to the people within the context of a covenant forged on Mount Sinai. Recall from chapter 11 how the pattern of suzerainty treaties structured the expression of this relationship. These covenants demanded that both parties assume responsibilities and make promises, with the primary burden, naturally, falling on the weaker member or the vassal. As portrayed by the writers, the god in this relationship demanded the absolute fidelity of the people in unequivocal terms. Predicated on the actions of YHWH to deliver the people from bondage in Egypt, the presumed display of divine largesse functions to make this command seem reasonable. Who better to trust with their fate and future?

Within this context, the biblical writers speak of God as jealous (see Exod 20:5; 34:14; Deut 4:24; 5:9; 6:15; 32:16, 19, 21). This image of a jealous covenant God sets the stage for one of the most powerful metaphors describing the relationship of Israel to the deity in the prophetic literature—marriage. Drawn from the context of the *bet av*, the metaphor portrays the deity as a husband and Israel as a wife. Linking the covenant with the deity to matrimony made sense for biblical writers addressing an audience of elite men. Because these men typically lived within the structure of a traditional household, they could readily relate what God expected of them to what they expected of a wife. And even though the metaphor places the Israelites, or the audience receiving this word, in the position of a woman, the message transmitted in these texts invites men to identify with God—not as a deity, but as a husband. In this manner, male readers and hearers can relate to the actions of the deity expressed in various texts.

Recall that proper functioning of the *bet av* depends on each member's understanding his or her obligations. The social order stays intact only as long as participants fulfill the duties incumbent on them. Chapter 4 demonstrated how inheritance and financial and social standing relied upon birth order and assurance of paternity. A woman's fidelity, then, and other men's respect for the holdings of a given man stood out as core values. And the law worked to protect these varied relationships. For the purposes of the metaphor, the focus on exclusivity and faithfulness in marriage not only shed light on the requirements of the covenant but also on the manner in which the deity expresses power.

The writings attributed to the prophet Hosea offer extensive use of marriage as a metaphor for the covenant relationship and provide a clear path to understanding how this language functions. In the text, YHWH commands

### Jealousy as a Feature of the Suzerain-Vassal Relationship

A modern definition of jealousy often centers on an immature emotional response to the loss of affection, an infidelity, or the fear of such loss. In a suzerainty treaty, this conception comes across as ludicrous; in the face of a clearly outlined series of retributions and an obvious power differential, why would the more dominant party "feel" anything toward a subservient king? To reveal an emotional attachment of this kind either demonstrates ego weakness in the suzerain—a need for acquiescence from lesser entities in order to support a fragile sense of self—or invests the relationship with far more reciprocity as the lesser party generates something in the ruler that leads to protective or possessive traits.

In the treaty context, jealousy springs from the need to keep vassals in line to maintain order. That is, in a world where suzerains compete for control, the success of any given leader rests largely on the stability of the treaties signed and so on the ability to hold vassal states to the terms of their agreements. The swaying of a signatory to another patron potentially results in disaster if others follow and the command of the guarantor comes into question. "Jealousy," therefore, suggests possessiveness not out of emotion or of ego-building but rather stemming from the requirements of sustaining supremacy among peers.

In the case of the deity in the Hebrew Bible, the competition occurs in both political and religious arenas. The god described in these texts seeks an exclusive relationship with the people of Israel, built on the premise of a greater capability than other gods. The events of the exodus serve, for the writers, as proof of the capability of YHWH to secure the destiny of the people.

Hosea to marry a whore and raise children, possibly not his own, to symbolize the departure of Israel from God (Hos 1:2). This demand likely insulted many in the text's original audience, given that no leader of a *bet av* would actively seek to bring infidelity into his household. Nor would he likely worship a god who demanded it. After all, such actions cause a family to deteriorate rapidly. Adultery threatens the stability of the household by challenging the authority of its head and introducing uncertainty into the lineage. Indeed, the name Hosea gives to the third child, "Lo-ammi" (Hos 1:8–9), or "Not my people," questions paternity.

In Hosea 2, the writers describe Israel metaphorically taking other lovers. These lovers, clearly identified in Hos 2:5, 12 as other gods that the woman claims provide the resources she needs for survival, symbolize Israel's idolatrous behavior. Moreover, such behavior within the context of a household shames her husband. To grasp exactly what that means requires a consideration of honor/shame cultures.

In such a culture, a head of household secures his status and earns honor in the community, at least in part, by controlling all of his holdings. This control extends to the behavior of those persons living under his care. Violations of that honor—termed "shame"—indicate disorder within his home and diminish opportunities for advantageous interactions with other households and the wider community. In order to rehabilitate his public reputation, he must visibly demonstrate his power or risk retribution on his household. In other words, if he fails to act to solve his problem, other senior males will move their families against the offending household in order to discourage such behavior and to reaffirm the authority of their positions.

In Hosea, then, the deity seeks to restore order after Israel's infidelities. First, the writers present God as promising stripping and exposure—actions suggesting punishment of a whore. Then the deity pledges to kill her via thirst—a threat more suggestive of bringing a drought on the land (Hos 2:3). Likewise, in Hos 2:9–10 the writers attribute to God the removal of life necessities, including grain, wine, wool, and flax. These items certainly might disappear in a water shortage, but the section concludes: "I will uncover her shame in the sight of her lovers, and no one shall rescue her out of my hand." Such language appears to go back to what happens to women who violate established norms. In order to work, the metaphor must connect with the

## Marriage as Metaphor

When using a marriage metaphor, the Hebrew Bible primarily focuses on troubled relationships. The prophetic literature in particular finds the idea of infidelity compelling in describing the behavior of the people toward the deity as well as in framing the divine response toward this wayward group.

The Hebrew Bible holds, however, that marriage within the *bet av* bears more than negative consequences for women. Writers sometimes generate images of profound pride and deep affection between God and Israel as male and female partners. Isaiah 62:3–5 gives voice to this vision of the marital experience:

> You [the Israelites] shall be a crown of beauty in the hand of the LORD,
>   and a royal diadem in the hand of your God.
> You shall no more be termed Forsaken,
>   and your land shall no more be termed Desolate;
> but you shall be called My Delight Is in Her,
>   and your land Married;
> for the LORD delights in you,
>   and your land shall be married.
> For as a young man marries a young woman,
>   so shall your builder marry you,
> and as the bridegroom rejoices over the bride,
>   so shall your God rejoice over you.

A positive evaluation of the bond between male and female in marriage, this text expresses the joy of God in this relationship.

A feminist critique of this text and others like it certainly identifies problems. For example, the primary actor in the drama—God—functions in the masculine role. The woman, by contrast, gains her apparently radiant beauty only as a result of her location within the firm grasp, and thus within the power, of the deity. Further, even as her married status apparently "rescues" her from a life without prospects, the delight and rejoicing mentioned both reside with God. Any choice, will, or desire that she might feel in the situation remains uncertain, since her perspective never receives mention.

## Honor Crimes

However tempting it is to consider honor crimes a relic of a distant past, these atrocities continue today. The United Nations estimates that over five thousand women die yearly as the result of such crimes. These women victims, from many different regions and religious faiths, suffer for a variety of reasons and with little legal recourse. Most cases go unreported, and the perpetrators face no punishment.

Honor crimes typically involve male relatives abusing or killing a woman perceived as shaming their family. Behaviors driving men to act include publicly acknowledging a man, divorcing, marrying a person of the woman's own choosing, or engaging in sexual intercourse without the benefit of marriage. A raped woman also often suffers further abuse or is killed, as are women who marry with an insufficient dowry. Accused women frequently take their own lives.

The fifty-seventh session of the United Nations General Assembly Third Committee passed a resolution on October 24, 2002, entitled "Working Towards the Elimination of Crimes Committed in the Name of Honor." See the full text online at http://www.soros.org/initiatives/women/news/honorkillings_20021024.

reality of the audience it addresses. So readers need to make sense of what uncovering shame before her lovers means with regard to the treatment of women as well as what it suggests with regard to the fate of Israel.

Some precedent exists for public stripping as a form of humiliating an accused adulteress (see Susanna 32, for example). But, as seen in chapter 6, the colloquialism of uncovering shame or nakedness generally makes reference to unsanctioned or inappropriate sexual activity. For a woman, such activity might include sex before marriage, adultery, or an incestuous relationship. By contrast, covering a woman's nakedness expresses taking a woman legally into your care as a wife and obtaining sexual access to her.

Thinking of the deity as uncovering Israel's shame in the sight of all her lovers, then, presents a number of difficulties for an interpreter. Two similar texts in Ezekiel, chapters 16 and 23, also employ this terminology in metaphorical punishment sequences for women who commit adultery. One particular passage, Ezek 16:36–43a, assists in critically analyzing the metaphor:

> "Because your vaginal secretions were poured out and your genitals exposed in your whorings with your lovers, and with all of the idols of your abominations—and also for the blood of your children that you gave to them, therefore, watch me, gathering all your lovers whom you pleased—all those you loved and all of those you hated—and I will gather them against you from all around, and I will expose your geni-

## Susanna

The book of Susanna is one of fifteen texts known as the Apocrypha, or "hidden books." It is one of three "additions" in this collection to the book of Daniel.

tals to them so that they will see all of your genitals. Then I will judge you with the judgments of adulterers and murderers, and I will put upon you the blood of violence and jealousy. And I will put you into their hands and they will tear down your platform and break down your high places and they will strip you of your clothes and they will take the articles of your beauty, and they will leave you naked and exposed. Then they will bring up a mob against you and they will stone you with stones and slice you open with their swords. And they will burn your houses with fire and bring against you judgments in the sight of many women. And I will make you stop whoring; also, you will not give payment again. Then I will quiet my rage against you and turn aside my jealousy from you and I will be calm and I will not be angry again. Because you have not remembered the days of your youth and have roused me in all of these things, so also watch, I will put your actions on your head," says the Lord, YHWH. "Have you not been the whore with all of your abominations?" (authors' translation)

In this text the woman accused of taking many lovers represents Jerusalem. A symbol of the city and of the Davidic state apparatus located within it, this woman forges alliances with other nations (16:23–34), worships idols (16:15–19), and sacrifices children (16:20–21). As a result of this infidelity, YHWH turns the city over to its enemies, and the text depicts its complete and utter destruction—described primarily in terms of what happens to people in the context of war.

Thus, when the writers present YHWH exposing the woman's nakedness to her lovers, the plural denotes multiple participants and the exposure of nakedness stands for sexual activity. In short, the text imagines an enraged husband instigating gang rape against his wife. Honor/shame cultures reveal similar punishment of women occurring within households. Further, the association of rape and war comes in other biblical materials where women receive mention as sexual "spoil" for victorious soldiers (see Judg 5:30).

## Women, Sexual Violence, and War

Experts estimate that between 20,000 and 50,000 women suffered rape in the Bosnia-Herzegovina conflict (1992–1995). In Sierra Leone, 50,000 to 64,000 internally displaced women experienced sexual abuse from men fighting in that country's conflict (1991–2002). In Rwanda, 250,000 to 300,000 women were raped during the genocide there (most in 1994). (All figures are from http://www.stoprapenow.org)

Gender-based violence, however, extends beyond abusive sexual penetration. It also includes acts such as sexual mutilation, purposeful infection with HIV/AIDS and other sexually transmitted infections (STI), and forced impregnation, abortion, trafficking, and prostitution. While many of these acts constitute war crimes under the Geneva Conventions of 1948, the Torture Convention of 1984, and as defined by the Nuremberg Charter and the Treaty creating the International Criminal Court, they often go unreported and unprosecuted.

The words and actions of the deity horrify modern readers. A god who initiates a gang rape to calm fury and appease jealousy (Ezek 16:42) seems incomprehensible. And a deity who acts against one woman to warn others against similar behavior (23:48) appears not only angry but also abusive, not only vengeful but also dangerously violent. But in the context of an honor/shame culture, such a punishment renders a desolate cuckold, raging over how Israel took other lovers and left the husband behind (Hos 2:13), honorable again. It shows him as a man who acts to reassert control over his household.

For many contemporary readers, however, the functioning of the honor/shame system makes no sense. Ezekiel 23:35, for example, like the other texts, identifies the woman's adulterous actions as the source of the man's rage. Blaming one's wife and calling her a whore, however, begs the question of why her husband would want her back. Striking out against the other men, who within this structure challenge the masculinity and standing of the husband, appears more sensible. Why no suggestion of this solution emerges demands an examination of both the metaphorical language and the reality it conveys.

According to the metaphor, a woman who takes another lover or lovers shames a husband by impugning his masculinity. Her unfaithfulness implies not only his lack of ability to control her actions, but it also questions fundamental aspects of how he fulfills his role. Does he provide adequately, for instance? Reading through the metaphor, Israel's religious and political disloyalty diminishes YHWH and requires YHWH's actions to restore proper relational balance. Just as a suzerain must ensure that vassals stay in line in order to maintain his standing regionally, so also the deity needs fidelity in order to demonstrate his ability as a god.

But again, the real affront to a man or to YHWH comes from other men or from rival gods. Only they truly challenge the offended party by infringing upon his property and thereby asserting his weakness in the male leadership role. The functioning of power comes to the forefront here. Taking on male competitors and their families could cause local disruptions between households, clans, or tribes. Instead, blaming the woman and inflicting punishment on her strikes out at an easy target. In the world of the *bet av*, she lacks any reasonable alternatives for survival apart from her husband. The restoration of the husband's honor comes without community consequences—even if it might result in her death. Unfortunately, when applying the metaphor, the Israelites could not escape the devastation inflicted upon them by other nations. But blaming the people for their own downfall absents YHWH from any responsibility for their fate or from any requirement to assist them as a patron in defeating far superior military forces. The restoration of YHWH's honor comes at the expense of the weaker parties—states destroyed and blamed for their own downfall.

The pervasiveness of this metaphor over the course of time indicates its utility to the writers and the community. The writers of Isaiah and Jeremiah join Hosea and Ezekiel in using this idea. Its value comes through the

### An "Old Testament" versus a "New Testament" God

When confronting troubling texts about God in the Hebrew Bible, many Christians refuse to see the deity as violent or ethically challenged. A simple explanation allows this dismissal: God only acts in such a manner in the Old Testament. With the coming of the Christ, God suddenly reveals a transformed divine character, marked by love, mercy, and grace.

This approach to understanding God ignores the complexity of the presentation of the divine in both the Hebrew Bible and in the New Testament. The writers of Exodus, for example, present God as describing God's self as merciful, gracious, slow to anger, and filled with steadfast love (Exod 34:6–7). Even in Hosea readers encounter YHWH imagined as a parent teaching a child to walk, feeding the child, and holding the child up lovingly against a cheek (Hos 11:3–4). Even though each of these texts turns to the possibility of punishment, they nonetheless express gentle and caring qualities in the deity.

Similarly, the image of God in the New Testament includes some disturbing descriptions of the divine. Revelation, for instance, presents the great supper of God as featuring the flesh of kings, their armies, and their horses (Rev 19:17–18). And the book of Hebrews depicts a vengeful God whom people should fear (Heb 10:30–31) and whom the writers liken to a consuming fire (12:29).

To reduce the presentation of the deity in either group of texts to a caricature may meet the religious needs of the reader, but it fails to take seriously what the texts say about God. It also denigrates the Jewish tradition as primitive while promoting Christianity as a more evolved religion. Such a reading should not receive serious attention.

commonness of the *bet av* as a social arrangement. The audience understood the responsibilities of husbands and wives in this context and accepted them as normative. But the continued pleading of the prophets for the people to change their behavior might mean the metaphor lacked effectiveness as a rhetoric of change. Or at least the hearers rarely equated their actions within the cult or politics to the actions of an adulterous wife. By contrast, when considering the metaphor as rejecting the claim of the deity's failure, it likely communicated clearly about the Israelites' responsibility for the downfall of the states of Israel and Judah. After all, a husband's acting decisively to restore his honor, even at the expense of the life of his wife, falls within the acceptable practices of those men to whom this text speaks.

*YHWH the King and the Divine Assembly*

The book of Isaiah describes YHWH as present in the Temple (Isa 6:1–4). As imagined in the text, the deity sits on a throne, wearing a robe that fills the Temple, and <u>seraphim</u> in attendance sing praises. The sound shakes the

### seraphim

Seraphim are celestial beings. The word *seraph* comes from the Hebrew verbal root "to burn." Numbers 21:6 depicts them as fiery serpents.

foundations of the building, and smoke fills the entire area. This picture of YHWH as an enthroned king served as a primary image for the divine. Within the ancient Near East, no other metaphor spoke as effectively to the authority wielded by the divine. Kings served as loci of power—the center around which military, civil, and religious control all moved. Imagining God enacting this role meant placing the deity in the highest office known in the human community. But this location in an earthly position did not diminish the standing of the divine. Given the distance of the king from the average person, the position and all that attended it retained a certain mystery appropriate to thinking about God.

Descriptions of the divine court, like the throne room of a human king, include others in attendance. While the writers of Isaiah envision an angelic entourage, 1 Kgs 22 presents Micaiah ben Imlah describing God as surrounded by the host of heaven (1 Kgs 22:19). In this case, as in others, "host" receives mention in the singular and probably originally related to celestial bodies. For example, in Deut 4:19 the writer mentions the sun, moon, and stars as part of this heavenly host before discouraging their worship (see also Deut 17:3; Isa 24:21–23; Jer 8:2). Other texts, such as 2 Kgs 17:16; 21:3, 5; 23:4; and perhaps Zeph 1:5, indicate the host functioning as an object of praise in association with the veneration of Baal and Asherah.

Worship of astral bodies certainly existed throughout the region. Deities ruled over these objects and thereby demonstrated their ability to manipulate the cosmic order. God as positioned in and in control of the heavenly sphere appears primary in many biblical texts; indeed, God is pictured as king over all of the created order (see also Job 38:7; Pss 29; 89:5–18). Such demonstrations of a deity's authority made a strong case that the deity deserved adoration and praise. As Ps 148 states in its opening, YHWH as king basks in the devoted attentions of angels, the host, and celestial entities.

## God Alone as King

Some biblical material about the development of the state indicates opposition to crowning an earthly ruler. At least part of the contentiousness, according to 1 Sam, rests on the fear that anointing a human king displaces God from that position. First Samuel 8:7, for example, relates a purported conversation between God and the prophet Samuel in which God claims the people who request a king have rejected God, not Samuel (see also 1 Sam 10:17–19).

One attempt to blunt the apparent displacement of God comes in language describing both kings David and Hezekiah. The use of the title "prince" (2 Sam 7:8; 2 Kgs 20:4–5; see also Isa 9:6; Jer 30:21; Ezek 12:10) implies that God remains in the role of king and that the earthly monarch functions in a lesser role. Being a prince, however, requires a father-son relationship. Psalm 2, a hymn celebrating the enthronement of a king (see chapter 11 for more commentary on this psalm), holds open that possibility with words of God telling the chosen monarch that he is the begotten son of the deity (Ps 2:7).

This "host" also relates to one of the more common designations for the deity: "YHWH *tsebaoth*," or "YHWH of hosts/armies" (see also "God of hosts" in 1 Kgs 19:10, 14; Ps 80:7, 14). Note here the plural instead of the singular. First Samuel 17:45 helps us understand the reference. In his battle with Goliath, the writers show David expressing his confidence by claiming that he represents the Lord of hosts, who happens also to be the God of the armies of Israel. Just as a king stakes a claim based on military might, so also God rules as king and heads a mighty army.

In the prophets, "YHWH of hosts" designates not only a king but also takes on aspects of a warrior. This nuance expresses how YHWH uses the hosts as a king marching armies into battle to enact power. For example, to describe the fate of Babylon, the writers of Isaiah picture YHWH of hosts gathering forces to go to war. While part of the text identifies the army as consecrated persons—perhaps indicating human fighters—other parts of the passage envision a more cosmic battle (Isa 13:3–13). The heavens in this latter portion tremble along with the earth as the deity expresses anger. Joshua 5:13–15 affirms that possibility of the hosts as heavenly beings when the writers depict Joshua meeting face-to-face with one of the leaders of the hosts of YHWH and bowing down in worship on the holy ground. Similarly, Judg 5:20 speaks of the stars of heaven taking part in battle. In other places, the action described comes at the hand of human armies. Jeremiah states plainly that the Lord of hosts will bring destruction to Jerusalem at the hand of enemy swords (Jer 19:3, 7).

In addition to the host, other figures occupy this divine assembly. In 1 Kgs 22, Micaiah ben Imlah describes a spirit coming forward (1 Kgs 22:21) in YHWH's court and volunteering to deliver a message. Likewise, a collection of holy ones surround God in Deut 33:2–3; Job 5:1; and Zech 14:5. Most famously, a figure called "the satan" shows up in Job 1–2 and Zech 3. As depicted in Job, this character emerges as one among multiple sons of God. Angels also appear; Isa 6 describes seraphim attending the deity, while Ezek 10 mentions cherubim.

Members of the divine assembly conduct the business over which God as king presides. The scenes in Job and Zechariah in particular talk about the throne room as a divine court of law. As a judge, God the king asserts control

### The Divine Warrior

The image of the divine warrior also occurs in Ugaritic texts about Cisjordanian deities. Baal, for example, uses the elements of the storm as a weapon: "Seven lightning bolts he casts, Eight magazines of thunder; He brandishes a spear of lightning" ("A Hymn to Baal Enthroned" [KTU 1.101], translated in Frank Moore Cross, *Canaanite Myth and Hebrew Epic: Essays in the History of the Religion of Israel* [Cambridge, MA: Harvard University Press, 1973]). Those tools defeat enemies such as Yamm, or the sea. Likewise, Anat (Baal's consort) battles Mot, or death. Her victory requires use of swords, sieves, and fire.

over the public order. Just as the king commands armies from this place, so also the king commands justice.

The deity also dispatches messengers from this assembly to communicate the divine will. The angel of the Lord (or *malak YHWH*) most often assumes this function. As seen in Exod 3, the angel of the Lord comes to Moses in the burning bush (3:2) in order to encourage Moses to lead the people out of Egypt. Likewise, this messenger appears to Hagar after she runs away from Sarai and persuades her to return home (Gen 16:7ff.). The angel of the Lord also comes to Israel in Judg 2:1 to chastise the people for their disobedience.

An emissary of the divine, this messenger angel communicates the full authority of the deity. Hagar, for example, equates her experience of this messenger with seeing God; according to the text, she names the Lord who spoke to her "El-roi"—the God she sees (Gen 16:13). And the writers of Exod 3 use the terms "angel of the Lord," "Lord," and "God" interchangeably. The "angel of the Lord" appears in the flaming bush in Exod 3:2, followed by "the Lord" turning to Moses and "God" speaking in Exod 3:4. This emissary of the divine king exerts the monarch's influence by projecting his command in diverse situations and to various locales. The *malak YHWH*

### The Satan

For westerners steeped in Christian traditions, "Satan" conjures up images of the devil—Lucifer, Beelzebub, the prince of darkness. Whether depicted as a fallen angel or as the locus of all evil, Christian understandings associate Satan with the fires of hell and the embodiment of a state of separation from things divine. Likewise, Muslim readers know Satan, or Shaytaan, as the figure that tempts human beings to sin.

The Hebrew Bible, however, presents quite a different image. *Satan* as a common noun only appears in three biblical texts: Job 1–2; Zech 3; and 1 Chr 21. In both Job and Zechariah, the Hebrew uses the noun *satan* preceded by the definite article *ha*, meaning "the *satan*" or "the adversary." This title defines the *satan* as a functionary in the divine court; the adversary serves God as a prosecutor, bringing humans up on charges of sin.

Only 1 Chr 21:1 lacks the definite article and uses *Satan* as a proper name. But that occurrence proves complicated. Second Samuel 24:1 reports the anger of YHWH toward Israel, whereas 1 Chr 21:1 states that *Satan* acts against Israel. Both cases result in David's taking a census. The differences between the two demonstrate a transition in the idea of God over the course of time. The writers of Chronicles, who retold the story from Samuel, hesitated to attribute problematic behavior to the deity, and so they transformed God's anger into Satan.

Nothing in any of these texts indicates anything like western ideas of a devil presiding over a fiery hell. Indeed, at least until quite late, the Hebrew text lacks any idea of an afterlife, much less a place of eternal punishment. These ideas began to take shape in Judaism in the second and first centuries B.C.E. and the first century C.E. Contemporary readers thus need to use caution and read Ha-Satan in the Hebrew Bible as nothing more than a prosecutor in the divine court.

performs this function by conveying the presence of the enthroned deity and thus symbolically extending the boundaries of the divine assembly.

An interesting twist in this role comes in the writings about the prophets. The writers show prophets such as Micaiah ben Imlah, Isaiah, Ezekiel, and Zechariah claiming rights of access to the divine assembly. From this location, they acquire the word of God to communicate to kings, other leaders, and the people. God's speech in Jer 23:21–22 describes succinctly how their presence in this throne room imbues their words with authority:

> I did not send the prophets,
>     yet they ran;
> I did not speak to them,
>     yet they prophesied.
> But if they had stood in my council,
>     then they would have proclaimed my words to my people,
>  and they would have turned them from their evil way,
>     and from the evil of their doings.

The formulaic phrase "thus says the LORD" serves as an indicator of the divine authority carried in their words (see Ezek 2:4–5 for a clear example of linking the prophetic word to this phrase).

Placing the deity in the position of king logically proceeds from living in a land under monarchic rule. The image of the king and his palace provided ample material for the writers to think about the court of the divine, especially during periods when the temple or a cult site stood adjacent to the palace. Isaiah 6:1, for example, describes the hem of God's robe as filling the Temple. And since the prophets often worked for the deity and in service of the state simultaneously, the locale provided a natural link between the court of the king and the court of the divine.

But the loss of Jerusalem, Judah, the king, and the temple-palace complex challenged this picture of the patron deity as monarch. If defeat annulled the possibilities of a smaller monarchy like Judah expressing power, the status of its patron god would also decline. God as king, then, lost some of its persuasiveness as a metaphor with no nation to rule. Although the idea of a monarch as model did not disappear, the close association drawn between the deity and the house of David resulted in problems for sustaining this image. The effect of human events required a revisioning of the deity. To respond, the writers turned to a newer political model exerting influence—emperor.

## God as Emperor

The smoldering ruins of the Jerusalem Temple and the subjection of the Israelites to foreign powers looked like the defeat of the God of Israel. The idea of a patron deity fighting to secure the safety of the people and to preserve their land could no longer hold. Only a reimagining of this God as operating on a much grander scale and working toward a far greater purpose could salvage the idea of a relationship between God and whatever "Israel" was to become. A succession of Assyrian, Babylonian, and Persian emperors modeled a transnational system of governance that influenced the emerging portrait of the divine.

Throughout the course of the Hebrew Bible, the writers stress God's authority over nature. The miraculous events associated with the narrative of the exodus, for example, reveal the deity as in control of rivers, seas, all types of flying insects, storms, darkness, bodies, and ultimately death (Exod 7:14–12:32). As the writers tell the story, even Pharaoh's officials recognize God's ability to manipulate the elements; they declare at the end of the third plague the actions of God's finger (8:19)! This same God also intervenes in political events, particularly as a source of military strength. Joshua 10:42, for example, declares Joshua victorious because YHWH fights for Israel. But the deity as "emperor" possessed significantly increased ability to shape events on both earthly and cosmic levels.

An emperor wields greater authority over more territory and thus requires accouterments to demonstrate his ability to maintain control. In the case of God, additional layers of bureaucrats appeared ready to accomplish the divine will, and their presence resulted in less direct access to the divine. Such a retinue of officials, human and divine, not only generated increased activity around the emperor but also bolstered the impression of his importance. This model of rule translated into a stepped-up emphasis on the singularity of God when speaking of the deity.

Perhaps most important to the Israelites, the failure of their kings to secure the safety of the people could have implied the weakness of the patron deity as well. As a result, the writers needed to present God as exercising dominion over rulers, nations, and other gods who controlled them politically and militarily. In other words, the biblical writers characterized God in order to claim positions in the power dynamics of history that appeared directly contrary to political reality. Such a bold move kept the story of the Israelites alive in multiple geographic locations and reshaped the manner in which these communities conceptualized God.

The book of Ezekiel opens with a presentation of the presence of YHWH and offers a good place to explore this new look at the deity. In this story, however, the prophet depicted stands not on the soil of Judah or Israel but on the banks of the river Chebar in Babylon (Ezek 1:1). And the vision describes not a static throne room but rather the chariot of God upon which an object appearing like a throne rests (1:26). The image of a ruler in his chariot occurred commonly in ancient Near Eastern iconography.

This divine chariot, however, incorporates some features distinct from typical royal chariots that speak also to the nature of the deity enthroned on it. Winged creatures with human forms and four faces—one each of a human, a lion, an ox, and an eagle—sit below to power the vehicle (1:6–12). These faces denote divine dominance over all aspects of the created order, given that they represent the highest ranking creatures in the realms of humanity, wild animals, domestic animals, and birds. The wheels of the vehicle, described as wheels within wheels (1:16), include tall rims filled with eyes (1:17), suggesting both motion and vision. The deity described as seated on this chariot possesses the ability to move in all four directions simultaneously (1:9), as well as the facility to monitor happenings all around with these multiple eyes. In this manner, the god the writers produce here resembles a figure of the region's emperors—majestic, mobile, and capable of keeping careful watch over the empire's holdings.

This image of YHWH clearly reconfigures the idea of a patron deity. The text implies that the prophet Ezekiel was taken into exile by the Babylonians with a group of prominent citizens and King Jehoiachin in 597 B.C.E. (1:1–2). Given the location of YHWH's dwelling place in the Temple in Jerusalem, one might expect that their removal from the city equates to removal from the presence of the divine. The writers of Ezekiel argue against such a view. In chapter 10, for example, the prophet sees this chariot-throne leaving a corrupted Temple through the east door (10:18–19). The disconnection of YHWH from Zion challenged a common perception about Jerusalem as the home of the divine and thus as an unconquerable city (see chapter 11). In Ezekiel, this deity moves where this deity will—even into the enemy territory of Babylon.

Mobility certainly presents YHWH as greater than the Temple and capable of dwelling outside of Jerusalem. But it does not offer any answers about the lack of a patron's ability to protect the city or the purported divine home. With the destruction of Jerusalem at the hands of invading armies and the annexation of the land by various empires, writers of texts such as Jeremiah, Ezekiel, Isa 40–55, Haggai, and Zechariah needed to defend YHWH against charges of weakness—and they took a rather brazen approach.

Jeremiah provides an interesting starting point. Instead of visualizing YHWH as fighting against all enemies on behalf of the Israelites, as claimed

---

### Omnipotence, Omniscience, and Omnipresence

In a creed adopted by Free Will Baptists in 1834, the section on God reads, in part, "The Scriptures teach that there is only one true and living God, who is a Spirit, self-existent, eternal, immutable, omnipresent, omniscient, omnipotent, independent, good, wise, holy, just, merciful; the Creator, Preserver, and Governor of the universe; the Redeemer, Saviour, Sanctifier, and Judge of men; and the only proper object of Divine worship." Such grand terms commonly express modern western ideas about the nature of the divine.

Hebrew as a language lacks such abstract words. Instead, it uses pictures of what happens in order to convey an idea. Recall from chapter 6 how Exod 4:14 says the "nose of the LORD burned against Moses" (authors' translation) to describe God's anger (see also Gen 30:2; Exod 32:19; Num 11:1). Likewise, images such as the chariot in Ezekiel serve the purpose of portraying in concrete terms an all-powerful, all-knowing, and all-present deity.

in stories such as the exodus, the writers imagined God as using Nebuchadnezzar, ruler of Babylon, to accomplish YHWH's judgment on the Israelites. Jeremiah 21:4–7, for example, says:

> Thus says the LORD, the God of Israel: I am going to turn back the weapons of war that are in your hands and with which you are fighting against the king of Babylon and against the Chaldeans who are besieging you outside the walls; and I will bring them together into the center of this city. I myself will fight against you with outstretched hand and mighty arm, in anger, in fury, and in great wrath. And I will strike down the inhabitants of this city, both human beings and animals; they shall die of a great pestilence. Afterward, says the LORD, I will give King Zedekiah of Judah, and his servants, and the people in this city—those who survive the pestilence, sword, and famine—into the hands of King Nebuchadrezzar of Babylon, into the hands of their enemies, into the hands of those who seek their lives. He shall strike them down with the edge of the sword; he shall not pity them, or spare them, or have compassion.

In other words, the hand and arm of YHWH that rescued the Israelites in Exodus becomes the invading Babylonian army here.

The twenty-seventh chapter of Jeremiah shows the writers pushing this line of thinking further (27:5–6). Nebuchadnezzar (the passage above uses a variant spelling) becomes YHWH's servant, and in this instance he joins figures such as Moses (Exod 14:31; Num 11:1; Josh 1:1; Mal 4:4), David (2 Sam 7:5; Isa 35:37; Jer 33:21; Ezek 34:23), and the people (Isa 41:8; Jer 30:10; Ezek 27:25) in that role. YHWH's imperial rule as the creator, and thus as the one in control of all things, grounds this claim.

The writers of Jeremiah blame the people's false worship (Jer 11:9–13; 17:1–4; 19:4–6), as do Ezekiel's writers (Ezek 6:1–7; 8:7–13), for YHWH's attack on the Israelites via Babylon. Covenant violation stands at the heart of the issue, and therein rests the brazenness of these writers. Political and military weakness gets erased by claims that the people's domination and suffering come, deservedly, from YHWH. That idea hearkens back to the deity as the offended head of the *bet av*. But what happens differently here comes in the assertion that YHWH does not fight against these enemy nations but rather co-opts their ability to dominate as a way to express divine power. The humiliating defeat of Israelite's deity by Nebuchadnezzar's army becomes not an act of the Babylonian ruler to extend his holdings, but the act of an angry god to punish a wayward people.

The writers of Isaiah 40–55 advance this line of thinking further with regard to the ruler Cyrus. Named God's "servant" in 44:26, "shepherd" in 44:28, and "anointed" (messiah) in 45:1, the text goes on to describe all of the actions that God performs for Cyrus to assure earthly dominance (see 44:1–4). While clearly acknowledging Cyrus's lack of relationship with, or even knowledge of, Israel's God, the writer nonetheless clearly states that the deity sponsors his victories and promotes his successes to serve the divine purpose. In this way, a defeated nation gets to redefine its status. The text presents this nation, which will be only a small cog in the Persian Empire, as powerful in actuality. The god of the exiles controls the emperor and works on their behalf. Cyrus receives credit for nothing; anything he achieves he owes to a deity he does not know.

What kind of God do the writers imagine making such a claim? The text of Isa 45 goes on to supply an answer: only one god exists (45:5–7). Israel's god no longer serves as one god among many; instead, a monotheistic ideal emerges. And if only a single divine entity exists, all of the things attributed to other deities now reside in the god of Israel. This god not only controls other kings but also the natural order—light and darkness—as well as something far more urgent to the lives of most people in that time, namely, good and evil (in the NRSV, "weal" and "woe"). Nothing humans know, the writer affirms, happens outside of this deity's will.

These images fit in well with the idea of God as an emperor deploying power. Like the suzerains of the past, a successful emperor relied on the

## The Hebrew Bible and the Cyrus Cylinder

Ezra 1:2–4 presents Cyrus as issuing the following edict:

> The LORD, the God of heaven, has given me all the kingdoms of the earth, and he has charged me to build him a house at Jerusalem in Judah. Any of those among you who are of his people—may their God be with them!—are now permitted to go up to Jerusalem in Judah, and rebuild the house of the LORD, the God of Israel—he is the God who is in Jerusalem; and let all survivors, in whatever place they reside, be assisted by the people of their place with silver and gold, with goods and with animals, besides freewill offerings for the house of God in Jerusalem.

Articulating Persian support for the reconstruction of the Temple, the edict declares that YHWH empowers Cyrus (see also Ezra 6:3–5).

The Cyrus Cylinder, discovered in 1879 in a Babylonian temple and now residing in the British Museum, relates Cyrus's perspective on these events. It spells out a similar imperial policy centered on support for local worship traditions:

> I am Kourosh [Cyrus], king of the world, great king, mighty king. . . . Now that I put the crown of kingdom of Persia [Iran], Babylon, and the nations of the four directions on the head with the help of [Ahura] Mazda, I announce that I will respect the traditions, customs, and religions of the nations of my empire and never let any of my governors and subordinates look down on or insult them while I am alive. . . . People are free to live in all regions and take up a job provided that they never violate others' rights.

Note how the biblical material subsumes Cyrus's policies and places them at the direction of YHWH. In this manner, the writers assert YHWH's control over political events shaping the lives of the Israelites and other peoples.

Shapour Suren-Pahlav, ed., "Cyrus [sic] Charter of Human Rights,"
http://www.iranchamber.com/history/cyrus/cyrus_charter.php.

loyalty of client states to secure power. As a result, this picture of a deity who parcels out work to local commanders—whether or not they know the emperor or have much of a personal stake in the success of the empire—accurately depicts the method of governance. Accomplishing the business of empire depends on a vast bureaucracy of officials and functionaries and the effective functioning of client states. Delegating authority allowed the emperor to intervene directly only when strictly necessary and yet to reap the benefits from the action of others.

When the divine emperor employs additional layers of intermediaries to conduct business, he concurrently withdraws far more from sight and reach. The scenes of the divine council again emerge as examples. In Zech 3, for instance, the "angel of the LORD" (rather than YHWH himself) and Ha-Satan come forward as the major actors in the court to debate the status of the priest Joshua. And the prophet, pictured in Isa 6 and 2 Kgs 19 as having unmediated access to the happenings in the throne room, now requires a guide to the process. Named "the angel who talked with me" in Zech 1:9, 13–14, 18, this being reveals the scene and, in most cases, assists in its interpretation. Similar passages appear in Daniel. Sometimes an unnamed heavenly being helps the human present to comprehend the visions described (7:15–16; 10:15–21). On other occasions, the angel Gabriel takes on the role of interpreter (8:15–16; 9:20–21).

The deity here reigns above a busy and active group of servants, but mostly remains out of sight and leaves the business of the divine court to the functionaries who accomplish its work. Ezekiel's chariot vision demonstrates the remoteness of this God:

> And above the dome over their heads there was something like a throne, in appearance like sapphire; and seated above the likeness of a throne was something that seemed like a human form. Upward from what appeared like the loins I saw something like gleaming amber, something that looked like fire enclosed all around; and downward from what looked like the loins I saw something that looked like fire, and there was a splendor all around. Like the bow in a cloud on a rainy day, such was the appearance of the splendor all around. (Ezek 1:26–28)

Note the nine uses of some form of the word "like." Description fails in large part due to distance. The writers can only pile modifier on modifier and conclude that this representation offers some semblance of the deity.

The insertion of space between the divine and human allows the writers to present God in a position of extraordinary power. No one can really see and thus no one can really know this deity, who is beyond human perception. Certainly other texts present God as unviewable. Moses asks, for example, to see the glory of God. Instead of viewing the face, however, Moses glimpses the deity's backside or goodness while shielded (Exod 33:17–23). Further, within the Temple, God dwelt in the Holy of Holies, separated off by a curtain and accessible only to the high priest one time per year (Exod

> ### The Strange Case of Esther
>
> Perhaps the most interesting case of divine distance comes in the book of Esther. There, in spite of a strong threat against the Judeans, God never appears. As the writers tell it, Esther and Mordecai must act to save their people. While the text includes mention of sackcloth and ashes for mourning (Esth 4:1–3) and fasting for strength (4:16–17), no prayers come forward and no divine intervention results. The Judeans here fight on their own behalf (9:5–6). If any God exists, the plight facing the people fails to provoke God to action.

30:10; Lev 16). But these cases spoke of God as present and yet hidden. The writers of Job go further, indicating that no one can locate this God (Job 37:23). The deity as imagined here resides apart from humanity—a situation that the character of Job himself alludes to by hoping to come to God's dwelling place (Job 23:3). Similarly, Isaiah concludes that no attempt to bring the divine closer can ultimately work in its assertion that YHWH uses heaven for a throne and earth for a footstool and cannot be limited to any house of human construction (Isa 66:1).

From this remote vantage point, the deity interacts with the human community quite differently. Just as emperors project their authority through edicts that communicate their will, God's presence also finds its revelation in words. As seen in chapter 12, the writers of Nehemiah describe Ezra as gathering the people, standing on a wooden platform, and reading the law aloud from early morning until midday (Neh 8). God's presence dwells with the people in the reading and interpreting of the divine word (8:8). In Job, the writers reveal the divine only in two wild whirlwinds of speech (Job 38:1–40:2 and 40:6–41:34). And this God speaks only of authority over all creation, refusing to respond to Job's human inquiries.

But even the divine in words sometimes remains obscure. The writers of Daniel show Daniel seeking to understand the outcome of the events he sees in a vision. The response he receives—to go away until the end because all things will remain secret (Dan 12:9)—offers no answers. God here refuses to reveal too much. An emperor (or a deity modeled on one) needs the aura of mystery. Too much familiarity reduces status by making the extraordinary appear ordinary and thus comprehensible.

## Conclusion

The deity encountered in the Hebrew Bible challenges us to consider the idea of power in an entirely different way. Readers might be tempted simply to declare, "In your hand are power and might, so that no one is able to withstand you" (2 Chr 20:6), or to say, "Once God has spoken; twice I have heard this: that power belongs to God" (Ps 62:11). But such easy pronouncements direct attention away from thinking about how power works.

Instead, the writers use what their environment offers to conceptualize God in positions from which power can be exercised. The divine character developed thus assumes names and characteristics of Cisjordanian deities. Likewise, the nature and actions of God borrow images from the social and political world, where the Israelites see power in play. Reading God as a character requires constantly shifting conceptions of the divine, because when the ideas about God fail the needs of their audience, the writers simply remake the deity to reflect the new power dynamic. And therein power circulates.

| | |
|---|---|
| **Suggested Biblical Readings** | Exodus 3:1–15 <br> Ezekiel 1–3, 16 <br> Hosea 1–3 <br> Nahum 1:1–5 |

**Discussion Questions**

1. Write your own description of what the word "god" means. Does it reflect a nontheistic or a theistic understanding? If theistic, is it monotheistic or henotheistic? Or do you see elements of monolatry in your understanding?
2. Consider how the writers of the Hebrew Bible used descriptions of a deity common in the Cisjordan to describe Israel's God while simultaneously instructing hearers not to worship other gods. Can you make sense of this contradiction? How?
3. List some metaphors used to describe the deity. How do they assist in understanding the nature or character of the divine? What kinds of limitations do you see in these metaphors?

**Suggestions for Further Reading**

DeMoor, Johannes C. *The Rise of Yahwism: The Roots of Israelite Monotheism.* Louvain, Belgium: Peeters, 1990.

Keel, Othmar, and Christoph Uelinger. *Gods, Goddesses, and Images of God in Ancient Israel.* Minneapolis: Fortress Press, 1998.

Smith, Mark S. *The Early History of God: Yahweh and Other Deities in Ancient Israel.* New York: Harper & Row, 1990.

Weems, Renita J. *Battered Love: Marriage, Sex, and Violence in the Hebrew Prophets.* Minneapolis: Fortress Press, 1995.

# 14. Considering Job

I read the book of Job last night, I don't think God comes out well in it.
—Virginia Woolf, "Letter to Lady Robert Cecil, 12 November 1922"

This textbook promised a diversity of approaches to the Hebrew Bible. So what better way to close than to consider the book of Job, a text that features a diversity of voices engaged in intense debate? This chapter does not resolve all the tensions that the book of Job opens. Rather, it provides a glimpse at the book from the various vantage points elaborated in the preceding chapters. This chapter asks two central questions: How does the book of Job construct its central character's identity? Where does it place this character in regard to power relations? After treating these topics, following the order in which they appear below, it offers a consideration of Job's restoration at the end of the story and ponders what that says about identity and power. Finally, a look at the way Job's "repentance" (42:1–6) forces readers to reconsider what they think of this character and the book that bears his name brings the chapter and the textbook to a close.

The book of Job follows a simple plot. One day, God points to God's "blameless and upright" servant Job, an unimaginably wealthy man (1:8). God's special prosecutor, Ha-Satan, claims that Job worships God because God has given him all this good stuff (1:9–10). They agree to a wager to see whether Job will abandon God if God takes away his wealth and health (1:12). So Job loses everything and ends up living on an ash heap (2:8). Three friends then come and attempt to determine why Job suffers (3:11). To them, these dire events look like punishment, so they blame some sin on Job's part. Job contradicts them and accuses God of attacking him despite his innocence. Job finally swears an oath that he has done nothing wrong, and demands a hearing before this God (Job 31). God responds from a whirlwind, but these responses focus on divine power and provide no clear answer to Job's plight (Job 38–41). Job then "repents," though what he regrets remains unclear (42:1–6). At the end, God restores Job, castigates Job's friends, and grants Job a long, blessed life (42:7–17).

The book of Job is a classic. It also ranks as one of the most difficult and troubling texts in the canon of western literature. Nothing here is simple. The book's central character suffers excruciating pain and, for his trouble, spends most of the book arguing with his friends about whether he deserves to be a boil-covered, ash heap–dwelling wreck of a man. One of the issues raised by the book, the question of innocent suffering, proves emotionally taxing. It seems like overkill to add Job's struggles to the daily flood of images and words attesting to the grotesque suffering of innocent people. The book's failure to provide a clear reply to the cries of its oppressed hero simply intensifies the frustration. Moreover, the dialogical pattern of the book is difficult: multiple voices counter one another, yell at one another, imagine different worlds. This text does not resolve easily; this story leaves a frustrating sting.

## Job: A Case of Identity Theft

When they [Job's friends] saw him from a distance, they did not recognize him, and they raised their voices and wept aloud. (2:12)

Chapter 3 of this book claimed that Exodus introduces Moses as a character with an uncertain identity. It then attempts to give Moses a stable identity but never quite succeeds. The authors of Job take a strongly different approach. They construct Job as a character with an extremely stable identity, then swiftly go about destroying it. By the book's second chapter, even Job's friends cannot recognize him! Both ways of telling a story show the import of these issues of identity. Exodus illustrates the importance of identity by having Moses develop one. The book of Job shows this importance by recording Job's struggle to regain his identity. The following briefly considers Job's identity by using the categories from the first section of this textbook: family, gender, body, ethnicity, and class.

### Family Man

The opening of the story presents Job as having an utterly stable identity. Job rules his *bet av* as the shining example of a patriarch. When readers first meet Job, he has seven sons and three daughters (1:2) and controls an immense amount of property (1:3–4). Each of his sons apparently has established his own *bet av*, but Job still treats his adult children as under his control. He presides over sacrifices, attempting to ensure that God will not judge them harshly for any sin they might have committed (1:5). In this act, Job also

**Fig. 14.1: William Blake's**
***Job and His Family***
*British artist William Blake focuses on the piety of Job and his family in this drawing. But Blake also captures Job's secure family position. Notice how only Job casts his eyes upward toward heaven, while all his children kneel and his wife clasps her hands in prayer. Job is clearly at the center. And the inclusion of the rising sun and setting moon nicely picks up on the stability of the cosmos, mirrored in the stable, pious family of Job.*

*(Collection of Robert N. Essick. Copyright © 2007 the William Blake Archive. Used with permission.)*

looks out for himself, since his own well-being, authority, and honor as patriarch depend on the well-being and moral rectitude of his children.

Recall that the *bet av* treated children differently than modern western cultures do. Children, at a certain level, simply provided one other way of measuring the prosperity of the *bet av*. So the book of Job lumps them in with Job's other possessions. When YHWH gives Ha-Satan power over all Job "has" (1:12), Ha-Satan dutifully goes out and arranges the destruction of Job's oxen, donkeys, and slaves (1:13–15), his sheep and slaves (1:16), his camels and slaves (1:17), and finally, his sons and daughters (1:18–19). While the placement of the children at the end of the list (and the mention of the children at the start of the list in 1:13) indicates their great importance, the story still classes them along with Job's other assets.

Job's wife also belongs to the *bet av*. But the book of Job expresses no interest in her response to the loss of her children and, in a real sense, her husband. She only gains a cameo role in the story when she suggests that Job should "curse God, and die" (2:9). Job dismisses his wife's comment as the blabbering of "any foolish woman" (2:10) and says little more about her. He mentions that she finds him repellent (19:17), and he uses her in the oath he swears to defend his integrity:

> If my heart has been enticed by a woman,
>     and I have lain in wait at my neighbor's door;
> then let my wife grind for another,
>     and let other men kneel over her.                    (31:9–10)

Job claims that if he has ever committed adultery (or perhaps even been tempted to commit adultery), then he should be punished by having his wife be used for other men's sexual gratification. The regulation of sexual relationships, vital for the continuing life of the *bet av*, appears here as Job projects his authority, as putative head of the household, to offer access to his wife's body. By this act, he defends his own position.

With the exception of his wife, the story renders Job bereft of most of the trappings of his life as head of a *bet av*. This loss removes a great deal of Job's established identity and his ability to control events and people around him. In Job 19:13–19, Job offers a veritable catalog of not so much the things, but the relationships, that God has taken away from him. He no longer enjoys the company of friends or the loyalty of servants. His family finds him loathsome. His age garners not respect but derision. This loss of status irritates Job greatly throughout his complaints.

### Job's wife

While the book of Job in the Masoretic Text lacks interest in Job's wife, the Septuagint includes a speech from her in which she focuses on the loss of their children and reveals that she has been working as a servant. Likewise, an early Jewish text (first century B.C.E. or C.E.), the *Testament of Job*, claims that Job's wife, whom it names Sitidos, hires herself out as a servant. According to this text, she dies before Job's restoration. Rabbinic traditions mention her death as well and add the detail that after his restoration Job marries Dinah, the daughter of Jacob. The early Christian writer John Chrysostom (ca. 400 C.E.) was less fond of Job's wife, claiming that God allowed her to live as a way to punish Job further.

### Job bereft

Job's loss of his children and his accompanying loss of identity reflect a possible meaning of Job's name. The Hebrew *Iyyov* could be related to the phrase *ey av*, meaning "Where is the father?"

### A Redeemer for Job?

Christian readers frequently take the *goel* in Job 19:25 as a "Redeemer" and thus see Job professing faith in (or at least anticipating) Christ. In addition, some Christians see Job's claim in 19:26 that he would see God "in my flesh" after "my skin has been thus destroyed" as evidence of a belief in a bodily resurrection. This interpretation appears in the aria "I Know That My Redeemer Liveth" from Handel's *Messiah*, which combines the King James Version of this passage ("I know that my Redeemer liveth, and that He shall stand at the latter day upon the earth. And though worms destroy this body, yet in my flesh shall I see God") with a selection from the New Testament ("For now is Christ risen from the dead, and become the firstfruits of them that slept" [1 Cor 15:20]).

But these interpretations are hardly certain: the Hebrew here is exceedingly obscure. The text reads literally something like this: "And I know my *goel* is living and after upon dust he will stand. And after my skin they cut this and from my flesh I will see Eloah [a name for God]." Biblical scholar H. H. Rowley, commenting on verse 26, claims that "the text of this verse is so difficult, and any convincing reconstruction is so unlikely, that it seems best not to attempt it" (*Job* [New Century Bible; Grand Rapids: Wm. B. Eerdmans Publishing Co., 1980], 140).

Interestingly, Job moves on in chapter 19 to conjure the *bet av* again, threatening God with the appearance of a *goel*. This *goel* was a "redeemer" who was to protect the interests of the head of the *bet av*, in this case Job, when he was under threat:

> For I know that my *goel* lives,
>     and that at the last he will stand upon the earth;
> and after my skin has been thus destroyed,
>     then in my flesh I shall see God.     (19:25–26)

The *goel* here will defend Job against God and ensure that Job will get what he wants: an audience with God that will vindicate him.

Here Job makes two interesting claims about the *bet av*. First, his *goel* will face off against God. This assumption places God as the head of the *bet av* who has harmed the *goel*'s relation, namely, Job. So God appears in the role of patriarch. The *bet av* serves as a source of identity for both Job and God. Second, Job, in an act of desperation, calls upon the identity he has lost. From the ashes of his *bet av*, he conjures up his *goel*. He looks to a system now destroyed—at least for him—to reconfirm his identity.

*Man's Man*

As noted in chapter 5, the Hebrew Bible constructs both femininity and masculinity. Since male characters dominate the book of Job, little information on femininity appears. Job's encounter with his wife implies that women tend toward foolishness (2:10). Job's wife here might also fall into the general category of "temptress," since she tries to persuade Job to take an action that would make God lose the bet with Ha-Satan (1:11; 2:5, 9). And

Job explicitly mentions women as a temptation in his oath (31:1–4, 9–12). But there is little else concerning femininity in the book of Job.

The text, however, emphasizes the vital role of masculinity in developing Job's identity. At the start of the book, Job is clearly masculine. Ten children demonstrate his sexual activity and his fertility. Later in his story, Job describes the virility that formerly marked his life: "My glory was fresh with me, and my bow ever new in my hand" (29:20). Here the "bow" serves as a euphemism for potency, especially male sexual potency. Being able to shoot swift arrows from a newly strung bow speaks to Job's ability to behave like a powerful *man*.

But now Job is less of a man and blames God for this loss. Job uses two images to describe the divine assault on his masculinity. First, he claims that God has physically attacked him, besting him in a street fight, a public demonstration of strength (30:18–19). Here his strength, a marker of masculinity, is clearly at issue. Job does not possess the brute force needed to avoid his fate.

Second, Job describes his loss of virility at the hands of God: "Because God has loosed my bowstring and humbled me, they [the rabble] have cast off restraint in my presence" (30:11). As in Job 29:20, the "bow" relates to male potency. By loosening Job's bowstring, God removes Job's ability to shoot arrows, to penetrate. But Job claims that God moves beyond that by "humbling" him, using the verb *anah* (humiliate) to describe God's action toward him. This word often refers to acts that modern readers label rape or humiliation through penetration (see Judg 19:24 and 20:5 and compare the intended humiliation in Gen 19:4–11). Job cannot penetrate, but finds himself penetrated by God (cf. Jer 20:7). So this text suggests that Job considers himself forcibly "rebranded" as a penetratee, not a penetrator.

Job sees God abusing him and facilitating abuse by others—the poor whom Job calls "rabble." Job wants to claim an identity over against these

## The Meaning of Penetration

In Job 30:11 the social meaning of penetration, especially the penetration of one male by another, comes to the fore. As an act, it has no set social meaning; its significance depends on a variety of societal understandings. Some ancient cultures associated masculinity with penetration and femininity with being penetrated. Thus, to be penetrated made one "feminine." Other ancient peoples tended to identify gender identities less as "masculine" and "feminine" and more as "penetrator" (active) and "penetratee" (passive). So if a person accustomed to being the penetrator assumed the role of penetratee, a severe dislocation of identity ensued.

In either way of understanding penetration, a forcibly penetrated male would suffer a disturbance of gender identity and would, in addition, be shamed by such a disturbance. This shaming helps explain the common practice in the ancient Near East of sexually humiliating defeated enemy soldiers, sometimes through rape (for a milder instance of sexually humiliating an enemy in the Hebrew Bible, see 2 Sam 10:4–5). Rape would serve to "rebrand" the soldier as "feminine" or as "passive."

people, who according to him are a "senseless disreputable brood" (30:8), lacking in wisdom. For Job, foolishness marks the feminine (recall his dismissal of his wife in 2:9–10). Job's verbal attack on this "rabble" (30:1–8, 12) represents an attempt to secure his identity over against these "unmen," these fools who should not count as men.

But they follow God's lead and physically attack Job (30:12–13). Although considered less than men due to their foolishness, they vaunt themselves over one who should be their better, who should be the "real man" in the scene. But they know a weak "man" when they see one. Job's attempts to restore his masculine identity come to naught.

## Disembodied Man

At the start of the story, Job offers sacrifices on behalf of his children (Job 1:5). Recall that Leviticus allows only those males who possess defect-free bodies to preside over sacrifices. So the story implies that Job possesses a priestly body, one free of flaw or defect. He is the "perfect" man (1:1).

This perfect body attracts the attention of the wagerers in heaven. When taking Job's possessions does not work, Ha-Satan suggests that Job's body holds the key to deciding the victor in the wager with God (2:4–5) and chooses boils as a fitting test. These "loathsome sores" (2:7) break out all over Job. More than painful and disgusting, these boils indicate that the boundaries of Job's body are breaking down. Job literally cannot control his body's "edges." His body oozes and leaks. Even scraping the boils cannot keep his body intact (2:8). Losing its ability to define Job's identity, his body instead represents Job's disordered state.

Job's lack of bodily boundaries, as well as physical and psychic pain, make him beg to go to Sheol. Death would end Job's pain, extinguishing what was left of his identity. Job would finally be disembodied. While he does not seem to consider suicide, he does occasionally wish for death (e.g., 7:15–16).

But at other points Job hangs on to life, simply to keep defending his integrity, to keep arguing with his friends and with God. If anyone ends this debate, it will be God, not Job. Indeed, although Job expects that God will end the discussion by killing him, he will not abandon the conversation (13:13–15). He wants to maintain his bodily identity, even as excruciating

---

### perfect

Many translations of Job 1:1 take the Hebrew word *tam* to mean "blameless" (NRSV, NIV). But the word also carries with it the sense of "complete" or "perfect" (KJV). Biblical scholars usually understand this sense of "completeness" to refer to Job's moral or spiritual integrity. But *tam* here may at least hint at Job's bodily integrity. In Ps 73:4, the NRSV translates *tam* as "sound," as it describes bodies in that text. And the male lover in the Song of Songs twice describes his beloved as "my dove, my perfect one [*tamati*]" (5:2; 6:9), using a feminine form of *tam*. It is unlikely that the singer here intends to praise her spiritual integrity.

**Fig. 14.2: William Blake's** *Job's Despair*
*In this rendering, Blake does not focus on the sorry state of Job's body but follows the book of Job's lead, as it does not spend a great deal of time discussing Job's bodily ailments. Blake represents Job's disordered state through the threatening cloud in the background and through the mushrooms and thorns found in the lower border.*
*(Collection of Robert N. Essick. Copyright © 2007 the William Blake Archive. Used with permission.)*

pain makes choosing death an understandable option. It seems the rigorous discussion of the theological issues at hand trumps Job's pain and sickness, reasonable excuses to seek death.

*The Other Man*

Regarding ethnic identity, the book of Job makes two moves that may seem odd. First, the text introduces Job as an <u>outsider</u>, a non-Israelite. Even before

### outsider

Job's outsider status connects to another possible meaning for the name *Iyyov*. Here it may relate to the Hebrew word *oyev*, meaning "enemy."

revealing Job's name, the text reports that he comes from the land of Uz. And the rest of the cast of characters is likewise non-Israelite: Eliphaz (a Temanite), Bildad (a Shuhite), Zophar (a Naamathite), and Elihu (a Buzite of the family of Ram). Strangely, in this piece of Israelite literature, no Israelite characters appear.

Given both the international focus of wisdom thinking and the universal problem of human suffering, it perhaps makes perfect sense to examine a major problem in wisdom through an international cast of characters. But it may also be that Job's status as "Other" allows him indirectly to raise problematic issues in Israelite covenant thought, since he is not a party to the covenant. For example, Deuteronomy, following the line of ancient Near Eastern suzerainty treaties, claims that Israel would prosper (be blessed) if they kept the covenant's strictures, while suffering (curses) awaited if they violated the rules of their suzerain, YHWH. This arrangement sounds similar to the way Job and his friends imagine the world to operate: there is an order to the universe that blesses the upright and punishes the disorderly. So Job as outsider can remain a "thought experiment," allowing indirect discussion and critique of national covenant thinking as well as a more direct discussion and critique of international wisdom categories.

The second odd aspect of the book of Job's treatment of ethnicity comes in the authors' lack of interest in destroying Job's ethnic identity. The authors remove other markers of identity (family, gender, body, and class) and then have Job spend the rest of the book literally trying to find himself. But they do not problematize Job's ethnicity in the story; after the introduction they never again mention his ethnic origins.

The only hint of a shift in Job's ethnic status comes in his mention of resident aliens, "inside-outsiders." Job, in his "former life," welcomed such people (31:32). These aliens would have depended upon Job as patron in the larger Uzite culture. In his "present" life, Job himself has become an "inside-outsider." The women who formerly served in his house now view *him* as a

## Where Are Job and His Friends From?

Uz appears as a place name in only three places in the Hebrew Bible (Job 1:1; Lam 4:21; Jer 25:20). In addition, several genealogies mention men named Uz (Gen 10:23; 22:21; 36:28; 1 Chr 1:17, 42). These occurrences suggest several possibilities for Uz's location: northwest Arabia near Edom, Edom itself, the Negev, the region of Aram. The Hebrew Bible associates Eliphaz's people of origin, the Temanites, with the Edomites (Jer 49:7). So the Temanites probably hailed from northwest Arabia near Edom. But the Hebrew Bible (and other ancient sources) fails to provide evidence for the geographic origins of Job's other friends. Perhaps the authors did not have precise geographical settings in mind but instead wished to show that these "others" are purely imaginary, that they are extremely "other." A contemporary author writing Job, then, could accomplish the same goal by claiming that Job came from Oz, not Uz!

foreigner (19:15). Job, once the defender of resident aliens, would now need a defender of his own. The book of Job, however, does not develop this possible shift in Job's ethnic identity beyond this brief mention.

*Rich Man, Poor Man*     At the beginning, the story presents Job as a man of extreme wealth. One cannot imagine a better picture of stability and security. His immense possessions make him "the greatest of all the people of the east" (1:3). In his reflection upon his old life, he explicitly links his wealth with his status in the community:

> Oh, that I were as in the months of old,
>     as in the days when God watched over me,
> . . . . . . . . . . . . . . . . . . . . . . . . . . . . . . . . . . .
> when my steps were washed with milk,
>     and the rock poured out for me streams of oil!
> When I went out to the gate of the city,
>     when I took my seat in the square,
> the young men saw me and withdrew,
>     and the aged rose up and stood;
> the nobles refrained from talking,
>     and laid their hands on their mouths;
> the voices of princes were hushed,
>     and their tongues stuck to the roof of their mouths.     (29:2, 6–10)

Job's steps being washed with milk indicates his possession of a huge dairy herd. The rock pouring out oil shows that Job owns olive groves as well as a press to extract oil from the olives they produce. The story pictures Job as drawing his position of honor, his identity, from these possessions. Indeed, they grant him such a strong identity, such preeminence, that other men naturally shut up in his presence.

While tying his own identity to wealth, Job denies putting his faith in riches. In addition, his wealth does not lead him to adopt nonstandard worship practices or lead him to venerate the sun and the moon (31:24–28). So Job's possessions (and by extension anyone's possessions) are an acceptable blessing from a benevolent God. This move on Job's part justifies his class status.

But when his stable identity as a wealthy landowner vanishes, Job again tries desperately to claim a marker of an identity now gone. He argues that the memory of his wealth and his acts of charity should at least garner some respect. But now he finds himself an object of disdain, especially by the poor (30:1). He lashes out at them as fools who cannot recognize that Job, while poor, should still receive a modicum of honor (30:1–8). In doing so, Job conjures up the "old days" as an attempt to secure his identity on the basis of the rules in place then. Job cannot admit that the world has changed, that his former honor has been effaced, that his works of charity have been cast into a land beyond memory.

Job suffers because he loses so much wealth and its honor. The book of Job implies that the poor suffer less. Never possessing much of anything, they certainly never hear the praise of the community that Job aches to hear again (29:11–13). The writers position the character of Job as swinging wildly between class extremes to convey the extraordinary nature of his fall. In doing this, they once again show the dissolution of Job's identity.

*Conclusion*

The book of Job demonstrates the vitality of identity by destroying its main character's identity. Job's sufferings are not merely painful; they also testify to Job's loss of existence. By the time his friends arrive, nothing much remains of Job. But the book also shows Job desperately attempting to project his former self. He imagines his dissolved *bet av* will yet provide a *goel* to secure his family status. He claims foolish men should still respect his utterly compromised masculinity. He refuses to abandon his oozing, disordered body. He asserts class status on the basis of his vanished wealth. But all these moves represent only wishful thinking; Job's identity has disintegrated.

## Job: Power Plays

Am I [Job] the Sea or the Dragon,
    that you [God] set a guard over me?
. . . . . . . . . . . . . . . . . . . . . . . . . . . . . . .
What are human beings, that you make so much of them,
    that you set your mind on them,
visit them every morning,
    test them every moment?                    (Job 7:12, 17–18)

David, exemplar for power in the Hebrew Bible, comes across as nothing if not a skillful negotiator, always locating himself advantageously in and among other powerful figures. The stories about David present him as largely "in charge" of these processes. This presentation makes him quite the hero but also (at some level) less believable as a character. Who gets to structure every contest so it goes their way?

Job would also seem to be an unbelievable character in some ways. Few people have ever met someone who is so blameless and upright. But while points of Job's identity are "over the top," his relation to power lacks the control imagined with David. The whole narrative concerns a wager made between two powerful figures: God and Ha-Satan. In other words, the book of Job defines its title character in a web of power relations. As a character, Job is very much a product of these power plays.

The book of Job shows great interest in the ways power operates, both in its characterization of God and in the various ways it challenges readers to think through ideologies and their expressions. This section looks at how each of the ways of presenting power previously examined intersect with the book of Job. The state presents power as operating in and through the person of the monarch, but in the case of Job the monarch in question is God. The book of Job constructs Job as a subject of God's kingdom and as subject to God's court of law.

But power involves more than the organization of politics. Power also involves the ways societies create meaning through ideologies. The book of Job addresses many of the various ideologies in the Hebrew Bible already considered. And power also involves how ideologies are expressed in society, namely, through media. In the book of Job, nature serves as a medium for ideological contestations. Finally, in the Hebrew Bible, one cannot speak of power without speaking of God, whom the text understands to occupy a central place in the exercise of power in the cosmos. The book of Job, of all the books in the Hebrew Bible, is most aware of the implications of divine power, from the arbitrary wager at its start to the mystifying blast from the whirlwind at its end.

## Living in God's Kingdom

The book of Job spends little time on the nuts and bolts of political organization. But the general absence of a royal government in the story does not mean that the story lacks an interest in the display of political power. Rather, the book places God as king and Job as a royal subject. And in the book's understanding of the monarchy, two major functions of government emerge: God's "royal court" (how God administers the divine government in general), and God's "court of law" (how God as king administers justice in particular).

### God's Royal Court

The story of Job begins with a series of scenes from God's throne room. Pictured as a monarch surrounded by his council, God calls a meeting for some purpose (Job 1:6). This meeting includes the council's special prosecutor, Ha-Satan. The discussion between God and Ha-Satan revolves around the question of Job's motivations. Ha-Satan poses a political question: Is the loyalty of a subject to the king simply a result of the king's beneficence? (1:9). If the king changes policy, will there be a revolt? Will the subject curse the king? God, as king, must know whether subjects will remain loyal; thus, the test begins.

In the course of the discussion with Ha-Satan, God raises a second political point. God admits to exercising royal power arbitrarily:

> The LORD said to Ha-Satan, "Have you considered my servant Job? There is no one like him on the earth, a blameless and upright man who fears God and turns away from evil. He still persists in his integrity, although you incited me against him, to destroy him *for no reason*." (2:3)

The picture here looks quite similar to the way the Hebrew Bible often describes emperors. Ahasuerus in Esther (1:21–22; 2:14, 17–18; 5:3, 6; 6:10;

7:2, 7–10; 8:2), the pharaohs in Genesis and Exodus (Gen 40:20–22; Exod 7:13; 8:15, 19, 32; 9:7, 34–35), and the various Persian emperors in Ezra and Nehemiah (Ezra 1:1–8; 4:17–22; 6:1–12; 7:12–26; Neh 2:1–8) favor whom they will favor and can change their minds quickly, with dire effects.

Just as arbitrary emperors raise issues of justice for subject peoples, when God acts "for no reason," God inevitably raises questions regarding divine justice. The question remains whether the book of Job, especially through its construction of Job's responses, ratifies this notion of divine and royal power. Will Job curse God as a king who violates standards of justice? Or will Job accept this royal power as a given, implicitly supporting the imperial status quo?

### God's Court of Law

Raising the question of divine justice locates readers in one particular place: God's court of law. The royal court in Judah made the king the guarantor of justice by co-opting the work of local courts that functioned "in the gate" (e.g., the story of Solomon and the two prostitutes in 1 Kgs 3:16–28). The book of Job frequently conjures the image of the divine court of law, most particularly in Job's incessant requests for a hearing before God the judge.

In many places in the book, Job assumes that he will gain a hearing with this royal figure, a hearing that will work in Job's favor: "There an upright person could reason with him, and I should be acquitted forever by my judge" (23:7). But Job imagines elsewhere that in this hearing before God the judge, God will also serve as prosecutor. In this situation the court proceedings are unlikely to result in his vindication:

> Though I am innocent, I cannot answer him;
>  I must appeal for mercy to my accuser.
> If I summoned him and he answered me,
>  I do not believe that he would listen to my voice.          (9:15–16)

So Job remains unsure whether God's court of law will act justly. This lack of certainty explains the book's somewhat contradictory portrayal of Job's attitude toward the divine court. The text pictures Job fulminating against God's lack of justice only in the context of repeated appeals for an audience with God as judge:

> Though I am innocent, my own mouth would condemn me;
>  though I am blameless, he [God] would prove me perverse
>  [in a court hearing].
> . . . . . . . . . . . . . . . . . . . . . . . . . . . . . . . . . . . . . . . . . . . . . . . . . . . . . .
> It is all one; therefore I say,
>  he destroys both the blameless and the wicked.
> When disaster brings sudden death,
>  he mocks at the calamity of the innocent.          (9:20, 22–23)

God's court of law is not necessarily a place where justice rules, yet it certainly provides a venue where God demonstrates power.

Job finally gets his day in court. And, much as Job expected, arbitrary power reigns. God treats Job to a massive display of royal power. God ignores the substance of Job's complaint, instead speaking at length about natural phenomena (38:4–38) and animals (38:39–39:30; 40:15–41:34). But how will Job respond to this mock hearing? At this point the text is not clear; Job's "repentance" reads ambiguously (42:1–6). So the question of royal power in Job must wait for a fuller treatment of Job's closing words.

*Thinking Through Job's Predicament: Ideological Approaches to Job*

Chapter 11 of this book argues that ideologies make a society possible by providing pictures of that society and of an individual's place within it. They make the ways power operates in and through society seem obvious and irrefutable. The book of Job relates in some sense to *three* of the four ideological complexes identified previously, exposing these ideological understandings to sharp critique. (The King-Zion complex does not appear as a focal concern in the book. A few places, such as Job 26:5–14, use imagery that fits with the mythological justification of royal and cultic power. But in general the book of Job shows no interest in the functioning of the cult or its relationship to the monarchy.)

### Job and the Sage-Order Complex

Since the book of Job originated in the Israelite wisdom tradition, readers might expect it to support the Sage-Order ideology, which affirms that there is an order to the world that supports living in certain hierarchical arrangements, especially those placing king above subject and father above children. Job's friends take the position that this order, sponsored by God, rewards the righteous and curses the wicked. Job's disordered state provides evidence of Job's inability to relate positively to God. So, Bildad suggests, Job needs to make amends and find his place in the divine order:

> If you will seek God
>    and make supplication to the Almighty,
> if you are pure and upright,
>    surely then he will rouse himself for you
>    and restore to you your rightful place.          (8:5–6)

But Bildad's ideology cannot apply to Job. Both the narrator and God describe Job as "upright" (1:1, 8), and upright people should not suffer like Job suffers. Job's situation as a suffering righteous man threatens his friends' (and wisdom's) understanding of the way the world really operates. Job has done everything possible to fit into the order of the world, yet he suffers more than the wicked. One is thus tempted to see Job as a piece of data that forces a reevaluation of the wisdom paradigm.

But Job's story produces no paradigm shift for wisdom. Critiquing the wisdom perspective is not necessarily the same thing as overthrowing it or discarding it. Job himself spends most of the book assuming that the world really does operate in an orderly fashion and ought not to curse him, an obviously righteous man (Job 31). In other words, Job continues to hold in his mind the picture of society that the wisdom ideology provides: the order of the world benefits the pious and punishes the wicked. A large part of Job's pain comes from his inability to reconcile the wisdom ideology that undergirds how he understands the world to his life of deep, seemingly endless suffering.

### Job and the Sinai-Nation Complex

The friends in the book of Job may not only be understood as typical sages, but they also appear similar to proponents of the Sinai-Nation ideological complex. Those persons supporting this complex encouraged the community to understand its own behavior as part of its relationship to YHWH. For the community to continue to exist, it must obey certain stipulations outlined in the law codes. Vassals must keep the treaty, else the suzerain will visit destruction upon them.

This general attitude appears in the book of Job, though with two major differences at the start. First, the book of Job concerns itself not with a community but rather with an individual (cf. Ezek 18). The writers of the book of Job focus on the circumstances of this one man, while the writers of Deuteronomy, in contrast, keep the nation as a whole in view.

Second, the book of Job lacks explicit interest in the actual stipulations seen in Deuteronomy and other covenant legislation. When Job swears an oath defending his righteous conduct (Job 31), he does not cite previously existing law codes to say, in essence, "I have kept the law," and on that basis demand just recompense. Instead, Job lists various actions he has not done, actions that, at most, allude to the covenant traditions. And when he does swear the oath, he also may indirectly refer to the covenant traditions in his use of curses as enforcement (31:21–22). So the book of Job echoes the covenant ideology in Job's particular selection of offenses and in the curse mechanism of enforcement. The book of Job shares ideological elements with the Sinai-Nation complex but does not express them in as thorough a way as it does elements of the Sage-Order complex.

The book of Job challenges the Sinai-Nation ideological complex by exposing its assumptions to critique. First, Job's experience raises the question of whether God has, in Israel's case, failed to apply fairly the curses that enforce the covenant. God has inflicted unjustified extreme sufferings upon Job. Job has maintained an exemplary life yet suffers like the worst sinner imaginable. If God cannot and will not enforce punishments fairly on Job, then the question arises whether God can and will enforce covenantal punishments fairly on Israel.

Second, Ha-Satan has claimed that Job's maintenance of a solid relationship with God simply arises from his blessed existence. According to Ha-Satan, Job's devotion to God is hardly unmotivated. It is grounded in the divine provision of blessings. This point of view also raises issues in

## Job's Oath and the Covenant in Deuteronomy

In his oath in chapter 31, Job mentions items that bear some relation to the stipulations of the covenant, especially in Deuteronomy. The allusions here are often fairly general, but they show how the book of Job might be in some relationship to covenant ideology.

| Action Job claims to have avoided | Compare to |
| --- | --- |
| Looking on a virgin—desire (v. 1) | Deut 5:21 |
| Falsity/deceit (v. 5) | Deut 5:20 |
| Adultery (v. 9) | Deut 5:18 |
| Rejecting the cause of his slaves (v. 13) | Deut 15:12–18; 23:15–16 |
| Withholding care from the poor, widows, and orphans (v. 16) | Deut 15:7–11; 24:14–22; 27:19 |
| Withholding clothing from the poor (v. 19) | Deut 24:12–13, 17 |
| Raising a hand against the orphan (v. 21) | Deut 24:17–22 |
| Trusting in gold and wealth (v. 24) | Deut 7:25; 8:11–14 |
| Worshiping the sun and moon (v. 26) | Deut 4:19; 17:3 |
| Rejoicing at the fall of enemies and cursing them (v. 29) | Deut 5:11 |
| Denying hospitality (v. 31) | Deut 10:18–19; 24:17–22; 27:19 |
| Concealed/secret sin (v. 33) | Deut 27:15–26 |
| Alienating land from its rightful owner; murder (vv. 38–39) | Lev 25:8–34; Num 27:9–11 |

covenantal understanding. Does God's blessing of Israel, God's sometimes-loyal vassals, corrupt the system? Perhaps Israel, even at its most "faithful" moments, wants only land and security rather than the satisfactions of a pious life. If Israel the "adulteress" shows loyalty to whatever god provides grain, wine, and oil (Hos 2:8), perhaps God's blessings simply encourage this frankly cynical calculus.

Finally, God acts "for no reason" (2:3). If the power of the suzerain, God, is that arbitrary, any treaty with that suzerain, then, proves worthless. If God can act this way, no one can know for certain that God will link a particular cause ("covenant violation" or "stipulation observance") and a particular effect ("curse" or "blessing"). The book of Job raises the question of whether this capricious deity deserves trust. The book of Job's construction of the relationship between Job (the supposed vassal) and God (the supposed suzerain) thus threatens to "disconfirm" covenant ideology.

### Job and the Empire-Colony Complex

While the book of Job raises difficulties with the Sage-Order and Sinai-Nation complexes, its relationship to the Empire-Colony complex lacks the same critical edge. The local elite in Jerusalem in the Persian and Greek periods sought to negotiate their place between imperial authorities and the local populace. Life in Jerusalem in this period was not easy. The Persians and the Greeks exploited the region, drawing off resources and damaging the local economy. One may see the book of Job's focus on questions of suffering, especially of the innocent, as part of the elite's active interest in the power relations between colony and empire. In other words, the book of Job does not critique the Empire-Colony complex as much as show it in action, supporting collaboration with the empire.

Job complains at length about his undeserved suffering, yet he never receives a direct answer to his questions. Instead, he receives an essay on the accomplishments of the divine ruler (38:1–40:2; 40:6–41:34). God controls chaotic forces such as Behemoth and Leviathan. Humans, including Job on his ash heap, had best be thankful for whatever they get. Job's problems are, it seems, way down on the divine emperor's "to do" list. Job gets an audience with God but no promise of attention, much less a solution. This picture of God fits very well with the lived social situation of the elite in Jerusalem. Yehud was not all that important in the imperial system and undoubtedly suffered greatly under imperial rule. Yet imperial rule was simply a given. And the empire, like God, could act "for no reason," and no explanations would be forthcoming.

Yet the book of Job at least validates the act of complaint against unjust suffering. The narrator shows God affirming this protest (42:7) and attacking the friends' attempts to explain Job's suffering as somehow justified. So why would the elite in Jerusalem wish to affirm Job's outcry? Perhaps they wished to play Job themselves, reserving the right at least to speak out in troubled times. But perhaps they, as collaborators with the empire, realized that a certain amount of ineffectual speaking out actually helped maintain the overall stability of the region.

Recall that Job, in pleading with God for a hearing, still assumes God's ability to resolve Job's situation, as well as God's interest in doing so. From God's perspective, Job may complain about the divine king, but he remains languishing on the ash heap, debating his friends. He is much too busy discussing matters to raise an army to storm the divine council meeting! Now think of the elite of Jerusalem as analogous to Job. If they cry out to the emperor for redress, they assume that the emperor is able and willing to answer. And they choose to spend their time and effort in correspondence with the emperor; they do not conspire to leave the empire. The book of Job, while admitting that the divine and imperial orders may be arbitrary, refuses to opt out of them, maintaining relationships with God and empire.

*Expressing the Order of Job: Creation as Medium*

If "empire" is alive and well in Job, with its attendant assumptions about the emperor's power over subjects and about his ability to act in whatever way he so desires, what media serve God's exercise of power? For the King-Zion ideology, the Temple communicates royal power. There is no such obvious social institution in the book of Job that broadcasts its own ideological understandings.

But another "institution" does serve to mediate these varied ideological perspectives: creation itself. The book of Job makes frequent use of imagery from nature. Crocodiles, hippopotami, and all the rest embody a particular power structure: God's orderly reign (38:1–39:30). So for the authors of Job, experiencing nature was hardly <u>an experience of freedom</u>, an escape from power, but a way to find oneself in a particular power relationship. The book of Job encourages readers to look to the created order for guidance in developing understandings of how society is meant to operate and how to live in society.

Job's friends understand nature as a field on which God's benevolent justice is played out. Bildad insists, for example, that Job would understand his plight if he would only recall that just as plants die for lack of water, those persons who forget God will perish (8:11–13). And Eliphaz claims that if Job would accept divine discipline, he would relate to nature rightly: "For

---

### an experience of freedom

Contrast the book of Job's estimate of nature with that of Henry David Thoreau: "I wish to speak a word for Nature, for absolute freedom and wildness, as contrasted with a freedom and culture merely civil,—to regard man as an inhabitant, or a part and parcel of Nature, rather than a member of society."

"Walking," in *The Writings of Henry David Thoreau*, vol. 9 (Boston: Houghton Mifflin, 1893), 251.

---

### Understanding Nature Ideologically

The book of Job is hardly unique in assuming nature as a medium for expressing power relations. Here are two examples from western intellectual traditions. Most western thinkers in the medieval and early modern periods viewed nature as a "great chain of being." In this arrangement, God was the topmost link, with all other things ranked below: angels (spiritual beings), humans (mixtures of flesh and spirit), animals (living things that move), plants (living things that cannot move), and, finally, rocks. Within these broader groupings, individual humans, animals, plants, and rocks were similarly differentiated. More spiritual or rational humans (such as European kings) ranked above more flesh-oriented persons (serfs). The "great chain of being" was thus a grand unchanging hierarchy in which everything (and everyone) had a place. Nature expressed the very sociopolitical hierarchy in which one had to live.

From the mid-nineteenth century on, most western thinkers embraced a much less static view of nature, derived from Darwin's insights regarding natural selection. Nature "selects" the features of organisms that best fit the demands of that organism's environment. Individual species rise and fall based on how well they relate to their natural contexts. Such a logic fits very well with market capitalism, encouraging the person viewing nature to see a contest for survival in which the organism most fitted to the demands of the "market" of nature would succeed. So nature becomes a medium for a particular ideological stance, helping persons learn how the world works and what their place in it is.

you shall be in league with the stones of the field, and the wild animals shall be at peace with you" (5:23). Nature is a medium of divine power; studying nature leads one to submit to this power. And Job shares his friends' perspective on nature. Job himself learns from nature that divine power cannot be resisted (9:4–10).

While Job and his friends define their respective positions using creation as a medium, God uses nature imagery to describe the arbitrary power of the divine emperor in the speeches from the whirlwind. God chooses to use a naturally occurring, yet chaotic, phenomenon—the whirlwind—in addressing Job. These divine speeches underline what the friends and Job have already assumed: all of creation indicates divine power, from rainstorms (38:28), to goats and deer (39:1–4), to ostriches (39:13–18), to sea dragons (41:1–34).

*Picturing God's Power*      The book of Job characterizes God as king through the political locations of royal court and law court. But the relationship between God and power is more complicated than that image can allow. One question helps clarify the issues of divine character and power: Why does God bring up the subject of Job?

### Divine Self-Interest

> The LORD said to Satan, "Have you considered my servant Job? There is no one like him on the earth, a blameless and upright man who fears God and turns away from evil." (1:8)

Notice a certain hubris here as God boasts about "my servant Job" in this meeting of the divine council. Job belongs to God, and God is quick to point out that Job reverences God. But Ha-Satan quickly calls God on it:

> Does Job fear God for nothing? Have you not put a fence around him and his house and all that he has, on every side? You have blessed the work of his hands, and his possessions have increased in the land. But stretch out your hand now, and touch all that he has, and he will curse you to your face. (1:9–11)

Ha-Satan claims that God has used divine power to make Job the wealthy head of a *bet av* and has gained in return Job's undying devotion. Ha-Satan also implies that God has introduced the subject of Job to point out how great God is, rather than what a great person Job is. After all, God is really praising God's own work. So Ha-Satan raises serious questions: Does God relate to Job truly to benefit Job or to reward human righteousness? Or does God relate to Job only to secure praise, to stroke the divine ego, to express the divine self-interest? These questions suggest that God's power is hardly absolute: God needs Job to demonstrate power.

### Divine Insecurity

Consider also that in the story God directs Ha-Satan's attention to Job. Perhaps God is unsure of Job's true motivation. Maybe God's immense power cannot secure a human subject's unmotivated devotion. Is divine power just a way to force the subject to "love" God? In this way of reading the story, God mentions Job to Ha-Satan in hopes that Ha-Satan will agree to a test of Job's devotion that will resolve divine insecurity.

The book of Job assumes that God needs to know Job's motives. So God, with Ha-Satan's encouragement, calls upon Job to prove that his devotion to God is more than a love of the stuff of earthly life—wealth, health, and family. Job must love God for God alone, must relate to the divine power absent that power's beneficial influence in his life. God here tries to be an ultimate being, a being whose power brings forth love no matter how that power is exercised, a being whose power is not subject to negotiation. But this supposedly powerful God, this king of all, may be more insecure than at first glance. If God is secure, why the test?

### God, Power, and the End of the Story

In the book of Job, God attempts to resolve these questions of divine self-interest and divine insecurity by taking action at the end of the story. God addresses Job from a whirlwind, a spinning mass of wind that leaves destruction in its wake. Job sought the divine presence and gets a visit from random, irrational power. If Job expected comfort from God, the tornado spinning toward him indicates that God intends merely to maintain power.

God speaks from the whirlwind (38:1–40:2; 40:6–41:34) in ways in keeping with this meteorological costume. Offering a soliloquy on divine power, God

**Fig. 14.3: Tornado Damage**
*A tornado in Fulton, Missouri, in April 2000 destroyed a mobile home, killing one person. Yet the tornado did little damage to nearby trees and left the trailer's satellite television dish untouched. A whirlwind is therefore a particularly fit image for immense power manifested with no seeming logic.*

asserts divine prerogatives and human inabilities. God claims that no one can contend with God (40:2) and thus attempts to end the circulation of power.

In the first speech from the whirlwind, God identifies God's self as the creator and controller of a world that Job cannot and will not comprehend. God piles up the examples: Job did not lay the foundation of the earth, cannot control the seas, is unable to make the sun rise, will never provide the weather, nor even understand animals. After Job comments that he cannot really answer God's attack (40:3–5), God keeps right on going in a second speech, focusing in a rather overbearing manner on God's power over two mythically powerful beasts: Behemoth and Leviathan.

God defines God's self in terms of abilities that Job cannot fathom. But God's speeches here utterly fail to answer Job's complaints. In fact, God relies on the power differential between them to silence Job:

> Gird up your loins like a man;
> I will question you, and you declare to me.
> Will you even put me in the wrong?
> Will you condemn me that you may be justified?
> Have you an arm like God,
> and can you thunder with a voice like his?                 (40:7–9)

**Fig. 14.4: Malcah Zeldis's *Job* (1999)**
*This folk art representation of Job's plight by Malcah Zeldis represents the question of power at the end of the divine speeches. Does God's hand reach out to Job, or is it a gesture silencing Job? Is Job's stance an act of supplication, or do his hands express an attempt to explain himself? Whatever the precise nuance of the gestures, the relationship between Job and God is the powerful center of the painting's action. The other characters (Job's wife, the friends, Ha-Satan) carefully watch the interaction between them.*

At the end of the speeches from the whirlwind, it seems that God clearly holds power. This God hardly needs Job to stroke the divine ego. And this God answers any hint of insecurity with a blast of divine words. God has challenged Job, demonstrated mastery over creation, and insisted that Job read nature as testifying to divine authority. By the end of the speeches, Job, bereft of his former identity, appears astonishingly small against the backdrop of the divine management of the cosmos.

Yet the book does not hold a single ideological position. So the question remains whether the end of the book of Job will point toward "closure," toward manufacturing a stable identity for Job and a stable power relationship among God, Job, and the world. The implications of the restoration of Job for issues of identity and power begin a consideration of this question, followed by a look at the perplexing account of Job's "repentance."

## Restoring Job

God's in His Heaven—All's right with the world!
—Robert Browning, "Pippa's Passes"

The ending of the book of Job takes on a magical air. God decides to call a halt to Job's suffering. And not only that, God decides that Job deserves twice as much as he had before (42:10). For some readers the restoration of Job's wealth comes as a great relief. Poor Job deserves this sort of break. And it is comforting to think that God and the world, in the last analysis, do demonstrate some kind of stability. But other readers feel cheated by this precise feature. Job's passionate and poignant grappling with suffering, and with the God who inflicts it, dissolves into a frustratingly bland "happy ending." This vision of a happy and stable life after the ash heap threatens to erase the difficult discussions and harsh language that dominate most of the book. Readers must decide between these two ways of reading. But looking carefully at the ways this ending both supports and threatens the book of Job's understandings of identity and power will help readers make judgments about the text.

### Reviving Job's Identity

By restoring Job, God attempts to reinstate Job's identity as it was before he began to suffer. This original identity, which the writers of the book of Job present as exceedingly stable, and which Job invokes out of desperation during his sufferings, now reappears. So the treatments of the various markers of identity in the ending of the book once again demonstrate their vitality.

Job regains status as head of a *bet av*, with new sheep, camels, oxen, donkeys, and children (42:12–13). As at the beginning of Job's story, children simply appear on the list of valued "possessions" of the patriarch. These ten children replace the ten dead children in the same way that the 14,000 sheep replace the 7,000 sheep. Job's giving his daughters an inheritance (42:15) puts the focus on Job's power, as head of the *bet av*, to determine the future of all elements of his household. Even Job's extended family and friends give Job sympathy as well as money (42:11).

These ten new children also show God's restoration of Job's masculinity. The story remains silent on who gives birth to all these children; Job's wife has vanished from the scene. Perhaps Job now has multiple wives, concubines, or slave girls. Or maybe Job's wife soldiers on in silence and obscurity, bearing children eleven through twenty. In any case, the focus remains clearly on Job's productivity, not that of the women involved.

Job's body, beyond what may be inferred about his restored sexual ability and availability, remains largely unmentioned in Job's restoration. The narrator <u>describes no healing</u>, despite the emphasis on Job's health in the opening scenes of the book. The reference to "all the evil that the LORD had brought upon him" in Job 42:11 provides the clearest indication that Job's bodily sufferings are past. It is not certain whether Job presides over the sacrifices for his friends in Job 42:8, but even a limited involvement in this action would hint that his perfect priestly body has returned. And his long life, seeing four generations of descendants, also indicates this.

While Job's ethnic background remains unmentioned here as throughout most of the book, Job's class status receives a great deal of emphasis at the book's close. Now twice as wealthy as before, Job collects gifts from his family and doles out inheritances. The demonstrations of sympathy in Job 42:11 probably include a requisite amount of deference from the rest of the community. Job is once more Job; he reclaims his class identity, his honor.

At the end of the story, the authors restore all the markers of identity that Job had lost. Job has reappeared as Job, the one leading an immense *bet av*, embodied in flesh that will live for one hundred and forty more years, fathering many more children, and possessing a huge amount of property. Job's restoration simply underlines the vital role that these markers of identity play in his story and in the Hebrew Bible as a whole. The authors insist that stability rules.

### describes no healing

The missing description of Job's healing inspired early interpreters to fill in that gap. In the *Testament of Job*, God gives Job three sashes. When Job "girds up his loins" with them, they cause his boils (and maggots) to disappear. These magical belts become Job's special gift to his three daughters and, when worn by them, allow them to sing in the language of angels, imparting heavenly wisdom.

**Fig. 14.5: William Blake's** *Every Man Also Gave Him a Piece of Money* *This drawing captures Job's reestablished class position. Job and his wife—Blake assumes her presence—sit under a tree, recalling the drawing of Job and his family before his suffering. Job has a certain confidence here. He may be grateful for the money offered by his relatives here, if the arm across his chest is a sign of gratitude. But, generally, Job is neither exuberantly thankful (there is no smile) nor utterly indifferent (he looks directly at the gift, not coyly averting his eyes). In contrast, his relatives look directly at him, making him the center of attention. Job, wealthy once more, again commands the attention of those around him.*

*(Collection of Robert N. Essick. Copyright © 2007 the William Blake Archive.)*

*Renegotiating Power*

The authors also attempt to present power as stable at the book's ending. The writers use the story of Job's restoration, just like the speeches from the whirlwind, to represent an attempt by God to monopolize power. First, restoring Job is an arbitrary, unexplained exercise of divine authority on behalf of order. Second, God expresses anger, a frequent indicator of divine power, while demanding a large sacrifice (42:7). Third, God monopolizes speech. Job does not speak at all in this section; the writers do not wish to report even the words he prayed for his friends! God is clearly the active principle in this story. So the end of the book seems to proclaim an end to power negotiations. God rules, and all is now well.

Yet one might well wonder how complete this supposed end of power is. The ending of the book of Job is not as tidy as it appears at first glance. Three loci of power relations at the end of the book of Job—the court, ideology, and the characterization of the deity—each undermines the "happily ever after" finish.

### The Court

God's arbitrary use of power in restoring Job indicates that the authors are once again imagining God as king. But while God may still be king, evidence of the court vanishes in the description of Job's restoration. Ha-Satan is gone, along with the rest of the divine council. Imagery from the court of law also disappears. In short, the end of the book loses the metaphorical development of God's "political" power seen in the book's first forty-one chapters. And because the courts vanish, no one ever knows who won the wager made in the royal court between God and Ha-Satan. YHWH's court of law also never returns a verdict in Job's court case. These matters vanish along with their court settings.

Perhaps the writers wish readers to believe that all has been answered. Thus, God has won the bet; Job has received a hearing and then groveled before God. But the writers do not say this explicitly. They refuse clearly to state that God has secured all power, ignoring the pointed questions about divine power raised by both Ha-Satan and Job rather than answering them. And they drop two hints that all might not be so secure in this new life for God and Job.

First, God admits that Job <u>spoke correctly</u>, while the friends have not. While Job accepts his new blessed life in silence, God introduces Job's former words into the scene while affirming them. So even amid all this new stuff, readers receive a reminder of Job's "old stuff"—his words that questioned, if not impugned, the divine character.

Second, the narrator now clearly identifies God, not Ha-Satan, as responsible for Job's suffering: "all the evil that the Lord had brought upon him" (42:11). At the tale's beginning, God places Job in Ha-Satan's power (1:12; 2:6). True, those early chapters do not absolve God (after all, God claims to have destroyed Job [2:3]), yet the figure of Ha-Satan helps distance God and God's power from the particulars of Job's situation. At the end,

---

### spoke correctly

The writers never disclose precisely what Job said that was correct in God's view. Was it Job's characterization of God as a "watcher of humanity" (7:20) and a thug (30:18–19)? Was it Job's occasional claims that God would vindicate him (23:7)? Was it Job's repentance (42:1–6)? Resolving the question of what words God cares to affirm would go a long way toward deciding just how destabilizing this affirmation of Job's words could be.

without Ha-Satan to take the fall, God the king must assume direct responsibility for acting arbitrarily. But if God can and does act this way, Job's questions about the justice of God the judge are once again in order.

### Ideology

The story of the restoration of Job attempts to resolve the ideological contestations present in much of the book, giving the book a tidy ideological finish. In the cases of the Sage-Order and Sinai-Nation complexes, the end of the book blunts the effect of the attacks seen earlier. Job, as righteous sufferer, does not fit with the assumptions of the Sage-Order complex regarding the way the order of the world is supposed to operate. But now Job no longer suffers. Righteous and blessed, he proves that his friends were right: God *does* bless the righteous. Job's place looks secure once more. That God gives him twice as much stuff as before ratifies the notion of a world in which people find their places and in which God ultimately rewards those who uphold God's notion of order.

Similarly, the end of the book of Job backs away from rejecting the Sinai-Nation ideology. The story of Job's restoration emphasizes Job's status as a vassal: God calls Job "my servant" four times in the first two verses of the story of the restoration (42:7–8). The vassal Job once again luxuriates in the blessings of the suzerain, God. Job, "blameless and upright" the whole way through and speaking correctly about YHWH (42:7), gets his due. Blessing once more fits with good behavior. And the dire threats against the friends for their misspeaking about God, alleviated only by sacrifice and Job's prayer, indicate that God intends to exact punishment for wrongdoing. This picture fits well with covenantal ideology.

Yet while the restoration may question the criticism of these ideologies, the restoration cannot finally erase all the effects of the rest of the book. Job's friends, who affirm the Sage-Order and covenantal ideologies, do not speak correctly about God (42:7). And the account of God's blessing of Job explicitly states that God brought "evil" upon him (42:11). God's attack on Job, as well as God's apparently unmotivated and sudden act in restoring Job, points toward a God who still acts "for no reason" (2:3). As long as the deity continues to exercise power arbitrarily, one cannot confidently state that a certain act will bring blessing or curse. And so one cannot assume a beneficent order of the universe that favors those who live in tune with it.

This very capriciousness of the restoration directs the reader toward the Empire-Colony complex that models God's power after the arbitrary rule of the emperor. Here, though Job will never know why, God's imperial power acts in his favor. Job's story and his complaints fit with the interests of the elite in Jerusalem who collaborated with the empire. The restoration also fits with these interests. God's restoration of Job presents arbitrary divine and imperial power in a favorable light. Thus the empire, despite causing potential and real suffering, may also change its attitude for no reason and bless the people in Yehud.

### Characterization of God

The question of God's arbitrary nature leads directly to issues of the divine exercise of power. The story of Job's restoration may indicate that God's power is secure and unquestionable. Yet the story also implies that God's power cannot finally cover the traces of the power negotiations present in most of the book. Two familiar categories for understanding divine power in Job—divine self-interest and divine insecurity—aid in the examination of God's character.

In restoring Job, God once again uses power as an expression of divine self-interest. God now ignores Ha-Satan's suggestion that blessing Job is simply a way to secure devotion. And Ha-Satan, conveniently, is no longer around to raise the issue. God once again boasts about Job, this time to Job's friends, while once again playing the role of Job's benefactor. And Job, in his prayer for his friends, reprises his role as devotee of God.

Differences, however, crop up between the beginning of Job's story and its end. Compare Job's sacrifices, for example. In chapter 1, Job, as a wealthy patriarch, sacrifices for his children. In chapter 42, even before he regains wealth, he intercedes with God for his friends. In fact, the writers link Job's restoration to this act of devotion: "The Lord restored the fortunes of Job when he had prayed for his friends" (42:10). Perhaps, then, Job demonstrates piety unmotivated by God's blessing. But this understanding fails, since Job's piety here comes at divine request, perhaps even from divine control. God knows what Job will do: "My servant Job shall pray for you, for I will accept his prayer not to deal with you according to your folly" (42:8). So divine power works to secure pious devotion. The divine self-interest remains in play here.

If the divine self-interest still functions in the restoration, do possible divine insecurities exist as well? In the first scenes in the book of Job, God, perhaps uncertain of Job's unmotivated devotion, sets up a test. And the story revolves around this question: Will Job love God no matter what God does?

The restoration effectively ends this test. One wonders about the results. Has this test allayed divine insecurities, permitting God to return to business as usual? Perhaps God can now use power on Job's behalf. God now knows for certain that Job will remain faithful even when God's power turns against him. Or perhaps God has simply decided to live with insecurities and doubts, covering them by giving Job even greater riches.

Any attempt to resolve this issue, then, must investigate Job's attitude toward God. Does Job accept his "old" role, affirming God's benevolent power? Or does Job still claim his words that question God's justice, forever skeptical of God's intentions? To examine power further, the characterization of Job at the book's end must be addressed. Working on power at the end of the book directs the reader to Job's response to God, his so-called repentance.

**Translating Power: Job's Final Ambiguity**

The book of Job advances no simple view of power. Does its title character confront power? Refuse it? Deny it? Or is he mesmerized by power? The essential text for determining Job's final relationship to power is Job 42:1–6, especially its final verse:

> Then Job answered the LORD: "I know that you can do all things,
>     and that no purpose of yours can be thwarted.
> 'Who is this that hides counsel without knowledge?'
> Therefore I have uttered what I did not understand,
>     things too wonderful for me, which I did not know.
> 'Hear, and I will speak;
>     I will question you, and you declare to me.'
> I had heard of you by the hearing of the ear,
>     but now my eye sees you;
> therefore I despise myself [*emas*],
>     and repent in [*nikhamti al*] dust and ashes [*afar vaefer*]."   (42:1–6)

This text bristles with difficulties, as do so many texts in the book of Job (and the Hebrew Bible as a whole).

A translator facing Job 42:6 finds words with wide varieties of meaning. The second verb in the phrase, *nikhamti*, followed by the preposition *al* may be translated as "I forswear," "I have changed my mind concerning," "I repent on account of/upon," or "I am consoled concerning." The first verb in the phrase, *emas*, also has a range of meanings ("despise," "reject," and "retract" are good candidates), and this verb lacks the expected direct object. What does Job "despise" or "reject"—himself, his words, God? The translator has to fill in the blank.

The concluding two words of the phrase, *afar vaefer*, clearly mean "dust and ashes." This ease of translation may relieve the translator, but the phrase still gives the reader difficulty. The dust and ashes may represent any number of things: the heap on which Job sits, the human condition, humiliation, mourning, and so forth. From the diverse connotations of its words, to its

---

### Translating Job

If you have been using another version while reading this chapter, you may have already seen that your translation does not always correspond to the NRSV, which is used in this textbook. The reason for these discrepancies is that there are numerous places in Job where translation is difficult, if not impossible. The book of Job includes many Hebrew words that do not appear elsewhere in the Hebrew Bible, making precise definitions difficult to secure. And the book of Job has apparently been damaged during its transmission, forcing scholars to emend the text in many locations to come up with a text that makes sense. Because of these factors, judgments about possible meanings of texts in Job are frequently provisional in nature.

unclear structure, to its metaphorical uncertainties, Job 42:6 defies the reader. This chart shows some of the possible elements. Feel free to create your own path through the text by selecting one word from each column.

| I retract | myself | and | I repent | concerning | dust and ashes (humiliation) |
| I reject | my words | but | I forswear | upon | dust and ashes (the human condition) |
| I despise | you | | I am consoled | on account of | dust and ashes (mourning) |
| | (omit) | | I change my mind | of | dust and ashes (the ash heap) |
| | | | (omit) | | |

Of course, not just any combination of words makes for a fitting translation, but by experimenting this way, you can see a number of viable translations of Job 42:6 emerging.

The way translators render this verse will help determine how Job addresses a highly authoritative God. Here are three possible translations, with some analysis of their implications for the characterization of Job and thus how the writers construct his relationship to divine power.

*"Therefore I despise myself and repent in dust and ashes"* (NRSV, NIV).

In this rendering, Job rejects his own self and his conduct throughout the book, on the basis of what he has learned in the speeches from the whirlwind. The dust and ashes represent Job's humiliation; Job repents with deep humility for what he did and said. This reading fits well with the beginning of Job's speech (42:1–3), in which Job affirms God's ability to do anything and calls to mind God's knowledge, which easily surpasses Job's. Job, admitting that God holds all the power, accepts a place in a stable power regime.

## Job repents

Some scholars relate the Hebrew name *Iyyov* to the Arabic root *'wb*, which means "penitent." The Qur'an calls Job *Aiyub* (not related to *'wb*) and characterizes him as patiently persevering in his suffering. He is "patient in adversity, an excellent devotee, always turning in repentance" (38:44). In this regard, the Qur'an's perspective is similar to that found in the New Testament book of James, which speaks of Job's "endurance" (5:11).

Once Job acknowledges his position, God uses immense power to reestablish Job's wealth and health.

*"Therefore I reject and forswear dust and ashes."*

Here Job forcefully abandons the role of mourner. This rendering relates well to the phrase directly preceding it: "I had heard of you by the hearing of the ear, but now my eye sees you" (42:5). Job has finally gotten what he desired: an audience with God. God came down from the heavenly courtroom and appeared at Job's ash heap. Because of this encounter, Job can cease behaving as a mournful sufferer.

In terms of power, this rendering presents a couple of choices. First, Job could decide that he will live with unanswered questions and will move on in an uncertain relationship with the deity. This interpretation assumes that Job would have considered the divine speeches not to be an answer to his plight but at least a divine response to it. God's power would thus be left intact, but questions about it would still be in order.

Second, Job could decide that he will joyfully embrace an altered divine power regime. This interpretation assumes that Job heard in God's mentions of Behemoth and Leviathan a claim from God that chaos always threatens the world and that God secures the world as much as possible. So Job will celebrate God's ability to provide what order there is. And God will demonstrate that even this threatened order can, at times, bless Job greatly.

*"I reject you and change my mind concerning dust and ashes."*

Here Job admits that the divine speeches have changed his thinking about his present location, that is, the ash heap. And as part of the rejection of this location, Job rejects his role as pious sufferer, as persecuted victim of God. This reading fits well with the other occurrence of the phrase "dust and ashes" in the book, used in the context of God's abusive conduct toward Job:

> He has cast me into the mire,
>     and I have become like dust and ashes.
> I cry to you and you do not answer me;
>     I stand, and you merely look at me.                    (30:19–20)

Here Job claims God has made him into "dust and ashes" and has not responded to his pleas.

But now God has responded to Job, although in a powerful and enigmatic way. Job answers God's power claims by rejecting being "dust and ashes," that is, being the victim of the divine. In doing so, Job refuses to participate in the "power game" that God has been playing. And in doing so, Job rejects God.

Job will no longer fight with his friends about God. He will no longer ratify God's power by complaining to God. By doing this, Job does not claim that God lacks power. But Job opts out of the dance of power that characterizes the dialogues and the divine speeches. In this case, then, God's restoration of Job attempts to inveigle him back into his role as pious beneficiary of divine power, the flip side of his pious sufferer role. While Job takes the benefits, he remains silent.

The various translations of Job 42:6 produce starkly different perspectives on Job's character and his relationship to power. They present a set of cogent options, none of which demands complete assent. There are no final answers to the questions raised in the book of Job. Attempting to state a single definitive answer inevitably reduces (or effaces) the ambiguities of the text. And even choosing which understanding of the text to affirm reveals at least as much about a reader's sensibilities as about the text itself.

## Conclusion?

The complexities and ambiguities that typify the book of Job appear throughout the Hebrew Bible. Written over the course of centuries, from a variety of social and ideological perspectives, the Hebrew Bible bears in it a remarkable diversity. Its characterization of God twists and turns. Its understanding of what it means to be Israelite shifts. Its analysis of how readers are to comprehend the world around them remains inconsistent. And its language often perplexes the modern reader.

In this textbook, we, its authors, have attempted to understand the Hebrew Bible by examining its interaction with questions of identity and power. And as with any of its readers, our attempts to comprehend its diversity and to decipher its language have resulted in a variety of conclusions. This variety makes bringing this textbook to a conclusion difficult. The Hebrew Bible cannot be summarized in a clever closing paragraph. So we, the writers, hope that this last paragraph is not a conclusion at all.

## Suggested Biblical Readings

Job 1–14, 19, 29–31, 38–42

## Discussion Questions

1. Think of other characters in the Hebrew Bible. How do they demonstrate the importance of identity? How do they relate to power?
2. Write a blog as if you were Job. How do you treat Job's identity? What would you do with the character of God?
3. If you could erase the happy ending of Job, would you? Why or why not? Now write your own ending to the book. How do you address the various problems that the book raises?

4. What translation of Job 42:6 do you favor? Compare this and other passages in Job in a variety of translations. How do these translations understand Job's character? God's?

5. Choose an instance of widespread innocent suffering in the world today. How do the various options in Job relate to the discussion of this issue in our culture (television, print media, radio, Internet sources)?

**Suggestions for Further Reading**

Good, Edwin. *In Turns of Tempest: A Reading of Job with a Translation.* Stanford, CA: Stanford University Press, 1990.

MacLeish, Archibald. *J. B.: A Play in Verse.* Boston: Houghton Mifflin, 1957.

Newsom, Carol. "The Book of Job: Introduction, Commentary, and Reflections." *The New Interpreter's Bible*, vol. 4, 317–637. Nashville: Abingdon Press, 1996.

Penchansky, David. *The Betrayal of God: Ideological Conflict in Job.* Louisville, KY: Westminster John Knox Press, 1990.

Simon, Neil. *God's Favorite: A New Comedy.* New York: Random House, 1975.

# List of Illustrations and Credits

1.1: Map of Ancient Cisjordan and Its Immediately Surrounding Regions: Courtesy of Karla Bohmbach  2

1.2: The Judean Hills around Jerusalem: Courtesy of Israel Ministry of Tourism (http://www.goisrael.com)  3

1.3: The Coastal Plain near Ashkelon: Courtesy of Don Polaski  5

1.4: The Elah Valley: Courtesy of Sandie Gravett  6

1.5: The Samarian Hills: Courtesy of Todd Bolen / BiblePlaces.com  6

1.6: The Jezreel Valley: Courtesy of Karla Bohmbach  7

1.7: The Galilean Highlands: Courtesy of Israel Ministry of Tourism (http://www.goisrael.com)  9

1.8: Mount Hermon, a Prominent Mountain Northeast of Galilee: Courtesy of Israel Ministry of Tourism (http://www.goisrael.com)  9

1.9: The Negev: Courtesy of Israel Ministry of Tourism (http://www.goisrael.com)  10

1.10: Part of the Ancient Road from Jerusalem to Jericho: Courtesy of Sandie Gravett  10

1.11: The Sea of Galilee: Courtesy of Todd Bolen/BiblePlaces.com  11

1.12: The Transjordanian Highlands from the Rift Valley: Courtesy of Don Polaski  11

1.13: The Jordan River Just South of the Sea of Galilee: Courtesy of Sandie Gravett  12

1.14: The Terrain Surrounding the Dead Sea: Courtesy of Israel Ministry of Tourism (http://www.goisrael.com)  14

1.15: Swimmers Floating in the Dead Sea: Courtesy of Karla Bohmbach  14

1.16: The Judean Wilderness on the West Side of the Dead Sea: Courtesy of Don Polaski  15

1.17: Salt Formations at the Dead Sea: Courtesy of Israel Ministry of Tourism (http://www.goisrael.com)  15

1.18: Map of the Ancient Near East: Courtesy of Karla Bohmbach  17

1.19: Neolithic Jericho: Courtesy of Don Polaski  22

1.20: Model of the Ziggurat at Ur: Courtesy of the Oriental Institute of the University of Chicago  24

2.1: *Biblia Hebraica Stuttgartensia.* Edited by Karl Elliger and Wilhelm Rudolph, Fifth Revised Edition, edited by Adrian Schenker, © 1977 and 1997 Deutsche Bibelgesellschaft, Stuttgart. Used by permission.  47

2.2: Chester Beatty Biblical Papyri VI (Rahlfs 963): Picture © The Trustees of the Chester Beatty Library, Dublin. Used by permission.  48

2.3: Qumran, Cave 4: Courtesy of Israel Ministry of Tourism (http://www.goisrael.com)  49

2.4: Qumran, Cave 4 Scroll Fragments: Courtesy of Israel Antiquities Authority  50

2.5: Great Isaiah Scroll from Qumran, Cave 1: Courtesy of Erich Lessing / Art Resource, NY  51

2.6: Selection from *The Eerdmans Analytical Concordance to the Revised Standard Version of the Bible*, 1988 © Wm. B. Eerdmans Publishing Company. Reproduced by permission of Wm. B. Eerdmans Publishing Company.  69

2.7 Marc Chagall's *Le Songe de Jacob*: Réunion des Musées Nationaux / Art Resource, NY; © 2008 Artists Rights Society (ARS), New York/ADAGP, Paris  71

3.1: *Moses Striking the Rock,* by Valerio Castello: Courtesy of Erich Lessing / Art Resource, NY  88

3.2: Michelangelo's *Moses*: Courtesy of Sandie Gravett  92

4.1: A Typical Modern Family? (1951 advertisement for Motorola televisions). © 2008 Motorola, Inc. Reprinted with permission. Photograph Courtesy AdAccess, Hartman Institute, Duke University   97

4.2: A Typical Biblical Israelite Family? Artist: Rhonda Root, Madaba Plains Project, Tell al-'Umaryi, © 1999   98

4.3: The Relationships in a Model *Bet Av*: Courtesy of Karla Bohmbach   99

4.4: Horned Altars from Megiddo: Courtesy of the Oriental Institute of the University of Chicago   119

4.5: Fertility Figurines: Photo © The Israel Museum, Jerusalem   119

4.6: Line Drawing of the Ketef Hinnom Tomb, Jerusalem: © Tracy Wellman, from *The Israelites*, by B. J. Isserlin, Thames & Hudson Inc., New York. Reproduced by permission of Thames & Hudson Ltd.   121

5.1: Cover of *Samson: Judge of Israel*: Used by permission of American Bible Society   136

5.2: Carl Bloch's, *Samson and the Philistines*: Reproduced with the permission of the Statens Museum for Kunst, Copenhagen. Photograph courtesy of SMK Foto.   139

5.3: Gustave Doré's *Samson Destroying the Temple*: Gustave Doré, *The Doré Bible Gallery*, pl. 27   140

5.4: Eugene Delacroix's *Jacob Wrestling with the Angel* (Detail): Scala / Art Resource, NY   144

5.5: A View of Ruth and Naomi's Relationship: *The Parting of Ruth and Naomi*, Lithograph card distributed by Charles E. Hires Company, 1890s.   152

5.6: Gustave Doré's *Ineffable God*: Gustave Doré, illus. *La divina commedia di Dante Alighieri*, Casa Editrici Sonziogno.   155

5.7: Wiligelmo da Modena's *Portrayal of Man and Woman*: Alinari / Art Resource, NY Photo: Ghigo Roli, 1999. Franco Cosimo Panini Editore © Management Fratelli Alinari.   161

6.1: *Venus of Willendorf*: Erich Lessing / Art Resource, NY   167

6.2: Peter Paul Rubens's *Three Graces*: Erich Lessing / Art Resource, NY   168

6.3: Meaning of the Body's Parts in the Hebrew Bible: Drawing © 2008 Susan P. M. Cherland   174

6.4: The "Ideal" Modern Female Body: Photo © istockphotos.com   180

6.5: The "Ideal" Modern Male Body: Photo © istockphotos.com   180

6.6: Circumcision in Ancient Egypt: Line drawing © 2008 John Lathan, after a painting from the tomb of Ankhmahor, Saqqara, Sixth Dynasty (2350–2000 B.C.E.)   190

6.7: William Blake's *The Ancient of Days*: Lessing J. Rosenwald Collection, Library of Congress. Copyright © 2008 the William Blake Archive. Used with permission.   193

7.1: Pruning the Family Tree of Genesis: Drawing © 2008 Susan P. M. Cherland   205

7.2: The Mesha Inscription: Courtesy of Erich Lessing / Art Resource, NY   226

8.1: Ancient Coins: Courtesy of Erich Lessing / Art Resource, NY   243

8.2: Samarian Ivory Plaque: Courtesy of Erich Lessing / Art Resource, NY   257

9.1: Michelangelo's *David*: Courtesy of Scala / Art Resource, NY   277

11.1: The King-Zion Complex: Courtesy of John Lathan   325

11.2: The Temple Mount / Harem al-Sharif as Seen from the Mount of Olives: Courtesy of Don Polaski   329

11.3: The Sinai-Nation Complex: Courtesy of John Lathan   343

11.4: The Sage-Order Complex: Courtesy of John Lathan   348

11.5: The Empire-Colony Complex: Courtesy of John Lathan   354

12.1: The Temple-Palace Complex: Based on Th. A. Busink, from *Der Tempel von Jerusalem von Salamo bis Herdoes*, vol. 1, *Der Tempel Salomos*, 160. Used by permission of E. J. Brill.   363

12.2: Artist's Representation of the First Temple: Th. A. Busink, from *Der Tempel von Jerusalem von Salamo bis Herdoes*, vol. 1, *Der Tempel Salomos*, vii. Used by permission of E. J. Brill.   364

12.3: Artist's Representation of the Bronze Sea: Th. A. Busink, from *Der Tempel von Jerusalem von Salamo bis Herdoes*, vol. 1, *Der Tempel Salomos*, 329. Used by permission of E. J. Brill.   365

12.4: Detail from the Sarcophagus of King Ahiram of Byblos: Line drawing © 2008 John Lathan, after the Sarcophagus of Ahiram (ca. 1250 B.C.E.), National Museum of Beirut    366

12.5: Plan of the Courtyards of Herod's Temple: Based on Th. A. Busink, *Der Tempel von Jerusalem von Salamo bis Herodes,* vol. 2, *Von Ezechiel bis Middot* (Leiden: Brill, 1980), 1179. Used by permission of E. J. Brill.    377

12.6: Line Drawing of the Merneptah Stele and "Israel": Excerpts from *The Bible in the British Museum,* by T. C. Mitchell. Copyright © 1988 by the Trustees of The British Museum, Paulist Press, Inc., New York / Mahwah, NJ. Reprinted by permission of Paulist Press, Inc. (http://www.paulistpress.com).    379

12.7: Amarna Letter 68: Picture © The Trustees of the British Museum. Used by permission.    380

12.8: The Gezer Calendar: http://www.holylandphotos.org    380

12.9: *Lmlk* Seal Impression: Courtesy of Israel Antiquities Authority    382

12.10: The Behistun Inscription: Courtesy of Alinari / Art Resource, NY    383

13.1: The Tanaach Cult Stand: Photo © The Israel Museum, Jerusalem    401

14.1: William Blake's *Job and His Family:* Collection of Robert N. Essick. Copyright © 2007 the William Blake Archive. Used with permission.    429

14.2: William Blake's *Job's Despair:* Collection of Robert N. Essick. Copyright © 2007 the William Blake Archive. Used with permission.    434

14.3: Tornado Damage: Photograph courtesy National Weather Service, St. Louis, MO    446

14.4: Malcah Zeldis's *Job:* Malcah Zeldis / Art Resource, NY; © 2008 Artists Right Society (ARS), New York    447

14.5: William Blake's *Every Man Also Gave Him a Piece of Money:* Collection of Robert N. Essick. Copyright © 2007 the William Blake Archive. Used with permission.    450

# Glossary

**Ammonites** An ethnic group in the Hebrew Bible described as descending from the incestuous union of Abraham's nephew Lot with his two daughters. The Ammonites lived across the Jordan River from the Israelites.

**anointing** The pouring of oil on the head marks a person's selection for service. In the Hebrew Bible, kings, prophets, and priests all are anointed. The Hebrew word for this practice becomes the English term "messiah," or "anointed one."

**anti-Semitism** Jew-hatred, expressed in discrimination and attacks against Jewish persons and communities. The Nazi program to exterminate Europe's Jews was the most virulent form of anti-Semitism.

**Aramaeans** An ethnic group in the Hebrew Bible described as descending from Abraham's brother Nahor. The Aramaeans lived to the northeast of the Israelites.

**ark of the covenant** A sacred box that purportedly carried items to symbolize the presence of YHWH with the people. Its contents supposedly included the tablets of the Ten Commandments, manna from the wilderness wandering, and Aaron's budding rod.

**Apocrypha** Early Jewish texts not accepted as authoritative in Judaism but accepted by some Christian groups.

**archaeology** The investigation of the material remains of a site or sites in order to describe a particular site's or region's culture.

**Assyria, Assyrians** A place and people located in northern Mesopotamia. Center of a powerful empire that dominated much of the ancient Near East, including the Cisjordan, from ca. the ninth to the seventh centuries B.C.E.

**axis mundi** A holy place assumed to be the meeting point of the divine and human realms.

**Babylonia, Babylonians** A place and people located in southern Mesopotamia. Center of a powerful empire that defeated the Assyrians and held sway over the ancient Near East from ca. 609 to 539 B.C.E.

**barter** An economic system based on the exchange of goods deemed of comparable worth; often used in societies without a money system.

**B.C.E.** Abbreviation for "before the Common Era"; a more religiously neutral time referent than B.C. (before Christ).

**bet av** Hebrew term meaning "house of the father"; denotes a social unit akin to a family, one in which the senior male has priority.

**bet em** Hebrew term meaning "house of the mother"; denotes a social unit akin to a family, one in which the senior female has priority.

**binary dualism** A perspective that divides the object of investigation into two irreducible and often opposing elements or principles. Western thought has a tradition of viewing the human person as a binary dualism of mind or spirit versus body, an approach not found in the Hebrew Bible.

**bride-price** A gift given by the bridegroom and/or his family to the bride's family; this economic transaction strengthens the bonds between the two families.

**Canaanites** An ethnic group, or collection of ethnic groups, indigenous to the Cisjordan. The Canaanites are featured prominently in the Hebrew Bible as providing the major contrast to Israelite ethnicity in the story of the settlement of the Israelites in the Cisjordan.

**canon** A body of literature that holds a special status for a particular community.

**circumcision** The removal of the foreskin from the penis, practiced by several peoples in the ancient Near East. In the Hebrew Bible, circumcision is one of the most prominent characteristics of Israelite identity.

**Cisjordan** The region on the west side of the Jordan River. The term functions as a less religiously or politically fraught way to name the territory claimed by the ancient Israelites.

**clan** A social group of related households often connected by a common ancestor or common characteristics; its size often consists of several hundred persons.

**collateral** An object or good, such as land, a building, or material goods, used as security for a loan.

**comparative ethnography** A subfield of anthropology. Anthropologists study present-day societies organized similarly to ancient or lesser known societies in order to understand better the structures and functions of the otherwise inaccessible or unknown society.

**corvée** A kind of taxation in the form of forced labor exacted by public or state authorities.

**covenant** Any agreement between two parties. In the Hebrew Bible, it especially denotes the relationship between God and the Israelites via Abraham, the relationship between God and Israel forged at Mount Sinai, or the relationship between God and the Davidic dynasty. A covenant depends on the integrity and commitment of the parties who negotiate it and promise to uphold its stipulations.

**covet** To desire or want something inordinately.

**debt slavery** A way of repaying a defaulted loan whereby a person is sold into servitude.

**dowry** In some societies a gift given by the bride's family to the bride on the occasion of her wedding; may function as her share of the family inheritance.

**dynamic equivalence** A type of translation that emphasizes readability in the target language.

**Edomites** An ethnic group in the Hebrew Bible, described as descending from Jacob's twin brother, Esau. The Edomites lived southeast of the Dead Sea and of the Israelites.

**Egyptians** An ethnic group featured prominently in the Hebrew Bible, the Egyptians provide the major contrast to Israelite ethnicity in the story of the exodus. The Egyptians lived in the Nile valley but historically also exerted considerable economic and political influence on the Cisjordan.

**endogamy** Marrying within a certain group, whether clan, tribe, people, or other group.

**eponymous ancestor** The putative ancestral figure from which an ethnic group, tribe, or family derives its name. The Israelites derived their name from their eponymous ancestor Jacob, who was also named Israel.

**ethnicity** A socially produced concept for constructing a sense of peoplehood based generally on a belief in common origin (descent) and on the practice of certain social behaviors believed to be unique to the group (culture).

**eunuch** A castrated male, often employed in the royal courts of the ancient Near East. The Hebrew term for eunuch (*saris*) could also simply signify a court official without necessarily implying castration.

**euphemism** The substitution of an innocuous or inoffensive expression for one that is unpleasant or might offend. Expressions that directly describe body processes such as elimination or sex are often replaced by euphemisms; for example, the Hebrew Bible often employs the euphemism "hand" or "flesh" for the penis.

**exile (Babylonian)** An event occurring in the sixth century B.C.E. whereby the Babylonians, after defeating the Judeans, took some of them captive and resettled them in Babylonia.

**exogamy** Marrying outside a certain group, whether clan, tribe, people, or other group.

**femininity** A culture's construction of what it means to be female within a particular social context.

**Fertile Crescent** A geographical region of fertility in the ancient Near East, broadly encompassing Egypt, the Cisjordan, Syria, and Mesopotamia.

**form criticism** A method of reading a text to find evidence of its origins in oral literature and its original social location.

**formal correspondence** A type of translation that emphasizes the precise linguistic forms of the original language.

**fornication** A general term for illicit sexual intercourse; it may include prostitution, adultery, pornography, and/or consensual sex between unmarried persons.

**gender binary** The distinct separation of masculine and feminine traits within a cultural context in order to distinguish male and female clearly and unequivocally.

**genocide** The attempt to exterminate an entire defined human group.

**gleaning** Gathering the grain or other crops left behind by harvesters.

*goel* Hebrew for "redeemer"; identifies a male who acts to preserve a *bet av* at risk of losing either its land or its lineage.

*Habiru* Small groups of people in the ancient Near East forced to move due to famine, war, disaster, debt, or other causes. They often settled on the margins of society. The people of ancient Israel could have originated in such a group.

**Hebrew** A designator for the people of Israel employed most often by Egyptian characters in the book of Exodus.

**hellenization** The cultural mixing of Greek and ancient Near Eastern elements, as in the ancient Near East in the aftermath of Alexander the Great's conquests in the fourth century B.C.E.

**henotheism** The purported allegiance to one god even while acknowledging the existence of or even worshiping other gods.

*herem* **(or ban)** Items that are to be destroyed in a religiously sanctioned or holy war, whether goods, animals, or people.

**historical criticism** A method of reading a text to determine its value as a historical source and its relationship to historical events.

**Hokmah** The Hebrew word for wisdom, it is also used to represent divine wisdom as a female figure.

**holiness** A state of separation from the instabilities of the human world. According to the Hebrew Bible, God exists in this kind of separation, so anyone approaching God must be holy.

**hyperfeminine** An overexaggerated presentation of qualities a culture typically associates with women.

**hypermasculine** An overexaggerated presentation of qualities a culture typically associates with men.

**ideology** A basic assumption or set of assumptions that explain the way the world operates and a person's place in it. It often operates covertly to structure persons' experiences of society and themselves.

**inside-outsiders** A term for non-Israelite minorities within Israelite society as they are portrayed in the Hebrew Bible.

**intersex persons** People born with or who develop mixed or ambiguous sexual physiology such as chromosomes, genitalia, and/or secondary sex characteristics that do not conform to exclusively male or female classifications.

**Ishmaelites** An ethnic group in the Hebrew Bible described as descending from Abraham's first son, Ishmael. The biblical texts associate the Ishmaelites with various peoples from northern Arabia.

**Ishtar** Babylonian goddess of fertility, love, and sexuality. She often, however, gets described as heartlessly destroying her male lovers.

**Israel, Israelites** Names a region (as well as an ancient kingdom and modern nation) located in the southern part of the area along the eastern Mediterranean; also some of the people living there. The Hebrew Bible concerns itself largely with this people's story and traditions. Also, occasionally, the term refers to the northern kingdom alone.

**jubilee** The release of debt slaves and the return of land to its original owners once every fifty years (see Lev 25).

**Judah** One of the tribes of Israel; also names the southern kingdom after the united monarchy divided in ca. 922 B.C.E.

**Judeans** The inhabitants of the kingdom of Judah; also names those living in the Persian province of Yehud after 539 B.C.E.

*Kethuvim* Hebrew for "writings"; a diverse assemblage of the books in the Tanakh outside the Torah and Prophets.

**latifundialization** From the Latin *latifundia* (large estates); refers to a process whereby land increasingly accrues into the hands of just a few owners.

**levirate marriage** The practice whereby a male relative marries a dead man's childless widow; the purpose is to conceive a male child then reckoned as the dead man's heir.

**Levite** A member of the biblical tribe of Levi, one of the twelve sons of Jacob. This term also makes reference to priests from this line who served at various shrines and then in the temple at Jerusalem. The Hebrew Bible shows them performing duties such as singing the psalms, constructing and maintaining the temple, and serving as guards.

**Marx, Karl** A nineteenth-century thinker who developed the theory of socialism; he analyzed the dynamics of wage labor and surplus capital and postulated the development of a two-tier class system (the bourgeoisie and the proletariat).

**masculinity** A culture's construction of what it means to be male within a particular social context.

**Masoretic Text (MT)** The version of the texts of the Hebrew Bible produced by Masoretes in the last half of the first millennium C.E. Used as the basis for most present English translations.

**matrilocality** When a couple takes up residence with the woman's family.

**media** The ways cultures transmit ideologies.

**messiah** The Hebrew word for an anointed one (see *anointing*); it can also refer to a figure who will lead the people of Israel in the time to come.

**metaphor** A way of speaking about a subject indirectly through a comparison that suggests a similarity. In the Hebrew Bible, for example, marriage serves as a metaphor for the relationship between God and Israel.

**Midianites** An ethnic group in the Hebrew Bible described as descending from the union of Abraham with Keturah. The Midianites lived in the northwestern corner of the Arabian peninsula, south of Edom.

**Moabites** An ethnic group in the Hebrew Bible described as descending from the incestuous union of Abraham's nephew Lot with one of his two daughters. The Moabites lived across the Dead Sea from the Israelites.

**monadic** Of or related to one; a way of describing the structure and function of the biblical *bet av* wherein one person (the senior male) functions as its center.

**monoculture** The practice of growing just one crop primarily for profit; generally done by elites. In ancient Israel the main cash crops were grapes and olives.

**monolatry** The claim that only one god deserves worship even while acknowledging that other deities exist.

**monotheism** The claim that only one god exists.

**nahalah** Hebrew term meaning "inheritance"; refers primarily to land claimed or owned by some social unit depicted in the Hebrew Bible, especially a *bet av* or clan.

**narrator** The "voice" telling the story in a text. Most often in the Hebrew Bible, this voice does not belong to a character within the story.

**nation** A group founded on a common ethnic, cultural, or social heritage.

**near neighbors** An ethnic group living in close enough proximity to one's own group that interaction is inevitable. Near neighbors can pose problems for the maintenance of ethnic boundaries.

**Nebuchadnezzar** Ruler of the Babylonians from 605 to 562 B.C.E.; invaded Judah, destroyed Jerusalem, and exiled many Judeans in 587/586 B.C.E.

**nephesh** The Hebrew Bible's concept of the person as a living, breathing, embodied being.

**Neviim** Hebrew for "prophets"; the books in the Tanakh bearing the names of prophets, as well as Joshua, Judges, Samuel, and Kings.

**New Criticism** A method of reading a text as a piece of literature with no reference to the author's intent or the reader's response; also called "close reading."

**Old Testament** Christian term for the Hebrew Bible.

**paraphrases** Loose renderings of texts that highly prize readability but tend to lose touch with the original language.

**particularistic** An adjective describing ideologies and practices that focus on the unique characteristics of a select group or individual.

**patriarchal** A system in which the senior males have supreme authority.

**patrilineal** Tracing descent through the paternal or male line.

**patrilocality** When a couple takes up residence with the man's family.

**Pentateuch** An alternate term for the Torah, based on the Greek for "five scrolls/books."

**Persia, Persians** A place and people located east of Mesopotamia in what is now Iran. Ruled an empire that dominated much of the ancient Near East from ca. 539 to 333 B.C.E.

**Philistines** An ethnic group featured prominently in the Hebrew Bible, the Philistines lived on the southern coastal plain of Cisjordan beginning ca. 1200 B.C.E. The biblical books of Judges and 1 and 2 Samuel depict the Israelites as having a combative relationship with them.

**pilgrimage** The practice of people traveling to a particular shrine, usually at a set time. In the

Hebrew Bible, Jerusalem and the temple are the focus of pilgrimage.

**polyandry** Having more than one husband at a time.

**polygyny** Having more than one wife at a time.

**postmodern** A broad term describing a wide variety of trends opposing or building beyond modernity. For the purposes of this textbook, it describes kinds of reading that focus on instability and fluctuation in meaning, opposing modernity's focus on a single interpretation of a text.

**priests** Those persons who officiate at shrines, presiding over sacrifices and providing a link between the deity and the rest of the populace.

**primogeniture** The privileging of the firstborn son in inheritance.

**primordial** An adjective describing something that exists at the beginning. Genesis 1–11 narrates a primordial history of humanity.

**prophets** Those persons who communicated the divine will to a particular audience. Prophets interacted with deities through media such as dreams, visions, ecstatic states, or even standing in the presence of the divine. The Hebrew Bible often presents the delivery of their message in the form of an oracle.

**Qumran** Settlement near the Dead Sea (ca. 150 B.C.E.–ca. 70 C.E.) whose residents practiced a strict form of Judaism. The Dead Sea Scrolls, including some of the earliest extant Hebrew manuscripts of the Hebrew Bible, were found here.

**race** A socially produced concept for categorizing humans largely on the basis of physically visible characteristics, such as skin color or facial features. Current genetic research indicates that these categories do not rest on empirical data.

**reader-response criticism** A method of reading a text with an emphasis upon how the text and reader interact to produce meaning.

**redaction criticism** A method of reading a text to explain the ways it was edited (redacted) as well as the purposes of the editor.

**resident aliens** This common English translation of the Hebrew *gerim* refers to various outsiders not reckoned as part of the kinship or landownership system of the Israelites.

**Sabbath** Derives from the Hebrew for "rest." This observance of a day of rest on the seventh day of the week is a practice characteristic of Israelite ethnic identity in the Hebrew Bible.

**sacrifices** Gifts, usually of animals, foodstuffs, and incense, offered before a deity at a shrine.

**scribes** Officials who wrote and who thus were essential to the operation of royal and imperial administrations. Scribes were responsible for much of the literature in the Hebrew Bible, many times as authors, and always as editors and copyists.

**Septuagint** (LXX) Versions of the texts of the Hebrew Bible in ancient Greek translation.

**Sheol** The underworld that the Hebrew Bible understands to be the abode of all the dead.

**sociological and anthropological approaches** These critical approaches use methods and theories from the social sciences to better understand human societies. They are based on the recognition that humans are social beings who organize themselves in patterned ways.

**source criticism** A method of reading a text to find possible original sources and the attempt to locate those sources in historical context.

**state** A politically organized series of institutions exercising authority over a defined territory and/or population.

**suzerainty treaties** Agreements between powerful kings (suzerains) and lesser kings (vassals) in the ancient Near East. These treaties served as a model for the Hebrew Bible's understanding of the Sinai covenant.

**Tanakh** Jewish term for the Hebrew Bible, based on the initial letters of its three sections: *Torah, Neviim,* and *Kethuvim.*

**Temple (Jerusalem)** The building in Jerusalem dedicated to the worship of YHWH.

**textual criticism** A method of comparing various manuscripts to determine their relationship with each other, often in order to produce a basic text for translation.

**theophoric name** A name that includes the name of a god, thereby honoring that deity and invoking protection.

***torah,* Torah** Hebrew for "law" or "instruction"; the first five books of the Hebrew Bible.

**tribe** A social group normally consisting of several thousand persons and centered around agriculture; smaller cross-cutting groups (military, economic, religious) may further bind the whole unit together.

**tribute** A kind of taxation imposed by a ruler, usually on a conquered people; may take a variety of forms: money, goods, forced labor.

**uncleanness** A state of human instability that renders a person unfit to be in the divine presence.

**universalistic** An adjective describing ideologies and practices that focus on the commonality of all human beings.

**wisdom** The results of an examination of the world that discloses an order, as well as reflection upon the ethical implications of that order.

**Yehud** Name of a Persian province in the southern Cisjordan; centered around Jerusalem, it served as the homeland for some Judeans from ca. 539 to 333 B.C.E.

**Zadokites** A priestly line serving in Jerusalem purportedly from the time of David and Solomon. These elites dominated the Temple cult at Jerusalem prior to the exile and, upon their return, regained control.

**Zion** The hill on which the Temple in Jerusalem was built, this term is often used as a shorthand reference for the Temple, especially in its ideological function.

# Index to Citations
# of the Hebrew Bible

**OLD TESTAMENT**

**Genesis**

| | | | | | |
|---|---|---|---|---|---|
| 1 | 176 | 3:17 | 162 | 11:7 | 204 |
| 1–11 | 235 | 3:18–19 | 162 | 11:8 | 204 |
| 1:1 | 43, 397 | 3:19 | 163 | 11:30 | 182 |
| 1:1–2:4a | 349 | 3:20 | 163 | 12 | 95, 209 |
| 1:27 | 158–59, 192, 194–95 | 3:22 | 163 | 12–35 | 108 |
| 1:28 | 106, 107, 203 | 3:23–24 | 163 | 12:2 | 209 |
| 1:31 | 241 | 4 | 22, 171, 202 | 12:2–3 | 407 |
| 2 | 160 | 4:1 | 163, 191 | 12:2–3, 7 | 205 |
| 2:2–3 | 101, 159 | 4:1–5 | 22 | 12:3 | 235 |
| 2:4b-3:24 | 133, 159 | 4:17 | 22 | 12:7 | 207 |
| 2:7 | 160, 171–72, 176 | 4:20–22 | 22 | 12:10–16 | 221 |
| 2:15 | 160 | 5 | 22 | 12:10–20 | 212 |
| 2:15–17 | 160 | 6–9 | 23, 202 | 13 | 209 |
| 2:18 | 160 | 6:1–4 | 202 | 13:14–17 | 205–7 |
| 2:19 | 161 | 7:12 | 101 | 13:15 | 217 |
| 2:20 | 161 | 7:16 | 194 | 14 | 57 |
| 2:21 | 161 | 8:21 | 176, 188, 194 | 14–16 | 221 |
| 2:21–22 | 192 | 9 | 216 | 14:1–4 | 222 |
| 2:23 | 161 | 9:1–7 | 107 | 14:13 | 211 |
| 2:24 | 151, 191 | 9:3–4 | 171 | 14:14 | 100 |
| 2:25 | 162, 188 | 9:16 | 206 | 14:18–20 | 211 |
| 3 | 162 | 9:20–27 | 188 | 14:19 | 221 |
| 3:1, 4 | 162 | 10 | 202, 203 | 14:19–20, 22 | 399 |
| 3:4 | 163 | 10–12 | 204 | 15 | 206, 234 |
| 3:6 | 162 | 10:4 | 203 | 15:4–5 | 221 |
| 3:6–7 | 188 | 10:5, 20, 31 | 202 | 15:5, 7, 18–19 | 205 |
| 3:7 | 162 | 10:6, 15–19 | 216 | 15:8 | 221 |
| 3:8 | 194 | 10:8–12 | 203 | 15:9–10 | 206 |
| 3:12 | 162 | 10:13–14 | 216 | 15:18–21 | 207 |
| 3:16 | 162 | 10:23 | 435 | 15:19 | 229 |
| | | 11 | 23, 203 | 16 | 209, 212 |
| | | 11:1–9 | 23, 202, 204 | 16:1–3 | 221 |
| | | 11:5 | 194 | 16:1, 4 | 222 |

**Genesis** (*continued*)

| | |
|---|---|
| 16 | 192 |
| 16:1–2 | 105 |
| 16:1–4 | 107 |
| 16:3 | 417 |
| 16:7ff | 418 |
| 16:10 | 209 |
| 16:13 | 399 |
| 16:23–30 | 221 |
| 17 | 206, 234 |
| 17:1 | 399, 408 |
| 17:4–8 | 205 |
| 17:5 | 206 |
| 17:5–6 | 108 |
| 17:6 | 208 |
| 17:7, 13, 19 | 206 |
| 17:9–12 | 206 |
| 17:9–13 | 208 |
| 17:9–14 | 89 |
| 17:12 | 208 |
| 17:12, 27 | 207 |
| 17:14 | 206, 208 |
| 17:15 | 206 |
| 17:15–21 | 108 |
| 17:15–22 | 112 |
| 17:16 | 208 |
| 17:18–21 | 208 |
| 17:20 | 209 |
| 17:23–27 | 206, 208 |
| 18 | 209 |
| 18:13 | 402 |
| 18:16–33 | 211 |
| 18:18 | 235 |
| 19 | 109, 110, 185 |
| 19:4–11 | 432 |
| 19:26 | 15 |
| 19:30–38 | 224 |
| 19:31–21 | 191 |
| 20 | 209, 221 |
| 20:1–18 | 221 |
| 20:14–17 | 211 |
| 21 | 185, 212 |
| 21:1–7 | 108 |
| 21:5–7 | 402 |
| 21:8–14 | 112 |
| 21:9–14 | 211 |
| 21:13 | 209 |
| 21:14 | 208 |
| 21:18 | 209 |
| 21:21 | 209 |
| 21:22–32 | 221 |
| 21:22–34 | 221 |
| 21:25–34 | 141 |
| 21:33 | 399 |
| 22 | 225, 245 |
| 22:1–2 | 44 |
| 22:1–19 | 55, 115 |
| 22:17 | 26, 108 |
| 22:17–18 | 205 |
| 22:21 | 435 |

| | |
|---|---|
| 23:1–20 | 122 |
| 24 | 104, 209, 246 |
| 24:3 | 211 |
| 24:3–4 | 211 |
| 24:10–31 | 141 |
| 24:28 | 102 |
| 24:59, 61 | 104 |
| 25 | 209 |
| 25:1–6 | 85, 209 |
| 25:8 | 171 |
| 25:8–10 | 122 |
| 25:8, 17 | 120 |
| 25:11 | 100 |
| 25:12–18 | 209 |
| 25:19–34 | 113 |
| 25:21 | 182 |
| 25:21–26 | 108 |
| 25:23 | 143 |
| 25:25 | 173 |
| 25:26 | 141, 402 |
| 25:27 | 141, 145 |
| 25:29–34 | 112, 141, 223 |
| 26 | 209 |
| 26:1–33 | 221 |
| 26:1, 8 | 221 |
| 26:6–11 | 221 |
| 26:12 | 100 |
| 26:12–33 | 141 |
| 26:24 | 116 |
| 26:26–31 | 221 |
| 26:26–33 | 209 |
| 26:34 | 141 |
| 27 | 209, 223, 246, 402 |
| 27:1–46 | 113, 223 |
| 27:3 | 141 |
| 27:5–17 | 142, 147 |
| 27:8 | 141 |
| 27:11 | 141 |
| 27:24 | 70 |
| 27:28 | 223 |
| 27:28–29, 30–40 | 223 |
| 27:29 | 141, 143 |
| 27:39 | 223 |
| 27:43 | 141 |
| 27:45 | 176 |
| 28 | 53, 54, 68 |
| 28:1 | 141, 211 |
| 28:3 | 399 |
| 28:10–11 | 70 |
| 28:10–22 | 62 |
| 28:11 | 69, 73 |
| 28:12 | 42, 70 |
| 28:13 | 116 |
| 28:13–15 | 69, 73 |
| 28:16 | 73 |
| 28:16–17 | 61, 69, 70 |
| 28:17 | 73 |
| 28:18 | 61, 70 |
| 28:19 | 51, 69, 73 |
| 28:20–22 | 69, 70, 142 |

| | |
|---|---|
| 28:22 | 73 |
| 29 | 104, 105 |
| 29–30 | 108, 209 |
| 29:9–12 | 142 |
| 29:10 | 141 |
| 29:15–30 | 142 |
| 29:20 | 142 |
| 29:31 | 182 |
| 30 | 192 |
| 30:1 | 108, 124 |
| 30:2 | 68, 421 |
| 30:3–13 | 107 |
| 30:16 | 142 |
| 30:25–43 | 223 |
| 30:30 | 143 |
| 30:43 | 143 |
| 31:5 | 116 |
| 31:14 | 229 |
| 31:19 | 405 |
| 31:34–35 | 117 |
| 31:36–42 | 143 |
| 31:42, 53 | 116 |
| 31:43 | 143 |
| 31:43–54 | 209 |
| 32 | 398, 399 |
| 32:3–5 | 143 |
| 32:3–21 | 143 |
| 32:9 | 116 |
| 32:13–21 | 143 |
| 32:24 | 143 |
| 32:24–26 | 398 |
| 32:24–30 | 195 |
| 32:27–28 | 81, 207 |
| 32:28 | 18, 143, 398 |
| 32:30 | 399 |
| 32:31 | 180 |
| 33:5–14 | 143 |
| 33:9 | 143 |
| 33:11 | 143 |
| 34 | 134, 185, 209, 230 |
| 34:2 | 210 |
| 34:3 | 151 |
| 34:4 | 223 |
| 34:4–17 | 246 |
| 34:13–17 | 144 |
| 34:16 | 211 |
| 34:25–29 | 144, 211 |
| 34:30 | 144 |
| 35:2 | 229 |
| 35:4 | 176 |
| 35:10 | 207 |
| 35:11 | 399, 408 |
| 35:14 | 219 |
| 35:16–20 | 108 |
| 35:18 | 143, 402 |
| 35:20 | 121 |
| 35:22 | 144 |
| 35:22–26 | 101 |
| 35:29 | 120 |
| 36 | 223 |

| | | | |
|---|---|---|---|
| 36:11, 15 | 229 | **Exodus** | |
| 36:28 | 435 | 1 | 81 |
| 37 | 262 | 1–2 | 210 |
| 37–50 | 212 | 1:1 | 81 |
| 37:2–4 | 113 | 1:1–5 | 100 |
| 37:3 | 189 | 1:5 | 178 |
| 37:6–7 | 100 | 1:8 | 213 |
| 37:12 | 100 | 1:9–10 | 214 |
| 37:23 | 189 | 1:9, 12, 13 | 81 |
| 37:31–35 | 145 | 1:11, 12 | 110 |
| 37:36 | 233 | 1:12 | 215 |
| 38 | 126, 135, 185, 247 | 1:15–20 | 81 |
| 38:14 | 189 | 1:15–21 | 215 |
| 38:21 | 111 | 1:15–22 | 81, 215 |
| 38:24 | 115 | 1:18 | 216 |
| 38:26 | 220 | 1:19 | 215–16 |
| 39–46 | 262 | 1:22 | 81 |
| 39:1 | 233 | 2:1 | 81 |
| 39:6 | 134, 173 | 2:2 | 81, 173 |
| 39:6–18 | 147 | 2:4, 7–8 | 81 |
| 40 | 68 | 2:5–6:10 | 81 |
| 40:2, 7 | 233 | 2:6–7 | 81 |
| 41 | 186 | 2:10 | 83 |
| 41:1–36 | 101 | 2:11 | 83 |
| 41:37–45 | 212 | 2:11–13 | 81 |
| 41:42 | 189 | 2:12 | 342 |
| 41:45 | 105 | 2:13 | 84 |
| 41:50–52 | 212 | 2:14 | 84 |
| 42:15 | 68 | 2:14–15 | 84 |
| 42:37 | 145 | 2:15 | 84 |
| 43:14 | 399 | 2:16–17 | 85, 141 |
| 43:30 | 68 | 2:19 | 85, 222 |
| 43:32 | 213 | 2:20–21 | 86 |
| 44:34 | 145 | 2:21 | 105 |
| 45:25–28 | 145 | 2:22 | 86 |
| 46:1–3 | 116 | 3 | 418 |
| 46:8–27 | 203 | 3:1 | 402 |
| 46:20 | 231 | 3:2 | 418 |
| 46:34 | 213 | 3:4 | 418 |
| 47:13–26 | 213 | 3:6 | 87 |
| 47:18–19 | 170 | 3:7, 10 | 87 |
| 47:29–48:22 | 113 | 3:8 | 217 |
| 48–49 | 246 | 3:11 | 80, 87 |
| 48:3 | 399 | 3:14 | 401 |
| 48:5 | 128 | 3:15, 16 | 403 |
| 48:13–20 | 183 | 3:18 | 81, 183 |
| 48:17–20 | 143 | 3:21–22 | 212 |
| 49:4 | 144 | 4:14 | 421 |
| 49:5–7 | 144 | 4:16 | 88 |
| 49:10 | 170 | 4:22–23 | 89 |
| 49:15, 17, 19 | 143 | 4:24 | 89 |
| 49:25 | 195 | 4:24–26 | 89 |
| 49:28 | 101 | 4:25 | 89 |
| 49:29 | 120 | 4:25–26 | 171 |
| 49:33 | 120, 122 | 4:26 | 89 |
| 50:1–14 | 93, 212 | 5:3 | 81 |
| 50:7–14 | 122 | 6:20 | 113 |
| 50:11 | 68 | 7–12 | 213 |
| 50:24–26 | 93 | 7:1 | 88 |
| 50:26 | 213 | 7:8–11:10 | 101 |

| | | | |
|---|---|---|---|
| 7:14–12:32 | 420 |
| 7:16 | 81 |
| 7:17 | 88 |
| 8:8, 19 | 88 |
| 8:10 | 88 |
| 8:19 | 420 |
| 8:23 | 213 |
| 9:1, 13 | 81 |
| 9:3, 16 | 88 |
| 9:4 | 213 |
| 9:27–28 | 88 |
| 10:3 | 81 |
| 10:7 | 88 |
| 10:9 | 118 |
| 10:16 | 88 |
| 11:2 | 212 |
| 11:7 | 213 |
| 12 | 213, 229 |
| 12:7 | 171 |
| 12:19, 48–49 | 228 |
| 12:26–27 | 116 |
| 12:35–36 | 212 |
| 12:38 | 230 |
| 12:49 | 228 |
| 13–14 | 222 |
| 13:14–15 | 116 |
| 13:19 | 93 |
| 14:10–14 | 213 |
| 14:10b–11 | 88 |
| 14:31 | 422 |
| 15:2 | 117 |
| 15:3 | 156 |
| 15:6 | 183 |
| 15:11 | 405 |
| 15:20–21 | 149 |
| 15:26 | 182 |
| 16:2–3 | 213 |
| 16:35 | 101 |
| 17:1–7 | 88 |
| 17:2 | 88 |
| 17:6a-c | 88 |
| 17:7 | 88 |
| 19:3 | 57 |
| 19:3–4 | 338 |
| 19:4–5 | 407 |
| 19:5–6 | 342 |
| 19:6 | 342 |
| 19:7–8 | 183 |
| 19:14 | 57 |
| 19:14–15 | 192 |
| 20:2 | 338 |
| 20:2–3 | 405 |
| 20:3 | 398 |
| 20:4–5 | 367 |
| 20:5 | 409 |
| 20:7, 16 | 176 |
| 20:8–10 | 245 |
| 20:8–11 | 101, 229 |
| 20:12 | 115 |
| 20:14 | 112 |

**Exodus** (*continued*)
| | |
|---|---|
| 20:17 | 244 |
| 20:18–21 | 344 |
| 20:19, 21 | 88 |
| 20:24 | 57 |
| 20:26 | 188 |
| 21:1–6 | 247 |
| 21:2 | 81 |
| 21:6 | 176 |
| 21:7 | 245 |
| 21:7–11 | 115, 247 |
| 21:13–14 | 342 |
| 21:15, 17 | 115 |
| 21:20–21 | 115, 245 |
| 21:28–36 | 245 |
| 22:5 | 245 |
| 22:16–17 | 109, 112 |
| 22:21–22 | 268 |
| 22:22 | 124 |
| 22:26–27 | 189 |
| 23 | 217 |
| 23:10–11 | 246 |
| 23:12 | 245 |
| 23:14–17 | 118 |
| 23:23–33 | 217 |
| 23:33 | 217 |
| 23:34 | 217 |
| 24 | 234, 343 |
| 24:1, 9 | 101 |
| 24:4 | 219 |
| 24:6 | 343 |
| 24:7 | 343 |
| 24:8 | 343 |
| 24:18 | 101 |
| 25:10–22 | 29, 286 |
| 26–27 | 115 |
| 28 | 189, 372 |
| 28:2, 40 | 372 |
| 28:40–43 | 372 |
| 28:42–43 | 188 |
| 28:43 | 189 |
| 29:38–41 | 187 |
| 30:10 | 425 |
| 31:18 | 194 |
| 32 | 286 |
| 32:2–4 | 176 |
| 32:4 | 405 |
| 32:5 | 405 |
| 32:7 | 88 |
| 32:10 | 176 |
| 32:19 | 421 |
| 32:25–29 | 266 |
| 33:11 | 175, 195 |
| 33:13 | 202 |
| 33:17–23 | 424 |
| 33:20 | 195 |
| 33:23 | 195 |
| 34 | 217 |
| 34:6–7 | 415 |
| 34:14 | 409 |

| | |
|---|---|
| 34:28 | 101 |
| 34:29–35 | 88 |
| 37:1–9 | 29 |

**Leviticus**
| | |
|---|---|
| 1 | 371 |
| 1–7 | 187 |
| 1:5 | 171 |
| 3:1–17 | 371 |
| 3:11 | 188 |
| 3:16 | 188 |
| 4 | 191 |
| 4:1–5:13 | 371 |
| 5:14–6:7 | 371 |
| 6:8–13 | 371 |
| 6:24–30 | 371 |
| 7:1–10 | 371 |
| 7:11–38 | 371 |
| 8:23–24 | 183 |
| 10:1–2 | 376 |
| 11 | 187 |
| 11:2–8 | 187 |
| 11:9–12 | 187 |
| 11:24–28 | 375 |
| 11:39 | 375 |
| 11:40 | 375 |
| 12–15 | 187 |
| 12:2–8 | 375 |
| 12:4–5 | 375 |
| 12:6–8 | 375 |
| 13–14 | 181 |
| 13:1–16 | 188 |
| 13:1–46 | 181 |
| 13:2–46 | 375 |
| 13:47–59 | 375 |
| 15 | 181, 374 |
| 15:1–3 | 374 |
| 15:2–15 | 375 |
| 15:2, 19 | 170 |
| 15:3 | 375 |
| 15:5–6 | 374 |
| 15:8 | 374 |
| 15:12 | 374 |
| 15:13 | 375 |
| 15:14 | 375 |
| 15:16–17 | 375 |
| 15:18 | 192, 375 |
| 15:19–24 | 190, 375 |
| 15:25–30 | 375 |
| 15:33 | 109 |
| 16 | 376, 425 |
| 16:4 | 188 |
| 16:6–7 | 376 |
| 16:15 | 171 |
| 16:15–19 | 376 |
| 16:26, 28 | 375 |
| 16:29 | 228 |
| 17:8 | 228 |
| 17:10–16 | 229 |
| 17:11, 14 | 171 |

| | |
|---|---|
| 17:15 | 375 |
| 17:15–16 | 230 |
| 18 | 170, 185, 188 |
| 18:3 | 201 |
| 18:6 | 188 |
| 18:6–18 | 109 |
| 18:6–23 | 184 |
| 18:19 | 109 |
| 18:20 | 112 |
| 18:21 | 225 |
| 18:22 | 154 |
| 18:22–23 | 109 |
| 18:24–30 | 389 |
| 18:26 | 229 |
| 19 | 403 |
| 19:9–10 | 153, 268 |
| 19:14 | 180 |
| 19:23–25 | 190 |
| 19:27–28 | 121, 175, 189 |
| 20 | 185, 188 |
| 20:2 | 229 |
| 20:2–5 | 225 |
| 20:10 | 49, 112 |
| 20:10–21 | 184 |
| 20:13 | 110, 154 |
| 20:18 | 109 |
| 20:26 | 201 |
| 21 | 179 |
| 21:5 | 121 |
| 21:6 | 188 |
| 21:10 | 181 |
| 21:18–20 | 179 |
| 22:17–25 | 187 |
| 22:18–19 | 228 |
| 22:25 | 188 |
| 23:22 | 153, 268 |
| 23:42 | 230 |
| 25 | 465 |
| 25:8–34 | 442 |
| 25:8–55 | 101 |
| 25:10–17 | 247 |
| 25:23 | 243 |
| 25:23–28 | 114 |
| 25:25–28 | 247 |
| 25:39 | 247 |
| 26:30 | 170 |

**Numbers**
| | |
|---|---|
| 1 | 341 |
| 1:2–3 | 126 |
| 2 | 341 |
| 2–3 | 128 |
| 5:11–31 | 192 |
| 6 | 175 |
| 6:22–27 | 175 |
| 8:5–26 | 266 |
| 9:14 | 228 |
| 11:1 | 421, 422 |
| 11:4 | 230 |
| 11:4–6, 18 | 213 |

| | | | | | |
|---|---|---|---|---|---|
| 11:12 | 157 | 5:11, 20 | 176 | 16:11, 14 | 228 |
| 11:25–30 | 310 | 5:12–14 | 245 | 16:21 | 400 |
| 12 | 113 | 5:12–15 | 229 | 16:22 | 219 |
| 12:1–2 | 154 | 5:14 | 229 | 17:3 | 416, 442 |
| 12:6–8 | 310 | 5:15 | 177 | 17:16–20 | 346 |
| 12:6–15 | 154 | 5:16 | 115 | 18:15–19 | 344 |
| 14:2–4 | 213 | 5:18 | 442 | 19 | 340 |
| 14:22–23 | 213 | 5:20 | 442 | 19–24 | 340 |
| 14:29 | 170 | 5:21 | 244, 442 | 19:4 | 340 |
| 15 | 228 | 6:4–9 | 175 | 19:7–8 | 341 |
| 15:32–36 | 229 | 6:5 | 172 | 19:14 | 114 |
| 16 | 373 | 6:7 | 116 | 20 | 341 |
| 16:13–14 | 213 | 6:14 | 405 | 20:2 | 341 |
| 19:7, 21 | 375 | 6:15 | 409 | 20:16–17 | 217 |
| 19:8, 10 | 375 | 6:20–24 | 116 | 20:16–18 | 217 |
| 19:10 | 228 | 7:1 | 217 | 21:10–14 | 109 |
| 19:11, 16 | 375 | 7:1–2 | 210 | 21:17 | 112, 217 |
| 19:14 | 375 | 7:1–4 | 232 | 21:18–21 | 115, 183 |
| 19:16 | 375 | 7:1–5 | 217 | 21:19 | 259 |
| 20:3–5 | 213 | 7:2 | 217 | 22:5 | 154, 189 |
| 20:17 | 33 | 7:3 | 231 | 22:11–12 | 189 |
| 21:4–9 | 182 | 7:3–4 | 219, 231, 389 | 22:13–19 | 192 |
| 21:6 | 415 | 7:6 | 234 | 22:13–22 | 112 |
| 21:8–9 | 367 | 7:7 | 202, 235 | 22:22–24 | 112 |
| 23:13 | 405 | 7:7–8 | 235 | 22:23–29 | 109 |
| 26 | 111, 127 | 7:11ff | 202 | 22:28–29 | 112, 191 |
| 26:1–2 | 126 | 7:13 | 241 | 22:29 | 104 |
| 26:64–65 | 213 | 7:25 | 442 | 23:1 | 154, 179, 233 |
| 27:1 | 125 | 8:11–14 | 442 | 23:1–8 | 233 |
| 27:1–11 | 113, 246 | 8:19 | 405 | 23:3 | 225, 388 |
| 27:9–11 | 442 | 9:6 | 235 | 23:3–6 | 232 |
| 28–29 | 187 | 9:14 | 202 | 23:3, 6 | 232 |
| 28:1–8 | 372 | 10:1–5 | 286 | 23:3–8 | 234 |
| 28:2 | 188 | 10:4 | 341 | 23:3, 6–8 | 230 |
| 30:1–15 | 245 | 10:8–9 | 266 | 23:6 | 231 |
| 30:3–16 | 124 | 10:18 | 268 | 23:7 | 224 |
| 33 | 217 | 10:18–19 | 442 | 23:15–16 | 442 |
| 33:11–16 | 217 | 10:20 | 151 | 24:3, 7 | 341 |
| 36:1, 10–12 | 125 | 11:16, 28 | 405 | 24:12–13, 17 | 442 |
| 36:1–12 | 113 | 11:19–21 | 116 | 24:14–22 | 442 |
| 36:2–12 | 246 | 11:22 | 151 | 24:17–22 | 442 |
| 36:6–9 | 114 | 12 | 315 | 24:19–21 | 124, 153 |
| | | 12:2–4 | 346 | 24:21 | 268 |
| **Deuteronomy** | | 12:5–12 | 118 | 25:5–10 | 126, 247 |
| 1:16 | 229 | 12:5–28 | 346 | 25:9–10 | 248 |
| 1:44 | 149 | 12:23 | 171 | 25:11–12 | 154 |
| 2:5, 12, 22 | 224 | 12:31 | 225 | 26:11 | 228 |
| 4:6 | 202 | 13:5 | 151 | 26:12 | 101 |
| 4:6–23 | 48 | 13:6–8 | 338 | 26:12–15 | 266 |
| 4:10, 12, 15 | 193 | 14 | 187 | 26:15 | 101 |
| 4:13 | 341 | 14:1 | 189 | 27:12–13 | 128 |
| 4:19 | 416, 442 | 14:1–2 | 121 | 27:15–16 | 442 |
| 4:24 | 409 | 14:21 | 230 | 27:16 | 115 |
| 4:29 | 172 | 14:22–29 | 266 | 27:17 | 114 |
| 4:32–40 | 234 | 14:26 | 368 | 27:18 | 180 |
| 4:39 | 220 | 15:7–11 | 442 | 27:19 | 442 |
| 5 | 341 | 15:9 | 175 | 28:23–24, 53 | 339 |
| 5:8–9 | 367 | 15:12–15 | 245 | 28:30 | 170 |
| 5:9 | 409 | 15:12–18 | 247, 442 | 28:43–44 | 230 |
| 5:11 | 442 | 15:17 | 176 | 29:4 | 177 |

**Deuteronomy** (*continued*)

| | |
|---|---|
| 30:19 | 339 |
| 31:17 | 175 |
| 31:24–26, 28 | 338 |
| 31:26 | 367 |
| 32 | 340 |
| 32–33 | 403 |
| 32–34 | 340 |
| 32:1 | 340 |
| 32:7 | 340 |
| 32:9–10 | 340 |
| 32:13–14 | 157 |
| 32:16, 19, 21 | 409 |
| 32:18 | 157 |
| 32:46–47 | 116 |
| 32:48–52 | 93 |
| 32:50 | 93, 120 |
| 33:2–3 | 417 |
| 33:3 | 340 |
| 33:6–25 | 128 |
| 33:26–39 | 160 |
| 34 | 92 |
| 34:1–6 | 93 |
| 34:6 | 93 |
| 34:10 | 344 |
| 34:10–12 | 92 |
| 34:28 | 341 |

**Joshua**

| | |
|---|---|
| 1–11 | 28 |
| 1–12 | 303 |
| 1:1 | 422 |
| 2 | 111, 219, 220 |
| 3 | 286 |
| 3:10 | 217 |
| 4:6–7 | 116 |
| 5:13–15 | 417 |
| 6 | 111, 219, 286 |
| 6:22–25 | 220 |
| 6:26 | 225 |
| 7:16–18 | 125 |
| 10:42 | 420 |
| 12–22 | 28 |
| 12:17, 24 | 230 |
| 13–21 | 303 |
| 14:13–14 | 229 |
| 15:13 | 229 |
| 15:16–19 | 105 |
| 15:63 | 219 |
| 16:10 | 219 |
| 17:2–3 | 230 |
| 17:3–6 | 246 |
| 17:12–13 | 219 |
| 17:18 | 218 |
| 18 | 315 |
| 18:1 | 29 |
| 19:51b | 29 |
| 20:4 | 259 |
| 21–23 | 116 |
| 22:19 | 243 |
| 23–24 | 28 |
| 23:16 | 405 |
| 24 | 315, 399 |
| 24:11–13 | 407 |
| 24:14 | 214 |
| 24:26 | 315 |
| 32:12 | 151 |

**Judges**

| | |
|---|---|
| 1 | 218 |
| 1:12–15 | 105 |
| 1:21 | 251 |
| 1:21, 27–36 | 219 |
| 1:27–28 | 251 |
| 1:28 | 218 |
| 2–16 | 303 |
| 2:10 | 120 |
| 2:13 | 399 |
| 2:18 | 310 |
| 3 | 222 |
| 3:1–6 | 219 |
| 3:5 | 217 |
| 3:9–10 | 310 |
| 3:12–30 | 225 |
| 3:15–29 | 182 |
| 4 | 310 |
| 4–5 | 149, 150 |
| 4:4 | 149 |
| 4:5 | 310 |
| 4:6–7 | 149, 310 |
| 4:8 | 149 |
| 4:17 | 149, 150 |
| 4:18–19 | 149, 150 |
| 4:21 | 150 |
| 5:2 | 138 |
| 5:4 | 403 |
| 5:4–5 | 156 |
| 5:4b-5 | 403 |
| 5:7 | 149 |
| 5:12 | 149 |
| 5:14–18 | 128 |
| 5:20 | 417 |
| 5:26–27 | 150 |
| 5:30 | 150, 413 |
| 5:31 | 150 |
| 6–8 | 307 |
| 6:8–10 | 310 |
| 6:11–18 | 310 |
| 6:15 | 125 |
| 6:32 | 400 |
| 6:33- 7:23 | 8 |
| 6:34–35 | 126 |
| 8:2 | 126 |
| 9 | 307, 315, 399 |
| 9:4 | 399 |
| 9:6 | 307 |
| 9:46 | 315, 399 |
| 10:13 | 405 |
| 11 | 306 |
| 11:1 | 107 |
| 11:3 | 268 |
| 11:4–6 | 306 |
| 11:4–11 | 183 |
| 11:7–8 | 306 |
| 11:11 | 307 |
| 11:29–40 | 115, 225, 245 |
| 11:39–40 | 116 |
| 13 | 135 |
| 13–16 | 175 |
| 14:1–4 | 141 |
| 14:2 | 138 |
| 14:3 | 137 |
| 14:6, 9 | 138 |
| 14:14 | 138 |
| 14:18 | 137 |
| 14:19 | 138 |
| 15:4 | 138 |
| 15:6 | 136 |
| 15:7 | 137 |
| 15:8 | 137 |
| 15:12–13 | 138 |
| 15:15 | 136, 138 |
| 15:18 | 137 |
| 16:3 | 136 |
| 16:4 | 137 |
| 16:7 | 136 |
| 16:9, 12, 14 | 138 |
| 16:11, 13, 17 | 136, 138 |
| 16:17, 22 | 138 |
| 16:21 | 139 |
| 16:22 | 139 |
| 16:25 | 139 |
| 16:26 | 139 |
| 16:28 | 136 |
| 16:30 | 140 |
| 16:31 | 135 |
| 17 | 344 |
| 17:4–5 | 117 |
| 18:30 | 344 |
| 19 | 107, 109, 110 |
| 19–21 | 29 |
| 19:24 | 432 |
| 20 | 210 |
| 20:5 | 432 |
| 21:16–24 | 306 |

**Ruth**

| | |
|---|---|
| 1:1–3 | 151 |
| 1:3–5 | 151 |
| 1:8 | 102, 151 |
| 1:12 | 151 |
| 1:14 | 151 |
| 1:16 | 117 |
| 1:16–18 | 151 |
| 1:17 | 120 |
| 2 | 268 |
| 2:2 | 152 |
| 2:8–9 | 152 |
| 2:10 | 152 |
| 2:12 | 153 |
| 2:14–16 | 152 |
| 3:3–4 | 153 |
| 3:4 | 153 |

| | | | | | |
|---|---|---|---|---|---|
| 3:7–8 | 153 | 11:5 | 284 | 24 | 15 |
| 3:9 | 153 | 11:6 | 310 | 24:3 | 170 |
| 4 | 247, 248 | 11:7 | 284 | 25:1–42 | 307 |
| 4:1 | 259 | 12–31 | 49 | 25:10 | 307 |
| 4:1–11 | 153 | 12:8 | 212 | 25:18 | 307 |
| 4:3 | 266 | 13 | 279, 307 | 25:18–31 | 147 |
| 4:13 | 105, 153 | 13:16 | 307 | 25:44 | 307 |
| 4:13–17 | 231 | 14:2 | 284 | 26:1 | 284 |
| 4:14–15, 17 | 154 | 14:3 | 307 | 26:5 | 307 |
| 4:15–17 | 153 | 14:47–48 | 307 | 27 | 222 |
| 4:17–18 | 281 | 14:50 | 307 | 27–30 | 299 |
| 4:18–22 | 154, 220 | 15 | 217, 279 | 28 | 120 |
| 4:22 | 225 | 15:3 | 210, 217, 279 | 28–29 | 120 |
| | | 15:18–22 | 222 | 29 | 8 |
| **1 Samuel** | | 15:32 | 53 | 30 | 307 |
| 1 | 118 | 16 | 278 | 30:26–31 | 307 |
| 1–2 | 108 | 16:1–13 | 281 | 30:29 | 229 |
| 1–3 | 29, 315 | 16:1–14 | 113 | 31 | 222 |
| 1:1–8 | 107 | 16:1, 18 | 280 | 31:1–2 | 307 |
| 1:2 | 182 | 16:6–7 | 173 | 31:8–13 | 299 |
| 1:4–9 | 118 | 16:11–13 | 302 | 31:10 | 170 |
| 1:14 | 368 | 16:12 | 134, 173, 282 | 55–58 | 49 |
| 2 | 372 | 16:14–23 | 182, 282, 310 | | |
| 2:4 | 141 | 16:43 | 288 | **2 Samuel** | |
| 2:22b | 29 | 17 | 7, 29, 49, 222, | 1 | 283 |
| 4 | 286 | | 276, 282 | 1:11–12 | 189 |
| 4–6 | 222 | 17:4 | 173 | 1:11–16 | 299 |
| 4–8 | 222 | 17:12 | 127 | 1:15 | 283 |
| 4:19–22 | 108 | 17:12, 58 | 280 | 2:4 | 281, 307 |
| 5:1–5 | 222 | 17:42 | 173 | 2:4–7 | 283 |
| 5:6–12 | 222, 223 | 17:45 | 417 | 2:8 | 400 |
| 7:2 | 286 | 18 | 222 | 3:1 | 304 |
| 8 | 253 | 18:1–5 | 282 | 3:2–5 | 31, 287 |
| 8–12 | 29 | 18:2 | 222 | 3:3 | 105 |
| 8–13 | 303 | 18:6–7 | 149 | 3:7 | 107 |
| 8:2, 6 | 252 | 18:6–7, 27, 29 | 299 | 3:12 | 298 |
| 8:3 | 278 | 18:6–9, 12–15, 30 | 282 | 3:12–16 | 280 |
| 8:5 | 278 | 18:7, 12–16 | 304 | 3:23–4:4 | 50 |
| 8:7 | 416 | 18:10–11 | 310 | 3:26–30 | 282 |
| 8:7–8, 10b-11 | 252 | 18:17–28 | 246 | 3:27 | 298 |
| 8:11–12 | 253 | 18:17–29 | 282, 307 | 3:31–38 | 283 |
| 8:11–13 | 252 | 18:18 | 280 | 4:4 | 181 |
| 8:11–17 | 294 | 18:20–29 | 104 | 4:5–8 | 282 |
| 8:14 | 253 | 18:31 | 110 | 4:5–12 | 299 |
| 8:15, 17 | 252 | 19:1–7 | 282 | 4:12 | 283 |
| 9:1–2 | 307 | 19:7 | 304 | 4:24–25 | 298 |
| 9:2 | 173 | 19:8–17 | 282 | 5 | 287 |
| 9:21 | 125 | 19:13, 16 | 117 | 5:2 | 282 |
| 10:1 | 278, 302 | 19:18–24 | 310 | 5:3 | 281, 307 |
| 10:5 | 309 | 19:20 | 309 | 5:6–10 | 251 |
| 10:8–14 | 279 | 20:1–42 | 282 | 5:7 | 251 |
| 10:9 | 278 | 20:5–6 | 120 | 5:8 | 181 |
| 10:10 | 310 | 20:28 | 280 | 5:14, 20 | 188 |
| 10:17–19 | 416 | 20:31 | 304 | 6 | 30, 296 |
| 10:20–21 | 125 | 21:4–5 | 192 | 6:2 | 286 |
| 10:21 | 127 | 21:6 | 284 | 6:5, 14–15 | 286 |
| 10:22–24 | 278 | 22:1 | 285 | 6:10–11 | 222 |
| 10:26 | 284 | 22:2 | 268 | 6:13, 18 | 286 |
| 10:26–11:1 | 52 | 22:7–8 | 307 | 6:16 | 181 |
| 10:27 | 294 | 23:17 | 304 | 6:19 | 286 |
| 11 | 284 | 23:19 | 284 | 6:23 | 287 |

**2 Samuel** (*continued*)

| | |
|---|---|
| 7 | 30, 325, 326 |
| 7, 12 | 301 |
| 7:1–17 | 293 |
| 7:5 | 422 |
| 7:8 | 416 |
| 7:10–11 | 407 |
| 7:11 | 287 |
| 7:13 | 325 |
| 7:14–15 | 276 |
| 7:16 | 287 |
| 7:23 | 405 |
| 8 | 250, 252 |
| 8:2 | 225 |
| 8:12 | 250 |
| 8:13–14 | 224 |
| 8:15 | 298 |
| 8:15–18 | 295 |
| 8:16–18 | 253 |
| 8:17 | 383 |
| 8:18 | 299 |
| 9 | 180 |
| 9:3, 13 | 181 |
| 9:6 | 400 |
| 9:17 | 297 |
| 10–11 | 11 |
| 10:4 | 175 |
| 10:4–5 | 432 |
| 11 | 185 |
| 11:8 | 170 |
| 11:14–27 | 298 |
| 11:27–12:15 | 309 |
| 12:7–23 | 108 |
| 13 | 210, 288 |
| 13:1–14 | 110 |
| 13:15 | 137 |
| 13:18 | 189 |
| 13:28–29 | 304 |
| 15 | 219 |
| 15–18 | 288, 304 |
| 15:10 | 307 |
| 15:18 | 299 |
| 15:25–26 | 296 |
| 16:5–8 | 307 |
| 16:20–22 | 107 |
| 17 | 296 |
| 18:14 | 298 |
| 19–20 | 304 |
| 19:5–7 | 298 |
| 19:11–15 | 307 |
| 19:16–20 | 307 |
| 19:24–30 | 307 |
| 19:32–35 | 183 |
| 19:43 | 128 |
| 20:1–2 | 308 |
| 20:2 | 151 |
| 20:3 | 107 |
| 20:4–22 | 308 |
| 20:7 | 299 |
| 20:23 | 298, 299 |
| 20:23–26 | 253, 295 |

| | |
|---|---|
| 20:25 | 297, 383 |
| 21:7–9 | 307 |
| 21:8–14 | 107 |
| 21:15–22 | 173 |
| 21:19 | 276 |
| 22 | 219 |
| 22:7 | 176 |
| 22:34, 37 | 181 |
| 24:1 | 418 |

**1 Kings**

| | |
|---|---|
| 1 | 294, 301 |
| 1–2 | 304 |
| 1:1–4 | 183 |
| 1:1–53 | 303 |
| 1:5–40 | 113 |
| 1:7 | 294 |
| 1:8 | 294 |
| 1:11–14 | 302 |
| 1:38, 44 | 299 |
| 2:5–6 | 298 |
| 2:11 | 101 |
| 2:13–18 | 302 |
| 2:13–46 | 303 |
| 2:24 | 293 |
| 2:26 | 370 |
| 2:28–35 | 298 |
| 3–11 | 262 |
| 3:1 | 303 |
| 3:16–28 | 111, 303, 439 |
| 3:26 | 178 |
| 4 | 299 |
| 4:1–6 | 253 |
| 4:1–19 | 295 |
| 4:5 | 301 |
| 4:6 | 301 |
| 4:7 | 300 |
| 4:7–19 | 299 |
| 4:7–19, 22–28 | 254 |
| 4:12 | 251 |
| 4:22–28 | 300 |
| 4:25 | 244, 262, 271 |
| 4:29–34 | 303 |
| 4:30–31 | 31 |
| 5 | 325, 326 |
| 5:4 | 325 |
| 5:5 | 325 |
| 5:8–16 | 254 |
| 5:11 | 325 |
| 5:12 | 325 |
| 5:13 | 252 |
| 5:13–17 | 325 |
| 5:13–18 | 252, 300 |
| 7 | 363 |
| 8 | 325, 326 |
| 8:20 | 325 |
| 8:21 | 29 |
| 8:23 | 220 |
| 8:25 | 326 |
| 8:26 | 303 |
| 8:48–49 | 328 |

| | |
|---|---|
| 8:53 | 212 |
| 8:62–64 | 326 |
| 8:62–66 | 363 |
| 8:63 | 187 |
| 9:5 | 293 |
| 9:10–14 | 300, 303 |
| 9:10–28 | 254 |
| 9:15–17 | 301 |
| 9:15–23 | 252 |
| 9:19 | 301 |
| 9:20–21 | 219 |
| 9:20–22 | 300 |
| 9:26–28 | 303 |
| 10:1–39 | 303 |
| 10:11, 14–29 | 254 |
| 10:23–25 | 30 |
| 10:27 | 30 |
| 11:1 | 105 |
| 11:1–3 | 303 |
| 11:1–8 | 231 |
| 11:1–13 | 303 |
| 11:2 | 151 |
| 11:3 | 31 |
| 11:14–40 | 303 |
| 11:26–40 | 300, 305, 315 |
| 11:28 | 300 |
| 11:29–32 | 302 |
| 11:31 | 128 |
| 11:42 | 101 |
| 12 | 286, 305 |
| 12:1, 25 | 399 |
| 12:25–33 | 313 |
| 12:25–13:5 | 61 |
| 13:20–32 | 121 |
| 14:3 | 182 |
| 14:9–10 | 315 |
| 14:16 | 365 |
| 14:19 | 298 |
| 14:23 | 400 |
| 14:25 | 19, 20 |
| 14:29 | 298 |
| 14:30 | 305 |
| 15:7, 23, 31 | 298 |
| 15:8 | 302, 365 |
| 15:10 | 302 |
| 15:11 | 293 |
| 15:13 | 302 |
| 15:25–32 | 305 |
| 15:26 | 315 |
| 15:33 | 400 |
| 15:34 | 293, 315 |
| 16:2, 19, 26 | 315 |
| 16:5, 14, 20, 27 | 298 |
| 16:8–14 | 305 |
| 16:9–10 | 298 |
| 16:15–20 | 305 |
| 16:19 | 293 |
| 16:29 | 19 |
| 16:34 | 225 |
| 17:5–6 | 309 |
| 17:8–16 | 310 |

| | | | | | |
|---|---|---|---|---|---|
| 17:12 | 269 | 12:3 | 118 | 22:18–20 | 386 |
| 17:17–24 | 182 | 12:4–5 | 297 | 23:1–2 | 387 |
| 17:18–16 | 269 | 12:11 | 347 | 23:4 | 416 |
| 18 | 400 | 12:18 | 365 | 23:4–20 | 346 |
| 18:3–4 | 315 | 13:2, 6, 11 | 293 | 23:10 | 225 |
| 18:17–40 | 118 | 14:3–4 | 346 | 23:11 | 233 |
| 18:20–40 | 314 | 14:4 | 118 | 23:15–18 | 61 |
| 18:21 | 399, 400 | 14:7 | 224 | 23:17 | 121 |
| 18:28 | 309 | 14:11–14 | 305 | 23:29 | 311 |
| 19:1–3 | 315 | 14:14 | 365 | 23:30 | 308 |
| 19:7 | 302 | 14:24 | 293 | 23:30–31 | 311 |
| 19:10, 14 | 417 | 15:4, 35 | 118 | 23:31–35 | 311 |
| 19:19 | 309 | 15:9 | 293 | 24:15 | 233 |
| 19:21 | 309 | 15:18, 24, 28 | 293 | 25:7 | 181 |
| 20:7–8 | 183 | 15:25 | 298 | 25:27–30 | 336 |
| 20:35 | 309 | 16:1–8 | 347 | 28:63–65 | 347 |
| 21 | 251 | 16:3 | 115, 225 | 30:1–4 | 347 |
| 21:1–29 | 114 | 16:8 | 365 | | |
| 21:3 | 114 | 16:10–16 | 296 | **1 Chronicles** | |
| 21:4 | 154 | 16:25–26 | 346 | 1:4–23 | 203 |
| 21:8–15 | 154 | 17:3 | 305 | 1:7 | 203 |
| 22 | 41, 417 | 17:8–16 | 272 | 1:17, 42 | 435 |
| 22:1–4 | 250 | 17:16 | 416 | 1:36 | 229 |
| 22:6 | 302 | 17:17 | 115 | 2:1–2 | 128 |
| 22:9 | 233 | 17:35 | 405 | 2:9–15 | 281 |
| 22:15 | 293 | 18:4 | 182, 367 | 6:1–81 | 373 |
| 22:19 | 156, 416 | 18:7 | 331 | 8:34 | 400 |
| 22:21 | 417 | 18:13–16 | 331 | 9:40 | 400 |
| 22:34–37 | 154 | 18:14 | 305 | 11:6 | 298 |
| 22:52 | 315 | 18:14–16 | 35 | 16:4–7, 37–42 | 336 |
| 29–36 | 250 | 18:16 | 365 | 21:1 | 418 |
| | | 18:18 | 253 | 22:1 | 336 |
| **2 Kings** | | 18:27 | 170, 178 | 22:2–5 | 336 |
| 1:2 | 182 | 18:31 | 265 | 29:2–5 | 336 |
| 1:8 | 309 | 19 | 424 | 29:14 | 199 |
| 2:3, 5, 7, 15 | 309 | 19:7 | 35 | | |
| 2:13–46 | 295 | 19:34 | 331 | **2 Chronicles** | |
| 3 | 225, 250 | 19:35 | 35 | 16:12 | 182 |
| 3:13 | 302 | 19:35–37 | 331 | 20:6 | 425 |
| 3:27 | 225, 245 | 20:1–5 | 182 | 36:22 | 298 |
| 4:1–7 | 115, 269, 310 | 20:4–5 | 416 | 36:22–23 | 336 |
| 4:1, 38 | 309 | 20:7 | 182 | 36:23 | 230 |
| 5:8–14 | 182 | 21:1–9 | 118 | | |
| 5:22 | 309 | 21:2 | 346 | **Ezra** | |
| 6:1 | 309 | 21:3, 5 | 416 | 1:1 | 298 |
| 8:6 | 233 | 21:6 | 115, 225 | 1:1–8 | 439 |
| 8:8 | 182 | 21:7 | 400 | 1:2–4 | 230, 423 |
| 8:20–22 | 224 | 21:23–24 | 308, 311 | 1:11 | 230 |
| 9:1 | 309 | 22 | 385 | 2:1 | 230 |
| 9:1–13 | 308, 315 | 22:2 | 293 | 2:36–63 | 373 |
| 9:11 | 308 | 22:3 | 311 | 2:69 | 242 |
| 9:12–13 | 308 | 22:3–7 | 385 | 4 | 231 |
| 9:30 | 146 | 22:3–10 | 297 | 4:17–22 | 439 |
| 9:30–37 | 154 | 22:4 | 297 | 6:1–12 | 439 |
| 9:32 | 233 | 22:4, 8 | 310 | 6:3–5 | 423 |
| 10:1–8 | 308 | 22:8 | 386 | 6:7–8 | 183 |
| 10:5 | 183 | 22:11–20 | 297 | 6:11 | 298 |
| 10:9–11 | 308 | 22:11, 14 | 311 | 7:6 | 386 |
| 10:32–33 | 305 | 22:14 | 310 | 7:11 | 386 |
| 11:13–16 | 308 | 22:14–20 | 310 | 7:11–26 | 318 |
| 11:18 | 311 | 22:16 | 386 | 7:12–26 | 386, 439 |
| | | | | 7:14 | 386 |

**Ezra** (*continued*)
| | |
|---|---|
| 7:25–26 | 386 |
| 7:26 | 387 |
| 9:1 | 230, 232, 234 |
| 9:1–10 | 185 |
| 9:1–10:44 | 319 |
| 9:2 | 230 |
| 9:10–12 | 231–32, 389 |
| 9:11 | 231 |
| 10:2–3 | 231 |
| 10:8 | 230 |
| 10:11 | 234 |
| 10:44 | 232 |

**Nehemiah**
| | |
|---|---|
| 2:1–8 | 439 |
| 2:1–10 | 317 |
| 5 | 265 |
| 5:1–5 | 115, 265 |
| 5:6–13 | 265 |
| 5:14–19 | 265 |
| 5:18 | 26 |
| 6:17–19 | 388 |
| 7:4–5 | 317 |
| 8 | 425 |
| 8:1 | 387 |
| 8:5 | 388 |
| 8:7–8 | 388 |
| 8:8 | 388, 425 |
| 8:12 | 388 |
| 9:2 | 230, 234 |
| 9:24 | 217 |
| 9:32–37 | 264 |
| 9:32, 36–37 | 264 |
| 9:36–37 | 170 |
| 10:28 | 234 |
| 11:1–2 | 317 |
| 13:1 | 388 |
| 13:1–3 | 232 |
| 13:3 | 230, 234 |
| 13:4–9, 28–29 | 319 |
| 13:15–18 | 229 |
| 13:19–22 | 319 |
| 13:23–27 | 319 |
| 13:23–31 | 185 |

**Esther**
| | |
|---|---|
| 1:1 | 146 |
| 1:8 | 147 |
| 1:10 | 355 |
| 1:12 | 146 |
| 1:17–18 | 146 |
| 1:19 | 355, 389 |
| 1:21 | 355 |
| 1:21–22 | 438 |
| 1:22 | 355, 389 |
| 2:2–4 | 145 |
| 2:5–7 | 148 |
| 2:7 | 145 |
| 2:8 | 298 |
| 2:8–9 | 145 |

| | |
|---|---|
| 2:10 | 145 |
| 2:10, 20 | 147 |
| 2:12 | 146 |
| 2:14, 17–18 | 438 |
| 2:15 | 146, 148 |
| 2:17 | 146 |
| 2:20 | 148 |
| 3:8–10 | 147 |
| 3:10 | 355 |
| 3:12 | 298 |
| 3:12–15 | 355 |
| 4:1–3 | 425 |
| 4:5 | 148 |
| 4:8–14 | 147 |
| 4:11 | 148 |
| 4:16 | 148 |
| 4:16–17 | 425 |
| 5:1 | 146 |
| 5:2 | 146, 147 |
| 5:3, 6 | 438 |
| 5:4 | 147 |
| 5:6 | 147 |
| 5:8 | 147 |
| 6:10 | 438 |
| 7:2 | 147 |
| 7:2–4 | 147 |
| 7:2, 7–10 | 439 |
| 7:7 | 147 |
| 7:8 | 147 |
| 7:10 | 148 |
| 8:1–2 | 389 |
| 8:2 | 148, 355, 439 |
| 8:3–6 | 148 |
| 8:8–14 | 355 |
| 8:8–9, 17 | 298 |
| 8:9 | 148 |
| 8:10 | 148 |
| 8:10–14 | 390 |
| 8:15 | 355 |
| 9:1, 13 | 298 |
| 9:5–6 | 425 |
| 9:13 | 148 |
| 9:13–14 | 355 |
| 9:20–23 | 390 |
| 9:29 | 390 |
| 9:29, 31 | 148 |
| 9:32 | 148 |
| 10:2 | 390 |
| 10:3 | 148 |
| 11:1 | 390 |

**Job**
| | |
|---|---|
| 1 | 453 |
| 1–2 | 417, 418 |
| 1:1 | 263, 433, 435 |
| 1:1, 8 | 440 |
| 1:2 | 428 |
| 1:2–3 | 263 |
| 1:3 | 436 |
| 1:3–4 | 428 |

| | |
|---|---|
| 1:5 | 428, 433 |
| 1:6 | 438 |
| 1:8 | 427, 445 |
| 1:9 | 438 |
| 1:9–10 | 427 |
| 1:9–11 | 445 |
| 1:11 | 431 |
| 1:12 | 427, 429, 451 |
| 1:13 | 429 |
| 1:13–15 | 429 |
| 1:16 | 429 |
| 1:17 | 429 |
| 1:18–19 | 429 |
| 2:3 | 438, 451, 452 |
| 2:4–5 | 433 |
| 2:5, 9 | 431 |
| 2:6 | 451 |
| 2:7 | 433 |
| 2:8 | 427, 433 |
| 2:9 | 430 |
| 2:9–10 | 433 |
| 2:10 | 430, 431 |
| 2:12 | 428 |
| 3:11 | 427 |
| 5:1 | 417 |
| 5:17 | 399 |
| 5:18 | 182 |
| 5:23 | 445 |
| 6:4 | 399 |
| 7:12, 17–18 | 437 |
| 7:15–16 | 433 |
| 7:20 | 451 |
| 8:3, 5 | 399 |
| 8:5–6 | 440 |
| 8:11–13 | 444 |
| 9:4–10 | 445 |
| 9:15–16 | 439 |
| 9:20, 22–23 | 439 |
| 10:20–22 | 171 |
| 13:13–15 | 433 |
| 19:13–19 | 430 |
| 19:13–22 | 181 |
| 19:15 | 436 |
| 19:17 | 430 |
| 19:25 | 431 |
| 19:25–26 | 431 |
| 19:26 | 431 |
| 23:3 | 425 |
| 23:7 | 439, 451 |
| 23:16 | 399 |
| 24:3 | 124 |
| 26:5–14 | 440 |
| 29:2, 6–10 | 436 |
| 29:11–13 | 437 |
| 29:12–13, 15–17 | 264 |
| 29:20 | 432 |
| 30:1 | 436 |
| 30:1–8 | 436 |
| 30:1–8, 12 | 433 |
| 30:8 | 433 |

| | | | |
|---|---|---|---|
| 30:11 | 432 | 19 | 262 |
| 30:12–13 | 433 | 22:21 | 4 |
| 30:18–19 | 432, 451 | 24:1 | 243 |
| 30:19–20 | 456 | 26:2 | 177 |
| 30:25 | 264 | 29 | 416 |
| 31 | 427, 441, 442 | 29:3 | 403 |
| 31:1–4, 9–12 | 432 | 29:7 | 403 |
| 31:9–10 | 430 | 29:8–9 | 9 |
| 31:10 | 139 | 31:2 | 194 |
| 31:13, 16–22, 32, 39 | 264 | 32:4 | 4 |
| 31:21–22 | 441 | 33:20 | 160 |
| 31:24–28 | 436 | 38:1–5 | 182 |
| 31:32 | 435 | 38:11–12 | 182 |
| 33:4 | 399 | 38:18 | 182 |
| 34:14–15 | 171 | 39:12 | 243 |
| 37:23 | 425 | 45:3 | 178 |
| 38–41 | 426 | 47:8 | 194 |
| 38:1–39:30 | 444 | 48 | 328, 330 |
| 38:1–40:2 | 425, 443, 446 | 48:1–2 | 328 |
| 38:4–38 | 440 | 48:12–14 | 329 |
| 38:7 | 416 | 49 | 262 |
| 38:28 | 445 | 50:12–13 | 188 |
| 38:39–39:30 | 440 | 51:5 | 176 |
| 38:44 | 455 | 51:10 | 177 |
| 39:1–4 | 445 | 57:2 | 399 |
| 39:13–18 | 445 | 60:2 | 10 |
| 40:2 | 447 | 62:11 | 425 |
| 40:3–5 | 447 | 63:1 | 4 |
| 40:6–41:34 | 425, 443, 446 | 68:4 | 403 |
| 40:7–9 | 447 | 73:4 | 433 |
| 40:15–41:34 | 440 | 74:12–15 | 363 |
| 41:1–34 | 445 | 74:13–14 | 327 |
| 42 | 453 | 77 | 403 |
| 42:1–3 | 455 | 78 | 214 |
| 42:1–6 | 427, 428, 440, 451, 454 | 78:35, 36 | 399 |
| 42:5 | 175, 456 | 80:7, 14 | 417 |
| 42:6 | 454, 455, 457, 458 | 82 | 398 |
| 42:7 | 443, 450, 452 | 82:1 | 156 |
| 42:7–8 | 452 | 86 | 406 |
| 42:7–17 | 428 | 86:8–10 | 407 |
| 42:8 | 449, 453 | 88:3–12 | 171 |
| 42:10 | 448, 453 | 89 | 326, 327 |
| 42:11 | 449, 451–52 | 89:3–4 | 326 |
| 42:12–13 | 448 | 89:5–18 | 326, 416 |
| 42:14 | 146 | 89:6–8 | 326 |
| 42:15 | 449 | 89:9 | 6, 326 |
| | | 89:10 | 326 |
| **Psalms** | | 89:11 | 326 |
| 1 | 262 | 89:18 | 326 |
| 2 | 327, 416 | 89:25 | 326 |
| 2:7 | 327, 416 | 89:26 | 327 |
| 8:3–4 | 4 | 89:26–36 | 128 |
| 8:6 | 178 | 89:27 | 327 |
| 11:4 | 194 | 89:36–37 | 326 |
| 16:7–10 | 168, 169 | 89:38–39 | 326 |
| 16:7b | 169 | 89:50–51 | 327 |
| 16:11 | 183 | 90:1–3 | 399 |
| 17:15 | 175 | 90:15 | 110 |
| 18:7 | 9 | 93:2 | 399 |
| 18:10 | 366 | 93:3–4 | 327 |

| | | | |
|---|---|---|---|
| 94:6 | 124 |
| 103:1 | 176 |
| 103:13 | 178 |
| 104:10–11 | 4 |
| 104:25–26 | 5 |
| 104:29 | 171 |
| 106 | 214 |
| 107:9 | 176 |
| 107:23–27 | 5 |
| 112 | 262 |
| 114 | 403 |
| 118:12 | 149 |
| 118:15 | 183 |
| 119:19 | 243 |
| 119:75 | 110 |
| 121:1 | 175 |
| 121:1–2 | 4, 160 |
| 121:1, 3 | 263 |
| 121:5–6 | 4 |
| 124:8 | 160 |
| 127:3–5 | 107 |
| 130:1–2 | 176 |
| 133:2 | 146 |
| 136 | 214 |
| 146:9 | 268 |
| 148 | 416 |
| 148:3, 9–10 | 4 |
| | |
| **Proverbs** | |
| 1:8 | 349 |
| 1:20–33 | 351 |
| 1:23–32 | 351 |
| 1:33 | 351 |
| 3:9–10 | 262 |
| 5:18–19 | 191 |
| 5:19 | 149 |
| 6:10–11 | 270 |
| 7:11 | 350 |
| 7:17 | 146 |
| 8:1–36 | 351 |
| 8:15–16 | 351 |
| 8:22 | 350 |
| 8:22–31 | 157 |
| 8:30–31 | 350 |
| 9:1–6 | 350 |
| 9:14–19 | 350 |
| 10:3 | 262 |
| 10:4 | 263, 270 |
| 10:5 | 263 |
| 10:17 | 349 |
| 10:22 | 262 |
| 10:31 | 349 |
| 11:12–13 | 350 |
| 11:13 | 349 |
| 11:24–25 | 263 |
| 12:11 | 263 |
| 12:18 | 176 |
| 12:27 | 263 |
| 13:18 | 270 |
| 13:21 | 262 |

**Proverbs** (*continued*)

| | |
|---|---|
| 13:25 | 262 |
| 14:21 | 263 |
| 14:23 | 270 |
| 15:1 | 262 |
| 15:6 | 262 |
| 15:31 | 176 |
| 16:14–15 | 351 |
| 17:5 | 271 |
| 18:21 | 176 |
| 19:17 | 263 |
| 20:20 | 115 |
| 21:5 | 270 |
| 21:17 | 270 |
| 22:2 | 271 |
| 22:4 | 263 |
| 22:9 | 263 |
| 22:17 | 176, 262 |
| 22:17–24:32 | 350 |
| 22:20–21 | 350 |
| 22:24 | 350 |
| 22:28 | 350 |
| 23:2 | 170 |
| 23:3–5 | 175 |
| 23:4–5 | 350 |
| 23:13–14 | 351 |
| 23:29–35 | 349 |
| 24:23 | 262 |
| 24:33–34 | 270 |
| 25:1 | 262 |
| 26:4–5 | 349 |
| 27:7–9 | 350 |
| 28:19 | 263, 270 |
| 28:20, 25 | 262 |
| 28:27 | 271 |
| 29:13 | 271 |
| 29:20 | 176 |
| 30:11, 17 | 115 |
| 30:24–28 | 349 |
| 31:10–31 | 116, 263 |
| 31:20 | 264 |

**Ecclesiastes**

| | |
|---|---|
| 1:1 | 352 |
| 1:3–9 | 352 |
| 2:15–17 | 352 |
| 3:1–8 | 352 |
| 3:11 | 352 |
| 4:1–2 | 353 |
| 5:10 | 264 |
| 5:10–6:9 | 264 |
| 5:12, 17 | 264 |
| 5:13–14 | 264 |
| 5:13–17 | 352 |
| 5:15–16 | 264 |
| 6:1–3 | 264 |
| 6:7, 9 | 264 |
| 7:16–18 | 352 |
| 8:15 | 352 |
| 9:8 | 146 |

| | |
|---|---|
| 9:11–12 | 352 |
| 12 | 196 |
| 12:1–7 | 173–75 |
| 12:3 | 139 |
| 12:7 | 171 |

**Song of Songs**

| | |
|---|---|
| 1:5 | 74 |
| 1:5–6 | 173 |
| 1:6 | 65, 74 |
| 1:10 | 42 |
| 1:13 | 146 |
| 3:4 | 65, 74, 102 |
| 3:14–15 | 268 |
| 4:1–7 | 60 |
| 4:2 | 60 |
| 4:9 | 74, 173, 175 |
| 4:11 | 173 |
| 5:2 | 433 |
| 5:2–6 | 74 |
| 5:4 | 170 |
| 5:5 | 146 |
| 5:7 | 74 |
| 5:10 | 173 |
| 5:10–15 | 171 |
| 5:10–16 | 60 |
| 5:11 | 173 |
| 5:13 | 173 |
| 5:14–15 | 173 |
| 6:4–10 | 60 |
| 6:5 | 173 |
| 6:6 | 60 |
| 6:9 | 433 |
| 6:13 (7:1 Heb.) | 42 |
| 7:1–2 | 60 |
| 7:1–5 | 60, 74, 173 |
| 7:9 | 173 |
| 8:2 | 65, 74, 102 |
| 8:8–9 | 65 |
| 8:10 | 60 |
| 28:11 | 68 |

**Isaiah**

| | |
|---|---|
| 1:2 | 124 |
| 1:8 | 333 |
| 1:12–13 | 260 |
| 1:16–17 | 260 |
| 1:23 | 259 |
| 2:3 | 324 |
| 3:16 | 258 |
| 3:18–23 | 257 |
| 3:20 | 146 |
| 5:8 | 114, 254 |
| 5:8–9 | 256 |
| 5:11–12 | 258 |
| 5:22 | 258 |
| 5:23 | 259 |
| 6 | 424 |
| 6:1 | 195, 419 |
| 6:1–2 | 156 |
| 6:1–4 | 261, 415 |

| | |
|---|---|
| 6:1–6 | 302 |
| 6:1–8 | 328 |
| 7 | 53, 62, 71, 72, 302 |
| 7:1 | 71 |
| 7:1–4 | 261 |
| 7:1–17 | 302 |
| 7:3 | 71 |
| 7:4 | 71 |
| 7:7 | 71 |
| 7:9 | 43, 63 |
| 7:10–17 | 62, 64 |
| 7:13 | 309 |
| 7:14 | 72 |
| 7:16 | 62, 71 |
| 7:17 | 63 |
| 7:18 | 149 |
| 7:18–25 | 62, 63, 72 |
| 7:19 | 64 |
| 7:20 | 64, 170 |
| 7:23–25 | 64 |
| 8:1–4 | 64 |
| 8:5–8 | 64 |
| 8:8, 10 | 72 |
| 8:16–17 | 384 |
| 9 | 331 |
| 9:1 (8:23 Heb.) | 33 |
| 9:2–7 | 64, 302 |
| 9:4–5 | 330 |
| 9:6 | 331, 416 |
| 9:6–7 | 330 |
| 9:7 | 331 |
| 10:2 | 259 |
| 10:21–22 | 72 |
| 10:32 | 333 |
| 11:1–9 | 302 |
| 13:3–13 | 417 |
| 13:16 | 170 |
| 14:9–11 | 171 |
| 16:1 | 333 |
| 16:5 | 302 |
| 19 | 216 |
| 19:25 | 216 |
| 20:1–5 | 188 |
| 22:12 | 189 |
| 22:15–16 | 302 |
| 24:21–23 | 416 |
| 25:8 | 327 |
| 30:8–9 | 384 |
| 34:3 | 170 |
| 35:5–6 | 180 |
| 35:37 | 422 |
| 36–39 | 302 |
| 36:12 | 170 |
| 36:16 | 244, 265, 271 |
| 37:1–2 | 261 |
| 37:2, 5 | 302 |
| 37:7 | 35 |
| 37:22 | 333 |
| 37:35 | 331 |
| 37:36 | 35 |

| | |
|---|---|
| 37:36–38 | 331 |
| 38:1–5 | 182 |
| 38:1–6 | 261 |
| 38:18–19 | 171 |
| 38:21 | 182 |
| 40–55 | 64, 421 |
| 41:10 | 183 |
| 41:26- 42:10 | 51 |
| 42:14 | 157 |
| 43:13 | 395 |
| 44:1–4 | 422 |
| 44:6 | 408 |
| 44:26 | 422 |
| 44:28 | 422 |
| 45 | 235, 423 |
| 45:1 | 64, 333, 422 |
| 45:5–7 | 423 |
| 45:6b-7 | 407 |
| 45:12–13 | 333 |
| 48 | 362 |
| 49:14 | 333 |
| 49:15 | 157, 178 |
| 50:5 | 176 |
| 51:3 | 328 |
| 51:15–16 | 333 |
| 51:16 | 324 |
| 52:1–3 | 333 |
| 52:2 | 333 |
| 56 | 234 |
| 56–66 | 232, 319 |
| 56:2–8 | 229 |
| 56:3–7 | 233 |
| 56:4–5 | 180 |
| 56:5 | 177 |
| 57:3 | 315 |
| 57:8 | 170 |
| 58:6–9 | 268 |
| 62:3–5 | 411 |
| 62:11 | 333 |
| 63:3, 6 | 178 |
| 66:1 | 177, 425 |

**Jeremiah**

| | |
|---|---|
| 1:1 | 261, 310, 311 |
| 1:2–3 | 58 |
| 2:7 | 243 |
| 2:20 | 315 |
| 3:6, 13 | 315 |
| 4:30 | 146 |
| 5:28 | 259 |
| 5:30–31 | 407 |
| 7 | 311 |
| 7, 26 | 359 |
| 7:3–4 | 345 |
| 7:6 | 268 |
| 7:9–10 | 345 |
| 7:13–15 | 345 |
| 7:16–20 | 118 |
| 7:29 | 189 |
| 8:2 | 416 |
| 8:8 | 383 |
| 9:17–22 | 121 |
| 9:21 | 327 |
| 9:24 | 207 |
| 9:26 | 175 |
| 11:4 | 212 |
| 11:9–13 | 422 |
| 11:13 | 400 |
| 11:19 | 312 |
| 13:11 | 151 |
| 13:18 | 303 |
| 13:22, 26 | 195 |
| 15:15–18 | 312 |
| 16:5–9 | 120 |
| 16:6 | 189 |
| 16:18 | 243 |
| 17:1–4 | 422 |
| 17:2 | 315 |
| 17:19–23 | 229 |
| 18:18–23 | 312 |
| 19:3, 7 | 417 |
| 19:4–6 | 422 |
| 19:5–6 | 225 |
| 20:1–2 | 261 |
| 20:7, 10 | 312 |
| 21:1 | 310 |
| 21:1–10 | 311 |
| 21:2-7 | 312 |
| 21:4–7 | 422 |
| 21:8–9 | 408 |
| 22:3 | 268 |
| 22:13–17 | 312 |
| 22:13–19 | 311 |
| 22:18–19 | 312 |
| 22:24 | 334 |
| 23:21–22 | 419 |
| 23:27 | 399 |
| 25:1–7 | 312 |
| 25:9 | 312 |
| 25:11–12 | 392 |
| 25:12 | 101 |
| 25:13 | 384 |
| 25:20 | 435 |
| 25:26 | 57 |
| 26 | 311 |
| 26:1 | 311 |
| 26:4 | 345 |
| 26:4–7 | 312 |
| 26:10–11 | 261 |
| 26:16, 24 | 261 |
| 26:17–19 | 345 |
| 26:20–23 | 312 |
| 26:24 | 311 |
| 27:1–28:17 | 311, 312 |
| 27:5–6 | 422 |
| 27:9–10, 14–18 | 312 |
| 28:1–4, 10–11 | 312 |
| 28:1–17 | 314 |
| 29:2 | 303 |
| 29:3 | 311 |
| 30:2 | 384 |
| 30:10 | 422 |
| 30:21 | 416 |
| 31:20 | 157 |
| 32:2–3 | 261 |
| 32:6–15 | 248 |
| 32:7 | 310 |
| 33:1 | 261 |
| 33:17 | 289 |
| 33:21 | 422 |
| 34:8–16 | 248 |
| 35:4 | 310 |
| 36 | 384 |
| 36:1–4, 32 | 58 |
| 36:4 | 383 |
| 36:5–7 | 385 |
| 36:9–19 | 261 |
| 36:10 | 311 |
| 36:11–13 | 311 |
| 36:15–18 | 385 |
| 36:19 | 311 |
| 36:20–26 | 315 |
| 36:22–25 | 384 |
| 36:29–30 | 385 |
| 36:32 | 384, 385 |
| 37:3 | 310 |
| 37:11–21 | 261 |
| 38:7–13 | 261 |
| 39:1–40:6 | 315 |
| 41:4–5 | 189 |
| 42:12 | 178 |
| 44 | 405 |
| 44:15–19 | 118, 120, 406 |
| 44:15–28 | 118 |
| 45:1 | 384 |
| 46 | 216 |
| 46:11 | 182 |
| 47:5 | 189 |
| 49:7 | 435 |
| 49:7–22 | 224 |
| 50:2 | 170 |
| 51:1 | 57 |
| 51:8–9 | 182 |
| 51:41 | 57 |

**Lamentations**

| | |
|---|---|
| 1:8 | 188 |
| 1:9 | 195 |
| 1:26–28 | 424 |
| 2:1, 4, 8, 10, 13, 18 | 333 |
| 2:3 | 183 |
| 2:11 | 177 |
| 4:7–8 | 173 |
| 4:21 | 435 |
| 5:10 | 173 |

**Ezekiel**

| | |
|---|---|
| 1 | 366 |
| 1:1 | 420 |
| 1:1–2 | 421 |
| 1:2–3 | 313 |

**Ezekiel** (*continued*)
| | |
|---|---|
| 1:6–12 | 420 |
| 1:9 | 421 |
| 1:16 | 421 |
| 1:17 | 421 |
| 1:26 | 420 |
| 1:26–27 | 194 |
| 2:4–5 | 418 |
| 5:5 | 328 |
| 6:1–7 | 422 |
| 6:13 | 315 |
| 8 | 407 |
| 8:1 | 313 |
| 8:7–13 | 422 |
| 10 | 417 |
| 10:18–19 | 421 |
| 11:1–4 | 313 |
| 12:1–5 | 313 |
| 12:10 | 416 |
| 14:1–3 | 313 |
| 16 | 188, 412 |
| 16:8 | 153, 170 |
| 16:15–19 | 413 |
| 16:20–21 | 413 |
| 16:23–34 | 413 |
| 16:36–43a | 412 |
| 16:42 | 414 |
| 16:49 | 268 |
| 17:1–22 | 313 |
| 18 | 441 |
| 20:1 | 313 |
| 20:5, 7 | 214 |
| 20:27–28 | 406 |
| 20:32 | 202 |
| 20:47 | 315 |
| 21:18–32 | 313 |
| 22:29 | 268 |
| 23 | 412 |
| 23:20 | 170 |
| 23:35 | 414 |
| 23:48 | 414 |
| 25:12–14 | 224 |
| 27:17 | 146 |
| 27:24–28 | 314 |
| 27:25 | 422 |
| 28:13–14 | 328 |
| 29:32 | 216 |
| 33:30–31 | 313 |
| 34:23 | 422 |
| 35 | 224 |
| 35:10–14 | 224 |
| 37:24–28 | 289 |
| 38:12 | 328 |
| 40–43 | 377 |
| 40–48 | 229, 313 |
| 43:7–9 | 314 |
| 43:18–27 | 314 |
| 44:7 | 188 |
| 44:10–14 | 314 |
| 44:15–16 | 314 |

| | |
|---|---|
| 44:20 | 175 |
| 46 | 314 |
| 47:21–23 | 229 |
| 48:1–7, 23–27 | 128 |
| 48:30–35 | 377 |

**Daniel**
| | |
|---|---|
| 1 | 233 |
| 1–6 | 355 |
| 1:1–2 | 356 |
| 3 | 357 |
| 3:16–18 | 357 |
| 4:30 | 357 |
| 4:36–37 | 357 |
| 5:19 | 356 |
| 6 | 357 |
| 6:5 | 390 |
| 6:10 | 391 |
| 6:22 | 391 |
| 6:26–27 | 391 |
| 7 | 357 |
| 7–12 | 355, 357, 358 |
| 7:6 | 357 |
| 7:9 | 195 |
| 7:10 | 392 |
| 7:15–16 | 424 |
| 7:17 | 357 |
| 7:25 | 357 |
| 7:27 | 357 |
| 8:11–14 | 372 |
| 8:15–16 | 424 |
| 9 | 392 |
| 9:20–21 | 424 |
| 9:24 | 392 |
| 10:15–21 | 424 |
| 11:33 | 358 |
| 11:34 | 358 |
| 12:1 | 392 |
| 12:1–2 | 359 |
| 12:2 | 358 |
| 12:4 | 392 |
| 12:4, 9 | 392 |
| 12:9 | 425 |
| 12:10 | 358 |

**Hosea**
| | |
|---|---|
| 1:2 | 410 |
| 1:8–9 | 410 |
| 2 | 188, 410 |
| 2:3 | 411, 442 |
| 2:5, 12 | 410 |
| 2:8 | 404, 442 |
| 2:9–10 | 411 |
| 2:13 | 414 |
| 2:16–17 | 404 |
| 2:16–20 | 156 |
| 4:4–6 | 314 |
| 4:7–14 | 314 |
| 4:18 | 258 |
| 5:1–7 | 314 |
| 9:1 | 153 |

| | |
|---|---|
| 10:15 | 61 |
| 11:1 | 214 |
| 11:3–4 | 157, 415 |
| 11:8 | 178 |
| 12:2–4, 12 | 214 |
| 12:7 | 260 |
| 12:9, 13 | 214 |
| 13:4 | 214 |

**Joel**
| | |
|---|---|
| 1–2 | 370 |

**Amos**
| | |
|---|---|
| 1:1 | 19, 261 |
| 1:3–2:16 | 313 |
| 2:5 | 313 |
| 2:6 | 260 |
| 2:6–8 | 313 |
| 2:8 | 258 |
| 2:10 | 214 |
| 3:1 | 214 |
| 3:2 | 234 |
| 3:9,14 | 313 |
| 3:15 | 256 |
| 4:1 | 258 |
| 4:1–3 | 313 |
| 4:1,4 | 313 |
| 5:4–7 | 61 |
| 5:5–6 | 313 |
| 5:10 | 259 |
| 5:10–15, 21–24 | 313 |
| 5:11 | 256 |
| 5:12 | 259 |
| 5:21–24 | 260 |
| 5:22 | 258 |
| 6:1 | 258, 313 |
| 6:1–7 | 313 |
| 6:4 | 258 |
| 7:9 | 118 |
| 7:10–13 | 313 |
| 7:10–17 | 314 |
| 7:13 | 313 |
| 7:14 | 261, 313 |
| 7:17 | 370 |
| 8:4–5 | 260 |
| 8:4–6 | 313 |
| 8:5b | 260 |
| 8:6 | 260 |
| 8:10 | 189 |
| 8:14 | 313 |
| 9:1 | 57 |
| 9:7 | 214 |

**Obadiah**
| | |
|---|---|
| 10–14 | 224 |

**Jonah**
| | |
|---|---|
| 4:11 | 183 |

**Micah**
| | |
|---|---|
| 1:1 | 261, 313 |
| 1:3–4 | 156 |

| | |
|---|---|
| 1:16 | 189 |
| 2:2 | 114 |
| 2:2, 4 | 313 |
| 2:8–9 | 313 |
| 3:1–3 | 260, 313, 314 |
| 3:9–11 | 314 |
| 3:11 | 259 |
| 3:12 | 313 |
| 4:4 | 244, 255, 271 |
| 4:8, 10, 13 | 333 |
| 6:6–8 | 188 |
| 6:10–11 | 260 |
| 7:3 | 259 |
| 8:1–9:11 | 314 |
| 10:1–22 | 314 |
| 11:22–25 | 314 |

**Nahum**

| | |
|---|---|
| 1:2 | 404 |
| 1:2–8 | 404 |
| 1:3 | 404 |
| 1:4 | 404 |
| 1:5 | 404 |
| 3:5 | 195 |
| 24 | 149 |

**Habakkuk**

| | |
|---|---|
| 1:4 | 259 |
| 2:2–3 | 384 |
| 3 | 403 |
| 3:3–6 | 156 |

**Zephaniah**

| | |
|---|---|
| 1:4–6 | 314 |
| 1:5 | 416 |
| 1:8–9 | 314 |
| 1:10–13 | 314 |
| 1:13 | 256 |
| 3:3–4 | 259 |

**Haggai**

| | |
|---|---|
| 2:7–9 | 334, 367 |
| 2:8 | 318 |
| 2:18–19 | 334 |
| 2:23 | 334 |

**Zechariah**

| | |
|---|---|
| 1:9, 13–14, 18 | 424 |
| 2:5 | 330 |
| 2:12 | 51 |

| | |
|---|---|
| 3 | 417, 418, 424 |
| 3:10 | 244, 255, 271 |
| 4:1–14 | 319 |
| 4:7 | 334 |
| 4:9 | 334 |
| 4:10 | 367 |
| 4:11–14 | 335 |
| 6:9–14 | 319 |
| 6:11 | 335 |
| 7:10 | 268 |
| 10:2–3 | 319 |
| 11:14–17 | 319 |
| 12:7–10 | 319 |
| 13:7–9 | 319 |
| 14 | 319 |
| 14:5 | 417 |

**Malachi**

| | |
|---|---|
| 1:2–3 | 224 |
| 1:7, 12 | 188 |
| 4:4 | 422 |

**APOCRYPHA**

**Sirach**

| | |
|---|---|
| 25:24 | 159 |
| 38:24–34 | 382 |
| 50:5–6, 11–13 | 373 |

**Susanna**

| | |
|---|---|
| 32 | 412 |

**1 Maccabees**

| | |
|---|---|
| 1:15 | 207 |
| 1:20–28 | 318 |

**2 Esdras**

| | |
|---|---|
| 3:16 | 224 |

**PSEUDEPIGRAPHA**

***Jubilees***

| | |
|---|---|
| 15:26–27 | 207 |

***4 Ezra***

| | |
|---|---|
| 3:16 | 224 |

**NEW TESTAMENT**

**Matthew**

| | |
|---|---|
| 1:5 | 220 |

| | |
|---|---|
| 1:22–23 | 72 |

**John**

| | |
|---|---|
| 1:51 | 54 |
| 6:32–33 | 55 |

**Romans**

| | |
|---|---|
| 1:3 | 289 |

**1 Corinthians**

| | |
|---|---|
| 7:18 | 207 |
| 15:20 | 431 |

**Galatians**

| | |
|---|---|
| 3:28 | 234 |
| 4:21–28 | 208 |

**1 Timothy**

| | |
|---|---|
| 2:11–14 | 158 |

**Hebrews**

| | |
|---|---|
| 10:30–31 | 415 |
| 12:16–17 | 224 |
| 12:29 | 415 |

**James**

| | |
|---|---|
| 5:11 | 455 |

**Revelation**

| | |
|---|---|
| 5:5 | 289 |
| 16:14, 16 | 7 |
| 19:17–18 | 415 |

**OTHER ANCIENT SOURCES**

***Antiquities***

| | |
|---|---|
| 12:5 | 207 |
| 13.372–73 | 374 |

***Qidd***

| | |
|---|---|
| 3:12 | 111 |

**Qumran**

| | |
|---|---|
| 11:3 | 52 |

**Qur'an**

| | |
|---|---|
| 5:18 | 234 |

***Yebam***

| | |
|---|---|
| 7:5 | 111 |

# Index of Subjects

Aaron, 86, 90, 113, 154, 310, 344, 386, 405
Abel, 22
Abimelech, 209, 221, 307, 399
Abraham, 25–27, 89, 99–100, 108, 205–8
Absalom, 31, 288, 296, 298–99, 304, 307
Adam, 22, 133, 158–61, 192, 194, 202
Adonijah, 31, 293–94, 298, 302, 304
adultery, 112, 185, 192, 276, 341–42, 410, 412, 430
Ahab, 19, 32, 154, 250–51, 308, 310, 315
Ahasuerus, 146, 148, 355, 389, 438
Ahaz, 34, 62–64, 71, 296–97, 309
Alexander the Great, 38, 207
altar, 35, 57, 117, 179, 188, 191, 296–97, 315, 343, 362, 365, 370, 372, 400, 405
Ammonites, 11, 52, 118, 185, 207, 209, 212, 231–32, 234, 284
Amnon, 110, 288, 304
Amos, 34, 213, 258, 261, 312–14, 346
anointed one, 289, 333–35
anointing, 278, 287, 310, 416
    ceremony, 281–83, 285
    with oil, 146
    for priests, 183
Antiochus, 38–39, 355, 357–58
Anti-Semitism, 67, 208, 234, 236
Aramaeans, 209, 250
ark of the covenant, 29, 30, 284, 286, 296, 315, 338
Armageddon, 7
apocalyptic, 39, 355–56, 359, 392

Apocrypha, 56, 412
apocryphal, xv
archaeology, 30, 67, 121
Asherah, 118, 398, 400–401, 405, 416
Assyria, 16, 33–4, 36, 64, 71, 203, 305, 331–33
Assyrian kingdom, 27
Assyrians, 26, 27, 29, 34–35, 63, 216, 265, 316, 330
axis mundi, 328, 368

Baal, 118, 225, 311, 314, 327, 329, 398–404, 416–17
Babylonia, 16, 36, 203
Babylonians, 27, 29, 37, 224, 234, 312, 316–17, 345, 348–49, 422
    *See* exile (Babylonian)
Barter, 242
Baruch, 383
Bathsheba, 185, 294, 298, 302, 336
B.C.E., xv, 19, 20
Benjamin, 108, 143–45
*bet av*, 65, 98–99, 100, 102–7, 110, 112, 114–18, 120–23, 125–26, 128–29, 140, 142–45, 150, 153, 156, 162, 185, 242, 244–50, 268, 284, 288, 294, 308, 361, 408–11, 414, 422, 429–30, 432, 437, 448–49
*bet em*, 65, 102
Bildad, 435, 440, 444
Bilhah, 100, 104, 107, 144, 209
binary dualism, 165
Boaz, 105, 152–53, 231
bride-price, 104–5, 112, 361

Cain, 22, 202
Caleb, 229
Canaanites, 75, 209, 216–20, 224
Canon, xv, 47, 383, 385, 389
    deuterocanodical, 56
circumcision, 90, 171, 186, 189–91, 205–11, 219
    Moses receiving, 89
Cisjordan, xv, 1, 16, 25–27, 33, 101, 328
    definition, 19
    map, 2
clan, 79, 111, 125, 127, 304, 306
collateral, 250, 254
comparative ethnography, 100
corveé, 252
covenant, 27–30, 34, 89–90, 108, 205–9, 215, 221, 234–35, 284, 326, 337, 338, 351, 422, 435, 441–42
    Sinai (covenant), 339–41, 345–47, 367, 409
covet, 33, 244, 251, 342
Cyrus, 37, 64, 316, 333–34, 422–23

Daniel, 355–59, 389, 391–92
Darius, 316–17, 334, 381, 388–91
David, 6–7, 15, 29, 30–32, 37, 49, 104–5, 110, 113, 134, 181, 188, 222, 250–52, 276–89, 293–94, 298–99, 302, 307–9, 323, 325–31, 333–36, 437
Dead Sea, 13–16, 21
Dead Sea Scrolls, 49, 335
Deborah, 28, 149–50, 310
debt slavery, 245

Delilah, 136–38
Dinah, 100, 134, 144, 210–11, 246, 430
Divine Assembly (God's throne room),
146, 310, 415–17, 419–20, 424, 438
dowry, 104–5, 412
dynamic equivalence, 43–45

Edomites, 207, 209, 223–24, 227
Eglon, 183, 222, 225
Egyptians, 27, 33, 86, 89, 199, 212–16,
378
Moses, 85
old Egypt, 24
pyramids, 120
time, 19
El, 397–400, 403–4
elder, 26, 28, 32, 101, 116, 183, 229, 259,
305–8, 310, 313
Eliezer, 57, 99, 113, 142, 246
Elihu, 435
Elijah, 33, 182, 269, 309–10, 400
Eliphaz, 435, 444
Elisha, 33, 182, 269, 308–10
Elkanah, 107, 118
Elohim, 61–63, 397–99, 405–6
empire, 25–26, 33, 38, 264–65, 316–17,
353–54, 357–58, 381, 383, 389,
408, 421, 424, 443, 452
endogamy, 105, 125
Ephraim, 128, 143, 157, 183, 212, 231, 306
eponymous, 220
Esau, 99, 113, 141–43, 223–24, 246, 402
Esther, 133, 135, 145–49, 186, 355,
389–91, 425
ethnicity, 79- 80, 199–236, 435
eunuch, 145, 148, 179–80, 233
euphemism, 170, 173, 432
for genitals, 89, 153, 169
for sexual intercourse, 191, 351
Eve, 22, 133, 158–59, 192, 202
Exile (Babylonian), 27, 36, 64, 101,
230–32, 311, 313–14, 316–17,
333–34, 347, 421
exogamy, 105, 125
Ezekiel, 308, 313–14, 407, 421, 424
Ezra, 38, 230, 232, 386–89

femininity, 132–35, 148–51, 162–63,
431–32
Fertile Crescent, 16
formal correspondence, 43–45
form criticism, 59–60
fornication, 112

gender binary, 133, 159
genocide, 36, 209–11, 217, 413
Gideon, 8, 28, 125–26, 400
gleaning, 124, 152–53, 268
goel, 126, 153, 246–48, 431, 437
Goliath, 6, 7, 29, 49, 222, 276, 282, 288

Habakkuk, 384
Habiru, 81
Hagar, 99, 104, 107, 113, 135, 208–9,
212, 418
Haggai, 319, 334, 366–67, 421
hair, 86, 121, 138–39, 141, 173, 175,
186, 189
Samson's hair, 138
Haman, 147–49, 355
Heber, 149–50
Hebrew, 81, 210
Hebron, 8, 136, 229, 285, 307, 401
hellenization, 38
henotheism, 405, 408
herem, 217
Hezekiah, 331–33, 365
historical criticism, 58, 66
Hokmah, 350–52
holiness, 296, 374–77, 402
homosexuality, 106, 109–10, 154,
184–85
Hosea, 214, 314, 404, 409–11, 415
Huldah, 310, 386
hyperfeminine, 133, 135, 145, 148–49
hypermasculine, 133, 135, 138, 148, 221

ideology, 74, 76–77, 154, 225–26, 241,
305, 323–59, 361–62, 367, 378,
441–42, 451–52
King-Zion, 377, 443
national existence, 66
sage order, 440
Sinai-Nation, 452
incest, 109–10, 185
inside-outsiders, 105, 208–9, 234–36,
266, 435
intermarriage, 185–86, 217, 219,
231–32, 319
intersex persons, 132, 159
Isaac, 25, 99–100, 104, 141–42, 208–9,
221, 223, 246, 402
Isaiah, 34, 62–63, 71–72, 261, 302, 309,
328, 331, 384, 414
Ishbaal, 282–83, 298, 304, 400
Ishmael, 99, 208–9, 211
Ishmaelites, 208–9
Ishtar, 145
Israel, 7, 17–19, 32, 80, 93, 304–6, 316,
343, 348, 399
Israelites, 5–6, 22, 27, 37, 81, 119, 200,
205, 213–36, 291, 349, 371

Jabin, 150
Jacob, 18, 25, 42, 51, 54–55, 61–62, 66,
68, 73–74, 113, 140–45, 203, 223,
399
Jael, 133, 135, 149–50
Jehoash, 297, 365
Jehoiakim, 36, 311, 315, 319, 421
Jehoram, 225, 250

Jehoshaphat, 250
Jehu, 308, 315
Jephthah, 107, 225, 245, 268, 306–7
Jeremiah, 58–59, 261, 310–15, 345,
383–85, 392, 405, 421–22
Jericho, 8, 21, 220, 286
Jerusalem, 1, 3–4, 6–10, 30–31, 35–39,
46, 74, 224, 230–31, 250–51, 261,
265, 297, 305, 312, 318–19, 324,
326, 332, 334, 354, 362, 407, 417,
421, 443
Jesse, 49, 280, 282
Jesus Christ, 20, 72, 289
Jethro, 141, 402
Jezebel, 154, 251, 315
Joab, 282, 293, 298
Job, 146, 181, 262–64, 425, 427–57
Jonathan, 110, 180–81, 282–83, 307,
400
Jordan River, 8, 11–13, 19, 307
Joseph, 93, 105–6, 113, 128, 143–45,
147, 212–13, 300
Josephus, 207, 318, 370–71, 374
Joshua, 28, 35, 37, 125, 214, 304, 335,
417, 420, 424
Josiah, 58, 64, 297, 311, 331, 346,
385–87
jubilee, 101, 207, 247
Judah, 27, 32, 34, 36–37, 230, 281, 316
Judeans, 37, 354

Kethuvim, 54
King Ahasuerus, 146, 148, 389
kosher, 39, 375

latifundialization, 254
Leah, 100, 104–5, 108, 142–43, 209
Levi, 134, 144, 211
Levirate marriage, 247
Levite, 85, 266–67, 372–73
life expectancy, 108, 183
literal translation, 68, 160, 168–69
Lot, 15, 99, 113, 185, 209, 225

Manasseh, 36, 128, 143, 183, 212, 231,
306, 346, 400
Marduk, 37, 329, 348–49
Marx, Karl, 240
masculinity, 132–35, 138, 140, 143, 431
God as masculine, 156
Masoretes, 46–47, 402
Masoretic Text, 47
matrilocality, 102
media, 361–93, 443
Menelaus, 39
Merab, 246, 280, 354
Mesha, 225–27
messiah, 289, 334–35
metaphor, 60, 169, 408–12, 414–15, 419
God as head of household, 397

Micah, 34, 255, 260–61, 272, 313, 344
Micaiah ben-Imlah, 33, 309–11, 416–17, 419
Michal, 104, 188, 246, 280, 282, 286–87
Midianites, 85
midrash, 54, 58
midwife, 215
Miriam, 113, 154, 310
Moabites, 224–27
monadic, 102, 106, 109, 124
monoculture, 249
monolatry, 405–6, 408
monotheism, 235, 407
Mordecai, 145, 147–48, 355, 389–90
Moses, 27–28, 57, 90, 92–94, 101, 105, 141, 157, 175, 183, 222, 340, 343–44, 400–401, 424, 428
Mount Sinai, 27, 57, 336, 344, 409
mourning, 121, 175, 179, 189, 212, 283, 425, 454

Nabol, 307
Naboth, 114, 154, 251
nahalah, 102
Naomi, 102, 117, 120, 124, 151–53, 266
narrator, 69–70
Nathan, 287, 294, 301–2, 309
nation, 31, 72, 93–94, 184, 199–200, 202, 284, 291, 304, 341
near neighbors, 213, 219, 224, 226
Nebuchadnezzar, 36, 311, 356–57, 422
Nehemiah, 37, 265, 319, 387–88
nephesh, 171–72, 176, 190
Neviim, 54, 308
New Criticism, 68
Noah, 23, 171, 188, 194, 203, 206, 216

Obed, 231
Old Testament, 54, 56, 415
Omri, 19, 227, 305, 320, 346
oracles, 59, 62–64, 216, 261, 313–14, 319, 331
Orpah, 151
orphans, 124–25, 153, 259, 267

paraphrases, 43, 46
particularistic, 235
patriarchal, 74, 102, 135, 183, 233
patrilineal, 102, 104, 111
patrilocal, 102
Pentateuch, 35, 61
Persia, 357
Persians, 231, 318–19, 334–35
   Persian Empire, 37–38, 316–17, 364, 389, 391
Pharaoh, 25–27, 80, 83–89, 101, 120, 209, 212–15, 228, 327, 365, 420, 439
Philistines, 5, 17, 29, 221–22
Phoenicians, 5
pilgrimage, 318, 368–70

polyandry, 109
polygyny, 109, 185
postmodern, 72, 77
Potiphar's wife, 147
priests, 29, 175, 179, 183, 187–89, 296–97, 314, 335, 343, 366–67, 370, 372, 374, 376
primogeniture, 112–13
primordial, 202, 206–7, 235
prophets, 33–34, 54, 182, 256, 259–62, 268–69, 301–2, 306, 308–15, 344, 383–84
prostitution, 111–12, 220, 268, 413
Ptolemy, 38
pyramids, 21, 23–24, 120

Qoheleth, 262, 352–53
Qumran, 49–53, 351

race, 79–80, 200
Rachel, 100, 104–5, 108, 121, 124, 142–44, 209, 402, 405
Rahab, 111, 219–20, 327
rape, 109–10, 133, 150, 188, 191, 412–14, 432
reader-response criticism, 70
Rebekah, 25, 99, 102, 104, 108, 113, 142
redaction criticism, 60–61, 64
Rehoboam, 32, 300
resident alien, 99, 228–30, 266
Reuben, 113, 142, 144
Rizpah, 107
Ruth, 105, 117, 120, 124, 151–54, 232, 248, 266, 281

Sabbath, 35, 37, 39, 57, 101, 229, 245, 342, 349
sacrifices, 187–88, 362–63, 371–72
sages, 348–53, 441
Samaria, 34, 257–58
Samaritans, 34–35
Samson, 28–29, 133, 135–40, 221–22
Samuel, 308–9, 416
Sarah, 25, 99, 104, 108, 185, 206, 208–9
Satan, 418
Saul, 15, 30, 49, 53, 104, 125, 127, 180–81, 219, 222, 246, 278–79, 282–83, 285–87, 304, 307
scribes, 23, 49, 51–52, 59, 256, 316, 318, 380–85, 387, 390, 392–93
Seleucids, 38
Sennacherib, 35, 332
Septuagint, 47, 202
Seth, 22
Shearjashub, 71–72
Sheol, 171, 433
Sheshbazzar, 37
Shiloh, 29, 307, 315, 345
shrine, 29, 61, 117–18, 127, 268, 275, 296–97, 306, 315, 318, 324, 326, 334, 368

Simeon, 128, 134, 144, 211
Sisera, 149–50
sociological and anthropological approaches, 96
Solomon, 30–32, 74, 105, 113, 262, 293–305, 325–26, 362, 365
source criticism, 61–62
state, 222, 291–321, 416
Sumerians, 24
Susanna, 412
suzerainty treaties, 337–39, 409, 435

Tamar, 110, 126, 135, 185, 220
Tanakh, xiii, 54, 56
Temple (Jerusalem), 30–31, 36–37, 252, 287, 333, 361–83, 385–88, 421
Ten Commandments (Decalogue), 27, 29, 101, 176, 244, 341–42, 345, 404
tetragrammaton, 401
textual criticism, 42, 46, 49, 53
theophoric name, 400
Torah, 54, 56, 58, 61, 63–64, 336–38, 387–89
tribe, 79, 125, 127–28, 200
   Judah (tribes of), 34, 281
   lost tribes, 34
   twelve tribes of Israel, 32, 127–28, 304
tribute, 34, 37, 242, 251–52, 264, 305, 316

uncleanness, 181, 192, 374- 76
   causes of, 375
universalistic, 216, 235
Uriah, 296, 298, 312, 336

Vashti, 146, 355

widows, 124–25, 151, 153, 179, 189, 259, 267–68
wisdom, 38, 157, 216, 261–64, 269–72, 348–52, 435, 440–41

Yehud, 37, 316–17, 334–35, 352, 375, 388–89, 443
   See Judeans
YHWH, 11, 27, 30, 61–62, 129, 156, 243, 312, 340–48, 350, 358, 362, 374, 400–10, 413–18, 420–25, 451

Zabdi, 125
Zabud, 295, 301
Zadokites, 314
Zechariah, 51, 305, 318, 329, 334–35, 366, 418–19, 421
Zedekiah, 36, 58, 181, 311–13
Zerah, 125
Zerubbabel, 37, 334–35
Zilpah, 100, 104, 107, 209
Zion, 324–36, 343–44, 346–48, 362–63
Zipporah, 86, 89, 105, 190
Zophar, 435